THE
ANNUAL REGISTER
Vol. 219
WORLD EVENTS IN
1977

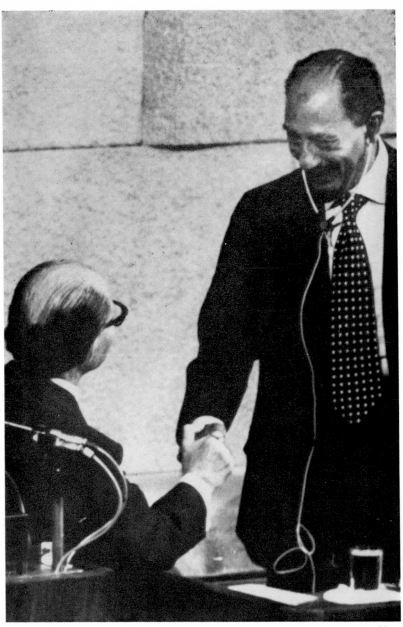

An historic meeting:
President Anwar Sadat of Egypt shakes hands with Prime Minister Menachem Begin of
Israel after addressing the Knesset on 20 November 1977.

THE
ANNUAL REGISTER

World Events in
1977

Edited by
H. V. HODSON

Assisted by
BISHAKHA BOSE

FIRST EDITED IN 1758
BY EDMUND BURKE

ST. MARTIN'S PRESS
NEW YORK
1978

Published in the United States by St. Martin's Press Inc. 1978
© Longman Group Limited 1978
Library of Congress Catalog Card Number 4–17979

PRINTED IN GREAT BRITAIN

CONTENTS

CONTENTS

ABBREVIATIONS

AID	Agency for International Development
ASEAN	Association of South-East Asian Nations
AR	Annual Register
CENTO	Central Treaty Organization
CERN	European Organization for Nuclear Research
CFA	Communauté Française Africaine
COMECON	Council for Mutual Economic Assistance
EC	European Community
ECA	Economic Commission for Africa (UN)
ECE	Economic Commission for Europe (UN)
ECLA	Economic Commission for Latin America (UN)
ECOSOC	United Nations Economic and Social Council
ECSC	European Coal and Steel Community
EEC	European Economic Community (Common Market)
EFTA	European Free Trade Association
ESCAP	Economic and Social Commission for Asia and the Pacific (UN)
EURATOM	European Atomic Energy Community
FAO	Food and Agriculture Organization
GATT	General Agreement on Tariffs and Trade
IAEA	International Atomic Energy Agency
IBRD	International Bank for Reconstruction and Development
ICAO	International Civil Aviation Organization
ICBM	Inter-Continental Ballistic Missile
IDA	International Development Association
IFC	International Finance Corporation
ILO	International Labour Organization
IMF	International Monetary Fund
LAFTA	Latin American Free Trade Association
LDCs	Less Developed Countries
MBFR	Mutual and Balanced Force Reductions
MDCs	More Developed Countries
NATO	North Atlantic Treaty Organization
OAS	Organization of American States
OAU	Organization of African Unity
OECD	Organization for Economic Co-operation and Development
OPEC	Organization of Petroleum Exporting Countries
SALT	Strategic Arms Limitation Talks
SEATO	South East Asia Treaty Organization
TUC	Trades Union Congress
UN	United Nations
UNCTAD	United Nations Conference on Trade and Development
UNDP	United Nations Development Programme
UNESCO	United Nations Educational, Scientific and Cultural Organization
UNFICYP	United Nations Peace-Keeping Force in Cyprus
UNRWA	United Nations Relief and Works Agency
VAT	Value Added Tax
WEU	Western European Union
WHO	World Health Organization

CONTRIBUTORS

Africa, East: Uganda, Tanzania, Kenya
WILLIAM TORDOFF, MA, PH.D
(Professor of Government, University of Manchester)

Africa, North: Algeria, Libya Morocco, Tunisia, Western Sahara
DR ROBIN BIDWELL
(Secretary, Middle East Centre, University of Cambridge)

Africa: French-speaking West and Central Africa, Equatorial Guinea;
O. E. WILTON-MARSHALL
(Writer on African affairs)

Africa: Ethiopia, Somalia, French Territory of the Afars and Issas
CHRISTOPHER CLAPHAM
(Senior Lecturer in Politics, University of Lancaster)

Africa; former Portuguese territories, Zaïre, Rwanda and Burundi
D. H. JONES, MA
(Senior Lecturer in African History, University of London)

Albania
ANTON LOGORECI, B.SC (ECON)
(Writer and broadcaster on communist affairs)

Arab States of the Middle East: Egypt, Jordan, Syria, Lebanon, Iraq
CHRISTOPHER GANDY
(Formerly UK Diplomatic Service, writer on Middle Eastern affairs)

Saudi Arabia, Yemen and Gulf States
R. M. BURRELL,
(Lecturer in the Contemporary History of the Near and Middle East School of Oriental and African Studies, University of London)

Australia
GEOFFREY SAWER, BA, LL.M
(Emeritus Professor of Law, Australian National University)

Bangladesh
KEVIN RAFFERTY
(Journalist and expert on Asian affairs)

Benelux countries
J. D. McLACHLAN
(Economic analyst and writer specializing in European countries)

Botswana; Lesotho; Swaziland
GERALD SHAW
(Chief Assistant Editor, *The Cape Times*)

Bulgaria
RADA NIKOLAEV
(Head of Bulgarian research section, *Radio Free Europe*)

Canada
BRUCE THORDARSON, BA, MA
(Writer on Canadian affairs)

Caribbean (Commonwealth)
SIR PHILIP SHERLOCK, KBE, LL.D, D.LITT, DCL
(Secretary-General, Association of Caribbean Universities and Research Institutes)

China
MICHAEL YAHUDA
(Lecturer in International Relations, London School of Economics and Political Science)

Cyprus
RICHARD SPEAREY
(Editor *Cyprus Mail*, and writer on Cyprus affairs)

Czechoslovakia
VLADIMIR V. KUSIN, PH.D
(Director, International Information Centre for Soviet and East European Studies, University of Glasgow)

France
MARTIN HARRISON
(Professor of Politics, University of Keele)

Gambia, The
ARNOLD HUGHES, BA
(Lecturer in Political Science, Centre of West African Studies, University of Birmingham)

Germany, West and East
H. N. CROSSLAND
(Freelance journalist, Bonn)

x

Ghana	D. G. AUSTIN
	(Professor of Government, University of Manchester)
Gibraltar	D. G. AUSTIN (see above)
Greece	RICHARD CLOGG, MA
	(King's College, University of London)
Hong Kong	A. S. B. OLVER, MA
	(Specialist in South East Asian affairs)
Hungary	GEORGE SCHÖPFLIN
	(Joint Lecturer in East European Political Institutions at the London School of Economics and the School of Slavonic and East European Studies)
India; Nepal; Afghanistan	KULDIP NAYAR
	(Editor, *The Indian Express*, New Delhi, and author)
Iran	KEITH MCLACHLAN, BA, PH.D
	(Lecturer in Geography with reference to the Near and Middle East, School of Oriental and African Studies, University of London)
Ireland, Northern	A. I. Q. STEWART, MA, PH.D
	(Reader in Irish History, Queen's University, Belfast)
Ireland, Republic of	LOUIS MCREDMOND, MA, BL
	(Head of Information in Radio Telefis Eireann, the Irish broadcasting service)
Israel	The Hon. Terence Prittie, MBE, MA
	(Director, Britain and Israel)
Italy	MURIEL GRINDROD, OBE
	(Writer on Italian affairs; formerly Assistant Editor, *The Annual Register*)
Japan	REGINALD CUDLIPP
	(Director, Anglo-Japanese Economic Institute)
Korea	PETER FINCH
	(Hon. Editor, *Bulletin of the Anglo-Korean Society* and writer on Korean affairs)
Latin America	PETER CALVERT, AM, MA, PH.D
	(Reader in Politics, University of Southampton)
Liberia; Malagasy Republic	O. E. WILTON-MARSHALL
	(Writer on African affairs)
Malawi	RALPH A. YOUNG
	(Lecturer in Government, University of Manchester)
Malaysia; Singapore; Brunei	MICHAEL LEIFER, BA, PH.D
	(Reader in International Relations, London School of Economics and Political Science)
Malta	D. G. AUSTIN
	(Professor of Government, University of Manchester)
Mongolia	ALAN SANDERS, FIL
	(British Broadcasting Corporation)
New Zealand	DR RODERIC ALLEY
	(School of Political Science and Public Administration, Victoria University of Wellington)
Nigeria	ARNOLD HUGHES, BA
	(Lecturer in Political Science, Centre of West African Studies, University of Birmingham)
Nordic States	T. K. DERRY, OBE, D.PHIL
	(Writer on Nordic history and current affairs)
Pakistan	P. T. ENSOR, B.SC(ECON), ICS (retd)
	(Writer on Pakistan affairs; Secretary, Overseas Investors Chamber of Commerce and Industry, Karachi)
Papua New Guinea	DAVID HEGARTY
	(Senior Lecturer Department of Political and Administrative Studies, University of Papua New Guinea)

Poland	Z. J. BLAZYNSKI (Writer and broadcaster on Polish and communist affairs)
Portugal	G. A. M. HILLS, BA, D.LIT (Writer and broadcaster on Iberian current affairs and history)
Rhodesia	R. W. BALDOCK (Editor-in-chief, Harvester Press; writer on African affairs).
Romania	SYLVIA M. FLORESCU (Specialist on Romanian affairs)
Rwanda and Burundi	D. H. JONES, MA (Senior Lecturer in African History, University of London)
Scandinavian States *see* Nordic States	
Scotland	PETER GOULDESBROUGH, MA, LL.B (An Assistant Keeper, Scottish Record Office)
Seychelles, BIOT, Mauritius	ROY LEWIS (Journalist and expert on African affairs)
Sierra Leone	ARNOLD HUGHES (see Nigeria)
South-East Asian States (except Malaysia, Singapore, Brunei)	A. S. B. OLVER, MA (Specialist in South-East Asian affairs)
South Africa	GERALD SHAW (Chief Assistant Editor, *The Cape Times*)
South Pacific	DR RODERIC ALLEY (see New Zealand)
Spain	G. A. M. HILLS (see Portugal)
Sri Lanka	JAMES JUPP, M.SC (ECON), PH.D (Visiting Professor in Political Science, University of Waterloo, Canada)
Sudan	DR AHMED AL-SHAHI (Lecturer in Social Anthropology, Department of Social Studies, University of Newcastle upon Tyne)
Switzerland	HERMANN BÖSCHENSTEIN, D.PH (Historian and Editor)
Taiwan	BRIAN HOOK, BA (Senior Lecturer in Chinese Studies, University of Leeds)
Turkey	A. J. A. MANGO, BA, PH.D (Orientalist and writer on current affairs in Turkey and the Near East)
United Kingdom	H. V. HODSON, MA (Formerly Editor, *The Sunday Times*)
USA	JAMES BISHOP (Editor, *The Illustrated London News*)
USSR	DR PHILIP HANSON, MA, PH.D (Senior Lecturer, Centre for Russian and East European Studies, University of Birmingham)
Vietnam	A. S. B. OLVER, MA (Specialist in S.E. Asian affairs)
Wales	PETER STEAD (Lecturer in History, University College of Swansea)
Yugoslavia	F. B. SINGLETON, MA (Chairman, Post-Graduate School of Yugoslav Studies, University of Bradford)
Zambia	RALPH A. YOUNG (Lecturer in Government, University of Manchester)

INTERNATIONAL ORGANIZATIONS AND CONFERENCES

African Conferences and Institutions	O. E. WILTON-MARSHALL (Writer on African affairs)
Caribbean Organizations	SIR PHILIP SHERLOCK, KBE, LLD, D.LITT, DCL (Secretary-General, Association of Caribbean Universities and Research Institutes)

Comecon	MICHAEL KASER, MA (Reader in Economics, Oxford, and Professorial Fellow of St Antony's College, Oxford)
Commonwealth, The	ALEXANDER MACLEOD (Editor, *The Round Table*)
Council of Europe; WEU; North Atlantic Assembly	DAVID BUCHAN (Brussels correspondent, *The Financial Times*)
Defence Negotiations and Organizations	JOHN C. GARNETT, B.SC(ECON), M.SC(ECON) (Department of International Politics, The University College of Wales, Aberystwyth)
European Community	DAVID BUCHAN (see above)
Nordic Council	T. K. DERRY, OBE, D.PHIL (Writer on Nordic history and current affairs)
South-East Asian Conferences and Institutions	A. S. B. OLVER, MA (Specialist in S.E. Asian affairs)
United Nations	MARY ALLSEBROOK, MA (Writer on international and UN matters)

THE ARTS

Architecture	GEORGE MANSELL, RIBA (Architectural writer)
Art	LADY VAIZEY (Art Critic, *The Sunday Times*)
Ballet	G. B. L. WILSON, MA (Ballet critic of *The Jewish Chronicle*, London, and *Dance News*, New York; author of the *Dictionary of Ballet*)
Cinema	ROGER MANVELL, PH.D, D.LITT, LITT.D (HON) (Director, British Film Academy 1947-59; Visiting Fellow, University of Sussex; Visiting Professor of Film, Boston University; author and critic)
Fashion	ANNE PRICE (Fashion Editor, *Country Life*)
Literature	DAVID HOLLOWAY (Literary Editor, *The Daily Telegraph*)
Music	FRANK GRANVILLE BARKER (Music critic and broadcaster)
Opera	RODNEY MILNES (Writer and broadcaster on opera)
Television and Radio	RICHARD LAST (Television critic, *The Daily Telegraph*)
Theatre	ERIC SHORTER (Drama critic, *The Daily Telegraph*)
New York Theatre	EDWARD G. GREER (Assistant Professor, Drama Department, Syracuse University, USA)

ECONOMIC AFFAIRS

International, UK and USA Economic Developments	PETER RIDDELL (Economics correspondent, *The Financial Times*)
Economic and Social Data	J. J. PRYOR (General Editor, *Financial Times Business News-letters*)

LAW

International Law	ROSALYN HIGGINS, MA, LL.B, JSD (Professor of International Law, University of Kent, Canterbury)
European Community Law	N. MARCH HUNNINGS, LL.M, PH.D (Editor, *Common Market Law Reports*)

Law in the United Kingdom

W. A. MCKEAN, PH.D
(Fellow of St John's College Cambridge)

RELIGION

GEOFFREY PARRINDER, MA, PH.D, DD, D.LITT (HON)
(Professor of the Comparative Study of Religions, University of London)

SCIENCE

Science, Medicine, and Technology
Technology

JOHN NEWELL, B.SC
(Assistant Editor, Science, Industry and Agriculture, BBC External Services)

Environment

GEOFFREY LEAN
(Editorial Staff, *The Observer*)

SPORT

DOUG GARDNER
(Sports journalist, *United Newspapers*)

PREFACE

PERHAPS the most significant feature of the Annual Register for 1977 is the selection of documents. They include two massive texts, the new Constitution of the USSR and the constitution of the Chinese Communist Party, both promulgated during the year. It seemed to the Editor and his advisers important that readers outside Russia and China should know under what terms those two vast and powerful countries, exhibiting different brands of marxism, are governed, however far constitutional forms may diverge from political practice. To that divergence another document, Charter 77 of Czechoslovak protesters, bears eloquent witness. All these indications have to be borne in mind in judging the fourth text we print, the Madrid declaration of the Spanish, French and Italian Communist leaders. Clearly the advance of Eurocommunism has to be seen in a context of political and social ideologies, much wider than that of its possible repercussions upon Nato and upon United States attitudes.

The only major change in organization of the Contents is the separation of Equatorial Africa from the more southerly belt of that Continent, where problems and events centre particularly upon the still white-ruled countries. The Malagasy Republic has been shifted from Part VI (Equatorial Africa) to Part VIII (Indian Ocean). Part XV, on the Arts, has been re-ordered to bring the performing arts, visual arts and literature into distinct chapters.

ACKNOWLEDGEMENTS

The Advisory Board again gratefully acknowledges its debt to the Royal Institute of International Affairs and other institutions for their advice and help with sources, references and the provision of documents, figures and maps. The Board, and the bodies which nominate its members, disclaim responsibility for any opinions expressed or the accuracy of any facts recorded in this volume.

THE ANNUAL REGISTER

200 years ago

24 February 1777. *The Marquis of Pombal dismissed.* It is hardly possible to conceive the joy that ran through the whole kingdom (of Portugal) from this change in the administration; for more than twenty years have the people of this country been grievously oppressed and afflicted . . . What numbers of all ranks has he shut up in dungeons, without their being guilty of any other crime than standing in his way! Figure to yourself these feeding on scanty portions of rotten sardines (a fish resembling our sprat) and broa (an inferior kind of bread) without ever being indulged with physicians or confessor; without any social intercourse, without even seeing the chearful face of man.

150 years ago

8 August 1827. *The death of George Canning.* At the very moment when he reached the pinnacle of his fortunes, he found himself left almost alone by those whom he had hoped to use as coadjutors . . . His care-worn appearance betrayed that the mind was ill at ease within: mind and body panted equally for repose. Soon after the rising of parliament he was visited by an attack of illness, which seemed, however, to yield to medical treatment, and he went down to the duke of Devonshire's seat at Chiswick, to seek tranquillity and enjoy a purer air. The disease returned; inflammation had commenced; . . . and Mr. Canning expired at Chiswick (the same house in which Mr. Fox had breathed his last), on the morning of the 8th of August, after having been prime minister for only four months . . . His fancy was elegant and prolific; his taste was exquisite; . . . he was never inflated or inane; it would scarcely be possible to select from his speeches a single sample of bombast . . . He was the most unyielding opponent of all the schemes which, for more than thirty years, had thrown the world into confusion under the name of reform: and he had done his country much good service in maintaining the integrity of her existing institutions.

100 years ago

9-10 December 1877. *The Russo-Turkish War.* Several of the Russian armies of invasion had been placed in jeopardy from deficient numbers and incompetent generals, but now, by the fall of Plevna, 100,000 men were set at liberty for offensive purposes. Besides these, large reinforcements had been brought into the field, and in the latter policy of the Russian war-direction, talent, not favouritism, placed officers in important commands. The Russians having, in fact, completely recovered from the critical position in which their own shortcomings and the successes of the Turks at Plevna in July and September had placed them, were now prepared to prosecute their onward march.

50 years ago

21 December 1927. *Greyhound racing.* A deputation of members of Parliament of all parties, headed by Mr. J. H. Thomas, waited on the Home Secretary to urge him to take steps for dealing with the evils attendant on the sport of greyhound racing. Introduced early in the year, this practice had soon become amazingly popular, and new tracks were continually being opened. The popularity of the entertainment was confessedly due, not to its merits as a sport, but to the facilities it afforded for gambling, and many people were afraid that it was developing into a social evil of the first magnitude. Mr. Thomas laid especial stress on the urgent need of preventing betting by children.

ANNUAL REGISTER

FOR THE YEAR 1977

EDITORIAL

THE twelve months whose events are recorded in this volume might be dubbed by many a year of violence. Internationally, it witnessed continued war in the Horn of Africa and Spanish Morocco, fresh war in Indo-China, and ghastly atrocities in Cambodia and Uganda, to name only two of the worst of many countries where murder, torture and other physical violence by rulers against the ruled was the prevailing mode of life. The terrorism and counter-terrorism of the 'war of liberation' in Rhodesia were intensified. Peaceful Bermuda erupted in riots. The world's news was stained by assassinations, kidnappings (which afflicted Italy terribly) and aeroplane hijacks, among which the most notorious were the abduction and murder of a West German industrialist, the South Moluccan seizure of a Dutch school and train, and the hijacking of a Lufthansa plane—in aid of terrorists already behind bars. Domestically, in the United Kingdom, although violence in Northern Ireland slackened from its peak it was still nauseating in detail and intolerable in scale; and violence in schools, among football crowds and in street demonstrations shocked the public and strained the forces of law and order. Figures of violent crime, here and elsewhere in the West, continued to rise.

Before we conclude, however, that throughout the world some disease of violence is endemic and increasing in clinical frequency we must do two things: we must put these events in historical perspective, and we must classify them into distinct phenomena which have different causes and different cures—if cures there be. The main classes, which can nevertheless overlap, are open international war, governmental violence, terrorism whether national or international (including hijacking and threats to hostages), individual violent crime for gain or sexual lust or other motive, and crowd violence however motivated.

Such a sorting-out reminds us that none of these violent symptoms is new, nor even, *prima facie*, conspicuously worse than in the past, though they may be taking novel forms. Two theatres of open warfare in Africa in 1977 have been mentioned: in neither of these was there a state of war as recognized in classical international law. Morocco, Mauritania and Algeria (through its protégé Polisario) fought in the Sahara without any open declaration which would entail both obligations and rights; Ethiopia was threatened not by frank invasion but by armed revolts from north and south notoriously supported by outside countries; Cambodia and

A

Vietnam fought fiercely long before the existence of war was admitted; Rhodesia was not legally at war with any of its neighbours, from whose territory and with whose aid aggression against it was mounted. The fact that these wars were not legally respectable did not make them less real or less devastating. It merely reflects the sad truth that to outlaw war by multinational peace pledges or United Nations charters does not change the conditions that lead to violent international action. The maintenance of global peace by a balance of deterrence—for which we must be thankful—can actually enlarge the risks of war (or warlike strife) between non-nuclear countries well aware that the great powers will not intervene to stop it lest they perilously confront each other.

We used to talk wistfully, in League of Nations days, of 'peaceful change' as the necessary corollary of the outlawry of war. The regrettable fact is that peaceful change, in the sense of anaesthetized territorial or governmental surgery, has happened only in the rarest circumstances, where powerful external countries have an interest in it and no interest in quarrelling over it. The map of the world has indeed been radically altered in the last thirty years by the new independence of four-score countries; but where this was not accomplished by violence it was achieved by the resignation of the former imperial powers which had lost either their capacity or their will to resist it.

Had white-ruled Rhodesia not unilaterally declared its independence the same pattern of change to popular self-rule would probably have been followed there too over the past 15 years. As it was, the pseudo-independent regime demonstrated the inefficacy of sanctions short of war—the international strategem of non-violence—and incurred illegal war which began to prove a more effective lever.

The illegitimacy of the regime did not legalize the external violence against it, let alone the methods thereof. The regime was illegal only in the sense that it rejected a nominal sovereign incapable of enforcing its sovereignty—a not unusual situation in modern history—and that it was not recognized by any but a very few other countries, contrary to the usual practice of accepting de-facto regimes at their effective value. The external violence was and is as much an affront to international law and order as was, say, the Indonesian attempt to overthrow the British colonial regime in Sabah or the American attempt to overthrow the Castro regime in Cuba at the Bay of Pigs. Yet that violent assault in southern Africa, using methods of terrorism, has been not only tolerated but actually applauded by Western countries which should have been the first to deplore it. It was even endorsed by the World and British Councils of (Christian!) Churches. If we do not like violence in the world scene we cannot afford to make exceptions on political or racial grounds. Where would that lead us in our domestic affairs?

That brings up the next category, governmental violence, by which is meant all forms of torture and cruel punishment, deprivation of life or liberty without trial and due process of law, physical brutality or coercion by official forces. This is indeed globally endemic. Scarcely a government in the world has clean hands. Repression in Chile is matched by repression in Soviet Russia. Britain itself is arraigned before the European Court of Human Rights for wrongful methods of interrogation in Northern Ireland: strong-arm police activity is notorious in most Western countries and accepted as a fact of life almost everywhere else. Amin's countless murders were but a grotesque and disgusting caricature of the physical force that had been used to sustain power in many pseudo-democratic countries in Asia, Africa and Latin America.

There are, of course, often sound excuses for the exercise of official violence, as well we know in Britain when subjected to Irish terrorism. Murderous men and women armed with guns and grenades cannot be confronted only with the weapons and behaviour of the rural policeman. Violence on one side induces violence on the other. And this works both ways. There is every excuse for violent action by reformists oppressed by violent regimes that allow no peaceable way of changing the existing order. The process of violence and counter-violence is self-escalating. But the example, the norm, is set by the top dogs, the governments: those who live by violence risk perishing by violence. The critical question is whether the world is more or less democratic than it was, say, 20 years ago— meaning by democracy not any particular electoral procedure or franchise but the existence of freedom of speech and association, equality before the law and a lawful means of changing the government by popular will, conditions which dissolve the excuse for violence. The answer is not obvious, but—remembering in the historical foreground Spain, Portugal and Greece—it is probably 'more democratic', that is to say, politically less violent.

Indeed one of the most notable and pleasing world-wide developments in 1977 was the rising clamour for 'human rights'. President Carter's idealist stand might not yet have had much clear effect, but it became a beacon for world opinion. Amnesty International gained the Nobel Prize for peace in recognition of its stalwart work for political prisoners. Charter 77 (reproduced in full in this volume) was a momentous effort of protest against violation of human rights, relevant not only to Czechoslovakia but to the whole communist world. The principles of human rights were held aloft by many participants in the Belgrade conference which reviewed the working of the Helsinki agreement. Positive progress in assertion of the basic rights of citizens in countries claiming to be civilized, rather than counter-violence, is the true response to political violence by governments.

Terrorism, a form of political violence, is a word often on our lips but seldom defined. Its essence is not mere violence, but coercion by terror, compelling people to do that which they would not otherwise do by dread of death, injury or pain, either for themselves or for others. It is obvious that the appropriate direct victims of terror are not those in official power or in armed forces, who are usually both well-protected and tough in resistance, but ordinary people, who are not—aircraft crew and passengers, African villagers, shoppers in Belfast or Birmingham, peaceable business men or their children who can be ransomed for money to serve the terrorists' cause. Terrorism is a specially hideous and shameful form of violence because its implicit object is to strike at the innocent, the unsuspecting and the weak.

Though not peculiarly a phenomenon of the present time (certainly not in the form of terrorization of civil populations, which is as old as war and revolution), it has today a shape, or shapes, and a prevalence which are both new and alarming. Its characteristic contemporary shapes are 'urban guerrilla war' and the seizure of individuals or the whole occupants of buildings or aircraft for ransom against threats to their lives and limbs, the ransom being either money or release of other terrorists or both. Clearly these methods reflect at the same time the vulnerability of complex modern life and the sophistication of terrorist organization.

The most dangerous perpetrators of terrorism are professionals at the game. Professionals are typically more interested in their skill and performance than in the use to which their output is directed: the professional scientist makes his discoveries regardless of whether the eventual product is a nuclear bomb or a power station, the professional surgeon operates with as much zeal to save the life of a criminal as that of a philanthropist. The typical professional terrorist has inchoate anti-establishment aims which can hardly be called ideals: the Baader–Meinhof Group and the Japanese United Red Army are professional terrorist organizations, rather than devotees of a particular cause. The causes they nominally espouse are so diverse, even self-contradictory, as to defy summation, except as destruction or nihilism. Security agencies believe them and the Latin American Junta de Coordinacion Revolutionaria to have a transnational centre in Paris for interchange of propaganda, training, planning and personnel. Their operations are circular: terrorism to release terrorists or to gain more funds for more terrorism, which thus becomes an end in itself.

Terrorism is a crime which can be met only by relentless confrontation. Its ostensible political objects are irrelevant, whether they be the overthrow of a regime in Africa, the creation of an all-Ireland republic, the independence of South Molucca, or the destruction of multinational companies. The defeat of the Lufthansa hijack in Mogadishu through international cooperation was a milestone in the defence of human life and civilized order, another mile forward from the Israeli rescue at Entebbe in 1975. Refuges for hijackers and other terrorists were, however, still open in Cuba, Libya and South Yemen.

Stern confrontation is requisite at the lowest as well as the highest levels. Thus in Northern Ireland, where terrorism has bred extortion rackets and with them has become a regular industry, the critical problem in 1977 was not a problem in politics but a problem in crime.

The growth in violent crime of a non-political, unorganized kind is certainly a disturbing feature of social statistics in most Western countries. The statistics may, however, exaggerate the reality. Much violence in the past went unrecorded, because it was internal to classes or areas where police interference was prudently minimal, or because the victims shirked complaint to the authorities, or because a great deal of juvenile crime was summarily punished, or because records were ill-kept. The novels of Dickens or Trollope do not suggest that the streets and parks of London were safer a century ago than they are now. Bill Sykes and his Nancy were far more typical of London's East End than they would be today. Nevertheless the rising curve of violent crime, in cities especially, over recent years is an inescapable fact.

Many explanations have been offered. If they are sought in social and economic conditions, the paradox is that crime advances while poverty lessens, housing standards rise and the welfare state provides for the disadvantaged. Though 'Satan finds work for idle hands to do', the curve of violent crime bears no affinity to the curve of unemployment. Drug-taking may be an ancillary cause, which generates its own cycle of crime, but it is not a primary cause: no one imagines that suppression of drug traffic would radically alter the overall crime patterns.

The most plausible explanations lie in the weakening of parental and school discipline, the uprooting of stable communities, the disappointment of overblown expectations, the permissiveness of latter-day social and moral codes, the decay of the work ethic and sense of personal responsibility, the insinuating example of violence on the television screen, and in some cases a decline in the capacity of the forces of law and order to police the streets and the conduct of likely wrong-doers. All these causes probably contribute. If we do not like the effects we must tackle the causes, all of them, though some may be ineluctable. The state cannot escape much of the responsibility: it makes the laws which ratify the permissive society, it controls most of the schools, it has a monopoly of urban planning, it musters the forces of law, order and punishment.

Clearly it has a special responsibility in respect of crowd violence. A few notorious contemporary examples do not prove that this phenomenon is waxing, or peculiar to the present. On the contrary, riots and the conflict of rival crowds were more frequent and more dangerous in past times, whether we look at episodes in British social history, at industrial warfare in America, at pogroms in Europe, or at intercommunal massacres in India. The misbehaviour of football spectators or the clash of pickets with police in an English strike is milk-and-water stuff by comparison with the past of crowd disorder.

One of the basic truths about violence as a condition of society is that our standards have risen. We no longer turn the pages indifferently on reports of violence as being 'only what you would expect' of slum-bred soccer supporters, or of the 'submerged tenth' in poor city neighbour-hoods, or of roughnecks on an industrial site, or of ignorant religious fanatics. The media, especially television, daily depict the violence to which we used to turn a near-blind eye. Instant communication tells us of violence anywhere in the world. Some sorts of violence are actually promoted by publicity, which is what their fomenters seek.

Man is by nature a violent as well as a social animal. By nature he fights for himself and his family, for his home, his territory, his tribe, his group. Through the millennia of his evolution, his innate violence has been tamed or canalized by a social order reinforced by the transcendental sanctions of religion. The social order of mankind itself has of necessity been upheld by forms of violence. Only very recently, on the evolutionary time-scale, has the imposed order been refined by laws, democracy, inter-national compacts and the rest of the apparatus of peace, order and social cohesion to a point where violence is the abhorred exception rather than the accepted rule. At any phase of the system's development, there is probably an irreducible minimum of violence, expressing that inborn strand in the character of mankind. In 1977 the world had obviously not yet secured that irreducible minimum, given its existing social and govern-mental institutions. But on a historical view the minimum had fallen and the approach to it had narrowed. The past year was one as much of consciousness of violence as of violence itself. It was a year in which concern for human rights, oppressed by violence, became a major inter-national issue, not a mere philanthropic plea. And that growth of con-sciousness, that heightening of conscience, may surely be counted an advance.

I HISTORY OF THE UNITED KINGDOM

Chapter 1

THE SILVER JUBILEE

In Britain and many parts of the Commonwealth, 1977 will be remembered as Jubilee year, when Queen Elizabeth II's loyal subjects celebrated the completion of 25 years of Her Majesty's reign. The Queen and her Consort the Duke of Edinburgh travelled widely in the Commonwealth, meeting the people not only in select bands at ceremonies and entertainments but also in streets and playing fields in friendly and informal 'walkabouts'. Such visits and personal contacts were made likewise in all the four countries of the United Kingdom (including the different regions of England), save Northern Ireland where walking among unfiltered crowds was omitted for the sake of Her Majesty's personal safety (see p. 48). In the hundred days which the Queen spent on her UK tours, she travelled 8,000 miles and kept 800 engagements.

The British celebrations, which by the Queen's express wish involved the least possible expenditure of public money in hard times, and included countless street parties and village functions up and down the country, reached their peak on 7 June. That Tuesday was declared an extra bank holiday, after the 'Whitsun' holiday (now divorced from the ecclesiastical calendar) on the previous day, when, late in the evening, the Queen lit a great bonfire in Windsor Great Park as a signal for starting similar conflagrations at beacon points throughout the Kingdom. On the Tuesday she drove in state with Prince Philip in the gold coach led by a grand procession from Buckingham Palace to St Paul's cathedral for a service of thanksgiving; walked thence to Guildhall for a luncheon given by the Lord Mayor, talking freely on the way with young and old people at the kerbside; and returned to the palace in an open carriage escorted by the Household Cavalry. A damp cold day deterred none of the enthusiastic crowds who cheered Her Majesty and the Prince on their way; *The Times* numbered them at a million, but as this would have meant an average of 50 deep on both sides of a three-mile route it must be taken as a symbolic rather than an actual figure. The rain held off until the moment the Queen reached home again, but even then a heavy shower seemed to send none away, and the countless millions who did actually watch the scene on television will never forget the sight of that huge throng packed round the Victoria Memorial and funnelled hundreds of yards back along the Mall, utterly cheerful and orderly, with homemade banners bearing such slogans as 'Liz Rules OK' or 'It's ERii Jubilee', cheering and waving insatiably as time and again the Queen and the Royal Family appeared on the balcony.

Close-ups of faces of all ages and colours showed not just dutiful loyalty but real happiness, the most memorable mark of all the celebrations, belying the illusion that economic difficulties had depressed the spirit of the British people. The great mass of them of all classes, indeed, showed by their ecstatic cheers, and the manifest joy of their celebrations, that Her Majesty was held in deep affection and the Monarchy in unshaken respect, not least because it demonstrated the virtues of stability, family solidarity and high moral standards which were specially treasured in an unsettled and permissive era.

Other grand occasions for the Silver Jubilee included a water pageant and fireworks on the Thames on 9 June, reviews of the Fleet at Spithead on 28 June, of the British Army of the Rhine in Germany on 7 July, and of the Royal Air Force. A succession of Jubilee tours of the Commonwealth in which the Queen travelled 56,000 miles was completed on 2 November when Her Majesty returned from Barbados in a British Airways Concorde.

In her speech at the Guildhall banquet, Queen Elizabeth said: 'When I was 21, I pledged my life to the service of our people and I asked for God's help to make good that vow. Although that vow was made "in my salad days when I was green in judgement" I do not regret nor retract one word of it.' It was in that spirit of service that Her Majesty desired the Silver Jubilee Appeal which was headed by the Prince of Wales to be devoted to the youth of the nation and Commonwealth, especially to helping young people to help themselves through service to the community. The Appeal had raised £13 million by the end of the year.

Chapter 2

A LIBERAL–LABOUR PACT

WHEN Parliament reassembled in January, the Government, on a strict party count, was in a minority in the House of Commons, and even with its usual fringe adherents (two Scottish Labour Party members, and two Roman Catholics from Northern Ireland) its majority was nil. Its lack of mastery of the House was signalled on 7 February when it was defeated by one vote on the second reading of its Redundancy Rebates Bill, which would have obliged employers to find 60 instead of 50 per cent of the statutory compensation paid to laid-off employees. But its first major defeat was on a matter of far greater importance.

The Bill to set up assemblies in Scotland and Wales, commonly called the Devolution Bill (see AR 1976, pp. 34-36), was making very slow progress in Committee, where the Government had to make a number of concessions, including a provision for consultative rather than binding referendums. The Government therefore moved on 22 February to impose a guillotine on the remaining stages. The motion was defeated by 312 votes to 283; the majority included 22 Labour MPs, and 15 more abstained. Without a guillotine it was obvious that the Bill would never carry through the House unless all other business were sacrificed, perhaps not even so. Although the Government continued to uphold its own devolution proposals it invited leaders of all parties to discuss 'how they might be improved, so that what finally reaches the statute book should reflect the widest possible agreement'. The talks took place, though the Scottish Nationalists (SNP) refused to take part, but evinced no more agreement than had been displayed in the Commons.

Both major parties were divided. The Tory leadership even appeared at one time to be back-pedalling on its commitment to a directly elected Scottish assembly without legislative powers; on the other hand, Mr Edward Heath, speaking in Glasgow on 15 April, went further than the Government in calling for revenue-raising powers for the Scottish assembly. If Parliament got it wrong again, he said, 'we shall not only fail the genuine aspirations of the people of Scotland but we shall also hasten the break-up of the United Kingdom'. On that point, the Queen herself was charged by Scottish Nationalists with expressing a political view when, acknowledging loyal addresses from the two Houses of Parliament on her Silver Jubilee on 4 May, she said: 'I can never forget that I was crowned Queen of the United Kingdom of Great Britain and Northern Ireland'. The next day, however, the Prime Minister coolly observed that Her Majesty was only reflecting Government policy.

On 26 July Mr Michael Foot, the Minister in charge of devolution, made a statement to the House of Commons. In the next session, separate Bills for Scotland and Wales would be introduced. Among other changes, the Judicial Committee of the Privy Council would be the sole tribunal to determine issues of *vires* and on those grounds would scrutinize Bills from the Scottish and Welsh assemblies before they received the Royal Assent. The Government would allow a free vote in Parliament on proportional representation. The block grants to finance devolved subjects would be based on a percentage formula that would be maintained for a period of years. No independent taxing powers would be granted in the Bill, but the Government would view sympathetically any proposals from the assemblies to supplement their block grants with tax revenue.

Meanwhile the Government's parliamentary weakness had been increasingly manifest. In February the examiners of private Bills in the House of Lords ruled that the Bill to nationalize aircraft manufacture and shipbuilding was 'hybrid' because of its discrimination among different firms; unable to press it through the consequent slow procedure, the Government decided to drop ship-repairing from it—the very issue on which the two Houses had been in conflict (see AR 1976, p. 19). Thus

A*

amended, it secured its third reading without a division on 15 March. To avoid risk of defection by the Labour left the Government shirked contesting an Opposition motion to adjourn the House after a debate on public spending on 17 March, and it was carried by 293 votes to none, the SNP providing the two No tellers. Mrs Thatcher described this as 'defeat with dishonour' and continued: 'No Government has ever sunk so low as this one in refusing to put its policies to the vote of the House of Commons on a matter so central to the function and purposes of Parliament'—a somewhat over-heated description of a manoeuvre in parliamentary tactics on both sides.

The Leader of the Opposition put down a no-confidence motion which was due for debate on 23 March. Defeat for the Government would clearly entail its resignation and a general election, and on the figures its parliamentary position was perilous. The state of the parties in the House of Commons was as follows: Labour 310, Scottish Labour 2, Conservatives 278, Liberals 13, Scottish National Party (SNP) 11, Plaid Cymru 3, United Ulster Unionists 8, Independent Ulster Unionists 2, SDLP (Northern Ireland) one, Irish Independent one, Speaker and chairmen of committees 4, vacant seats 2. A bare majority, if all available members went into the lobbies, required 315 votes. Although Mr Enoch Powell was reported to be urging his Ulster Unionist colleagues to support the Government, their votes were unreliable. The Government therefore entered into negotiation with the Liberals.

On the day of the vote the Prime Minister and the Liberal leader, Mr David Steel, issued a joint statement. A joint consultative committee would be set up, under the chairmanship of Mr Michael Foot, Leader of the House, to examine Government policies before they were presented to Parliament, together with Liberal proposals, though its existence would not commit either side; there would also be regular meetings between the Prime Minister and Mr Steel and between the Chancellor of the Exchequer and the Liberals' chief economic spokesman. The Cabinet undertook to introduce a Bill for direct elections to the European Parliament in the current session and to consult the Liberals on the electoral method, taking full account of their commitment to proportional representation and allowing a free vote on this issue; to make progress on devolution in consultation with the Liberals, again putting PR to a free vote; to provide time for the Housing (Homeless Persons) Bill, favoured by the Liberals; and to restrict the Local Authorities (Works) Bill (later dropped) to legalizing existing 'direct labour' activities. For their part, the Liberal Party would work with the Government in pursuit of economic recovery at least until the end of the current parliamentary session, when both sides would consider whether the experiment had been of sufficient benefit to the country to be prolonged.

Four members of the Cabinet (Messrs Benn, Millan, Orme and Shore) were reported without denial to have opposed the 'Lib-Lab' pact but to have agreed to abide by a majority decision. Mrs Thatcher denounced it as 'shabby, devious manipulations'. Mr Steel claimed that it had 'stopped socialism' so long as it lasted. Its advantage to a Government which was teetering on the edge of an election that it appeared bound to lose, and which had already carried most of the socialist measures in its current programme, was obvious, but its effect on the electoral popularity of the Liberals was yet very much in doubt. Its first fruit was a victory for the Government in the no-confidence debate by 322 votes to 298.

The first by-election of the year, caused by the appointment of Mr Christopher Tugendhat to be a European Commissioner, had been in the safe Conservative seat of Cities of London and Westminster, where on a low poll the Tory majority was increased by over 2,000, with a swing of nearly 10 per cent from Labour. On 31 March, at Stechford, the seat likewise vacated by Mr Roy Jenkins (see AR 1976, p. 16), with a swing of 17·4 per cent, the Conservatives captured the seat from Labour. Simultaneous by-elections, caused by the resignation of Mr David Marquand and the death of Mr Anthony Crosland (see p. 37 and OBITUARY), were held on 29 April at Ashfield and Grimsby, both previously safe Labour seats. On current electoral form, the Conservatives had expected to win Grimsby, but not Ashfield, a mining constituency: the reverse happened. At Ashfield, with a swing of over 20 per cent, a Labour majority of 22,915 was converted to a Conservative majority of 264; at Grimsby, with a swing of 13·8 per cent, the Labour majority fell from 6,982 to 520.

In all three constituencies, in the first tests after the Lib-Lab pact, the Liberals fared disastrously, losing 2,959 votes at Stechford, 3,579 at Ashfield and 6,359 at Grimsby. The irregular result at Grimsby, a major fishing port, was attributed partly to anti-Common Market feeling, rife in the area and adopted by the Labour candidate. At Saffron Walden, on 7 July, following the death of Mr Peter Kirk (see OBITUARY), although the Liberals easily held their second place to the Conservatives, they saw their share of the poll reduced by 5 per cent: 4½ per cent voted for an anti-EEC candidate. At Ladywood, Birmingham, a small constituency with a large immigrant element, in a poll of only 42·6 per cent of the electorate on 18 August, Labour held the seat by a majority reduced from 9,739 to 3,825, a swing of about 10 per cent to the Conservatives. All the rest of the ten candidates lost their deposits, the Liberal vote falling from 3,086 to 534, fewer than the 888 (5·7 per cent of the total vote) given to the National Front (fascist-racialist) candidate. At Stechford, too, the National Front had beaten the Liberals into fourth place. So far, those critics of the Lib-Lab pact were vindicated who held that it would make former Liberal supporters think they might as well vote Labour, or, if they shrank from that, abstain or vote Conservative.

Direct elections to the European Parliament, together with their method, were an issue on which members of both the Labour and Conservative parties were divided. On the Government side particularly, a large number of MPs, who had opposed Britain's continued membership of the European Community in 1975 (see AR 1975, pp. 12-19), and who had never swallowed the verdict of the referendum and Parliament and would regurgitate it if they could—'false democrats', Mr Roy Jenkins called them—were hostile to any move that would enhance the Community's prestige and parliamentary independence; a much smaller minority of Conservatives thought likewise, and in both parties there were many opposed to any form of proportional representation for Strasbourg —a Liberal plank—because they feared it might become a precedent for similar reform at Westminster.

The European Assembly Elections Bill was published on 24 June. The Bill itself embraced a form of proportional representation, the regional list system, allocating Scotland 8 seats, Wales 4, Northern Ireland 3 and the English regions 66; but the 'first-past-the-post' system was also presented as an alternative electoral method. The second reading was carried on 7 July by 394 votes to 147; no fewer than six Cabinet members and 26 junior Ministers voted with the minority.

On 28 July, in an exchange of letters between Mr Steel and Mr Callaghan, the Lib-Lab pact was renewed for the coming session 'so long as the objectives set out in the Chancellor's statement of 15 July are sustained by the Government' (see p. 21). This implied that Liberal support would be withdrawn if the Government failed to get overall union consent to its pay strategy or made significant exceptions in the public sector. Among the particular measures required of the Government were reintroduction of the European Elections Bill, which the Government would use its best endeavours to carry into law in time for the Community's target date; the promotion of new legislation for devolution to Scotland and Wales on the lines indicated by Mr Foot on 26 July (see p. 9); and continued consultations with the Liberals 'with a view to determining the priorities in the Queen's speech' and other matters. In reply the Prime Minister wrote: 'I confirm the Government's position on the particular issues to which you refer, and agree that we should continue consultations already begun on other possible measures that might be brought forward in the next session.'

One Liberal MP, Mr Cyril Smith, dissented from this fresh concordat, and another, Mr Jo Grimond, while acquiescing, had written to Mr Steel: 'I am against renewing the pact . . . The long-run danger which I see is that the more Liberals collaborate with Labour the more difficult it will be to break out.' Speaking on 17 June, Mr Steel had justified his policy in these terms: 'In the autumn we shall either be fighting an election on the basis that the Labour Party has proved unable to govern in a purposeful and coherent way, or else we shall be sustaining a Government in office with an agreed programme which will include some Liberal content.' A Tory victory, he went on, could lead to social disorder.

The future of the pact was naturally the focus of debate at the Liberal Party's annual Assembly in the week beginning 26 September. Despite a warning from the Association of Liberal Councillors that because of it the party was 'bleeding to death', the Assembly approved continuance of the pact by a large majority on a show of hands, with a rider demanding that all Ministers and a majority of Labour MPs should vote for PR in elections to the European Parliament. Mr Steel told delegates that the pact 'marked the beginning of the return to sanity in this divided country', and added: 'We have begun to change, just slightly, the way in which Britain is run. Now we have to demonstrate that if this much can be done by a tiny band of Liberals outside Government how much more could be done by a larger group inside the next Government, and still more by a Liberal Government itself.' In debate Mr Cyril Smith had said that the Prime Minister could 'pull the rug from under us any time' by calling an election: since Labour was in a minority the Liberals could have done more by exerting their muscle outside the Government. After the vote he resigned as Liberal spokesman on employment and declared that he would not campaign nationally for the party.

The Liberal Assembly had been preceded by the secession of Mr Peter Hain, the militant anti-racialist Young Liberal leader (see AR 1976, p. 12), to the Labour Party. The Tory conference was preceded by a much more significant translation, that of Mr Reginald Prentice, MP, a member of Mr Wilson's and Mr Callaghan's Cabinets until December 1976 (see AR 1975, p. 7 and 1976, p. 20), who resigned from Labour and joined the Conservatives on 8 October, saying 'I was forced to the conclusion that the only way we can prevent this country going on a further lurch down the marxist road is for the Labour Party to be soundly defeated at the next election.' Mrs Thatcher welcomed him into her fold but Labour supporters were outraged and demanded that Mr Prentice resign his Commons seat, which he refused to do: a former Labour Chief Whip called him a 'nauseating traitor'. Another eminent defector from the Labour Party was Mr Paul Johnson, for many years editor of the radical weekly, *The Statesman*.

The highlight of the Tory conference was a rousing final speech by Mrs Thatcher, who echoed Mr Prentice by exclaiming 'Britain beware! The signpost reads "this way to the total socialist state".' But amid her denunciation of controls and restrictions she insisted that a Conservative Government would be 'a truly moderate government' and that confrontation with the unions was far from inevitable. 'A strong and responsible trade union movement is essential to this country and its rights must be respected', she said; but 'the belief that those rights take precedence over all other rights and even over the law itself could be fatal'. She went on to restate a thought which she had surprisingly thrown out in a television interview on 18 September. If, she said at Blackpool a month later, a few men with great power were to hold the nation to ransom, it would be the Government's duty to act through Parliament. The conflict would be one between the unions and the people. 'It is in that context, and that context only, that I have suggested a referendum to test public opinion. In these special circumstances I say "let the people speak". I hope and believe the situation will never arise.'

All the party conferences, of which the Liberals' was the first, had a pre-election atmosphere. In this respect the mood of the Labour Party had altogether changed since the bad days of the summer by-elections. The respite afforded by the Lib-Lab pact had witnessed a dramatic change in Britain's financial fortunes, though not in its industrial performance (see p. 27). No doubt largely in consequence, opinion polls showed a sharp decline in the margin of electoral superiority of Conservatives over Labour. Through the recess Ministers had been making speeches stressing at the same time the need to continue existing policies of restraint and the glowing opportunities of the future, with hints of fiscal benefits soon to come. 'We can begin to look the world in the face', said Mr Callaghan at Bristol on 16 September, 'with a sound currency, a strong balance of payments, a falling inflation rate and a people with determination to succeed'. 'We need to look ahead', he continued, 'not for one or two good months, but to a whole five-year perspective in which we will restore Britain's industrial strength and competitiveness'.

The Labour Party conference, held at Brighton at the beginning of October, carried by an overwhelming majority a composite motion supporting the Government's economic strategy. Addressing the conference the Prime Minister said that the Government's priority was to vanquish inflation and unemployment and to use the revenues from North Sea oil strategically to modernize British industry. 'Back us or sack us', was his call, and the answer was not in doubt.

Seeking to check inflation through control of public expenditure and the money supply was not the only respect in which the Government displeased its left-wing supporters by borrowing conservative clothes. Other such matters included worker participation in industrial management, housing, transport and local government finance. The report of the committee on 'industrial democracy' under Lord Bullock was published on 26 January. The majority report recommended compelling companies employing 2,000 workers or more to compose their boards of equal numbers of worker representatives elected by trade unions and ownership representatives elected by shareholders plus a number (less than one-third of the board) of co-opted directors. The idea of supervising boards with worker representatives, distinct from boards of management, as practised in West Germany and elsewhere, was rejected. A minority report, signed by the three employer members of the committee, claimed that the proposed form of 'industrial democracy' would be seen by many trade unionists as a means of changing the structure of society by bringing industry under union control.

On 28 January the Prime Minister promised that the Government would bring in a Bill on industrial democracy 'by the summer'. This promise was not fulfilled. Action on the Bullock report was delayed by two main obstacles. Politically, not only the Tories but also the Liberals, having their own ideas on co-partnership in industry, were opposed to the majority recommendation, especially to the election of board members by the unions rather than the workers directly. Opposition was also encountered from both sides of industry. Management was united in its hostility, but many trade unionists were also highly doubtful, fearing that worker directors would become part of the managerial complex rather than champions of their constituents, and that the unions would be hamstrung in their traditional posture of contest with management. The Prime Minister suggested to leaders of the Confederation of British Industry on 15 February that Bullock be put aside in favour of worker participation below board level, and on 24 February Mr Edmund Dell, Secretary of State for Trade, told the Society for Long-Range Planning: 'It will be the Government's best endeavour to come forward with proposals that command widespread acceptance. It will be widely agreed that management must not be hindered in its efforts to achieve success for the company.'

On 19 May the Government published a 'green paper' (consultative document) on local government finance. It rejected proposals for a local income tax or other new source of revenue to replace rates, but offered reform of the rates system, under which capital valuation of property would replace hypothetical rental as the basis of tax from 1982 onwards, with the probable result of raising domestic rates at the bottom and top ends of the housing scale, lowering them in the middle. This was followed by a white paper on transport and a consultative paper (long delayed by political in-fighting) on housing on 27 and 28 June. The prime themes on transport, said Secretary of State William Rodgers in the House of Commons, were maintaining public transport, especially in rural areas, and enlarged responsibility and powers for local authorities. There was no question of major cuts on the railways, which had been widely feared. A 'modest and selective' road programme would be maintained at the current year's reduced level. The Opposition spokesman on transport, Mr Norman Fowler, observed that the white paper was as significant for what it omitted as for what it contained—no nationalization of ports, no extended public ownership of road haulage, no penalties on the use of motor cars, no deliberate shift of traffic from roads to rail and water transport.

The proposed housing policy was equally conservative. Responsibility for housing should be transferred from central to local government.

Council rents should be raised in step with incomes. A better balance should be struck between building new houses and repairing old ones. No change was indicated in the tax relief on mortgage interest, which had been held by many on the left to give an unfair subsidy to home-owners. Greater opportunities should be afforded for people to buy their own homes, including special financial help for first-time purchasers. A financial intermediary was suggested to raise 'stabilization funds' for building societies whose interest rates would otherwise be at the mercy of fluctuating terms and volume of their deposits. Mr Michael Heseltine, the Conservative spokesman on the environment, called the consultative paper 'a damp squib, spluttering in the right direction'.

The Labour Party's national executive committee decided on 26 October to abstain from policy-making for 12 months. The general secretary of the party remarked that there was already enough policy to occupy Labour Governments for a decade. A different view was that of Mrs Thatcher. British feelings after better economic news, she said on 2 November, were like those of the children of Israel after the crossing of the Red Sea (an oblique reference to the label of Labour's 'Moses' which had been attached to Mr Callaghan); they were so relieved not to be drowned that they forgot the 40 years in the wilderness still to be faced.

Measures promised in the Queen's speech at the opening of the new session of Parliament on 3 November included separate devolution Bills for Scotland and Wales, a European Assembly Elections Bill, a Bill to give financial help to first-time home-buyers, and legislation on transport policy, aid to inner cities, redundancy payments to shipyard workers, and the reorganization of broadcasting following the report of a commission under Lord Annan (see Pt. XV, Ch. 1). Consideration would be given to measures to help small businesses.

The devolution Bills were immediately introduced, and on 14 November the Scotland Bill received a second reading by 307 votes to 263, the Wales Bill by 295 votes to 264 on the following day. On 16 November motions to impose a guillotine on both Bills were carried by majorities of 26 and 27. The objectors included nine Labour MPs, but seven who had voted against the guillotine in February went into the Aye lobby.

However, the Government received a shock when at the start of the committee stage the House by 199 votes to 184 threw out Clause I of the Scotland Bill which asserted that its provisions did not affect the unity of the United Kingdom, for different reasons the Liberals and the Scottish and Welsh nationalists voting with the Tories. A few days later, after many clauses had already gone undebated under the time-table, the House repeated, by 290 votes to 107, the opposition it had shown on the earlier devolution Bill to proportional representation for the Scottish Assembly.

When Parliament rose for the Christmas recess the Commons had reached Clause 38 of the Scotland Bill. Mr Pym, for the Opposition, protested that in a single day, thanks to the guillotine, the Committee had passed without debate clauses on such vital matters as the overriding powers of the UK Government on Bills and executive orders, the size of the Scottish Assembly and the position of the House of Lords.

In a by-election on 24 November at Bournemouth, East, caused by the resignation of a Tory MP, the swing to the Conservatives was 8·7 per cent: the Liberal vote, on a reduced poll, fell by two-thirds, and although the Labour vote also dropped drastically it sufficed to displace the Liberals from second place. Nevertheless Mr Steel claimed that it was still his party's paramount duty in the national interest to continue to support the Government. He held to that claim despite a severe jolt sustained on 13 December when the House of Commons on a free vote rejected by 319 votes to 222 the method of proportional representation proposed for the first elections to the European Parliament, notwithstanding the argument that the first-past-the-post system on which the House insisted must mean a breach of Britain's pledge to enable elections to take place in 1978. Four Cabinet Ministers voted against PR, and among all Labour MPs fewer than half voted for it. Nevertheless on the following day, after declaring earlier that those facts were calculated to destroy the pact, the majority of Liberal MPs resolved to continue to support it, accepting Mr Steel's view that it would be madness, by ending it, to force a general election on the issue of PR for Europe. A special Liberal Assembly was called for 21 January to debate the future of the pact, and Mr Steel made it clear that he would then stake his leadership on its continuance.

Observers of Parliament judged that, whatever the merits of the pact for the Liberals, its necessity for the Government had declined. For until the devolution Bills were through they could count on the general support of the Scottish and Welsh nationalists, and their legislative programme involved no measures likely to incur the united hostility of all non-Labour parties. Moreover if they could ride out until after the spring 1978 Budget the Prime Minister could choose his own date for a general election, regardless of the Liberals, in a favourable economic climate.

The Government suffered a defeat, though not an injurious one, in the reaction to revelations by a committee under Mr Justice Fay that grave financial mishandling had been committed by the Crown Agents, a body set up to make purchases for overseas Commonwealth governments which had plunged into property and fringe-banking business. The Ministry of Overseas Development, the Treasury and the Bank of England were implicitly criticized for failure to check or expose these operations. The Government proposed a secret inquiry to fix responsibility, a Labour MP successfully called for an emergency debate, and on 5 December by 158 votes to 126 the House rejected the Government's proposal on the grounds that the gross misuse of public money and allegations of official cover-up required public investigation. The Prime Minister was thus constrained to set up a tribunal under the Act of 1921, meeting in public and taking evidence on oath.

Despite such incidents and its precarious parliamentary position, the Government's confidence steadily grew in the latter part of the year. Instead of struggling to survive economically as well as politically, it was able to launch a public debate on the use to which the expected huge revenues from North Sea oil should be put in the coming five or ten years, a debate in which repaying past international indebtedness, investing abroad (including help to poorer countries), modernizing British industrial capital, absorbing unemployment, raising workers' living standards and strengthening the welfare state would be the main contenders. Attitudes towards socialism apart, Mr Callaghan had established himself as a popular Prime Minister, calm, cheerful, determined and in control of the dissident left of his party and Cabinet.

While Mr Callaghan's popularity grew, Sir Harold Wilson's public image, tarnished by his last controversial honours list and revelations in the Crossman diaries and elsewhere of an alleged 'kitchen Cabinet' at 10 Downing Street under his regime, was further dimmed. On 16 March Lord Brayley, whom Wilson had brought from the political shadows to ministerial office and the House of Lords, died when on bail on charges of conspiracy to defraud the company of which he had been chairman and of stealing money from it. And on 22 September Sir Eric Miller, former chairman of the Peachey Property company, who had figured in Sir Harold's resignation honours, committed suicide after a Department of Trade investigation into Peachey's affairs had led to police inquiries and exposure of Sir Eric's heavy indebtedness. As a prophylactic against future such scandals, a strong new political honours scrutiny committee was set up in May and gave notice that it meant to take its duties seriously. A third volume of the Crossman diaries, published in October, revealed that in 1968 Wilson had rejected the idea of a committee to check his honours list, because, he had said, they might make difficulties about his choices, for instance, of one of his economic advisers for a peerage, 'or on the other hand about some person they had never heard of'. Beyond doubt these episodes served to discredit and debase the whole honours system.

Chapter 3

WAGES AND PRICES

AT the end of 1976 a fainting pound had been revived by the grant of an IMF credit of £2,300 million backed by a 'letter of intent' pledging the Government to a regime of economic orthodoxy, which was partly embodied in Mr Healey's December 'mini-Budget' (see AR 1976, pp. 26-27). On 10 January the patient was further helped to its feet by the Bank for International Settlements, which opened for the Bank of England a $3,000 million credit facility available for two years and repayable over four. The Bank of England also negotiated a $1,500 million loan from a consortium of British, West German and American banks, the advances from the 'Group of Ten' in the previous summer having had to be repaid (see AR 1976, p. 23). The news that the international balance on current account had been in the black in December 1976 had an additional resuscitating effect.

At the start of 1976, the pound had been worth $2.024; a year later it stood at $1.702. Dearer imports caused by its decline were a major cause of the Government's failure to achieve its objectives in curbing price inflation (see AR 1976, p. 24, and p. 27 below).

The continued rise in the cost of living was one of two major influences upon the Government's endeavour to maintain a policy of wage restraint. The other was the mounting clamour of skilled, clerical, managerial and professional workers against the erosion of their 'differentials' for skill, training and responsibility. The schemes of voluntary restraint on wage claims accepted in the so-called 'social contract' between the Labour Government and the Trades Union Congress for the two years ending 31 July 1977 had been deliberately weighted in favour of the lower-paid. In the first year, wage and salary increases had been limited to a flat £6 per week, with a freeze above £8,500 per annum, in the second year to an average of 4½ per cent or £4 per week, whichever was the higher (see AR 1975, p. 32, and 1976, p. 23). These maxima, which inevitably became the norm, were observed almost universally, though 'wages drift' was higher than had been expected.

The dialogue between the Government and unions was conducted partly in organized discussions, partly in a succession of public speeches or statements by either side. Speaking at an overseas bankers' dinner on 31 January, Mr Healey, Chancellor of the Exchequer, said that fighting unemployment and cutting inflation were the Government's two main economic targets, and the one could not be achieved without the other. Unemployment would rise sharply if there were no third round of pay restraint. The Chancellor confessed that failure to make the necessary financial adjustments in the previous summer had had grave consequences, but claimed that his December measures (see AR 1976, p. 27) had transformed the situation and that the financial corner had been turned. In the House of Commons on 10 February the Prime Minister described a third year of pay restraint as 'inevitable policy'. 'Prices are the crux of the matter now', wrote Mr Jack Jones, retiring general secretary of the Transport and General Workers Union and principal architect of the original 'social contract', in his union's magazine in February, and on

3 March he called on the Government to introduce an immediate statutory price freeze in order to prevent a wages explosion. Mr Joe Gormley, president of the miners' union, however, dismissed the idea of a prices freeze as 'completely unrealistic'. There was not a cat in hell's chance of the miners' accepting a third year of pay restraint, he said.

On 29 March Mr Healey introduced his regular Budget. While offering £1,290 million in tax reliefs with immediate effect, he made a reduction in the basic rate of income tax from 35 to 33 per cent in the £, costing £960 million, dependent upon the acceptance of a new round of pay restraint. The Chancellor raised petrol duty by 5p a gallon, car licence duty by £10 a year and the tax on tobacco by the equivalent of 4p on 20 cigarettes. The temporary employment subsidy was prolonged through 1977-78 at a cost of £214 million, and an additional £100 million over two years was to be made available to local councils for construction in inner cities. The public sector borrowing requirement (PSBR) in 1977-78 would be about £7,500 million against £9,000 million forecast for the previous year (the actual out-turn was some £1,000 million less). Mrs Thatcher's immediate comment was that Mr Healey was in effect apologizing for the damage he had done in his previous nine maxi- and mini-Budgets: he boasted of removing 845,000 people from income tax by raising the threshold, but over a million had been brought within its grasp during his Chancellorship.

In the course of debate on the Finance Bill the Government suffered two major defeats. As early as 4 April the Chancellor had bowed to Liberal opposition to the increased petrol tax, which the Liberals held was a severe blow to rural communities, by announcing that the Government would accept a majority decision in Committee of the whole House, the petrol tax being separated from the tax on heavy oil. On 5 May a Liberal amendment stopping collection of extra petrol tax from 5 August was carried with Tory support. The Chief Secretary to the Treasury, declaring the Government's reluctant concurrence, said that the vote was dictated by party arithmetic and that the House might have to get used to that sort of thing. Then on 14 June the Government were defeated on seven amendments to the Finance Bill (known, from the two Labour members who promoted them, as the Rooker–Wise amendments), having the effect of reducing revenue by £450 million per annum through raising income tax reliefs and tying them in future to the cost of living.

The Chancellor's intention to cut income tax by 2p in the pound was thus seriously weakened by budgetary considerations, quite apart from the condition of agreement by the unions to a third phase of pay policy. The prospect of any such agreement, too, was swiftly fading.

On 3 April a meeting of 1,700 shop stewards of British Leyland declared its total opposition to a continuation of any pay policy. Mr Clive Jenkins, the highly vocal leader of the Association of Scientific, Technical and Managerial Staffs (ASTMS), referring on 6 April to the idea floated by the Government that industries or firms should be allotted an overall total, or 'kitty', of pay rises, to be distributed among different grades through collective bargaining, said 'kitty bargaining is for tabby-cats'. On 17 April Mr Jack Jones said that there must be a very early return to free collective bargaining: price control would be a vital factor in winning restraint by unions—a line followed shortly afterwards by Mr Hugh Scanlon, retiring leader of the engineers' union, AUEW. The Government did indeed introduce and carry a measure to tighten control of prices and give extra powers to the Price Commission, but this did little to stem the tide. On 6 July the annual conference of Mr Jones's usually moderate union voted, against the advice of its leaders, for unrestricted pay bargaining, and even for an end to the 'twelve-months rule' establishing a minimum of a year between successive pay settlements for any group.

After meeting the TUC economic committee on 13 April Mr Healey said: 'I am determined rather than confident that there will be a pay policy.' Speaking to a conference of the shop workers' union on 24 April he described the combination of inflation and unemployment as 'in the most fundamental sense a test of the ability of free trade unionism and democratic socialism to meet the challenge of the modern world'. His forecast, he said, that inflation would fall to 13 per cent in the last quarter of 1977 and to single figures in the second quarter of 1978 was based on the assumption that the increase in earnings would not rise into double figures in the next 12 months. The Prime Minister, after presenting a Labour Party rally in Wales on 2 July with an ecstatic portrait of Britain's future if Labour stayed in power, hinted that the first task was to beat inflation. 'Until we do, every wage rise which is not met from higher production is a ticket to the dole queue.'

The TUC economic committee met the Prime Minister and his colleagues on 12 and 13 July only to tell them that no third year of pay restraint was possible in view of rank-and-file opposition, and that the most the TUC leaders could offer was to back the 12-months rule. They had already expressed their hostility to attempts of a number of unions to evade it by postponing Phase 2 settlements in order to free their hands for quick big improvements in Phase 3.

On 15 July the Chancellor made a statement on pay policy and related fiscal measures to the House of Commons. The total increase in the national wages bill in the coming August–July period, he said, ought not to exceed 10 per cent. (This implied a substantially smaller rise in basic wages.) If the rate were as high as 15 per cent 'we would not get inflation down to 10 per cent at all, and it would be rising steadily through the second half of next year and into 1979'. Companies breaching the guidelines would be penalized through government purchasing policy and the price code. The Government would do everything possible to ensure that full account of the guidance was taken throughout the public sector. In debate the Prime Minister promised explicitly that the Government would keep the increase in earnings to no more than 10 per cent in 1977-78 in all those areas where it had direct control or influence: later the director general of the Confederation of British Industry declared: 'If the Government holds the line in the public sector the private sector in industry will do its damnedest to hold the line as well.'

Income tax, Mr Healey told the Commons on 15 July, would be cut by half the amount mentioned in his Budget, to 34p in the £. To offset wages policy, personal tax allowances and child benefits would be raised, the milk subsidy would be increased and the income limit for free school meals raised. These measures meant no net change in the PSBR, and strict control over public expenditure would continue.

The TUC economic committee, while ignoring the stated percentage limit, promptly endorsed the Chancellor's broad purpose. All its power and influence would be used to see that unions adhered to the 12-months rule. If unions made claims on the basis of making good the ground apparently lost since 1975 great difficulties would be caused. A group in a strong negotiating position might conceivably succeed in such an aim, but it would be at the expense of weaker groups. 'It would be quite impossible for trade unionists as a whole to do so without adding to the inflationary pressure.' The 'social contract' was not dead, averred the Prime Minister and the TUC's general secretary when jointly presenting on 27 July a document entitled *The next three years and into the 80's*: it was only taking a new form. A return to collective bargaining did not destroy the basis of Labour–union cooperation. The document called for a growth rate of 3 per cent per annum, a million more jobs to be found within three years, more training and retraining of workers, planning agreements with big firms, and limits on imports in key industrial sectors.

Already many groups of workers, both the more and the less favoured under past pay policy, were launching demands far beyond the 1977-78 guidelines. Railwaymen, for example, were calling for a 63 per cent rise, dockers and farm workers for around 59 per cent, the union of public employees for 30 per cent, ASTMS for up to 34 per cent, car workers for upwards of 20 per cent. The miners were sticking to a claim of £135 per week for face-workers, a rise of 90 per cent.

Policemen were another group demanding much higher pay. Negotiations between them and the Home Office broke down in February, and a growing demand for the right to strike was reported, a demand overwhelmingly endorsed by the Police Federation in a vote on 24 May. At the Federation's conference, on the following day, the Home Secretary was booed and his speech heard in silence. He told them there was nothing he could do on pay in Phase 2, but 'in the next round I am prepared to play my part in putting right all that has gone wrong between us since

July 1976'. The Federation's chairman, Mr James Jardine, declared: 'We want the full purchasing power of the Willink standard set in 1960' by a Royal Commission (see AR 1960, p. 55) 'to be restored to the police. This would require an increase of more than £15 immediately. We want a proper career structure and decent differentials.' Conservative leaders, while acquiescing in the Government's general pay policy, which they were doubtless thankful they had not the responsibility for enforcing, frequently expressed their favour for treating the police as a special case.

The police demand for 'decent differentials' was typical of a rising tide of revolt against the compression of pay scales and the frozen distortions of the 'wages explosion' of 1974-75. The official review body on doctors' and dentists' remuneration, awarding a rise of £4 per week under Phase 2 on 26 May, warned that it might not be able to carry the professions unless a 'rational and orderly pay structure' was restored. On 18 and 19 July representatives of general practitioners called for industrial action if they did not get a 15 per cent pay rise after Phase 2 was ended, and hospital consultants, likewise threatening industrial action, denounced the pay policy as 'a sham policy loaded against the weakest and those with a social conscience', including doctors, nurses, teachers and the police—an outburst which Secretary of State Ennals called 'deplorable and pointless'. The erosion of differentials in industry was well illustrated by a survey published in April which showed that while average wages for all workers had risen by 11·86 per cent in 1976, managerial pay had risen by only 1·8 per cent. At the top levels, it was reported around the same time that members of the boards of nationalized industries had seen the real values of their net salaries halved since 1972-73. On 5 August organizations representing a quarter of a million professional and salaried staff, including doctors, aimed a memorial at the Chancellor of the Exchequer protesting against the anomalies caused by two years of pay restraint. Such people, they said, had been prepared to accept disproportionate contributions to checking inflation, but continuance of policies which discriminated against them was now unacceptable.

Government spokesmen hammered away at their wage-holding policy. Thus the Prime Minister said in a radio interview on 31 July that if unions succeeded in getting high wage increases to make good lost purchasing power the result would be hyper-inflation. The Government had deliberately arranged such a loss as a necessary adjustment to the rise in oil prices—a somewhat disingenuous account, since a year and a half of wages spree under the Labour Government had intervened between the rise in oil prices and Phase 1 of the pay policy. Interviewed on 10 August Mr Healey said that the general level of pay settlements would have to be around 5 or 6 per cent. It was up to employers to judge whether productivity deals beyond such norms were genuinely self-financing. If unions in nationalized industries insisted on excessive increases the money would not be provided to pay them. The Government was prepared to fight any strikes in the public sector for claims outside the limit.

The crunch came at the annual Congress of the TUC at Blackpool in the first week of September. Addressing it as a guest speaker, the Prime Minister, in confident mood, declared that cooperation between the Government and the unions must not be allowed to wither away. He would have liked to have a third year of the social contract, but 'I am told it is not on'. Nevertheless he insisted that the 10 per cent overall limit on pay increases must be observed. On 7 September the Congress debated a resolution instructing general council to seek an immediate return to free collective bargaining, but confirming support for the 12-months rule, and calling for further reflation of the economy to reduce unemployment. The resolution was moved by Mr Hugh Scanlon, the engineering workers' leader, despite the naked opposition of large sections of his union to the 12-months rule, and opposed by the transport workers union despite the personal commitment of its leader to the rule, and was carried by the unexpectedly large majority of 7,130,000 to 4,344,000 on a card vote.

Now came the test of actual settlements. The first case to earn national notoriety was that of James Mackie and Sons, a Belfast engineering firm with 4,000 workers, which had agreed to a 22 per cent pay rise. On 20 September the Government warned the firm that unless it renegotiated the deal within the guidelines it would forfeit its export credit guarantees, a threat *pour encourager les autres* which drew much rebuke as using an official facility for a purpose totally different from that for which it had been provided by Parliament. The company and the unions stood their ground. Much weightier was the case of the Ford Motor Company, not only because of its size and its place in the crucial car manufacturing industry but also because the parent multinational company had decided, in face of strong competitive pressure from Belgium, Germany and the Netherlands, to site a new £180 million engine plant in Wales and might change its mind if labour trouble supervened. After an offer within the guidelines had been rejected by the Ford unions, the company's 'final offer', ranging from 10·5 to 13·2 with an average of just over 12 per cent, was referred by the shop stewards, without approval, to plant voting by members. All plants voted for acceptance, to the Government's relief, though the settlement was clearly beyond the guidelines. On 27 October, a day after the Metropolitan Police Commissioner had said that the police were closer to a strike than at any time since 1919, the Police Federation accepted a previously-scorned 10 per cent rise in pay, on condition that a far-reaching independent inquiry into the pay, status and conditions of the police was immediately set up under the chairmanship of the eminent judge Lord Edmund-Davis.

The early response to a third year of wage restraint was encouraging enough for the Chancellor to give further tax relief in an economic package or mini-Budget which he opened on 26 October. But the more directly relevant financial impulse was a great improvement in the balance of payments and an excess of government spending over revenue much less than had been forecast. Mr Healey raised personal tax allowances, granted a £10 Christmas bonus to old-age pensioners, allocated £9 million for police training and equipment and handed out other benefits to small firms, the disabled and overseas aid. The estimated cost of these concessions, together with an increase of government building expenditure of £400 million in 1978-79, was £3,347 million over 18 months, of which £1,090 million would fall in the current tax year. The Chancellor promised more in his April 1978 Budget if wage settlements remained moderate.

The measures clearly involved a modest degree of reflation—much less than the Labour left and the TUC had been demanding. The Treasury estimated that they would raise domestic output by $\frac{1}{2}$ per cent by the first quarter of 1978, making possible a $3\frac{1}{2}$ per cent growth rate in that year. The Opposition spokesman Sir Geoffrey Howe called the package 'a Budget of repentance' and Conservatives hammered away at the fact that the real value of tax allowances was still much less than it had been before Labour took office and inflation soared. The most striking utterances in the Commons debate, however, were those in which Mr Healey expressed thoughts which might have been those of any sound Tory. 'Public investment will not help the economy unless it produces a real return in terms of saleable goods at the prices they cost to produce', and 'an increase in living standards generated by tax reductions is infinitely better for the economy, employment and trade than an increase in living standards generated by excessive wage increases'.

On the wage front the mini-Budget was swiftly followed by developments in contrary directions. In October British Leyland workers voted decisively, in plant ballots, to accept in principle the company's plan to rationalize its wage structure through a single, all-union, nationwide annual negotiation, which it regarded as vital to permanent improvement of its industrial relations, then in such a sorry state that many thousands of workers were currently laid off and the financial position was desperate. The plan had been opposed not only by many Leyland shop stewards but also by the leaders of the Transport and General Workers, the largest union in the company. Unfortunately it involved breaches of the pay guidelines which caused its deferment. A week later the miners voted equally decisively in a pithead ballot to reject a National Coal Board offer of a productivity scheme which could have raised earnings by up to £20 a week, and resumed their demand (see p. 22) for huge straight wage increases and other concessions. Meanwhile workers in power stations, against the advice of their unions, were operating a work-to-rule and overtime ban, as sanction for a demand for costly 'fringe benefits', action which strained electric supply and caused local black-outs at peak times to the injury as much of industry as of the public. On 11 November their shop stewards voted for a return to work without having gained any of their main objectives, their leader exclaiming, 'We have lost the battle and should accept the fact. The Government, the public and the TUC are all against us.'

On 14 November 43,000 members of the Fire Brigades Union began an official strike in support of demands for higher pay and shorter hours far in excess of the 10 per cent guideline. This was the first confrontation with a public service union and the Government were determined not to give way. As the Prime Minister told a conference of the electricians' union on 23 November, 'wherever the Government or the local authorities are engaged in wage negotiations, everyone watches like a hawk, ready to pounce if the Government breaks its own guidelines'. Contingents of the three armed forces, mainly 10,000 soldiers, were drafted for emergency firefighting duty in cities. Opposition leaders, while deploring the strike and promising its support for the emergency measures, sought to make some capital out of it. The Government, said Mr William Whitelaw, deputy leader of the Conservatives, had driven the armed services, the police and now the firemen to an unprecedented pitch of discontent. There must be another look at the pay of all who risked their lives for the country.

Indeed, while public opinion polls showed majority sympathy for the firemen, popular attention began to switch to the substantially worse pay and conditions of the men and women in the armed forces who were striving to do their work. On 9 December the Government accepted a Tory private member's motion calling for betterment of the pay and conditions of the armed services as soon as pay policy permitted. They undertook that recommendations of a review body would be accepted, though they might have to be phased. Public sympathy for the firemen began to ebb as their strike continued. The TUC general purposes committee voted not to support the strike because its objective would entail a breach of the 12-months rule: a TUC campaign against the 10 per cent policy would be fruitless because 'the Government is not likely to be deflected from its present course of action'. Firemen's leaders called this a betrayal. On 9 December they rejected, against TUC advice, a settlement offered by the Government, which, while confining an immediate pay rise to 10 per cent, promised that after November 1978 firemen's pay would be linked by stages to that of the top quartile of industrial workers, an undertaking exceptionally proof against any adverse changes in the economy. The strike continued into the New Year.

The Government's firm defence of its strategy had been fortified by acceptance of settlements at or near the 10 per cent mark by local authority manual workers, merchant seamen, busmen and others in the public and private sectors. (It seemed to be conveniently forgotten that 10 per cent had been laid down as the maximum for earnings, not the minimum or norm for basic wages, always slower to rise than actual pay packets.) Early confrontation with the miners was averted when the NUM executive voted to adhere to the 12-months rule, which deferred their high wage demand to March. But the most striking development on that front was the acceptance by pit after pit of local productivity agreements giving substantial extra pay at once in return for output, thus undermining the balloted rejection of a national productivity offer. Mr Scargill, the Yorkshire miners' leader who had led the campaign against productivity agreements because they would 'set pit against pit and man against man', described the majority vote of the NUM executive to countenance local productivity schemes as 'one of the most disastrous decisions in the history of the union'. Even in his own area pits were jumping on the productivity bandwagon.

Meanwhile there had been a change in the general economic circumstances. A rapidly improving balance of payments (the current account for the year showed a net credit, estimated at £59 million, for the first time since 1973) and a huge inflow of foreign funds caused the UK's currency reserves to rise to over $20,000 million—a record figure—in October, and on the last day of that month the Bank of England ceased its policy of selling sterling to hold down the pound's value. Immediately the pound rose 6·3c to $1.8405. At the end of 1977 it stood at $1.917 and at 65·2 per cent of its 1971 value in terms of a basket of sound currencies, against 44·1 per cent at the beginning of the year. While this appreciation made British exports dearer and imports cheaper, it greatly helped to keep down the rate of price inflation. The year-on-year increase of the retail price index in December was 12·1 per cent; still more significantly, wholesale (factory input) prices had virtually stabilized.

The Government's posture in face of its international creditors became assured rather than suppliant. In a new letter of intent to the IMF published on 15 December the Chancellor of the Exchequer undertook only that the Government would continue the anti-inflationary thrust of its policies. He expected the Public Sector Borrowing Requirement to be around £8,600 million in 1977-78. He believed a 3½ per cent annual growth rate in the second half of 1977 through 1978 was possible. Another consequence of the inflow of money had been a dramatic fall in interest rates. By rapid steps the Bank of England's minimum lending rate was cut from 14½ per cent at the start of the year to 5 per cent in October, to revert to 7 per cent in late November. This stimulus to investment acted slowly, however, and unemployment remained high—1,371,000 in Britain in December (seasonally adjusted) or 5·9 per cent of the workforce, although this represented a small improvement on the previous month.

Chapter 4

THE GRUNWICK AFFAIR

EVEN before the end of Phase 2, the strike record in 1977 was bad, after two good years. More than a million days were lost in March alone. The car industry was, as usual, particularly hard hit, both by strikes of its own workers and by stoppages in ancillary industries, notably electrical component manufacture in July and August, most of them reactions to pay restraint or demands by skilled groups like toolroom workers for special treatment or separate negotiation. Such a demand also led to a damaging strike of aircraft maintenance engineers, and at the peak of holiday movement in August air traffic was disrupted by a go-slow and subsequent strike by assistant air traffic controllers demanding payment of an increase of pay negotiated in 1975 but frozen by Phases 1 and 2 of the pay policy. Port Talbot steelworks were brought to a halt for ten weeks in April–June by a strike of 520 electricians. Strikes by power workers, lift engineers and firemen, among others, directly hit the public in the autumn. The total of working days lost through industrial action in 1977 was 9,985,000, far from a record but much higher than in the previous two years.

The most extraordinary industrial dispute of the year, however, occurred in a small company in a far from essential industry, the north London firm of Grunwick, processors of films. It began on 23 August 1976, when a number of workers walked out, to be joined by others to a total of about one-fifth of the work-force. The strike was essentially for the right to be represented by a union in negotiation with management, none of the workers having hitherto been members of a union. The majority of the Grunwick workers were Indian and Pakistani immigrants, mostly women. The strikers found a willing union in the Association of Professional, Executive, Clerical and Computer Staff (APEX). The company was advised that if it wished to avoid the risk of compulsory reinstatement of some of the strikers it must dismiss all of them, which it did. Shortly afterwards APEX successfully sought to enlist the support of the trade union movement generally in a contest which it evidently could not win on its own, for the factory continued operating with a workforce who showed no signs of wanting to strike or join a union.

The dispute reached the status of a national *cause célèbre* in two ways. First, at the instance of APEX, postal workers began early in 1977 to 'black' Grunwick mail, contrary to a legal decision (later overturned by the House of Lords) in the case of *Gouriet* v *Union of Postal Workers*, which concerned an attempted 'blacking' of mail for South Africa (see Pt. XIII, Ch. 2, Law in the UK). This interference with the mail was not officially supported by the UPW, and eventually ceased, after various vicissitudes, including the suspension of some recalcitrant postal sorters. Secondly, in June members of other unions from different parts of the country took part in a sequence of mass pickets of the Grunwick factory. (Three Government Ministers had appeared at different times on the picket lines.) These were met by large forces of police endeavouring to protect workers entering and leaving the factory, subject to the pickets' right of peaceful persuasion, and inevitably led to violence: on 14 June there were 84 arrests and on 23 June, when 2,500 picketers appeared and a policeman was severely injured, there were 53, including Mr Scargill, the militant leader of the Yorkshire miners, who was later cleared.

The mediation of the Advisory Conciliation and Arbitration Service (ACAS) was offered but rejected by the company. However, APEX exercised its statutory right to have ACAS determine the issue of recognition of a union for purposes of collective bargaining, a determination not binding in law. ACAS, having polled the dismissed strikers but not the workers presently employed, particulars of whom the company refused its request to supply, recommended recognition. The Grunwick management sought a declaration that the finding was invalid, was rebuffed in the High Court (Lord Widgery, LCJ) but succeeded in the Court of Appeal, where Lord Denning, MR, described ACAS's partial poll as a 'fatal mistake'. ACAS appealed to the House of Lords (see Pt. XIV, Ch. 2).

The next stage was the Government's appointment of a Court of Inquiry consisting of Mr Justice Scarman (later elevated to Lord Justice), a trade unionist and the chief industrial relations executive of British Leyland. Its report was published on 26 August. After reviewing the history of the dispute and rapping both parties on the knuckles for heightening the confrontation, it recommended that the strikers be reinstated or, if no vacancies existed, be financially compensated, and that the company give effect to its own declaration of willingness to allow any worker with a grievance to be represented by a union to which he or she belonged. The key question of union recognition for collective bargaining purposes was left to be settled after the House of Lords decision in the ACAS case.

Since this little local dispute had taken the shape of a contest of general principle, the most important part of the Scarman report was its reflections on the clash of rights and freedoms claimed respectively by the contestants. Those, it said, with which the company's stance was associated were the right to conduct a legitimate business within the law as one judged best, the freedom to refuse to join a union and the right to free choice of employment. Those with which the union's stance was associated were the right to join a union, the freedom of peaceful assembly (picketing) and the right to just and favourable conditions of work. All these rights and freedoms on both sides, the report observed, were enshrined in the European Convention of Human Rights, the Universal Declaration of Human Rights or the European Social Charter. The report continued:

All rights and freedoms for which each side contends are recognized by English law, but failing agreement their adjustment to each other is to be sought by the processes of conciliation and arbitration under the guidance of ACAS. The sanctions of the law (such as they are) are indirect and are not those associated with the execution or enforcement of a judgment delivered by a court of law.

In short, the Scarman inquiry passed the dispute back to the contestants and ACAS, with certain recommendations having no legal force.

The union, APEX, accepted the report and offered to negotiate in a conciliatory way on its implementation, promising in particular not to seek a closed shop. The Grunwick management, however, in the person of Mr George Ward, managing director, flatly rejected the recommendations on reinstatement or compensation for the strikers, on the grounds that no vacancies existed and that the loyal work-force would refuse to work alongside those who had been harassing their lives and threatening their jobs for the past year. Mr Ward went further, denouncing the court of inquiry as having been established for a political purpose and having reached conclusions unrelated to its findings of fact, which he claimed wholly substantiated Grunwick's case. The philosophy behind the report, declared Mr Ward,

is the philosophy of the corporate state. . . . The report makes constant references to Grunwick's scrupulous observance of the law and praises the company for this. But the praise is qualified . . . Grunwick is held to have behaved according to the 'letter of the law', but somehow to have fallen short of apprehending the niceties of 'the policy of the law' as the Government and powerful vested interests would wish that policy to be. But when this 'policy of the law' is examined, it turns out to have nothing to do with law of any description and everything to do with conciliating trade unions. . . . Perhaps Britain would be happier if the individual had less freedom, though Grunwick does not think so. But it is a matter for the British people as a whole through their representatives in Parliament and not for courts of inquiry. So long as an area of freedom exists, a good citizen has every right to enjoy it.

Thus a dispute over a few workers in a small factory was elevated to a controversy on fundamental political, constitutional and social issues.

The politicians were not slow to engage in it. Mr Booth, Secretary for Employment, vehemently denied that the Scarman inquiry was biased towards collectivism or was in any way political. Sir Keith Joseph, Opposition spokesman on industry, speaking on 1 September, criticized the Scarman report as either naive or slipshod in important respects. Mr James Prior, however, Opposition spokesman on employment, claiming to speak with the voice of the Shadow Cabinet and Mrs Thatcher, who was abroad, defended the Scarman inquiry and called for mediation. Later Sir Keith palliated this conflict of views as a difference of emphasis, his being on a point of principle, Mr Prior's being on pragmatic concerns; in particular, he agreed (as did Mrs Thatcher) with Mr Prior's view that experience had shown it was impossible to ban the closed shop by law.

The reconciliation was reinforced by the publication, before the Tory party conference (see p. 13), of an official Conservative pamphlet called

The Right Approach to the Economy, to which both Sir Keith and Mr Prior appended their names. It argued that a legal ban on closed shops could be not only ineffective but even harmful, but that closed shops must be subject to certain conditions, including a secret ballot of all workers, no enforcement against workers already employed, and exemption for individuals with strong convictions against joining a union, with a right of legal appeal. This compromise policy was adopted by the conference with scarcely any dissent.

The Grunwick strike—which was not itself about the closed shop—meanwhile continued. The APEX leadership eschewed any further invitation to mass picketing, but called on the whole trade union movement for support; and on 6 September the Trades Union Congress in Blackpool carried unanimously, though evidently with little enthusiasm, a motion admonishing all affiliated unions to continue and intensify financial and practical aid, and inviting the International Confederation of Free Trade Unions to help in stopping Grunwick's overseas business. The local strike committee, against the wish of APEX, went on with plans for mass picketing, and even attempted in mid-October to cut off Grunwick's water by vainly trying to persuade repair workers not to make good an interrupted supply. The mass picketing inevitably led to more violence, notably on 7 November when 42 police and scores of demonstrators from a crowd of 4,000 or more were injured and 113 people were arrested. At the end of November it was reported that the strike committee had voted against seeking any more mass pickets. Their case was not helped by a finding of the Central Arbitration Committee on 12 December that pay and conditions at Grunwick were not, as alleged by APEX, lower than those of similar workers elsewhere; but the strikers retorted that substantial improvements in the past year had been the result of their action.

A further blow fell on them when the unanimous judgment of five Law Lords was published on 14 December. While sympathizing with the dilemma of ACAS, the House unanimously upheld the Court of Appeal. Grunwick, said Lord Diplock, had done nothing unlawful. An employer was under no obligation to cooperate with ACAS in its consultations or inquiries in a recognition issue.

As the year ended, the strike was still in force, but mass picketing had ceased, the company continued in full operation, and the affair had ceased to agitate the general public.

Chapter 5

SOME DOMESTIC UPSETS

Vicissitudes of the Press

THE newspaper press suffered much from labour troubles in 1977. At different times *The Times* (13 January and 4 to 10 March), *Financial Times* (5 to 23 August), *Sun*, *Mirror* and *Daily Express* were stopped from publication by union action. On two occasions (*Times* on 13 January and *Sun* on 30 July) the cause was printers' objection to certain editorial matter critical of Fleet Street unions, action which the Press Council condemned as tantamount to censorship.

Blows for press freedom, however, were struck by the courts when, on 14 October, the Court of Appeal lifted a High Court ban on newspaper serialization of a book about the financier Jim Slater (who earlier in the year had been successfully defended against extradition to Singapore on charges of financial misconduct) and when the Appeal Court ruled on 29 November that a printing union had no right to prevent the *Daily Express* from printing extra copies to fill demand created by stoppage of the *Mirror*—a traditional ploy of newspaper unions. In the former case Lord Denning, Master of the Rolls, observed: 'The press should be free to publish fair comment on matters of public importance, and no court should grant an injunction to restrain a newspaper from doing so, except in the most extreme circumstances.' On an earlier occasion—a claim by distributors of *Private Eye* that libel writs taken out against them were an abuse of legal process—Lord Denning declared that 'the freedom of the press depends on keeping open the channels of distribution', but he was overruled by the majority of the Court of Appeal, Lord Justice Scarman remarking that injury to the freedom of the press was a matter for Parliament; the Courts had to administer the law. (The *Private Eye* action— see AR 1976, p. 393, and Pt. XIV, Ch. 2—was settled by all parties in May, with an apology and a contribution to the costs of the plaintiff, who withdrew his suit for criminal libel.)

The report of the Royal Commission on the Press was published on 9 July. It rejected all the forms of state aid or control which had been proposed in evidence from the political left, and was content to recommend a strengthening of the Press Council and the drafting of a code to regulate the closed shop in the press—a task which continued to baffle the rival representatives of editors and unions, especially the National Union of Journalists (NUJ). The closed shop issue was at the core of the most prolonged press strike of the year, at Darlington, where members of the NUJ refused to work with a newcomer who belonged to the Institute of Journalists and a number of former NUJ members who had joined the IJ.

For many weeks the 107-year-old *Northern Echo* and the *Evening Dispatch* were brought out by a skeleton staff, until, following a decision by a TUC committee to support the strike, printers refused to cross the picket lines and publication stopped on 2 August. On 6 December, however, the printers decided to return to work and publication was resumed; the general secretary of the National Graphical Association declared: 'We have no intention of ending up with a situation in which the NUJ has achieved its closed shop at Darlington with no newspapers in which to operate it.'

An equally tough line was taken by the new proprietors of Beaverbrook Newspapers—Trafalgar House, who bought the loss-making company from the Beaverbrook family for £14 million at the end of June—in face of industrial action by engineers in September. The engineers were treated as having dismissed themselves by breaking their contracts, and within a week they were back virtually on management's terms. Beaverbrook's managing director, Mr Jocelyn Stevens, who had said that Trafalgar House were not prepared to invest more money in the business unless discipline and order were restored to industrial relations, hailed the settlement as calculated to 'speed and create confidence throughout the industry' and predicted a new style of management in Fleet Street. Mr Victor Mathews, managing director of Trafalgar House, had declared at the time of the take-over: 'I am here to make profits, but I am also here to keep going a very important newspaper group'—he had undertaken to maintain all three Beaverbrook titles, the *Daily* and *Sunday Express* and *Evening Standard*, whose possible demise or merger with its rival the *Evening News* had caused wide consternation—and added 'By and large the editors will have complete freedom as long as they agree with the policy I have laid down', a formula applicable to every proprietor–editor relationship in history.

Racial problems

Relations between people of different races in Britain, though generally friendly, caused some pangs, and there were not lacking those who for political ends made the worst of them. Mr Enoch Powell continued to affront liberal opinion with his prophecies of doom. Civil war was in prospect, he declared in January, through 'the occupation, more and more intense, of key areas and key functions in the heartlands of the kingdom' by immigrant peoples differentiated by colour and culture. Some on the left fumed that he ought to be prosecuted for inciting racial hatred, but the authorities prudently held their hand. There had been much political pressure for the establishment of a register of those family dependents of previous immigrants who could in the future claim to join them; but the Home Secretary told Parliament in February that, having studied the

B

report of a committee on the problem under Lord Franks, he rejected the proposition of a register as unfair, expensive and impracticable. At the end of March a select committee of the Commons on race relations reported that one group, young blacks from the West Indies, presented a critical challenge. They were an acute case of the socially and economically disadvantaged, for whom the Government was urged to frame a comprehensive strategy.

A belief that inter-racial strife was more provoked than spontaneous gained some support from events. The most serious disturbance of the year occurred on an August Saturday in Lewisham, a London area with many black inhabitants, when a march by the extreme right National Front clashed with members of the extreme left Socialist Workers Party, and 56 policemen and many others were injured. From such diverse figures as the general secretary of the TUC and the chairman (a former Tory MP) of the Commission on Racial Equality came demands that all such marches should be banned; but the Home Secretary, Mr Rees, refused thus to curtail a traditional civil liberty, and was backed by the opposition spokesman on home affairs, Mr Whitelaw. The new Commissioner of Metropolitan Police, Mr David McNee, declared: 'I have no intention of abdicating my responsibility in face of groups who threaten to achieve their ends by violent means, come what may.' This was his attitude to the Notting Hill (Caribbean) Carnival which despite the nasty experience of the previous year (see AR 1976, pp. 30-31) was again held on the August bank holiday. The Carnival itself was generally peaceful and happy, but at its end groups of black youths raised mayhem, robbing and breaking shop windows, and many people were hurt and 53 arrested. Mrs Thatcher on television took the occasion to denounce the destroyers of democracy, the fascists and communists who wanted to destroy society: the courts should have powers to impose heavy penalties for violence and hooliganism at street demonstrations. At the Labour Party conference in October Mr Rees urged its members not to confuse racism with public order. He hinted that the Government would legislate for stricter controls over marches and meetings designed to incite hatred against a racial group, but no such measures figured in the subsequent Queen's Speech.

The controversy took a new slant when on 7 December the Labour Party devoted the whole of one of its regular party political broadcasts to an attack on the National Front. Many people thought that Labour had over-reacted to certain advances which the Front had made in by-elections (see p. 11), that it was clearly still a very long way from gaining a single parliamentary seat, and that this publicity would only play the Front's own game. The counter-argument was that fascist movements which would destroy Britain's free way of life must be exposed and destroyed before they gained respectability and weight under cover of civil liberty by playing upon popular prejudices and fears.

Appointments

Mr George Barlow to succeed Sir William Ryland as chairman of the Post Office.

Mr David McNee to succeed Sir Robert Mark as Commissioner of Metropolitan Police.

Professor Bernard Williams, professor of philosophy at Cambridge, to chair an inquiry into the laws on obscenity.

Mr Leslie Murphy, deputy chairman, to succeed Lord Ryder as chairman of the National Enterprise Board.

Sir Ian Barcroft to succeed Sir Douglas Allen as Head of the Home Civil Service.

Chapter 6

FOREIGN AND COMMONWEALTH AFFAIRS

BRITAIN held the ministerial chairmanship of the European Community in 1976-77. The general opinion both in Britain and elsewhere in Europe was that its performance was undistinguished. Personalities apart, this was no doubt due partly to preoccupation with domestic economic difficulties which weakened Britain's international prestige; partly to a lack of concerted enthusiasm for Europe in the Cabinet, several of its members who chaired Ministerial meetings in Brussels having been hostile to membership of the Community; partly also to the classic partition of British external interests between the Continent on the one side and the Commonwealth and the United States on the other.

Thus after a two-day visit to Washington in March the Prime Minister exulted over the 'coordination' of policies that he had achieved with President Carter and the evident strength of the 'special relationship' between Britain and the United States, a conclusion warmly welcomed by the leader of the opposition. On all major issues, Mr Callaghan told the House of Commons, the two countries were following similar paths. The Government's reaction to President Carter's démarche on nuclear power in April (see p. 64) was equivocal. Muffled on the proposal to stop reprocessing of nuclear fuel in the US and to scrap plans for a new generation of fast breeder reactors—both issues on which British intentions, subject to the findings of a public inquiry into a proposed big new reactor at Windscale, might well be different—the Prime Minister welcomed the effort to arrest proliferation of nuclear capacity and offered full co-operation in stopping the spread of nuclear material. Following the Carter initiative on human rights (see p. 62), the Foreign Secretary said on 3 March: 'It is no part of the Government's policy to promote campaigns of democratization. . . . Equally, the Communist countries must recognize that concern for human rights is an integral part of foreign policy in the Western democracies. . . . We have to balance morality with reality.'

Coming down to brass tacks, it took months of tough, cliff-hanging negotiation to reach at the last possible moment a new Anglo-American pact concerning mutual landing and related rights for civil aircraft to replace one that expired on 21 June. The outcome, though balanced, was far from pleasing to all British interests. And the conflict over landing rights for Concorde simmered and bubbled through most of the year. At last, on 17 October, the United States Supreme Court ruled that landing rights at Kennedy airport, New York, for an experimental period must no longer be withheld, and on 19 and 20 October the first Concorde landed and took off there, recording noise levels well below the maximum allowed for subsonic aircraft. A commercial service London or Paris/New York opened on 22 November, and a service London/Singapore on 9 December, to be promptly frustrated by the refusal of Malaysia to grant over-flying rights.

Mr Carter had a cordial public reception when he visited Britain in May for an economic 'summit' and broke away for a tour of the industrial north-east. The summit itself voiced aspirations for a trade revival led by the strongest economies, aspirations which by the end of the year had been largely disappointed. The Commonwealth Prime Ministers' conference, held in London and Scotland in early June (see Pt. X, Ch. 2), registered several important deflections of British policy, particularly over Rhodesia (see p. 38), though it contributed nothing new save many words to furthering the cause of a 'new international economic order' on which many poorer countries of the Commonwealth set great store.

Conflicts with the EEC on particular problems recurred. In Brussels on 1 March Mr Silkin, Secretary for Agriculture and Fisheries, said it was absurd that the Community should be stockpiling butter and then selling it at bargain prices to the Russians. Britain's traditional policy of sub-sidizing producers while keeping food prices low continued to conflict with the EEC's Common Agriculture Policy (CAP). Mr Silkin, in face of strong opposition from British farmers as well as Europe, stalwartly refused to accept devaluation of the 'green pound', used to convert CAP prices into sterling. In May the European Court of Justice ordered Britain to cease forthwith paying its subsidy to pig producers, though a definitive order would await a full hearing on the alleged conflict with Community law. In April, after a long squabble over an uplift of EEC farm prices, Britain accepted compromise figures little different from those which the Minister had previously denounced as inflationary. The popular standing of the EEC was not enhanced by a proposal that would have barred the name 'ice cream' from the normal British product because it contained little or no cream—'what about shoe cream?' people asked—but this example of bureaucratic logic was fortunately modified.

Disputes over fisheries simmered through the year. In January Denmark formally protested against the British claim to fishing limits based on Rockall (see AR 1976, map on p. 39). In May the European Commission rejected British and Irish proposals for an exclusive national 50-mile fishing zone. On 27 June, after EEC disagreement, Britain unilaterally imposed a ban on herring fishing in the North Sea, and imposed heavy fines on Dutch trawlers; but three weeks later the Community concurred in a temporary ban and later extended it indefinitely.

The controversy over direct elections to the European Parliament belonged as much to domestic politics as to foreign affairs (see pp. 10 and 17). But it helped to provoke an anti-Community campaign of considerable weight. The left-wing *Tribune* (whose name attached to a parliamentary Labour group) launched in May a campaign for withdrawal from the EEC. A former chairman of the Tribune group, Mr Arthur Latham, declared that 'an anti-Common Market platform could be an election winner'. Some of the by-elections indeed showed signs that the Common Market was again becoming an electoral issue (see p. 11). On 2 June Mr Benn, Secretary of State for Power, introducing a pamphlet sponsored by the Labour Common Market Safeguards Committee, while silent on direct elections, declared: 'The prospects for Labour in the next general election may well depend more on how a future Labour Government intends to approach the Common Market than on any other single issue.' His Cabinet colleague, Dr David Owen, retorted in a speech the following day: 'We must not continue to argue whether we should or should not be members of the European Community. Indeed we should put our viewpoint in that Community clearly, firmly and resolutely.' This policy line was elaborated and reinforced by the Prime Minister in a long letter to the secretary-general of the Labour Party which was published on the eve of the party conference. Firmly ruling out any question of withdrawal, he laid down objectives to be worked for from within, including maintenance of national governmental and parliamentary authority, freedom for members to pursue their own economic, industrial and regional aims, and radical reform of the CAP. 'We do not envisage any significant increase in the powers of the European Parliament.' Of these objectives Herr Genscher, West German Foreign Minister, was reported to have said at a ministerial meeting in Brussels on 9 October that Britain's aim seemed to be both to belong to Europe and to undermine it.

Dr David Owen had become Foreign and Commonwealth Secretary on 21 February in succession to Mr Anthony Crosland, who had died in office two days earlier (see OBITUARY), after setting a distinct and realistic stamp upon British foreign policy. A medical practitioner turned social-democratic politician, at 38 Dr Owen was the youngest Foreign Secretary since Anthony Eden. He had been Minister of State with special responsibility for European affairs and was an ardent supporter of the Community. He brought to overseas affairs a sense of freshness and a persuasive public personality. (For other simultaneous Ministerial changes, see DOCUMENTS.)

One of Dr Owen's earliest deeds in office aroused passionate controversy. On 11 May it was announced that Sir Peter Ramsbotham, a distinguished career diplomat, was to be abruptly replaced as ambassador in Washington by Mr Peter Jay, a young economic journalist of acknowledged brilliance, son of a former Labour Cabinet Minister and son-in-law of the present Prime Minister. The taint of nepotism faded, and the right of a Foreign Secretary to choose an ambassador attuned, in his belief, to Government attitudes and the needs of the time was acknowledged, but in Parliament and outside there were heated protests at the treatment of Sir Peter Ramsbotham, a successful and popular envoy, now removed to the Governorship of Bermuda, especially at the mendacious innuendo apparently whispered to journalists in the back rooms of 10 Downing Street that he was 'old-fashioned' and 'fuddy-duddy'. He himself behaved with impeccable tact and modesty.

It was Africa that created most problems for Dr Owen during the year. He was immediately confronted with the need for decisions about President Amin's bloody regime in Uganda (see Pt. VI, Ch. 1). Diplomatic relations had been broken (see AR 1976, p. 220)—the last few British officials were withdrawn in June—but Uganda was still a member of the Commonwealth, and public outcry was to be expected if Amin attended the Prime Ministers' conference in June. 'I do not think we would regard it as a slight', Mr Callaghan caustically told the Commons on 22 February, 'if he stayed away'. In the event, neither he nor any other Ugandans came to the Commonwealth conference, which broke all precedents in condemning the Uganda regime (see Pt. X, Ch. 2), but not before he had kept everyone on tenterhooks, even fostering reports that he was on his way to London *via* a neighbouring country, and had displayed his conceited eccentricity by proposing that the conference should consider the annual rotation of the Headship of the Commonwealth among its members' heads of state, a plan that would have brought him in due course into the place occupied by the Queen.

Rhodesia, however, presented a much harder problem. The adjourned Geneva conference (see AR 1976, pp. 41 and 250-1) was never reconvened, Mr Richard's tour of southern Africa having brought flat rejection of the Kissinger plan by both Mr Smith and the leaders of the Patriotic Front. In April Dr Owen visited southern Africa, where, contrary to policy previously expressed by the Prime Minister, he decided to go to Rhodesia itself. He hoped that his talks would lead to proposals for a new constitution to be put to Parliament in the session starting in November. Meanwhile the immediate aim was to stop people from thinking that armed struggle was the only solution.

The Commonwealth conference marked a distinct shift in British

Government policy towards approval of the guerrilla campaign. In its final communique it noted that 'the armed struggle has become complementary to other efforts, including a negotiated settlement'—which ever since UDI in 1965 had been the policy of successive British Governments. The rest of the text on Rhodesia was couched in such terms as to approve capitulation to the guerrillas' demands, including the immediate displacement of the Smith regime and the dismantling of its security forces.

After talking about Rhodesia with Mr Cyrus Vance, the US Secretary of State, in London, Dr Owen set out on his second mission to southern Africa on 25 August, accompanied for most of it by Mr Andrew Young, permanent US representative at the UN. The proposals published on 1 September, on the morrow of Mr Smith's triumph at a general election which Dr Owen had gratuitously deplored, though expressed as British policy were universally regarded as an agreed Anglo-American plan. Their main features were the immediate return to 'legality' by demission of all governmental authority to a resident British commissioner, named as Field Marshal Lord Carver; the creation by him of a Zimbabwe national army—based, Dr Owen said, on 'the liberation forces'; the introduction of a United Nations force during the transition period; the adoption of a democratic constitution, depicted in outline, with universal adult franchise and a Bill of Rights, under which independence would be granted before the end of 1978; and a development fund to be provided by Britain and the United States. The reception of the plan in Rhodesia was discouraging (see Pt. VII, Ch. 2). Lord Carver's exploratory talks on the spot with both white and black leaders appeared to meet with sharp rebuff, on the one side mainly in opposition to the plan for the security forces, on the other to the transitional regime including elections before independence.

The Foreign Secretary's reaction to Mr Smith's effort to reach an internal settlement, launched on 2 December, was cautious. And of a massive Rhodesian raid into Mozambique, reported at the end of November, he mildly observed that it underlined the need for an internationally acceptable settlement: British policy seemed to be returning to its previous stance of seeking whatever settlement could be shown to be approved by the peoples of Rhodesia, and treating the violent coercion as an incentive for such a settlement rather than an alternative road to a transfer of power.

Meanwhile the situation in South Africa (see Pt. VII, Ch. 3) had engaged Dr Owen's even more urgent attention. After Dr Vorster's Government had suppressed a number of anti-apartheid organizations and journals and incarcerated many black leaders on 19 October, the British ambassador to the Republic was recalled for consultations. On 4 November Britain voted for a UN Security Council resolution imposing a mandatory arms embargo on South Africa, but it had joined with the USA and France in previously vetoing mandatory economic sanctions.

Among other developments in foreign and Commonwealth affairs, agreement to reopen formal negotiations with Argentina about the Falkland Islands was announced on 26 April. A contingent of troops was airlifted to Belize in July, and naval units stood by, to deter, successfully, a Guatemalan irredentist threat. An international arbitration on undersea rights in the Western approaches awarded on 25 July an equal partition of the area between Britain and France (see INTERNATIONAL LAW). On 4 December 200 men of the Royal Regiment of Fusiliers were flown to Bermuda to back up local security forces in quelling riots that had followed the execution of two black men convicted of several murders, including in one case that of the former Governor, Sir Richard Sharples and his ADC in December 1972. The local Prerogative of Mercy Committee and Bermudian Ministers had advised against reprieve, and the Foreign Secretary concluded that he had no alternative but to advise Her Majesty not to intervene: abolition of capital punishment was, he said, a matter for the Parliament of Bermuda.

At the second annual meeting between the French President and the Prime Minister (see AR 1976, p. 42), held at Chequers on 12 and 13 December, President Giscard d'Estaing and Mr Callaghan agreed to set up an Anglo-French committee of officials to study industrial cooperation and identify new areas for practicable joint projects.

A report by Sir Kenneth Berrill, head of the Central Policy Review Staff (known popularly as the Downing Street 'think tank') on Britain's overseas representation was published on 2 August. Among its more controversial recommendations were:

More concentration on economic policy and export promotion, with appropriate administrative changes: fewer reports on foreign policy and greater use of emissaries from London.

Big reductions in British defence staff in Washington, Ottawa and Canberra.

A reduction in British information services overseas, including abolition of the British Council as a separate organization abroad: confinement of BBC external services to communist and Third World countries.

The disposal of expensive historic buildings occupied by posts abroad.

The closure of 20 missions in independent countries.

A 50 per cent cut in entertaining.

Less research work and storage of information.

The creation of a Foreign Service Group in Whitehall combining both home civil servants and the diplomatic service.

Protests from the diplomatic establishment were to have been expected, but they were strongly reinforced by pleas from publishers, business executives and others who paid tribute to the value of political and cultural work abroad and from many defenders of BBC overseas services who rejected the report's apparent view that friendly nations can be taken for granted and only the peoples of unfriendly or doubtful ones need to be persuaded.

The strongest popular objection, however, was to the report's premise that for economic reasons 'the UK's ability to influence events in the world has declined and there is very little that diplomatic activity and international public relations can do to disguise the fact. . . . It will almost certainly take longer than a decade for the UK to recapture an appreciable amount of the ground lost since the war. In our view, over the time horizon of this review, the scale and pattern of the UK's overseas representation should be broadly that implied by its present relative position in the world'. These dicta were challenged, not so much upon the regrettable economic facts behind them, as upon the deductions drawn therefrom. International influence, it was argued, did not stem only from economic power, any more than in an earlier era it had stemmed only from military might. The critics observed that, if the UK 'is now on a par in terms of world status with the three other medium-sized countries in the European Community', this situation was paralleled in the nineteenth century, perhaps the heyday of British diplomacy. They claimed that its links with the Commonwealth and the United States enhanced this historic European status. It was part of the business of diplomacy, in which the British were highly skilled, to redress shortcomings in military or economic muscle.

In a debate on the Berrill report in the House of Lords on 23 November it was attacked from all sides, including Labour peers, though it had a few supporters too. Replying for the Government, Lord Goronwy-Roberts, Minister of State, while cautious because, he said, they were studying it in detail, made clear that they had already rejected its major conclusions.

Chapter 7

SCOTLAND

On 22 February the defeat of a guillotine motion by a majority of 29 (see p. 9) meant the end of the original Devolution Bill, but the Liberal–Labour pact in March included a promise of support for a guillotine procedure on a redrafted Bill. In May, however, the Scottish Conservative conference abandoned its former commitment to a directly-elected Assembly. The Government's new proposals envisaged separate Bills for Scotland and Wales. The new Scotland Bill, which provided for a referendum in Scotland before any Act should come into force, was still being debated when Parliament adjourned at Christmas.

In the Scottish district council elections on 3 May Labour had a net loss of 120 seats, the Scottish National Party a gain of 96, the Conservatives a gain of 21 and the Liberals a gain of 14. Labour lost control in Glasgow, Dundee and Aberdeen and the Conservatives won control in Edinburgh. In Glasgow, where no party had an overall majority, a Conservative

B*

administration eventually took office, but with a Labour Lord Provost. Later in the year the SNP had two more gains in district by-elections and one in a regional by-election.

In January the unemployed total of 183,000 was again the highest recorded since the beginning of World War II, representing 8·4 per cent as against a UK percentage of 6·1. A White Paper on government expenditure in February provided for an increased grant to the Scottish Development Agency, but Scottish institutions pointed out that selective assistance to industry in place of Regional Employment Premium was likely to have a bad effect on Scotland, which had been receiving a considerable proportion of payments under REP. The unemployment figure, higher still in the summer, by the end of the year had again fallen to the January percentage, but Scotland was the only area to show a rise in December.

The Piper oilfield went formally on stream with the inauguration of the Flotta terminal in January. The Mesa Petroleum Company decided in March to apply for the development of the Brora field in the Cromarty Firth and Shell/Esso and the Conoco group made similar decisions in June and July in relation to the Fulmar and Murchison fields respectively. In the latter case it was also announced that the platform order would go to the Ardersier yard, from which a platform jacket was towed out for the Heather field in May. In February the Nigg yard had won a contract for a platform, but the towing-out of a platform for the Brent field for completion in Norway left the Ardyne Point yard empty in July. In August the Marathon yard at Clydebank announced orders for two rigs, one of which had previously been ordered speculatively by the British National Oil Corporation. In September the Methil yard won a share in building a platform for the Tartan field. BNOC was given an important role in February in the granting of licences for new oil exploration, and the claim of the Irish Republic for oil-prospecting areas off Mull was ignored.

An unusual industrial dispute started on 15 April when the pilots at Bristow Helicopters Ltd. at Aberdeen went on strike over the sacking of a pilot for refusing a transfer, but the strike ended on 2 June with an agreement for a public inquiry. The report of the inquiry, published in September, threw some blame both on the company and on the British Airline Pilots Association. The Boilermakers Society had agreed to the ending of demarcation at Govan Shipbuilders in January, and car workers at Linwood in December accepted a package of recommendations aimed at ending the sort of industrial strife which had caused a two-week strike in October and November and delayed production of a new Chrysler car.

Some criminal sentences continued to reflect the close connexion between Scotland and Northern Ireland. Members of the Orange Order were imprisoned in March and June for possession of arms and explosives. In May an Ulster Defence Association member was sentenced for attempting to send explosives to Ulster and in August a sentence was passed under the Prevention of Terrorism Act for collecting money for the Ulster Volunteer Force. Seven members of a Glasgow crime syndicate were sentenced to a total of 74 years' imprisonment in November.

There were legal innovations in the fields of licensing and marriage. The first licences for the opening of public houses on Sunday were granted in October. The Marriage (Scotland) Act made the calling of banns unnecessary and legalized non-Christian religious marriages from the beginning of 1978. In July Sheriff Peter Thomson was dismissed by the Secretary of State for 'political activities' in publishing a pamphlet, *Scottish Plebiscite*. The dismissal was endorsed by the House of Commons after a debate in December.

There was much controversy over proposals published by the Secretary of State in January for the reduction of the number of colleges of education from ten to six by closures and amalgamations. They were rejected by the House of Commons by a narrow majority in April and in December it was announced that all the colleges would be retained, but with reduced intakes and alternative use of parts of their facilities. Three major educational reports appeared during the year. In August the Pack report dealt with truancy and indiscipline. In September the Munn and Dunning reports dealt with the secondary curriculum and a proposed new Certificate of Education at the end of the fourth year.

Mr John Drummond, assistant head of music and the arts at the BBC, was appointed director of the Edinburgh Festival, to succeed Mr Peter Diamond in 1978. A great Scottish mountaineer died in January when Dougal Haston was killed while skiing near his home in Switzerland. The Scottish football team was the only UK team to win a place in the finals of the World Cup to be played in Argentina in 1978.

Chapter 8

WALES

FOR Wales, 1977 was a year in which industrial news firmly eclipsed the debate on the Principality's constitutional status. There was a polarization between the Wales TUC and the opposition parties, who pointed to the unemployment total of 91,000, and Government supporters who claimed that their regional policies and the Welsh Development Agency were creating new jobs in Wales. The Government's case was boosted by two announcements which were seen as forming a turning-point in the history of the Welsh economy. In March the British Steel Corporation seemed to have ended a period of uncertainty in the Welsh steel industry when it announced that it would be investing £835 million to double the capacity of the Port Talbot works and that the works at Shotton would be reprieved at least until 1983. Then in September the Ford Motor Company indicated that, having considered several European alternatives, they would be developing a £180 million engine plant at Bridgend which would eventually employ 2,500 workmen. These developments, taken with the completion of a further 30 miles of motorway in South Wales, seemed to promise a new prosperity and diversity for the regional economy.

The economic optimism of high summer soon gave way to a new pessimism. The Port Talbot announcement was almost immediately followed by a ten-week strike of electricians which caused 7,000 men to be laid off; the British Steel Corporation later disclosed a half-yearly loss of £80 million on its Welsh activities and the year ended with a world recession in steel which highlighted the high cost and low productivity of the Welsh steel sector. By December it was clear that not only would the £835 million investment have to be delayed, but there was also a question-mark over the whole future of an industry which remained the largest employer of labour in Wales.

Devolution, which had loomed large in the Wales of 1976, rather faded as an issue in 1977. Many thought that the possibility of a Welsh assembly had been ended once and for all in February when, with two Welsh Labour MPs voting against and three abstaining, the Government lost its crucial guillotine motion (see p. 9). Even its obvious intention to press on with devolution and the introduction of a Welsh Bill did not engender a public debate. Devolution seemed to have become a strictly parliamentary matter, and there was a general feeling that in Wales at least the story of devolution would end with the promised referendum.

The retreat of devolution did not preclude continued decentralization. Never before had the Secretary of State and the Welsh Office been so prominent in Welsh life. During the year the former indicated that he would be assuming responsibility within Wales for agriculture and fisheries, urban aid, higher education (except the university) and the work of the Manpower Services Commission. The Queen's Jubilee was widely celebrated in Wales, and a three-day royal visit was concluded by a procession through the streets of Cardiff with the Queen travelling in an open coach accompanied by a Sovereign's escort of the Household Cavalry. It was adjudged one of the Welsh capital's most splendid days.

Welsh domestic affairs saw a keen preoccupation with cultural matters. Several reports having identified another crisis for the Welsh language, the recommendation of the Annan Committee on Broadcasting (see Pt. XV, Ch. 2) that provision of a fourth channel for Wales be made a priority inevitably established Welsh-language broadcasting as a controversial issue. The Government accepted the urgent need for a Welsh-language channel but there were still protests over the lack of action and a strong feeling that a specifically Welsh body should be established to run the fourth channel in Wales. The Welsh Arts Council found itself in the public eye as never before; there was so much criticism of its artistic policies and so much talk of bias and favouritism that its chairman, Lady Anglesey, announced that the council would organize a public conference in 1978. The year's greatest artistic successes were achieved by the Welsh National Opera Company but there was continued disappointment at the failure to provide this splendid company with a purpose-designed opera house in Cardiff. As ever, sport was well to the fore in the Principality, and the successes of the Welsh rugby and soccer sides were a reminder of how much the current sense of Welsh identity is related to devolution in sport.

Chapter 9

NORTHERN IRELAND

THE year saw a dramatic change in the Northern Ireland situation, and a sharp drop in the level of violence. A total of 111 people lost their lives by violence, compared with 297 in 1976. Civilian deaths were down, although security forces' casualties were only slightly reduced. The number of bombings, shootings and armed robberies fell significantly, while the police reported a record total of persons charged and convicted of serious crimes. The success of the Royal Ulster Constabulary (RUC) in swiftly apprehending law-breakers was the most encouraging sign of a return to the rule of law. Violence from Protestant sources virtually ceased by mid-summer, after the breaking-up of units of the Ulster Volunteer Force (UVF), leaving the security forces free to concentrate on the IRA, which was finding it increasingly difficult to obtain recruits, arms, explosives and money, and rapidly losing support among the Catholic community.

On the political front, however, there was little sign of any progress towards the restoration of devolved government. With local parties and politicians in disarray, direct rule continued with remarkably little complaint. At the end of the year the Secretary of State reported that he detected no groundswell of opposition to it. This was partly to be explained by the improving security situation, and partly by a change of attitude by the British Government, which began to show more sensitivity to the Province's peculiar tensions. The personality of the Secretary of State, Mr Roy Mason, was no small factor in creating an improved psychological climate. His qualities of shrewdness, tenacity and resoluteness, allied to a Yorkshire taste for blunt speech, could scarcely have been more congenial to the average Ulsterman, and on at least two occasions he showed courage and political acumen of a high order.

Although the violence was to decrease as the year progressed, there was little sign of this in January. The year began as bloodily as any of the previous seven. Within hours, terrorism had claimed its first victim when a 15-month-old baby was killed in its mother's arms by a car-bomb. Later in the day a woman visiting friends in Belfast lost both legs when she returned to her parked car, and a youth of 18 lost an arm when a motorcycle bomb exploded outside his father's public house. It was a routine day of Ulster violence. In the weeks and months which followed, the killing of soldiers, policemen, UDR men and prison officers continued, while millions of pounds worth of property was destroyed by bombs. A sinister extension of terror appeared on 2 February when Mr Jeffrey Agate, the 58-year-old English manager of the giant American Du Pont factory at Maydown, Co. Londonderry, was shot dead by the IRA. A series of attacks on prominent businessmen followed, and on 14 March a Yorkshire businessman, Mr James Nicholson, on a day visit to the Strathearn Audio plant in West Belfast, was shot dead as he left the factory.

In March and April the Province lost two of its most eminent personalities. Lord Faulkner, the best known and most experienced of the Ulster politicians, was killed in a hunting accident in Co. Down on 3 March (see OBITUARY). Although he had recently retired from active politics, his untimely death emphasized the political vacuum in Northern Ireland. On 17 April Cardinal Conway, the Roman Catholic Archbishop of Armagh and Primate of all Ireland, died at his Armagh residence (see OBITUARY). Cardinal Conway had not wearied in condemning violence and calling for Christian reconciliation. In August it was announced that his successor was to be the historian, Dr Tomas O Fiaich of Maynooth College. Dr O Fiaich, a Crossmaglen man, made no secret of his republican sympathies, but repudiated violence.

Despite signs of an improvement in the security situation, the violence in the early months of the year still continued at a sufficiently high level to cause resentment in some sections of the loyalist population, who called for more determined action by the Government against the IRA. The most vocal proponents of this case were the Rev. Ian Paisley, leader of the Democratic Unionist Party (DUP), and Mr Ernest Baird, formerly of Vanguard. In April they threatened that if no measures were taken they would organize a strike, similar to that of May 1974, in order to force the Government's hand. The groups in favour of such a strike organized themselves into a United Ulster Action Council (UUAC), which on 25 April issued an ultimatum to the Secretary of State, giving him seven days to comply with their demands for a return to self-government and an all-out offensive against the IRA. Mr Mason met the challenge with characteristic determination, spelling out to the workers the economic consequences of another damaging stoppage and grimly promising that enough troops and police would be available to maintain the rule of law. A spearhead battalion of 1,200 troops was flown in, and all police leave cancelled. Housewives stocked their larders and the population prepared to endure a repeat of the May 1974 crisis (see AR 1974, pp. 68-69).

The strike began at midnight on 2 May. From the outset it was clear that it did not have undivided loyalist support. The UUAC plans had been criticized by the Official Unionists, Vanguard and the Orange Order, and a majority of the Belfast shipyard workers had voted against a stoppage. Thousands of people went to work as usual, often defying threats of intimidation; factories stayed open and electricity supplies were maintained. The port of Larne was closed, however, and, as the days went by, the strike pickets became more aggressive. The RUC reported that it had removed 300 roadblocks, arrested 23 people and received 1,000 complaints of intimidation in the first three days. The success or failure of the strike came to depend on the attitude of the workers in the Ballylumford power station which supplied much of the Province's electricity. Though subjected to intolerable pressure, the power workers twice refused pleas by the strikers to close down the generators, saying that they would produce power for as long as other workers ignored the strike call.

By 8 May there were signs that the strike was collapsing. Two days later the leaders appeared at Ballymena among their most enthusiastic supporters—loyalist farmers who sealed off the town with their tractors and farm machinery. Heavy troop reinforcements and armour moving towards the town seemed to indicate that the Government would not flinch from the implied challenge, though ironically it supported Dr Paisley's case, since such military strength was patently not being used against IRA strongholds. The police took no action when Dr Paisley refused to call off the blockade, but later, as tension eased, he and Mr Baird were swiftly arrested, and then released, on a minor charge of obstruction, to be heard at some date in the future. On 12 May sailings from Larne resumed, and next day the strike was ended. A beaming Mr Mason told the Ulster workers that they could stand 'ten feet tall'.

Most loyalists seem to have taken the view that the circumstances were not those prevailing in 1974, and that this time the Government was right, while the Catholic community had had a clear demonstration that the RUC was an impartial law-keeping force. The strike cleared the air, and improved the political atmosphere, though it cost three lives, and 41 policemen were injured. In defying the call to strike, many workers had been concerned about the economic consequences; figures released in the summer showed that 13 per cent of the population was unemployed, about twice the ratio in the rest of the UK. Mr Mason and Mr Don Concannon, the Industry Minister, visited the United States and countries in Europe to encourage new investment in Ulster.

The local government elections on 19 May resulted in the return of 167 Official Unionists, 108 Social Democratic Labour Party (SDLP), 73 DUP and 71 Alliance Party. Other parties were virtually eliminated. Later in the year the United Ulster Unionist Coalition broke up with the defection of Dr Paisley's DUP, and Mr Craig announced the dissolution of Vanguard, most of the members becoming Official Unionists.

In June nine members of the illegal UVF were gaoled for a total of 108 years for serious terrorist offences after the longest trial in Northern Ireland legal history. Three policemen were shot dead in an IRA ambush in Co. Tyrone. On 8 June Mr Mason announced the withdrawal of the spearhead battalion, but promised that the RUC would be augmented by 1,200, and the full-time Ulster Defence Regiment (UDR) increased to 2,500. New anti-terrorist squads were to be created. The return of Mr Lynch and the Fianna Fail party to power in the Republic gave rise to fears in the North that the IRA would be strengthened, as the previous Administration had acted vigorously against them.

The highlight of the year was undoubtedly the Queen's Silver Jubilee visit to the Province in August. Nationalist leaders criticized the timing of the visit as 'insensitive', since it coincided with the anniversary of the introduction of internment in 1971. The IRA, aided by rising agitation in the English press, made an all-out effort to have the visit cancelled by threats of bombing and civil disturbance, but the royal yacht Britannia arrived in Belfast Lough at dawn on 10 August. While the Duke of Edinburgh toured the Belfast shipyards, the Queen held an investiture at Hillsborough and met representatives of all walks of life in Ulster. On the second day of her visit the Queen was flown by helicopter to the new University of Ulster at Coleraine to meet young people from many parts of the Province. During the afternoon Prince Andrew arrived unannounced to join his parents, to the delight of the assembled guests. The warmth and friendliness of the Queen's personality, and her obvious concern for Northern Ireland, made a profound impression on its people, and in her Christmas broadcast she again spoke of her hopes for peace and reconciliation there.

The visit was a political triumph for the Secretary of State, demonstrating the Government's ability to control and contain civil disorder. In a last desperate effort to achieve a propaganda success, the IRA warned of bombs placed on the university campus, and held the Secretary of State responsible for the lives of the children gathered there. Again, Mr Mason showed immense political courage in advising no change in the schedule. Members of the SDLP refused to attend the reception, Republicans regarded the visit as provocative, and Unionists read into it a reaffirmation of the link with Britain.

In September the US President, Mr Carter, made a guarded statement on Northern Ireland, backing power-sharing as a solution, and offering industrial investment incentives for peace. But a round of talks held by Mr Mason and the local politicians in November achieved no agreement, and was not indeed regarded as likely to achieve anything while direct rule was working so well.

September was the first month since 1968 in which no civilian was killed. The day of the massive car bomb had gone, but the IRA were now making effective use of firebombs which caused considerable damage. The firemen's strike in November gave the green light for a Province-wide firebomb blitz, which continued with varying success to the end of the year. In November Lieut.-General Timothy Creasey, a counter-insurgency expert, was appointed G.O.C. Northern Ireland.

On 10 December the Nobel Peace Prize of £80,000 was awarded to Mrs Betty Williams and Miss Mairead Corrigan, founders of the Peace Movement. A week later, their return to Belfast was marred by a lukewarm reception. Relatively few of the Peace People turned out to greet them, the city council declined to offer them a civic reception and dignitaries of the Roman Catholic Church stayed away. On 21 December the Prime Minister, Mr Callaghan, made a brief visit to Belfast, met Christmas shoppers and assured them that the tide had turned against the terrorists. On the same day the army defused most of the firebombs planted in seven of Ulster's top hotels. The road accident figures for 1977 were among the worst on record; 352 people were killed, more than three times those killed by terrorism.

At the end of the year, the Secretary of State declared, with cautious optimism, 'The atmosphere has undergone change for the better, and I am determined that it will improve still further. The message for 1978 is one of real hope.'

II THE AMERICAS AND THE CARIBBEAN

Chapter 1

THE UNITED STATES OF AMERICA

PRESIDENT CARTER took office early in the year on a tide of great expectations. Most of them remained unfulfilled by the end of 1977, which turned out to be a year more of words than achievement, particularly in domestic affairs. As a result Mr Carter's popularity sagged considerably—from around 75 per cent who thought he was doing a good job in the first months to less than 50 per cent as he came to the end of his first presidential year, according to one poll. But if he lost some of the ebullience he showed on his inauguration day, when he strode hand-in-hand with his wife down Pennsylvania Avenue, the good intentions remained and he was still confident that he would, in time, get his measures passed by a reluctant Congress.

Mr Carter's political achievement in getting himself elected in 1976 was that he recognized, and cleverly exploited, the American people's desire for a new face, for a change in the style of national leadership. His difficulty as President in 1977 lay in this same fact of his newness, of his position, as in a phrase he coined in his campaign, as an outsider. He put forward during the year a hefty programme of legislation, much of it quite revolutionary, but the new guard of loyal Georgians who had been brought in to staff the White House failed to find the right political levers in Washington to get many of the measures through the legislative process. Undoubtedly the greatest setback to the new Administration was the fate of the Energy Bill, which the President declared to be his top priority for the year. In spite of his strong personal campaign, and his clearly expressed conviction of its importance, he failed to persuade his countrymen that there was any real need to turn down their thermostats, switch to smaller cars or adopt other un-American habits. The Senate took its lead from this popular apathy and severely mauled the Bill, which had failed to emerge from Congress by the end of the year. Other proposed reforms, including those for the tax system and the welfare programme, were also delayed.

At the same time, the President could point to some achievements. His $22,000 million package for stimulating the economy, which failed to make its expected recovery during the year, was passed, as were plans for government reorganization. And on foreign affairs, particularly in his relentless championship of human rights, he forced the world—allies included—to face issues which in the past had generally been ignored for the sake of diplomatic comfort. Whether such doses of truth would in the end contribute towards the creation of the stable, just and peaceful world order that Mr Carter defined as his objective in his message on inauguration day could not be determined from the experience of this somewhat confusing year.

HOME AFFAIRS. Soon after he won the presidential election on 2 November 1976 Mr Carter declared that he intended that his Administration would 'work intimately with Congress on a bipartisan basis' to achieve the various goals he had espoused during his campaign. Early in the new year, and even before his inauguration, he was given rude notice that Congress was not disposed to be all that bipartisan, and certainly had no desire to be particularly intimate with the new Administration, when one of the President-elect's key nominations, that of Mr Theodore Sorensen as Director of the Central Intelligence Agency, ran into trouble in the Senate.

Mr Carter was advised by members of the Senate's intelligence committee to withdraw the nomination when it was revealed that Mr Sorensen had removed from the White House in 1964 a number of classified documents which he then used in his book *Kennedy*, later donating the papers to a library and claiming a tax deduction on their estimated value. On 17 January Mr Sorensen appeared before the Senate committee and, after delivering a spirited defence of his record and his opinions, announced that he was withdrawing. To have continued fighting for the post, he said, which would have been his natural inclination, 'would only handicap the new Administration if I were rejected, or handicap my effectiveness as Director if I am confirmed'. Mr Carter said he deeply regretted the situation, adding that the Administration and the intelligence community had lost the services of an extremely talented and dedicated man. On 7 February Admiral Stansfield Turner was nominated as Director of the CIA in Mr Sorensen's place, and his nomination was confirmed by Congress. The incident was an early setback to Mr Carter, but not one that did any lasting damage, and it provided a useful warning that Congress would not be uncritical of a new and unknown President.

Mr Carter had arrived in Washington with surprisingly few commitments, and when he came to give his inaugural address after being sworn in as 39th President on 20 January he was again content to speak mainly in generalities, echoing the moralistic tone of his campaign. At the same time he emphasized the limitations of government. 'We have learnt that "more" is not necessarily "better" ', he said, 'that even our great nation has its recognized limits, and that we can neither answer all questions nor solve all problems. We cannot afford to do everything, nor can we afford to lack boldness as we meet the future. So together, in a spirit of individual sacrifice for the common good, we must simply do our best.

'Our nation can be strong abroad only if it is strong at home, and we know that the best way to enhance freedom in other lands is to demonstrate here that our democratic system is worthy of emulation. To be true to ourselves, we must be true to others. We will not behave in foreign places so as to violate our rules and standards here at home, for we know that the trust which our nation earns is essential to its strength.'

Mr Carter concluded by setting out what he hoped people might say about America when his time as President had ended:

That we had remembered the words of Micah and renewed our search for humility, mercy and justice;

That we had torn down the barriers that separated those of different races and region and religion, and, where there had been mistrust, built unity, with a respect for diversity;

That we had found productive work for those able to perform it;

That we had strengthened the American family, which is the basis of our society;

That we had ensured respect for the law, and equal treatment under the law, for the weak and the powerful, the rich and the poor;

And that we had enabled our people to be proud of their own Government once again.

President Carter's first formal act in office was to issue his promised pardon for Vietnam war conscription evaders, or 'draft dodgers', which he did on 21 January. His first unofficial act was to lower the thermostats controlling the heat in the White House to 65 degrees Fahrenheit, a reduction of some five degrees from their previous level, in the interests of fuel economy. It was an act that heralded what was to be the President's prime domestic concern throughout the year—the development of an effective energy policy and conservation programme. He was to have difficulty in persuading his fellow-countrymen that it was necessary, in spite of an extremely cold spell of weather in the early part of the year when the Federal Government found itself unable to move swiftly and effectively to help the distressed areas, but it was not for lack of determination on his part. He launched his campaign officially on 1 March, when he proposed the establishment of a Department of Energy which would employ some 20,000 people and have an annual budget of $10,000 million. The head of the new Department, with a seat in the Cabinet, was to be the President's Special Assistant for Energy Policy, Dr James Schlesinger, and the Department would comprise the Federal Energy Administration, the Energy Research and Development Administration, the Federal Power Commission and the energy divisions of some 20 other government agencies, as well as the energy responsibilities previously exercised by the Departments of Defense and the Interior. It was, as Mr Carter acknowledged, a major and ambitious reorganization of government, and one which he held to have been long overdue.

The President addressed the nation on the subject on 18 April, declaring in a special television broadcast that the need to reduce energy consumption was, with the exception of preventing war, 'the greatest challenge our country will face during our lifetimes'. He said that, if nothing was done now, then within ten years America would not be able to import enough oil from any country at an acceptable price. He pointed out that the country wasted more energy than it imported, and that Americans used twice as much energy per person as the West Germans, or the Japanese, or the Swedes. 'The energy crisis has not yet overwhelmed us', he said, 'but it will if we do not act quickly. Further delay can affect our strength and our power as a nation. If we fail to act soon, we will face an economic, social and political crisis that will threaten our free institutions.'

The President announced that he was about to present to Congress a programme designed to reduce the annual growth rate in US energy demand from its current level of more than 4 per cent a year to less than 2 per cent by 1985. By then it was intended that petrol consumption should have been reduced to 10 per cent below current levels and oil imports cut by half to six million barrels a day. Other objectives were an increase of coal output by two-thirds, the establishment of a strategic petroleum reserve equal to six months' US consumption, the insulation of 90 per cent of all American homes and the use of solar energy in 2,500,000 houses. Mr Carter concluded his address by asking the American people to support his proposals, which he recognized might require sacrifices. 'Other generations of Americans have faced and mastered great challenges', he said. 'I have faith that meeting this challenge will make our own lives even richer. If you will join me so that we can work together with patriotism and courage, we will again prove that our great nation can lead the world into an age of peace, independence and freedom.'

Two days later, on 20 April, the President presented his energy plans, which proved to be numerous and complex, to Congress, asking them to help 'devise and implement' them. Deciding against any new immediate tax on petrol, the President proposed instead that the Government should set targets providing for a gradual rise in consumption until 1980, and for a gradual decline after 1982. If American motorists used more than 1 per cent above the target in any year after 1977, then in the following year they would have to pay a federal tax of 5 cents a gallon, a tax that could rise to a maximum of 50 cents by 1989. Any money raised by the tax would be returned through income tax credits and direct payments to people who did not owe taxes, the amount of the rebates being the same for everyone. Motorists driving large, petrol-hungry cars would be additionally penalized by means of a complex formula of excise taxes and rebates geared to the miles-per-gallon achieved by their cars. Under this proposed formula a car doing 12 miles to the gallon would pay a tax of $449 in 1978 but $2,488 by 1985, whereas the purchaser of a car which could do 39 miles per gallon would receive in 1978 a rebate of $473, which would rise to $493 by 1985.

To discourage oil consumption the President proposed the gradual lifting of controlled US-refined oil prices to the world market level, which White House officials estimated would add about $75 to the energy bills of every American by 1980. But people who heated their homes with oil would get back every dollar that the tax added to heating bills, and other revenue raised by the tax would be refunded to consumers in much the same way as the petrol tax. Natural gas, which was the nation's cheapest fuel, and which was consequently rapidly depleting, would become more expensive, and prices would be federally controlled so that they became equal throughout the country. Conversion of industrial plants to coal would be encouraged by tax credits, and by the imposition of higher taxes on users who failed to make the change. Tax rebates would be offered to householders who insulated their homes, and those who installed solar heating devices would receive a 40 per cent tax credit on the first $1,000 spent, and 25 per cent on the next $6,400.

When he stood before Congress to announce his plans the President said he expected little applause, and he got what he expected. Mr Carter was asking Americans to change their way of life, which had for so long been based on the most profligate use of energy, and not because of any immediate crisis but because one would develop in five or ten years' time. It was not a popular programme, and even those Congressmen who accepted the logic of the President's appeal recognized that it would be difficult for him to obtain the necessary legislation. The Speaker of the House of Representatives, Mr Thomas P. O'Neill, said after Mr Carter's speech that the passage of the programme would involve 'the toughest fight the Congress has ever had'.

Mr O'Neill was right. After three months little progress had been made, and the public's attention had begun to wander. Mr Carter expressed his disappointment to a group of newspaper editors in Washington on 31 July. 'I am concerned that the public has not responded well, and I think voluntary compliance is probably not adequate at all', he said. Four days later the House of Representatives killed the proposals to raise petrol taxes by 339 votes to 82, though the House was generally in favour of most of the President's plans. However, on 20 September, as other parts of the programme continued to wind their way through the Senate, the finance and energy committees of that body voted against the crude oil equalization tax proposals. On 4 October the Senate voted, by 50 to 46, in favour of phasing out federal controls over natural gas prices, thus knocking out another main pillar of the President's energy programme.

The programme was now in deep trouble, and the President reacted angrily by denouncing the US oil companies who were, he said, trying to rob American consumers and seeking 'the biggest rip-off in history'. He believed that it was the oil lobby, whose shadow was 'hovering over Capitol Hill', that was mainly responsible for influencing Senators to emasculate his energy Bills, though the Senators themselves clearly had other things in mind as well—not least the fact that the President, in spite of many earnest appeals, had failed to rouse public opinion. He had also, so many of his critics maintained, failed to spend enough time wooing

sceptical Congressmen, some of whom resented his apparent attempts to
by-pass Congress by appealing directly to the people.

If this was Mr Carter's intention he could have hoped to succeed only
by creating an enormous groundswell of support. As it was, the autumn
opinion polls showed that Mr Carter had lost a good deal of the popular
support he had enjoyed earlier in the year, and Congressmen, who in the
main owed him nothing and were not in need of his help (which electorally
was not worth much anyway), could afford to play it their own way. The
President hinted that he would veto legislation that did not conform to the
programme he originally presented, declared that he would start again in
the following year if the programme was not passed, postponed a visit to
seven countries and went on television again to reiterate the importance of
his energy proposals and to emphasize that what was being measured was
'the strength and will of our nation, whether we can acknowledge a threat
and meet a serious challenge together'. The answer was not to be provided
in 1977.

Preoccupation with the energy programme postponed action on most
of the President's other main domestic proposals, including his plan for
overhauling the American welfare system, which he published on 6 August.
Under his scheme the three existing main welfare programmes—aid to
families with dependent children (AFDC), supplemental security income
(SSI) to the old, the blind and the disabled, and the food stamp programme—were to be abolished. In their place there would be two new
basic payments—an income supplement for the old, the blind, the disabled
and single-parent families with young children, and a work benefit, linked
to work requirements and incentives, for other poor people. In his message
to Congress Mr Carter said he had concluded that the existing system
could not be cured by minor modifications: it 'is neither rational nor is
it fair, and is anti-work and anti-family'. His proposals were based on a
belief in the importance of jobs rather than welfare, and in holding families
together. Their cost was estimated to be $30,700 million, compared with
current expenditure of $26,300 million on welfare. The President had
originally ordered the Department of Health, Education and Welfare to
devise a new system that would not cost any more, but he defended the
increased cost on the grounds that it would improve the original plan, and
'not be incompatible with that dream to balance the budget by 1981'.

The President also presented to Congress during the year a proposal
for reforming the electoral laws by abolishing the electoral college system
and providing for the financing of congressional elections out of public
funds. Paying for presidential elections out of government funds was one
of the reforms that had followed the Watergate scandals, but proposals
that congressional elections should be funded in the same way had not
been supported by Congress, largely no doubt because incumbents found
it easier to raise funds to defend their seats than unknown candidates did

to challenge them. Proposals to reform the presidential election system had not in the past been successful, but even though the process of amending the Constitution was a protracted one it seemed that Mr Carter's plan might in the end get through. Certainly Congress was not unresponsive.

Under the Constitution as it stood, voters in presidential elections chose electors, who in turn voted for the President. Because candidates with the most popular votes in particular states took every electoral college vote it sometimes came about that a presidential candidate with a majority of popular votes found himself defeated by a rival who had accumulated more electoral college votes. This happened on several occasions during the nineteenth century, and was only narrowly avoided in the 1976 election; for if Mr Gerald Ford had carried Ohio and Hawaii, which he nearly did, he would have won the election, even though he would have been some two million behind Mr Carter in the popular vote. Mr Carter's plan was to ensure that in future Presidents would be elected directly.

A significant item of legislation that was enacted before the end of the year was the Unlawful Corporate Payments Bill, which the President signed on 20 December. The Bill was designed to put a stop to the bribing of officials in foreign countries by American firms seeking to win overseas orders, a practice which had become common, as had been revealed by congressional inquiries (see AR 1976, pp. 66-67) and by the Securities and Exchange Commission, who found that more than 300 American companies had paid hundreds of millions of dollars to officials and political parties in a good many countries. Under the Bill companies became liable to fines of up to $1 million for such acts, and individuals also risked fines of up to $10,000, or five years' imprisonment, or both.

The affairs of Mr Bert Lance, the Director of the Office of Management and Budget, became a matter of great concern in Washington during the summer months, and for a while seemed to paralyze the Administration's capacity for concentrating on anything else. Mr Lance, an old and trusted friend of the President, had been, before his appointment to Mr Carter's Administration, a banker in Georgia. On taking up his government post he had been required to sell his shares in the Bank of Georgia, and it was this that led to his difficulties. The value of the bank's shares had dropped sharply on his departure as its president, and it was revealed that he stood to lose some $1,500,000 on the sale. A second and more damaging discovery was that he had borrowed the money to buy his shares from a Chicago bank which had a close relationship with the National Bank of Georgia. Various allegations of dubious practices by Mr Lance were made in the American press, and on 21 September Mr Lance announced his resignation. The President said that he had accepted it with the greatest sense of sorrow and regret, and that nothing he had heard had shaken his faith in Lance's ability and integrity.

In his letter of resignation Mr Lance said there were three matters which had preoccupied him. The first was that his own name and reputation should be cleared: he believed that this had been done. The second was that people should be willing to make sacrifices to serve their country. 'This I can still say, and say proudly.' Thirdly, he believed in the 'absolute need for government to be able to attract good people from the private sector'. Mr Carter, who was visibly distressed by the affair when he spoke about it at a press conference, said that a lot of the problem had been brought about by his own insistence on the highest ethical standards for his colleagues, and he acknowledged that the affair might have damaged his credibility. To many observers there was indeed much that was reminiscent of the old-style Washington politics that Mr Carter had so persistently promised to change. As successor to Mr Lance the President, on 27 December, appointed Mr James McIntyre, Mr Lance's deputy, and formerly a budget director for the state of Georgia.

Echoes of the old Washington continued to be heard from time to time during the year. On 18 January the Justice Department announced that it was dropping charges against Mr Robert Mardian, the former Assistant Attorney-General, for his alleged part in the Watergate cover-up. In May further revelations about Watergate came from hitherto unpublished White House tapes which recorded a conversation between the then President Nixon and his special counsel, Mr Charles Coulson, in which it was shown that Mr Nixon was talking of the need to stonewall on the investigation only three days after the Watergate burglary took place. The tapes had been made available to the American press by Mr David Frost, who had interviewed Mr Nixon at length for a television series that began on 4 May. During the course of the interviews Mr Nixon insisted that he had committed no crime, but confessed to making untrue statements, and said he had 'let the American people down'. On 23 May the Supreme Court declined to hear the appeals of Mr John Mitchell, the former Attorney-General, Mr H. R. Haldeman, former White House chief of staff, and Mr John Ehrlichman, former director of domestic affairs in the White House, and on 22 June Mitchell and Haldeman began serving their sentences (Ehrlichman already having started his). Their sentences were from 30 months to eight years, but on 4 October Judge Sirica reduced these to one to four years in response to their admissions of guilt.

The Supreme Court also ruled during the year that Mr Nixon was not entitled to control the tapes and documents from his last years in the White House. Congress had passed an Act in 1974 denying Nixon his archives, but the former President had argued that it had no right to deprive him of his property. By a vote of 7 to 2 the Court upheld the constitutionality of Congress's Act, and on 9 August the tapes and documents were moved into the National Archives.

New York City captured the nation's interest in July, not because of its bright lights but because of their total absence. On 15 July three power lines and a transformer were hit by lightning in quick succession, cutting the city off from its sources of power in up-state New York. The city was plunged into darkness, and chaos, for 24 hours. During this period looters went on the rampage in some parts of the city, and damage to property was estimated at about $100 million. More than 3,400 people were arrested, and 426 policemen were injured by looters who in some cases could not understand why they were being stopped. Furniture, electronic and liquor stores were emptied, and then in many cases set on fire. The incident demonstrated again the vulnerability of this city, as American commentators were quick to emphasize. The city's own leading newspaper, the *New York Times*, referred to the 'social overload' that had been put upon the city by the combination of high unemployment among minority groups and by its shrinking services. 'We did not spend enough of our ingenuity and affluence to solve the problems the riots of the sixties made evident', the paper declared. 'It is a sad but profoundly important lesson for New York—and for the nation.'

The nation in fact did not seem to be all that interested in New York's other problems, not least among which was the continuing threat of bankruptcy. In March the city had once again found itself unable to meet its bills for the month, needing $200 million for these plus $1,000 million which it was being forced by court order to pay to noteholders. The word from Washington was that the President was in favour of extending existing federal loans, but not of providing more cash while local banks, politicians and trade unions continued to squabble about how to find new sources of funds. After further financial contortions the Mayor of New York, Mr Abraham Beame, was able to announce that he had found enough cash to pay off the most pressing bills, and once again the crisis passed, though for how long was not made clear. For Mr Beame, who had been Mayor since 1974, the problem became less personal when he was defeated in the mayoral Democratic Party primary election on 8 September. The party's nomination went instead to Mr Edward Koch, a 52-year-old bachelor, who duly inherited the city's problems when he won the election on 8 November.

The city of Washington experienced a problem of a different kind in March, when armed men, members of a Black Muslim sect, seized three buildings. One was the city's town hall, known as the District Building, which was a few blocks away from the White House; the second was the headquarters of B'nai B'rith, the Jewish charity; and the third was the Islamic Centre and Mosque on Embassy Row. One man was killed, several injured and scores of people held hostage during the three incidents. The men involved in the attack identified themselves as members of the Hanafi Muslim sect, and one of their demands was that five men convicted of murdering seven Hanafis, including five children, in 1973 should be handed over to them, together with the murderer of Malcolm X, a leader of the Black Muslims, who was killed in 1965. Two days later, on 11 March, the terrorists surrendered after negotiations conducted with the aid of three Muslim ambassadors in Washington—those of Iran, Egypt and Pakistan.

Capital punishment returned to the USA in 1977 when, on 17 January, Gary Gilmore, a convicted murderer, was executed by firing squad in the Utah state prison. The execution was the first for nearly ten years, and had been stayed three times in spite of Gilmore's own declared wish that it should go ahead. In 1976 the Supreme Court had ruled that capital punishment need not always be unconstitutional (see AR 1976, pp. 67-68).

ECONOMIC AFFAIRS. For most of 1977 the USA battled grimly on the economic front with uncomfortably high unemployment, rapidly rising trade and balance of payments deficits, a declining dollar and fears of growing inflation. The Government found itself trying to conduct an uneasy balancing act between those who demanded greater stimulus for the economy and those who saw the inflationary fires beginning to smoulder, while the demands seemed to be growing, both at home and abroad, for a reversal of free trade policies. Mr Robert Strauss, who on 1 March was nominated by the President as his Special Representative for Trade Negotiations, said shortly after taking office that the world, still staggering out of a deep recession, was faced with growing protectionist demands. 'We are going to have to work as hard as we can just to keep the world as open as it is', he said. The economic summit in London, which opened on 5 May, was seen by the Americans as an opportunity to stimulate the declining growth rates of many of the industrialized countries. Seeing itself as the only major trading country pursuing an expansionist policy at home, the Americans sought to persuade the others, particularly Japan and West Germany, to stimulate their economies in order to provide bigger markets for their trading partners. Both countries undertook to take steps to boost their economies, but neither in fact managed to increase their rates of growth during the year to the extent promised at the summit.

Japan, in particular, became a source of economic irritation to America as its exports expanded to the extent that during the year it sold some $7,000 million worth of goods more than it bought. Mr James Reston, the columnist of the *New York Times*, decided, after a visit to Japan, that it was 'hard to avoid the conclusion that the Japanese are outselling us at least partly because they are outworking us. And also because they are working together for reasons shared by their government, their managers, planners and workers.' Other Americans viewed the situation with less detachment, and the US steel industry filed a number of dumping actions in the courts against Japanese steel companies.

American steel companies strongly urged the Government to impose protectionist tariffs and quotas, but the Administration rejected their appeals and proposed instead, in a programme presented to Congress on 6 December, a 'reference price system' that would allow imports to be priced at or above a level based on Japanese production costs. The White House stated that its primary objective was 'to assist the steel industry in a manner which will stimulate efficiency and enable the industry to compete fairly'.

Even before he had been inaugurated Mr Carter had revealed, on 7 January, that he planned to stimulate the economy as a whole by reducing taxation and increasing federal expenditure. More precise details were presented to the House of Representatives' budget committee on 27 January by Mr Bert Lance, Mr Michael Blumenthal, the Secretary of the Treasury, and Mr Charles Schultze, chairman of the Council of Economic Advisers, and these were formally put before Congress on 31 January. The President's package proposed that there should be a rebate of $50 paid to all taxpayers and dependents on their 1976 tax payments, that a similar payment of $50 would be awarded to all social security beneficiaries and recipients of supplementary security income payments, that flat-rate tax deductions would replace the existing ranges of $1,700 to $2,400 for single persons and of $2,100 to $2,800 for married couples, that there would be alternative benefits for industry of either an increase from 10 to 12 per cent in the investment tax credit or a credit against income tax equal to 4 per cent of employers' social security taxes, that there would be an expansion of the public service employment programme, the emergency public works programme and employment training expenditure, and that there would be an increase of disbursements under the revenue-sharing programme. These proposals were estimated to cost more than $31,000 million for the two fiscal years 1977 and 1978.

On 22 February Mr Carter presented to Congress an amended version of the Budget for 1977-78 originally put forward by President Ford on 17 January, three days before his term of office ended. The effect of Mr Carter's amendments, which incorporated his 'economic stimulus package', was to increase the estimated expenditure from $411,200 million to $417,400 million and reduce income from $354,000 million to $349,400 million, which increased the estimated deficit for the year from $57,200 million to $68,000 million. In the fiscal year 1978 Mr Carter's estimated budget deficit was $57,700 million, compared with Mr Ford's forecast of $47,000 million. Though Mr Carter emphasized that the Budget was still essentially his predecessor's, since he had had time to make only limited revisions, there were some significant changes quite apart from the stimulus package. He had, for example, restored all the cuts in domestic social assistance programmes, and had abandoned Mr Ford's proposal to increase social security taxes as well as cutting $800 million from the defence programme.

The President's stimulus package was criticized by some influential economists because of its inflationary aspects. The heavyweight among these critics was Dr Arthur Burns, chairman of the US Federal Reserve Board, who said, in an address to the joint economic committees of Congress on 23 February, that the President's plan to distribute cash tax rebates would weaken business confidence. 'All these rebate cheques—throwing them out from airplanes—I think we should just calm down. . . . What this country now badly needs is an anti-inflation policy.' Though the tax rebate scheme was passed, in a modified version, by the House of Representatives, and by the Senate finance committee, it ran into more determined opposition in the Senate as a whole, and on 14 April the President abandoned it. The official reason given was that the $50 rebates were no longer required because of recent gains in the country's economic situation. Mr Carter pointed out that when the rebates were requested the unemployment rate was running at about 8 per cent and the economy growing at an annual rate of only 3·2 per cent. Since then unemployment had fallen to 7·3 per cent, and looked like falling further, while the rate of economic growth had almost doubled. Mr Carter also asked the Senate to drop the plan for alternative tax credits related to increased business investment. The Senate accepted these changes and on 23 May the Bill was passed and signed into law.

The economic indicators continued to fluctuate, however, and the unexpectedly fast growth rate achieved in the first quarter of the year slowly declined for the rest of the year. The rate of unemployment continued high, though it gradually dropped to 6·9 per cent in November and 6·4 per cent in December. There was still no agreement on what should be done, and Dr Burns continued to be critical of the Government's policies. He returned publicly to the attack on 27 October, charging Congress and the Administration with failure to adopt policies that could create an environment likely to encourage investment and so ensure sustained economic growth. At the end of the year Mr Carter announced that he would not reappoint Dr Burns as chairman of the Federal Reserve Board when his term of office ran out at the end of January 1978, and appointed to replace him Mr William Miller, a director of the Federal Reserve Bank in Boston and chairman of the Textron conglomerate.

Earlier in the year, on 15 April, the President had defined his longer-term economic objectives, aimed mainly at reducing the nation's inflation rate by some two percentage points to about 4 per cent by the end of 1979, while at the same time making further significant progress in reducing the unemployment level and balancing the federal budget by 1981. He made it clear that he did not believe the Government could achieve this on its own. 'No one should look to the Government for easy answers', he said, 'because there are none, and Government cannot do the job alone. We face difficult choices ahead in energy and other areas of national importance. However, I believe that government, business and labour together can, as an interim goal, reasonably aim at reducing the rate of inflation by two percentage points by the end of 1979, while still vigorously pursuing our commitment to full employment. All segments of the American economy must cooperate if we are to get inflation under control. In the long run that is the only path to more jobs, stable prices, and greater real income for all our people.'

The President had also planned to put forward proposals for a fundamental and comprehensive reform of the American tax system during the year, but because of delays to his other legislative programmes in Congress he postponed action on this part of his economic reforms.

By the end of the year the monthly trade deficit had improved slightly from the record level of $3,100 million reached in October, but the figure for the year was nearly $30,000 million, largely caused by oil imports, which cost $45,000 million in 1977. This was putting great pressure on the dollar, which in the last two weeks of the year fell steadily against most foreign currencies. An announcement by the President that he would 'intervene to the extent necessary to counter disorderly conditions in the exchange markets' checked the slide briefly, but in the last days of the year, following Mr Carter's announcement on 28 December of his dismissal of Dr Burns, the value of the dollar began to fall again and it seemed clear that the US was going to have to intervene in a market which was again becoming thoroughly disorderly.

FOREIGN AFFAIRS. President Carter took the opportunity of his inauguration to issue, in addition to the customary message to his own countrymen, a special address to the citizens of the world. He recognized, he said, that they, too, though they had had no part in the American election, would be affected by the decisions he made, and he thought therefore that they were entitled to know how the power and the influence of the United States would be exercised by the new Government. 'I want to assure you', Mr Carter said, 'that the relations of the United States with the other countries and peoples of the world will be guided during our administration by our desire to shape a world order that is more responsive to human aspirations. The United States will meet its obligation to help create a stable, just and peaceful world order.'

That the new President intended this to be more than diplomatic waffle quickly became evident from the strong stand he took on the American commitment to human rights, as defined in the Charter of the United Nations and in the Helsinki accord of 1975. The new Administration adopted a much more robust policy in drawing attention to other countries' shortcomings in this respect than had its recent predecessors. The first example of this change came in January, when the State Department commended the Soviet scientist, Andrei Sakharov, for his championship of human rights in the Soviet Union. On 1 February Mr Carter received the Soviet ambassador in Washington, Mr Anatoly Dobrynin, and told him that the US would not back down from publicly expressing its concern for human rights, and six days later the US formally expressed its 'profound concern' over the treatment of Alexander Ginsburg, who had been imprisoned in Russia by the KGB. Later in February Mr Carter wrote a letter to Dr Sakharov, which was handed to him at the US embassy in Moscow. In his letter, which was in reply to one written by Dr Sakharov shortly after Mr Carter's inauguration, the President assured Dr Sakharov that 'the American people and our Government will continue our firm commitment to promote respect for human rights not only in our country but also abroad. We shall use our good offices to seek the release of prisoners of conscience, and we will continue our efforts to shape a world responsive to human aspirations in which nationals of differing countries and histories can live side by side in peace and justice.'

Mr Carter followed up his unprecedented action in writing to a Soviet dissident by cutting American aid to Argentina, Ethiopia and Uruguay because of violations of human rights in those countries. His unconventional and aggressive approach unnerved some of America's allies and did not please the Soviet Union, whose leaders regarded themselves, inevitably, as the President's main target. They tried, as Mr James Reston put it in the *New York Times*, sneering at his defence of human rights 'as if it were a dreary Sunday school lesson out of Plains, Georgia', but they showed that they took it more deeply than that by their rebuff to Mr Cyrus Vance, the Secretary of State, when he visited Moscow in March for strategic arms limitation talks (SALT). Mr Vance went to Moscow with two proposals, but both were flatly rejected by Mr Brezhnev (see Pt. XI, Ch. 3). Though the question of human rights was not raised during Mr Vance's talks, there seemed little doubt that it had contributed to what the Americans identified as a considerable hardening of Soviet attitudes.

Deadlock in the SALT negotiations did not deter the US from trying to limit the spread of conventional weapons as well as nuclear capability. The Administration had confirmed, on 17 February, that the US would not supply the CBU 72 concussion bomb to any foreign country. The bomb, generally recognized as the most deadly non-nuclear weapon in existence, carried a volatile fuel which sprayed from the bomb and ignited, and Israel had been among the countries that hoped to gain possession of it. On 19 May the President announced a programme for limiting official sales of conventional arms, exempting only Nato countries, Australia, New Zealand, Japan and Israel. In future, he said, sales would be made only when the President judged them to be required by American national security or for 'the safety of our close friends'. Outstanding commitments, which totalled about $32,000 million, would be met, but he planned to reduce sales in the next fiscal year.

The President laid down three guidelines for future policy: first,

America would not be the first to introduce advanced weapons into a region where they would create significantly higher combat capability in that region; second, there would be a prohibition on the supply of advanced weapons systems solely for the use of other countries; and third, American embassies and military representatives abroad would cease promoting the sale of arms. Mr Carter said he recognized that the US alone could not curb international arms dealing, but declared that he was initiating a policy of restraint 'in the full understanding that actual reductions in the world-wide traffic in arms will require multilateral cooperation. Because we dominate the world market to such a degree, I believe that the United States can and should take the first step.'

The President also made a major change in American nuclear power policy by renouncing the commercial use of plutonium, and by appealing to Britain, Japan, France, West Germany and the Soviet Union to join in a new international effort to prevent the further proliferation of nuclear explosive capability by way of power plant reactors. Though he emphasized that these countries had a perfect right to go ahead and continue with their own reprocessing efforts, he noted that several other unnamed countries were 'on the verge' of acquiring the ability to make nuclear bombs.

Mr Carter met with some criticism for failing to urge other countries to follow the American lead in abandoning the commercial use of plutonium themselves, and evidence was produced in the US to show that he had intended to make such a plea, but had changed his mind at the last moment, apparently under pressure from some of America's allies. Two of them, France and West Germany, had already entered into contracts, with Pakistan and Brazil respectively, to supply nuclear equipment and materials, and these proved to be the one subject on which the allies failed to agree when they met at the summit in London in May. They agreed to differ on the subject, after setting up an inquiry into the matter, but both France and Germany made plain that they did not intend to give up their contracts, in spite of the American President's appeal.

On 30 June Mr Carter ended a long controversy by cancelling production of the American B1 bomber, a supersonic swing-wing aircraft with a range sufficient to fly intercontinental missions and to return. Three research and development models had already been built, and Mr Carter had earlier approved the building of five operational bombers, but these would not now be completed. The President's decision meant that the American manned bomber force would now be replaced by the Cruise missile, which cost about $1 million each compared with $100 million for each B1. The Cruise missile, which would not become available until early in the 1980s, was designed to fly at about 600 mph at a height of no more than 100 ft, following the contours of the Earth and having an accuracy of 100 ft whatever the range. American reliance on this missile did not improve the chances of progress in the SALT negotiations with the Soviet

Union, which remained intensely suspicious of the missile. The Soviet leaders accused the President of stepping up the arms race as well as continuing to resent his persistent emphasis on human rights—emphasis which the Americans maintained at the Belgrade conference which met in the latter half of the year to review the Helsinki agreements of 1975.

In an address to the UN General Assembly on 4 October Mr Carter declared that the US was willing to go as far as possible, consistent with security, on limiting nuclear weapons, and would, on a reciprocal basis, reduce them 'by 10 per cent, by 20 per cent, even by 50 per cent'. He went on: 'I hereby solemnly declare on behalf of the United States that we will not use nuclear weapons except in self-defence—that is, in circumstances of an actual nuclear or conventional attack on the United States, our territories or armed forces, or such an attack on our allies.' His efforts to come to some accord with the Soviet leaders met with no positive response during the year, however. They clearly found the new American President more than a little disconcerting.

During his election campaign in 1976 Mr Carter said on a number of occasions that he would never give up complete control or practical control of the Panama Canal Zone. He ran into some difficulties at home, therefore, when his Administration announced that it had concluded negotiations with Panama on a new treaty which would give Panama full control of both the canal and the Canal Zone by the year 2000, and though both he and the Panamanian President had signed the treaty on 7 September the US Senate had still not ratified it by the end of the year. The agreement comprised two treaties—one covering the operation of the canal and its defence until 1999, the second guaranteeing its permanent neutrality. They were to replace the treaty signed in 1903. Negotiations had begun 13 years earlier, during President Lyndon Johnson's term of office, and had continued in spite of differences which at times erupted into violence and bloodshed. Under the treaty guaranteeing the permanent neutrality of the canal American warships were given the permanent right of expeditious passage for warships, regardless of their means of propulsion, origin, destination, armament or cargo. Under the basic treaty handing over the canal to Panama in AD 2000 the two countries undertook to study the feasibility of a new sea-level canal and, if they agreed such a canal was necessary, to negotiate mutually agreeable terms for its construction. The USA would, in addition, have the right throughout the 23 years of the basic treaty's term to add a third lane of locks to increase the capacity of the existing canal. Mr Carter said the agreement heralded a new sense of partnership between Americans and Panamanians, and marked 'the commitment of the United States to the belief that fairness, not force, should lie at the heart of our dealings with the nations of the world'.

The Administration hoped that settlement of the Panama Canal dispute would also lead to improved relations with other Latin American

C

nations, many of whose heads of state came to Washington to witness the signing ceremony in the headquarters of the Organization of American States. A number of Latin American countries were uneasy at the strong line taken by the US Government on human rights, and there were some frank exchanges on the subject, notably when the Chilean President, General Pinochet, visited Mr Carter. Afterwards Mr Carter said that the Chilean leader had recognized that his country's reputation had been very poor in the field of human rights, and had reported that the situation was improving.

The USA also endeavoured to improve relations with Cuba during the year, though hampered by the Cuban Government's activities in Africa. On 27 April the two countries concluded an agreement on fishing limits, following the visit to Havana of Mr Clarence Todding, the Assistant Secretary of State for Latin America—the first by an American government official since the breaking-off of relations in 1961. The rapprochement was taken a small step further in June, when it was announced that Cuba and the USA would exchange diplomats, though below ambassador level. However, towards the end of the year the USA made it clear that there could be no possibility of re-establishing full diplomatic relations while the Cuban military presence in Angola, Ethiopia and other African countries continued to expand. The American estimate was that Cuba had sent between 4,000 and 6,000 additional troops to Angola in the second half of 1977, increasing the Cuban strength in that country to about 19,000 troops plus 4,000 civilian advisers. The State Department regarded the Cuban presence in Angola, and in 11 other African countries, as a deliberate policy of intervention in Africa along lines similar to those pursued by Cuba in Latin America in the 1960s.

The USA was active in trying to promote a settlement in Rhodesia during the year, though in a supporting role to Britain rather than as the principal. Mr Cyrus Vance, the new Secretary of State, warned Rhodesia, at his first press conference in Washington on 31 January, that it could not count on American assistance either in trying to prevent majority rule or in excluding nationalist leaders from their internal negotiations. American policy was consistent in supporting a peaceful settlement leading to majority rule in 1978. But the problem was seen to embrace more than just Rhodesia, and when the Vice-President, Mr Walter Mondale, saw the South African Prime Minister, Mr Vorster, in Vienna, he sought not only to gain South African agreement to put pressure on Mr Smith's Government in Rhodesia but also to persuade the South African Government to make changes within its own country. And Mr Andrew Young, the US representative at the UN, carried the same message when he visited Johannesburg.

Mr Vance explained America's concern when he spoke to the convention of the National Association for the Advancement of Coloured

People in St Louis on 1 July. He said the choice between a negotiated settlement and a violent solution in Rhodesia had to be made immediately. The conflict was growing, and the risk of increased foreign involvement in the racial disputes of southern Africa was real. The US intended to use its influence, as an impartial mediator, to pursue attempts to solve the problems of Rhodesia, Namibia and South Africa itself at the same time. A policy of leaving apartheid alone for the moment would not work. 'It would be blind to the reality that the beginning of progress must be made soon in South Africa if there is to be a possibility of peaceful solutions in the longer run', he said. 'It could mislead the South Africans about our real concerns. It would prejudice our relations with our African friends. It would be a disservice to our own beliefs and it would discourage those of all races who are working for peaceful progress within South Africa.'

Relations with South Africa deteriorated in October, following the restrictions imposed on black and white opponents of Dr Vorster's policies, and the American ambassador, Mr William Bowdler, was recalled to Washington for consultations. President Carter announced that the USA was ready to support a United Nations ban on the sale of arms to South Africa, and, after joining with Britain and France to veto the first motion to this effect because it included economic sanctions as well, voted, on 4 November, for the UN resolution imposing mandatory sanctions on the sale of arms.

In the Middle East the USA strove without success for most of the year to narrow the gap between the negotiating positions of Israel and the Arab countries in the hope of getting both sides together at Geneva. Mr Cyrus Vance toured the Middle East in February, but failed to make any progress. In March President Carter put forward the outlines of an American plan for peace in the Middle East based on the idea that Israel's defence lines might extend beyond its ultimate permanent frontier for an agreed period, which might be anything between two and eight years. Israel would eventually withdraw to the 1967 borders, with some minor adjustments, but would first be surrounded by a broad band of demilitarized zones, policed by international forces, while confidence was established between Israelis and Arabs through trade and tourism and the ending of the declared state of war. Mr Carter said the three requirements for a solution of the Arab-Israel problem were the need for a commitment to a complete peace, delineation of borders, and agreement on the 'highly controversial' Palestine issue. His thoughts were not received with any marked enthusiasm in the Middle East, any more than was a joint declaration on the subject issued by the US and Soviet Governments, as joint chairmen of the Geneva conference, on 1 October, in which the USA for the first time conceded that a resolution of the Palestine question should ensure 'the legitimate rights' of the Palestinian people.

The USA was taken by surprise by Mr Sadat's decision to visit

Jerusalem in November. It nevertheless welcomed Mr Sadat's initiative, though in somewhat cautious terms because it did not wish to be seen apparently supporting a bilateral agreement between Egypt and Israel, for fear of jeopardizing a more comprehensive settlement in the Middle East. Mr Vance in December set off to the Middle East again, this time to try to persuade other Arab nations to modify their anger with Egypt, and to attend the follow-up meetings. He was unsuccessful, and at the end of the year the chief American concern was to try to secure some tangible concession from Israel in response to Mr Sadat's dramatic gesture.

In the Far East the USA caused some concern during the year by deciding to withdraw its ground troops from South Korea. This had in fact been pledged by Mr Carter during his election campaign, and the decision to implement the promise was announced by the Vice-President, Mr Walter Mondale, during a tour of the Far East early in the year. Mr Mondale said the troops, who numbered some 41,000, would be withdrawn in a carefully phased programme, and that after that the USA would maintain a strong air capability in the area. Elsewhere, America upset the order of things by leaving the International Labour Organization, as it had announced it proposed to do some two years earlier. Dr Ray Marshall, the Secretary of Labor, said that American efforts to restore the ILO to its original principles had failed, and that the USA had withdrawn because the ILO applied unequal standards to its various members, because it made charges against countries without proper evidence, because extraneous political matters were frequently injected into labour matters, and because many countries could not produce independent labour or employer organizations, although national delegations were supposed to include separate representatives of government, management and labour.

One of the longest-running sagas of the year was the Anglo-French effort to persuade the city of New York to accept the Concorde supersonic airliner. It became an issue of diplomacy at the highest level; for both Mr James Callaghan, the British Prime Minister, and M Giscard d'Estaing, the President of France, took opportunities to raise it with Mr Carter, who could only explain that he had no authority to direct the Port Authority of New York to allow Concorde to land at Kennedy airport, even though the Federal Government had said that it should be given a trial period of 16 months, as it had been at Dulles airport in Washington. In the end it became a legal issue, and again at the highest level, for it was not until the Supreme Court ruled in its favour that Concorde was finally permitted to fly into New York. It began to do so regularly, and rather more quietly than had been expected, on 22 November.

Chapter 2

CANADA

NATIONAL unity and the economy were the themes which dominated events in Canada during 1977. While economic problems brought increasing public criticism upon the Government of Prime Minister Pierre Trudeau, the country's perception of his ability to deal with the challenge to national unity caused his overall popularity to rise during the year.

The impact of the Parti Québécois's triumph in the November 1976 election in the province of Quebec (see AR 1976, pp. 77-78) was felt throughout 1977. On 25 January, in his first major speech since the election victory, Premier René Lévesque told the Economic Club of New York that the independence of Quebec was 'as natural and irreversible as growth itself'. The Premier's trip was designed to reassure US bankers and investors that the new Government would not imperil their interests, and to ensure their continued support of the fragile Quebec economy. Mr Lévesque told his audience, which reacted somewhat sceptically, that his goal was to establish for Quebec a 'common market' relationship with Canada, a relationship which he also described during the year as 'sovereignty-association'.

The Quebec business community, both Canadian and multinational, also reacted negatively to the new Government. More than a hundred firms transferred either part or all of their operations out of Quebec during the year; most went to Ontario, although some re-established in the United States. A feature article in the US business magazine *Fortune* concluded in October that separation would be economically disastrous for the province and had already resulted in a massive flight of people, business and capital from Quebec.

The Quebec Government's language policy was a prime concern of many businessmen, although it appeared to be fairly well accepted by the majority of the French-speaking population of the province. As announced by the Minister of Cultural Development, Dr Camille Laurin, the new legislation limited access to English-language schools to children who had at least one parent who had been educated in English in Quebec; all others would be required to attend French-language schools. Firms with more than fifty employees would be required to obtain 'francization' certificates attesting to their ability to use French in all internal communications and with the public. All public signs were, as well, to appear in French only. On 24 August the Government tabled its White Paper on referendums, setting out the ground rules for the plebiscite, expected in 1979, under which Quebeckers would be asked to express their desire for or against independence. The White Paper indicated that the exact wording of the referendum would be proposed by the Government.

During the year the Federal Government began to counter-attack in an attempt to seize the initiative from the Parti Québécois. Prime Minister Trudeau proposed on several occasions a constitutional amendment to guarantee minority language rights across the country. In August the ten provincial premiers, including Mr Lévesque, directed their Ministers of Education to review the state of minority language instruction in each province in an attempt to provide second-language instruction where warranted by numbers. Premier Lévesque rejected, however, the federal proposal that such a guarantee be included in a revised constitution, on the grounds that education was a matter solely of provincial jurisdiction.

The Prime Minister received support from all parties for the speech he delivered to the US Congress on 22 February during his visit to the President, Mr Jimmy Carter. Mr Trudeau told Congress, in a speech clearly aimed at Canadians, that Canada's unity would not be fractured: 'Revisions will take place; accommodations will be made. We shall succeed.' For his part, President Carter told a Canadian journalist that the stability of Canada was of crucial importance to the United States and that he would personally prefer to see Canada remain united.

In March the Prime Minister called for an investigation of alleged pro-separatist bias in the French-language network of the publicly-owned Canadian Broadcasting Corporation. The Government also appointed a task force on Canadian unity, headed by two prominent former Liberal and Conservative politicians, to hold hearings and provide recommendations on the national unity issue; the task force soon identified its job as one of finding a third option somewhere between the constitutional status quo and the Parti Québécois's proposal for sovereignty-association. On 19 October the Prime Minister surprised the country by announcing his intention to introduce legislation that would enable the Federal Government to hold its own referendum, which he said would be legally binding, on some aspects of the national unity question. He left unanswered the questions whether this referendum would take place only in Quebec or also in the rest of the country, and when it would be held.

The continuing skirmishes between Ottawa and Quebec City also affected Canada's external relations. At the conclusion of a three-day visit to France in May Mr Trudeau said he was convinced that the French Government would do nothing to interfere in Canada's internal affairs. However, during a visit to France in November, Premier Lévesque was made a grand officer of the Legion of Honour, in violation of Canadian requirements that the Government give prior authorization for any award from a foreign Government to a Canadian citizen. The French President also told Mr Lévesque that Quebec could be assured of France's 'understanding, confidence, and support' along whatever road it decided to follow. At the same time, the Canadian Government was proposing to African members of *la francophonie* that a conference of government leaders from all French-speaking nations be held during the next year. If organized outside the aegis of the Agence de Coopération Culturelle et Technique, Quebec would not be entitled to independent representation at such a session, which Canadian officials viewed as a francophone equivalent of the regular Commonwealth heads of government meetings.

The Queen also became involved in Canada's internal problems during her six-day silver jubilee visit in October. In a speech on 16 October, which was written by the Canadian Government, she said that one of Canada's greatest assets was that it had two basic traditions, English and French. In the Speech from the Throne, which everyone recognizes is a Government statement, Queen Elizabeth said that the Government was prepared to work with the ten provinces on constitutional reform in pursuit of a 'new federalism'.

The national unity issue tended to obscure in part the serious problems which continued to plague the Canadian economy. October marked the second anniversary of the Government's programme of wage and price controls. Although the 1975 rate of inflation, 10·8 per cent, had been reduced to 5·8 per cent by December 1976, it rose again to approximately 7·5 per cent during 1977. Both changes were largely attributable to the cost of food and energy. Despite a series of consultative meetings in the first half of the year, the Government was unable to obtain the agreement of both labour and business for a programme to phase out the wage and price controls, due to expire in December 1978. In August the Canadian Labour Congress announced that it would proceed no further with the tripartite discussions. In September the former Finance Minister, Mr John Turner, said that the Government should begin immediately to phase out controls in order to remove economic uncertainty and restore investor confidence.

Unemployment remained a major problem as well, rising from a 1976 average of 7·3 per cent to 8·3 per cent in the autumn, when major lay-offs were announced in the mining industry. The 15-24 age group remained particularly hard-hit, experiencing a national unemployment rate of 15·3 per cent. The statistics emphasized the degree of regional economic disparity in the country; for Quebec and the four Atlantic provinces experienced unemployment rates over 10 per cent during most of the year. At the same time the Canadian dollar dropped some 12 points in relation to the US dollar; this was in part a response to the unrealistically high level of the Canadian currency in 1976, but also an indirect result of the economic uncertainty caused by the Parti Québécois victory. By October the dollar was trading at 89·88 US cents, its lowest point since 1939, and the Bank of Canada was obliged to arrange a stand-by line of credit of $1,500 million in US currency.

The Government's only formal Budget of the year, brought down on 31 March, emphasized the need for voluntary restraint if inflation were to be controlled without increasing unemployment. The Government provided

$100 million for additional direct job-creation programmes, increased the federal tax credit, and extended the corporate investment tax credit. In a major economic and fiscal statement on 20 October the new Minister of Finance, Mr Jean Chrétien, announced that wage and price controls would be phased out after 14 April 1978 and that a monitoring agency would be created to replace the Anti-Inflation Board. The Minister, hampered by his commitment to restrain government spending, announced only minor personal income tax reductions, the provision of an additional $150 million for direct job creation, and a $100 million subsidy programme to encourage the private sector to expand and create new jobs.

Debate over the construction of a northern gas pipeline occupied the country's attention during much of the year. On 9 May the inquiry headed by Mr Justice Thomas Berger recommended that no pipeline be built along the Mackenzie River valley for ten years, until native land claims had been settled, and that for environmental reasons there be a permanent ban on construction across the Northern Yukon. Two months later the National Energy Board concluded, after 18 months of hearings, that construction of a pipeline along the Alaska Highway would hold social and economic costs to tolerable levels, but that construction along the Mackenzie River valley would be environmentally unacceptable. The combined weight of these two reports dealt a death blow to the proposals of the Canadian Arctic Gas Pipeline Limited, a fifteen-member consortium of Canadian and US energy giants, in favour of Foothills Pipeline Limited, a much smaller, Canadian-owned company. On 8 September President Carter endorsed the Alaska Highway route, and two weeks later Canadian and US negotiators signed a pipeline agreement. The Foothills president, Mr Robert Blair, expressed the hope that the pipeline would be in service by 1983 to bring natural gas from Alaska, through Canada, to the US. It was estimated that this project would cost $10,000 million and result in the creation of 2,200 new jobs, even if it never became necessary to add a spur line to bring gas from the Canadian Arctic to Canadian markets.

Although Prime Minister Trudeau's Government had trailed the Progressive Conservative (PC) opposition by more than 10 percentage points in the opinion polls before the election of the Parti Québécois in 1976, its recovery began shortly thereafter and continued into 1977. By July, a Gallup poll gave the Liberals 51 per cent of the popular vote, compared to 27 per cent for the Conservatives. A prominent PC Member of Parliament, Mr Jack Horner, crossed the floor to join the Liberal Party in April, and in May the Liberals won five of six federal by-elections, including four of five ridings in Quebec. Even the announcement on 26 May that the Prime Minister and his wife were separating after six years of marriage had a favourable effect on his personal popularity.

Despite much pressure to call a general election in the autumn, the Prime Minister resisted. On 16 September he announced a Cabinet shuffle in which Jean Chrétien became the country's first French-Canadian Minister of Finance, replacing Donald Macdonald, who wished to leave the Cabinet for family reasons. Mr Marc Lalonde, one of the Prime Minister's closest advisers, was appointed to the newly-created portfolio of Minister of State for Federal-Provincial Relations, while Mr Horner received the important Ministry of Industry, Trade and Commerce.

The most encouraging development for the new leader of the Progressive Conservative Party, Mr Joe Clark, was the 93·1 per cent vote of confidence that he received at his party's national conference in November. Throughout the year Mr Clark attempted to emphasize the troubles of the economy in the hope that the electorate would soon tire of the national unity issue, on which his party, with only four MPs elected from Quebec in the last election, remained on the defensive. The opposition was provided with an opportunity to embarrass the Government when it was revealed that the Royal Canadian Mounted Police (RCMP) had been involved in illegal activities such as electronic surveillance and mail interception, primarily in Quebec. Although the issue dominated question time in Parliament for two weeks in November, the Government was able to refer all revelations of illegality to the Royal Commission of inquiry that it had appointed in July. The opposition parties accused the Government of evading the principle of ministerial responsibility for the illegal RCMP actions; however, it soon became apparent that public opinion was solidly on the side of the besieged police force. Another potentially significant development, the introduction of television coverage of Parliament in the autumn, was credited with improving, at least initially, the public image of the Leader of the Opposition.

The Progressive Conservative Party's fortunes were considerably brighter at the provincial level. Although the Ontario PC party, led by Premier William Davis, failed for the second time in 21 months to obtain a parliamentary majority, it was returned to office in a minority position. The New Democratic Party (NDP), which had been the official opposition since 1975, was narrowly replaced in that role by the Liberals. In Manitoba, Premier Edward Shreyer's eight-year-old NDP Government was defeated on 11 October by the Progressive Conservatives under Mr Sterling Lyon, who campaigned on a strong free-enterprise platform based on tax cuts and reductions in government spending.

Canada's external relations, while enlivened by the Ottawa–Quebec feud, were focused on a relatively small number of themes. At the Conference on International Economic Cooperation in Paris, Canada offered to write off $254 million of foreign-aid debts and proposed to contribute an additional $51 million to a fund designed to relieve the debt burdens of the world's poorest countries. In December, on the occasion of the first general parliamentary debate on Canada's external relations in over 20 years, the Government announced the termination of all publicly-

C*

assisted commercial activities in South Africa, including a withdrawal of Canada's commercial counsellors, cessation of government insurance for exports to South Africa, and the development of a 'code of ethics' for Canadian firms operating in that country. Canada's continued practice of selling nuclear technology and supplies to foreign nations was criticized by opposition parties in spite of the Government's attempts to develop better safeguards, which in turn aroused the resentment of some Western European nations which desired either nuclear technology or uranium from Canada.

Chapter 3

LATIN AMERICA

ARGENTINA—BOLIVIA—BRAZIL—CHILE—COLOMBIA—ECUADOR—
PARAGUAY—PERU—URUGUAY—VENEZUELA—CENTRAL AMERICA AND
PANAMA—CUBA—THE DOMINICAN REPUBLIC AND HAITI—MEXICO

ARGENTINA

WHEN on 1 April President Jorge R. Videla spoke to the nation on the anniversary of the army's seizure of power in March 1976 (see AR 1976, p. 80), it was to indicate that the Junta felt it could now proceed to normalize the political situation and install a democratic regime. For this purpose, he had earlier told journalists in March, a dialogue would be opened between the armed forces and civilian representatives. This would, in fact, form the third stage of a three-stage plan for the restoration of 'democratic, representative and federative government'.

The year began with the threat of terrorism still very much present behind unrest at the rapidly rising cost of living. In February widespread disruption was occasioned by a go-slow called by the Light and Power Union when it was required to increase its members' hours of work from 35 to 42 per week. The terrorist threat came from two sides. On the one hand, there was the Peronista formation known as the Montoneros which, it was disclosed on 26 April, had for some time been financed by investments made in the stock market under a syndicate led by Sr David Graiver, formerly Under Secretary of Social Welfare under the 1971-73 Government of President Lanusse. On the other stood the marxist Revolutionary Army of the People (ERP), believed to have been responsible for an attack on the aircraft carrying President Videla by a bomb planted on the runway at Buenos Aires on 18 February.

The Government admitted that its countermeasures had been severe, justifying them by the claim that it was at war, but from Amnesty International, in a report published on 22 March, there came documented charges that between 5,000 and 6,000 political prisoners were being detained in 'punitive conditions', while over 2,000 had disappeared since March 1976. A number of prisoners had been released in December 1976, and government statements said that the total number released since the coup exceeded 1,500.

International sympathy was not, however, accorded to the Government by the new Administration of President Carter in the United States. When on 24 February Secretary of State Cyrus Vance announced the reduction of military aid to Argentina because of violations of human rights, the response of the Argentine Government was on 29 February to reject altogether all US military aid. The following day Uruguay followed suit, though in its case aid had already been withheld by the United States in September 1976. On 15 June the Government did, however, allow all political prisoners who had not been charged to leave the country. Not long afterwards there were indications from the high command of the ERP in Rome that they would be prepared to lay down their arms if a democratic government could be restored, though the kidnapping of Sr Héctor Hidalgo Solá, the Argentine ambassador to Venezuela, while on holiday in Buenos Aires in July, because as a member of the Radical Party (UCR) he had cooperated with the Government, was an indicator of the difficulties yet to be overcome.

At the year's end, ex-President María Estela ('Isabel') Martínez de Perón was still in detention; the bodies of her late husband and that of his first wife Eva had been disinterred from the Presidential residence, Los Olivos, by order of General Videla; and his predecessor, Sr Héctor de Campora, was still in asylum in the Mexican embassy in Buenos Aires waiting for a safe-conduct to leave the country.

The Government meanwhile had been disturbed by the award of the Beagle Channel islands to Chile (see p. 78), but had shown itself willing to enter into serious discussions with the British Government on the future of the Falkland Islands. The action of an admiral in ordering his ship to open fire on a Soviet vessel was not regarded as indicating a general spirit of belligerency in the navy.

BOLIVIA

The Bolivian Government remained under considerable pressure at the beginning of the year as the result of the failure of its initiative to gain its long-hoped-for access to the sea by an agreement with Chile, whose terms had proved too severe to be acceptable to military and public opinion. Political moves suggested that President Hugo Banzer Suárez was endeavouring to attain constitutional status by elections to be held in 1978, probably as a civilian. His request to retire from the army, the key step in the civilianization of his Government, led to a crisis at the end of November. After the three service chiefs had submitted their resignations, the President in a surprise broadcast on 1 December announced that he would not be a candidate after all, and that his decision was 'firm and irreversible'. It was followed by the decision to retire some 100 senior officers in order to permit promotions in the junior ranks of the armed forces. Speculation that the new President to be chosen in July 1978 would be a military dignitary was confirmed by the announcement by ex-President Luis Adolfo Siles Salinas, the last previous civilian President (see AR 1969, p. 182), that he would not be a candidate either.

From 2 August two Indian languages, Quechua, spoken by 44 per cent of the population, and Aymara, spoken by 30 per cent, would become official languages alongside Spanish. They would be taught in schools from 1979 and could be used in judicial proceedings.

BRAZIL

The country entered the year in a new spirit of optimism based on the attainment of an 11 per cent growth rate in 1976, a halving of the trade deficit and some increase in the reserves. Coffee production was still down by 60 per cent, but revenue from it held up very satisfactorily, though towards the end of the year there were signs that the Government might incur heavy losses by its policy of withholding stocks in view of consumer resistance in the importing countries. Agriculture was generally affected by a long drought, while the development of off-shore oil, while keenly pursued during the year, had yet to produce results just when the very small existing wells showed signs of exhaustion.

Politically the Government entered the year apparently very much determined to retain control, and to discourage criticism. On 8 February the Minister of Industry and Trade, Senhor Severo Fagundo Gomes, resigned because he had called for a more open political debate, and was replaced by Senhor Angelo Calmon de Sá, President of the Bank of Brazil. The opposition Brazilian Democratic Movement (MDB) used its substantial size in Congress to block a constitutional amendment to reform the judiciary, since it neither safeguarded magistrates from dismissal nor reinstated the right of habeas corpus suspended in 1968. The response of President Ernesto Geisel, acting under the emergency powers of the National Security Council, empowered by Institutional Act No. 5, was to close Congress down on 1 April. On 14 April it was reconvened, after the President had on the previous day enacted the proposed change by decree. Other decrees extended the Presidential term from five years to six, allowed future constitutional amendments to be enacted by a simple rather than a two-thirds majority of Congress, provided for state governors and one-third of the Senate to be elected indirectly, and prohibited any candidate for office from presenting issues on either radio or television. This last decree was generally known as the 'lei Falcão', after Dr Armando Ribeiro Falcão, the Minister of Justice, who had instituted it for the 1976 municipal elections.

Denunciation of the moves came from several quarters. Cardinal Aloisio Lorschneider denounced the change in regard to constitutional amendment because he feared, correctly, that it would be followed by an amendment permitting divorce (23 June). The leader of the MDB in the Deputies was deprived of his political rights for ten years for his criticism. A series of student demonstrations, banned by Dr Falcão, were dispersed with difficulty. On 31 May a formal strike began at the University of Brasília, when the Rector suspended nine students, and on 4 June no less than 800 were arrested at the University of Minas Gerais. Above all, in a new and significant development, in a manifesto signed by a number of colonels on 27 May, elements within the army itself called for more political rights, a new provisional government, and the holding of fresh elections.

Deep political divisions, brought about by long participation in government by the army, were further shown up in October when President Geisel dismissed General Sylvio Frota, Minister of War and a prominent leader of the right, because of the effects of his campaign for succession to the Presidency. General Frota responded with hot accusations that the President himself was 'soft on communism'. For evidence he called on examples of Brazil's extreme pragmatism in foreign policy, including the recognition of China, Cuba, Angola and the Palestine Liberation Organization. In this field, however, the most important development during the year had been Brazil's denunciation of the military aid agreement with the United States on 3 March, by which the Government both demonstrated its independence of President Carter's human rights campaign and rid itself of its obligations at very low cost. At the beginning of December, there opened the first meeting of the proposed Amazon Pact, attended by representatives of Bolivia, Ecuador, Guyana, Peru, Surinam and Venezuela.

CHILE

In a year which saw the continued gradual improvement of economic conditions, there were signs that the collective pressure of international disapproval, shown once more in Chile's censure by the UN General Assembly in December, was making a regime now apparently stable and to some extent accepted take more heed of its appearance. At the end of

1976, President Augusto Pinochet Ugarte had told an interviewer on Colombian television that his country was 'an authoritarian democracy' and would not revert to 'the outdated system of representative democracy'. On 12 March, the junta issued a decree dissolving all remaining political parties, claiming that there had been a plot by the Christian Democrats to overthrow the Government. The state of siege was extended for another six months, with new provisions for the censorship of mail and a ban on foreign magazines. The Government's charges appeared to refer to the proposals of two of the Christian Democratic Party's leaders for the restoration of civilian government issued during a major reconstruction of the Cabinet.

The letter had been earlier disturbed by the resignation of Sr Jorge Cauas, who as Minister of Finance had been credited with laying the foundations of economic recovery. He had been replaced by Sr Sergio de Castro. On 11 April, with the effect of President Carter's initiative now evident, the Minister of Justice, Sr Renato Damiliano Bonfante, who had been appointed only a month previously, was forced to resign because of his remarks about church leaders who in late March had criticized publicly the unrepresentative character of the Government. On 19 June Jorge Montes, said to be the last political prisoner in custody, was exchanged for 11 political prisoners from East Germany, after a qualified general pardon for exiles had been issued on 22 May. Moves by the United States to end its aid programme to Chile were forestalled on 28 June, when the Government formally renounced all aid from any external source.

By the time the President announced proposals for a partial return to civilian rule in the late 1980s, with the transition beginning in 1981, the statement, on 10 July, was widely expected. During the rest of the year, with the rate of inflation dropping back towards the 70 per cent mark, the Government appeared confident, and the President's address to the nation on 11 September, after an evidently friendly visit to the United States, reflected this. Earlier, in January, he had visited the area claimed by Chile in Antarctica, and on 2 May had welcomed and accepted the decision of the International Court of Justice to award the Beagle Channel islands to Chile, namely Picton, Lennox and Nueva islands, at the eastern entrance to the channel (see Pt. xiv, Ch. 1).

COLOMBIA

The country continued to enjoy the benefit of the high world price of coffee, but also its problems. By September the annual rate of inflation had reached nearly 50 per cent, and was one of the factors leading on 14 September to a general strike called by a conjunction of the four principal trade union federations. The Government, which had maintained a state of siege since 25 October 1976, had in August declared strike organization illegal and prohibited all public references to strikes; on 6 September it declared the strike itself illegal. Despite a two-day curfew in the capital, severe conflicts with security forces resulted in 18 deaths and some 4,000 arrests. There were also clashes later at the state oil refinery at Barrancabermeja, Department of Santander, and the terrorist group M-19 reminded the Government of their existence by kidnapping a former Minister of Agriculture, Hugo Ferreira Neira.

For his handling of the strike, Dr Rafael Pardo Buelvas, the Conservative Minister of the Interior, was censured by Congress and resigned on 22 September. The President then reshuffled his Cabinet, appointing to the Interior another Conservative, Dr Alfredo Araújo Grau. The Minister of Defence, General Abraham Varón Valencia, the non-party member, remained at his post and the balance of the coalition was not disturbed. Indeed, for both the major political parties it was a year of unification for the 1978 elections, at which not only would a new Electoral Law, passed on 22 April, be used, but the Congressional would precede the Presidential elections, thus enabling the Liberals to abide by the result of the earlier elections in choosing a joint Presidential candidate. Early in November the two factions of the Conservative Party also united to back the candidature of a former Minister of Labour, Sr Belisario Betancur, aged 57, from a mining family in Antioquía.

ECUADOR

A series of resignations of members of the Cabinet towards the end of 1976 was continued on 8 February by that of Colonel René Vargas Pazzos, Minister of Natural Resources and Energy, seen as a 'progressive'. After the compulsory retirement of the head of the military academy, General Solón Espinosa, on 28 December 1976, General Luis Guillermo Durán Arcentales, army chief of staff, dominated the Government, and was widely expected to become President in elections announced for 1978. Ex-President José María Velasco Ibarra stated that he would not return to be a candidate, and gave his blessing to the Democratic Action Party led by his nephew, Sr Jaime Acosta Velasco. All would, however, depend on a referendum on the revision of the Constitution to be held in January 1978.

At home, there was scattered evidence of opposition to the military Government. A one-day general strike on 18 May led to clashes in which one person was killed. Three more died when after another strike the Government dissolved the teachers' union; 220 teachers were then dismissed, and the leaders of each strike imprisoned for two years apiece. Abroad, tension with Peru was somewhat abated by the decision earlier in the year by the United States to veto the sale to Ecuador by Israel of

24 Kfir long-range aircraft (with American engines), the sale of which had been negotiated at the end of the previous year after Peru had purchased 36 Su-22 fighter-bombers from the Soviet Union.

PARAGUAY

Elections were held on 6 February for 60 members of the Constitutional Convention to revise the 1967 Constitution in order that President Alfredo Stroessner could in 1978 stand for a further term. The result was the expected substantial majority, some 69 per cent of the electorate, for the governing Colorado Party. The state of siege, renewed periodically since 1954, was lifted for 24 hours to permit the elections to take place. Three days previously, three Communist leaders, including the Party's Secretary General, Sr Antonio Maidana, who had been in prison since 1958, were released.

Relations with the outside world were dominated by progress in hydro-electric development and the need to resolve fundamental technical difficulties. Brazil, which had earlier agreed to run its plant at Itaipú on a continuous basis, so that a constant flow would be available to the Argentine-Paraguayan plant downstream, early in November averted the most serious possibility of conflict by the unilateral decision to install two sets of turbines at Itaipú, so that Paraguay could maintain the 50-cycle standard it shared with Argentina rather than convert to the 60-cycle standard of Brazil.

PERU

It was announced on 5 February that the country would return to civilian rule under a new Constitution between 1977 and 1980. The new 'Tupac Amaru' Plan, it was said, would consolidate the revolutionary process, and the country would not 'move towards communism nor, in reaction, turn back to outdated forms of prerevolutionary capitalism'. It appeared that following a Christmas amnesty there were 'only' 100 political prisoners in Peru. However, on 8 January four prominent military figures who had supported the manifesto of the Revolutionary Socialist Party (PSR) were deported. They included General Leónidas Rodríguez Figueroa, one of the promoters of the 1968 revolution, and Admiral Jorge Dellapiane Ocampo, former Minister of Industry and Commerce. Between 3 and 5 March General Jorge Videla, President of Argentina, made a state visit to Lima, at the end of which an agreement was signed by which Argentine technology would be used to build a 10-mW research reactor, Peru's first, at an estimated cost of US$50 million. On 22 April it was stated that President Francisco Morales Bermúdez, now 56 but due to retire from the army in 1978, would remain as President to guide the process of institutionalization.

However, at this point economic problems again became more salient than political ones. The cost of living was continuing to rise at a rate calculated as 52·5 per cent in the 12 months to June. The IMF had proposed strict deflationary measures. Opposition to these by the Minister of the Economy, Dr Luis Barúa Castañeda, the only civilian in the Cabinet, caused him to resign on 13 May. He was replaced by Sr Walter Piazza Tanguis, a businessman and engineer, who announced on 10 June a new economic plan, including a 50 per cent rise in the price of petrol and severe budgetary economies, but resigned in turn on 6 July when he failed to gain military approval for further deflationary measures. He was replaced by a soldier, General Alcibíades Saenz Barsallo, but the President of the Central Bank then resigned.

Meanwhile those measures which the Government had taken had resulted in widespread demonstrations, which began in Cuzco on 17 June and did not abate until late in July, and in the course of which 17 died. They culminated in a general strike in the principal cities at the end of June, which the Government countered by the arrest of most of the prominent labour leaders. Strikes then spread to the mining sector, causing further disruption, and it was only the decision to announce on 12 July a series of humanitarian moves, beginning with a 10 per cent cut in the price of bread and pasta, and a general wage increase, that began the appeasement of public and in particular labour opinion.

At this point, too, the Central Bank was ordered to stop the series of mini-devaluations initiated in July 1976, leaving the sol standing at 80.88 to one US dollar. At the end of the year the size of the foreign debt and the need to renegotiate it remained a serious problem for the future. Strikes and demonstrations continued in the aftermath of the disturbances, and the publication of the new Electoral Law in November was the first step in arrangements for the selection of a Constituent Assembly in July 1978.

At the end of December the death was announced of General Juan Velasco Alvarado, aged 67, leader of the revolution of 1968 and President of Peru from 1968 until his deposition in 1975 (see OBITUARY).

URUGUAY

Like other states of the 'Southern Cone' (see pp. 75, 77 and 84), Uruguay renounced United States military aid following President Carter's initiative, and it was reported that at Montevideo in May high military officers from Argentina, Bolivia, Brazil, Chile, Paraguay, Peru and Uruguay met to concert opposition to it. As with the other countries, however, the year was marked by further steps towards the restoration of institutional government, after early signs of pressure towards the retention of authoritarian government. Thus at the end of January an Institutional Act No. 6 set up a new Ministry of Justice, designed to replace the Supreme Court by an executive organ, and Sr Fernando Bayardo Bengoa was appointed Attorney General. On 16 February Sr Antonio Mas, aged 28, a former leader of the Tupumaros, was sentenced to 30 years plus between 7 and 15 years imprisonment for his part in the kidnapping and murder of Mr Dan Mitrione (see AR 1970, p. 85) and the kidnapping of Mr (later Sir) Geoffrey Jackson, the British ambassador (see AR 1971, pp. 12-13 and 89). On his release he was to be deported to Spain. Already, however, divisions in the army had become manifest, and in March and April purges were conducted, including that of General Dardo Grossi, the military attache in Washington, before President Aparicio Méndez stated at a press conference on 21 May that a return to constitutionalism was intended.

After Institutional Acts No. 7 and 8 had permitted the Government to dismiss civil servants without charge, and, on 1 July, to dismiss judges at will for the coming four years, though with a new Court of Justice to act as supreme tribunal, the President announced on 9 August that he had 'adopted the proposal of the Junta' that general elections be held in 1981 in which the traditional parties would be permitted to participate, although, as became clear later in the month, under a new Constitution by which they would select a single candidate approved by the armed forces.

VENEZUELA

At the beginning of January President Carlos Andrés Pérez demonstrated the strength of his political position by reshuffling his Cabinet. Another major reconstruction took place in July, and was followed by the appointment of new chiefs of staff. Economically the country continued in a strong position, with revenue up despite a further fall of 1·9 per cent in oil production. The choice of Luis Piñerúa by the governing Acción Democrática as its candidate for the Presidential succession in August focused internal political attention on the contest between him and his most significant rival, Sr Luis Herrera Campins of the opposition COPEI.

For the President, therefore, it was a year marked above all else by the continuing zeal with which he pursued a dynamic, radical foreign policy. From 11 to 14 May President Videla of Argentina visited Venezuela to enlist the President's support against what the Argentines saw as the expansionism of Brazil. To the Venezuelan Congress, on 9 September, at the end of his two-day state visit, King Juan Carlos of Spain affirmed that Latin America now had a high priority in his country's foreign policy. Agreements were signed for joint projects to the value of US$1,300 million.

The President himself had been much embarrassed by a report in the *New York Times* on 19 February that he had, while Minister of the Interior in the early 1960s, received payments from the US Central Intelligence Agency, and he had shown his displeasure by recalling his ambassador. On 24 February President Carter described the allegations as 'groundless and mischievous', and the President in his state visit to Washington from 28 June to 3 July took the opportunity to urge intensification of the campaign for human rights and a settlement with Panama.

CENTRAL AMERICA AND PANAMA

For Central America, the tradition of unity, as manifested by the royal visit of King Juan Carlos of Spain to Guatemala, Honduras, El Salvador and Costa Rica, between 10 and 16 September, and to PANAMA on 16-17 September, showed signs of strain. The King expressed support in Panama for Guatemala's claim to Belize, while the Panamanian President affirmed in turn his support for Spain's claim to Gibraltar. However, earlier, on 8 May, in a diplomatic *volte-face*, President Omar Torrijos during a stopover in Belize had expressed support for that territory's rightful claim to independence. Diplomatic relations with Panama were severed by Guatemala on 19 May, Panamanian interests in Guatemala being taken over by the embassy of Costa Rica, where the Government, under the pressure of international opinion, was modifying its earlier support for the formal claims of Guatemala by stating that it thought they should take second place to the wishes of the inhabitants of Belize, though its Foreign Minister on 25 August joined with his fellows from the other Central American states in reaffirming their original position.

Negotiations with the United States on the conclusion of a new Panama Canal treaty, which had earlier cost the resignation of Sr Aquilino Boyd, the Foreign Minister (9 February), were continued by his successor, Sr Nicolás González Revilla, and received the support of all the Central American states, together with the Presidents of Colombia and Mexico. They concluded triumphantly for Panama on 7 September with the signing of the new treaty by Presidents Carter and Torrijos (see p. 65), following which the President made a tour of Western Europe and Israel to secure diplomatic support for its ratification by the United States Senate.

COSTA RICA restored diplomatic relations with Cuba on 21 February, the first Latin American country to do so since the Organization of American States (OAS) 'freedom of action' resolution of October 1975. In May a General Staff was created to coordinate the Ministries of Interior, of Public Security and of the Presidency with the police forces. But the dominant theme of the year was the opening of the Presidential election campaign in September. In view of the continued presence in the country of Mr Robert Vesco, the United States financier, which was adversely affecting support for the ruling Party of National Liberation (PLN), President Daniel Oduber, who had admitted him in the first place, ordered him to leave the country on 10 June, a few days after the Minister of Economy, Industry and Commerce, Sr Jorge Sánchez Méndez, had resigned from the Cabinet to run the campaign of the PLN candidate, Sr Luis Alberto Monge. Among the five other candidates, Sr Guillermo Villalobos Arce, of the Party of National Unification (PUN), presented the most serious challenge, and Sr Rodrigo Gutiérrez Saenz represented a new left-wing coalition with the first direct communist participation since the Party was legalized in May 1975.

In NICARAGUA criticism of the Government became more open, and in December President Anastasio Somoza, in a Cabinet reshuffle, replaced General Roger Bermúdez Ballesteros as Minister of Information by Sr Rafael Cano. In HONDURAS in January the leaders of the armed forces were replaced, and Colonel Omar Antonio Zelaya Reyes succeeded General Mario Carcama Chinchilla as Minister of Defence. Other changes followed the denial of rumours that left-wing feeling had been aroused by the more right-wing tone of the Government's recent actions. At the year's end the Government, accused by El Salvador of new border incidents, denied that the disturbances had any official sanction, and the two Governments showed their goodwill by deposition of their ratifications of the 1976 mediation agreement in Washington.

Both at home and abroad, EL SALVADOR was seen to move well to the right. Like Guatemala, it joined the 'Southern Cone' countries in formally renouncing military aid after criticism of its position on human rights. When the new President, Carlos Humberto Romero, took office on 1 July, the clergy boycotted the ceremony in protest against the arrest and torture of priests, particularly Jesuits, who were the target of threats from a paramilitary organization known as the White Warriors Union (UGB). Violence had surrounded the elections on 20 February which had returned the candidate of the ruling Party of National Conciliation (PCN). The body of the Foreign Minister, Sr Mauricio Borgonovo Pohl, aged 38, who had been kidnapped on 19 April by the Popular Liberation Front (FPL), was found on 11 May at Santa Tecla, after the Government had refused to free 37 prisoners.

GUATEMALA, where terrorist incidents in late 1976 continued in the new year, displayed fresh energy in the pursuit of its claim to Belize (see p. 91), due to pressure from Vice-President Mario Sandoval Alarcón, head of the ruling Movement of National Liberation (MLN). A new law promulgated in July made it a capital offence to question the validity of the claim, and was followed by accusations of conspiracy between Britain and left-wing states following Panama's change of view on the issue (see p. 83). In February, General David Caminos Barrios, former chief of staff, had replaced General Otto Spiegler Noriega as Minister of Defence. In July a new military build-up on the frontier was countered by Britain's reinforcing the Belize garrison; the commander in the Petén said his forces would not leave, but would invade Belize if it became independent. The kidnapping of the Salvadorean ambassador, Colonel Eduardo Casanova Sandóval, on 29 May, by the insurgent Guerrilla Army of the Poor (EGP) —he was released unharmed two days later, after a communique had been broadcast—was a reminder that the Guatemalan military position was more fragile than it appeared.

CUBA

In Cuba, 1977 was above all seen as a year of 'growing influence in the international arena'. From 28 February, for more than five weeks, President Fidel Castro Ruz made an extensive tour of socialist countries in Africa, the Middle East and Europe, during which he reaffirmed the right of Cuba to aid liberation movements throughout the world. On 16 October he paid a six-day state visit to Jamaica. Praised for his fight against colonialism and neocolonialism, and decorated with Jamaica's highest order, President Castro promised increased aid. A week previously, President Samora Machel of Mozambique had followed President Agostinho Neto of Angola in visiting Cuba, and in December General Raul Castro Ruz, Minister of the Revolutionary Armed Forces, attended the first congress of the PLM in Angola.

His words on that occasion were echoed by his brother, closing the annual three-day session of the National People's Power Assembly. Cuba, he said, which had begun regular bilateral discussions with the United States in September, would not change its relations with the USSR and the socialist camp. The United States, moreover, had no right to criticize the stationing of Cuban soldiers in Angola. 'Solidarity with the peoples of Africa and the aid that Cuba is giving them and will continue to give also to the movements of African liberation', he continued, 'cannot be negotiated because they are part of the principles of the Cuban revolution'. Nevertheless, agreements signed with the United States on maritime limits and cultural exchange did indicate a further thaw in relations, as did the reopening of direct air communications on 20 December.

At home, on the 16th anniversary of their foundation, the Committees for the Defence of the Revolution, with five million members, held their first congress, and preparations for the XIIth World Youth Festival to be held in Havana in 1978 generated much enthusiasm.

DOMINICAN REPUBLIC AND HAITI

In the DOMINICAN REPUBLIC Cabinet changes early in the year brought Rear-Admiral Ramón Emilio Jiménez Reyes Hizo to the Ministry of Foreign Affairs and General Juan Beauchamps Javier to the Ministry for the Armed Forces. Student demonstrations at the latter appointment led to the occupation by soldiers of the Autonomous University of Santo Domingo in March. Political activity intensified in anticipation of the coming elections, in which the main opposition party, the Dominican Revolutionary Party (PRD), decided to take part. Following its legalization in November the Communist Party appeared likely to do so too.

Tension with HAITI brought charges of border violations. Haiti was suffering from its most severe drought on record, which had brought widespread famine, increased by soil erosion, and had brought to a halt nine-tenths of the country's industry. Since the appointment of M Pierre Biamby as Minister of Interior and Defence in April 1976 there had been many arrests of political opponents, including many returning exiles, and a US congressional report issued in January strengthened criticisms. In a Cabinet reshuffle on 28 May M Biamby was replaced by M Aurélien C. Jeanty, with M Michel Fièvre at the Ministry of Justice.

MEXICO

The year began in uneasy calm as the new Government of President José López Portillo took stock of the difficult situation following the effective devaluation of the peso by over 100 per cent. The increase in federal expenditure over actual 1976 was held below 40 per cent in the Budget, and in the course of the year the Government's economic strategy of strict adherence to IMF norms, combined with rapid expansion of oil production, proved successful, though growth for the year was only 2 per cent against a population increase of 3 per cent, some 6 million of Mexico's 18 million labour force being unemployed. Casualties in the Cabinet were Carlos Tello Macias, Secretary of Budget, who favoured an expansionist policy, and towards the end of the year the Secretary of Hacienda (Finance), Julio Rodolfo Moctezuma Cid, who opposed early reflation. The new President also replaced Sr Porfirio Muñoz Ledo by Carlos Sansores Pérez as president of the ruling Party of the Institutionalized Revolution (PRI).

In foreign policy, relations with the United States were improved by the visit of the President to Washington between 13 and 17 February, where he urged Congress to support a new world economic order, and American Jewish organizations agreed to lift their boycott of Mexican tourism. Then on 28 March diplomatic relations were resumed with Spain in an historic move welcomed even by the Republican Government in Exile which alone Mexico had recognized since 1939. Trouble came, however, when ex-President Gustavo Díaz Ordaz was named as the first ambassador. The writers Carlos Fuentes, ambassador in Paris, and Octavio Paz, ambassador to India, both resigned in protest. At the end of July, after he had made public criticism of ex-President Echeverría's Spanish policy, Sr Díaz Ordaz presented his resignation for reasons of health, while in the meantime Sr Echeverría had himself been sent to Paris on 30 June as ambassador to Unesco, though he too had returned to Mexico unexpectedly at the end of July after attacks had begun on a number of his leading supporters. One of these, Alberto Rios Camarena, had shortly beforehand been arrested in Miami on charges of embezzling over US$4·3 million for PRI funds from the Bahia de Banderas Trust of Nayarit.

Another former Secretary of Agriculture, Felix Barra García, was arrested in connexion with the controversial expropriation of 250,000 hectares in the Yaqui Valley in Sonora (see AR 1976, p. 93), but told a court on 28 August that he had confessed only under threat of torture. In a Solomonic judgment the President had ruled in May that the land had been illegally expropriated, since it was small property, but that it would not be restored to its former owners, who would be compensated instead: 752 proprietors received 679 million pesos for 37,660 hectares in August. A final political shock was the resignation in the same month of the President of the Chamber of Deputies, Augusto Gómez Villanueva, who though accused of submitting false expenses claims was given the embassy in Rome.

The ability of the Government to use a firm hand was not in doubt after 7 July when a strike by non-academic staff at the National University (UNAM) was ended by occupation of the campus. After the Presidential address at the beginning of September had announced the adoption of the West German system of proportional representation for Congress in order to increase opposition representation, evidence of deeper dissent was shown by the explosion of some 23 bombs in the capital, Guadalajara and Oaxaca, where the State Governor, Manuel Zarate Arquino, had been dismissed on 3 March. Five people were injured.

Chapter 4

THE CARIBBEAN

COMMONWEALTH CARIBBEAN—TRINIDAD AND TOBAGO—GUYANA—
JAMAICA—BELIZE AND ANGUILLA—BARBADOS—ANTIGUA AND ST KITTS-NEVIS
—ST LUCIA—DOMINICA—ST VINCENT AND GRENADA—SURINAM

COMMONWEALTH CARIBBEAN

THE ancient Carib god Huracan must have gone on a journey, for no storm warnings troubled the islands during 1977. But there was turbulence enough, with recurring crises that had their origins in a depressed economy and were exacerbated by ideological differences.

Rich in oil, Trinidad and Tobago prospered; but even there inflation proved to be a problem. The other English-speaking countries were all hard hit by the cost of energy, which multiplied between 1975 and 1977. It cost more to grow food, run factories and to move people and goods to markets and ports. While the cost of production increased, the prices of most primary commodities fell. Anxiety about the future of the sugar industry grew with the spread of the dreaded smut disease which, during the year, moved from the eastern Caribbean into the canefields of Jamaica. The resource-base was eroded by a fall in production and by the spread of plant diseases. The land fed fewer mouths, and there were more mouths to feed because of the high rate of population growth.

The reality came home when basic foods disappeared from the shelves of shops. The shortages kept recurring, for the Caribbean had become more of a food-deficit area than it had ever been. The traditional remedy was to import more food from North America, but foreign reserves had dwindled and there was less money available for this.

The Caribbean community was divided also by ideological differences. Contrary forces were at work. Those which expressed themselves through common action showed weakness, those which fostered closer friendships with other countries committed to similar political doctrines showed strength. There was a strengthening also of attitudes that involved identification with the Third World, closer association with African countries, a rejection of many of the values and models of the highly industrialized countries of the West, and in some places a rejection of, and hostility to, 'whiteness'.

The whole region was greatly concerned over discussions about the Law of the Sea. The proposal to allow countries bordering on the sea a 200-mile exclusive economic limit would produce chaos in the Caribbean, where, as Dr Eric Williams, Prime Minister of Trinidad and Tobago, insisted, many national jurisdictions were involved, and independent nations lay close to each other. He urged that the Caribbean should be treated as a special area.

The Caribbean turned its eyes from the sea to Washington in mid-December. The World Bank sponsored a meeting there involving donor countries and international funding agencies on the one hand and the Caribbean countries in need of aid on the other. The conference noted with growing concern the serious economic problems that these countries faced as a result of the slow-down of the world economy, increases in import prices, a weak demand for Caribbean products and 'the deep-rooted structural problems of small island economies'. It pointed out that in many countries per-capita production and incomes had declined, and recognized the need for a larger flow of external assistance over the next five years. It decided that a Caribbean Group for Economic Cooperation (CGEC) should be set up in the spring of 1978 to deal with the needs of individual countries and to examine specific proposals for regional cooperation. For the region as a whole, this was the most hopeful happening of the year.

TRINIDAD AND TOBAGO

Little of the general depression touched Trinidad and Tobago, whose foreign reserves ranked with the highest group in the Commonwealth. The island's manufacturing industry expanded and land prices rose sharply, causing the banks to curb the current speculation in land by making mortgages difficult. The buoyancy of the economy resulted in a general feeling of optimism. Below the surface, however, there were indications of trouble. Money, that most sensitive of migrants, started to move out in such quantity that the Government was forced to introduce currency restrictions. Most startling of all was a great fire that devoured the commercial heart of Port of Spain a few days before Christmas. It was generally thought to have been the work of a small band of guerrillas.

GUYANA

Guyana and Jamaica were at the other end of the spectrum. Both countries had set themselves the task of restructuring the society to make it more egalitarian, less dependent on imports, freer from any threat of dominance by foreign corporations.

Guyana's strivings toward a planned economy were made more painful by a long strike in the sugar industry. The state-owned Guyana Sugar Corporation was forced to cut back its estimate of sugar production from 312,000 tons to 260,000, the cut-back representing a loss of G$30 million in foreign reserves. As a result the Government restricted the already small inflow of consumer goods by a further 10 per cent. The country's near-monopoly of the world market for sale of calcined bauxite meant less because of a world-wide slow-down in the steel industry.

JAMAICA

Mr Michael Manley, Prime Minister, having scored a resounding victory over the Jamaica Labour Party in December 1976, set out brave plans for the country, but, after a brief euphoric period, Jamaica found itself beset by grave economic difficulties. Foreign reserves were down almost to vanishing-point. Imports were severely cut, and an emergency production plan adopted, which had as its short-term objective the maximization of productive employment opportunities, and as a long-term objective enlarging the nation's pool of skilled persons. The Government made strenuous efforts to borrow money wherever it could, among its creditors being Trinidad and Tobago and Barbados. It sought the assistance of the international agencies, including the International Development Fund, and undertook to devalue its currency by 37 per cent. The economic difficulties were compounded by an upsurge in crimes of violence, including rape, assault and murder. The flow of skilled and professional people from the country continued, and the country became more sharply divided by political differences.

A report on the Production Plan, which was tabled in the House of Representatives on 13 December, made dismal reading. It complained of the absence of a reliable system for estimating employment in agriculture and the construction industry, and of a lack of progress in providing for the vocational and technical training of workers, and expressed the view that the employment situation had deteriorated. Toward the end of the year a ray of hope appeared on the horizon, with the prospect of a revival of the tourist industry and the hope of larger foreign reserves.

Mr Manley gave considerable time to consolidating his country's position of leadership in the Third World. In President Carter's words, he became a powerful voice of these countries, pressing for a new economic order and for a more equitable sharing of the world's wealth. Adhering to its policy of non-alignment, Jamaica opened an embassy in Moscow, sent trade missions to the countries of Eastern Europe and at the same time muted the rhetoric of hostility to the United States. Mrs Rosalyn Carter, Mr Andrew Young, President Machel and Dr Fidel Castro were among the distinguished visitors to the island.

Split by political differences, the nation found an occasion for unity in the death of its only surviving national hero, Sir Alexander Bustamante (see OBITUARY). A leader of towering personality, he had dominated the political scene from 1935 to the time of his retirement in 1968, and, with his cousin Norman Manley, had brought the Jamaican nation into being.

BELIZE AND ANGUILLA

Events in Barbados and the other English-speaking islands of the eastern Caribbean as well as in Belize appeared less spectacular. After some hurrying to and fro of British and Guatemalan troops the flurry on the border between Belize and Guatemala died down. In meetings of the Organization of American States the new members from the Commonwealth Caribbean were emphatic about the right of their sister community to decide whether or not it wished to be part of Guatemala. More than a thousand miles away, on the north-eastern rim of the archipelago, the name of Anguilla briefly reappeared in the headlines, when Mr Ronald Webster, who had led the movement for secession from St Kitts-Nevis-Anguilla, gave way to local political pressure and resigned. The British Commissioner named Mr Jeremiah Gumbs to succeed him.

BARBADOS

The recently elected Prime Minister of Barbados, Mr Tom Adams, followed a conservative course. The island was achieving the miraculous in carrying 1,500 people to the square mile, maintaining stability and maintaining also a relatively high standard of living, the per capita income being EC$2,700. Tourism, light industry and sugar were the chief money-earners, and Barbadians overseas sent back sizeable remittances. The chief problem was the high rate of unemployment. About 32 per cent of the labour force between 16 and 25 was unemployed. The attempt to contain inflation was made more difficult because the economy was so completely at the mercy of external markets. Despite the difficulties, however, some progress was made and the Central Bank reported a modest increase in production and a slow climb out of the depressed conditions of 1975.

ANTIGUA AND ST KITTS-NEVIS

Antigua, which had endured the eccentricities of the Walter Government for five years, settled back into the experienced hands of Mr Vere Bird with a measure of relief. Tourism showed signs of revival, and the economy brightened. Mr Bird kept his election promise of abolishing personal income tax. The loss in revenue was made good by increasing the hotel tax and the stamp duty on the transfer of real estate and on capital gains.

Tranquillity reigned also in neighbouring St Kitts-Nevis. The cries of independence for Nevis became less strident and the Government appeared more responsive to that island's appeals. It purchased the St Kitts Basseterre sugar factory, thus taking control of the whole of the island's sugar production.

ST LUCIA

On the other hand, political tension increased in St Lucia, where the St Lucia Labour Party (SLP) maintained a running battle with Mr John Compton's United Workers Party (UWP), which was in power. Mr Compton had promised at election time to take his country into independence. In preparation for this he had set about establishing a Division of External Affairs, with the help of the Government of Trinidad and Tobago. His Government issued a Green Paper setting out the advantages of independence, and a select committee of the House of Representatives was appointed to draft a constitution. A period of national consultation followed. The SLP boycotted the whole affair and published a Red Paper emphasizing that the decision about independence was one that the people should take.

DOMINICA

Dominica, long looked down upon as the Cinderella of the Caribbean Commonwealth, suffered from a bitter dispute between the Government and the civil service, which nearly brought the activities of the island to a standstill. The island, 305 square miles in area, is larger than Barbados and Grenada combined. It had been severely handicapped by lack of a good system of communication. With funding from the Caribbean Development Bank and the Canadian International Development Agency, three cargo sheds were built at the deep-sea harbour for the storage of in-transit and locally produced goods. Banana production fell, but only by about 1,000 tons. All told, the gloom was not as deep as in some of the other islands.

ST VINCENT AND GRENADA

In St Vincent the Premier, Mr Milton Cato, had promised to take his country into independence, but in power he walked carefully. The reason became clear when his development plan was made public; for it all depended on loans from the Caribbean Development Bank, the British

Development Division and local business. The Government Savings Bank was reorganized and set up as the National Commercial Bank. It was difficult to see how a small island of 150 square miles with 100,000 people and an annual budget of EC$40 million could achieve meaningful independence. The neighbouring island of Grenada, now independent and with its economy in shambles, did not provide any encouragement.

SURINAM

The first general election since Surinam achieved independence (see AR 1976, p. 96) was held on 31 October 1977. The main contestants were the ruling National Party Alliance led by Mr Henck Arron, the Prime Minister, a partnership of Mr Arron's Surinam National Party (NPS), the (mainly Hindu) Reformed Progressive Party (HPP), the Progressive Surinam People's Party (PSV) and the (Javanese) Kaum-Tani Persuatan Indonesia (KPTI); and the opposition United Democratic Party, a left-inclined alliance of five groups headed by Mr Jaggernath Lachmon's Progressive Reform Party. The election had been precipitated by the resignation of two Ministers, Mr Willy Soemita, who was gaoled in September for corruption, and Mr Soejadin André Soeperman, followed by the temporary alienation of the KTPI, to which Mr Soemita belonged, from the Government coalition, leaving it without a majority. After the impending election had been announced in July, the Nationalist Republican Party (PNR) led by Mr Eddie Bruma, holding five seats and three ministerial posts, was ejected from the coalition, to be replaced by the HPP, which held one seat.

Despite that defection, the National Party Alliance won the election with 22 seats in the Staten (legislative assembly), against 17 for the United Democratic Party, a victory insufficient, however, to give Mr Arron the two-thirds majority needed for constitutional changes. All other groups were eliminated from the Staten, including Mr Bruma's PNR.

Surinam became the 25th member of the Organization of American States on 22 February.

III THE USSR, EASTERN EUROPE AND MONGOLIA

Chapter 1

THE USSR

THE sixtieth anniversary of the Bolshevik Revolution saw Lenin's heirs forced more frequently on the defensive than had been usual in the previous few years. The anniversary was marked, it is true, by the adoption of a new Constitution. It was also marked by the adoption of a new President (or at any rate an almost-new President, since Mr Brezhnev had occupied this ceremonial post once before). On the other hand, the Kremlin's treatment of its unofficial internal opposition was subjected to far more public criticism by foreign governments than had previously been the case; Eurocommunists continued to make similar attacks, and the expulsions of Soviet advisers from the Sudan and Somalia were significant setbacks.

On the economic front, growth was relatively slow; there was a mediocre harvest, and machinery orders to Western suppliers had to be cut back. The Soviet leaders may, however, have found some consolation in observing the faltering recovery and continued disarray of the major Western economies.

DOMESTIC AFFAIRS.—*Government and Society*. In the course of the year, Mr Leonid Brezhnev's personal ascendancy was more than ever apparent. On 16 June he was elected Chairman of the Praesidium of the Supreme Soviet of the USSR. In other words, he added the role of head of state to that of Party leader. His assumption of the primarily decorative post of President added nothing to his effective power. It was noteworthy, however, as a mark of his current pre-eminence; no previous Soviet party leader had combined the two posts at one time.

This accretion of honours was facilitated by the new Soviet Constitution. The latter was published in draft on 4 June and, with some minor amendments, approved by the Supreme Soviet on 7 October (see DOCUMENTS). Official consideration and formulation of a new Constitution had begun as long ago as 1962. The timing of its eventual adoption was probably in part designed to mark the sixtieth anniversary of the Revolution; Mr Brezhnev also wished, no doubt, to ensure that the new Soviet Constitution would be firmly associated with his name.

Like the previous Soviet Constitutions of 1924 and 1936, the 1977 Constitution was designed to do more than describe formal institutions, procedures and rights. Its drafting also incorporated a statement of the principles guiding Soviet society at its current stage of development. In this and other respects there was considerable continuity with the 1936

Constitution, but there were also some notable new features. Amongst these were the following. First, the leading role of the Communist Party in Soviet society was clearly and formally enunciated (see Article 6). Second, the citizen's rights (e.g. to work, to health care, to housing, to education) were spelt out at greater length than before, but it was explicitly stated that they must be exercised only to the extent that they do not 'harm the interests of society and the state'. Third, some of the language of the Helsinki Final Act (see AR 1975, pp. 474-79) was incorporated in the article characterizing the relations of the USSR with other states.

Several provisions of the new Constitution were attacked by Soviet civil-rights activists. This was on the grounds that they reduced the scope for defending a citizen's civil rights by an appeal to the Constitution. The success of such appeals under the previous Constitution, however, was hardly sufficient to encourage a belief in their practical utility.

The new constitutional provision which eased Mr Brezhnev's assumption of the Presidency was the creation of a post of First Deputy Chairman of the Praesidium of the Supreme Soviet. This enabled a deputy to be appointed who could take most of the burden of routine protocol duties from the new head of state. The man appointed was Mr Vasily Kuznetsov, the 76-year-old First Deputy Minister of Foreign Affairs. One item in Mr Kuznetsov's biography was unusual for a high-ranking Soviet official: he had studied mineral engineering in the USA in 1931-33, and had worked for a time at the Ford River Rouge plant in Detroit. Despite Mr Kuznetsov's elevation both to his new post and to candidate membership of the Politburo in early October, he remained, for practical purposes, a second-rank member of the Soviet leadership.

One minor impediment to Mr Brezhnev's becoming head of state was that the position was already occupied by President Podgorny. The 74-year-old Podgorny was dropped from the Politburo in May and retired from the Presidency in June. This operation was conducted with the minimum of courtesy, and the reasons for it remained a matter of speculation among Western observers. Was Mr Podgorny removed solely because he was in the way? Or were there also serious disputes between the two men over policy or personal power?

President Brezhnev was not seen in public after 8 December, and failed to attend either the USSR Supreme Soviet meeting of 14 December or the RSFSR Supreme Soviet meeting of 21 December. As usual, rumours proliferated of his impending demise. He was officially reported, however, to have spoken to a closed plenary meeting of the Party Central Committee on 13 December, and subsequently to have suffered nothing more than a mild attack of influenza.

President Brezhnev's last public appearance of the year, on 8 December, was at the funeral of one of the most notable Soviet military men of World War II, Marshal Aleksandr Vassilyevsky (see OBITUARY).

The Economy. The Soviet economy continued to expand, but at a rate that was low by past Soviet standards. The problem of coping with this slowdown continued to loom large in Soviet policy-making, both domestic and international.

The official Soviet figures for 1976 were published early in 1977, and preliminary results for 1977 were published in part near the end of the year. The extent of the recent slowdown in Soviet growth was indicated by the following Soviet official data. Western re-calculations of Soviet output would generally yield somewhat lower growth rates throughout, but the pattern of deceleration would be similar.

USSR: Economic growth rates (per cent; annual average growth rates for five-year periods; increases over previous year for individual years)

	1966-70	1971-75	1976-80 Plan	1976 actual	1977 actual
National income utilized	7.1	5.1	4.7	5.0	3.2
Gross industrial output	8.5	7.4	6.3	4.8	5.7

Sources: Soviet annual statistical handbooks and central press.

The slow growth of national income in 1977 was the result primarily of another poor year for Soviet agriculture. Adverse weather during harvesting contributed to a mediocre grain harvest of about 194 million tonnes, well down from the record 1976 harvest of 224 million tonnes. The livestock sector, meanwhile, was still recovering from the effects of reduced feed supplies following the 1975 harvest failure. Thus some of the annual-plan targets for off-farm deliveries of livestock products were met, but others were not. Meat, in particular, remained in short supply in cities.

The approach of Soviet policymakers to these problems remained essentially unchanged. Leaders maintained their commitment to channelling very large quantities of resources into agriculture. In a speech of 2 November President Brezhnev clearly restated the policy goals of improved domestic food supplies and (in the long run) a restoration of the nation's agricultural self-sufficiency. To this end the annual plan for 1978, announced in December, maintained the allocation of over a quarter of total investment to agriculture.

For the industrial sector, the leadership and the planners continued to emphasize improvements in quality and efficiency. There was a major campaign to reduce wastage and promote recycling in the use of iron and steel. The regrouping of industrial enterprises into production associations (see AR 1975, p. 101) continued; in the course of the year more than two-fifths of industrial sales came from factories reorganized in this way. The growth of industrial investment continued to be held to modest rates in the 1978 plan, with sharper restrictions than before on the starting of large new construction projects.

During the year several joint resolutions of the Central Committee of the Party and of the USSR Council of Ministers were aimed directly or indirectly at improving living standards. In January and February there were resolutions on increasing the output of consumer durables and strengthening quality control generally; in July there was a resolution on improvements in the retail distribution system; in October there were resolutions calling for improvements in health services and for increased incentives to skilled agricultural workers to remain in agriculture. Meanwhile the transition to the new minimum monthly wage of 70 rubles (about £54 at official exchange rates) was completed during the year.

One innovation in economic policy was the raising, at the beginning of the year, of prices for certain consumer goods and services. In general, action of this kind was desirable for the sake of reducing the fiscal burden of subsidies and the frequently large discrepancies between supply and demand for particular products. (For example, it was stated in February that beef retailing in the Central Region at 2 rubles a kilo carried a subsidy of 1·5 rubles a kilo, and that the total budget subsidy in 1975 on meat and dairy produce had been almost 19,000 million rubles). The politically sensitive nature of any corrective action, however, was reflected in the extremely limited scope of the January price rises. They applied to relatively few items, all of which could be characterized as luxuries: certain carpets, glassware, silk fabrics, books and taxi, air and passenger-ship fares. The action was seen by some observers, however, as either a precedent or a trial run for more consequential price rises at some future date.

The pressures for more efficient resource allocation derived in part from the knowledge that growth would continue to slow down unless substantial counter-measures were taken. A major study prepared by the US Central Intelligence Agency in July gave an especially bleak forecast. Much of the CIA analysis (e.g. of the prospective slowing of the growth of the Soviet labour force to below 1 per cent a year from 1982) was uncontroversial, and was probably shared by Soviet economists and officials. The report was controversial, however, in its projection of a fall in Soviet oil production in the late 1970s or early 1980s—a fall that would place major additional constraints on future Soviet growth. This projection was disputed by several Western specialists; Soviet official plans for oil production beyond 1980 remained undisclosed.

There was abundant evidence, however, of continued Soviet concern over the general economic prospects. A number of proposals for both a greater decentralization of economic decision-making and a reorganization of the central planning machinery were published during the year. The notion of radical decentralization, to a system of so-called 'market socialism', remained a heresy and did not figure in any of the published reform proposals. The advocacy of limited decentralization, however, was a common feature of most proposals.

D

In foreign economic relations, the improvement in the hard-currency trade balance that began in 1976 was continued in 1977. It seemed probable that the overall Soviet hard-currency trade deficit, having risen to more than $6,000 million in 1975 and having remained above $5,000 million in 1976, would be of the order of $3,000 million in 1977. This improvement was the result of a number of factors: determined Soviet efforts to promote hard-currency exports; some recovery in Western economic activity and import demand; a reduction in grain imports because of the good 1976 harvest, and a cutback in Soviet ordering of Western machinery.

The remaining gap was bridged in part by a combination of arms sales, gold sales and earnings from tourism and shipping (the latter promoted by aggressive rate-cutting in liner trades, which provoked continuing strong protest from Western shipping concerns). Borrowing on a substantial scale from Western banks and governments remained a necessity, however, in part because of the burden of repaying past loans. Doubts about the desirability, for the West, of this lending were voiced by a number of Western economists and politicians.

Dissent and Emigration. The Soviet authorities continued to pursue a selective policy, combining exile, imprisonment and consignment to mental hospitals, against civil-rights activists. The knowledge that the Belgrade review of the implementation of the Helsinki Final Act would begin in the autumn seemed to influence the authorities' tactics throughout the year. So did the strong public criticism by President Carter of Soviet infringements of civil liberties.

One apparent aim of the authorities was to destroy the unofficial groups set up in the USSR to monitor Soviet observance of the Helsinki accords. Early in January searches and questioning were instituted against leading members of the 12-member Group for the Observance of the Helsinki Accords in the Soviet Union. In February Dr Yuri Orlov and Mr Aleksandr Ginzburg were arrested and another member, Miss Lyudmila Alekseeva, was given permission to emigrate. At about the same time, members of related 'Helsinki' groups in the Ukraine, Georgia and Lithuania were arrested. In March another member of the main group, Mr Anatoly Shcharansky, was also arrested. This pattern of selective arrests and either permitted or enforced emigration was repeated throughout the year.

During the spring and early summer President Carter on several occasions publicly criticized the Soviet Government for actions of this sort. His criticism drew strong counter-attacks from the Soviet media, and the confrontation contributed to a worsening of Soviet–US relations during the first half of the year (see below). The Soviet authorities appeared nonetheless to be treading warily in their handling of dissidents under international scrutiny: they clearly wanted both to curb dissident activities and to maintain a productive working relationship with the US Government.

An example of the Soviet authorities' problems was provided when Mr Shcharansky's name was linked in the Soviet press with the CIA, and the possibility of his being charged with treason was leaked. On 13 June President Carter stated publicly that he was convinced Shcharansky had never worked for the CIA. This meant that these charges could be preferred against Mr Shcharansky only at the risk of a severe worsening of Soviet–US relations. The Soviet Government's response was to continue to hold Mr Shcharansky under arrest but to delay preferring charges against him for the time being. Along with a number of other dissidents arrested earlier in 1977, he continued to be held, possibly for tactical reasons, while Soviet 'human rights' infringements were criticized at the Belgrade review and complex negotiations on other matters were pursued with the USA.

Emigration, similarly, appeared to be subject either to tactical manipulation or to vacillation on the part of the authorities. In 1976 the total number of emigrants (mostly Jewish) permitted to leave the USSR had been 13,254. During 1977 the monthly rate rose from about 1,000 to almost 2,000 in October; an annual total of about 17,000 seemed possible. This rate was such as to soften criticism slightly at Belgrade, and to hold out the prospect of further increases to meet demands made earlier by the US Congress.

The authorities' actions weakened but did not destroy the dissident movement. As well-known activists were arrested or exiled, new activists came forward to replace them. Equally important were the moves to develop links between the various 'opposition' groups (religious groups, nationalists, Jewish 'refuseniks' and civil-rights activists). These moves may well have worried the Soviet authorities at least as much as criticism from abroad.

A mysterious explosion on the Moscow Metro on 8 January, in which seven people were reported to have died, was expected by some observers to provide a pretext for a general witch-hunt against opposition groups. It did indeed coincide with the start of the drive against the 'Helsinki' groups; but the reasons for the explosion remained obscure, and arrests made during the year were not publicly connected with it.

The possible adoption of 'dissident' tactics by other citizens must also have been a source of concern for the Soviet authorities. There were two conspicuous examples of this during the year, when 'press conferences' with Western journalists were called by Soviet citizens with specific grievances against the Soviet authorities. On 17 November Corresponding Member of the USSR Academy of Sciences Sergei M. Polikanov, a department head at the Nuclear Research Institute at Dubna, used this device to publicize an individual grievance not explicitly related to a general criticism of the Soviet system: he objected to the authorities' refusal to allow him to take his family with him on a one-year spell of work at the European nuclear research centre in Geneva.

Soon after this it was reported that six Soviet workers who had lost their jobs and had suffered in other ways after making complaints against their immediate superiors had told their stories to a group of Western newsmen. The subjects of their original complaints had ranged from neglect of work-safety precautions in a Donbass coalmine to misappropriation of funds in a Party restaurant in Volgograd.

Arts and Sciences. The beginning of the year was marked by a literary incident of a familiar kind: the Moscow University philosopher, Aleksandr Zinoviev, was dismissed from his job because of an allegorical novel he had written, satirizing Soviet society. Entitled *Yawning Heights*, it had been published (in Russian) in Switzerland at the very end of 1976. The book was notable for its ridicule not only of official doctrine and official practice but also of some aspects of the dissident movement. It was remarkable, also, for a use of slang and word-play which seemed likely to make effective translation difficult, if not impossible.

A more orthodox Soviet writer, though nevertheless one of some distinction, died on 15 July. Konstantin Fedin, born in 1892, one of the few remaining writers whose work had been published before the Revolution, had at one time been associated with Maxim Gorky and Yevgenii Zamyatin. One of his best novels was *Cities and Years* which expressed the ambivalent feelings of many intellectuals about the Revolution. This was published in 1924, a year when ambivalence was still permitted. Succumbing later to 'socialist realism', he was well-known as a war correspondent in World War II, and subsequently served as chairman of the Writers' Union.

In the field of technology there were some conspicuous achievements. In the Soviet space programme manned space flights took place in February, October and December. The October exercise was timed to coincide with the twentieth anniversary of Sputnik I. It was probably also intended that the two cosmonauts involved would be orbiting on the day of the sixtieth anniversary of the Revolution (7 November)—and perhaps that they would try to break the American-held manned-orbiting record of 84 days. The mission was abandoned, however, when the cosmonauts were unable to dock their Soyuz craft with the Salyut-6 orbiting station. A repeat attempt at such a link-up in December, however, was successful.

At lower altitudes, a new stage was reached in the Soviet supersonic transport programme (see AR 1975, p. 102 and 1976, p. 103), when on 1 November the Tu-144 flew its first passengers from Moscow to Alma-Ata and back. It carried 80 passengers at a fare one-third higher than normal, and covered 2,025 miles in two hours. The flight came four years after the date when the Tu-144 was originally planned to enter commercial service, and Western journalists who were on the plane reported that the noise in the cabin during the flight made conversation difficult. Observers on the ground reported, on the one hand, an 'ear-shattering roar' on take-off and, on the other, a decibel level similar to that of Concorde. Whether those two observations were mutually consistent would be decided in America.

FOREIGN POLICY.—*Relations with other socialist countries.* There was no evidence of improved relations with the post-Mao leadership in Peking. President Brezhnev continued to claim that the Soviet Union wanted normal, good-neighbourly relations with China, but in June he lent his authority to a mounting war of words between the two countries. Chinese officials praised the Sudan for its expulsion of Soviet advisers, and in July they claimed that the build-up of Soviet troops on the Sino-Soviet border had reached a million. This did not, however, preclude a minor improvement in border relations in September when the Soviets reopened to Chinese vessels a channel at the Amur–Ussuri river junction that had been kept closed to them for ten years.

Relations with Yugoslavia were as tortuous as ever (see also pp. 118-9). In August President Tito visited Moscow and appeared to obtain some concessions in the form of a joint communique stressing mutual respect for sovereignty and for different varieties of socialism. The Soviet side apparently dropped requests for a naval base and rights to overfly Yugoslavia with military material, which Tito had refused the previous year. Instead President Brezhnev pinned a number of medals on the Yugoslav leader and—apparently—hoped for the best.

The mood of strained joviality between Moscow and Belgrade became rather more unhappy later in the year, however, when the memoirs of a former Yugoslav ambassador to Moscow were published. Ten thousand copies of the first volume of Mr Veljko Micunovic's memoirs, covering his 1956-58 spell in Moscow, sold out rapidly in Yugoslavia. Someone must nonetheless have succeeded in procuring a copy for the Kremlin. The Soviet leaders were distressed by Mr Micunovic's description of past Soviet intrigues against Yugoslavia and by his harsh depiction of (among others) Mr Mikhail Suslov and Mr Boris Ponomarev. An official Soviet protest was sent to Belgrade about the book. The Yugoslav reply was to promise a second printing soon.

Eurocommunism continued to be seen as a threat to Soviet power in Eastern Europe. That there was some justification for this fear was indicated by the Romanian Party paper, *Scinteia*, when it defended several arguments in Santiago Carrillo's *Eurocommunism and the State* in its issue of 5 July. The question of how best to respond to this threat, however, was a matter on which the Soviet leadership appeared to some Western commentators to be divided. An incident that seemed to support this view occurred at the Kremlin anniversary ceremonies of 2-3 November. Sr Carrillo had been invited to attend, and did so. He claimed, however, that he was prevented from delivering a speech. This was officially denied.

Relations with the non-communist world. In 1977 Soviet foreign policy was dominated to an unusual extent by bilateral relations with the USA. Even at the 35-nation Belgrade review of the Helsinki Final Act (which was adjourned on 21 December) American criticism of Moscow on civil-rights matters was the most prominent feature of the proceedings.

Early in the year officials of the Carter Administration claimed that civil-rights issues were 'separable' from other subjects of Soviet–US negotiation. In the course of the year, however, SALT, civil rights and the general climate of Soviet–US relations seemed to become increasingly hard to disentangle.

At the beginning of April, negotiations broke down in Moscow on a SALT-II agreement. With the SALT-I agreement due to expire on 3 October, President Brezhnev and a variety of Soviet spokesmen first expressed their anger at a 'Messianic' and provocative US approach to bilateral relations, and then signalled their readiness to resume negotiations on a practical basis. In September an informal extension of the SALT-I agreement was negotiated and substantial progress was made in SALT-II.

The major difficulties over the US Cruise missile and the Soviet Backfire bomber were compounded by controversy over US development of the neutron bomb and Soviet deployment of the mobile SS50 missile. (Both these latter weapons raised issues of concern to Western Europe.) A tentative outline SALT II agreement was nonetheless reached, and Soviet–US relations were improving towards the end of the year.

Trade between the two countries still languished, however. The extent of linkage between civil-rights, strategic and trade issues was illustrated on 10 November when President Carter was reported to have used a meeting with the Soviet Minister of Foreign Trade to bring pressure on the Soviet authorities over the treatment of dissidents.

In Africa it was a year of reverses for Moscow after the success in Angola in 1976. Soviet military advisers were expelled from the Sudan in May. In November Soviet attempts to side with both parties in the Somali–Ethiopian conflict finally led Somalia to expel all Soviet advisers and to close down Soviet naval facilities. Consequently, during December, Soviet supplies of arms and advisers to Ethiopia were sharply increased as ruble bets were placed, perforce, on Addis Ababa.

Chapter 2

THE GERMAN DEMOCRATIC REPUBLIC—POLAND—CZECHOSLOVAKIA—
HUNGARY—ROMANIA—BULGARIA—YUGOSLAVIA—ALBANIA—MONGOLIA

THE GERMAN DEMOCRATIC REPUBLIC

A manifesto purporting to have been written by a group of 'democratic and humanistic thinking communists' in East Germany reached the West in December, and was published by the West German magazine *Der Spiegel*. It created something of a sensation. The authors said they had formed the Federation of Democratic German Communists, and they appealed to like-minded comrades in West Berlin and West Germany to join them. Their aims, they explained, were not confined to East Germany alone, but were rather to bring about the reunification of Germany, a nation in which social democrats, socialists and democratic communists would outnumber 'conservative forces'. This goal demanded an offensive national policy.

The 'humanistic communists' would have Nato forces withdrawn from Western Europe. West Germany would leave Nato, and East Germany the Warsaw Pact. A reunified Germany, its neutrality guaranteed by the United Nations, would be totally disarmed. The Party leadership in East Berlin said the manifesto was no more than a bad joke, got up by West German intelligence with the connivance of West German correspondents in East Berlin. Some balanced Western observers thought it was genuine, and probably composed by a small group of young, disillusioned communist officials who were sickened by the stodgy, Soviet brand of East German communism and inspired by men like Professor Robert Havemann, a long-standing critic of the regime who was under house arrest, and Herr Rudolf Bahro, the economist who was awaiting trial on a charge of spying after his book, *The Alternative*, was published in the West.

East Germany made a relatively small concession to the demand for human rights before the Belgrade follow-up conference on European security and cooperation started on 4 October. A group of 90 political prisoners was freed and sent to West Germany. Most of them, like the majority of East Germany's estimated 6,000 political prisoners, had been imprisoned for trying to escape to the West. This was good business for the East German Government because West Germany paid about DM40,000 for each released prisoner. These prisoners-for-cash exchanges had been going on for some time, and about 1,200 political prisoners were let out of East Germany each year. The East German Government justified the arrangement on the grounds that the money it got from West Germany was compensation for its investment in the education of the people it let go. But it showed no signs of liberalizing its emigration policy in other respects. Unless they were old age pensioners or had urgent family business requiring their presence in the West, other East Germans did not get exit visas. Thirty or so intellectuals who were expelled during the year for dissident activity were in a different category from the political prisoners. West Germany did not pay cash for their release. Taking a cue from the Russians, the East German Government simply decided to get them out of the country as part of its policy of neutralizing its opponents by dispersing them.

A riot which occurred in East Berlin on 7 October was serious enough to bring the police into action with water canon and batons. The incident was dismissed by the East German authorities as the work of drunken rowdies. The trouble started when police sealed off an area around the Alexanderplatz in East Berlin, where a crowd had gathered for a pop concert; the fans chanted the name of Wolf Biermann, the singer deprived of his East German citizenship in 1976 for writing protest songs.

A report published by Amnesty International in September pointed out that the East German state retained 'censorship of the press and communications, a heavily guarded frontier with West Germany, including the Berlin Wall, and severe restrictions on freedom of movement, expression and association'. However, despite signs of de-liberalization it was not thought that the hawks in East Berlin had necessarily got the upper hand. Herr Erich Honecker, the East German Communist Party leader, was regarded as a relative dove, an impression strengthened perhaps by his statement in January that the relationship between the two German states should be guided by commonsense and goodwill.

The East Germans even made it clear they would be prepared to consider further 'easements' in their relations with West Germany—but at a price. They said it was illogical for the West German Government, having recognized the sovereignty of East Germany, to hold on to the myth of only one German citizenship. This allowed East Germans in any part of the world to be issued with a West German passport with the minimum of formality. The East Germans contended that sometimes their citizens were bribed to accept such a passport, and claimed that if this anomaly were removed the border with the West would become more permeable and relations more normal.

East Germany's draft economic plan for 1978 set targets which appeared completely unrealistic—an average increase of 30 per cent in exports to the capitalist countries, and a decrease of 5 per cent in imports from these countries. This goal was believed to be a consequence of the Soviet Union's insistence that East Germany must drastically reduce its indebtedness to the West, put at the colossal sum of DM13,300 million. Moscow feared that this risky credit business was not only economically unsound, but could also force East Germany to surrender some of its political independence in its dealings with the West.

The authorities went to considerable lengths to meet their insatiable appetite for hard Western currencies. They greatly extended the chain of Intershops, where a wide variety of high-quality Western goods could be bought—with Western money. In doing so they provoked heavy criticism from some of those people who had none. Nonetheless the East German Government had reason to feel fairly satisfied with some economic developments in the first two years of the five-year plan (1976-80). Rates of growth were close to expectations. Wages and pensions were increased according to plan, and working hours were marginally reduced. The Government also succeeded, albeit with ever larger subsidies, in stabilizing rents and the price of basic foods. Honecker, however, did not disguise the country's economic problems. The cost of raw materials had risen much higher than the price of industrial goods, he said, and the extra burden could be met only by stepping up economic growth.

It was announced in December that the Volkswagen concern had contracted to deliver 10,000 models of the Golf car to East Germany. Under the deal, the East Germans would not pay cash, but would supply Volkswagen with some DM90 million worth of machine tools and motor car accessories. The Golf, priced at DM10-15,000 in West Germany, was expected to cost about DM30,000 in East Germany. Still, the agreement was regarded as a breakthrough to the East European market generally.

East Germany was notably active in the field of foreign policy towards the end of the year. Honecker and the Prime Minister, Herr Willi Stoph, visited North Korea and Vietnam, and, more surprisingly, the Philippines, a state which was persecuting communists. The Foreign Minister, Herr Oskar Fischer, became the first East German Minister to visit Japan. The Chairman of the Volkskammer, the East German Parliament, Herr Horst Sindermann, went to West Africa and Angola. Herr Werner Lamberz, a member of the Politburo, visited Libya. There were specific reasons for some of these visits. In Libya the East Germans talked about oil, in Japan about trade, in Angola about the situation in Southern Africa. But such missions also demonstrated East Germany's determination to play a bigger international role, and to break away from thinking in tightly restricted East–West terms.

POLAND

In an atmosphere of economic and political tension the Polish Communist Party's policies became confused in 1977. The leadership was deeply shaken by the June 1976 events (see AR 1976, p. 110), the breakdown of communications between rulers and ruled, mishandling and gross political misjudgments. Mr Gierek, his image tarnished, had to tread carefully between conflicting trends within the Party and widespread

D*

dissent in the country. The leadership's very continuance depended on what it could do or would be prepared to do under strong pressure from society.

On the economic front Gierek turned for help to private enterprise. Modifying existing agricultural policies, the Central Committee plenum in January guaranteed private farmers permanent prospects of development. They would be able to buy additional land without limitations provided that they could increase production. In November a pension scheme was passed by the Sejm (Parliament) under which retiring farmers benefited whether they turned their farms over to the State or passed them to their children. The December 1976 legislation encouraging the expansion of private enterprise was followed in November 1977 by a decision to lease about 60 per cent of state shops to private individuals who would keep the profits.

However, the food supply deteriorated, following another poor harvest and the reluctance of farmers to sell more to the state. Prime Minister Jaroszewicz admitted in October that meat supply was below demand despite huge imports of meat and grain. No one could tell how the workers would react. Work stoppages in Silesian mines in protest against meat shortages sounded a danger signal. Cardinal Wyszynski appealed to the authorities to end the 'humiliation' of people queuing for hours to buy foodstuffs.

In October Gierek admitted that the 'economic manoeuvre' of shifting resources from capital investment to consumer goods and housing (see AR 1976, p. 111) had not been implemented, though two million people had been waiting for flats, some for 15 years. He blamed Party organizations, trade unions and management for sluggishness and resistance to change, and condemned widespread corruption, speculation, favouritism and low productivity. The completion of unfinished projects must be given absolute priority. In 1976 only 31 of 92 important projects were completed. The 1978 plan foresaw less growth in industrial output, an increase of 6·7 per cent in agricultural production, 10 per cent in consumer supplies and 13 per cent in services. Gierek warned that non-fulfilment of the plan would have serious social and political consequences. Poor export performance produced a deficit of $3,000 million with the West and Poland's indebtedness rose to $12,000 million.

Dissension within the Party on the issue of centralized economic management surfaced when the editor of the Party weekly *Polityka* *Rakowski* argued that the present excessive centralization limited individual initiative and killed personal responsibility. He was accused of 'revisionism'.

It was in the political arena that the intra-Party conflicts, between advocates of further repression and those who insisted on freer information and independent channels for consultation, resulted in erratic policies. Demands for a public enquiry into the June 1976 events, signed by 1,500 prominent representatives of society, were rejected. But the opposition movement grew in strength. The Committee for the Defence of Workers, KOR (see AR 1976, p. 111), transformed into a Social Self-Defence Committee, opposed political, religious and racial discrimination, claiming a thousand activists in the country, as did a separate Human Rights Defence Committee. These and two other groups, including the Democratic Movement, covered the whole political spectrum from radical left to nationalist right. While recognizing the limitations of Poland's geo-political situation, they demanded respect for human rights, as guaranteed by the Constitution, and reforms within the system, including some political pluralism and participation of truly representative bodies in decision-making processes. Over 50 unofficial publications, giving names and addresses of dissenters, claimed a circulation of 100,000.

Initially Gierek maintained an attitude of qualified tolerance and encouraged harsher criticisms in the media. Controversial films by famous Polish directors were released, ridiculing Stalinist methods and glorifying previously condemned pre-war Polish leaders. Attacked indirectly at the Party plenum in April for his softer policies, Gierek called for unmasking and opposing 'class enemies' who found 'few allies' in Poland, but promised to deepen 'socialist democracy'. Press criticism linked Polish dissenters with West German 'revanchists' and expatriate organizations. The writer Kijowski said: 'A mendacious world has arisen. That is its main basic structural fault.'

In May the mysterious death of a Krakow university student, regarded as a political murder by his colleagues and as an accident by the authorities, provoked a peaceful demonstration by 5,000 students and the formation of a Students Solidarity Committee to replace the official students organization. Minister Kaliski warned them against 'indulging in sterile arguments about freedom and civil rights'. Students emerged as yet another group pressing for reforms.

Eleven KOR members, accused of links with foreign organizations allegedly hostile to Poland, were held for three months' investigative detention. Fourteen prominent people subsequently went on hunger strike in a Warsaw church. Faced with massive protests from the Church, intellectuals, Western writers and Italian communists, the Government declared an amnesty in July, releasing KOR members and five remaining workers still imprisoned for participating in the June 1976 demonstrations. KOR spokesman Kuron called it 'an act of political realism'. The anti-dissenter campaign stopped, but occasional house searches and confiscation of reprographic equipment continued.

Gierek announced that 'for the first time conditions have been created for the actual implementation of human rights and factual democracy', but rejected any 'politicizing' activity which sowed confusion in people's minds. Under the strong impact of Eurocommunism on the intelligentsia and some

Party leaders, the press admitted that political pluralism, while 'progressive' in capitalist society, was unacceptable in Poland where 'confrontation of political systems' might result.

The Church constantly and publicly raised the unresolved issues of discrimination against believers, atheistic ideological offensives, freedom of religious instruction and permits for building new churches (18 were granted in Warsaw). It demanded access to the media, which 'persistently propagated a godless ideology and the cult of robot man'. Cardinal Wyszynski warned the leadership that the Church, the main protector of human rights, would oppose religious and political repression and that the authorities could not rely on the Church as a stabilizing force and yet constantly ignore its demands.

In the key political event of the year, regarded as a herald of a new modus vivendi, Cardinal Wyszynski met Gierek for the first time on 29 October. They exchanged views on 'the most important problems of the nation and the Church which are of great significance for the unity of Poles in the work of shaping the prosperity of the country'. Gierek sought help in calming the public mood in a situation fraught with danger, and the Primate, while stressing certain conditions, accepted that in such times the 'demands of Polish *raison d'état* must be clearly seen' (6 November). During his audience with the Pope (1 December) Gierek recognized the Pontiff as a great figure in contemporary history and the Pope promised to support the Government's efforts to create a prosperous Poland.

Over the year Gierek and Jaroszewicz met all East European leaders to reassure them about developments in Poland. Gierek fully maintained his Western connexion. He had talks with President Giscard d'Estaing in Paris and Signor Andreotti in Rome, while Chancellor Schmidt, Herr Brandt and the King of the Belgians visited Warsaw. On 29 December President Carter arrived in Poland, the only communist country he visited on his seven-capital tour. These contacts raised hopes of easing the Polish economic situation and provided welcome publicity for Gierek, who was anxious to divert public opinion from growing internal difficulties.

CZECHOSLOVAKIA

This was the year of Charter 77 (see DOCUMENTS), a petition criticizing the violation of human rights and international commitments by the Czechoslovak Government and initiating a civic movement to observe and publicize official malpractices. The number of signatories increased from 242 at the time of its promulgation in the first days of January to nearly 1,000 by the end of the year. The Charter contrasted cases of oppression with the two international covenants on human rights to which the Czechoslovak Government had acceded and the principles of the Helsinki Final Act.

In addition to the original Charter, a number of separate documentary collections of infringements were made public by the activists, relating to education, labour relations, religion, literature and art, police harassment and other forms of victimization. While not setting out a programme of political change, the Charter successfully challenged the official claim that 'normalcy' had been restored after the military defeat of the Prague Spring in 1968. The Charter signatories and supporters were men and women of varying political and religious persuasions and derived from all walks of life. The movement received publicity and support in the West, including some influential communist circles, and aroused solidarity moves among dissidents in several East European countries.

The authorities called the Charter a cynical and cold-blooded attempt to throw a peaceful country into confusion at the behest of the bourgeoisie, the counter-revolution, the Western intelligence services and Zionism. An intensive vilification campaign in the media lasted for six months, and supporters of the Charter suffered loss of jobs, demotions and other forms of repression. The chief ideologues of the other European communist countries, meeting in Sofia in March, were said to criticize the Czechoslovak leadership for an awkward handling of the affair. Sustained front-page publicity certainly made the Charter's existence and aims known to all citizens of Czechoslovakia, a feat which its authors could not hope to achieve with the limited *samizdat* means at their disposal. The artificially inflated campaign of signatures against the Charter also bore doubtful fruit, as many people, especially workers, refused to denounce a text which they had officially not been permitted to read.

There were arrests and several trials in connexion with the Charter, but the authorities refrained from citing adherence to the document in court. Instead, the charges against Vladimír Laštůvka and Aleš Macháček in Ústí (September) and against Ota Ornest, Jiří Lederer, Václav Havel and František Pavlíček in Prague (October) centred on 'connexion with emigrés', with sentences up to three and a half years' imprisonment. Police surveillance imposed on leading dissidents was tighter than ever before. When the Dutch Foreign Minister, on an official visit in Prague, received Professor Jan Patočka, a spokesman for the Charter movement, the 77-year-old philosopher was subjected to lengthy police interrogations which led to his death of brain haemorrhage on 13 March (see OBITUARY).

The Charter movement survived the year; new spokesmen emerged and, although some signatories had been forced into emigration, more young people appeared to be joining the Charter community despite the repressions, bringing with them more radical ideas about the future of the protest movement.

The country's foreign relations consisted of the usual mixture of trade, ceremony and ideology. Mr Husák, the President and Party leader, visited the USSR twice, Poland, Iraq, Romania, Hungary and East Germany. On the last occasion, in October, he signed a new friendship treaty with the GDR although the previous one still had ten years to run. The so-called Brezhnev Doctrine was now included and there was no longer a reference to possible reunification of Germany. Czechoslovak politicians and journalists took a prominent place in the orchestrated campaign against Eurocommunism in general and the Spanish leader Sr Carrillo in particular. Mr Gierek was the only top communist leader to visit Prague, but most East European Prime Ministers came. Among the more exotic visitors were Mr Joshua Nkomo of the Zimbabwe Patriotic Front in April, and Mr Sam Nuyoma of SWAPO, Namibia, in December. Officials of the Palestine Liberation Organization met the Israeli (pro-Moscow) Communist Party representatives in Prague in May for the first time. The Belgrade follow-up conference on European security and cooperation was greeted with official assertions that Czechoslovakia fulfilled its obligations deriving from Helsinki to the hilt while the West was guilty on almost every count.

Only three working sessions of the Communist Party central committee were held, each lasting a single day. The March plenum discussed the building trade; in May the chief topic was the supply of goods to the internal market; and a regular economic survey was carried out in December. The last session effected the only significant personnel change of the year, resulting from the death in November of Jan Baryl, a non-voting member of the Party praesidium. He was replaced by Miloš Jakeš, until then chairman of the Party control and auditing commission, whose elevation to the praesidium was seen by observers as important in view of his dogmatic reputation.

Economically, the overall indices of the plan were being met while signs of unease mounted. National income grew by 4·5 per cent against 1976, but a number of important branches failed to meet export and internal targets. Productivity increased less than wage growth warranted, and investment programmes fell short by 1,000 million crowns. Complaints were also voiced about increasing production costs and loss-making exports. Wholesale prices were restructured from 1 January after a year's delay, largely an accounting exercise designed to bring down excessive profit margins in some branches. As the new prices reflected the increased cost of imported raw materials, the overall price level fell by only 2·6 per cent. A more drastic movement was brought about in July when a number of retail prices were marked up and down. Increases were particularly noticeable in cotton and wool textiles (34 per cent), chocolate (33 per cent) and coffee (50 per cent). Reductions affected badly selling and overpriced items. The consumer reacted fairly placidly, but there were several panic buying waves during the year, the latest one, in November and December, leading to a depletion of the stock of salt and spices.

Agriculture had a good year in that the largest ever amount of cereals was harvested (10·4 million tons, 30 per cent more than in the bad year of 1976 and slightly over the record crop of 1974), but the humidity content in grain was up to 30 per cent and drying facilities could not cope. Poor quality of bread and other bakery products was admitted. Vegetable plans were only 93 per cent met and the fruit plan remained 26 per cent below target.

Most of the cultural and art unions held their separate Czech and Slovak congresses (a quinquennial event) and finally constituted themselves into federative Czechoslovak bodies. Observers generally agreed that the standard of cultural achievement remained inconspicuous and certainly below the country's intellectual potential.

Mgr František Tomášek, 78, the Apostolic Administrator of Prague, had been made Cardinal *in pectore* in 1976 and this appointment was announced in June 1977. After protracted negotiations of several years an agreement with the Vatican was reached in September according to which the Holy See could reorganize the Slovak dioceses so that their boundaries should coincide with those of Czechoslovakia and a Slovak church province be formed for the first time. Since the agreement had not been made public by the end of the year and remained unratified, it was not known whether the Government would make reciprocal concessions on the crucial issues of filling vacant bishoprics, lifting the quota system in theological seminaries, discontinuing premature retirement of priests, imprisonment of clergymen and discrimination against children who attend religious classes.

The spell of high birth-rate due to the maturing to fertility age of large post-war age groups and to the Government's social policy culminated on 28 March when the 15 millionth inhabitant was estimated to be born. With the rest of his compatriots, if with less interest than most of them, he or she saw the year going out on a combined note of reasonable prosperity and ideological tension, not near enough to the critical point which would dissatisfy those for whom survival is a programme, but disturbing to others.

HUNGARY

The year was marked by a much more active foreign policy than Hungary had had for a number of years and by the emergence of a certain amount of dissident activity. In foreign policy, Hungary had exchanges at head of state or head of government level with Austria, Italy, France, West Germany, Poland, the GDR and Czechoslovakia among others. The most significant were the visits to Italy and West Germany by the Party leader, János Kádár; these were his first trips to Nato countries and in themselves indicated Hungary's intention of pursuing a more forward foreign policy.

While in Italy, Kádár also visited the Pope. From the Hungarian point of view, the most striking event was perhaps the decision by the United States to return the Crown of St Stephen, an object of semi-mystical veneration in the Hungarian political tradition and one which traditionally conferred legitimacy through possession. Hungary's communist rulers had been resolute in seeking its return from the US, where it had been held since 1945.

The Hungarian Party also played an autonomous role in the debate over Eurocommunism. Whilst the Hungarian standpoint did not, for obvious reasons, run directly counter to the Soviet line, nevertheless the cautious approval given to the emergence of Eurocommunism was a sign of the Hungarian Party's preference for a measure of freedom in pursuing its own affairs. During the first part of the year, the Hungarian press published a number of statements considerably at variance with the line on Eurocommunism taken by the Czechoslovak and Bulgarian parties, for example. Instead of denouncing it as anti-Soviet, the Hungarians stressed the right of each party to resolve its problems as it saw fit. There was a cautious withdrawal from these positions during the summer, especially after Soviet attacks on Santiago Carrillo's study 'Eurocommunism and the State', and thereafter Hungarian spokesmen began to place emphasis on the international obligations of Communist Parties, *i.e.* the necessity to give support to the Soviet Union.

There was an important development in Hungary's relations with Romania, which had been increasingly strained over Hungarian resentment at Romania's policies towards the around two million Hungarians of Transylvania. In June, Kádár held his first-ever bilateral meeting with the Romanian head of state and Party, Nicolae Ceauşescu; the latter, it was reported, refused to go to Budapest, so the meeting was held on either side of the border, at Debrecen in Hungary and at Oradea in Romania. A major concession by the Romanians was their acceptance that Hungary had a certain political *locus standi* in the matter of the Hungarian minority; in other words, that it was no longer exclusively a question of Romanian internal politics. The Hungarian side made clear its anxiety to improve cultural contacts between Hungarians in both states. The two sides agreed on the establishment of consulates in Debrecen and Cluj, and the zone for the small frontier-traffic agreement was extended. However, towards the end of the year there were reports of dissatisfaction in Budapest with the way in which these agreements were being implemented in Romania.

The manifestation of dissent among Hungarian intellectuals owed something to both domestic and international factors. The first such event, the sending of a letter of solidarity with Charter 77 (see p. 108), was thus expressly triggered off by a foreign development. The letter was signed by 34 intellectuals, many of them known for having belonged to the New Left; however, about a third of the signatories stood entirely outside the marxist current, thus giving the letter a somewhat greater significance. In September, two substantial volumes of *samizdat* writings began circulating in Hungary. One of these contained reassessments of the meaning of marxism in Hungarian society by members of the New Left, and suggested that, in general, they no longer viewed marxist ideology as an adequate guide to current realities. The other volume was made up of writings which had been submitted for official publication but had been rejected for no discernible reason. The aim of this volume was to show how censorship operated in Hungary and to give a medium of publication to the authors whose works had been turned down.

Both parliament and the Central Committee met four times during the year. Parliament passed legislation on citizens' suggestions and complaints and on amendments to the Civil Code. The Central Committee heard a report on housing construction between 1961 and 1975, during which over a million housing units had been built and one-third of the population was in modern housing; however, the housing shortage was still acute in places, especially in Budapest, and about 1·5 million remained on the housing list.

The Committee's October session considered a report that Hungarian industrial growth had to depend exclusively on higher productivity, that the deterioration in the terms of trade was causing serious problems and that an increase in the quality of output was essential to meet higher standards in both Western and Eastern markets. The December session was given provisional figures on the implementation of the plan for 1977, and in general the year was seen as a good one, much better than 1976. Real wages went up by 3 to 3·5 per cent (somewhat higher than planned), whilst consumer prices were on target at 3·8 to 4 per cent higher; industrial growth was derived almost entirely from higher productivity; agricultural output was satisfactory; but the volume of investment was unexpectedly high, a danger sign for the future, as too much capital was being tied up in unfinished projects.

There was some improvement in church–state relations. For the first time since 1945, the entire episcopate was able to pay an *ad limina* visit to the Vatican; the Pope expressed himself fairly optimistically about the situation of the church after Kádár's visit, and in the autumn it was announced that agreement had been reached between church and state negotiators over religious education on church premises and a number of other, minor matters. For the Protestant churches, the visit to Hungary by Billy Graham was a spectacular event. He preached to an open-air congregation of 30,000 and expressed himself satisfied with his first trip to a communist country.

ROMANIA

For the Romanians the overriding event of 1977 was the severe earthquake (9 degrees on the Richter scale) that occurred on 4 March, destroying most of the centre of Bucharest and many of the surrounding villages. The official figure of 5,000 dead was certainly well below the actual number of victims.

In August miners in the Jiu Valley coalfields went on strike, demanding higher wages, improved housing and better food supplies. This was the first case of industrial action in Romania since the communists came to power and no mention of it was made by the Romanian media. Apparently the miners organized a sit-in in the pits, whence they were eventually evicted by the army. Some of them were arrested, while others were forcibly transferred with their families to distant parts of the country. On 12 December the Minister of Mines was removed from his post.

A Plenum of the Party Central Committee (CC) was held on 28-30 June. In addition to decisions regarding a gradual increase in earnings between 1977-80 for certain categories of wage-earners and pensioners, and improvement of education of all grades, two significant measures were announced: (1) abolition of censorship of the press, radio, television, theatre, cinema, literary, scientific and artistic works, hitherto exercised by a central state authority, and (2) abolition of custodial sentences for minor offences committed by juveniles up to the age of 21 and the immediate release of youths imprisoned for such offences.

The abolition of censorship was hailed as a democratic and liberal measure by writers, artists and publicists, who pointed out that 'outside' censorship acted as a brake on artistic creation. Nevertheless, in his speech to the Plenum, President Ceauşescu stated: 'We are not abolishing control of the media; we are abolishing a certain type of bureaucratic, administrative censorship and reinforcing the direct responsibility borne by Party activists for all that is written, published, printed, performed and distributed.' The Censorship Board was replaced by a network of steering councils, responsible to the CC Ideological Commission and the propaganda, press and radio–television sections of the CC, set up in all branches of the media, consisting solely of Party activists who would be responsible for the ideological and political content and the quality of the output. Thus the steering councils in no way differ from the former Censorship Board, which was also made up exclusively of Party activists.

According to Ceauşescu, custodial sentences for minor juvenile delinquency were abolished on the basis of 'marxist–leninist teaching on the subsidence of conflicts and differences between social classes and the inevitable *rapprochement* between the latter, as opposed to Stalin's anti-marxist and anti-scientific concept, *i.e.* that the consolidation of socialism results in an intensification of the class struggle, which entails still more repressive measures.' The President continued: 'We must do away with this false conception once and for all. We cannot allow tens of thousands of youths to waste their time in prison when they could be usefully employed in constructive work, where the workers themselves would educate them far more efficaciously than the Interior Ministry's re-education centres.' That was obviously the reason for this act of clemency, whereby some 18,000 youths were set free and assigned to large-scale projects, such as the underground railway system presently under construction in Bucharest and resumption of work on the notorious Danube–Black Sea canal project, suspended in 1953 after it had served as an extermination camp where *circa* 100,000 political prisoners lost their lives. However, press reports suggested that numerous youths had absconded from the work-sites to which they had been assigned and had returned to their former delinquency.

In November the Government declared an amnesty pardoning all penal offences committed prior to the date of the decree, except war crimes and crimes against humanity, treason, espionage, murder and serious theft of state property. As the amnesty did not differentiate between political and common-law crimes, it enabled most of the hundreds of thousands of victims of successive communist repressions to regain their place in society without the stigma of a political conviction. Indeed, the decree laid down that the names of persons with one or several previous convictions were to be removed from police records forthwith.

Another aspect of this idea of 'national reconciliation' based on the consolidation of socialism in Romania was contained in a law passed by the National Assembly in November, abolishing the courtesy titles of Mr Mrs and Miss between people at work and replacing them by 'Comrade' or 'Citizen'.

The National Conference of the Party was held in Bucharest on 8-10 December. It consisted exclusively of the reading of a 250,000-word report by Ceauşescu and its endorsement by 360 speakers among the 2,000 delegates. The main points in the report were: (1) the necessity of stepping up the production targets laid down in the 1976-80 five-year plan, industrial output from 10 to $11\frac{1}{2}$ per cent and agricultural production from 7 to 9 per cent; (2) a shift of emphasis in production from quantity to quality, in order to help Romanian exports; (3) postponement until 1983 of a gradual reduction in the working week from 48 to 44 hours; (4) a forthcoming reform of existing legislation to bring it into line with the principle that a person is presumed to be innocent until proved guilty.

At the end of November the Romanian dissident writer, Paul Goma, arrived in Paris with his wife and son, at the invitation of the French section of the International PEN Club. He had been granted a passport for one year. At a press conference he disclosed that before his departure an official had warned him not to make any statements against the Government or its leader. Nevertheless, Goma attacked the brutal police methods used by the tyrannical regime. He read out the names of miners and engineers who were sent to prison, labour camps or psychiatric hospitals as a result of the miners' strike and stated that 4,000 miners' families had been transported by the authorities to a distant region where they had no jobs or contacts. Referring to his arrest earlier in the year, after he had signed a collective protest against infringement of human rights in Romania, he said that he had initially been charged with treason and homosexuality, but later the latter charge was changed to conspiracy. Finally both charges were dropped prior to the opening of the Belgrade conference. Although he made it clear that he intended to return to Romania, it seemed highly improbable that he would be allowed to do so.

BULGARIA

The main political event in Bulgaria occurred in May: a plenum of the Central Committee (CC) of the Bulgarian Communist Party (BCP) ousted Politburo member and CC secretary Boris Velchev, considered as second in rank after Party leader Todor Zhivkov, from all his Party positions, including CC membership. No reason was given, except for a formula claiming 'reasons of expediency', tantamount to a grave political accusation. Velchev's downfall was followed by the replacement of the head of the CC organizational department and a purge in the district Party committee in Yambol, where his influence apparently had been strong. An extensive reshuffle of ambassadors abroad also seemed connected with Velchev's dismissal, although his son Vladimir, ambassador to London, was not affected by it.

The second major political event followed on 19 December when another CC plenum elected three new Politburo members: Minister of National Defence Dobri Dzhurov and Minister of Foreign Affairs Petar Mladenov, both until then Politburo candidate members, and Ognyan Doynov, a CC secretary who preserved this post and thus became one of the most important Party figures. This move brought the recently much-reduced Politburo again to 11 members, the same as after the 10th Congress (1971). The plenum also elected three additional CC secretaries: Petar Dyulgerov, Dimitar Stanishev and Georgi Atanasov, heads of the CC organizational, foreign relations, and record-keeping departments respectively. In a most unusual move it also expanded the CC to 171 by adding 19 new members, the majority of them Ministers, deputy Ministers, and Party officials. The same plenum also decided to hold a national Party conference in April 1978 and to exchange the Party membership cards between 1978 and 1980.

The domestic scene was dominated by continued references to the July 1976 plenum which had called for 'irreconcilability with existing short-comings' and for 'application of the leninist principles of management'. Among ensuing concrete measures was an internal streamlining of ministries; this helped to reduce managerial, administrative and office personnel, which had been another imperative demand of the July plenum. Some 30 to 40 per cent of such personnel was to be cut by March 1977, but by the end of the year the difficult process had not yet been completed.

A decree on a new system of wages, issued in February, introduced the principle that everybody should be paid only for the work he actually had done. The system was tested during the year in many industries and offices, but overall application was postponed until 1 January 1978.

In October it was revealed that in a written report Zhivkov had recommended 'a new approach' to planning, consisting, *inter alia*, of a better combination of centralized planning with planning 'from the bottom toward the top', by way of so-called supplementary plans proposed by the workers' collectives. The new approach was applied immediately upon elaboration of the 1978 plans. The importance attributed to planning and organization of labour was demonstrated by the summoning of the national Party conference for April 1978 to deal with these two very issues.

An attempt at improving insufficient supply of foodstuffs was made by two decrees, one encouraging personal plot farming and the other providing for a system of local and regional self-sufficiency in staple foods.

According to preliminary data, overall economic growth slowed down in 1977 and most plan targets were not fulfilled. Agricultural production, in particular, was rather poor, although it varied strongly for individual crops and regions. Natural disasters and adverse weather were blamed for the general setback. They were said to have caused losses worth 1,500 million leva, including some 350-400 million leva of damage caused by two major earthquakes: one on 4 March in Northern Bulgaria which claimed an admitted 125 lives and one on 3 November in the Rhodope mountains which was said to have had no fatal victims.

The year of the Belgrade follow-up conference brought a positive solution by Bulgarian authorities to a number of family reunification cases. Applications for travel abroad were also handled less restrictively. An unknown number of people, however, remained in prison on political charges. No spectacular manifestations of political dissidence became known; some isolated and rather tame cases attracted little attention abroad.

The cultural scene was marked by two major events: the third congress of Bulgarian culture in May, at which much was spoken but little of interest was decided, and the national conference of young writers in November–December, which conveyed a positive picture of the state and the prospects of young literature. Talent, originality and even mastery exist among the young and most of the shortcomings for which they were criticized were in respect of Party policy. In June Bulgaria organized an international conference of writers on peace, intended as a propaganda event in advance of Belgrade.

Neither Todor Zhivkov nor Premier Stanko Todorov made any official visit to non-communist countries, except for an African tour by the Premier in November, nor did any top politician from the West visit Bulgaria. An official visit by both leaders to Moscow in May–June was accorded great significance and seemed to have resulted in important decisions on further Bulgarian-Soviet rapprochement.

In the Balkans Bulgaria continued to obstruct multilateral initiatives, but maintained good relations with its two southern, non-communist neighbours. A new agreement on repatriation of ethnic Turks from Bulgaria reached in November was the most positive result of extensive talks with Turkey.

In foreign trade efforts continued to balance exchanges with the West through reduced imports and increased exports and through other forms of cooperation.

YUGOSLAVIA

President Tito's activities were at the centre of public attention on many occasions during the year. In addition to the public celebration of his 85th birthday and the 40th anniversary of his assumption of the post of Secretary-General of the Communist Party, he attracted world-wide attention by undertaking one of his most important foreign tours. In August he visited the USSR, North Korea and the People's Republic of China (see also p. 121). A month after this arduous journey he again went abroad to visit France, Portugal and Algeria. In November he rested from public activities on medical advice, but returned to active duty in early December. On 3 December he joined President Ceauşescu at the Romanian border to attend the formal opening of Djerdap II, the second phase of the joint Yugoslav-Romanian hydro-electric and river regulation scheme across the Danube at the Iron Gate, and on 6 December he received the British Conservative leader, Mrs Thatcher.

The absence from public life of the President's wife, Jovanka, since June caused so much speculation in the Western press that the authorities took the unusual step of commenting officially. Their denials that she was ill or that there was any political significance in her withdrawal merely encouraged further rumours. The mystery was deepened by the continued use of the opening phrase 'Jovanka and I' in official messages of condolence which the President issued during the rest of the year.

An amnesty involving 723 persons was granted to mark Republic Day,

29 November. Of these, 218 had been convicted of political offences. The best known of those released from prison were Mihajlo Mihajlov, who had served two years of his seven years' sentence (see AR 1975, p. 123) and several former Cominform supporters. A few days before the announcement of the amnesty it was made known that another Cominformist, Mileta Perović, who disappeared in August whilst travelling between Israel and France, was in custody and would be put on trial.

During the long-drawn-out discussions at the Belgrade conference on European peace and security, which occupied most of the second half of the year, there were a number of incidents involving Western protesters against alleged violations of human rights by the Soviet Union and the Warsaw Pact allies. These were firmly but quietly dealt with by the Yugoslav police and frontier guards.

Industrial output rose more than 3 per cent above the planned target of 7 per cent and there was a good harvest, but the chronic weaknesses of the economy continued to cause anxiety. The slight balance of payments surplus of 1976 was turned into a massive $1,500 million deficit. This was attributable mainly to the large trade deficit with Western countries, especially with the EEC, from which export earnings reached only 37 per cent of the cost of imports from the Community. The Federal Executive Council was so alarmed that on 17 November it issued a memorandum which was sent to all Community members, urging them to take concrete steps to implement the joint Yugoslav-EEC declaration of December 1976. There were unofficial hints that, if the EEC was unable to help, the Yugoslavs might be forced to consider 'a gradual reorientation of trade towards those countries with whom we have . . . a more balanced and equal economic cooperation'—*i.e.* Comecon and the Third World. However, a Yugoslav-Soviet trade agreement signed on 18 October did not envisage a significant rise in the volume of trade, and a promised increase in Soviet credits did no more than keep pace with price rises. Comecon's share in Yugoslavia's foreign trade declined slightly, but there was a significant growth in trade with the Third World. An attempt to develop closer trading relations with the Efta countries was welcomed at the Vienna conference of Efta in May, but produced no concrete results.

Inflation began to rise again after the sharp fall during the previous year. Despite a 3 per cent rise in the numbers employed in the public sector, to a total of over 5 million workers, unemployment rose to over 700,000.

The problems of illiquidity within the economy and the failure of enterprises to obey the regulations laid down in 1976 for the settlement of debts provoked much criticism from political leaders, one of whom declared that almost every other enterprise flouted the law.

On 18 January the Prime Minister Džemal Bijedić was killed in an air crash near Sarajevo. President Tito cut short a visit to Tripoli in order to participate in the appointment of the new Premier, the Montenegrin Veselin Djuranović. In May a new Vice-President, Stevan Doronjski, the representative of the autonomous province of Vojvodina, replaced the Montenegrin Vidoje Žarković.

ALBANIA

The year was dominated by the gradual decline in the country's close relations with China, its only ally and source of economic aid for 16 years. This chain of events was set in motion by Mao Tse-tung's death in September 1976 and the subsequent removal from office of his widow Chiang Ch'ing and her radical associates, officially branded as the 'gang of four'. By the beginning of 1977 it had become fairly clear that the Albanian communist regime was finding it difficult to give loyal support to the new leadership in China or to come to terms with its domestic and external policies. One of the causes of the regime's reluctance to adjust itself to the post-Mao era was its previous expectation that the Chinese radical faction, to whose revolutionary doctrines the Albanian leaders were wholeheartedly committed, would assume power after Mao's death. When it became clear that this was not likely to happen, the Albanians showed themselves unwilling to comply with the political realities of the new situation in China.

In May a Chinese parliamentary delegation headed by Saifudin, a vice-chairman of the standing committee of the National People's Congress, paid a visit to Romania and Yugoslavia but not Albania. This in itself was a sign that all was not well between the new Chinese leadership and its small ally in the Balkans. During his stay in Yugoslavia the Chinese spokesman praised President Tito's policy of non-alignment as well as his achievements in such spheres as national unity and military defence against foreign encroachments. The visit marked an important change in China's earlier unfriendly attitude towards Yugoslavia, but roused suspicions in Albania, whose leaders had continued to regard Yugoslavia's brand of communism as 'revisionist' and its policy of non-alignment as a sham.

The Albanian leadership expressed its misgivings about these developments in highly abstract ideological terms. On 7 July *Zëri i Popullit* (Voice of the People), the official newspaper of the Albanian Workers' Party, published an editorial under the title 'The theory and practice of revolution'. This contained a sharp rebuttal of the theory of the Three Worlds, expressed by Chairman Mao, which enjoyed the full support of Hua Kuo-feng and his associates. The theory envisaged the world divided into three broad groupings: first, the two super-powers, the United States and the Soviet Union; second, the industrialized countries of Western Europe, Japan and Canada; third, the developing nations of Europe, Africa, Asia and Latin America. This analysis maintained that communist regimes and parties, in their struggle to bring about revolutionary change and national liberation throughout the world, should foster ties between the second and third groupings in order to thwart the imperialistic ambitions of the two super-powers.

The Albanian newspaper editorial objected to this on the grounds that it gave rise to dangerous illusions—that the nations of the second and third groupings really shared common interests, that the United States was a less aggressive power than the Soviet Union, that the non-aligned countries were genuinely independent. The Albanian embassy in Peking took the highly provocative step of delivering copies of the editorial to other embassies and to foreign correspondents working in the Chinese capital. The article consequently got worldwide publicity, making it clear that the alliance between the largest and the smallest communist countries of the world had entered a critical phase. The Chinese reacted obliquely by issuing several statements reaffirming the soundness of their analysis.

Albania's suspicions and fears about the new trends of Chinese foreign policy were further increased in September when President Tito of Yugoslavia paid an official visit to China, where he had talks with Hua Kuo-feng and other leaders. His friendly reception in Peking brought to a close China's long and bitter quarrel with Yugoslavia. The Albanian leadership expressed its anger about this development by giving publicity to an article first published in Albania in September 1963 in which Nikita Khrushchev was criticized for paying a visit to Belgrade that same year. Copies of this article were also distributed by the Albanian embassy in Peking during President Tito's stay there.

During the summer there were reports that the Chinese Government had decided to reduce its economic aid to Albania and withdraw its technical advisers working there. Although both sides were quick to deny rumours concerning the advisers, they were silent on the issue of economic aid. This suggested that the actual amount of Chinese aid had probably been scaled down.

Replying to repeated Albanian attacks on Chinese policies, the *People's Daily*, the Chinese Communist Party newspaper, carried an editorial at the beginning of November setting forth at great length the current official views on the theory of the Three Worlds. The article reiterated the familiar arguments for the theory (arguments which, it said, had been opposed by the 'gang of four') and maintained that the Soviet Union was a greater menace to world peace than the United States. A few days later, the Albanian Prime Minister, Mehmet Shehu, addressing a meeting in Tirana, said that the theory of the Three Worlds was counter-revolutionary because it tended to preserve the international status quo and favour the interests of the United States and its allies.

What these ideological arguments really indicated was that the

Albanian leaders had decided not to follow China's example of opening to the United States and Western Europe or of establishing closer ties with Yugoslavia. According to them, those policies might suit China's national interests but if adopted by Albania they would seriously impair the marxist-leninist orthodoxy and political stability of its regime. So, even though there had been no official rupture between China and Albania, their relations had nevertheless reached a very low ebb indeed.

MONGOLIA

The quadrennial elections to the People's Great Hural (the unicameral national assembly), held in June 1977, brought about no significant change in the composition of the Mongolian Government. It was claimed that all but one of the registered voters had gone to the polls, and that 99·99 per cent of the votes had been for the official candidates. The candidates, one per constituency, were proposed for election by their local Mongolian People's Revolutionary Party (MPRP), trade union or administrative body, and approved by a Central Election Commission chaired by an MPRP Politburo member, Sampilyn Jalan-aajav.

Reflecting the steady 3 per cent growth in Mongolia's population (which reached around 1,530,000 at mid-year), 354 deputies were elected to the ninth Hural, 18 more than to the eighth in 1973. As usual, around 70 per cent of the candidates, mostly workers and herdsmen, became Hural deputies for the first time, while the remainder, mostly officials of the ruling MPRP and the MPR Government, were re-elected.

At the new Hural's first session, Yumjaagiyn Tsedenbal, concurrently First Secretary of the MPRP Central Committee, was re-elected Chairman of the Hural Presidium, that is, President of the MPR, a post he had held since he quit the premiership in 1974. The post of First Vice-Chairman of the Presidium, which had been especially created in 1972 for Sonomyn Luvsan, apparently as a device to prevent him from becoming Chairman in place of Tsedenbal, was discontinued. The one Vice-Chairman of the Presidium, Tsagaanlamyn Dügersüren, was given an ambassadorship, and two new Vice-Chairmen were appointed—Sampilyn Jalan-aajav (for the first time) and Namsrayn Luvsanravdan (for the third time); both were members of the MPRP Politburo, while Dügersüren had left the Politburo in 1971.

Damdiny Gombojav, promoted a candidate member of the Politburo and secretary of the MPRP Central Committee in June 1976, surrendered his government post of Vice-Premier just before the Hural session, and also passed the chairmanship of the Council of Ministers' Comecon affairs commission to Vice-Premier Myatavyn Peljee. In June 1977 Gombojav was re-elected chairman of the presidium of the central council of the Mongolian-Soviet Friendship Society, a large and important body for promoting the country's political purity and guarding against anti-Soviet sentiment.

The Hural election campaign was used by President Tsedenbal as the occasion for a restatement of Mongolia's policy towards China and an attack on the Hua Kuo-feng leadership in Peking. Speaking in his constituency, Tsedenbal expressed disappointment that after Mao Tse-tung's death there had been no 'critical re-evaluation' of what he called China's 'anti-popular, anti-socialist policy of nationalism, great-power chauvinism and expansionism'. The new leadership of China had proclaimed anti-Sovietism and militarism as programme tasks, pursued a policy of intensive militarization and fanned up 'war hysteria', Tsedenbal said. It was therefore the duty of all who cared for peace, freedom and socialism to struggle against 'reactionary Maoism'.

The 'alarming' situation in Mongolia's animal husbandry, remarked upon by Tsedenbal in December 1976, worsened rather than improved. A period of severe weather in January and February 1977, combined with the neglect and haphazard preparations for winter in 1976, spelled disaster. The Mongolian press admitted that the situation was as bad as it had been in the winter of 1967-68, when 3·8 million animals perished, although it said that livestock losses were fewer this time. Nonetheless, the many local reports of livestock dying of cold, starvation and thirst, combined with the continuing lack of national statistics for the herds, could only confirm the need for Tsedenbal's appeal to rural working people for 'great efforts' to overcome these difficulties.

As a measure of the crisis, it was noticeable during 1977 that the Mongolian media gave much publicity to personal instructions issued by 'the chief' (Tsedenbal *darga*), as well as the more usual resolutions and decrees of the MPRP Central Committee and MPR Council of Ministers. In particular, Tsedenbal said that the livestock losses of 1976 and 1977 must be made up by the end of the five-year plan (1976-80). He described this task as a 'matter of particular state and economic importance', and demanded that the 'appropriate conclusions be drawn from the considerable harm done to the national economy by the loss of many livestock'. These losses, he claimed, were the result of 'shortcomings' in the countryside 'during the temporary weather difficulties'—in other words, negligence as much as the climate.

Mongolia's livestock breeders managed to raise from birth in 1977 only 7·2 million head, compared with the planned 9·3 million. Although the same plan target was also set for 1978, in October 1977 the MPR Council of Ministers was obliged to say that regional reports indicated that preparations for the winter were unsatisfactory. It was estimated at the end of 1977 that the herds had dwindled to around 22 million head.

Mongolia's grain harvest in 1977, according to Premier Jambyn

Batmönh, was '11 per cent greater than the average for the five-year period 1971-75'—that is to say, about 407,000 tons, some 100,000 tons short of the target for the year. Batmönh also said that potato and vegetable production was 41 per cent up on the average for the same period—*i.e.* over 61,000 tons, which was 16,000 tons below the annual plan. Provisional figures indicated that the rise in gross industrial production in 1977 was very low, amounting to only 3·3 per cent, compared with a plan of 5·6 per cent and the achievement of 7·3 per cent in 1976.

At the joint Mongolian-Soviet mining and concentrating combine based on the Erdenetiyn-ovoo copper and molybdenum deposit—described as one of the world's ten biggest—preparations approached completion for the launching of stage one of the combine in 1978. Under a contract signed in August 1977 on Soviet aid for development of Baganuur open-cast coalmine, the first stage of the mine was to go into full production by 1984, and its eventual capacity was to reach six million tons a year. It was agreed that in 1978 a high-tension power line and a 97 km railway line would be built between Baganuur and the capital Ulan Bator.

In September an agreement was concluded with the USSR which provided for a permanent 'plenipotentiary representation' of the Soviet Ministry of Finance in its Mongolian counterpart, to help it 'utilize its financial resources rationally'. The process of Mongolia's political and economic 'drawing together' with the Soviet Union, much vaunted by Tsedenbal, had thus brought the country to a new stage of dependence on the Kremlin planners.

IV WESTERN, CENTRAL AND SOUTHERN EUROPE

Chapter 1

FRANCE—THE FEDERAL REPUBLIC OF GERMANY—ITALY—BELGIUM—
THE NETHERLANDS—LUXEMBOURG—REPUBLIC OF IRELAND

FRANCE

POLITICALLY and economically 1977 was for France a year of changing fortunes. It began with deepening acrimony and pessimism on the Government side as the left made the running in the polls, the prospect of victory papering over its manifold divisions. Exasperated by the drift and defeatism, the ex-Prime Minister, M Jacques Chirac, seized the initiative in January by declaring his candidacy for the recently restored post of Mayor of Paris. As M Giscard d'Estaing was backing his worthy but colourless Minister of Industry, M Michel d'Ornano, this was as much a challenge to the President as to the left. But, rejecting all appeals to step down, M Chirac campaigned on two fronts with characteristic aggression and efficiency.

Although French politics retain a strong strain of localism, all parties treated the March municipal elections as a dress rehearsal for the 1978 parliamentary campaign. In a hard-fought battle, honours went clearly to the left, which emerged controlling 159 of the 221 urban areas with over 30,000 inhabitants, in place of 103. The left-wing alliance had held well, scoring significant gains in almost every region. Prospects for a left-wing Government in 1978 had never seemed brighter.

For the President's supporters defeat was due to the disruptive activities of M Chirac. But, having brushed M d'Ornano aside at the first ballot and taken 60 per cent of the vote on the second, M Chirac retorted that his fighting campaign had shown the way to stem the socialo-communist tide. With inflation and unemployment running high the Government's poor showing also had more obvious explanations. However, a Cabinet reshuffle followed hard on the heels of defeat. M Raymond Barre remained as Prime Minister and Finance Minister, but the three political heavyweights of the previous Cabinet, MM Poniatowski, Guichard and Lecanuet, all lost their places. There were few new faces or first-rank politicians in the new team; rather the President had turned to still more technocrats in the hope of avoiding political infighting and of turning the economy round in time to reap the reward from a duly grateful electorate. He also appeared to be banking on the left's collapsing from its internal contradictions.

M Chirac rejected such Fabian tactics. While the Prime Minister concentrated on the economy and the President stayed withdrawn and remote he asserted his claim to be the Government's standard-bearer, tirelessly urging on his own supporters and flaying the 'socialo-communists'. But he was scarcely less of a thorn in the Government's flesh. A constant stream of critical comments on its performance was allied with a determination to rub home its dependence on the Gaullists' goodwill. M Barre's new Cabinet won a grudging confidence vote in the Assembly at the end of April by only 271 votes to 186 after a much publicized plea by M Chirac that his Rassemblement pour la République (RPR) should not cause a political crisis. There were further clashes over direct elections to the European Parliament, defence and, above all, M Barre's repeated refusal to reflate. Yet, despite the ill-tempered bickering and jockeying for position on the Government side, the divisions over personalities and tactics rather than basic principles never seemed unbridgeable.

Not so on the left. It had seemed in the early months that the socialist-communist alliance would hold firm until the parliamentary elections with no more than occasional bouts of acrimony, to which it had been prone since the beginning. The Socialists were irritated in May when *l'Humanité* published a calculation that implementation of the Common Programme of the left would cost £40,000 million, on the eve of a television encounter between M Barre and M Mitterrand from which the Prime Minister emerged the happier. Then in June the Communists saw M Mitterrand's tough handling of his own left wing at the party congress as an unpromising augury for his future treatment of them in office. There was further annoyance when the Communists abruptly changed their line on nuclear weapons without consultation (see p. 130).

Differences came to a head, however, over negotiations to up-date the 1972 Common Programme. While there were serious disagreements over defence, foreign policy and minimum wages, the final stumbling-block proved to be nationalization. The two parties were agreed that a left-wing Government would undertake large-scale nationalization immediately after taking office, but not on what to take over and how. The Communists listed 729 companies, the Socialists 277 (the effective gap being much less than the numbers suggested). In September the smallest of the three partners, the Left Radicals, walked out of the talks, their leader, M Robert Fabre, declaring that he would have no part in any irreversible slide into 'statism or collectivism'. A week later negotiations between the Socialists and Communists broke down in turn over the issue of nationalizing sub-sidiaries. From then on, while proclaiming their devotion to unity and the Common Programme, both parties plunged deeper and deeper into mutual recrimination.

Immediately after the suspension of talks came the senatorial elections. Held by indirect suffrage, the results reflected the local government successes of the spring rather than the current situation, and the left parties took roughly 40 per cent of the seats which were up for renewal in place of 30 per cent. But while, electorally, the alliance held, politically it had collapsed. During the autumn the President's popularity revived at the polls, some of which were now pointing to a Government victory in March.

Economically, the year began amid qualified optimism. If unemployment was high at 1,036,000 and the foreign trade balance bleak, the franc was stable and inflation falling, aided by the New Year cuts in VAT. Although M Barre's adamant refusal to recognize the political 'realities' of election year by reflating infuriated the RPR as much as (and for quite different reasons) it annoyed the left, his tough but commonsense handling of the economy was surprisingly popular. In February there was a modest series of measures to aid exports and reduce the unacceptably high costs of energy imports. There were also plans to put £500 million of public money into the ailing steel industry in return for 20 per cent of the equity. Even so, 14,000 jobs would go, and feeling ran high in Alsace, the heartland of steelmaking. But, as throughout Europe, the industry was to end the year deeper in crisis, with the Government threatening unilateral action unless the European Community could curb imports. In June the difficulties of another problem industry, aircraft construction, was tackled when the Government took a 34 per cent holding in the Dassault company. Textiles and shipbuilding, too, remained racked by problems despite government aid.

Nevertheless, in April the Barre plan was said to be 'on course', and measures were announced to improve employment prospects by creating some 20,000 new public sector jobs, to encourage immigrants to return home, and to encourage employment of school leavers (under-25s constituting a quarter of the total unemployed); family allowances were also raised. But gloom soon returned. The April inflation figures were bad; investment was flagging and production falling, while the spectre of a left-wing victory had sent the stock market to a 16-year low. By June unemployment was up 19 per cent on the previous year, at 1,150,000, and the trade deficit for the first half was over £900 million. While resisting renewed demands for reflation, in July M Barre announced fresh energy economy measures, and then at the end of August there was further 'support' for the economy in the form of lower interest rates, grants to low income families, and help to the building and civil engineering industries which had suffered badly from austerity cutbacks. The total package was costed at nearly £600 million. Then in the Budget, published in early September, Fifth Republic orthodoxy was breached with an acknowledged shortfall of about £1,000 million.

Nevertheless this was scarcely an electioneering Budget. Expenditure (on the optimistic assumption of 6·5 per cent inflation) was to rise 12·5 per cent to £44,700 million, partly covered by higher petrol and tobacco taxes. Defence and justice were the modestly favoured spending areas. If the declared aim of the Budget was to improve competitiveness, this would take time to bear fruit. Meanwhile, unemployment reached a record 1,205,000 in October. Moreover, while the Budget assumed that the unions would accept a pegging of workers' purchasing power, during the autumn there was a revival of industrial militancy as diminishing hopes of an election victory for the left lessened some of the unions' earlier inhibitions. In addition to a ritual one-day national strike against austerity on 1 December, there were disputes on the railways and in electricity supply, despite the announcement of higher pensions and increases in the minimum wage and civil service pay. And, although the Prime Minister's reputation had taken a knock when he tried to force the bakers into reducing the cost of *croissants* in November, by the close of the year there were greater grounds for optimism than had once seemed likely.

To be sure, unemployment remained woefully high at 1,145,000, investment was still marking time, and the franc was weak. But the foreign trade deficit had fallen from £2,000 million to £1,700 million, GDP was up 3 per cent (though 4·8 per cent had been forecast), and inflation at 9·0 per cent was at least little different from 1976—though a fall to 6·5 per cent had been forecast. Moreover, average hourly earnings rose 2 per cent in real terms over the year. Pensioners had kept well ahead of inflation with 22 per cent rises for those on the basic rate.

Beyond the immediate crisis there was the nagging energy problem, France being heavily dependent on imported energy. The three series of energy economy measures announced during the year attracted mounting scepticism. Earlier nuclear power had seemed the solution. But, although M Giscard d'Estaing declared flatly in July 'there is no alternative to nuclear power', difficulties persisted. In the March local elections a significant ecological movement emerged to take 10 per cent of the vote in Paris—enough to ensure that environmental concerns were particularly in the mind of electorally-minded politicians. In August clashes at the site of the new Super-Phénix reactor at Creys-Malville left one person dead and a hundred or more injured. Moreover, the technical and financial problems of nuclear power were also causing mounting concern as capital costs rocketed.

In 1977 internal political preoccupations took priority over external policy—though foreign affairs had a way of entangling themselves with the election skirmishing. With the creation in June of the Republic of Djibouti the long history of French colonization of the African mainland finally closed. Not that this spelled the end of French involvement in Africa. On the contrary, a sizeable garrison remained in Djibouti. In February M Giscard d'Estaing visited Mali, announcing a strengthening of the embargo on arms sales to South Africa. And in March the French air force supplied transport to ferry Moroccan troops to Zäire to crush a small-scale invasion, while in July Chad received air transport help to combat its long-standing rebellion. In August M Louis de Guiringaud, the Foreign Minister, embarked on a tour designed to strengthen France's rather sketchy links with anglophone Africa. But his visit came to an early end in Tanzania when an apology was refused for the noisy demonstrations against French policy towards South Africa on his arrival. In November delivery of four naval vessels to South Africa was cancelled in line with United Nations policy.

France was caught awkwardly by the West Saharan dispute, its support for Morocco and Mauritania inflaming the always touchy relationship with Algeria (which was to deteriorate further with the murder of an Algerian by right-wing extremists in Paris at the end of the year). In October eight French civilians were captured by Polisario forces and held in Algeria. French aircraft were promptly dispatched to the region for 'exercises', and joined in operational sorties against Polisario. When the prisoners were released at Christmas during a visit to Algiers by the communist leader M Georges Marchais this was taken as a deliberate snub to President Giscard d'Estaing by President Boumédienne, and led to bitter mutual accusations of electioneering with hostages.

There was also controversy over two very different extradition cases. At the New Year the security services picked up Abu Daoud, a Palestinian wanted for questioning over the Munich massacre of 1972. Amid a storm of protest, first at his arrest and then at his release, the German request for extradition was dismissed on a technicality. Abu Daoud went free. Not so Klaus Croissant, one of the Baader–Meinhof group's defence counsel, himself wanted for offences related to terrorism. When extradition was granted he was shipped back to Germany with astonishing rapidity, amid allegations that in both cases the judicial machine had served as the pliant handmaid of the executive. The Croissant incident gave a further fillip to the anti-German mood in some political and intellectual circles, which seemed to owe as much to envy as to opposition to the German handling of terrorism. But at government level there was close support for the Germans on the terrorism issue, and the regular meetings between President Giscard d'Estaing and Herr Schmidt maintained the cordiality of the 'special relationship' within the EEC.

Both men remained reserved in the face of President Carter's stress on human rights; in July M Giscard d'Estaing made plain his view that Mr Carter's insistence was 'jeopardizing detente'. Nevertheless, he himself was obliged to give some weight to human rights during Mr Brezhnev's visit in June which, partly in consequence, had little concrete outcome. But then, in a year of busy diplomatic journeying, there were few major developments. Much was hoped of President Giscard d'Estaing's visit to Saudi Arabia in January, but it produced only a minor oil supply pact and agreement to establish a nuclear research centre. In October the Premier

E

of Quebec, M René Levesque, was received with quite exceptional honours by all shades of political opinion. But although the occasion left the Canadian Government smarting (see p. 70) French support remained, as always, more moral than material.

As always defence matters caused controversy. During the year it was announced that France was to develop her own Cruise missiles and military reconnaissance satellites. The Defence Minister, M Yvon Bourges, promised that by 1982 firepower would be quadrupled. This was not sufficient to mollify many of the Gaullists, who suspected the Government of favouring conventional forces at the expense of the nuclear 'panoply'. The Government came under great pressure during the Budget debate in November to authorize construction of a sixth nuclear submarine. For different reasons the opposition was sceptical of the state of effectiveness of the armed forces. Nevertheless, in May the Communist Party announced the reversal of its long-standing hostility to the nuclear strike force, declaring that the nuclear forces were the only effective deterrent available. This abrupt change caught the Socialists unprepared, and M Mitterrand's immediate response was to suggest a referendum on the issue—something which could be staged only after a constitutional amendment. Yet although there were strong anti-nuclear feelings within the Socialist ranks it seemed that the parties might be moving to a greater measure of consensus on the matter.

THE FEDERAL REPUBLIC OF GERMANY

INTERNAL AFFAIRS. The year was likely to be best remembered for an outbreak of terrorism which presented the constitutional state with the most serious challenge it had had to face in its relatively short history. With the arrest of the ringleaders of the Baader–Meinhof gang in the summer of 1972 it was hoped that West Germany had got on top of terrorism. But the events of 1977 showed that a new generation of terrorists, more ruthless than their predecessors, had sprung up— fanatically dedicated to destroying the Rechtsstaat, the state based on the rule of law.

On 7 April Herr Siegfried Buback, the country's chief public prosecutor, was murdered on the way to his office in Karlsruhe. His driver and a motor mechanic travelling with him were also killed. A terrorist group known as the Red Army Faction (RAF) claimed responsibility. On 30 July Herr Jürgen Ponto, chairman of the Dresdner Bank, was killed while resisting the attempts of a group of terrorists to kidnap him at his home near Frankfurt. On 5 September terrorists kidnapped the President of the Employers' Federation, Herr Hanns-Martin Schleyer (see OBITUARY), in Cologne, and shot dead his driver and three bodyguards. Six weeks later, after the Government had refused to give in to the kidnappers' demands, Schleyer's body was found in the boot of a car which had been abandoned in the French town of Mühlhausen. He had been shot through the head.

The kidnappers threatened to kill Schleyer unless 11 terrorists were freed from West German prisons and flown to a country of their choice. They included the three members of the original Baader–Meinhof gang, Andreas Baader, Jan-Carl Raspe and Gudrun Ensslin, who had been sentenced to life imprisonment in April for terrorist crimes.

The Government, a coalition of the Social Democratic Party (SPD) and the Free Democratic Party (FDP), imposed a news blackout over its negotiations with the kidnappers, but it was soon reasonably clear that it had no intention of surrendering. Then, on 13 October, Arab terrorists launched an operation to support their German comrades. The Arabs, two men and two women, hijacked a Lufthansa Boeing 737 aircraft, with 86 passengers and five crew on board, on a flight from Majorca to Frankfurt. The plane was forced to fly to Rome, then to Cyprus, Dubai and Aden, where the pilot was murdered, and finally, with the co-pilot at the controls, to Mogadishu in Somalia. There, after nightfall on 17 October, it was stormed by a unit of Germany's crack anti-terrorist force, GSG 9, with the aid of some British experts and equipment.

All the hostages were freed, most of them physically unharmed. Three terrorists were killed, and the fourth seriously injured. The Government of Somalia had given permission for the attack to be launched. But the West German Government's relief at the outcome of the raid was quickly over-shadowed by the news that Baader, Raspe and Ensslin had committed suicide in their cells at Stammheim gaol, near Stuttgart. Baader and Raspe had shot themselves, Ensslin had hanged herself from a window, and Irmgard Möller, another terrorist, had stabbed herself with a knife, but not fatally. Not only had Baader and Raspe been able to conceal pistols in their cells, Raspe also had a transistor radio, and had managed to construct a primitive radio circuit to enable the prisoners to communicate with one another. The Stammheim affair was all the more alarming because it happened at a time when terrorist prisoners throughout the country had been barred from contact with each other and the world outside under a special law. This controversial measure had been passed by the Federal Parliament after the Schleyer kidnapping. In particular it attracted criticism because it deprived prisoners of access to defence counsel.

Schleyer's body was found on 19 October, and immediately the hunt for the terrorists began. In the aftermath of the violence a heated public discussion about the causes of terrorism took place, and there was a clamour for more law and order. Politicians, writers and clergymen who had tried to analyze terrorism or who dared to question the sort of society in which it had grown up were frequently condemned as sympathizers with the terrorists. Since terrorism gained a foothold in West Germany in the late 1960s the internal security forces had become markedly stronger and more effective. But the opposition, composed of the Christian Democratic Union (CDU) and the Bavarian Christian Social Union (CSU), insisted that still more legislation was needed. One of its main proposals was that in certain cases a judge should be allowed to monitor conversations between a defence lawyer and his client. It was strongly suspected, with good reason, that many lawyers representing terrorists had a conspiratorial relationship with their clients and acted as couriers, enabling prisoners to maintain contact with each other and with terrorists still at large.

However, the way in which the Government handled the situation greatly enhanced the reputation of the Federal Chancellor, Herr Helmut Schmidt. He had been put to the test, and was not found wanting. Although the German terrorists had shown they could count on international support, so had Schmidt. He succeeded more than any other statesman so far in persuading the civilized world that terrorism was an international problem, the solution of which required international cooperation. More-over he managed to ensure that his every move had the support not only of his Cabinet colleagues, but also of the leaders of all the political parties represented in the Bundestag.

Certainly the Chancellor, whose reputation as a man of action had been suffering in the face of obstinate unemployment and falling economic growth, needed a boost. The economic recovery that was sustained from the middle of 1975 to the middle of 1976 practically came to a standstill in 1977. The stimulative measures finally agreed by the Government, after long discussions and controversies, were aimed at supporting all the important sources of demand in the economy. Private consumption and investment were to be encouraged by means of tax reliefs, to be introduced at the beginning of 1978. These would inject at least DM10,000 million into the economy. Further, the Government launched a DM16,500 million investment programme to help the chronically sick building industry. Original hopes that unemployment would average about 900,000 during 1977, beginning a steady decline to about half that number by the end of the decade, were dashed. At the end of the year the unemployment total reached 1,100,000, and the prospects for the labour market in 1978 were bleak.

Uncertainty about the country's nuclear energy programme grew during the year. 'Bürgerinitiativen'—citizens' initiatives got up by the environmentalists—played a big part in wrecking it. The future of the fast breeder reactor being built at Kalkar on the Lower Rhine, a joint venture with the Belgians and the Dutch, depended on the Federal Constitutional Court, which had been asked to rule whether fast breeder reactors con-formed to West Germany's Basic Law. Work on six other, light water, reactors was held up by litigation; a dozen were still being built and nine, generating a total of 6,340 MW, about 2 per cent of West Germany's primary energy needs, were actually in operation. In March Germany's plan to generate 45,000 MW of nuclear energy by 1985 was slashed by a third. Later it became clear that the new target was wildly optimistic.

The most controversial point on the agenda of both coalition party conferences in November was the nuclear energy programme. A substantial number of delegates at both conferences wanted the programme stopped until the go-ahead was given for a nuclear disposal and reprocessing plant at Gorleben in Lower Saxony. But in the event the Free Democrats accepted that there should be no moratorium in the building programme, while the Social Democrats agreed on a compromise which stopped short of calling for a halt, but nonetheless gave priority to the construction of coal-fired power stations. A demonstration in Dortmund by 40,000 trade unionists in favour of safe nuclear energy greatly helped the SPD leadership in bringing through this compromise solution.

In the late summer the West Germans indulged in an orgy of introspection. Whole pages of newspapers were devoted to reports about how Germany looked to foreign eyes. This preoccupation with the theme of the 'ugly German' was prompted by three main factors: Germany's refusal to extradite Herbert Kappler, the former Nazi police chief of Rome who in August escaped from a hospital in Rome where he was serving a life sentence for war crimes; a revival of German interest in the Nazi period, inspired by a film and several books about Hitler and dubbed the 'Hitler wave'; and a letter to the Chancellor from his predecessor, Herr Willy Brandt, expressing concern about the activities of right-wing extremists. The Nazi past still accounted for a considerable measure of anti-German feeling. The Third Reich was close enough for millions of Europeans to have vivid personal memories of an unparalleled outbreak of German madness. But history alone could not account for recurring outbursts of anti-German feeling. Many people harboured envy and resentment of Germany's economic power, and were suspicious of the political and even of the military power that was assumed to go with it.

Judging by a report leaked to the press in December, it appeared that a secretary in the Defence Ministry, Frau Renate Lutze, who had been arrested on suspicion of spying for East Germany 18 months previously, was one of the most successful spies ever to operate in West Germany. It seemed she was even a bigger fish than Herr Günter Guillaume, the Chancellery aide whose arrest in 1974 caused the resignation of Herr Brandt as Chancellor. With the cooperation of her husband and another man, both employed at the Ministry, she was suspected of providing East German intelligence with copies of about a thousand documents from the Ministry's files, many of them top secret. They included an analysis of the Bundeswehr, detailing its strengths and weaknesses; a report on the

Bundeswehr's short, medium and long-term planning; an evaluation of the Nato command post exercise, Wintex 75; plans for the development of a tank for the 1990s; an analysis of the 'enemy situation', revealing Nato's knowledge of the Warsaw Pact's military strength; a paper about the Bundeswehr's probable response to an international emergency in Central Europe, including arrangements for refugees; and proposed West German defence budgets for years ahead, in detail.

FOREIGN AFFAIRS. The Federal Chancellor's visit to Washington in July for talks with President Carter helped to iron out differences between the West German and United States Governments. Some friction in this relationship had been caused by Germany's undertaking to supply Brazil with eight nuclear power stations, a uranium enrichment plant and an installation for reprocessing spent fuel elements. The Carter Administration was opposed to this transfer of the technology for the entire nuclear fuel cycle, especially the reprocessing plant producing plutonium that could be used to make nuclear warheads. Germany argued that its credibility as an exporter of advanced technology was at stake, and it also suspected that America, not content with being a super-power in weaponry, wanted to dominate the West in the peaceful uses of atomic energy. The German Government refused to back down on the deal.

Schmidt's Government was also sceptical about President Carter's stand on human rights. It feared that the spectacular championship of dissidents in the communist world might not only make the communist regimes more repressive, but also hamper the West's negotiations with them. The German Government claimed that its own quiet diplomacy had produced tangible, if modest, results. A total of 55,400 people of German origin were allowed to leave Eastern European countries in 1977, compared with 44,402 in 1976 and 19,657 in 1975.

The third bone of contention between Schmidt and President Carter concerned the economy. President Carter's Administration regarded Germany as a main obstacle to revitalizing the world economy because, in Washington's view, it did not do enough to reflate. Schmidt was unmoved by the charge, and his Ministers reeled off a list of good deeds the Germans had done to help their partners' economies. In the tough recession year of 1975, they said, all other industrial countries cut back their imports by about 7 per cent, while Germany's went up by 3 per cent. As for reflation, it sounded to German ears too much like inflation to be acceptable.

The Chancellor paid a five-day visit to Poland in November, and during his cordial talks with the Polish leader, Edward Gierek, emphasized the need for progress in the negotiations for a balanced reduction of military forces in East and West. Schmidt said that in their own interests the small and medium-sized states of Europe should themselves make a contribution to detente and 'not merely look passively over the Atlantic or towards the

Urals'. Gierek, however, was preoccupied with the pressing economic problems of his country (see p. 106). His main interest lay in persuading the Germans to accept increased imports from Poland, to help Poles pay off their enormous debts to the West. The Chancellor was sympathetic, but offered no firm commitment.

A visit by the Chancellor to Italy, planned for the late summer, was postponed at Rome's suggestion in view of the Italians' hostile reaction to Germany's refusal to extradite Herr Kappler (see pp. 133 and 138). Eventually the Chancellor went to Rome in November and his talks with the Prime Minister, Signor Giulio Andreotti, did much to restore good relations between the two countries. The 'irritations of the past', said Schmidt, had been played up by extremists, and were best forgotten. Andreotti said that public opinion in Italy was in no sense anti-German, but he added that Kappler's crimes could not be forgotten after 33 years—not even after 300 years.

ITALY

By the year's end the single-party Christian Democrat Government under Giulio Andreotti had survived for 17 months—in itself something of an achievement judged by the usual standards of shortlived Italian Governments. Its continuance was dependent on the benevolent support, or rather abstention from opposition in Parliament, of the Communist Party and the four smaller democratic parties. The success of this experiment, initiated after the general election of June 1976, had brought a big increase in the Communist vote, was due largely to two factors: the astute leadership of Signor Andreotti and the cautious forbearance of the Communist Party leader, Enrico Berlinguer. A third factor was the situation in the country itself: both leaders realized that they were bound together by the need to put up a united fight against inflation and extremist terrorism.

These two were the main preoccupations in the early part of the year. On the economic side, the Government was engaged in negotiating a loan from the International Monetary Fund (see p. 138). And President Giovanni Leone had already warned in his New Year speech against increasing crime and violence.

Sociologists had been saying for months that the explosive situation among school-leavers and students, caused by overcrowding in the universities and prospective unemployment, must break out soon. It did so on 2 February in Rome University, where a sit-in was sparked off by the shooting of a student by a right-wing gang. Unrest among students continued throughout February in Rome and other universities, their protests being directed partly against failure to implement long-overdue reforms. But, unlike the student risings of 1968-69, left-wing students' protest now took a new turn in attacking the Communist Party for its 'betrayal' in agreeing to support the establishment party. On 17 February the Communist trade union leader Luciano Lama was heckled and shouted down at Rome University when he urged students to abandon their occupation of the campus.

On 11 March violence moved to Bologna, where street barricades were set up and a left-wing student was shot dead by a policeman under attack. Such disorders were something new in Bologna, hitherto the showpiece for efficient administration under a Communist town council. The mayor attributed them to deliberate right-wing attempts to discredit the administration now that the Communist Party was coming nearer to playing a definite role in government; and a similar tactic could be seen at the end of the year in Rome (also under a Communist mayor) when right-wing extremists staged a number of petrol-bomb attacks on buildings. The student violence reached its climax in May, when clashes between demonstrators and the police occurred in several main towns and in Rome University a policeman was killed during an attempt to evict extremists who had occupied several faculties.

Terrorist action with a political flavour was also carried on by other extremist groups, in particular by the left-wing Red Brigade. In an attempt to hold up the trial of their captured leader Renato Curcio they shot and killed, on 28 April, the chairman of the Turin lawyers' association and terrorized the lay judges into postponing Curcio's trial—which, however, was held in Milan in June despite intimidation. He got a seven-year sentence. On 1 July Antonio Lo Muscio, leader of another left-wing gang, NAP (Nuclei Armati Proletarii), associated with the Red Brigade, was shot dead in a gunfight with carabinieri in Rome. In their efforts to spread terror the Red Brigaders resorted to shooting in the legs or kneecap a number of fairly prominent persons, including medium-level Christian Democrat politicians, industrialists and journalists. Among their journalist victims thus injured was Indro Montanelli, the well-known writer and editor of *Giornale Nuovo*; and in November for the first time they shot to kill when their attack caused the death of Carlo Casalegno, deputy editor of the Turin daily *La Stampa*.

Kidnappings against extortionate ransom continued throughout the year, by December numbering over 70 victims. In some cases their perpetrators were linked with Mafia gangs from Calabria operating in the more prosperous north and centre. In Calabria itself, according to one high official, the state's authority was 'about zero'; the revived Mafia was running protection rackets and bringing in the young for whom there was small prospect of employment. Local profiteers competed for contracts for the construction of Italy's fifth steel plant at Gioia Tauro, on the Calabrian coast. Strong protests were aroused when it was suggested that the scheme might be abandoned owing to changes in the world steel situation.

Against this background of violence and terrorism, coupled with a still serious economic situation, the Communists and Socialists at the end of April stated that they could no longer support the Government without having a say in official policies. The Christian Democrat Party therefore authorized its leaders to negotiate a common programme with the supporting parties. By the end of June discussions between the six party leaders had produced a programme covering all the main domestic problems, including law and order, economic legislation aimed to increase production, and reforms in local government and in education. The Communist leader Berlinguer still pressed for a broadly-based Government of democratic unity with his party in it. But on 4 July all six parties signed an agreement on the programme and a week later it was debated in Parliament. For the first time in the Republic's history, it was presented not by the Prime Minister but by the leaders of the parliamentary parties concerned, thus emphasizing the historic nature of this consensus; for such inter-party agreement, comprising the Communists as well as the other democratic parties, had not been known since the immediate post-war days. The programme was approved on 15 July by an overwhelming majority of 442 to 77, with 79 abstentions.

After the summer recess, however, violence and terrorism revived, and the economic situation, which had shown some slight signs of improvement, still caused grave concern especially in the sphere of unemployment. Early in December Communist headquarters issued a statement contrasting the gravity of the country's crisis with the inadequacies of the minority Government and putting forward the idea of a 'Government of unity and national solidarity' which would include the Communists and Socialists as well as the Christian Democrats. The Socialists were much more uncompromising in their demand for such a Government. And the small Republican Party under its influential leader Ugo La Malfa declared that rather than abstaining it would go into opposition in the imminent vote on the 1978 Budget.

Signor Andreotti's response was to present, in mid-December, a package of economic proposals for the Budget which he discussed with the leaders both of the six parties and of the trade unions. These talks had produced no agreement by the year's end. The trade unions threatened to stage a one-day general strike in January 1978, and the Communist Party spokesman Giorgio Napoletano said the proposals contained insufficient guarantees for cuts in public spending and no concrete plans for increasing productivity and employment. Signor Andreotti himself was prepared to make some changes in his Government, but his party was deeply divided as to what form any new Communist role might take. The Government's fall might precipitate a general election—and that, at least, none of the parties wanted.

On the economic side, the early part of the year was taken up with

E*

negotiations for the long-sought standby credit of $530 million from the IMF—in itself not a large sum, but its granting would mark international approval of the Government's efforts to curb inflation and help to clear the way for a $500 million loan from the EEC. In February a further package of anti-inflationary measures, additional to those of October 1976, was introduced, aiming to meet the IMF requirement of reducing labour costs. In early March IMF negotiators spent a fortnight in Italy investigating the economy, and on 17 March they handed to Signor Andreotti a draft Letter of Intent outlining conditions for granting the credit. These involved restrictions on the Treasury deficit and other public sector deficits and on public expenditure; a fall in the rate of inflation to 16 per cent in 1977 and to 10 per cent in 1978; and restriction of labour cost increases to 16 per cent in 1977 and further reductions in 1978. The trade unions resisted any attempt to tamper with threshold-indexed wage increases; but the conditions secured parliamentary approval early in April.

The economy showed some slight improvement in the following months. Inflation fell from around 21 to 18 per cent, industrial production rose (though it later flagged), and from May onwards the serious balance of payments deficit was turned into a small surplus—though this was achieved largely as a result of restrictions on imports. But the number of unemployed remained at around $1\frac{1}{2}$ million, two-thirds of whom were reckoned to be in the 15-29 age groups.

The IMF had already warned in August that Italy must make greater efforts to curb public spending. By December, when the 1978 Budget came under discussion, it was already apparent that all hopes of fulfilling the original commitment of limiting the budget deficit to 14,450,000 million lire had been abandoned, for the deficit now seemed likely to be around 26,000,000 million, which the Government aimed to pare down to 19,000,000 million. While retrenchment proposals were being discussed a temporary Budget up to March 1978 was approved. The big loss-making state or para-statal corporations represented a serious drag on the economy.

Signor Andreotti received a warm welcome from President Carter when he visited Washington (25-28 July) and outlined Italy's measures against inflation, securing promises of US aid for its nuclear power programme. He also went to Canada in November, when agreements were signed for exchanges in nuclear technology. On 1 December he met the West German Chancellor Helmut Schmidt in Verona. This meeting had been postponed from August because of difficulties arising from the abduction from a Rome hospital to the Federal Republic, on 15 August, of the former SS Colonel Herbert Kappler, who was serving a life sentence in Rome for war crimes (he had ordered the Fosse Ardeatine massacres of 1944). Italy demanded his extradition, which Germany could not see its way to granting.

On 2-3 March the Communist Party leader Enrico Berlinguer met the

French and Spanish Communist Party leaders in Madrid for discussions on their respective approaches to Eurocommunism (see DOCUMENTS). At the Moscow celebrations of the Russian Revolution's 60th anniversary in November he made a six-minute speech in which he said that each Communist Party should follow the particular factors and conditions of its own country. He and Mr Brezhnev appeared to have agreed to limit the area of disagreement between them.

BELGIUM

Early in the year it became clear that the coalition Government led by Mr Tindemans could not survive the departure of one of its participants, the Rassemblement Wallon, three of whose Ministers in the Government had defected to the Liberal Party. The Socialists, hopeful of large gains in a general election, refused to accept an invitation to join the coalition, leaving Mr Tindemans with the support of only 105 of the 212 members of the Lower House.

On 9 March the Prime Minister announced that a general election would be held on 17 April. The election campaign was unremarkable, tending to revolve, as always, around the intercommunal problem. However, it was notable that there was less intercommunal hostility during the campaign than had been feared after the excesses of the previous October's municipal elections. The Social Christians were again returned as the largest party, with 80 seats (a gain of 8). The success of the Social Christians derived mainly from the general recognition that the party leader, Mr Tindemans, was the right man to take Belgium towards a devolved federal system of government. Among the other parties, only the Socialists made any real progress, winning three additional seats. The extremist parties, including the Communists, all lost ground, except the Brussels-based Front Démocratique des Francophones (FDF), which increased its representation from 9 to 10.

Mr Tindemans, given the task of forming a new Government, at first sought to create a grand coalition of Social Christians, Socialists and Liberals. His obvious intention was to ease the shift towards a federal constitution. However, the refusal of the Socialists to serve with the Liberals dashed this hope. Instead, after several weeks of negotiations, the Social Christians, the Socialists and the two communal parties—the Volksunie and the FDF—agreed on a far-reaching devolution programme and enabled Mr Tindemans to form a new Administration in which the Flemish Social Christians had six ministries, the Walloon Social Christians four, the Socialists nine, the FDF two and the Volksunie two. The new coalition took office on 3 June.

The new devolution programme was based on a complex arrangement to resolve the vexed question of the status of the Brussels region, consensus having been easily reached on federalized government for Flanders and Wallonia. It was eventually agreed that the Brussels region would have a regional council of its own. In addition, the thorny problem of French-speakers in suburbs of Brussels that lay within Flanders was resolved by giving the French parity of rights in six communes where they were numerically predominant and, in a byzantine twist, by allowing French-speakers in ten other communes (where they were numerous but had no special privileges) to take out notional domicile within Brussels and have their civil rights 'relocated', leaving their real residential location technically entirely Flemish. Those arrangements represented a big concession by the Flemish population in return for an agreement by the French-speaking community not to redraw the Brussels boundary. In Belgian terms, the outcome was momentous.

As the year opened, the economy appeared to be pulling out of the business recession, with most indicators showing an improvement. However, during the second quarter demand clearly weakened and by September, after allowing for the effects of the holiday period, it was apparent that the recovery had lost most of its momentum. Consumer demand, which had been one of the main forces behind the recovery, was affected by the very high level of unemployment, which remained over 10 per cent of the labour force throughout the year. Investment by industry was lower in real terms than two years earlier, and the Government's efforts to offset this deficiency had no quick impact in terms of job creation. Exports were affected by the continuing slackness of demand in Belgium's main export markets.

In the face of this deterioration, industrial production began to fall after mid-year. The decline of the steel and textile industries intensified, requiring substantial financial aid from the Government in order to mitigate the loss of jobs. Inflation, however, had come under control and ceased to be the main preoccupation of the authorities, permitting them to concentrate their efforts on promoting re-expansion.

THE NETHERLANDS

Until almost the end, 1977 was a year of continuous political crisis. Mr Den Uyl, the leader of the Labour Party and Prime Minister of the coalition Government, very early found himself in difficulties when seeking the acceptance by the Lower House of his own party's draft Bill on land reform, aimed primarily at curbing speculation. With a general election due on 25 May, the Labour Party's main coalition partner declined to support the land reform Bill and Mr Den Uyl, in no position to continue, resigned in March.

Contrary to the general expectation, the general election resulted in a large gain, by Dutch standards, for the Labour Party, which increased its representation by 10 seats to 53 in a 150-seat chamber. However, this increase by no means betokened an unambiguous swing to the left, since other socialist parties lost ground. The right-wing Liberal Party took 28 seats against 22 in the previous Parliament. The centrist Christian Democrats (a new party formed in 1976 by the Catholics and the two main Protestant parties, the Anti-Revolutionary Party and the Christian Historical Union) won 49 seats, one more than at the previous elections. Among the small parties, Democrats '66 (progressive liberals) did well, but all the others dropped back to insignificance.

As leader of what had become the largest party, Mr Den Uyl was invited by the Queen to form a new coalition Government. However, the Labour Party, emboldened by its success at the polls, attempted to impose its proposals for profit redistribution, land reform, increased powers for works councils and changes in the abortion laws on the Christian Democrats, its most likely coalition partner. This proved too much for the latter to accept, and this first attempt to form a Government failed on 14 July, ostensibly because of disagreement over the profit-sharing proposal. A mediator, appointed by Queen Juliana, succeeded in bringing about a compromise solution on this issue, but almost immediately the Labour Party's plans for new abortion legislation proved unacceptable to the Christian Democrats and efforts to form a new Government came to a halt in August. On this occasion a way ahead was reopened when the proposed legislation was put off for the time being.

It then seemed that the only remaining problem—the distribution of ministries between the Labour Party, the Christian Democrats and Democrats '66—could be resolved easily. However, the Christian Democrats insisted on parity of ministries with the Labour Party, especially since the Prime Minister was *ex officio* entitled to two votes in the Cabinet. After three further crises, Mr Den Uyl accepted the Christian Democrats' demand, only to find that his own party, which at its annual conference had swung further to the left, rejected its leader's intention. At this stage, early in November, Mr Den Uyl withdrew from his attempt to form a Government.

As the year drew to a close, the Christian Democrats and the Liberals sought to establish a basis for a new Government that would command 77 of the 150 seats in the Lower House. After protracted negotiations, on 17 December Mr Andreas Van Agt, the leader of the Christian Democrats, became Prime Minister of a centre-right coalition Government with the Liberals. The new Government's prospects seemed unfavourable; for although it commanded a technical majority of seats seven left-wing Christian Democrat members said that they did not support the new Government's programme. The Labour Party and Democrats '66 stated they would oppose Mr Van Agt.

The Netherlands had its share of terrorism in 1977. Most notably, in May South Moluccan terrorists took hostages, including schoolchildren, in an attack on a train and a school. Though the schoolchildren were released after four days, the remaining hostages were held under threat for 18 days, when an armed assault by government forces achieved their release, but only at the cost of the lives of two hostages and six terrorists. The South Moluccans went on trial at Assen in September, to the accompaniment of new acts of terrorism by their supporters. In addition, members of the German Red Army faction who had sought refuge in the Netherlands were involved in other acts of violence.

With only a caretaker Government in office, there were no new economic policy initiatives to counter the recession in the economy. Industrial output declined during the year as orders diminished. Unemployment remained high. Inflation, however, was kept under control.

LUXEMBOURG

Economic difficulties were severe throughout 1977. The recession affected virtually every section of the economy, but for the steel industry the deterioration came near to being catastrophic in face of high local production costs and a massive decline in demand for steel by West Germany and France, Luxembourg's main export markets. The problems of ARBED, the big steel company whose operations are vital to the Grand Duchy's economy, were a major preoccupation of the authorities. The main hope for future viability was placed in a plan to reduce the industry's labour force to about 17,000 from the 1977 figure of 21,200.

The long-heralded changes in the legislation controlling the activities of the 6,000 holding companies incorporated in Luxembourg to take advantage of tax concessions were enacted in June after being in preparation for three years. The fundamental intention was, by setting higher minimum capital requirements, to discourage small holding companies, sometimes with dubious affiliations, which made little or no contribution to Luxembourg's standing as an international financial centre, and, as mainly 'nameplate' operations, created very few jobs for local people.

Politically, it was a quiet year for Mr Gaston Thorn's centre-left coalition Government of Liberals and Socialists.

REPUBLIC OF IRELAND

The health of the national economy, threatened by heavy trade deficits and conflicting sectional demands, dominated public policy throughout the year. Despite the national wage agreement approved in February, which provided pay rises between the limits of £4 and £8.26, industrial disputes disrupted a number of sectors from the telephone and telex services to electricity supplies and the national airline. Comparatively few man-hours were lost through these sporadic stoppages, however, and income tax relief coupled with improved social welfare benefits in the January Budget brought tangible economic improvement. In the first quarter of the year inflation dropped by 4 per cent to a rate of 16·70 per cent. At the end of June, EEC figures showed the Irish rate to be lower than those of Britain and Italy. Substantial grants from the EEC Social Fund and higher yields from taxation, including revenue from new taxes on wealth and on farmers, combined with wage restraint to stimulate this modest but real movement out of recession.

Nonetheless, discontent continued. Industrial and agricultural interests resented the burden of tax which this policy imposed on them, while housewives and workers generally took more note of the continuing rise in prices than of the fall in the inflation rate. These factors played a major part in the defeat of the Government at the general election in June.

The coalition Government of the Fine Gael and Labour Parties had been in office for over four years when the Taoiseach (Prime Minister), Mr Liam Cosgrave, called the election. Most commentators judged its chance of survival to be good. The timing seemed right, given the improvement in the economic indices and the seasonal fall in unemployment, which might have been swollen by jobless school-leavers later in the year. During the preceding months, the Government had been seen to fight strenuously for the needs of Irish farmers and fishermen at the EEC. If it had failed to halt the spiralling prices, the Government had contained the increases by wide-ranging subsidies. Special interests had been catered for by the Minister for the Gaeltacht (Irish-speaking regions), Mr Tom O'Donnell, the Minister for Health and Social Welfare, Mr Brendan Corish, and others. The Government parties took their stand on the record and made few promises of popular appeal. The opposition Fianna Fail party, led by the former Taoiseach, Mr Jack Lynch, built its campaign round the grievances of the public regarding taxation, living costs, poor employment prospects and the growing crime rate. It promised the abolition of motor tax and rates on private houses as well as an increase in the level of tax-free earnings and a special grant for first-time house purchasers.

This programme carried Fianna Fail to victory. The party won 84 of the 148 seats in the Dail, giving Mr Lynch the largest majority ever enjoyed by an Irish head of government. Three coalition Ministers lost their seats: Dr Conor Cruise O'Brien, Mr Patrick Cooney and Mr Justin Keating. Mr Cosgrave resigned the leadership of Fine Gael and was replaced by the outgoing Foreign Minister, Dr Garret FitzGerald, who became Leader of the Opposition. The Labour Party also acquired a new leader in Mr Frank Cluskey, who had been a junior Minister in the coalition Government. Whether Fianna Fail had won because of its specific promises, its broader sympathy with popular grievances or an unsuspected deep-running dissatisfaction with the coalition was still being debated at the end of the year. With hindsight, many agreed that the . coalition had contributed to its own downfall during its final year of office by single-minded law-and-order policies, which weakened constitutional guarantees against arbitrary arrest and detention, and by its failure to protect the head of state when he was subjected to ministerial insult (see AR 1976, pp. 147-48).

The new Government took office in July. Mr Lynch's principal colleagues included Mr George Colley, Minister for Finance, Dr Martin O'Donoghue, Minister for Economic Planning, Mr Charles Haughey, Minister for Health, and Mr John Wilson, Minister for Education. Mr Haughey had been dismissed as Minister for Finance from the Fianna Fail Administration in 1970 by Mr Lynch, who charged him with not fully subscribing to the then Government's policy on Northern Ireland (see AR 1970, pp. 173-74). His return to office was seen as recognition of the grassroots support which he retained within the party. The most active member of the new Government initially was Mr Brian Lenihan, Minister for Fisheries. He found himself under the same pressures as the coalition, with Irish fishermen demanding extensive protection against foreign intrusion in traditional Irish waters while the EEC rejected measures which it considered to be discriminatory against member countries of the Common Market. Restrictions on mesh sizes for nets proved no more acceptable to Brussels than the coalition's restrictions on boat sizes. Each was argued on the ground of conservation needs. Each ran into EEC objections that Irish fishermen were less disadvantaged than others. The process of compromise between the Government and the EEC Commission was still in train at the end of the year, with the Government tactically holding to a demand for a 50-mile exclusive limit in the Republic's favour.

Few steps of any significance were undertaken in regard to the political situation in Northern Ireland. In January, the Fianna Fail party repeated its opposition to changes in the Republic's constitution which would remove the clauses implying a right to jurisdiction over the North. Fianna Fail also argued the need for a British commitment to phased withdrawal from Northern Ireland, while the coalition parties continued to propose a power-sharing local administration for the area, involving participation by representatives of the unionist and nationalist communities. The change of Government in the Republic brought no new initiatives. In practice, a bi-partisan stand on the part of Government and Opposition in the Dail remained in force and contacts were maintained with the British authorities in the interest of a *modus vivendi* until fresh approaches towards a long-term solution became evident in Northern Ireland.

The new Government also committed itself to prosecution of the final stages of the torture proceedings against Britain at the European Court of Human Rights in Strasbourg. The Republic itself came under criticism from the British Prime Minister, Mr Callaghan, for its refusal to sign the European Convention on the Suppression of Terrorism. This refusal reflected major concern over the state of security within the Republic, where bank raids and robberies with violence occurred with unprecedented frequency throughout the year. In the absence of sufficient convictions it could not be said with accuracy how many of these crimes were the work of politically-motivated subversive organizations. The police, already stretched beyond their strength by the demands of patrol duty along the border with Northern Ireland, had also to cope with an increase of urban vandalism in Dublin and other cities.

The problems of internal security were highlighted in February by allegations in the *Irish Times* that suspects under interrogation had been subjected to physical violence by a special unit of police investigators. The police as well as the then Minister for Justice, Mr Patrick Cooney, denied the allegations but these were followed in April by public questioning of the validity of fingerprint evidence offered by the police in cases before the Special Criminal Court. The Director of Public Prosecutions was still examining the fingerprint charges at the end of the year. In October, the Government released details of an Amnesty International report which found *prima facie* proof of police brutality and called for an impartial inquiry. None of these recriminations elicited extensive concern on the part of the public, whose sympathies lay with the hard-pressed police force and who tended to suspect the motives of some of the complainants who spoke to the newspapers or to Amnesty. The courts vindicated the police in several cases where assault charges were brought by private individuals. There remained sufficient anxiety to persuade the Government to drop the emergency measure allowing the police to hold certain suspects for seven days without charge. The Government also appointed a three-man committee in October with a neatly-balanced brief to advise on safeguards for suspects in police custody and on protection for the police against false allegations.

Meanwhile, the intake of new recruits to the police force had become evident on the ground, and the incidence of crime appeared to be falling in the weeks before Christmas. A hunger strike by members of the Provisional IRA serving sentences in Portlaoise prison during March and April won no concessions from the Government. Eight British soldiers, who had been arrested on the Republic's side of the border, were fined £100 each by the Special Criminal Court for illegal possession of firearms. The Court sentenced the man charged with murdering a British army officer, Captain Robert Nairac, who had been kidnapped in County Armagh and was found shot dead in the Republic, to life imprisonment in November.

Cardinal William Conway, Archbishop of Armagh and Primate of All Ireland, died in April (see OBITUARY) and was succeeded in October by Monsignor Tomás O Fiaich, a renowned historian and President of Saint Patrick's College, Maynooth. The appointment of Monsignor O Fiaich as the spiritual leader of Irish Roman Catholics was warmly welcomed by the national press and the Protestant churches in the Republic. Much indignation was expressed at criticism of the appointment voiced by elements in the British Conservative Party and the British media, who claimed to be disturbed by the new Archbishop's commitment to Gaelic culture and his personal aspiration for a united Ireland. Archbishop O Fiaich himself caused some speculation about a possible change of official attitudes within the Irish Church when he told the *Belfast Telegraph* in October that he favoured replacement of the Republic's constitution by a 'very short basic document' and that he approved complete separation of church and state. There was no response from the state and contentious questions on divorce, contraception and education remained unresolved.

The Roman Catholic bishops published a major pastoral letter in September on 'The Work of Justice' which, among other matters, pointed to the unhappy state of industrial relations in the Republic. This was dramatically confirmed in the closing months of the year, when a prolonged dispute between two trade unions led to the closure of the Dutch-owned Ferenka factory in Limerick with the loss of 1,400 jobs. At a time when unemployment still totalled the ominous figure for the Republic of 100,000, and when other foreign concerns were suffering similar problems, the undoubted contributory negligence of the parent firm in Holland offered little ground for complacency.

Chapter 2

DENMARK—ICELAND—NORWAY—SWEDEN—FINLAND—AUSTRIA—
SWITZERLAND

DENMARK

A new 'crisis agreement' was duly attempted (see AR 1976, p. 150), but Mr Anker Jørgensen could find no alternative to a further election, which was held on 15 February and produced the following results (previous representation in brackets):

Social Democrats	65	(53)
Socialist People's Party	7	(9)
Communists	7	(7)
Left Socialists	5	(4)

Conservatives	15 (10)
Venstre (Liberal Left)	21 (42)
Radikale Venstre (Radical Left)	6 (13)
Christian People's Party	6 (9)
Retsforbundet (single-tax Radicals)	6 (0)
Progressives	26 (24)
Centre Democrats	11 (4)

In addition to the eleven parties which reached the Rigsdag, at least nine others tried to attract the minimum of support for admission to the contest; one bore the hopeful name 'An earthly paradise'. The main losers in the election were the Liberal Left, whose leader, Mr Poul Hartling, was in November appointed UN High Commissioner for Refugees. Mr Jørgensen's Social Democratic Government—the eleventh minority Ministry out of a total of 14 since World War II—had clearly received a mandate to carry on, and he tried to strengthen its position by two non-party additions: an architect as Minister of Housing and a woman professor of clinical psychology with an interest in Unesco and refugee questions, Lise Østergaard, as a Minister without portfolio assisting the Foreign Office.

The economic difficulties continued to mount. On 1 April Denmark (like Norway) made a 3 per cent devaluation on account of action taken by Sweden (see p. 149). In the same month almost all the newspapers were stopped for three weeks by the printers in pursuit of a bitter conflict over technical changes in *Berlingske Tidende*, which brought a Conservative organ dating from 1749 to the verge of final collapse. In May the committee of the Economic Council warned the Government that unemployment would not reach its peak before 1979 and that in the current year the balance of payments would show no improvement. By 6 September yet another compromise solution had been found for the needs of the economy, involving 30 new measures; these had the approval of all parties in the middle of the political spectrum, though not of the extreme left or of the anti-taxation Progressives. Nevertheless, when the Finance Minister (Mr K. Heinesen) introduced the 1978 Budget into the Folketing on 30 November, he drew a gloomy picture of the prospects for a country which had had an unfavourable balance of payments every year since 1963 and was almost 100 per cent dependent on imported energy resources.

The institution of a separate post of suffragan bishop for the Faeroes was among the extravagances denounced by the Progressives, albeit the diocesan bishop of Copenhagen had found time to visit the islands on only five occasions since the Reformation.

ICELAND

The two-year fishing agreement for West German trawlers expired on 28 November, whereupon the Icelanders achieved the full control over fisheries which had long been their aim. Although some concessions were still available to Belgian, Norwegian and especially to Faeroese fishermen, the main emphasis was now laid upon measures to conserve the stock of cod, no catch whatever being allowed during a 12-day period in December. For this reason there was thought to be no likelihood of any immediate fisheries agreement with the European Community.

Icelandic foreign relations continued to be carefully balanced between East and West. In April a Communist member of the Allting proposed to call in Swedish experts to conduct a neutral inquiry into the alleged presence of nuclear weapons at Keflavik. In July the West German Chancellor paid an official visit to the island, but a couple of months later Mr G. Hallgrímsson was the first Icelandic Premier to pay a similar visit to the Soviet Union. In November it became known that the Chinese were sending ships for 8,000 tons of aluminium, of which they had bought 3,000 tons earlier in the year.

NORWAY

Relations with Norway's mighty neighbour in the far north continued to be disquieting, not least because it was brought to light in January that a minor woman official of the Foreign Ministry had been passing secret information to the Russians for nearly 18 years. In June the Government established a 200-mile fisheries zone round Svalbard, but the exercise of sovereignty over an archipelago one-fifth the size of mainland Norway still involved thorny problems. For example, the Norwegians exercised their surveillance by means of one small helicopter, whereas the Russians had five large ones on the station, nominally for the purpose of ferrying workers between Barentsburg and their new mining development at Pyramiden. The immediate problem, however, was that of the Barents Sea fisheries, where the Norwegian zone (see AR 1976, p. 152) overlapped with the Russian, announced on 25 May. On 11 November a 'grey zone' agreement, valid until 1 July 1978, enabled both parties to go on fishing without risk of a confrontation, but this was not to prejudice the final settlement. On 6 December the Norwegian position over Svalbard, the Barents Sea and West German participation in Nato activities on Norwegian soil were among the subjects raised by Mr Kosygin with the Nordic Premiers at the Finnish jubilee celebrations (see p. 151). The tone of his harangue, delivered in a side room whilst 2,000 other guests were dancing, was such that the Prime Minister of Denmark (according to an interview cited by *Aftenposten*) 'had to say to Kosygin, "Take it easy." '

The quadrennial elections to the Storting on 12 September resulted as follows (previous representation in brackets):

Centre (Agrarians)	12 (21)
Christian People's Party	22 (20)
Venstre (Left)	2 (2)
Conservatives	41 (29)
New People's Party ('New Left')	0 (1)
Progressives (formerly Lange's Party)	0 (4)
Labour	76 (62)
Socialist Left (SV)	2 (16)

The non-socialists polled 4·8 per cent more votes than their opponents and were for a few hectic hours believed to be the winners, but they lacked unity in a situation in which one voter in four had changed party. With five parties in the field, they were not even agreed on a future Premier. The minority Labour Government remained in office, and could rely on SV's support for such socializing measures as public control of private banks (to take effect on 1 January 1978) and a proposed levy on all successful business concerns in order to subsidize below-average wages paid elsewhere. By December it was clear that oil profits would not accrue fast enough to tide Norway over the prolonged depression in world trade, and that social costs must therefore be consistent with the saleability of Norwegian exports.

A serious blow-out on the Bravo platform of the Ekofisk oilfield led to the tightening-up of safety regulations. One consequence was the likelihood of further delay in the investigation of oil prospects north of 62° under the auspices of the Oil and Energy Department to be inaugurated at New Year.

SWEDEN

The krona was devalued by 6 per cent in April and by a further 10 per cent on 29 August, when Sweden left the currency 'snake'. These measures failed, however, to give a sufficient fillip to the exports of the country which had so long been 'the America of Europe', its high labour costs counterbalanced by a far-advanced technology. Under the influence of the general crisis in steel, shipbuilding and textiles, the first three-quarters of the year showed a fall of 2 per cent in GNP. The Grand Old Man of Swedish business life, Mr Marcus Wallenberg, was believed to be responsible for a merger of record size, which placed the 100,000 employees of the motor industry under a single ultimate authority. Soon afterwards an export rival was bought up at twice its market value by Electrolux, another Wallenberg concern but one which employed twice as many of its

76,000 workers abroad as in Sweden. On 8 November the Government announced its 50 per cent participation in a new company which was to restore Sweden's position in the steel trade. But when the year ended Mr K. Fälldin and his colleagues still faced acute problems of inflation and unemployment.

Nevertheless, opinion polls indicated that the coalition Government still enjoyed slightly more direct party support than did the Social Democrats. In February–March the other opposition party had split, two of its 17 representatives in the Riksdag seceding to form the 'Labour Party Communists', who would have no truck with Eurocommunism. Their stronghold was among the miners and ironworkers of the far north, but by October support had apparently dwindled to 0·5 per cent of the electorate, as compared with 4·5 per cent supporting the original 'Communist Left' party.

An important defence problem arose from the report of a committee on future policy regarding fighter aircraft, the choice lying between six divisions of the existing Viggen A 20 and nine of the B3LA design, with two Viggen divisions also retained in service. Although fighters of the proposed new design would be slower than the Viggen and therefore unable to engage an enemy far out at sea, the commander-in-chief pointed to 'features which may make it somewhat better than the alternative' and it was definitely preferred by the head of the air force. In the view of the committee, the abandonment of the B3LA would mean the end of Swedish technological advance in this sphere. The Social Democrats, however, were against the development of any new fighter aircraft, and the Prime Minister told journalists that it would be 'unwise' to have a major political struggle over this question.

FINLAND

From early March until mid-May Finnish life was disturbed by a wave of strikes, involving about 300,000 workers and extending even to the electricity supply. In February unemployment amounted to 5·9 per cent, and it subsequently reached the record total of 157,700. On 29 March the Government's pay proposals were supported by a majority of 96 to 2 in the Eduskunta, but the Social Democrats had abstained from the vote of confidence for fear of losing ground to the Communists in the trade unions. Agreement was eventually reached on wage increases of up to 16 per cent spread over a period of two years. The Finnish mark, which had been devalued by 5·7 per cent on 5 April, was reduced by a further 3 per cent on 1 September in order to maintain competition against Swedish exports, cheapened by the fall in the krona. In November legislators were presented with a 15-year programme for increased bilateral trade with the Soviet

Union. It was claimed that this relationship already provided employment for at least 120,000 Finns, including 35,000 in the metal-working industries; only the Conservatives ventured to suggest that commercial dependence upon the larger power might lead to other forms of dependence.

On 15 May, two days before President Kekkonen's departure on a visit to Russia, he succeeded in establishing a majority Government under Mr K. Sorsa (see AR 1975, pp. 152-53), with Mr P. Värynen, the 31-year-old 'coming man' of the Centre Party, as Foreign Minister. Three posts additional to the premiership went to Social Democrats and a total of five to the Centre, but the most notable inclusion was that of four Communists, among them their secretary-general, Mr Arvo Aalto. Given the support of the Stalinist wing of the Communist Party, the new Cabinet had fully three-quarters of the Finnish Parliament behind it. But it remained uncertain whether the majority could hold together, even until the Presidential election in 1978. On 7 December the precarious economic situation obliged the Government to launch a new programme, which would postpone the agreed wage increases of March to October and those of October to February whilst also increasing ministerial control over prices.

Thus the sixtieth anniversary of Finland's proclamation of independence was celebrated on 6 December in conditions of continuing uncertainty. Since 1917 there had been one new Cabinet for every year; no party had ever achieved a majority; and numerous caretaker Administrations had held office under Presidential authority. In his election campaign, endorsed by six political parties and formally launched in October, President Kekkonen stressed the dependence of his office upon the higher constitutional authority of the Eduskunta. Yet the man in the street might be excused for believing that the Presidency was indeed a key office, his re-election to which at the age of 78 was required by their mighty neighbour, with whose leaders he enjoyed such consistently good relations (see AR 1972, p. 160). At the opening of parliament in February, Kekkonen had uttered a sharp warning against any presumption that changed world conditions might be 'reflected in the foreign policy of Finland'. On two later occasions he engaged in historical observations of an equally pointed nature. At a festivity in honour of Russia's October Revolution, he spoke of the sympathy which Lenin had shown for Finnish independence in 1901 and 1913 as well as in its recognition by the Council of People's Commissars on 31 December 1917, so that he 'deserved the undivided respect of the people of Finland and a permanent place in its history'. A month later he was inviting another Helsinki audience to see the war crimes trials, by which the political leaders of 1941-44 were consigned to prison at Russian behest, as 'a test of political maturity' which had prepared the way for the happy Finno-Soviet relations of later decades.

AUSTRIA

Autumn 1977 was the halfway mark for Dr Bruno Kreisky's second one-party Government, and the Bürgenland regional assembly elections on 2 October produced a gratifying vote of confidence for the Federal Chancellor. The Austrian Socialist Party (SPÖ) won 51·9 per cent of the vote, for the first time achieving an absolute majority of seats in this assembly.

The Government was only temporarily affected by the controversy in January over the Defence Minister's responsibility for an arms deal that had violated Austria's neutrality law and had included material from army stocks. Brigadier Karl Lütgendorf resigned on 30 May, after a parliamentary commission reported that he had failed to give Parliament or Dr Kreisky the full facts. He was replaced by Otto Rösch, formerly Minister of the Interior. Herr Rösch was succeeded by Erwin Lanc, previously Minister of Transport, and Herr Lanc by a State Secretary in the Federal Chancellery, Karl Lausecker.

The economy continued to perform fairly well in 1977. Real GNP rose by 4 per cent in the first half of the year, inflation dropped in August to 5·5 per cent on a yearly basis, and unemployment stayed at a mere 1·8 per cent. Unplanned shortfalls in successive federal budgets coupled with spectacular increases in the balance of payments deficit, however, signalled a serious threat to Austria's industrial peace, rapid growth and increasing affluence. Between January and September 1977 Austria's visible trade deficit reached an all-time peak of 51,000 million Austrian schillings (£1·75 billion), 31 per cent more than in the same period of 1976. Tourism, which in 1975 still covered 96 per cent of the trade deficit, covered only 56 per cent in 1976 and 47 per cent in the first eight months of 1977. Consequently the deficit on current account almost doubled during this period and external reserves fell by AS10,000 million.

After tightening monetary and fiscal policies somewhat in June, the Government announced on 3 October a package of austerity measures aimed at raising an additional AS14,500 million in 1978. VAT on luxury items was increased from 18 to 30 per cent, a special levy on transit lorry traffic was announced, social security contributions were raised and company tax concessions reduced. Controls were imposed on textile and agricultural imports, and income tax cuts demanded by the unions were postponed. The 1978 Budget introduced by the Finance Minister, Dr Hannes Androsch, on 18 October still envisaged a deficit of AS40,600 million, and allowed for increased expenditure on education, the police and the army. Dr Androsch's plans were based on a projected growth rate of 2 to 2·5 per cent in 1978. His optimism was not shared by outside observers, since Austria's production costs were now level with those of its German and Swiss competitors and its industries were much less efficient and well organized.

For the moment the electorate was less preoccupied with the economy than with public order. In Vienna there were thirty armed bank robberies in the first six months of the year, some with terrorist connexions, and dramatic kidnappings in November and December. Violent incidents also occurred in Carinthia, but all-party cooperation over minority rights for the Slovenes probably contributed to a calmer atmosphere in that province. Disputes between various Croat, Czech and Hungarian factions delayed the establishment of the advisory councils proposed for these ethnic groups, while the Slovenes boycotted their council on the grounds that participation would prejudice their chances of getting the 1976 minorities legislation repealed by the Constitutional Court. A law passed on 31 May made Slovene an official language in 14 districts, and required bilingual place-name signs in 91 localities in eight districts. The first signs went up at the end of June, drawing protests from extremist German speakers and from places with a Slovene minority too small to qualify for them.

Although acrimonious public exchanges were avoided, relations with Yugoslavia remained cool on the Slovene issue. The Czechs objected strongly at the beginning of the year to Dr Kreisky's support for their human rights campaigners, and in May to a Sudeten German rally in Vienna. The Government tabled proposals on energy and transport questions at the Helsinki follow-up conference in Belgrade (see Pt. XI) and realized a long-standing ambition when the UN agreed (in December 1976) to transfer four organizations from New York and Geneva to the purpose built UN City in Vienna. Concern was felt over Italian failure to observe the agreed timetable for implementation of measures agreed on behalf of the German-speaking population of South Tyrol, but its expression was muted.

SWITZERLAND

In 1977 the economic revival in Switzerland undoubtedly became more marked than in 1976. The committee for economic questions, a highly competent body of scientists, industrialists and representatives of the trade unions, reported that 'in late autumn 1977 we can clearly see that the lowest level of the recession has been passed and the economy is slowly recovering'. In spite of the high value of the Swiss currency there was an export boom, while the building industry was still suffering badly. Unemployment fell back to 0·3 per cent of the working population, or between 7,000 and 8,000, while 500,000 foreign workers were still employed. An unemployment rate of this kind was unique in Western Europe. Although the country, particularly the usually sunny southern area, had a wet and cold summer, the figures for tourism were surprisingly satisfactory.

Politically a degree of unrest was shown by a steadily increasing number of initiatives asking for constitutional reforms. The Swiss citizens were four times called to the polls to decide on 14 issues by referendum. The most important decision was the rejection (12 June) of the new Value Added Tax, a system approaching that of the EEC, thus leaving the Federal State's deficit budget unresolved. It was evident that the majority wanted first a reduction of expenditure and state activity. When the Government and Parliament proposed reductions of various subsidies the left-wing groups asked for a referendum, but on 4 December the economy measures were accepted. On the same day a Socialist initiative for heavier taxes on high incomes was refused. In any case the Federal Council, unwilling to tolerate deficit spending, was preparing new taxes. The liquidity of the money market and low interest rates facilitated public borrowing, but the majority of Parliament and public were against any postponement of a restoration of the financial balance.

Two constitutional initiatives which were rejected provoked a lively campaign. On 25 September, by 995,000 to 929,000, the citizens rejected legitimization of abortion in the first 12 weeks of pregnancy. The leading opponents of any such freedom were the Roman Catholics and some strongly Protestant circles. The second initiative which was rejected, on 4 December, by the tremendous majority of 887,000 to 534,000, concerned the introduction of compulsory civil instead of military service for con-scientious objectors. Amongst 30,000 recruits were 300 to 400 religious or political objectors refusing any military service, even in the unarmed Red Cross units. Government and Parliament were ready to give way, provided that each case was examined by a commission. But the great majority of the Swiss people rejected the idea of qualifying the traditional duty of any healthy Swiss to join the army.

The minimum figures of 30,000 signatures for a referendum and 50,000 for a constitutional initiative were raised to 50,000 and 100,000 and the collection of signatures for initiatives limited to 18 months from the start of the attempt. This measure, which was opposed by the left-wing parties but accepted by the majority of the people, was designed to restrict the flood of popular initiatives and demands for a referendum. The slogan of 'democratization' seemed to be losing its attraction. Thus the initiative of the trade unions for reducing working hours missed the goal.

Two events in the business world provoked an unusual uproar in public opinion. The Chiasso (Tessin) branch of the Crédit Suisse, one of the oldest and best-known big banks of Switzerland, incurred heavy losses in Italian business speculations, and the majority of the shares of the famous shoe business Bally changed hands until the leading Swiss gun factory

Buehrle took over control. The losses of the Crédit Suisse were expected to lead to a new banking law.

At the end of the year two of the seven members of the Federal Government, Ernst Brugger, Socialist, head of the Department for Economy, and Pierre Graber, Liberal-Radical, head of the Foreign Department, left office, for reasons of age and health respectively. In their place Parliament elected State Councillors Pierre Aubert, of the Canton of Neuchatel, a well-known Socialist lawyer and delegate to the Council of Europe, and Fritz Honegger, Radical-Liberal director of the chamber of commerce in Zürich. Thus the coalition of two Socialists, two Liberal-Radicals, two Roman Catholics or Christian Democrats and one member of the People's (Farmers') Party was unchanged. The Socialist Willy Ritschard, a former trade union leader, was triumphantly elected President for 1978.

In view of various demonstrations against nuclear power stations and of international terrorism Parliament accepted the draft of a new law creating a police force composed of cantonal contingents but under Federal control. A referendum launched against it by the extreme left-wing groups would proceed in 1978. Federal referendum at the end of September approved the creation of a new Swiss Canton of the Jura a year later, after a struggle of more than 25 years, thus partly correcting a decision of the Congress of Vienna in 1815, when the former Principality of French-speaking Jura was given to the German-speaking Canton of Berne.

Chapter 3

SPAIN—PORTUGAL—MALTA—GIBRALTAR—GREECE—CYPRUS—TURKEY

SPAIN

THE results of the December 1976 referendum on the Political Reform Law (see AR 1976, p. 161) showed how little support there was either for the preservation intact of the Franco system or for *ruptura*, its destruction at a single blow. The issue now to be determined was whether there was to be superficial change or metamorphosis. The Law was *para* (for), not *de* (of) Political Reform. Therefore any or all of its provisions could be interpreted as transient. It enabled the existing structure to be transformed, piece by piece, into something totally different—without a break in government or a breach of legality (whether or not the existing legality was held to be legitimate).

The Law's potential as the instrument for peaceful establishment of a new order was realized fully by the *bunker* and the advocates of violent revolution alike, and they sought to prevent it by acts of terrorism. On 24 January, an extreme left organization, already holding Antonio de Oriol prisoner (see AR 1976, p. 161), kidnapped the Judge Advocate General, General Emilio Villaescusa, and an organization of the extreme right killed five lawyers assembled in a labour union office. Three paramilitary policemen were killed in other incidents. At their funeral, some officers of the armed services publicly insulted the Vice-Premier, General Gutiérrez Mellado, and others took part in anti-Government demonstrations elsewhere. General Mellado and other senior officers issued strong warnings against indiscipline. The Prime Minister, Adolfo Suárez, appealed for calm and unity in the fight against terrorism. He was backed by the leaders of many political parties, and the director general of the Civil Guard assured him of the loyalty of that force to the King and Government.

Suárez reaffirmed his determination to democratize Spain. No major party from right-of-centre leftwards had applied for legalization under the terms of the June 1976 Law on the right to political association. None was prepared to concede to the Government the right to judge whether its statutes complied with the Law or not. The Government now changed the Law: as from 10 February the Ministry of the Interior was either to declare a party legalized within ten days of the submission of its statutes, or refer to the Supreme Tribunal those of any party suspected of being subject to orders from abroad and of having as its aim the establishment of a totalitarian regime. The Socialist Workers' Party was the first off the mark, and by the end of May over 250 parties had followed its lead.

The Communist Party submitted on 11 February a set of statutes hurriedly drafted in accordance with the principles of Santiago Carrillo's 'Eurocommunism' rather than marxist-leninism. The Ministry referred them to the Tribunal, which saw nothing illegal in them and ruled that judgment as to their sincerity, not being a matter of law, was outside their competence. The Government decided to declare the Party legal on 9 April, Holy Saturday, when those opposed to the legalization were on holiday and the risk of immediate concerted action was at its minimum. There were some demonstrations in Madrid. Manuel Fraga Iribarne, then emerging as the leader of the conservative right, called the legalization 'a grave political error and a juridical farce'. A meeting of army generals issued a communique stating that they accepted the decision 'with revulsion' and only because of their 'spirit of patriotism and duty'. In signing it, however, they committed themselves, some perhaps unwittingly, as a point of honour not to plot against the Government, and some came to attribute their 'revulsion' as being over the way in which the Government had acted over the matter and not over the legalization as such.

In the eight-week period between the application and the declaration of legality, the Government had allowed Carrillo to hold a conference in Madrid with the other two leading Eurocommunists, Marchais of France and Berlinguer of Italy (see DOCUMENTS). Carrillo had not only publicly condemned the suppression of human rights in the Soviet Union, but also committed himself and his party to the pursuance of communism only within the rules of parliamentary democracy. His book 'Eurocommunism and the State' was to be on sale shortly afterwards.

After consultations with the leaders of the legalized parties, the Government issued on 15 March a decree-law setting out the rules for the elections to the new Cortes promised in the Law for Political Reform: 15 June was to be the election day; voting was to be by party lists; the 207 elective seats in the Senate were allocated basically four per province, and election to them was to be by simple majority. The 350 seats in the Lower House (*Congreso*) were distributed two per province basic plus one per 144,500 inhabitants in the province. Election to them was to be according to the D'Hondt proportional representation system.

The moribund Cortes approved this decree-law according to Franco's rules, and on 30 March gave its assent to a Bill to legalize labour organizations other than those of the *Movimiento*. The *Movimiento*, Franco's principal instrument for the control of political thought and action, was declared dissolved on 1 April. On 14 May, Alfonso XIII's heir Don Juan renounced his claim to the throne of Spain in favour of his son Juan Carlos, who thereupon became King of Spain by inheritance and not merely by grace of Franco.

The chosen electoral list and proportional representation systems made advisable alliances among the smaller parties. Several of those which wanted the restoration of authoritarian and right-wing rule came together under the title Alianza Nacional. Seven, agreed upon the need for only superficial changes to the Franco system and joined in an *Alianza Popular* under Fraga. Fifteen assorted Liberal, Social Democrat and Christian Democrat groups formed a Democratic Centre Union (UCD). Suárez took over its leadership on the eve of the opening of the campaign. The main-stream left-inclined Christian Democrats and other Social Democrats decided to submit their own separate lists. So did the Socialist Workers' Party (PSOE) and Tierno Galván's strictly marxist Popular Socialist Party (PSP). The Communist Party (PCE) refused any link with parties to the left of them. In Euzkadi (the Basque provinces) and Catalonia all parties to the left of the UCD stressed their advocacy of autonomy more than their position in the ideological spectrum. In all 4,467 candidates belonging to 194 separate parties, but mostly in 18 coalitions, ran for the 350 seats in the Lower House. Almost 1,500 stood for election to the Senate.

Throughout the three weeks' campaign there was freedom of assembly and of spoken and printed word. All the major parties had access to television and radio. The emphasis in all propaganda was on personalities rather than party programmes, a feature which was possibly to the advantage of Suárez and the equally photogenic leader of the PSOE,

Felipe González. Terrorists killed two policemen in Barcelona and another in San Sebastian, and kidnapped a prominent Basque industrialist, Javier Ybarra. The Government did its best to pacify Euzkadi by releasing from prison almost all ETA men convicted of terrorist acts. Some 17 convicted or pending trial for assassination accepted an offer of release if they went into exile.

The poll numbered 78·2 per cent of the electorate. Of that percentage 34·3 per cent voted for the UCD candidates to Congress, of whom 165 were declared elected, 28·5 per cent for the PSOE (118 seats), 9 per cent for the Spanish Communist Party and its Catalan affiliate (20 seats) and 8·2 per cent for the Alianza Popular (16 seats). Alianza Nacional polled less than 1 per cent and did not qualify for a single seat.

Suárez, having been confirmed by the King as Premier, abolished the Ministry of Information, coalesced the separate service ministries into a single one of Defence, under General Gutierrez Mellado, and created a new Ministry of Economy to which he appointed a widely respected economist, Enrique Fuentes Quintana. The Government took office with a new simple oath of allegiance to the King and Country and no reference to the Principles of the Movimiento. So also in July did the new Senators and Congressmen.

Political expediency had inhibited Governments since 1974 from taking action against outflow of capital, neglect of investment, serious inflation and growing unemployment. Calculations in June projected a deficit of $5,000 million for 1977 and $12,000 million for the three years 1975-77, and a final inflation figure of over 30 per cent for 1977. Already 6 per cent of the labour force was unemployed. Fuentes proposed price controls, a limit on increases in executive salaries, a wealth tax and heavier taxes on higher incomes and luxury consumer goods. The wealthy reacted strongly. Fuentes also asked labour organizations to show restraint in their wage demands. On 12 July the Government devalued the peseta by 19·65 per cent. The left, and PSOE in particular, emphasized the foreseeable consequences of the devaluation on people of modest means— rises in the cost of petroleum products and imported food. They were therefore not prepared to cooperate with the Government.

Since *de facto* now (and *de jure* in the new constitution being drafted by a parliamentary Commission) the Government was to be answerable to Parliament, and its party, the UCD, had no overall majority, the Government had need of allies. Left-of-centre members of UCD would have seceded from it had Suárez turned to the Alianza Popular. PCE advocated a 'Government of national concentration', but PSOE, whose leaders looked on themselves as a viable 'alternative Government', would have none of it. Nor would the Basque Nationalist Party and the Catalan Pacte Democratic (with 8 and 11 seats respectively), albeit their position in the political spectrum was essentially that of the UCD. The election results had shown that nothing mattered more to Catalans and Basques than the recovery of their lost autonomy.

It was evident that the drafting of a constitution whose wording would be acceptable to both the marxist and non-marxist members of the Commission was going to take months. Definitive Statutes of Autonomy could not antecede its passage through the Cortes. Suárez invited the self-exiled President of the Catalan (Republican) Generalitat, Josep Tarradellas, to Madrid, and on 27 June they agreed in principle on the establishment of a new provisional Generalitat, details of which were entrusted to Tarradellas, a representative of Suárez and the Catalan members of parliament. Dissention among the Catalans, rather than differences with Suárez, delayed final agreement till 27 September.

A similar arrangement for Euzkadi took longer to complete. On 7 October a Bill was published to declare all Spaniards absolved of guilt and punishment for any political offence, even assassination, committed before the referendum. The following day ETA killed a government official and his bodyguard in Guernica. The text of the provisional Statute of Autonomy for Euzkadi was published on 26 November, and on that day ETA killed a major of the paramilitary *Policía Armada*. Faced with the consequent tension in the police forces, the Government delayed the approval, by decree, of the Statute till 30 December.

The delays in satisfying the Catalans and Basques led Suárez into another way of ensuring widespread support for the economic measures recommended by Fuentes. On 10 October he invited the leaders of all the parties in parliament to a conference at his office, the Moncloa Palace. After two weeks of bargaining a two-part pact emerged. The first part was socio-economic. Wage and salary increases in 1978 were to be limited to 22 per cent, and the growth of money supply to 17 per cent. Firms forced by labour union pressure to concede increases of more than 20 per cent would be allowed to dismiss up to 5 per cent of staff. In exchange the Government undertook to tax the wealthy more heavily, increase social security benefits and old-age pensions, spend more on schooling and housing, exercise greater control over state investment and expenditure and draft, by June 1978, a law on worker participation in the administration of publicly-owned enterprises.

All parties signed that first part, but Alianza Popular refused to sign the second. In this the signatories agreed on the deletion from all extant legislation of whatever was contrary to democratic practice or human rights: henceforward adultery by a woman would cease to be a criminal offence; the courts alone would rule on the legality of a particular publication, assembly of people or association. The Government was to put an inter-party Board of Control over the state radio and television networks, and reorganize the 'forces of public order'.

At the end of November the result of the work of the inter-party

Commission on the Constitution was leaked to the press. Spain was to be a parliamentary democracy under a monarch. During the year it had in fact come a long way towards democracy, and by common consent, including Carrillo's, the motive force had been the King, who had been greeted enthusiastically by crowds everywhere he had gone, and whose wishes most officers in command of troops were prepared to accept.

PORTUGAL

Portugal's trade deficit in 1976 came to $1,100 million, somewhat less than had been predicted earlier in the year, but still serious. The United States granted Portugal a $300 million emergency loan in January, and Dr Kissinger expressed the hope that the Portuguese Government and people would make the necessary effort during the year to strengthen their economy sufficiently to persuade the United States to increase the loan to $750 million, and other nations to lend Portugal a similar amount. The IMF recommended a 20 to 25 per cent devaluation of the escudo. In February it was devalued by 15 per cent, and in a one-hour television broadcast the Prime Minister, Dr Soares, tried to persuade workers to limit their demands for higher wages to a 15 per cent increase, and to accept the need for austerity and greater productivity. Portugal was now importing 50 per cent of its food and 85 per cent of its animal fodder.

Dr Soares toured the capitals of the European Economic Community and was sympathetically received. The Governments of West Germany and Britain in particular intimated that they judged the possible political benefits from the admission of Portugal into the Community more important than the economic problems that this would inflict on it, and Portugal formally applied to join. In the United States the Carter Administration informed Dr Soares that the US would provide $550 million of the projected $1,500 million loan, if it materialized.

After long negotiations it was announced in June that the US would be prepared to advance $300 million only, West Germany $200 million and Britain, France, Italy, Japan, the Netherlands, Norway, Sweden and Venezuela a further $250 million between them, always provided that Portugal fulfilled the IMF's conditions for a credit of $40 million—a floating escudo, a reduction in imports, an increase in exports and measures to reduce the inflation rate from its then level of 34 per cent. The promised loan might have been larger had Soares not alienated possible Arab lenders by recognizing socialist-led Israel in May.

Dr Soares had been facing grave difficulties at home. The Communist Party (PCP) had attracted only 17·7 per cent of the vote at the December 1976 municipal elections, and 14·5 per cent at the general elections of the previous June, but it remained in control of Intersindical, to which

85 per cent of organized labour belonged. The wheat-growing Alentejo district was in effect its fief, and its position was decisive in most of the workers' committees in the businesses and factories taken over from their owners in the early days of the revolution. It repeatedly made it clear to Soares that the price of its cooperation in the enforcement of the austerity measures and the appeal for greater productivity was a share in government, with a view to a further step towards marxist socialism. Such a step, however, was hardly likely to attract financial help from non-communist nations. In May it was the turn of the two major parties to the right of Soares's Socialists (PSP)—the Social Democrats and Centre Democrats—to suggest a coalition with them. Soares's reply was to reassert his contention that only the PSP alone could govern Portugal. The PCP decided on a show of strength, a rally in Lisbon in June of some 200,000 members of Intersindical, and on a series of strikes.

A new agricultural reform Bill promised by Soares was published in early July. The Communist Party mounted a major propaganda campaign against its provisions: farms of less than 30 hectares (or slightly larger if of poor soil), were to be returned to their original owners, and no original owner was to be left wholly dispossessed. After a four-day acrimonious debate the Assembly passed the Bill on 22 July by 166 votes to 88, the Socialists (with exceptions) and the Social Democrats voting for, and the Communists and Centre Democrats against, the latter considering the redress inadequate. After the vote the Communists challenged the law as contrary to the Constitution, which explicitly committed Portuguese Governments to progress towards socialism. The Supreme Court rejected the Communist plea on 11 August. Soares stated that in future the Government would favour cooperative over collective farming in the million hectares of the Alentejo district. Those lands had yielded on average little over two tonnes of wheat per hectare when farmed privately, but the yields from collectives had been even lower.

In the meantime there had been another fierce debate—over a Bill to indemnify those who had lost land, factories or businesses during the revolution. They were to be compensated for their losses in government bonds redeemable after eight to 22 years. The Communists now called on the President to order general elections or at least dismiss Soares for his 'anti-democratic policies, incompetence, intolerance and ties with imperialistic capitalism'.

On 7 September, eleven days before the agricultural reform law was due to come into effect, explosive and incendiary devices in the six major offices of the Institute of Agrarian Reform destroyed the records of land tenure, and made the implementation of the law difficult if not impossible.

The balance of payments deficit grew, even though the devalued escudo attracted a greater number of tourists than in the previous year. In October and November President Eanes tried to persuade the four major parties

F

into 'a Government of national salvation'. There was personal antipathy between Soares and the leader of the Social Democrats, Sa Carneiro. The Social Democrat and Centre Democrat Parties would not cooperate with the Communists, while the Communists were prepared to support only what, in their opinion, was 'true socialist government'. Even a private conference, such as that then being held between the Spanish parties in Madrid, was out of the question. On 8 December Soares faced a vote of confidence in the Assembly. He declared a willingness to share government with non-partisan technocrats, but with no-one else. The offer proved unacceptable to any member of the Assembly not of his party, and he lost the vote by 159 to 100.

MALTA

Throughout the year, Dom Mintoff's Labour Party Government consolidated its hold on the country, following its election victory in September 1976 (see AR 1976, p. 165). On 27 December 1976, Dr Buttigieg, formerly Minister of Justice and Parliamentary Affairs, was elected President of the Republic by 33 votes to 31. A week later Dr Borg Olivier gave up control of the Nationalist Party after 25 years as its leader and after two consecutive defeats by the Labour Party. He was replaced on 16 January by Dr Edward Fenech Adami, a law graduate of the University of Malta, in a close contest with the party's general secretary, Dr Guido de Marco.

The extension of party power led the Government into conflict with professional groups in the island, and brought the most notable feature of the year, namely, the long quarrel with the Medical Association of Malta. Matters came to a head in May. A dispute between the Minister of Health and the Association began on issues of registration and was exacerbated by the Government's dismissal of almost all doctors from government hospitals for refusing to comply with ministerial instructions: they were replaced by doctors from Libya, Czechoslovakia and Yugoslavia. The dismissals affected the incumbents of six consultant posts at St Luke's Hospital, including the professors of medicine, surgery and gynaecology who held joint university/government appointments. As a result, there was no formal teaching of clinical medicine after the end of May, nor were the University's external examiners allowed to conduct final examinations at the hospital for the Joint Board of the Royal College of Physicians and Surgeons in London. The 37 students who were due to take the examination on 26 September travelled to Britain at their own cost and in opposition to the Government. The dispute was still unresolved as the year ended, and student unrest persisted. The Government's reply was to formulate, and to try and secure the agreement of teachers at the Royal University to, a system of 'student–worker education'.

Mr Mintoff continued to urge on neighbouring states the need for a peaceful and, ultimately, a 'neutral Mediterranean', and on 24 to 27 August he visited Madrid to try and enlist the help of the newly-installed Spanish Government. On a wider front, two minor protocols were signed on 4 March, confirming the existing financial and trading arrangements with the EEC. The Government also entered into further negotiations with Brussels in June: no formal agreement was reached on full economic cooperation but the present, preferential articles of association were extended until 31 December 1980.

GIBRALTAR

Still the saga of blockade, talks, meetings, press statements and refutations continued. On 5-7 September, Dr Owen visited Madrid, the first Foreign and Commonwealth Secretary to do so since Sir Alec Douglas-Home in May 1961. Discussions ranged over Spain's application to join the EEC and the new Spanish Government's attitude towards Gibraltar. Dr Owen, at a press conference, said that, although he had asked the Spanish Government to lift the 1969 blockade of goods, labour and communications, EEC membership and Gibraltar were not to be set against each other. There was, he thought, a new 'degree of sensitivity and understanding' in Madrid, but still no immediate prospect of direct negotiations. Later that month, Mr Frank Judd, Minister of State, flew to Gibraltar to talk with Sir Joshua Hassan and the opposition leaders, and with Mr Peter Triay's small splinter 'party for the autonomy of Gibraltar' which had been formed on 7 September.

The theme of regional autonomy was very much in the Spanish air, and when Sr Suarez went to London in October he talked of the probability of 'a negotiated statute respecting the identity, culture and special characteristics of the Gibraltar people' which might eventually 'bring about the reintegration of Gibraltar into Spanish territory in accordance with UN resolutions'. But that was for the future and for a total settlement. In the meantime, the blockade must continue, and the new Government would stand by its programme of 12 July which included the aim of 'restoring Spain's territorial integrity'. Democracy meant autonomy for Catalonia and other regions but it also included an autonomous Gibraltar. On 3 November Sir Joshua Hassan and Mr Maurice Xiberras, a leader of the former Integration with Britain Party, flew to London with the Governor, Marshal of the RAF Sir John Grundy, for still more talks.

On the Rock itself, civil unrest over pay policy continued. On 14 September the board of inquiry presided over by Professor George Bain of the University of Warwick produced its recommendations for settling the dispute among some 300 civil servants. There should be a lump-sum payment and the backdating of agreed salary increases. On 21 December, however, Dr John Gilbert, Minister of State for Defence, had to visit Gibraltar when the Civil and Public Servants Association, still in dispute, threatened to cut communications with London.

On 25 November, on a visit to Paris, King Hassan of Morocco announced that 'when Spain recovers Gibraltar we shall retrieve Ceuta and Melilla', the two Spanish cities on the north coast of Africa. The Spanish Government, however, refused to allow such parallels to be drawn. There were rumours of a possible ground of agreement, under EEC or Nato auspices, in terms of Spanish or Anglo-Spanish sovereignty over the Rock and a continuing British or British/Nato defence base, but by the end of the year there was still no recorded change of position.

GREECE

Undoubtedly the most important event in Greece in 1977 was the holding of national elections on 20 November. According to the provisions of the 1975 Constitution these need not have been held before November 1978, four years after the previous elections. After some months of speculation the Prime Minister, Constantine Karamanlis, announced on 20 September that elections would be held one year early on the grounds that during the coming year crucial decisions would have to be made over Cyprus, over Greco-Turkish relations in general and over Greece's application for accelerated membership of the EEC, and that such decisions could be made only by a Government armed with a fresh mandate. All the opposition parties, with the exception of Andreas Papandreou's Panhellenic Socialist Movement (PASOK), opposed the early holding of elections but nonetheless a vigorous and, by common consent, fairly conducted election campaign was soon under way.

On the far right a new political party entered the Greek political spectrum. This was the Ethniki Parataxis (National Rally), founded by Stephanos Stephanopoulos, the Prime Minister of the 'apostate' Centre Union Government of 1965-66. The National Rally aimed to attract the support of royalists, unhappy about the abolition of the monarchy in 1974, and, by holding out the hope of an amnesty for the country's gaoled ex-dictators, that of erstwhile supporters of the Colonels' junta. The National Rally also favoured Greece's immediate return to Nato.

The moderate right was represented by Karamanlis's own New Democracy Party, which had won a landslide victory in the November 1974 elections. A new party on the centre right was Constantine Mitsotakis's New Liberals, who claimed to inherit the mantle of the Venizelist Liberals. Moderate socialism was represented by George Mavros's Union of the Democratic Centre (EDIK), the outcome of the fusion of the Centre Union and the New Forces group. A more flamboyant brand of populist socialism was represented by PASOK, while the far left was represented by numerous groups the most important of which were the Moscow-oriented Greek Communist Party (KKE) and the Alliance of Progressive and Left-Wing Forces. The Alliance consisted of five small groups; the Communist Party of the Interior (Eurocommunists), the United Democratic Left (EDA), Socialist Initiative, Socialist Progress and Christian Democracy.

That Mr Karamanlis would retain a commanding majority in the new parliament was never much in doubt, given the system of reinforced, proportional representation in operation, although this had been somewhat modified to favour smaller parties by increasing the number of seats allocated in the first distribution. The ruling New Democracy Party duly retained control of 172 seats in the 300-seat parliament, securing a 41·85 per cent of the vote in contrast to the 54 per cent gained in 1974. The result that surprised most observers was the substantial gains made by Papandreou's PASOK, which almost doubled its share of the vote from 13·6 to 25·33 per cent and its seats from 12 to 93. By contrast the share obtained by Mavros's social democratic Union of the Democratic Centre slumped from 20·5 per cent (60 seats) to 11·95 per cent (15 seats). Mavros resigned the leadership of the party, which was entrusted to a three-man committee, chaired by Ioannis Zigdis, pending the election of a new leader at the forthcoming party congress. With a 9·36 per cent share of the vote the orthodox Communists gained 11 seats. The National Rally, with 6·82 per cent, gained five seats, the Alliance of Progressive and Left Wing Forces with 2·72 per cent gained two seats. Mitsotakis's New Liberals gained 1·08 per cent of the vote and two seats.

The combined right-wing vote (National Rally, New Democracy and the New Liberals) at 50 per cent registered only a small decline since 1974, while the combined left-wing vote (PASOK, Communist Party, Alliance of Progressive and Left Wing Forces) at 37 per cent was by far the highest in Greek electoral history. It was clear that most of PASOK's increased share of the vote was gained at the expense of the Union of the Democratic Centre. The upswing in the PASOK vote was interpreted more as representing a protest vote by those Greeks who felt let down by their traditional allies in the United States and in Europe than as necessarily signifying any great upsurge in support for Mr Papandreou's brand of radical populist socialism. It also reflected the superior electoral organization of PASOK. Moreover, as memories of the dictatorship faded, the appeal of Karamanlis as the one man who stood between democracy and a return of the tanks was somewhat diminished.

But one thing was clear, namely, that the post-war consensus between Government and 'official' opposition on many aspects of the country's foreign and domestic policies had ended. For Papandreou advocated a total Greek withdrawal from Nato and urged a policy of 'anti-imperialist' non-alignment, linked with a hard line towards Turkey over Cyprus and Greek rights in the Aegean. Papandreou also rejected Karamanlis's total commitment (shared by the Union of the Democratic Centre) to full Greek membership of the EEC, arguing instead for an association agreement on the Norwegian model. To a degree Karamanlis's electoral strategy back-fired, for he was no longer able to argue that an overwhelming majority of the electorate favoured Greek entry into the EEC. In the new Government Panayiotis Papaligouras moved from Coordination to Foreign Affairs, with George Rallis moving from Education to Coordination. Some observers detected a tilt to the right in the composition of the new Government.

In foreign affairs little progress was made in resolving Greece's various bilateral disagreements with Turkey in matters such as air traffic control and the delimitation of the two countries' respective continental shelves in the Aegean. Nor was any progress registered towards a settlement of the Cyprus dispute, despite the high hopes which many Greeks had placed in the election of Jimmy Carter as President of the USA. In July an agreement was initialled between the Greek and United States Governments defining, more restrictively than had been the case before 1974, US rights to use facilities at four military installations in Greece, but by year's end this had not been ratified. Negotiations for Greece's accelerated accession to the EEC continued throughout the year. In February the President of the Commission, Mr Roy Jenkins, stated in the European Parliament that the Greek issue was regarded as settled and that the Commission was fully committed to negotiations leading to Greek membership. Progress in the detailed negotiations, however, was hampered by French and Italian fears of the effect of Greek agricultural exports on their own Mediterranean produce.

During the summer the tourist boom showed signs of slowing down, through customer resistance to increased hotel charges. Early in November parts of Athens were affected by severe flooding. First estimates of the damage were assessed at over 600 million drachmas. The rate of inflation in Greece during 1977 was 13 per cent, while daily wage rates increased by 27 per cent for women and 16 per cent for men. Per-capita income reached the level of $2,500 per annum. The experimental three-month introduction in February of a continuous working day, from 9.00 a.m. to 5.30 p.m., instead of separate morning and early evening periods, inter-spersed by a lengthy siesta, provoked protest strikes by shopkeepers.

CYPRUS

The death of Archbishop Makarios on 3 August (see OBITUARY) shook the country, coming as it did during a crucial period in relations between the Greek and Turkish Cypriot communities. Cyprus had known no other leader since the Republic was founded in 1960 and his unexpected death left a vacuum in Greek-Cypriot politics. In accordance with the Constitution the Leader (Speaker) of the House of Representatives, Mr Spyros Kyprianou, became Acting President. On 13 August all the main Greek-Cypriot political parties, in the interest of national unity, agreed that Mr Kyprianou be acclaimed President to serve the remainder of President Makarios's term of office, which would have expired in February 1978. When the Archbishop died the leader of the Turkish-Cypriot community, Mr Rauf Denktash, warned that his successor would be regarded as leader of the Greek-Cypriot community only and not head of the Republic.

Intercommunal relations started the year on a note of hope following an historic meeting between Archbishop Makarios and Mr Denktash on 27 January, their first meeting in 14 years. They met again on neutral ground in Nicosia on 12 February, in the presence of UN Secretary-General Kurt Waldheim. The four-hour meeting was described by Archbishop Makarios as the first positive step towards a Cyprus settlement. The two leaders agreed to resume intercommunal talks and to seek an 'independent, non-aligned, bi-communal federal republic'.

But the new spirit spoken of by Dr Waldheim soured during successive meetings of the negotiators and no real progress was made. At a meeting in Vienna on 31 March, again in the presence of Dr Waldheim, the talks bogged down on the second day after the two sides had tabled widely divergent proposals. The Turkish side was accused of seeking a 'loose confederation', not a federation. The Greek side presented a map which provided for the Turkish community to occupy less than 20 per cent of the island, compared with the 40 per cent they actually controlled. Mr Denktash dismissed it as 'unrealistic and unreasonable'. Greek proposals for a bicommunal federal state were rejected by Turkish-Cypriot negotiator Mr Umit Suleiman Onan because the regional powers envisaged were 'so limited they do not exist'. Dr Waldheim handed over to his Special Representative for Cyprus, Mr Perez de Cuellar (whose term of office eventually ended on 1 December), but after a further week of talks there was complete deadlock. The negotiators left Vienna—their only agreement being to resume talks in Nicosia. They met there three times in May and June but made no further progress. The Turkish side maintained its stand for 'federation by evolution' and insisted that the two communities should develop separate economies.

On 8 June the UN Security Council, on the recommendation of Dr

Waldheim, granted a further six-month extension of the mandate for UN forces in Cyprus. This was again renewed on 15 December.

Turkey's caretaker Premier at the time, Mr Bulent Ecevit, announced on 20 July that the Turks were preparing to reopen the modern part of Famagusta, known as Varosha. This was once the island's main tourist resort but had been closed off since falling into Turkish hands during the 1974 invasion. Mr Ecevit made it clear that he wished to dispel the impression that because the area had been kept closed it was intended to return it to the Greek-Cypriots as a concession in any settlement. Archbishop Makarios said that materialization of such a plan would remove all hope of an early settlement. He accused Turkey of ruthlessly going ahead with plans to partition the island. Dr Waldheim also expressed concern. In reply, Mr Denktash said the question of Varosha was solely a Turkish affair since it was within the Turkish Federated State of Cyprus.

On 24 August Cyprus called for an urgent session of the UN Security Council, prompted by fears over Famagusta and in the light of Turkey's continued non-compliance with previous UN resolutions. Foreign Minister John Christophides told the Security Council that colonization of Varosha would be the *coup de grace* for the intercommunal talks. The Turkish-Cypriot envoy, Mr Vedat Celik, replied that the Turkish-Cypriots were still in favour of talks and denied there had been any resettlement of Varosha; although one hotel had been reopened as a catering institute it did not warrant an emergency meeting of the Security Council. After two weeks of behind-the-scene consultations a resolution was passed expressing concern at recent developments and calling on the parties to resume negotiations and refrain from unilateral actions.

At the UN General Assembly, in November, after a three-day debate on Cyprus, a resolution recommended the Security Council to adopt 'all practical means' to promote implementation of previous resolutions. This was welcomed by the Greek side but Mr Denktash said it would make resumption of the intercommunal talks even more difficult. Resolutions which were contrary to realities could not, he said, be binding on the Turkish-Cypriots. On 3 December Dr Waldheim said he would not try to reconvene the stalemated intercommunal talks until he had assurances from both sides that they were prepared to negotiate 'concretely and substantially' on all major aspects of the problem.

The former Bishop Khrysostomos of Paphos became Archbishop for life in succession to Archbishop Makarios on 12 September after a protracted election by clergy and laymen.

The economy took a tremendous leap forward during the year. The Minister of Commerce and Industry, Mr Andreas Pierides, told the annual meeting of the Chamber of Commerce and Industry on 14 December that the economy was firmly on the road of rapid growth. Domestic production continued to grow at a relatively high rate and was expected to reach

C£270 million by the end of the year, an increase of more than 10 per cent at constant prices compared with 1976, but about 13 per cent lower than the figure for 1973, the year before the invasion. Exports for the first nine months of the year were, at C£105·4 million, 40 per cent up on the same period of the previous year. Imports increased by 55 per cent to C£185·5 million, the trade gap widening to C£80·1 million from C£44·4 million.

The Government's second emergency economic action plan, announced on 7 October, envisaged government development expenditure for the ensuing year of C£60·3 million, compared with C£46·6 million in the previous plan. The emphasis was shifted from labour-intensive to capital-intensive projects. The target rate of growth was set at 8·5 per cent.

After many calls for an investigation into missing persons the matter was taken up in the Third Committee of the UN Assembly on 11 December and the Greek and Turkish sides agreed to set up a joint investigative committee, to include a representative of the International Red Cross. The Greek-Cypriots claimed there were more than 2,000 missing persons. The investigation would also include Turkish-Cypriots missing since the outbreak of intercommunal hostilities in 1963. Agreement was reached in principle but there were still differences to be settled over modalities.

Calls for a renewed purge against supporters of the 1974 coup continued to be made, particularly by the left-wing parties. The alleged successor of General Grivas as leader of Eoka B, Lefteris Papadoloulos, was convicted of seditious conspiracy and preparing warlike operations against the Government and gaoled for life. Ioannis Ktimatis and Neoptolemos Leftis were gaoled for seven and five years respectively on 21 June for taking part in riots outside the US embassy in August 1974 but were acquitted of killing the ambassador, Mr Rodger Davies.

On 15 December President Kyprianou's 21-year-old son, Achilleas, was kidnapped by Eoka B activists seeking amnesty for Eoka B men and coupists. He was freed four days later after the Government had promised immunity from arrest for the kidnappers, but had made no other concessions. The incident adversely affected the right-wing Democratic Rally Party, whose leader, Mr Glafcos Clerides, withdrew his candidature in the Presidential election to be held in February 1978.

TURKEY

Turkey had a difficult year. The trade gap widened; inflation and unemployment increased; so also did the number of political assassinations. The Prime Minister, Mr Süleyman Demirel, leader of the Justice Party (JP), advanced to 5 June the general elections which were due in October. The decision was supported by the opposition Republican People's Party

F*

(RPP), but ran against the wishes of Mr Demirel's main coalition partner, the religious National Salvation Party (NSP).

Both main parties appealed for a clear-cut majority. The JP campaigned against both the RPP and the NSP, while the RPP concentrated on the issue of law and order, blaming one of Mr Demirel's coalition partners, the extreme right-wing Nationalist Action Party (NAP) of Colonel (retired) Alpaslan Türkeş, for the wave of political killings. There was shooting at several of the provincial rallies addressed by the RPP leader, Mr Bülent Ecevit, but the worst violence occurred at a national rally organized on 1 May in Istanbul by the Confederation of Revolutionary Trade Unions (DISK). The rally was fired on by extremists, described as Maoist, and in the panic which followed more than 30 people were killed.

The two main parties strengthened their position in the elections, but neither won a clear majority. The left-of-centre RPP led with 41 per cent of the poll, winning 213 seats in the 450-member Assembly (against 185 in 1973). Among right-wing parties there was a significant shift. The JP increased its representation from 149 to 189 seats (with 37 per cent of the poll), and the NAP from 3 to 16 (with 6 per cent), while the NSP dropped from 48 to 24 (with 9 per cent), the liberal Republican Reliance Party (RRP) from 13 to 3, and the Democratic Party (DP), a breakaway from the JP, from 45 to 1. In the elections held simultaneously for one-third of the elected seats in the Senate, the RPP won 28 seats (and the absolute majority in the new chamber), the JP 21 and the NSP one seat.

Although he failed to secure the support of any other party, Mr Ecevit accepted the mandate given to him by the President of the Republic Mr Fahri Korutürk, and formed a minority RPP Administration on 21 June. His Government was, however, short-lived. On 3 July it was defeated in the Assembly and resigned.

Mr Demirel thereupon reformed his Nationalist Front coalition, but without the RRP. The coalition assumed office on 21 July and was endorsed by the Assembly on 1 August by 229 votes to 219. But the 16 JP Ministers, the eight Ministers from the NSP and the five from the NAP found it hard to agree on the policy to follow in the economic crisis, and even on administrative appointments. True, on 8 September a package of austerity measures was introduced, but, at the insistence of the NSP, the devaluation of the Turkish lira was limited to 10 per cent, while inflation was estimated at 30 per cent.

The foreign payments position continued to worsen. By the end of September, imports had increased by 19 per cent over the previous year to $4,400 million, while exports had dropped over 20 per cent to $1,200 million. By the end of the year, Turkey's short-term debts to foreign suppliers were put at some $2,000 million, and the country lived from hand to mouth, with sporadic shortages of essential imports, including petrol. The NSP still insisted on large-scale industrial investment, and on

17 November the Government fixed the growth target for the fourth five-year plan at an unrealistic 8·5 per cent per annum. In the circumstances no agreement could be reached with the IMF mission which the Government had invited to Turkey.

Political violence increased. More than 200 people were killed between the formation of the second Nationalist Front coalition and the end of the year. University education, which had been almost totally disrupted in the 1976-77 academic year, fared no better when the new term started in November. Once again the opposition put the main blame on the NAP, whose leader, Colonel Türkeş was again Deputy Prime Minister, although NAP offices throughout the country were themselves the targets of a spate of bombings by leftist extremists.

The Assembly could not elect a Speaker and was, as a result, paralyzed until 17 November, when Mr Cahit Karakaş of the RPP was elected by the narrow majority of 227 votes, with the help of NAP Deputies. Thereafter important decisions were delayed until after the local government elections on 11 December.

These showed little underlying change in political preferences. In elections to provincial councils, based on the national electoral register, the RPP increased its share of the poll marginally to 42 per cent, while the JP held 37 per cent. However, because of its urban bias, the RPP won the mayoralties of almost all important cities. Much attention was given to the success of the NAP in electing several mayors in Central Anatolian towns, but the party's overall share of the poll was little changed at 6·7 per cent. The NSP dropped further to 6·8 per cent.

The political stalemate was finally broken by a revolt within the Justice Party. Unhappy at the disproportionate power wielded within the coalition by the NSP and the NAP, and the Government's consequent difficulty in reaching decisions, 12 Deputies resigned from the JP, thus depriving the Nationalist Front of its parliamentary majority. The majority of the JP decided, however, to stay in power until voted out by the Assembly. This finally occurred on 31 December, when a vote of no-confidence tabled by the RPP was carried by 228 votes to 218. The 12 former members of the JP, two members of the RRP and the sole remaining Deputy of the Democratic Party voted against the JP, as a result of a previous decision to cooperate in a successor Administration under Mr Ecevit. Mr Demirel resigned as soon as the result of the vote was announced, and President Korutürk called on Mr Ecevit to form the new Government.

Harassed by the opposition and internally divided, the two Nationalist Front Governments could achieve little in foreign affairs. Their main effort was directed at securing Western and particularly US aid. However, the US-Turkish defence cooperation agreement, providing for the disbursement of $1,000 million in US military aid, remained blocked in Congress in the absence of any Turkish concessions over Cyprus. As a stop-gap measure US military credits were increased to $175 million. Meetings between Turkish and Greek Foreign Ministers in Brussels and New York did not lead to any progress. But the agreement to refrain from action likely to increase tension held, and Turkey did not resume prospecting for oil in disputed Aegean waters. In September both Turkey and Greece took part in Nato exercises, joining forces for the first time since 1974.

Mr Demirel found it hard to pursue a coherent policy in the Arab world. When, at the beginning of December, he sent his Foreign Minister Mr Caglayangil to Egypt, he was denounced not only by his partners in the NSP and NAP, but even by his JP Minister of Energy, Mr Kamuran Inan, whose main concern was to maintain oil supplies from Iraq. An oil pipeline from Kirkuk to Yumurtalik, near Iskenderun in Turkey, was inaugurated in January, but the flow of oil was delayed by payment difficulties, and, on one occasion, interrupted by sabotage.

V THE MIDDLE EAST AND NORTH AFRICA

Chapter 1

ISRAEL

FOR Israel, the outstanding event of 1977 was the start of peace negotiations with Egypt—the first such direct talks with any Arab neighbour since the State of Israel came into existence in 1948. (See also pp. 179-80.)

That sensational development was triggered by the invitation sent on 15 November by the Israeli Prime Minister, Menachem Begin to President Sadat of Egypt to come to Jerusalem, after the latter had indicated his readiness to meet Israel's leader face to face. Sadat at once accepted and arrived in Jerusalem on 19 November. The next day he spoke in the Knesset (Israel's Parliament), renouncing belligerency and calling for a peace settlement which would include Israeli withdrawal from Arab territories occupied in 1967 and the creation of a Palestinian Arab state there. Sadat was given a warm welcome in Jerusalem and Begin offered him the hand of friendship, while reminding him of Israel's need for security within an overall Middle East settlement.

The first early development from the Sadat visit was the holding of Israeli-Egyptian talks at official level in Cairo in mid-December, which established standing joint political and military committees to examine all aspects of a future peace settlement. The second development was the return visit of Begin to Ismailia, on the Suez Canal, on 25 December. At this meeting the basis of an agreement was found for Israeli withdrawal from the Sinai peninsula, to be undertaken in stages. Differences remained over the Palestinian Arab question. Begin was prepared to see an 'autonomous' Palestinian entity established, subject to a continuing Israeli military presence over a period of up to 20 years. Sadat wanted a fully-fledged Palestinian Arab state on the West Bank and in the Gaza Strip.

Apart from the tremendous psychological breakthrough of the Sadat visit, there were other consequences. President Sadat declared that he was ready to negotiate with Israel on his own, if other Arab states continued to hang back. Begin stated that he would not refuse a separate peace treaty with Egypt. Israeli journalists were allowed into both Cairo and Ismailia, for the first time in Israel's existence. Telephonic communication was re-established between Egypt and the Israeli-occupied West Bank. Begin followed up the Jerusalem meeting with visits to Washington and London, where he received assurances of diplomatic help in the peace-making process.

These developments received a rapturous welcome from the people of Israel, and a more guarded one from the political parties. After the first burst of enthusiasm it became understood that Israel stood only on the threshold of peace negotiations, and that the road to peace would be long and difficult. There were some expressions of concern in Begin's own Likud Party that he would be forced to make dangerous concessions. Overwhelming support for a peace policy was, however, pledged in the Knesset.

The Egyptian-Israeli diplomatic breakthrough came as a complete surprise, both to Israel and in the outside world. The Foreign Minister, Moshe Dayan, had indeed made a cryptic statement on 12 August that peace negotiations had, in effect, already begun. And from 25 to 30 August Begin was in Romania, where there were rumours that President Ceauşescu had offered to mediate in the Middle East dispute. But diplomatic interest had been concentrated on the possible reconvening of the Geneva peace conference, which had met only briefly after the 1973 war. It had been with Geneva in view that in January Israel's Labour Party offered a withdrawal from the West Bank in return for full peace.

One obstacle to peace negotiations was the refusal of the Palestine Liberation Organization (PLO), reaffirmed on several occasions during the year, to modify its National Covenant, which called for the destruction of the state of Israel. The PLO took part in the Tripoli conference called in December by the 'rejectionist' Arab states—Libya, Syria, Algeria and the South Yemen—which totally rejected the Sadat–Begin peace initiative. The Israeli reaction to the PLO line was to refuse PLO participation in a reconvened Geneva conference or, indeed, in any future peace talks. Begin repeated his Government's unalterable opposition to meeting with the PLO after his meetings with Sadat. Israel was worried even by US President Carter's statement in March that 'the Palestinians' were entitled to a homeland.

On 19 May the US and the Soviet Union agreed to press for a resumption of the Geneva conference. On 27 June Carter warned Israel against refusing to make any territorial concessions on the West Bank and Gaza, and on 29 June Begin, newly elected as Israel's Prime Minister, said that his country was ready to negotiate in Geneva, without prior conditions of any kind. Carter's response was to declare on 6 July that a Middle East peace must be full and comprehensive, not another patched-up armistice. On 1 August the US State Department agreed that since the PLO refused Israel's right to exist and rejected UN Resolutions 242 and 338 (laying down principles for peace talks, and urging direct inter-state negotiations) it was not a suitable participant at Geneva. At the year's end the situation was that the Geneva conference could be reconvened at any time in 1978, but that the bilateral talks between Egypt and Israel were due to continue, while there were hopes that other bilateral talks with Israel's neighbours, notably Jordan, might shortly begin. A US-Israeli working paper for procedures at Geneva was agreed on 4 October.

Israel's critics maintained that a further obstacle to peace was Israel's policy in the occupied territories. During 1977 some rioting occurred on the West Bank, and there were bomb explosions both there and in East Jerusalem. In July the Begin Government 'legalized' three Jewish settlements on the West Bank which had been declared unofficial by the previous Labour Government, and authorized the establishment of five new Jewish settlements. On 14 and 15 August Israel announced measures to 'equalize' living standards in occupied territories with those in Israel 'proper', by increasing health and other social benefits. But whatever good effect this announcement might have had was nullified by a statement on 2 September by the Minister of Agriculture, Arik Sharon, that there was a long-term plan to settle up to two million Jews in occupied territories by the year 2000. In his talks with Sadat, Begin insisted on the 'right' of Jews to settle in the occupied territories, but conceded that Arabs should also be free to settle in Israel. This was taken to be an oblique proposal for at least some Palestinian Arab refugees to return to parts of Israel proper.

The moves towards peace at the end of 1977 were all the more remarkable in view of the change of Government which took place as a result of the elections of 15 May. Until then Israel had been ruled for 29 years by Labour-led Governments. Early in 1977 the Government led by Itzhak Rabin ran into increasing difficulties. It already lacked a clear working majority in the Knesset; outside Parliament it began to lose support to the newly-formed Democratic Movement for Change (DMC) led by the archaeologist Yigal Yadin. A number of financial scandals resulted in the suicide of the Minister of Housing, Avraham Ofer, and a five-year prison sentence on the designated Governor of the Bank of Israel, Asher Yadlin. There were a growing number of crippling strikes, and the poor economic situation forced the Government to order virtually monthly devaluation of the currency by 2 per cent. On 23 February Rabin only narrowly defeated Shimon Peres in the leadership contest at the Labour Party convention.

On 15 March came a bombshell for the Government. The Prime Minister's wife, Leah Rabin, made an apology on television for having contravened currency regulations by holding a dollar account in the US; on 17 April a court fined her I£250,000 (about £15,000). In the meantime, Rabin had admitted knowledge of the bank account and had resigned on 8 April. He was succeeded as Labour Party leader by his rival, Shimon Peres, who also became Prime Minister with a caretaker Cabinet. A great deal of sympathy for Rabin was expressed in the country; most people felt that he had been guilty only of a technical misdemeanour. Even so, Labour was expected to lose some support in the 15 May elections, although it was regarded as sure to remain the strongest party.

The election results were a shock. Out of the 120 seats in the Knesset, Begin's Likud Party won 43 and the Labour Party only 32, beaten into second place for the first time in Israel's history. Labour lost votes to Likud, but even more to DMC, which secured 15 seats at its first attempt.

The National Religious Party (NRP) gained 12 seats, the remaining 18 seats being divided among splinter groups.

Begin had been confirmed as leader of his party by a 90 per cent vote on 23 March. When asked to form the new Israeli Government by President Katzir he proposed an alliance of all the major parties. Labour, however, refused to join him, while Yadin, whom he offered the post of Deputy Prime Minister, reluctantly declined after lengthy negotiations. The NRP agreed to join the Government, and a surprise recruit was Moshe Dayan as Foreign Minister; his whole political life had been spent with one or other group within the Labour 'Alignment'. On 20 June the Knesset approved the new Government by 63 votes to 53 and heard a low-key policy statement. A minor consolation for Labour was the result, on 21 June, of the Histadrut (trade union) elections: Labour retained control, with 56 per cent of the vote.

Begin was widely regarded as a 'hawk' and his success was not welcomed in the outside world, where the UN Secretary-General, Kurt Waldheim, described it as a blow to the cause of peace. The EEC leaders reacted by calling on 29 June for a 'national home' for the Palestinian Arabs. But Begin showed immediately that he had leadership qualities. In July he introduced new austerity measures, bringing a 25 per cent increase in the cost of basic foodstuffs, increased bus and train fares and cuts in the defence budget. Because he acted without hesitation, there was little grumbling. His ten-day visit to the US in mid-July was strikingly successful, and there was general approval of his instant response to rocket attacks on settlements in northern Israel: PLO bases in Lebanon were immediately bombed from the air. In spite of health worries—he was in hospital with heart trouble in October and again in December—Begin was proving himself a leader, and on 19 October his Government was strengthened by the acquisition of DMC support. Yadin became Deputy Prime Minister and the DMC was given three other Cabinet posts. With a comfortable parliamentary majority, Begin floated the Israeli £ on 28 October, abolished export incentives and the foreign travel tax, eased currency restrictions and increased VAT from 8 to 12 per cent. These measures brought a 40 per cent devaluation of the Israeli £, but also the promise of a major export drive in 1978. At the end of the year Mr Begin's Government was far more secure than had been believed possible, and public opinion polls showed firm support for him in the country.

South-east India was devastated by floods in the wake of a cyclone in November 1977: survivors gaze from their village's sole remaining, stone-built dwelling at the ruins of palm-thatched houses.

In the gilt state coach escorted by the Household Cavalry, HM Queen Elizabeth II and her Consort Prince Philip leave Buckingham Palace for St Paul's to give thanks for 25 years of her reign on 7 June 1977.

After the Jubilee service of thanksgiving at St Paul's on 7 June, the Queen walked to Guildhall and talked with many people in the crowd who cheered her ecstatically.

As Wimbledon celebrated its centenary in the Queen's Jubilee year, it was fitting that the women's singles title should have been won by the British player Virginia Wade, seen here with the trophy.

Chapter 2

THE ARAB WORLD—EGYPT—JORDAN—SYRIA—
LEBANON—IRAQ

THE ARAB WORLD

By December 1976 the Lebanese cease-fire had reconciled and restrained the front-line Arabs, giving hope for a Middle East settlement. A year later divisions were deeper than ever and Syria was leading the rejectionist pack against Egypt. Even before President Sadat's Jerusalem visit in December Egypt and Syria, the natural leaders, had been drifting apart. This breach overshadowed the customary feuds between Syria and Iraq, Libya and Egypt, Algeria and Morocco.

This was the more regrettable for the Arabs because under its new Administration the USA seemed readier to help them than ever before. Secretary of State Vance visited the Middle East three times and the President met the heads of state of Egypt, Syria, Jordan and Saudi Arabia. The US now advocated Israeli withdrawal to 1967 borders, a homeland for the Palestinians and their representation at the peace conference.

The obstacles came partly from Israel. Its policy in south Lebanon had embittered Syria, which henceforward was less and less ready to moderate the PLO or cooperate with the US. The change of Israeli Government in May did not help. Meanwhile the Palestinians themselves competed in intransigent bravura. Their nominal leader, Yassir Arafat, often displayed readiness to compromise but allowed himself to be regularly contradicted and disowned.

In January, interviewed by *Al Ahram*, he said that the PLO was ready to attend a peace conference and accept a Palestinian state on the West Bank—a big advance on the PLO's theoretical aim of a bi-national Palestine and the end of Israel. In March the Palestine National Council (the PLO's parliament) met in Cairo but failed formally to drop this doctrine (which the head of its Political Department restated on 17 March) or to accept UN Resolution 242 which recognized Israel. Though not ideal for the Palestinians, whom it failed to mention, Resolution 242 had nevertheless been accepted by all the front-line states. Also on 17 March President Carter advocated a Palestinian homeland, which became, to Israeli chagrin, a theme of US policy.

On 27 May Mr Begin's Likud Party won the Israel elections (see p. 175): he immediately claimed the West Bank for Israel and began to support and multiply the Jewish settlements there.

In June and July the PLO was much occupied by the search for an agreement with Lebanon and Syria about its own future in Lebanon. This was reached on 25 July and there seemed to be hope that the PLO would now find some way of accepting UN Resolution 242. On 28 July President Carter said that the Palestinians must be represented at Geneva, but they must also recognize Israel's right to exist, and this theme was repeated, despite an automatic negative reflex by the PLO, by Secretary Vance on 7 August and in a State Department communique on 12 September. But on 8 August Begin declared that Israel could never negotiate with the PLO even if they did accept Israel. His policy of settlements on Arab soil came under increasing criticism at the UN and from the US: they were, said the State Department on 18 August, illegal, a word which the President repeated on 23 August.

The US had also abandoned the attempt to exclude the Soviet Union from discussions. In May Mr Vance had agreed with Mr Gromyko at Geneva on the need to resume the Geneva peace conference and on 1 October a joint US-Soviet statement recognized as 'key issues' the 'withdrawal of Israeli forces from territories occupied in the 1967 conflict' and 'resolution of the Palestine question by ensuring the legitimate rights of the Palestinian people' and advocated resumption of the Geneva conference by 1 December.

This offended Israel. A frenzied US-Israeli negotiation followed and produced a document about procedures and terms of reference, but not objectives, for Geneva: Israel conceded Palestinian, but not PLO, representation, but gained by reinstating a reference to Resolutions 242 and 338. To the Arabs this document seemed a step backwards from the US-Soviet agreement. The PLO denounced it and Arab leaders hurried to and fro in inconclusive debate.

All this, by further deferring the Geneva conference, let alone peace itself, distressed President Sadat, who ever since his internal troubles in January had been desperate for a settlement. He had already, with minimal consultation, launched two initiatives designed to hurry things on: in January, when he proposed linking the putative Palestinian state to Jordan, an idea pleasing to Israel, and in August, when he suggested a meeting of Arab and Israeli Foreign Ministers to prepare for Geneva. But now, on 9 November, he suddenly offered to visit Jerusalem. The fortunes of this initiative are related separately.

In oil matters the divisions at OPEC's December 1976 meeting produced differential increases in Middle East oil prices in January 1977, when Saudi Arabia and the UAE raised theirs by only 5 per cent against the others' 10 per cent. After much diplomacy the gap was closed in July, when the two odd men out raised prices by another 5 per cent and the rest kept theirs steady. Later the world glut and an Iranian *volte-face* strengthened the more cautious group, despite the arguments furnished to their opponents by the decline in the dollar and thus in real prices paid. At OPEC's December meeting in Caracas, Venezuela, supported by Iraq, Libya and Algeria, failed to secure agreement on a rise, to which Saudi

Arabia as ever and now Iran were opposed, and prices consequently seemed likely to remain unaltered until the next meeting.

On 4 September Djibouti, on attaining independence, was admitted to the Arab League as its twenty-second member.

SADAT'S PEACE INITIATIVE

How did the initiative start? Sadat denied having sounded Israel first, but reports connected it with his recent visit to Romania, friendly with Arabs and Israelis alike. The Israeli invitation came through the US Government, whom Sadat had apparently not consulted beforehand.

In addressing the Israeli Knesset on 20 November Sadat deplored the failure to reconvene Geneva; rejected a separate peace with Israel or one without the Palestinians (without naming the PLO); insisted on complete Israeli withdrawal to 1967 frontiers; mentioned the recent US recognition of legitimate Palestinian rights, meaning, he said, self-determination and statehood; and wanted all Middle Eastern states to enjoy peace within boundaries safeguarded by international guarantees. Mr Begin's reply was effusive but non-committal.

However orthodox Sadat's proposals, he had infuriated President Asad and the PLO. They had not been consulted: the visit, which Israel deliberately loaded with ceremonial, implied, they held, recognition of Israel and abandoned the military option. They and the four rejectionist states raged together and met in Tripoli on 2 December to 'hate Sadat'; but no constructive proposals, or even a Syrian-Iraqi reconciliation, emerged. King Hussein praised Sadat's courage and visited him: Sudan backed him loyally: Saudi Arabia, Lebanon and the Gulf states lay low. Sadat now smartly broke relations with Syria and the rejectionist states.

The next step was a meeting of officials in Cairo, to which the US and Soviet Governments, the UN Secretary-General and the front-line Arab states were invited. Neither Syria nor the PLO would attend, nor would Jordan or Lebanon come unless they did. The Russians refused: the US Government hesitated, and postponed the meeting to 14 December (after another visit by Mr Vance). It discussed only procedure for subsequent meetings, but was notable for the friendly popular reception of Israeli journalists in Cairo.

Meanwhile the world awaited Israel's response to Sadat, who had won sympathy. Subordinating Cairo to Washington, Begin flew there to explain, and selectively publicize, his proposals, claiming for them Presidential and Congressional approval. On return he had them approved by his own party caucus. All that was yet publicly known for certain was his proposed 'administrative autonomy' (not independence) for the West Bank.

Begin's next meeting with Sadat, in Ismailia on 25 December, was not a success. No agreed communique accompanied his departure next day:

the two had agreed only to establish two ministerial committees, one political and one military, to meet in January.

On 28 December the proposals were approved by the Knesset and officially published. For the central Palestinian problem Israel proposed an autonomous area, comprising Judaea and Samaria (i.e. the West Bank) plus Gaza, under an autonomous executive (headquarters Bethlehem) elected by all its residents, its powers excluding security and public order, which Israel would retain: freedom of residents to choose Israel or Jordan citizenship: freedom for Israelis to buy land and operate businesses: freedom for those choosing Israel citizenship to buy land in Israel proper: a commission representing Israel, Jordan and the autonomous authority to 'set norms for' (not to control) the immigration of Arab refugees 'in reasonable numbers': Israel to maintain her 'claim and right' to sovereignty, which would, however, remain 'open': freedom of access in Jerusalem for the three religions to their respective shrines (which they already had): and a review of these principles after five years.

No authorized text covered other territorial proposals. Published reports were silent about the future of occupied Syrian territory. Though Israel claimed no sovereignty in Sinai, Begin assured its Jewish settlers that Israel would continue to administer them. Existing military dispositions would last 'a few years', after which Israeli forces would regain the 1967 frontier: freedom of navigation in the Tiran straits would be guaranteed by an irremovable UN force or a joint Egyptian-Israeli one.

Sadat found these proposals disappointing, as indeed they were. The autonomous area, with its Israeli garrison, could hardly be considered even a 'Palestinian homeland' and risked being absorbed into Israel proper, through massive Jewish land purchases followed by Palestinian emigration, which neither the review nor the indeterminate sovereignty clauses would prevent: the Sinai proposals seemed severely to limit Egyptian sovereignty there, even when (date uncertain) Israeli troops withdrew, and there was nothing to tempt Syria into negotiation.

On 28 December President Carter dealt Sadat a heavier blow by welcoming the Begin proposals and opposing an independent Palestinian state: his preferred homeland attached to Jordan was unacceptable, on any reasonable guess, to Palestinians and thus to King Hussein, who wanted no unwilling subjects and whose Government had already condemned the Begin plan. On 31 December it was announced that President Carter, after seeing King Hussein in Teheran, would visit Sadat on 4 January 1978.

Sadat's expression of disappointment at Carter's reward for his support of US policy and the risks this entailed was dignified, but his future seemed bleak. True, he might still choose a separate peace which he said Begin had offered in Jerusalem. This would alienate the Saudi and other Gulf Governments, on whose money Egypt now heavily depended: still, Sadat's enthusiastic reception on his return from Israel seemed to confirm that the Egyptians were eager for peace, and unwilling to be sacrificed again for non-Egyptian causes. The military option had anyhow been effectively closed by the increase in Israel's relative military strength since 1973.

THE ARAB REPUBLIC OF EGYPT

Almost throughout the year, 1977 belied the hopes with which it started. Economic grievances caused serious rioting. The Geneva conference came no nearer resumption, relations with the Soviet Union worsened, those with the USA were politically unproductive, there was a brief war with Libya and growing coolness with Syria. Then suddenly in November President Anwar Sadat abandoned the Arab consensus for bilateral negotiation with Israel. Despite his courage and confidence and the popular welcome for his initiative, the Israeli, and seemingly the US, response was disappointing.

Sadat visited the USA from 3 to 6 April without securing satisfaction on a Middle East settlement or on arms supplies (though Congress eventually allowed the sale of $200 million of transport aircraft), nor did Mr Vance's visits to Egypt in February and August materially alter things. However, US goodwill had one solid advantage—aid estimated at $1,000 million per annum.

To differences with the Soviet Union over arms, debts and Egypt's denunciation of the treaty of friendship were added Soviet support and arms for Libya, Egypt's bitterest enemy. The Foreign Minister vainly visited Moscow from 8 to 11 June. Gromyko, Sadat later reported, said 'It's all over': no arms except for hard currency. Cotton shipments and debt repayments to Russia, and Soviet coke shipments to Egypt, were reduced or interrupted.

Libya was blamed for sabotage in Egypt and made counter-charges. Egypt called Libya a Soviet catspaw and on 28 April *Sawt al Arab* demanded Colonel Qadafi's overthrow. The 250,000 Egyptians working in Libya suffered: by August they were reported to have fallen to 100,000.

Troops were naturally concentrated on the frontier. After border incidents, protest notes and a Libyan reprisal raid, Egypt attacked Libya on 21 July by land and air. Next day Sadat said that having 'taught Qadafi a lesson' Egyptian troops had left. Air attacks were, however, resumed on 23 and 24 July. After mediation by Algeria, Kuwait and the PLO, Sadat ordered a cease-fire on 24 July, but throughout August troops guarded the frontier: Libyans and Russians accused Egypt of planning fresh attacks. Libyan hostility brought together Egypt and Sudan, another Libyan target.

Throughout 1977 Sadat was searching for peace with Israel. He was not helped by the PLO's refusal to accept Israel's right to exist, and

President Carter's advances towards the Arab position were insufficient to get the Geneva conference resumed. Nor did Sadat get much support from his nominal ally Syria for his proposed group of Foreign Ministers to prepare the return to Geneva. Egypt took the lead from Syria at the UN in September by denouncing Jewish colonization of the West Bank. On 21 October the Foreign Minister again defined the Egyptian position: Israel must evacuate all occupied territory and allow the Palestinians an independent state.

On 28 October Sadat left for Iran and Romania to recruit support for reconvening the Geneva conference and perhaps initiated his next surprising step. On 9 November he told the Egyptian National Assembly that 'Israel will be astonished when it hears that I am ready to go to the Knesset'. This offer, which Israel accepted, isolated Sadat from Syria and many other Arab states and caused his Foreign Minister and his hurriedly found replacement to resign. The subsequent events are related elsewhere (see pp. 179-81). On 5 December Egypt broke with Syria, Libya, Algeria, Iraq and South Yemen and on 7 December closed the Soviet, East German, Hungarian, Polish and Czech cultural centres.

At home 1977 started badly. In January an attempt to follow the IMF's anti-inflationary advice by halving food and transport subsidies was followed on 18 and 19 January by widespread riots, with 43 admitted deaths. Government allegations of communist and Soviet inspiration were unconvincing. Many hundreds were arrested and eventually tried. Strikes and political activity, except by authorized parties, were forbidden, after a referendum on 10 February. Press freedom was restricted and the advance towards pluralist democracy halted. In renewed agitation by Islamic fundamentalists, the Muslim Brothers were outflanked by the *Jama'at al takfir wa'l hijra* (roughly 'Society for Atonement and Renewal') which in July kidnapped and murdered a former Minister who had opposed them. Its leader and hundreds of others were arrested: a cell was found in the army. On 28 August the press announced the detection of two even wilder Muslim groups. It was doubtless this fundamentalist revival which prompted the discussion of legislation to restore Shari'a punishments and penalize apostasy from Islam, but Sadat demonstrated his sympathy with the Copts, who felt threatened.

Egypt's finances continued alarming, and short-term obligations could be met only by diverting Gulf money intended for development. In April foreign debts were estimated at $12,000 million and constantly increasing. There were a few less gloomy items: the Suez–Mediterranean pipeline began operating successfully, without prejudicing the Canal itself, which was reported to be carrying twice the 1967 tonnage and earning $450 million per annum. Tourist earnings were increasing, the 1976 total being 80 per cent above that of 1975, and in September deposits of uranium and a big aquifer in the desert were reported to have been discovered.

JORDAN

Jordan remained in 1977 distinct from the other confrontation states. Unlike Egypt and Syria (despite close links with the latter) it was not anxious to recover for itself territory lost in 1967, nor did it suffer, like Lebanon, from a Palestinian military presence. King Hussein's main object appeared to be the unspectacular development of his truncated realm—a process easily ruined by war or subversion—and his policy was to work for a lasting peace without provoking Palestinian or other Arab extremists or allowing his authority to be weakened.

This he could best do, in this resembling President Sadat, by influencing the US towards persuading Israel to offer a settlement which the Arabs could honourably accept. His visit to the US from 25 April to 14 May was thus his centrepiece, supported by regular interviews with Western publicity media. At Atlanta on 20 April he declared himself encouraged by his talk with President Carter, once he had been reassured that the Palestinian homeland, of which the President had spoken on 17 March, was not to be the East Bank of the Jordan as Hussein had feared. But throughout the year he warned against over-optimism: the Arabs were now militarily weaker and less united than in 1973 and so less favourably situated for negotiation. Jordan evidently thought it mistaken, from both these points of view, to cut Soviet links as Sadat had done and several Jordanian-Soviet visits were exchanged.

King Hussein's concern for Arab unity and for Jordan's internal security presumably determined his attitude to the PLO, which alone, according to the Rabat decision of 1974, could speak for the Palestinians. Though Sadat urged some link between Jordan and the putative Palestinian state, Hussein maintained that any such link must depend on Palestinian will and initiative: nor could he yet consider any return of PLO forces to Jordan, whence he had expelled them in 1970. He doubtless judged that any revision of the Rabat principle in Jordan's favour would entail the re-admission of these forces. In March Hussein went to Cairo for the meeting of Arab and African leaders, had a meeting with Yassir Arafat (the first since 1970) and was applauded by the Palestinian delegation. Similar considerations informed his policy towards the West Bank, which was to maintain morale there without encouraging suspicions that he was aiming at re-incorporating it in Jordan. An interesting illustration of this policy was the large financial encouragement offered to developing independent power supplies there to prevent integration in the Israeli grid.

The policy of integration with Syria continued and fields covered by it included civil aviation, power supplies, laws on investment and the dissemination of news.

However, Hussein suffered two severe setbacks from Israel and Egypt.

In May the new Likud Government rejected a peaceful Arab recovery of former Palestine territory; in November Sadat suddenly put Arab unity into question with his visit to Jerusalem. This deeply embarrassed Jordan, whose closest ally, Syria, was enraged by Sadat's unilateral action. Hussein, though applauding Sadat's courage and visiting him, joined neither his conference in Cairo nor the rejectionist meetings in Libya.

At home the King suffered a tragic loss when Queen Alia, his third wife, died in a helicopter crash on 9 February. Later that month the *Washington Post* reported that the CIA had paid Hussein several million dollars since 1957. This disclosure seemed to embarrass him less than one might have expected: he explained that the money, which had been to assist Jordan's counter-espionage, had been paid in his name only as a matter of convenience.

Economically Jordan continued towards the viability which 1967 had seemed to destroy for ever. Whereas the Government criticized the Gulf oil producers for their inadequate aid to the confrontation states, the US Congress agreed in June to provide $93 million and the various Arab development funds, especially Kuwait's, provided large sums, mainly for the phosphate industry. Foreign exchange came also from tourism ($204 million in 1976) and remittances from the 200,000 or so Jordanians abroad (up to $300 million). An important trade and aid agreement was made with the EEC.

But there were shadows. Phosphate exports, though larger in volume, earned 41 per cent less because of a collapse in world prices and Jordanian agricultural decline increased food imports. Thus the visible deficit had risen by 30 per cent from 1975 to 1976 and the overall payments surplus had fallen from nearly $200 million to $10·8 million. Inflation appeared to be running at about 14 per cent. Other causes for concern were the growth of Amman at the expense of the countryside and the brain-drain of qualified Jordanians abroad, which led the Government to raise specialist salaries by from 40 to 100 per cent.

SYRIA

For Syria, 1977 was a difficult year. In Lebanon fighting in the south and mutual intolerance between Lebanese factions prolonged Syria's expensive commitment. As President Sadat of Egypt became desperate for some advance towards peace, he and President Hafez al Asad drifted apart. Asad, suspicious of the Israelis and the US, rebuilt bridges to the PLO and the Soviet Union. Sadat's direct approach to Israel in November enraged Asad and threw him into the arms of the rejectionists.

At first the euphoria of triumph in Lebanon and rapprochement with Egypt continued and Asad's prescription for a Middle East settlement resembled Sadat's. But Israel's attitude to the largely Syrian Arab Deterrent Force (ADF) in Lebanon soon caused difficulty. On 16 January the Israeli chief of staff alleged that Syrian troops in Lebanon threatened Israel and on 26 January Israel protested at their entering Nabatiya. After US intervention troops were withdrawn. With Syria thus forbidden, and Lebanon unable, to pacify the south, the conflict there continued, delaying the restoration of communal harmony elsewhere in Lebanon and preventing a Syrian withdrawal. Israeli intervention also aggravated the conflict and helped to frustrate the enforcement of the vital 1969 Cairo agreement regulating the Palestinian presence in Lebanon (see LEBANON).

Asad therefore evinced less enthusiasm than Sadat for peace-making with Israel. Though ready for demilitarized zones he was less prepared to recognize Israel, and readier to accept that, if negotiations failed, another war was inevitable.

This contrast showed in dealings with the super-powers. Asad's meeting with President Carter on 9 May brought the Geneva conference no closer, nor did several visits (in February and August) by Secretary Vance. Asad's April visit to Moscow had been more decisive. Though reportedly declining Soviet requests for bases, Asad, unlike Sadat, had not broken with the Soviet Government. True, Syria, whose intervention in Lebanon had pained the Soviets, had also found its flow of arms reduced: but now, after Moscow, Syria received tanks and aircraft. Asad declared that Soviet-Syrian relations were 'emerging from a difficult phase'.

As Israel's interference in Lebanon continued, Asad warmed to the Palestinians and cooled to Sadat, who failed to consult him before proposing in August a meeting of Foreign Ministers to prepare a Geneva resumption. In early September, the Syrian suggestion that the UN should expel Israel and institute sanctions was criticized by Egypt as unrealistic and rejected, as was Syria's proposal for an immediate Arab summit: and Zuhair Muhsin, leader of Syria's Palestinian protegés, compared Sadat to Nuri Sa'id, former bugbear of Arab nationalists.

A quarrel with Egypt was thus brewing even before Sadat, without consulting Syria, suggested visiting Israel and went there, despite Asad's strong opposition expressed during Sadat's visit to Damascus on 16 November. As this nightmare approached—for Egypt's withdrawal would leave Syria facing Israel's forces alone—Asad's hostility hardened, threatening rupture with Egypt and producing a rapprochement at Tripoli with the rejectionists, Libyan, Algerian and others, who had but lately been vilifying him. However, even this did not reconcile Syria with Iraq, which walked out.

As in 1977, Iraq organized subversion in Syria: the rector of Damascus university and various senior officers died and yet another attempt in Abu Dhabi on the Syrian Foreign Minister killed his UAE host. Iraq also penalized Syria by keeping the Kirkuk–Banias pipeline closed.

Nor were Syria's relations entirely satisfactory with the Gulf oil states. In April the Central Bank revealed that their aid had fallen by 48 per cent from 1975 to 1976. In June it was rumoured that Saudi Arabia had reduced her 1977 aid by 80 per cent 'to discourage Syrian ambitions'.

With Jordan relations appeared happy. Gradual integration continued field by field (see p. 183). However, King Hussein's milder attitude to Sadat's initiative differed widely from Asad's, though no obvious strain had appeared between the two by the end of the year.

Internally, too, 1977 was trying. The cost of the Lebanon operation (about $85 million per month) was not fully covered by other states: the 1977 budget expenditure of $4,625 million included 20 per cent for defence: and the Lebanese commitment was doubtless partly responsible for Iraqi hostility and thus for the Iraqi campaign of subversion. Some attributed it, however, to resentment of the dominance of Asad's own Alawite community, which though only 11 per cent of the population apparently filled over 70 per cent of the higher military commands.

The Lebanese commitment also diverted Asad from domestic matters and in August, after an election which the Ba'ath coalition won on a humiliatingly low poll, there began a campaign against irresponsibility, negligence and corruption. New legislation and courts were to punish 'economic offences', especially over government contracts. These attacks were not against Asad, who had given the state all his property, but affected the Prime Minister and those who had joined the Ba'ath after Asad's coup in 1970. In September it was reported that 30 senior officials and ex-Ministers had been detained.

Other internal misfortunes were a cholera epidemic, which by mid-September had caused 68 deaths, and a fall from ten to eight million tons in the output of Syria's oilfields, which made Syria withdraw its application to join OPEC.

LEBANON

Civil war divisions remained. Israeli objections prevented the Arab Deterrent Force (ADF) from pacifying the south and Lebanon lacked forces adequate to the task. Leftist, mainly Palestinian, militias continued skirmishing there with Maronites, whom Israel openly supported. These southern hostilities and sectarian outrages elsewhere kept the Lebanese communities apart and thus delayed the necessary new constitutional arrangement. President Elias Sarkis and Prime Minister Salim al Hoss advocated a unified, secularized administration: the extremer Maronites demanded partition, which Muslims opposed. This hampered reconstruction: investors and friendly Governments needed stability before undertaking large expenditures.

Except in the south, the ADF had soon restored a semblance of order, but when, in January, Syrian troops of the ADF entered Nabatiya to start pacifying the south, Israeli protests, conveyed through the US, forced a withdrawal. Serious fighting soon started between Palestinians and rightists.

Theoretically the Lebanese army ought to have filled the gap, but it could not do so without radical reorganization. This was delayed by Maronite fears of reduced dominance of the army by Maronite officers. The Lebanese Front, an umbrella covering, but not uniting, Shamounists and Falangists (they came to blows in July), attacked the Government in February for planning to discharge 'patriotic', *i.e.* partisan, officers.

On 27 February Sarkis suggested UN policing. This proposal went no further: President Asad of Syria admitted his preference for the ADF. The Lebanese Foreign Minister declared on 1 March that his Government could not control the south. To Israeli support for the southern Maronites, the Syrians reacted by supporting the Palestinians again.

Meanwhile the ADF often had full hands elsewhere collecting weapons and preventing clashes between Maronite and non-Maronite areas or between rival gangs of Palestinians. On 16 March persons unknown assassinated the left-wing Druze leader Kamal Jumblatt (see OBITUARY). Reprisals against Christians followed.

Lebanese politics centred round the Cairo agreement, made in 1969 between Lebanon and the PLO to avoid armed Palestinians intervening in Lebanese affairs, or provoking Israeli retaliation, by removing them from the frontier and the Beirut streets and limiting their numbers and armament. The Maronites, however, wanted to interpret it in such a way as to remove Palestinians from the Lebanon. On 2 April the Prime Minister said the Government would if necessary impose its own interpretation. However, on 27 May a Lebanese Front communique advocated denouncing the Cairo agreement, since the PLO had refused to observe it, and thus depriving the Palestinian presence of legal justification.

So national reconciliation made no progress. On 13 May ex-President Chamoun demanded partition into two provinces each with its own president, parliament and law courts, though others, Muslim and Maronite, appealed for inter-communal understanding. On 10 May the Prime Minister admitted that 'morally' the country was already partitioned: but, provided political unity were safeguarded, there could be 'administrative decentralization'. Kuwaiti and Saudi spokesmen said (4 and 11 May) that material reconstruction must await a political settlement: as the Prime Minister commented, internal dissensions were delaying aid.

In June and July Syria and other Arab countries urged the application of the Cairo agreement, on 17 July Syrian-Palestinian agreement was reported on a Palestinian withdrawal from the south, and on 25 July the Lebanon, Syria and the PLO, meeting at Shtoura, concurred on the application of the Cairo agreement. Early in August began the partial disarming of the Palestinians and their removal into the refugee camps. However, this excluded the south, where fighting intensified in August: repeated Israeli intervention led President Carter on 16 August to appeal for Israeli restraint. Syria blamed Israel for the agreement's non-application.

Meanwhile on 21 August a typical Lebanese tragedy diverted attention. At a requiem mass near Beirut shooting broke out between Druzes and Maronites, another setback to intercommunal peace.

In September the southern fighting, with Israeli participation, intensified. On 26 September, after US mediation, Israeli forces began to leave and Lebanese forces, though still outside the area, were preparing to take over the southern barracks. The Palestinians were due to pull back on 1 November. However, Israel insisted on keeping the frontier open to protect her Christian allies, some Palestinian commanders resisted orders to withdraw, shelling continued across the frontier and the Lebanese army move never took place. The Israeli air force began raids on Lebanon and the worst was on 9 November when 100 people were reported killed.

This air raid coincided with President Sadat's offer to visit Israel and in Beirut henceforward Palestinians organized a violent anti-Egyptian campaign, which the Syrian forces did not prevent. Lebanon naturally followed Jordan in staying away from the Arab-Israeli talks arranged by Sadat on 14 December.

Meanwhile reconstruction and recovery rather hung fire. In July a report from the Arab League's industrial development centre neatly summarized the difficulties of Lebanese industry, once a flourishing supplier to home and Arab export markets. Its capital had lost 15 per cent by physical destruction and another 35 per cent by disruption: its markets had contracted, especially abroad: its work-force had fallen, many foreign workers having left and Lebanese not daring to cross inter-communal boundaries: communications and power supplies had deteriorated. Foreign aid concentrated on relief rather than reconstruction, though Kuwait helped rebuild the airport and Abu Dhabi the port and power system, while Saudi Arabia facilitated the renewal of oil supplies.

IRAQ

The Ba'ath maintained its strong hold and its obsessive hostilities. Even when President Sadat's Jerusalem visit reunited Arab extremists, Iraq would not join them.

At home the Government faced, or provoked, a February clash with Shia processions in Najaf and Kerbela, which it blamed on Syrian intrigue. Eight people were executed after trial by a special tribunal. Meanwhile

Kurdish troubles continued: the mass deportations had left bitterness. In January and February foreigners working in Kurdistan were taken hostage by rebels, detained till late March and liberated only after an army offensive: on 4 April ten Kurds were executed. Some 40,000 were simultaneously allowed to go home: but, according to Kurdish rebel sources in Europe, villages in regions bordering Turkey and Iran were bulldozed in July and others in the autumn. However, appearances were kept up: on 1 October the President opened a new session of the Legislative Council of the 'autonomous region' (Kurdistan), in November the secretary of the Kurdish Democratic Party was made a Minister of State, and on 8 December the Revolutionary Command Council (RCC) proclaimed an amnesty for all Iraqi refugees abroad, including Kurds, provided they returned within two months.

There were several sudden organizational changes. On 23 January the Cabinet was enlarged by a third to find posts for all the Ba'ath Party leadership: on 23 March two Ministers were dismissed for 'negligence', probably meaning insufficient severity on the tribunal mentioned above. On 4 September the Ministers added in January were removed to the RCC, which grew from five to twenty-two members. Some ascribed these changes to a struggle between the army, relying on the ailing President Ahmad Hassan al Bakr, who surrendered the defence portfolio on 15 October, and the Ba'ath, led by Sadam Hussain (sometimes confusingly called Takriti, a geographical adjective of origin shared by many Ba'ath leaders, including the President himself), the RCC's vice-president, whose power was waxing.

There was also a dichotomy in foreign policy. On the one hand, hostility to Syria persisted, inspiring a campaign of violence against the Damascus Government, which retaliated in kind and by supporting the Kurds. Only President Asad's removal, it appeared, would end Iraqi enmity. Opposition to peacemaking with Israel was also violent: even Iraq's Soviet friends could not persuade Saddam Hussain (in Moscow from 31 January to 2 February) to favour a Geneva conference. After the Israeli Likud's electoral victory in May, he declared that Iraq would never recognize Israel. Iraq was now, more than Libya, the base for Palestinian and allied terrorists, probably including the Lufthansa hijackers in October (see p. 131). Asad's split with Egypt confronted Iraq with the choice of welcoming him among the militants or isolating itself, which it did at Tripoli in December (see ARAB WORLD), refusing to sign the Tripoli declaration, ostensibly because it avoided denouncing UN Resolution 242. Before this, Iraq had caused indignation by executing Jordanian and Egyptian students for alleged espionage.

On the other hand, away from Syria and Palestine, Iraq's policy appeared pragmatic. Most remarkable was the continued closeness with Iran, many visits being exchanged, including one by the Shah's twin sister in March, and various cooperation agreements signed. Visits were also exchanged with 'reactionary' Oman and Saudi Arabia. The little local difficulty with Kuwait, whose frontiers Iraq still refused formally to acknowledge and had repeatedly violated, was suspended by a temporary understanding in early July, though the border commission provided for met only in November. Iraq also refused to join Libya in following the Soviet example by switching support towards marxist Ethiopia.

Economic and oil affairs were also handled pragmatically. Iraq did not, on 1 July, raise its oil price by 5 per cent as it had threatened, and instead froze it for six months. Like other producers, Iraq was feeling the glut: the Turkish pipeline, inaugurated in January, found few clients save Turks, who were bad payers and sometimes cut off. True, in November the Oil Minister was talking of demanding an OPEC rise of 23 per cent and restriction of production, but he returned from Caracas without them. Large contracts continued to go to capitalist countries like the US and West Germany: Japan provided the steel for the Soviet pipeline from Basra to Baghdad, opened in March.

In October a census showed that the population was now 12 million, having increased by over 50 per cent in 20 years: 63 per cent was now urban, Baghdad alone holding over 25 per cent of the total population.

Chapter 3

SAUDI ARABIA—YEMEN ARAB REPUBLIC—PEOPLE'S DEMOCRATIC REPUBLIC OF YEMEN—KUWAIT—BAHREIN—QATAR—UNITED ARAB EMIRATES—OMAN

SAUDI ARABIA

DURING the year there was some speculation that King Khalid was considering abdication on the grounds of poor health, but after repeated medical treatment in London he appeared to be much better. Considerable uncertainty was felt about the wider ramifications of the succession issue. The present Crown Prince, Fahd, would almost certainly become King, but there seemed to be little agreement within the family about who should be the next Crown Prince. It was widely believed that Prince Fahd wished the post to go to one of his full brothers, either Sultan or Salman. These two names were apparently opposed by other members of the family, and it was reported that Prince Abdullah, a half-brother of Prince Fahd, was also seeking to become Crown Prince. The dissension appeared to be unresolved at the end of the year.

There were unconfirmed indications of a minor coup attempt at Tabuk air base in the north of the country in mid-June. No details were released but two Saudi Arabian pilots were reported to have fled to seek asylum in Iraq when the plot was discovered. Significant evidence accumulated during the year that the authorities were seeking to enforce Islamic practices; several important visitors to the country were reminded that the first goal in the Government's current five-year development plan was to maintain the religious and moral values of Islam.

In foreign affairs the Government continued to take an active interest in a wide range of issues. Relations with its neighbours in the Arabian peninsula and deep involvement in the Arab-Israeli dispute continued to be prominent factors in Saudi Arabian foreign policy. The Government was also concerned in attempts to mediate in the dispute between Syria and Iraq and it continued to keep a careful eye on both the Saharan dispute and the internal situation in Lebanon. The Government also took an active role in the so-called 'North–South dialogue' between the rich and poor nations of the world. Events in the Horn of Africa further demanded considerable attention. Saudi Arabia remained staunchly anti-communist and welcomed the expulsion of the Russians from Somalia, but the growing Russian presence in Ethiopia caused much disquiet in Riyadh.

Opposition to the spread of communism was also largely responsible for Saudi Arabia's efforts in 1976 and in 1977 to limit any rise in the price of crude oil. The Government feared that any increase might cause further economic dislocation in the developed world; in particular it was aware that such disruption could lead to the emergence of communist-dominated Governments in a number of western European states.

In January the price of Saudi Arabian crude oil was increased by approximately 5 per cent and by a similar amount in July. The other OPEC members increased their oil prices by approximately 10 per cent in January, but sluggish world demand meant that the further increase of 5 per cent which had been promised for July was abandoned. It had gradually become clear that Saudi Arabia alone was unable to dominate OPEC, as it did not yet have the ability to increase its oil output to that critical level at which it could dictate prices. It was, however, certainly the most powerful single member of OPEC, and when at the meeting in December it was joined by Iran in the desire to hold oil prices stable it became clear that these two countries would either get their way or OPEC would be in serious danger of disintegration.

Oil output was restricted temporarily by a serious fire in the Abqaiq oil field during early May. A pumping station, pipelines and ancillary plant were destroyed. Full production in the area was not resumed until the autumn. The authorities endeavoured in the autumn to try to restrict the production of the lighter grades of oil and to increase exports of medium and heavy crudes.

Oil continued to be by far the largest source of government revenue, estimates for the financial year 1977-78 ranging as high as $38,000 million. It was announced that government expenditure for the year was expected to reach the level of $31,510 million. Income was estimated to be $41,440 million, showing a planned surplus of $9,930 million. In 1976-77 expenditures had been lower than planned and the actual surplus for that year was believed to have been over $6,500 million. In the current fiscal year it was planned to spend some $12,150 million on infrastructural projects.

The foreign assets held by the Saudi Arabian Monetary Authority continued to grow, and in the middle of the year they were estimated to be in excess of $50,000 million. One American report calculated that the reserves would continue to grow and would exceed $130,000 million by 1980-81. In August it was announced that Saudi Arabia was going to contribute $2,100 million to the so-called 'Witteveen facility' of the IMF. By the end of the year Saudi Arabia had become the second largest creditor of the IMF, after the USA, and there was renewed speculation that the Government would seek the right to appoint one of the 20 directors of that organization.

YEMEN ARAB REPUBLIC

The most important political event of the year was the triple assassination on 11 October of the head of state and chairman of the Military Command Council, Colonel Ibrahim al-Hamdi, his brother Colonel Abdullah al-Hamdi and his brother-in-law Colonel Ali Kannas, who commanded the armoured wing of the army. (Colonel al-Hamdi had come to power in a bloodless coup on 13 June 1974—see AR 1974, p. 220). No arrests were reported and the incident remained shrouded in mystery and surrounded by rumour.

The new head of state was Lieut.-Colonel Ahmad al-Ghashmi, a member of the powerful Hashid tribe from the north. He declared that the YAR was to be governed by a three-man Presidential Council with himself as chairman. The other two members were to be Mr Abdul Aziz Abdul Ghani, who continued in office as Prime Minister, and Major Abdullah Abdul Alim, the commander of the paratroop forces. There were reports of attempts on the life of al-Ghashmi a few days after the triple assassination, but otherwise the transfer of power seemed to have been effected with relatively little disturbance.

The assassinations had been preceded by a period of tribal unrest which had resulted in military action during July against dissident tribesmen in and around the northern towns of Sada and Khamir. Observers in Sanaa and Beirut suggested that the killing of the head of state and his two relatives was linked with this unrest and that responsibility lay with conservative tribal leaders in the north who had been alarmed by al-Hamdi's recent and apparently determined policy of trying to improve relations between the YAR and the marxist regime in the People's Democratic Republic of Yemen. The fact that the assassination took place just before al-Hamdi was due to visit Aden for celebrations marking the tenth anniversary of the independence of the PDRY added to the credibility of this explanation.

Another assassination had already occurred on 10 April in London when Abdullah al-Hajari, a former Prime Minister, was shot together with his wife and an official from the YAR Embassy. This killing was believed to have been the work of radical groups who disapproved of Hajari's right-wing and pro-royalist views. Hajari is believed to have preferred the fostering of close links between the YAR and Saudi Arabia, and to have opposed the development of better relations between Sanaa and Aden.

The politics of the YAR remained of considerable interest to the Government of Saudi Arabia; for there were believed to be over a million YAR citizens working in that country. If the unification of the two Yemens was to take place under a radical or revolutionary regime then the Saudi Arabian authorities feared that the immigrants from the YAR would prove to be a fertile source of political agitation and discontent. It was generally believed that the new YAR head of state would seek to develop close relations with Saudi Arabia and that any improvement in relations with the PDRY would proceed only slowly.

The earnings of Yemenis working outside the country continued to be a very important source of foreign exchange income for the YAR. Remittances from Yemenis abroad were believed to have exceeded $800 million in 1977; some authorities put the figure as high as $1,000 million. Useful as such remittances were, doubts were again expressed about this continuing migration and the harmful impact which it was having on the supply of labour within the YAR. In particular a shortage of labour was having bad effects on the traditional agricultural sector, and food imports grew at an accelerated rate in 1977. Indeed, imports of all commodities increased sharply and the major port of Hodeida became one of the most congested in the world, delays of over 150 days being reported. Part of the difficulty was due to an insufficient number of berths but another problem was the tendency of importers, as elsewhere in the Arabian peninsula, to use port warehouses as a cheap or free form of storage for their goods.

The YAR continued to receive considerable economic aid from Saudi Arabia as Riyadh sought to maintain anti-communist governments along the shores of the Red Sea. Aid was also received from other Arab governments including Kuwait and the United Arab Emirates. Hopes of finding oil in commercial quantities were again disappointed. It was believed that no active petroleum exploration ventures were being pursued at the end of the year. In late August, however, it was announced that large deposits of copper had been discovered in the south and that the YAR hoped to become one of the world's largest exporters of that ore. It remained to be seen whether the deposits were sufficiently attractive to encourage the large foreign investment necessary before these hopes could be fulfilled, as the scale of financing was known to be beyond the domestic resources of the country.

PEOPLE'S DEMOCRATIC REPUBLIC OF YEMEN

There were few signs of fundamental change either in external political alignments or in the authoritarian nature of the country's political system during the year. The first ambassador from Saudi Arabia arrived in Aden in April and the President of the PDRY, Salim Rubai Ali, visited Riyadh in July, but there was little evidence that the Government wished to diminish its close relationships with the countries of the communist bloc and in particular with the USSR, the German Democratic Republic and Cuba. It had been hoped that the apparent ending of the guerrilla war in the neighbouring Dhofar province of Oman would lead to better relations between Aden and Muscat but no appreciable improvement was observed. The first nine months of the year did see an apparently sustained attempt at promoting closer relations with the Yemen Arab Republic and a series of meetings took place, at least one of which, in mid-February, involved the two heads of state. The assassination of the chairman of the Command Council of the YAR made any further progress difficult (see p. 192).

In March it was announced that a new law had been introduced making the carrying of identity cards compulsory for all PDRY citizens. It was also reported that in future no one would be able to take a job with the government or civil service without such a card.

The domestic economy remained weak and depressed. The former British Petroleum refinery at Little Aden was sold by the company to the Yemen National Oil Company in May. It was reported that crude oil supplies were being received by the refinery from Kuwait, Saudi Arabia and the USSR, but the refinery was believed to be still operating at much below its maximum capacity. The bunkering of ships at Aden has not yet recovered from the effects of the closure of the Suez Canal between 1967 and 1975, but the Soviet navy continued to use the port for supplying its ships on patrol in the Indian Ocean. The USSR and Czechoslovakia provided aid for onshore oil and mineral exploration during the year but no significant discoveries were reported.

KUWAIT

The most important political event of the year was the death on 31 December of the ruler, Sheikh Sabah al Salim al Sabah (see OBITUARY). Sheikh Sabah had been in charge of the affairs of Kuwait during the years when its oil wealth grew immeasurably and the creation of an effective welfare state owed much to his personal efforts and guidance. He was succeeded by his first cousin, Sheikh Jabir al Ahmad al Jabir al Sabah, who had been appointed Crown Prince in May 1966.

The year had been a quiet one politically. The National Assembly remained in suspension, and although it was reported that work on a new constitution was proceeding no date was announced for the recall of the Assembly. Press censorship remained in force, but turned out to be less irksome in practice than some commentators had predicted. The newspaper *Al Talia* was again suspended for a period of three months.

Tension increased between Kuwait and Iraq and the frontier between them was closed intermittently between February and June. The basic cause of the dispute was an unresolved claim by Iraq to part of Kuwait's territory. The renewal of this dispute was one of the reasons which encouraged Kuwait to remain on good terms with Saudi Arabia; at the same time the dispute was said to have been responsible for prompting the Government to announce an increase of $1,500 million in the arms budget. New equipment would be purchased from Britain, France, the USA and the USSR. The decision to seek anti-aircraft missiles from Moscow was unexpected, and the Government showed uncertainty as to whether it would permit a Russian military team to enter Kuwait for training purposes. The alternative solution of sending Kuwaitis to undergo training in the USSR was regarded by the authorities as undesirable. As well as developing its army and air force it was announced that Kuwait's small navy would also be expanded. New shore facilities were to be built by a Japanese firm while assistance with training was sought from Pakistan.

Economically Kuwait continued its policy of limiting oil production to two million barrels per day or less. In some local quarters the view was expressed that the production limit should be even lower to permit the effective life of the country's oil reserves to be extended still further. Oil revenues continued to account for over 90 per cent of the Government's development budget.

The planning authorities continued to avoid schemes for the creation of heavy industry on the grounds that such plans would encourage, or even require, greater immigration; less than half the population being native-born, such a further influx was generally regarded as undesirable. Plans were, however, announced for an expansion of the capital-intensive petro-chemical industry. Port delays were reduced significantly during the year.

Banking and allied services continued to flourish and it was felt that much of the financial business which had moved to Kuwait—and to Bahrein—from Lebanon during that country's civil war was unlikely to return very quickly to Beirut. The Kuwait Fund for Arab Economic Development further enhanced its prestige and experience in the granting of foreign aid, and the country continued to devote a significantly high percentage of its GNP to such schemes both in the Arab world and beyond.

BAHREIN

The National Assembly remained suspended throughout 1977, nor were any indications given as to when it might be reconvened. The domestic political scene remained tranquil, however, and several observers concluded that as long as the economy and trade continued to prosper the absence of a parliament was unlikely to be a cause for serious and sustained complaint.

The Government had begun to take action to curb the high rate of inflation in 1976 and these efforts continued, with some success, in 1977. The rate of increase in the price of land and housing was reduced, and there were some reports that rents had actually begun to fall, but a shortage of housing remained a major economic weakness. Determined efforts by the Government also reduced the degree of port congestion, much of which had been due to long delays in the clearing of imports from the docks. Plans for the construction of a causeway linking Bahrein and Saudi Arabia went ahead and it was predicted that tenders for construction would be sought in the early months of 1978.

The offshore banking units scheme was further expanded; assets of the units which had been established by June were said to exceed $6,500 million. The units had already achieved a good reputation for the handling of short-term loans and there was little fear that any revival of Lebanese economic fortunes would lead to the loss of this business to Beirut.

Oil output remained at the low level of about 60,000 barrels per day, as Bahrein's wells were in the final stages of production and the refinery continued to rely on crude oil supplies from Saudi Arabia. On 30 September the dry dock owned and operated by the Arab Shipbuilding and Repair Yard began operations. The dock could handle ships of up to 500,000 tons deadweight and the operating company was owned by Bahrein, Saudi Arabia, the UAE, Qatar and Kuwait. With the addition of the dry dock to the already operating oil refinery and aluminium smelting plant Bahrein's current plans for heavy industrial expansion had come to an end and no further schemes in this sector were envisaged.

QATAR

The political scene was again quiet in 1977 and most attention was focused on the domestic economy. For its size Qatar had embraced one of the most ambitious development plans in the Arabian peninsula, and in 1977 the development budget was increased by over 40 per cent to $1,590 million. Emphasis was again given to both infrastructure and industry, with particular stress on housing, education and electricity supply.

The cost of these plans was the fundamental reason why Qatar decided at the beginning of the year to implement the full 10 per cent oil price rise called for by OPEC. This surprised several observers, for Qatar had usually kept in close step with Saudi Arabia, which had raised oil prices by only 5 per cent. Oil continued to provide some 98 per cent of government income. Although the low level of world demand meant that oil output was considerably less in 1977 than it had been in 1976, questions began to be asked as to whether or not Qatar might decide to modify its developmental plans and adopt a policy already followed by Kuwait in setting a limit on oil production in order to extend the life of its reserves. At current levels of production it was calculated that Qatar's oil reserves would last for between 30 and 35 years. Any massive new discoveries capable of improving this forecast seemed unlikely.

On 3 April the natural gas liquefaction plant at Umm Said was badly damaged by fire and explosion but plans were quickly drawn up for its reconstruction. In March an agreement was announced whereby the Government took full ownership of Shell Qatar, an oil company in which it had had a 60 per cent stake since 1974. Compensation was paid and a new company was established under which management and technical services would continue to be provided by the Shell company on a fee basis.

UNITED ARAB EMIRATES

The year 1977 saw some significant movement in the direction of stronger federal control over the affairs of the member states. Sheikh Zaid of Abu Dhabi was re-elected as President of the UAE after extracting promises from the other rulers that greater efforts would be made towards the unification, under federal control, of police, intelligence, immigration and information services. The success which had been achieved in the unification of the armed forces of some of the member states strengthened hopes that these new policies would be accomplished smoothly. There was certainly considerable indigenous discontent about the high level of illegal immigration. Some estimates stated that less than one-third of the population of the UAE was native-born, and measures to unify immigration services were welcomed by local inhabitants.

The UAE's temporary constitution was extended for a further five-year period from January 1977, but here too several changes were introduced which foreshadowed a movement towards stronger federal control. A new and smaller federal Cabinet was sworn in on 4 January and a new National Assembly was appointed in February. Abu Dhabi and Dubai each had eight seats in the Assembly, Sharjah and Ras al Khaimah each had six, while Fujairah, Ajman, and Umm al Qaiwain each had four. Of the 40 members 16 had served in the Assembly which had been dissolved in December 1976.

Sheikh Zaid again sought to encourage the other members of the UAE to make a greater contribution to the federation's budget. In the past Abu Dhabi had been responsible for providing over 90 per cent of central funds and it was felt that other members, particularly Dubai, ought to shoulder a greater share of financial responsibility.

The 1977 federal budget was not as large as some observers had expected. After allowances had been made for the facts that some expenditures had been transferred from member states to the federation, and that the local annual rate of inflation was believed to be in excess of 30 per cent, it was calculated that the 1977 budget was actually smaller in real terms than that of the previous year.

This slowing in developmental expenditure was due in part to long-term constraints such as a continuing shortage of skilled labour and the traditional nature of much local administration, but it was also partly due to a deliberate policy of trying to limit the alarming growth in inflation. Prices of food, housing and land had risen very rapidly, and during 1977 a determined effort was made by the federal Government to freeze both rents and the price of essential foodstuffs. The credit squeeze which resulted was an unexpected and in some respects a disturbing phenomenon. It resulted in the closure of a handful of banks, and life was made difficult for some local merchants and entrepreneurs, particularly those who had over-invested in speculative constructional projects. Although members of the local mercantile community objected to these government decisions there was considerable indigenous support for them.

The pace of development was to some extent reduced, but there was still little visible sign of any effective coordination of the member states' economic planning. Each state appeared to be unwilling to modify its plans for industrialization and the wasteful duplication of projects continued. Port congestion was less than in 1976, but the distribution of goods from the docks remained poor. The UAE, in common with Saudi Arabia, increased oil prices by approximately 5 per cent in January and by a similar amount in July. The second rise brought local oil prices in line with those of other OPEC states.

OMAN

During a quiet year in Omani politics there was no renewed outbreak of fighting in the Dhofar province, where several former leaders of the guerrilla movement surrendered to the Sultan's forces. As it became clear that the Government had indeed achieved a lasting victory some of the Iranian troops who had been sent to Oman to assist the Sultan were withdrawn. Some, however, remained in the country and in December the Sultan and the Shah, in a joint statement, reaffirmed their determination to continue close cooperation in protecting the security of oil tanker routes through the Strait of Hormuz. The two rulers also promised to assist each other in the fight against internal subversion.

Defence continued to be a major preoccupation of the Sultan and expenditure on it accounted for some 40 per cent of the national budget. The withdrawal of RAF personnel from Salalah and Masirah was completed by 31 March (see AR 1976, p. 202). Official sources made strong and repeated denials that the military facilities at Masirah island would be leased to the USA but it remained possible for American forces to be granted occasional use of those facilities.

The withdrawal of most of the Iranian troops allowed Oman to improve its relations with several Arab states, the notable exception being the People's Democratic Republic of Yemen with which relations remained extremely cool. Oman was one of the few Arab states to express open approval of President Sadat's peace initiative in November.

As the danger of internal subversion and guerrilla activities retreated, the Sultan found that financial aid was slightly less forthcoming from some of his richer Arab neighbours; much attention was accordingly given to Oman's economic future. Oil production in 1976 had reached a level of 366,000 barrels per day but by July 1977 had dropped to 333,000 barrels per day. An exploration venture off Oman's territory in Ras Musandam failed to find petroleum in commercial quantities. Renewed exploration efforts were begun in the Dhofar province now that the danger of guerrilla attacks had been reduced and several small oilfields in that region were brought into production during the year. But prospects for major oil discoveries remained bleak and oil companies believed that the level of proved oil reserves was unlikely to rise much beyond the current level of 6,000 million barrels. It seemed that Oman might be the first major state in the Gulf region, after Bahrein, to have to face the problem of diminishing oil output.

Chapter 4

SUDAN—LIBYA—TUNISIA—WESTERN SAHARA—ALGERIA—MOROCCO

SUDAN

PRESIDENT NIMEIRI was re-elected for a second six-year term after gaining 99·1 per cent of votes in April's referendum. Despite continuing political unrest the President saw the need for national reconciliation between his regime and the different political factions of the opposition. After a meeting with the leader of the National Front, Al-Sadiq Al-Mahdi, in July in Port Sudan, the President decreed a general amnesty for Sudanese political detainees and dissidents living abroad. The aims of the National Front were to consolidate the North–South accord, to put an end to violence in Sudanese politics, to achieve cooperation between civilian and military authorities and to work for the development of the Sudan. In September Al-Sadiq Al-Mahdi returned to the Sudan to negotiate the terms of a national reconciliation, which was welcomed by Sudanese although its outcome remained to be seen.

Sudan's relations with Russia deteriorated while those with Western countries grew. The Government expelled Russian military experts and reduced the size of the Soviet embassy staff and, though it had been wholly dependent on Soviet arms since 1970, efforts were made to acquire Western arms financed mainly by Saudi Arabia and Abu Dhabi. The American Government approved the sale of six military transport planes. France also agreed to sell fighter planes and air defence material to the Sudan.

The strained relations with Libya continued and President Nimeiri accused the Libyan Government of backing Ethiopia against the Sudanese regime and the Eritrean Liberation Movement, for which he had declared his support. Relations with Ethiopia declined because of Sudan's support of Somalia in its military conflict with Ethiopia over the Ogaden region; Sudan and Ethiopia recalled their ambassadors.

The Sudan, with Saudi Arabia, Jordan, Egypt and Syria, was involved in diplomatic manoeuvres over the strategic importance of the Horn of Africa and the security of the Red Sea. In March a mini-summit was held in Taaz between Sudan, Somalia, North and South Yemen with the object of guaranteeing the Red Sea area against Israeli and super-power interests. President Nimeiri pledged his support to President Mobutu of Zaïre when the southern Zaïrean region of Shaba was invaded. After a visit by President Idi Amin of Uganda, it was agreed that Uganda should export coffee and import petroleum products through the Sudan.

Egypt, Syria and Sudan signed in Khartoum a joint political command agreement aimed at protecting the Sudan from Libya and Ethiopia in case of military conflict. In October a joint meeting of the Egyptian and Sudanese People's Assemblies was held in Cairo to discuss political, economic, educational and cultural cooperation. The following month President Nimeiri visited Egypt to congratulate President Sadat on his peace mission to Israel.

Nimeiri visited China for the second time (the first being in 1970) and China pledged support for the new six-year plan, which included a new bridge over the Blue Nile at Sennar, a clothing factory, and two Nile fishing projects, as well as an extension to the rice scheme at Malakal. The French Government promised 400 million francs to meet part of the escalating cost of the Kenana sugar project; a further 26 million francs was to pay for transporting the digging equipment for the Jonglei canal.

The year witnessed the second conference of the Sudan Socialist

Union's National Congress. With a view to wider participation the number of delegates increased from 1,758 in 1974 to 2,000 in 1977, and positions from basic units to the executive committee were filled through elections.

In February, a minor ministerial re-shuffle took place. Dr Mansur Khalid became Foreign Minister while retaining his post of assistant to the President for coordination, and Mr Abd Al-Wahab Ibrahim took over the Interior Ministry while retaining his old post of Chief of Public Security. In May the President decreed the dissolution of the Ministry of People's Local Government, to be replaced by an Office in the Republican Presidency, a move towards decentralization and increasing popular participation in government at local level. In a second major re-shuffle in August nine Ministers and Ministers of State were removed. The President assumed the post of Prime Minister and the finance and economy portfolio. The former Prime Minister became the Foreign Minister and Dr Mansur Khalid, who held various ministerial positions, was removed from the Cabinet.

In face of worsening inflation the 1977-78 Budget emphasized curbing public expenditure, increasing revenue and solving the problem of loss-making public corporations. Development projects, particularly in the agricultural and communication sectors, were allocated £S307 million. Defence expenditure rose from £S58 million to £S82·6 million and an additional sum of £S20·8 million was allocated for the Southern Region. Record revenue from cotton was expected to ease Sudan's balance of payments difficulties. The People's Assembly ratified the agreement setting up the Arab Authority for Investment and Agricultural Development. This aimed to increase Sudan's agricultural output and to diversify its exports away from cotton, with a capital of 150 million Kuwaiti dinars and $510 million. A joint venture to develop the chrome deposits in the Ingessena Hills was agreed between the Government and two Japanese companies, the latter investing between $50 million and $60 million. The Netherlands granted 40 million guilders towards financial aid and technical cooperation. Lonrho, stockholder and hitherto manager of the Kenana sugar project, had its management contract terminated. The Arab Investment Company contributed a loan of $10·25 million towards the Kenana sugar project. Further, the Saudi Development Fund made loans to the amount of $26 million to finance various telecommunication projects and the Western Savanna agriculture project. The administration and the public services in Sudan were put under strain by the growing numbers of qualified Sudanese taking up employment abroad, notably in Saudi Arabia, Kuwait and the Trucial States.

The five-year experiment in regional autonomy in the South brought, according to General Joseph Lagu, stability and peace. The gradual re-construction of the South continued and President Nimeiri announced

G*

that the sum of $517 million, to be spent over six years, had been earmarked for development. However, the Southern Region was not free of trouble. On 2 February Juba airport was attacked and occupied by some mutinous members of the air defence force until forces loyal to the Government crushed the mutiny. The aim of the plot was to separate the Southern Region from the rest of the Sudan. A state Security Court tried 99 men but the accused were included in the general amnesty proclaimed in July.

Sudan's problems of desert encroachment were highlighted during a UN conference, held in August in Nairobi, on the environment and desertification. It was estimated that the desert was advancing at the rate of five to six km a year in northern and western Sudan and measures to prevent this were put forward. During the conference, the Jonglei canal project, to be built at an estimated cost of £S70 million financed equally by Egypt and Sudan, came under attack by environmentalists who claimed that the project would increase desertification.

LIBYA

For a few days Libya found itself actually at war with its great neigh-bour and it remained clear the Presidents Sadat and Qadafi cannot peacefully coexist. In February Qadafi said that it would take 50 years to normalize relations after the 'high-treason' of the 'hangman Sadat', while in March it seemed that (with monotonous regularity) Libyan agents were being arrested in Egypt on sabotage missions. The Egyptian War Minister, General Gamassi, said that his army was looking westwards and the press trumpeted that Qadafi was planning to annex the Western Desert with the aid of 7,000 Cubans. Each side complained to the Arab League and Russia warned Sadat against any adventure. Qadafi founded the Egyptian Liberation Front and financed attacks on Sadat in the Lebanese press. Both sides agreed to cease propaganda early in June but a few days later Qadafi said that the wounds were too deep to heal thus quickly.

On 21 July Sadat attacked across the border, claiming that he would teach 'the crazy red agent' a lesson that he would never forget. Airfields and radar installations (allegedly used by the Russians for monitoring the American Sixth Fleet) were bombed and the Libyans claimed that US forces were helping the Egyptians in large-scale operations, with enormous casualties such as 2,000 in a day at Jaghbub. The Sudanese were also said to be aiding Sadat, while Qadafi was supposed to have recruited 500 Palestinians. The PLO leader Yassir Arafat flew to and fro and soon there was an informal cease-fire. On 24 August prisoners were exchanged and the matter rested there. Sadat probably thought that the Libyan people would rise to overthrow the regime and certainly for a few days Qadafi was shaken, uncertain whether he could trust his forces and calling for a people's war. Sadat's visit to Israel brought forth a new crescendo of denunciation and a meeting of the 'rejectionist front' in Tripoli.

The clash showed Libyan isolation within the Arab world; for only Algeria supported Libya and the controlled press called for a new approach to North Africa at the expense of the Arab east. One of the first beneficiaries was Tunisia, which in May had found itself on the brink of war with Libya over the demarcation of coastal waters believed to contain oil. For a few days warships prowled around an American-owned rig, one fleet ordering it out and the other threatening it if it obeyed. A compromise over this was followed by a series of agreements—Libya would help Tunisia by taking some of its agricultural produce and surplus workers. In the interests of North African fellowship, too, Qadafi showed unusual discretion in refusing to welcome an SADR delegation from Western Sahara to the Revolution celebrations. In the east he restored relations with Jordan, and common hostility to Sadat's Israeli policy enabled him to bury a quarrel with Syria over alleged ill-treatment of its nationals.

At intervals Chad complained that Libya was occupying some 27,000 square miles of its territory (an area believed rich in uranium) and threatening its independence. The actual position in this remote area was obscure but Qadafi was believed to be building a base there with Russian help.

The Libyan Foreign Minister said that his country was spending $2 million a year on liberation movements, and during the year Tripoli entertained most of the militant African leaders, particularly those involved in Rhodesia. Qadafi supported Muslim minorities everywhere, particularly in the Philippines, but not in Eritrea where, doubtless in deference to Russian wishes, he declared himself for the Christian Ethiopians.

The alliance with Russia was a natural marriage of convenience; for Libya felt isolated from the rest of the Arabs while Russia was excluded from the peace-making diplomacy of Kissinger and Vance. In June there were new agreements on developing atomic energy, engineering, agriculture etc.: King Hassan said there were 7,000 Soviet citizens in Libya.

Very close relations had been established with Yugoslavia, which had provided some 10,000 technicians, particularly in the medical field. Visits were exchanged with President Tito, who appeared to be acting as mentor to the young Colonel. Another mentor was Castro, who paid a prolonged visit in the spring. Relations with the West continued bad, Libya being listed among the potential enemies of the US, and in September two American oil companies were nationalized. France was attacked for making itself the gendarme of Africa and there was no follow-up to the big deal with Fiat announced in December 1976 (see AR 1976, p. 207).

In internal affairs the first two months were devoted to preparations for the General People's Congress which was held in March at Sebha amidst resounding slogans that the Arabs had invented socialism and that

Nasser personally had proclaimed Qadafi his true heir. The demand was for committees everywhere running everything and culminating in the 26 members of the General People's Committee of which Qadafi was Secretary-General. This was proclaimed a new era and 'the greatest event in the history of mankind'; as a symbol, the name of the state was changed for the second time in six months. Now it became the Socialist People's Libyan Arab Jamahariyyah—a word specially coined for the occasion and best rendered 'Massdom'. Qadafi claimed that the word 'Republic' discredited. Libya (the inelegant acronym SPLAJ did not catch on) was hailed as the first true democracy since Athens, with the Qur'ān as its legal guide, all man-made law being invalid. The concept of armed forces was replaced by that of a nation in arms. As a further bonus Qadafi announced that Part II of his *Green Book* would provide the final solution of the problem of economics: unfortunately publication has been delayed.

There are few countries where political theory and practice differ so widely. All domestic opposition is treated as treason and in April there were the first executions for 23 years. Libya was reported to hold more political prisoners in proportion to its population than any other country.

Oil production increased and economically Libya had a good year. Ambitious plans were laid to make Tripoli the largest port in North Africa and to shift the balance away from oil to petro-chemicals and other products. In 1977, 20 new industrial plants were opened. There were hopes that the country would be self-supporting in food by 1980, and 30,000 British hens were imported by air to assist the process. A Revolution Day march saw the first appearance of women in a parade.

TUNISIA

Tunisia, once the most stable of all North African countries, had a year of unprecedented unrest. Habib Bourguiba has towered over his fellows and the Constitution was tailored to fit him. Now the question was whether the establishment was capable of a smooth succession. Bourguiba's Tunisia had failed to move with the times, fossilizing into a gerontocracy deriving its legitimacy from the struggle for independence now nearly a quarter of a century past.

The Destour Party brooked no rivals but in June a group of dissatisfied intellectuals was allowed to create a National Council for the Defence of Civil Liberties, calling for a general amnesty for political offences. The university students were also unhappy and there were several sharp clashes in which people believed to be government informers were thrashed. In May 80 junior magistrates struck for greater judicial freedom as well as for better pay: in November a teachers' strike closed the schools. Both the intellectuals and the young had come to see in the trade union movement

(UGTT), 650,000 strong and aggressively led by Habib Achour, the strongest force in the country for economic and social change.

Despite substantial pay rises in January, the first since 1971, there were 41 strikes (39 of them unofficial) in the next six months. In October a dispute in a textile factory got so far out of hand that for the first time since 1969 troops had to assist the police. The Prime Minister, Hedi Nouira, saw these strikes as a trial of strength and Achour as a personal enemy.

The unrest was intimately bound up with the struggle for the succession. Nouira, Bourguiba's nominated heir, was ageing, colourless and unpopular, deriving support mainly from the Party *apparatchiks*. Taha Belkhodja, his Interior Minister, was believed to be more liberal, favouring concessions to the UGTT. Ahmed Mestiri, dismissed from the Ministry of the Interior in 1971, had considerable support for views that were roughly social democratic. Muhammad Masmoudi, disgraced from the Foreign Ministry after an abortive agreement on unity with Libya, returned from two years' exile and proclaimed himself the spiritual son of Bourguiba and, more importantly, the champion of the UGTT. He and his ally Achour were several times received by Qadafi, while another 'dark horse', the exiled Ben Salah, was believed to enjoy Algerian support.

At the end of December events reached a crisis. Nouira called for strong measures against the UGTT and dismissed Belkhodja who had refused to support them. Six other members of the Cabinet thereupon resigned and were replaced mostly by technocrats without political following: it was said that their skills were needed to deal with economic difficulties arising from too rapid expansion. An interesting feature of the reshuffle was the re-emergence of Bourguiba's son as special adviser: he was thereupon regarded as another potential candidate.

The UGTT was not slow to see these events as a challenge and the year ended with a series of strike calls: there was little doubt that the UGTT had acquired some weapons. There were fears that civil war would break out in this once peaceful land or that it could be averted only by a military takeover.

Economically the situation was no more encouraging. The fifth five-year plan announced in July called for an annual growth rate of $7\frac{1}{2}$ per cent, self-sufficiency in food and 234,000 new jobs, but economists agreed that it was too ambitious. In the meanwhile EEC restrictions had damaged exports and unemployment was rife. Bourguiba was able to do little more than call for birth-control.

In foreign affairs, apart from the clash with Libya (see p. 203), there was talk of a deal with the US which would give arms in return for bases.

WESTERN SAHARA

It became increasingly clear that the Saharan Arab Democratic Republic (SADR) was, in the words of the Moroccan communist Ali Yata, merely 'a gang of Moroccan and Mauritanian mercenaries in the pay of the regime in Algeria'. It had no existence on the ground, although selected correspondents were driven into a patch of desert, informed that they were in the liberated Sahara and returned with pictures of women brandishing carbines. Native Saharans were in the minority on its guiding council and in its forces, which were reported to include Cubans, Vietnamese and East Germans. King Hassan stated that Algerian regulars had been captured, as well as boys of fifteen.

The SADR made no diplomatic progress and added only the Seychelles to the nine countries which recognized it. Its neighbours like Mali, the Arab League and even the Russians, preferring to cultivate good relations with Rabat, stood aloof. A decision by the OAU in July to discuss the Saharan question at a special summit in Lusaka was a diplomatic defeat for Morocco but one that was nullified as the meeting never took place.

The main military activities of the SADR seem to have taken place in the imagination of its communique writers, broadcasting from Algiers: massive casualties were claimed, 15,000 in a year. What fighting there was took place against Mauritania as the weaker of the two enemies and because the leaders of the SADR were mostly Mauritanians who had quarrelled with the Daddah regime: King Hassan said that they had offered him peace in return for a free hand against Nouakchott. The most successful attack was on the iron ore mining centre of Zouerate in May. Two French citizens were killed and six made hostages, or, as the SADR claimed, prisoners of war. Moroccan troops moved in to support the Mauritanians, who had started the war with an army of 2,000 men. In November, after attempts to free the hostages through Algerian mediation had failed, President Giscard sent 200 special troops to 'help Mauritanian citizens when their lives are in danger, if requested by the Mauritanian Government'. In December French aircraft were also in action against a raiding column.

From the Moroccan point of view, the situation was annoying and expensive rather than dangerous. There was no weakening of resolve and, to quote Ali Yata again, 'the Moroccan character of the Sahara is not negotiable'. The army was chafing at the restrictions put upon it by the King's caution, and in November he recognized this by saying that his troops would be authorized to cross the Algerian frontier in hot pursuit in defence of his own realm or even of Mauritania: his patience was exhausted and if the Algerians wanted war they could have it. Boumédienne reacted with outrage at the idea that anyone should be allowed to hit him back.

There were attempts by African and Arab leaders to mediate. In December the Saudis promised to finance massive development of a semi-autonomous Sahara under Moroccan sovereignty. In return Morocco would renounce its old claims to Tindouf. Although Boumédienne could hardly wish for a prolonged war, the difficulty was to find a peace formula which would save his face.

ALGERIA

February saw the culmination of the process begun the previous year to provide the regime with a respectable constitutional façade. Parliamentary elections were held with exactly three candidates, all chosen by the only permitted party, the FLN, for each seat. A quarter of those elected were teachers, with a very small percentage of peasants. Nine out of 36 women candidates were successful.

In May occurred the first major Cabinet reshuffle since President Boumédienne seized power in 1965. There were 14 new Ministers, practically all technocrats. Despite speculation to the contrary the President retained the office of Prime Minister while adding to his powers by taking over control of the police, the civil service and religious affairs.

In the worst labour unrest since independence there were some 160 strikes in July and August. Unlike its neighbours, the trade union movement (UGTA) was totally subservient to the state and provided no means of redress against evident and increasing inequality. Boumédienne had to admit that many grievances were genuine and decreed a general increase in wages averaging 20 per cent, although some groups received up to 80 per cent.

The regime continued its attempt to combine socialism with Islam. The weekly rest day was changed to Friday and the educational system was further arabized.

In foreign affairs relations with France became icy as a result of French policy in the Sahara. In contrast they warmed with the US which received an Algerian ambassador for the first time since 1967 and doubled its investment in two years. In October the Government refused to hand over to the Japanese a group of Red Army hijackers and the ransom that they had extorted (see JAPAN). Sadat's visit to Israel was zestfully denounced and earlier in the year Boumédienne threatened to intervene if the attack on the Libyans were not called off.

Algeria's oil, it had been estimated, would run dry in 20 years, and $250 million spent on exploration failed to find new fields. On the other hand Algeria possessed 12 per cent of the world's natural gas reserves. Contracts with Holland and West Germany worth $7,500 million were signed; full development of exports to the US hung fire as Congress doubted the wisdom of becoming too dependent upon a single source. A project for a gas pipe line from Hassi R'mel to Bologna was revived in October. As this would pass across Tunisia it would have important political effects. Another was suggested to Spain across Morocco.

Boumédienne had long harnessed all resources to the development of heavy industry, with the result that Algeria had become the most industrialized country in the Arab world although, through technical inefficiency, full production was rarely attained. Agriculture suffered as a result and the new four-year plan announced in October raised its priority. An agreement was signed with the Canadian Pacific Railway for study of the possibility of a further 1,500 km of line. The building of eight new universities, technologically biased, was announced.

The involvement in the Sahara cast its shadow over the year and the lack of success damaged Algerian prestige. Its costliness was unpopular and naturally was at the expense of a further much-needed raising of living standards.

MOROCCO

Morocco continued the progress begun in 1976 towards giving all political groups a voice in decision-making. In November there had been elections for the municipalities and in January the next layer was added to the pyramid by those for the provincial assemblies, which, with the representatives of the professional bodies, would receive a third of the parliamentary seats. Again the Independents were largely successful. In March, in preparation for a national election, press censorship was ended and the secretaries-general of the four main parties were brought into the Cabinet to guarantee fair play.

The elections were remarkably fair and free by African standards and, in striking contrast to Algeria, nine parties provided 1,022 candidates (75 per cent of them under 45) for 176 seats. The Party for Progress and Socialism, led by the veteran communist Ali Yata (who was elected for Casablanca), fielded a team of 90. The result was a triumph for the Independents (81 seats), mostly supporters of the King campaigning under the slogan 'Hassanism is our doctrine'. The traditional Istiqlal (45 seats) took satisfaction that it was still the largest single party. Only the left-wing USFP (16 seats) claimed that its candidates had been harassed. Its leader Abderrahim Bouabid, who had foolishly challenged a popular local notable, was defeated to the embarrassment of the Government.

In October the King swore in a new Cabinet which satisfied nearly everyone, instructing them that they must 'realize that they represent various views and parties'. He returned to this theme when opening Parliament, quoting the Qur'ān about 'a people of the middle way' and calling for 'agreement through dialogue'.

As a monarchy Morocco had suffered a bad press amongst international 'progressives' who would have praised King Hassan had he been a revolutionary who had seized power in a bloody coup. He had shown a mastery of politics, moving with great skill to enlarge his basis of support while encouraging a young elite, many of whom were brought into Parliament through safe rural seats. He had shown that he could appeal to the people over the heads of the politicians, and even the communists regarded him as preferable to the only conceivable alternative, a military takeover. Meanwhile, despite an ostentatious display of democracy, he had kept all real power in the hands of himself and his closest associates. The revelation at a trial in Casablanca that there had been a plot to establish a republic under a Jewish mining engineer evoked general amusement and most of those sentenced were later pardoned.

Until November little was said publicly about the military side of what was happening in the Sahara (see p. 206) and all stress was upon development there, in which the public participated with a loan of 1,000 million dirhams. There were announcements that new schools and harbours had been built, that 65,000 nomads had been settled and that plans were being considered for a railway from Marrakesh to el-Ayoun and for electrification through digging an eight-mile channel from the ocean to a 162 square mile depression. However, in May it was reported that Morocco was buying $500 million worth of arms from Western Europe, and the 1978 Budget envisaged further increases in military expenditure with inevitable cuts elsewhere.

Inflation ran at 20 per cent, exports of fruit and textiles to the EEC were restricted and there was labour unrest. Morocco, needing to import 80 per cent of its energy, hoped that the development of shale oil might prove economically practical. In the meanwhile BP and other companies were intending to prospect off the coast at Soueira and el-Ayoun.

Phosphates, the main export, did not recover their peak, but an agreement was signed with Russia which would take five million tonnes a year and provide a loan for a new opencast mine, a railway and a port. Relations with Russia were friendly and improved still further when the US announced that it would give up its military facilities in Morocco.

The King, who had committed himself to recognition of Israel once the Palestinians had been satisfied, declared that he was 'heart and soul' with Sadat in his mission to Jerusalem, although he had been taken aback that the President had not consulted him in advance 'to spare him embarrassment'.

Morocco was extremely embarrassed by the events of 16 January in Benin: its participation was censured by a Commission of the OAU. There was further disagreement with the Organization in February when a SADR delegation was admitted to the Lomé conference: Morocco decided to boycott it and to avoid even African sporting events. However, its African reputation was restored by its effective intervention in Zaïre to 'evict invading mercenaries' at the request of President Mobutu. Its tough well-disciplined troops were able to return after a few weeks with their task accomplished.

VI EQUATORIAL AFRICA

Chapter 1

ETHIOPIA—SOMALIA—DJIBOUTI—KENYA—TANZANIA—UGANDA

ETHIOPIA

LONGSTANDING tensions in the Horn of Africa broke into open warfare between Ethiopia and Somalia, leaving most of south-eastern Ethiopia in Somali hands at the end of the year. Elsewhere in Ethiopia, opposition to the Provisional Military Government (Derg) was evident in Addis Ababa and the provinces, and in Eritrea the combined guerrilla forces restricted Ethiopian troops to a shrinking number of urban strongholds. At the centre, Colonel Mengistu Haile-Maryam emerged as the undisputed strong man, killing his immediate rivals and maintaining his regime by a reign of terror in which many thousands died. Externally, a close alliance with the Soviet Union, reversing Ethiopia's previous dependence on the United States, furnished the armaments essential to the Government's survival.

The uneasy triumvirate which had run the Derg since November 1974 was shattered on 3 February when the Chairman, Brigadier General Tafari Bante, was killed in a gun fight with the supporters of the First Vice-Chairman, Colonel Mengistu; this was apparently provoked by a re-organization of the Derg which reduced Mengistu's importance. The Second Vice-Chairman, Colonel Atnafu Abate, whose relations with Mengistu had been strained for some time, was executed on 12 November. This dissension at the highest level of the Government was reflected in a further fragmentation of its supporters. The pro-Derg political organization Meison came into conflict with the Government from August onwards, and the leader of one of the principal Addis Ababa urban associations (*kebelle*) on which the Government relied for support in the towns was executed in April; he was accused of personally murdering 24 people. Measures taken against the regime's suspected opponents became increasingly brutal and indiscriminating. Some 2,000 people were believed to have been killed in the aftermath of the leadership struggles of early February. In late April and early May, a concerted campaign was undertaken by *kebelle* leaders and the Government's counter-insurgency Flame Division against students and other suspected sympathizers with the marxist underground Ethiopian People's Revolutionary Party (EPRP), in the course of which about a thousand died.

Violence in Addis Ababa continued at a high level for the rest of the year, and intensified after Colonel Atnafu's execution in November, when Colonel Mengistu stated 'it is a historical obligation to clean up vigilantly

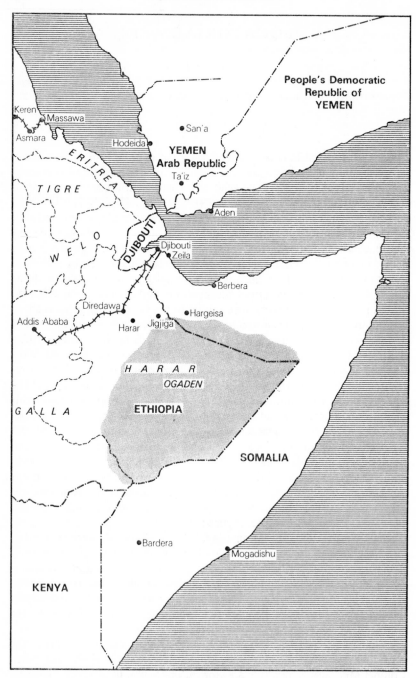

The Horn of Africa

using the revolutionary sword', and called for a 'red terror' against reactionaries. Opponents of the regime assassinated several of its leading advisers. Amnesty International estimated that at least 10,000 political killings, the great majority by government forces, took place in the first 11 months of the year, and there were further massacres in Addis Ababa in December. Large numbers of political prisoners were held under appalling conditions, Amnesty International accepting an estimate of 30,000 arrests since 1974 as 'probably not greatly exaggerated'. Ejigayahu Asfa-Wossen, grand-daughter of Emperor Haile-Selassie, was among those who died in prison; her six children found refuge abroad, as did many thousands of other Ethiopians.

It was difficult to gain reliable information about conditions in the countryside, but government claims to have liquidated 'bandits', 'feudalists' and 'anarchists' indicated widespread conflict in all but a few provinces. The main centres of opposition were in the northern provinces of Tigre, Begemder and Wollo, adjoining Eritrea, and in the south-east, encompassing not only the Somali irredentist movement but also Afar and Galla/Oromo groups. In Eritrea, the guerrilla forces consolidated their control of the entire province except for a few isolated Ethiopian garrisons. These fell steadily throughout the year: Keror and Om Hager on the Sudanese border in January, Nakfa in March, Tessenei in April, the major fortress of Keren in July, and Adi Caieh, south of Asmara, in December. By the end of the year only four strongholds remained in Ethiopian hands, and the capital Asmara depended entirely on airborne supplies.

The guerrillas' effectiveness was increased by a unity agreement between the two principal movements, the Eritrean Liberation Front (ELF) and the Eritrean People's Liberation Front (EPLF), in October, though the third group, the Popular Liberation Forces (PLF), did not take part. The guerrillas obtained increased external assistance, including the open support of President Nimeiri's Government in the Sudan, as well as Kuwait and United Arab Emirates. Libya, however, withdrew its backing, in step with Soviet policy, and in May President Qadafi urged the Eritreans to abandon their struggle on the grounds that the Ethiopian Government had brought justice and equality.

While events in Eritrea belied the assumption that a marxist Government in Ethiopia could make peace with marxist guerrilla movements, hopes of a Pax Sovietica in the south-east proved equally vain. Ethiopia's former links with the USA had become increasingly strained since 1974, and in March President Castro of Cuba visited both Somalia and Ethiopia in an attempt to reconcile the territorial dispute between them under Soviet protection. The proposed plan was, however, rejected by the Somalis, while Ethiopia-Soviet links grew closer. Colonel Mengistu visited Russia in May, shortly after the expulsion of the US Military Mission from Ethiopia and the suspension of American arms sales. As Soviet military advisers started to arrive in Ethiopia, in some cases transferred directly from Somalia, the Western Somalia Liberation Front (WSLF) launched an attack on Ethiopian forces in the Somali-inhabited Ogaden region towards the end of July. The WSLF was distinct from the Somali Government, and President Siyad had previously curbed its activities, but when war broke out amidst anti-Ethiopian and anti-Soviet fervour he had no option but to commit troops and armaments unofficially to the campaign.

The Ogaden, garrisoned by isolated Ethiopian detachments, fell within a week, leaving the Somalis with the much more difficult task of capturing the main bases at Jigjiga, Harar and Diredawa. An attack on Diredawa in mid-August, in which Somali tanks were engaged, was repulsed, but Jigjiga and the strategic Marda Pass fell in mid-September, partly as a result of dissension among Ethiopian troops. Massive shipments of Soviet arms, arriving from July onwards, helped the Ethiopians to stabilize the situation; although fighting continued round Harar and Diredawa, neither city fell, and by the end of the year the Ethiopians were in a position to start launching counter-attacks.

SOMALIA

In 1977 Somalia sharply broke the Soviet links which had been the mainstay of the country's defence policy since shortly after independence, and took the plunge in attempting to regain by force the Somali-inhabited areas of Ethiopia (see above). A rising tide of anti-Soviet feeling, in which Russian civilians were killed, culminated on 13 November in the expulsion of thousands of Soviet experts, renunciation of the treaty of friendship with the USSR, and withdrawal of all military facilities. At the same time, Somalia broke diplomatic relations with Cuba, which President Siyad Barre accused of supplying 15,000 troops to fight with the Ethiopians.

The Western powers, including the USA, UK, France and West Germany, refused to supply Somalia with arms so long as the fighting with Ethiopia continued, but the deficiency was to some extent made up by anti-Soviet Arab states, especially Saudi Arabia. Agricultural and health aid from the United States was resumed in December, however, and Somalia enjoyed increased aid and enormous popularity in West Germany, after allowing German troops to fly to Mogadishu to storm a Lufthansa aircraft hijacked there in October (see p. 131).

DJIBOUTI

The French Territory of the Afars and Issas became the Republic of Djibouti on 27 June, and in so doing exchanged its former status as the last French colony on the African continent for that of the smallest and poorest independent African state. Arrangements for independence were completed at a meeting of Djibouti representatives with the French Government in Paris in March. Independence was subsequently approved by over 98 per cent of the voters in a referendum on 8 May, while at the same time 92 per cent approved the single list of 65 candidates presented for the Assembly. This apparently overwhelming support, however, was tempered by a high abstention rate among Afars, who were outnumbered by Issas in the Assembly list.

The veteran Issa Somali politician Hassan Gouled became Prime Minister, and at independence President. He chose a carefully balanced Cabinet including eight Issas, seven Afars and an Arab. The new state was admitted to the UN and OAU, and applied for membership of the Arab League. More immediately important, the new Government signed agreements with France to retain 4,500 French troops and maintain French financial aid; aid was also provided by Saudi Arabia.

The first six months of independence were mercifully uneventful, in view of predictions that internal ethnic conflict and external intervention would swiftly follow, and Djibouti avoided involvement in the Somali-Ethiopian war which broke out in July. On 5 December, however, a bomb attack on a night club frequented by French soldiers indicated the continuing tensions. The economy remained extremely depressed, especially as a result of the cutting of the Djibouti–Addis Ababa railway line by Afar separatists opposed to the Ethiopian regime.

KENYA

In January many MPs competed in branch elections of the Kenya African National Union (KANU). However, national party elections scheduled for 3 April were indefinitely postponed, apparently because of acute organizational problems. The competition had already been intense: while President Kenyatta had been unopposed as party president, the other eight posts had attracted some 50 candidates. Mr Oginga Odinga, party and national Vice-President until 1966, had been debarred by KANU headquarters from standing for election to his former party post. The issue of land hunger, which he had exploited as opposition leader, remained politically explosive, but strong vested interests within the Government and the administration made it unlikely that a ceiling would be placed on individual land ownership.

Mr George Anyona, MP for Kitutu East and an outspoken critic of the Government (see AR 1976, p. 218), was detained in May. The next month George Githii resigned his post as editor-in-chief of the English-language *Daily Nation* (circulation 79,000) after a disagreement with the newspaper's main shareholder, the Aga Khan. The sacking in November of Mr David M. Kimani, personnel manager of the *Nation* group of newspapers, prompted the workers to stage a sit-in protest; more than 450 employees were dismissed and trade union officials were among those arrested. The *Sunday Nation* was now facing stiff competition from the *Nairobi Times*, a privately-owned Sunday newspaper committed to upholding human rights and constitutionalism, which was launched with government blessing in October by Mr Hilary Ng'weno, editor and publisher of the successful news magazine *The Weekly Review* since February 1975.

After Tanzania closed its border with Kenya in February, top officials of the two countries met to discuss points of difference, including the release by Tanzania of Kenya-registered vehicles and light aircraft and the freeing by Kenya of East African Community (EAC) property, such as the passenger ship *Victoria*, used by Tanzania. These negotiations failed and on 18 April Tanzania announced that it had sealed its border 'completely and permanently'. The Community effectively collapsed in 1977 (see Pt. XI, Ch. 6). President Kenyatta nominated Dr Robert Ouko, former East African Minister for Common Market and Economic Affairs, as an MP and appointed him to his Cabinet as Minister in charge of those EAC services which had been incorporated into the Kenyan civil service. The Government also took steps to establish a Court of Appeal for Kenya to replace the East African Court of Appeal. Relations with Tanzania remained cool as the institutional ties between them weakened, and were exacerbated by border incidents. Despite attempts to salvage some inter-state cooperation, the border was still closed at the end of the year.

Relations with Uganda, though better than in 1976, continued to be poor. Despite the Memorandum of Understanding reached at Nairobi in August 1976 (see AR 1976, p. 217), Uganda refused in September to pay compensation to the relatives of Kenyans who had lost their lives and property in Uganda. Relations with Somalia were strained after an incident at a northern border post in June, when six Kenyan policemen were killed. The Government condemned the seizure of much of the Ethiopian province of Ogaden by Somali insurgents and in October President Kenyatta stated that any attack by Somalia on Kenya would be repulsed. However, diplomatic relations with Somalia were maintained.

In April and May floods caused by torrential rains caused many deaths and extensive damage to property. The Government banned all hunting and said that in future only photographic safaris would be allowed. The International Louis Leakey Memorial Institute for African Prehistory was opened in Nairobi in September. The Attorney-General gave notice in November of local government elections to be held in June 1978 and of a general election in 1979.

TANZANIA

A new party, *Chama cha Mapinduzi* (the Revolutionary Party), was inaugurated in February after the merger of the Tanganyika African National Union (TANU) and the Afro-Shirazi Party (ASP) of Zanzibar. President Nyerere was elected chairman and Mr Aboud Jumbe, the Zanzibari leader and Tanzanian Vice-President, was made vice-chairman. The constitution of CCM was modelled on that of TANU and provided for a well-articulated structure with national, regional, district, branch and cell levels. After a register of the 1·5 million members had been compiled, a series of elections for leaders at the various levels culminated in October with the election by the national conference of 40 members to the national executive, which then elected 30 members to the central committee. There was a marked turnover of leaders, with preference given to younger and better educated men. The party chairman and vice-chairman served *ex-officio* on the central committee, to which ten members were nominated by the chairman. In the absence of any incompatibility rule such as Zambia enforced, five Ministers (apart from the President and Vice-President) belonged to this key committee. So, too, did Mr I. M. Kaduma, the vice-chancellor of the University of Dar es Salaam: his nomination convinced university students that President Nyerere, the University Chancellor, would not intervene to redress their grievances over student suspensions and dismissals (seven senior staff members had been removed in May).

A new Constitution for the United Republic, replacing the Interim Constitution of 1965, was adopted in April by a Constituent Assembly meeting in Dar es Salaam. For the first time Zanzibar, which would retain its separate government, was to elect representatives to the Union Parliament, ten members to sit alongside 96 constituency members elected from the mainland and 100 other members—50 from each part of the Republic. The ten Zanzibari MPs were elected in December. In the urban constituency of Stone Town, Mr A. H. Pandu, Zanzibar's Chief Justice and the presiding judge at the treason trial which followed the assassination of Shaikh Abeid Karume (see AR 1972, p. 237), was overwhelmingly defeated by Mr J. R. Nasibu, a journalist who was himself detained during Shaikh Karume's rule; most of the 81 people tried came from Stone Town.

In 'The Arusha Declaration—Ten Years After', President Nyerere reported in January that about 13,065,000 people were living together in 7,684 villages. While this was 'a tremendous achievement', Tanzania was still 'neither socialist, nor self-reliant' and great inequalities between citizens persisted; on the other hand, the national drift towards the growth of a class society had been arrested and reversed.

The 1974 decision to achieve universal primary education for all children was vigorously pursued, though the target date set (the end of 1977) proved unrealistic. Further changes in the decentralized system of government were impending; more manpower and other resources would be channelled downwards, to village level. The foreign exchange position improved, but productivity remained low. In October President Nyerere told government and parastatal leaders to encourage and support privately-owned small industries which produced essential commodities and thereby saved foreign exchange.

President Nyerere continued as chairman of the front-line Presidents and gave his full backing to the (Rhodesian) Patriotic Front. He gave qualified support to the Anglo-American proposals for a Rhodesian settlement and reiterated that one-man-one-vote elections should be held before independence. His disagreement with President Kaunda of Zambia on this point was reflected in a brief, but acrimonious, exchange between the newspaper editors of the two countries in late November. The Tanzanian Government denied responsibility for the collapse of the East African Community (see Pt. XI, Ch. 6). In June Mr Edward Sokoine, Prime Minister since February, told the National Assembly that the Government was still committed to its maintenance. Early the next month Mr Aboud Jumbe, the Vice-President, led a 15-man delegation to Kampala in a fruitless bid to salvage what remained of the Community. Tanzania refused to reopen its border with Kenya, closed in February.

Tanzania recognized the new Government of the Seychelles, under Mr Albert Réné, on 13 June and reinforced its close links with Mozambique: the third session of the Mozambique-Tanzania permanent commission for cooperation was held in Dar es Salaam in November. The Lutheran World Federation held its sixth assembly in Dar es Salaam in June and elected a Tanzanian, Bishop Josiah Kibira, as its president. President Nyerere made an official visit to the United States in August, as well as private visits to Canada and Jamaica. Visitors to Tanzania included the Presidents of Cuba and the Soviet Union, and the Nigerian head of state. Another visitor— M Louis de Guiringaud, the French Foreign Minister, who also visited Kenya—called off his scheduled four-day stay in Tanzania in August when 200 students at Dar es Salaam airport protested with impunity against French arms sales to South Africa and the Tanzanian Government refused to apologize.

UGANDA

In January General Mustafa Adrisi, the Defence Minister, was made Vice-President, the first to be appointed since President Amin seized power in January 1971 (see AR 1971, pp. 230-31). With the death of two Ministers the following month, none of the original Cabinet of 17 was still in office.

The Cabinet, in any case, lacked any real power and was subservient to the Defence Council. The dreaded State Research Bureau, Uganda's secret police, was an arm of the latter but was said to operate under the President's direct control.

After the discovery of a plot to assassinate President Amin in February there were reports of wholesale killings and arrests, especially of members of the Acholi and Langi tribes. Among those arrested and subsequently killed were two Cabinet Ministers and Dr Janani Luwum, the Anglican Archbishop (himself an Acholi), who had recently led the other Anglican bishops in publicly denouncing the abuse of power by the security forces. The Archbishop's murder (officially accidental death) in captivity provoked a wave of international protest, but limited action.

A number of Ugandan groups emerged in Africa, Britain and America; in November some of them merged to form, in Lusaka, the Ugandan National Movement. A prominent British-based group, the Uganda Freedom Committee, pressed the British Government to end Britain's economic links with Uganda, which accounted for some 30 per cent of Ugandan trade and bolstered an economy subject to rampant inflation and said to be tottering from mismanagement despite the high price paid for coffee, Uganda's principal export. The British Government wanted to terminate the shuttle service between Stansted airport and Entebbe but claimed that three international agreements prevented it from taking unilateral action. In June the EEC imposed selective economic sanctions against Uganda, beginning with the freezing of aid worth £6·5 million, and Britain recalled the two Foreign Office officials attached to the French embassy in Kampala (see AR 1976, p. 220). In September the NAAFI terminated its contract with the Ugandan armed forces and the following month, in the face of growing American business connexions with Uganda, a group of Congressmen urged a total American trade embargo. Though tighter visa restrictions were imposed on Ugandans wishing to enter the United States (to train as helicopter pilots, for example), the Administration's view was that, official bilateral links with Uganda having been severed, economic sanctions should be imposed through the UN. The latter's Human Rights Commission in Geneva had already received, but done nothing about, a damning report on the Amin regime by the International Commission of Jurists. The Organization of African Unity (OAU) also took no action, but the Commonwealth Conference of heads of government at its meeting in London in June issued a unanimous statement strongly critical of President Amin's rule (see Pt. XI, Ch. 2).

Within Uganda, following the death of Archbishop Luwum, four Anglican bishops and hundreds of refugees fled the country, and Dr Brian Herd, Bishop of Karamoja and the only white bishop, was deported to Britain. Several Ministers—including the former Ministers of Health, Justice and Information—sought political asylum abroad. Twenty-seven religious sects and groups, including the Salvation Army, were banned in September, and over 350 Christians were seized by the military at Masake, south-west of Kampala, early in November, after the killing of a Muslim businessman. Robert Scanlon, a British-born engineer who had become a Ugandan citizen in 1975, was arrested in June on a charge of spying and was believed to have been killed.

The Right Rev. Silvano Wani, Bishop of Madi and West Nile, was elected Anglican Archbishop in March and was enthroned in May. In the latter month Ghana suspended diplomatic relations with Uganda. President Amin negotiated with Tanzania over the moribund EAC and in November proposed that Uganda, Egypt and the Sudan should federate. In the same month the Information Ministers of 28 of the 49 member-states of the OAU met in Kampala to consider setting up a Pan-African News Agency (PANA); Kenya and Ethiopia, as well as Uganda, applied to house its headquarters.

Chapter 2

GHANA—NIGERIA—SIERRA LEONE—THE GAMBIA—LIBERIA

GHANA

THE year was dominated by debates over the proposals for a return to civilian rule put forward by the head of state and Chairman of the Supreme Military Council, General I. K. Acheampong. The notion of a 'Union Government to which everybody will belong' was first aired by Acheampong on 10 October 1976: it was given formal expression in a public speech on 10 January 1977 through the appointment of an Ad Hoc Committee on Union Government. Guidelines for the Committee, which was charged to collect and formulate views on a new form of constitution, were drawn up by Acheampong himself. They were based on two main assumptions, as the General made clear at a press conference on 14 January: (1) no party politics, since they had 'brought division, nepotism and all other evils'; (2) a mixed civilian-military form of government: 'talking about civilian rule, I do not really mean full civilian rule. There must be military-police participation if you want to see any peace and harmony in this country.'

The Ad Hoc Committee began its deliberations in Accra on 26 January and held its final meeting in Kumasi on 15 July. The chairman was Dr G. Koranteng-Addow, Attorney-General and Commissioner for Justice. The 17 members included chiefs, academics, former politicians (notably Mr Joe Appiah), two army officers and two women representatives. Their deliberations were beset with difficulties. The main proposal was not debated but endorsed, and any dissent was suppressed. On 16 March, for example, the *Pioneer* newspaper carried a report that 'Mr Daniel Kwaku Adjiraku, a private businessman, who stoutly declared he was wholly opposed to Union Government was quickly ordered by the chairman to go back to his seat. The chairman seriously remarked that his Committee was appointed to collect views and proposals for the formation of a Union Government. If, therefore, any one was against Union Government then that person could not help the Committee in its task in any way.'

The work of the Committee was also accompanied by demonstrations for and against the idea. Market women, trade unionists, Moslems and the Ghana Peace and Solidarity Council professed to be in favour; the Ghana Bar Association held an emergency meeting on 26 February and issued a statement declaring the Ad Hoc Committee to be a sham, 'unreservedly condemning the proposals for Union Government', and calling for a full return to civilian rule 'on the basis of political parties'. On 13 May, students in the three universities (Legon, Kumasi and Cape Coast) staged a mass protest against food shortages and the Union Government proposal. All three institutions were closed by the Government, reopened on 11 June, and closed once more three days later.

Many of those from whom the committee sought an opinion replied that they were not interested in constitutional reform but in the worsening economic situation. Inflation ran at over 60 per cent, imports fell drastically, a gross shortage of consumer goods emptied the shops, and food prices spiralled. A tuber of yam now cost nearly £2, yet wages were well under £40 a month. Across the Volta, in Upper and Northern Ghana, people went very hungry indeed, some to the point of starvation; but the Government refused to admit that there was any need for emergency measures. A large part of the problem lay in the Government's refusal to devalue the cedi, for which there was now a black market at almost five times its depreciated value. General Acheampong remembered, no doubt, that it was Dr Busia's 40 per cent devaluation at the end of 1971 which provoked the military's intervention on 13 January 1972; but among the effects of procrastination were the large-scale smuggling of cocoa across the border and a pervasive unrest not among Ghanaians generally but within the army itself. Rumours of attempted coups were common enough, and in June Colonel George Minyala (a former Commissioner for Industries) and Attoh Quarshie (a businessman and journalist of long standing) were detained.

Such arrests without trial brought a further quarrel between the Supreme Military Council and the Bar Association. Acheampong insisted that there were no political prisoners. Lawyers maintained that there were some 450 detainees in the maximum security prison at Nsawam and others elsewhere, of whom a number had been behind bars since the 1972 coup. On 13 December the Bar Association, through its human rights committee, obtained a writ of habeas corpus from the Accra High Court for the release of 175 of the prisoners. The Government ignored the court order, the Bar Association cited the military authorities for contempt of the High Court, and the outcome was still in doubt at the end of the year.

Meanwhile, preparations were put in hand for the return to civilian-military rule. A time-table of advance was issued with the report of the Ad Hoc Committee: a referendum to be held on 30 March 1978, a Constitutional Commission to be appointed in the last week of April and a Constituent Assembly by the end of November 1978, elections on 15 June 1979, and the 'induction into office of the new Government on 1 July 1979'. Thus launched, the ship of state entered the new year under strict orders from its military helmsman who (it was generally assumed) expected to remain on the bridge long after this voyage was safely completed.

NIGERIA

The tragic events of the previous year (see AR 1976, p. 223) were not allowed to slow down the Government's approach to a return to civilian rule in 1979. In January, elections and nominations to the new local governments were completed and a further round of national elections took place in August to choose 203 members of the new Constituent Assembly. As with the local elections, no overt political campaigning was permitted; the electorate was confined to local councillors, formed into electoral colleges. Public employees, members of the security forces, senior traditional office-holders and those found guilty of corrupt acts were barred from standing. State representation, based principally on population, ranged from 8 to 16 seats. Many seats in the northern states were uncontested but in the south there was intense competition in many areas. While those elected provided a fair cross-section of the country's ethnic groups, women and ordinary working people were under-represented. Businessmen, professional people and ex-politicians were numerous, but they included an encouraging number of younger persons. Equally encouraging was the relative absence of acrimony over the selection procedures and the final choice of representatives. The Government nominated a further 20 persons to represent various national categories, and a handful of ex-officio members was appointed as well, including the Assembly's Chairman, Justice Udoma.

Burning issues emerging from the constitutional debates were the creation of more states, the place of Muslim (Shariah) law at the federal level, freedom of the press, and the powers of the proposed head of state. Detailed discussion of the draft constitution was preceded by several weeks of general discussion of principles when the Constituent Assembly met in October. A return of political parties would have to await completion of the Assembly's deliberations, although preliminary work on the registration of an estimated electorate of 40 million commenced in the latter half of the year.

The progress towards civil rule did not prevent public criticism of the Government. There was widespread unrest in universities and schools; part of the student criticism, as expressed in the 'Kano Declaration' of the National Union of Nigerian Students, was directed at members of the military Government, who were accused of 'Gowonism'. Support for such charges was provided by frequent official exhortations to exercise probity and by the frequent dismissals and prosecution of civil servants and military personnel, which on the other hand showed the determination of the authorities to curb such dishonest behaviour. Trade unionists also clashed with the administration on a number of occasions. Restrictions on strikes did not prevent them from taking place, and the Government's decision to dismiss a number of leading trade unionists on grounds of corruption and the removal of official recognition from all save 70 of the 1,000 trade unions in the country created further conflict. The continuation of the 'wage-freeze' while inflation remained at over 20 per cent inevitably contributed to industrial unrest.

That all was not well with the economy despite the Government's impressive record of investment was indicated in the trade figures and the July Budget. Falling demand for oil on the world market and an unchecked demand for imports led to a decline in foreign reserves. The Government was also faced with an increase in the estimated cost of the third development plan from 30,000 million naira to 42,000 million. Admitting that public spending was a major source of the country's economic difficulties, the Government imposed large cuts on federal and state spending, curtailed the importation of luxury goods (notably of champagne, although in fact 41 million naira was spent on beer imports alone in 1976), and tightened currency controls. Equally revealing was the official decision to raise loans for further development through the World Bank and commercial institutions.

In other respects the performance of the economy and measures to modernize it were deemed successful. Industrial investment continued unabated and an increasing quantity of locally manufactured goods was marketed, including 54,000 motor vehicles. The international trade exhibition at Lagos in November–December saw an attempt to promote Nigerian-made industrial products, rather than raw materials and handicrafts or foreign manufactures. A new port was opened at Tin Can Island near the existing harbour at Lagos, but overcoming hold-ups in the supply of petrol would have to await the completion of a national pipe-line system. Some recovery in agricultural production was recorded but food imports continued to be a major drain on foreign reserves. The persisting effects of drought were to be seen in the virtual extinction of the groundnut trade

(Nigeria now being an importer) and a fall in the water level at the Kainji Dam, necessitating a reduction in its output of electricity. Several ambitious power and irrigation schemes were under construction but it would be some time before their benefits would be felt. The Nigerian Enterprises Promotion Decree (1977) consolidated previous legislation in this area and placed no less than 40 per cent of the equity of all business enterprises in indigenous hands.

Nigeria maintained its customary stance as a champion of black peoples and as a spokesman of the developing countries in their economic confrontation with the advanced industrial states. Numerous policy statements were made about the racialist regimes of southern Africa, and diplomatic and practical support was offered to the Rhodesian Patriotic Front, the Swapo guerrilla movement in Namibia and the black majority in South Africa. Western countries trading with South Africa or providing it with arms came in for particular censure; France was singled out for providing naval equipment and nuclear facilities as well as for its continued role in the domestic affairs of African states. Anglo-American initiatives over Rhodesia were given qualified support by the Nigerian Government and a noticeable improvement in relations with the UK and USA was detectable. A new British High Commissioner was appointed to Lagos and several official exchanges took place during the year. The new Carter Administration was given a cautious welcome and General Obasanjo's visit to Washington in October was deemed a success by both sides. President Carter's return visit to Lagos was postponed until spring 1978.

Even so, it was made clear that in future Nigeria's trading partners would have to choose between that country's still growing market and commerce with South Africa: an Economic Intelligence Unit was set up to monitor those trade links. Both at the World Conference for Action against Apartheid in Lagos and in the UN Security Council, Nigerian spokesmen urged the imposition of trade sanctions against South Africa, including a total oil embargo, for which the active and concerted support of the Arab oil-producing states would be necessary; the Nigerian view appeared to be that a number of Arab states were insufficiently active in African issues despite African support for the Arab position in the Middle East. Nigeria denied seeking to become the African continent's 'policeman'; instead the role of peacemaker was stressed, and to this purpose Lagos sought to mediate in the disputes between Libya and Chad and in the Horn of Africa. On a lighter note Nigeria, after a delay of some seven years, successfully hosted the second World Festival of Black and African Arts (FESTAC) in January, the occasion being used to reaffirm the solidarity of black peoples, including Australasians, besides presenting their cultural attainments to the world.

SIERRA LEONE

Violence in Freetown in January between student opponents of the Government and its supporters spread into the interior and necessitated a reimposition of a State of Emergency. It also helped bring forward elections planned for 1978. Promises of a fair contest did not seem borne out by the unusually high number of All People's Party (Government) candidates returned unopposed and the frequent charges of electoral irregularities and intimidation levelled by the United National Alliance, a coalition of the Sierra Leone People's Party, the Democratic National Party and the Independent candidates. In a popularly elected Parliament of 85, the 15 seats won by the SLPP were the only ones gained by the combined opposition. The Government had 51 candidates returned unopposed, eight of these being returned later in the year in the Bo constituencies where unrest had prevented elections taking place in May. By December SLPP strength in Parliament was eroded by a defection to the Government party and by the expulsion of three other MPs held in detention. Despite the questionable nature of the elections, President Siaka Stevens interpreted their result as evidence of national support for a one-party state; Western press reports of the event were condemned and blame for the disturbances was placed on the SLPP. In protest against government action, the SLPP boycotted the elections to the reconstituted Freetown city council in December. It also lent its support to a London-based opposition movement, the Association for the Restoration and Maintenance of Democracy in Sierra Leone, led by a former Governor-General, Sir Baanj Tejan-Sie, and a former army leader, Colonel Ambrose Genda.

The chronic economic difficulties of past years eased a little in response to tighter fiscal control, debt rescheduling, and an upturn in the value of sterling and commodity prices. Even so, the prospects for mineral extraction, the mainstay of the economy, remained uncertain. Assistance from the EEC and the African Development Fund enabled the Government to press forward its policies of rural development and extension of basic social services. Satisfaction continued to be expressed with the Mano River Union with neighbouring Liberia and, following the standardization of customs tariffs, plans for joint industrial development were disclosed.

THE GAMBIA

General elections were held on 4 to 5 April, resulting in a massive majority for the ruling People's Progressive Party led by the President, Sir Dawda Jawara. The Government won 27 of the 34 contested seats and the following month took another two seats in a by-election and a postponed

H

contest. The traditional opposition, the United Party, was in a state of disarray and fielded only a handful of candidates, two of whom were successful though one died immediately after the elections. Of the two new parties formed in 1975, the National Liberation Party, little more than the personal following of its leader, Pap Secka, failed badly and won no seats; on the other hand, the National Convention Party, led by former Vice-President Sherif Dibba, and itself a splinter movement from the governing party, did rather better, for its five seats now made it the effective opposition in the new legislature. The elections drew a very high turn-out but were conducted in a calm and fair manner, in contrast to those in neighbouring Sierra Leone in May. Two Ministers were defeated in the elections and a major Cabinet reshuffle took place in April. Despite criticism it was clear that the electorate preferred Sir Dawda's Administration and tended to regard the opposition forces as lacking in credibility or being sectionally motivated.

The economic situation was less satisfactory. A reappearance of Sahelian drought badly affected Gambian agriculture; cereals production fell, together with groundnut sales, and a number of emergency measures had to be taken. Successful appeals for relief assistance were made to outside powers and bodies; IMF Special Drawing Rights were called upon to help redress the trade deficit; and a range of duties were increased in the summer Budget. On a more hopeful note, the tourist trade showed an increase over the previous season despite a slow start, and considerable hopes were pinned on the publicity given The Gambia by the American book and television success, 'Roots'. Jufure, the village to which the author Alex Hayley traced his origins, was declared a 'national monument'.

Relations with Senegal also remained good, technical cooperation between the two countries being strengthened. It was indicated that the much-discussed trans-Gambian bridge would now take the form of a barrage in order to combine river control with the road crossing. Together with Guinea-Bissau, a joint appeal was made to the European Economic Community for funds to provide an inter-state highway. Road construction and planning featured prominently also in The Gambia's plans for rural development, together with an emphasis on improved yields of foodstuffs and export crops.

LIBERIA

President Tolbert, installed in 1976 for an eight-year term, continued to consolidate his economy at home and to enlarge his international contacts and reputation. In 1977 he finally broke relations with Taiwan and established them with the People's Republic of China. Nearer home he concluded six economic agreements with his powerful neighbour

Guinea, and continued to pursue good relations with his other neighbour Sierra Leone in the context of the Mano River Union.

On the economic front, although Liberia saw its earnings from iron ore reduced by poor world prices, the President was able in his budget to report that improved tax collection had meant higher revenue than in the previous year, while real gross national product had also risen, making Liberia one of the richest countries in the Third World in terms of income per head.

Chapter 3

SENEGAL—MAURITANIA—MALI—GUINEA—IVORY COAST—UPPER VOLTA—
TOGO—BENIN—NIGER—COMORO STATE—EQUATORIAL GUINEA—CHAD—
CAMEROON—GABON—CONGO—CENTRAL AFRICAN EMPIRE

SENEGAL

THE year saw a concentration on politics in preparation for the parliamentary and presidential elections due in February 1978. The tripartite multi-party system introduced by President Leopold Sedar Senghor in 1976 saw a consolidation, at least in respect of two of the three parties—the former Union Progressiste Sénégalaise, now called simply the Socialist Party, and the Parti Démocratique Sénégalaise (PDS). The third party, the Parti Africain de l'Indépendance (PAI), officially designated as the marxist-leninist party, was much less flourishing, partly because its selected leader, Mahjemout Diop, had broken from the bulk of his former followers, so that the real PAI remained in the clandestine state to which it had been consigned since 1960. An important radical grouping, the Rassemblement Démocratique Nationale (RND), led by Cheikh Anta Diop, remained unrecognized constitutionally, although permitted to exist, and a wide range of members of Senegal's hyper-active intellectual elite combined to condemn what it called 'pseudo-democracy'.

Notwithstanding these complaints, Senegal continued to enjoy a period of freedom unequalled anywhere else in francophone Africa, with a multitude of newspapers and journals, often extremely critical of the Government, selling in the streets, notably a satirical review *Le Politicien*, whose editor, Mam Less Dia, spent a month in prison charged with publishing stolen documents which incriminated a local businessman.

Economically it was a mediocre year, partly because the kind of service economy that Senegal's leaders had been trying to develop with some success had suffered in the world recession, and partly because Senegal's export earnings still depended to a great extent on groundnuts, the main crop. The summer's rains were disappointing, so that not only would export earnings be down for the 1977-78 season, but lower food production necessitated importing more foodstuffs.

MAURITANIA

The year was dominated by the war in the Western Sahara, where elements of the Front Polisario were fighting for the formerly Spanish territory, partitioned in 1976 with Spanish blessing between Morocco and Mauritania (see p. 206). The Polisario, supported by Algeria, seemed to have chosen Mauritania as the principal battleground, perhaps because its structures were more fragile than Morocco's, and therefore more vulnerable. In the summer of 1977 a general offensive was launched against Mauritania with an attack on the iron-mining site of Zouerate. Though one of the best-defended towns in the country, the Polisario were able to hold it for several hours. The result was the mass withdrawal of French technicians from the town, and the arrival of 600 Moroccan troops to protect Zouerate. Two weeks later a Morocco-Mauritania defence agreement was signed, providing for increased Moroccan military support to Mauritania and coordination of defence planning. Nonetheless Polisario kept up the military pressure, and during the OAU summit in Libreville in July (from which Polisario representatives had been excluded) there was a shell attack on the Mauritanian capital, Nouakchott, similar to that which had taken place the previous summer. The intention was to show that the guerrillas could move anywhere in Mauritania, and enjoyed a certain support among the local population.

The increasing Moroccan presence and the cost of the war (which had made Mauritania's economic situation extremely precarious) had certainly brought discontent among the local population, and in August President Moktar Ould Daddah streamlined his Government, limiting the power of the pro-Morocco lobby and promoting Colonel M'barek to be Defence Minister; this was an important concession to the army, which had grown from 1,500 to 17,000 in the two years of war. At the same time he turned increasingly to the French to counterbalance the Moroccan influence, mindful of the fact that 15 years previously Morocco had been officially claiming Mauritania as part of Greater Morocco, and that there were still important elements in Morocco who regarded the Sahara war as a useful way of entering Mauritania legitimately.

In the early 1970s Mauritania had tried to disengage from the French sphere of influence, had revised its cooperation agreements, broken its defence agreement, nationalized French mining interests and left the franc zone. In the war situation, however, the Mauritanians were obliged to go back on their tracks, and the French were drawn in willy-nilly because of the death of two Frenchmen and the kidnapping of six others during the Zouerate raid. In October it was revealed in Paris that French aircraft from the base in Dakar had been lending logistic support to the Mauritanian army (this was justified by the taking of French hostages by Polisario) and there were rumours that they had been involved in action. In the middle of December the hostages were released, apparently through the intervention of French Communist Party leader Georges Marchais during a visit to Algiers, although President Giscard d'Estaing claimed that it was due to his own tough line with the Polisario.

MALI

Although the year began encouragingly with the full panoply of a state visit by President Giscard d'Estaing (the first by a French President to an independent Mali) the regime ran into economic trouble from a new Sahelian drought, and political trouble after the death in May of the first President, Modibo Keita, from its refusing to announce the death officially or to accord him due honours. Anti-Government demonstrations at the funeral led to wide arrests and a tense political atmosphere, which set back attempts by the military Government to introduce constitutional single-party rule. The party structure, called the Union Démocratique du Peuple Malien (UDPM), remained feeble, and in some areas notional, although it was still intended to hold elections in 1979. Large-scale release of those arrested earlier, plus nearly all the supporters of the late President, before the end of the year indicated a certain return to calm, but major question-marks over the future remained.

GUINEA

This was the year of the official reconciliation between France and Guinea, already begun in the previous year. A French ambassador, in the person of M André Lewin (formerly special mediator between the two countries for the UN Secretary-General), was sent to Conakry, and Guinea's main embassy in Western Europe was moved from Rome to Paris. The reconciliation marked the end of various disputes between the two countries in the field of back payments by France to Guinean war veterans, Guinea's debts to France, and compensation for expropriations at the time of independence. President Sekou Touré had two main interests, securing investment to exploit Guinea's formidable reserves of bauxite, and neutralizing Guinean opposition groups based in France. He recognized that opposition to him still existed even within the country after a number of demonstrations in August, spearheaded by women's groups which had previously been among his most enthusiastic supporters. However, he pursued his detente with France, although a promised visit by President Giscard d'Estaing did not materialize. Some commentators suggested that the visit was being linked by the French to a parallel reconciliation with the two 'grand old men' of francophone Africa, President Senghor of Senegal and President Houphouet-Boigny of Ivory Coast. At the end of the year a number of political detainees were released.

IVORY COAST

Politically, the supremacy of President Félix Houphouet-Boigny, now aged 72, continued to make itself felt. In a far-reaching ministerial re-shuffle in July, four of the most powerful figures in the Government (and the names most frequently mentioned as successors to the 'old man') were dropped and replaced by comparative unknowns. They were the Finance Minister Konan Bedié, the Foreign Minister Assouan Usher, the Planning Minister Mohammed Diawara and the Agriculture Minister Abdoulaye Sawadogo. The changes were designed not only to show the President was still in control, but also to answer mounting domestic criticisms of inertia and corruption through the whole administration. The President followed the reshuffle with the announcement that he was presenting all his own estates to the nation.

Economically it was an encouraging year, with the country well placed to take advantage from the world boom in coffee prices, and every sign that the impact of the world economic recession had been mastered. Near the end of the year, too, it was announced that offshore oil had been discovered in commercial quantities.

UPPER VOLTA

Faced with a continuing disappointing economic situation, and growing signs of political and social unrest, Upper Volta's military rulers per-severed with their plans for a return to civilian rule, although the pro-gramme took longer than had been originally foreseen. A referendum on a new constitution providing for civilian government in six months was eventually held on 28 November with the participation of seven political parties. The constitution was approved by 69·9 per cent of voters and 98·7 per cent of votes cast.

TOGO

This was another year of poor relations with Ghana, due to smuggling and the activities of Togo-based supporters of secession in Ghana's Volta region, which often seemed to have official Togolese support. However, in November measures reinforcing border controls were announced. This coincided with the revelation of a plot to assassinate President Eyadema, using British mercenaries. It was stated that friendly Governments tipped off the Togolese authorities; one of these was apparently the British Government itself.

BENIN

The year 1977 began dramatically with a bizarre attempted invasion of Cotonou by a group of 'mercenaries' of mixed nationality who arrived by air early on the morning of Sunday 16 January. Despite investigations by teams from both the UN and the OAU, many mysteries about the invasion remained. A captured Guinean participant told an outlandish tale of training camps in Morocco, implicating Togo, Gabon and France (in particular a French security officer working in Libreville). This led to a serious row at the OAU Ministers' meeting in Lomé in February, and a boycotting by Benin of the OAU Libreville summit in July. Enigma remained as to how much local resistance there was to the attack, since the half-dozen or so deaths were of local civilians, and as to what had made the invaders withdraw in the aircraft in which they had come. There were widespread reports of arrests and purges after the event, but no members of the Government or leading members of the regime were affected. The instigator of the operation was reported to be the former Benin ambassador in Brussels, Gratien Pognon, and it was widely believed that it failed because a fifth column inside the country, including presumably some elements of the army, failed to appear.

The invasion was followed by a period of intense witch-hunting, and by popular mobilization, a People's Militia being formed by the ruling party to assist the army in resisting any future such attempted coups. A new marxist-leninist constitution was promulgated in May, establishing a revolutionary popular dictatorship, but retaining certain rights to private property.

NIGER

The drought which wrought such havoc in 1973 struck again, with not quite such intensity but nevertheless provoking concern about what would happen when the effects were really felt in 1978. Revenue from uranium (of which Niger was the largest producer in black Africa) continued to rise, and France, the principal importer, continued to watch political developments closely. President Seyni Kountché seemed firmly in control, although unable to release the man he overthrew, Hamani Diori, despite campaigns by Diori's many friends in Europe. Kountché's main military rival, former Vice-President Major Sani Sido, died in prison in Agades in July.

COMORO STATE

The isolation of the Comoro Islands (now renamed 'The Comoro State') from the mainstream of former French colonies continued to grow worse, since the dispute with France over the continued French presence on the island of Mayotte, which the Comorians claimed, remained unresolved. The matter was discussed at the OAU (a committee on Mayotte already existed) and at the UN General Assembly, but the French continued to base their arguments on the 1976 referendum in Mayotte in favour of staying with France.

In the meantime the withdrawal of all French personnel as well as aid and technical assistance continued to have a disadvantageous effect on the Comorian economy. Its health was not aided by the decision of President Ali Soilih to burn all the French colonial records and sack a large number of Comorian civil servants and replace them with 'untainted' teenagers. An attempt to overthrow Soilih's Government in the autumn led to demonstrations in the capital, Moroni, of solidarity from other islands.

EQUATORIAL GUINEA

The little-known but nonetheless deplorable regime of President Francisco Macias Nguena continued its unpalatable, unpublicized way. The country's former colonizer, Spain, suspended relations in March because of a 'slanderous attack' on Spain by Macias. Spanish aid in education and air transport continued for humanitarian reasons, and the Equatorial Guinea ambassador in Madrid remained at his post. The only remaining Western embassy was that of France, which had important business interests. Apparent Soviet influence was counterbalanced during the year by President Macias's long visit to China.

CHAD

In January Mme Françoise Claustre, the French archaeologist, and her husband Pierre were released from captivity by a group of rebels in Northern Chad. She had been held since her kidnapping in April 1974, he since the summer of 1975 when he went on an ill-fated rescue bid. The release appeared to have been made possible by the replacement, as head of the Toubou rebel group holding her, of Hissène Habre by Goukouny Oueddei, eldest son of the Derde, traditional ruler of the Toubou. Goukouny had been for some time a protégé of the Libyan leader Colonel Qadafi, who then intervened to claim maximum credit for himself. It appeared that the two prisoners were in Tripoli for a couple of weeks before their release was actually announced. Some observers related this delay to pressure being put on France at the same time by Arab leaders to release the Palestinian Abu Daoud.

The intervention of the Libyan leader, whose relations with France had always been fairly good, did not lead to any relaxation of his support for the rebellion in Chad. This retained its characteristic confusion, due to the many factions, most of which related loosely to the Frolinat movement (Chad National Liberation Front). In March Frolinat's 'Vulcan Force' in the north-eastern province of Ennedi suffered a setback with the death, in a car-crash in Libya, of General Barglani, its commander, who had been one of Frolinat's original founders, an event which led most of his followers to accept the leadership of Goukouny. At the same time there were reports that Abba Siddick, who at one time had pretensions to lead Frolinat, had moved from Algiers to Khartoum and was negotiating with the Government of President Malloum, although by the end of the year this had come to nothing.

In June the Libyan-based elements started a new offensive in the north, where Libyan troops had already occupied a 100 km strip of Chadian territory. The Malloum Government appealed for international assistance, and took the issue to the OAU summit, where a mediation committee was set up. At the same time it was announced that French aircraft had provided some logistic support for the Chad troops fighting the rebels, and there were reports of increased French military technical assistance. There was no doubt that by the end of the year the situation was still serious, Frolinat being perhaps better coordinated and supplied than ever before, and large tracts of territory being out of the control of the Ndjamena authorities, including even garrisons such as Aouzou and Bazdai in the far north.

CAMEROON

After the strikes and social unrest of 1976, this was a quiet year, concentrating on economic development and consolidating national unity.

GABON

Much of the year was concentrated on foreign policy questions, as President Oumar Bongo became chairman of the OAU in July (see Pt. XI,

H*

Ch. 6). This involved extensive travel and a number of mediation attempts (Chad-Libya, Sahara). The OAU summit itself had entailed considerable prestige expenditure, and although Gabon was an oil producer it became increasingly clear during the year that the period of vast surpluses was tailing off, and that Gabon was in for a period of belt-tightening.

CONGO

On 18 March President Marien Ngouabi was assassinated, during the penetration of the presidential compound by an armed commando raid led by an ex-army captain called Kikadidi, who subsequently disappeared. The assassination created an extremely tense atmosphere, and the next day the widely-esteemed Archbishop of Brazzaville, Cardinal Emile Biayenda, was killed by members of Ngouabi's own family, apparently as a revenge killing because the Cardinal had called on Ngouabi shortly before the assassination. Then the former President Alphonse Massemba-Debat, whom Ngouabi had ousted in 1968, was tried for masterminding the killing and was shot within 48 hours (see OBITUARY). Behind the brutal reprisals it was possible to detect the old ethnic animosities that had occasionally riven the Congo in the past, but had tended to go under the surface after the 1963 revolution—both Biayenda and Massemba-Debat were from the southern Bakongo grouping, about 40 per cent of the population, while Ngouabi, like most of the army, was a northerner.

That all was not as simple as it looked, however, became clear when it emerged that the man who actually shot Ngouabi was a northerner called Raphael Ontsou, from his own security entourage, who had allegedly been suborned by the plotters. The assassination also triggered a struggle for power between two northerners within the ruling military junta, in which the front runner, Major Sasso-Nguesso, a former head of Security, was defeated by Colonel Yhombi-Opango, the most senior army officer, who enjoyed considerable prestige with the rank and file. It took two weeks for the name of the new head of state to be announced. Less of an ideologue than Ngouabi, Yhombi-Opango immediately started mending international fences—reopening diplomatic relations with the US and visiting Paris to secure a deal over compensation for the closed potash mine at Holle. Later in the year he seemed increasingly caught in the same toils as Ngouabi, a top-heavy and avaricious bureaucracy, a determinedly left-leaning intelligentsia and an ailing economy, made worse by disappointing oil revenues. The expulsion of several hundred West Africans accused of currency offences was thus symptomatic of a certain general malaise.

CENTRAL AFRICAN EMPIRE

The dominating event of the year was the coronation of Emperor Bokassa the First by himself at the imperial court of Berengo before 3,500 guests. He also crowned his wife as Empress Catherine. Apart from the piquant details (the gold crown with 2,000 diamonds in it, the giant eagle-shaped throne, the open coach with six dapple-grey horses imported from Normandy, the intentional pastiche of Napoleon's coronation) the main interest of the affair was the caustic international reaction to an event reputed to have cost as much as $30 million, or one-fifth of national income. No head of state attended, and even many African states failed to send any representatives. Press commentary was universally hostile or at least sadly satirical. The United States announced that it would phase out its aid programme to the CAE, accusing the Emperor of human rights violations. Much of the cost of the event was reputedly born by France, which had a powerful sphere of influence in the CAE, as well as an interest in exploiting its considerable reserves of uranium.

VII CENTRAL AND SOUTHERN AFRICA

Chapter 1

THE REPUBLIC OF ZAÏRE—RWANDA AND BURUNDI—GUINEA-BISSAU AND
CAPE VERDE—SÃO TOME AND PRINCIPE—MOZAMBIQUE—ANGOLA

THE REPUBLIC OF ZAÏRE

THE year brought the strongest challenge yet to the already badly shaken regime of President Mobutu, and to the unity of this huge and ethnically fragmented country. Relations with Belgium were once more improving, and the President visited Brussels in January. Yet there was no alleviation of the economic crisis, dating from the 1974 collapse of copper prices, which had been aggravated by erratic policies of Zaïreanization. Inflation roaring at 30-50 per cent, increasing food shortages and gross corruption in the top-heavy bureaucracy fed popular discontent. Above all, the President still faced the explosive consequences of having backed the wrong side in the Angolan civil war. On 6 January Zaïre formally recognized the Angolan Government and agreed with it upon an exchange of ambassadors, but guerrillas of the defeated Front for the National Liberation of Angola (FNLA) remained under arms on Zaïrean soil and were alleged in February to have carried out raids into northern Angola and the oil-rich Cabinda Enclave.

With the collapse of Katanga's secession in 1964, elements of the provincial gendarmerie had withdrawn into Angola, where they had successively served the colonial and independent governments. On 8 March this force, some 2,000 strong, was permitted to launch an invasion of Shaba (the former Katanga), in the name of General Mbumba's Congo National Liberation Front. Probably intended by Angola as no more than a diversion, this attack met with quite unexpected success. The demoralized Zaïrean army offered little resistance and within three weeks the Katangese were closing in on Kolwezi, the western headquarters of the copper industry, more than 200 miles beyond the frontier. It was admitted that the invaders had sympathizers in high places and were in touch with the still unsubmitted rebels in Kivu province. Diplomatic relations with Cuba were suspended on 4 April and with East Germany on 2 May, on the grounds of their alleged complicity. Angola and Cuba continued to deny direct involvement, but the danger to the wider peace of the region was apparent.

Despite the successes claimed for pygmy irregulars, armed with poisoned arrows, the regime appeared to be crumbling from within. President Mobutu was obliged to deny rumours of his impending resignation and to appeal to friendly powers for assistance. More or less active gestures of support were obtained from Belgium, Egypt (which lent a number of pilots), Sudan, Uganda, the Central African Empire, Togo and China. The United States backed Nigerian efforts at mediation. The day was saved, however, by King Hassan of Morocco who, with the loan of French transport planes, dispatched 1,500 veteran troops to the threatened province between 7 and 10 April (a move which had the approval of Sir Seewoosagur Ramgoolam, the Prime Minister of Mauritius and current chairman of the OAU). The Katangan threat then melted away without serious fighting. Government forces, stiffened by the Moroccans, recaptured the important railway town of Mutshatsha on 25 April. On 21 May they regained the border town of Dilolo, the original invasion point; Kapanga, the last town held by the insurgents, fell on 26 May.

The immediate crisis was over. Its gravity, and the extent of the incompetence and disaffection which it had revealed, could be measured by the subsequent reactions of the Government. There was a drastic purge of high-ranking army officers, and the President, who already held the portfolios of National Defence and Security, assumed personal responsibility for the general staff. A major restructuring of government, under which two Vice-Presidents were each to assume overall responsibility for a large group of ministries, had taken place in February, but now, at the beginning of July, gave way to far more sweeping reform. Zaïre, while remaining a one-party state, was to embark on a process of democratization at every level of government. Open elections were to be held for local councils, the 270 seats of the National Assembly and the majority of places in the Political Bureau of the single party, the People's Revolutionary Movement. Meanwhile the new office of First Commissioner— i.e., Prime Minister—in a caretaker Government was allotted to Mr Mpinga, a former professor of political science.

In August the Foreign Minister, Mr Nguza, and the Mwata Yamvo, paramount chief of the Lunda tribe to which most of the Katangese force belonged, were arrested on treason charges related to the invasion. The death sentence passed upon the former in September was commuted to life imprisonment; the latter was wisely granted clemency and placed on probation.

The promised elections took place from 8 to 23 October. They brought many new faces to the Assembly, but no major changes to the top leadership. The President was confirmed in office for a further seven-year term. His meeting with President Giscard d'Estaing in Paris in October was followed by a visit to Kinshasa by M Galley, the French Minister of Development. At the party congress in November the President again attacked corruption and recalled his decision to decentralize the economy.

Zaïre's international position remained precarious. President Mobutu was still giving covert support to the dissident factions in Angola and complaining of intrigues against his regime directed from Algeria, Angola and Mozambique. Further elements in a threatening situation were the emergence in Brussels in September of a new opposition Party for the National Conscience, founded by Mr Mbawo-Mpyp, and the revelation that a West German firm had established an experimental rocket-firing range in Shaba. The country's chronic indebtedness was another problem. Zaïre did well until the summer with payments into its account with the Bank for International Settlements, but thereafter again fell behind in both interest and amortization payments. Zaïre's major creditors agreed in November to reschedule debts of more than $2 million.

RWANDA AND BURUNDI

In January the Supreme Revolutionary Council of Burundi fixed the mandate of President Bagaza at five years, after which time it was planned to return to civilian rule. President Bagaza visited Saudi Arabia in November.

President Habyalimana of Rwanda served as the chairman of OCAM, and visited Gabon in April. He received a notably warm welcome when he visited Dar es Salaam in July to negotiate the permanent settlement in Tanzania of the numerous Rwandan refugees who had fled there from the tribal conflicts of recent years. The announcement of plans to develop a road, and perhaps a rail, link between the two countries evoked threatening noises from President Amin of Uganda. There was also to be a feasibility study of a hydro-electric dam at Rusumo falls which would supply both countries.

Both Presidents met Mr Andrew Young at Zanzibar in February, and both countries were represented at the Franco-African summit conference at Dakar in April. In October it was announced that Burundi was to receive $2·9 million and Rwanda $5·6 million from the European Development Fund.

GUINEA-BISSAU AND CAPE VERDE

Since independence it had been the declared policy of the Party for the Independence of Guinea and Cape Verde (PAIGC), which was the single recognized party in both countries, to work for an early union between them. In January President Pereira of Cape Verde, in his capacity as secretary-general of the party, presided over the inauguration in Bissau of the Guinea-Bissau–Cape Verde Unity Council, which was described as a major step to this end.

After elections in Guinea-Bissau in February Mr Luis Cabral was re-elected by the National Assembly on 18 March to a further four-year term as President of the Council of State. Some minor governmental changes followed, but the Prime Minister, Mr Mendes, and other leading Ministers retained their offices. There were signs, however, both of clandestine opposition to the regime and of personal and policy differences within the leadership. The pragmatists were evenly balanced by the hard-line marxists, who disliked the Government's policy of decentralization and concentration on agricultural improvements, and these disagreements were aggravated by jealousy of the prominence in Guinea-Bissau of such Cape Verdeans as President Cabral and Mr Mendes. On 3 March Mr Rafael Barbosa, a former president of the party's Central Committee, was pronounced guilty of treason, the death sentence being subsequently commuted to one of 15 years' imprisonment.

It was no doubt the factional struggle behind the scenes which led to the postponement until November of the first party conference since independence, originally scheduled for July. When it finally met it sounded a significant note of caution against over-precipitate moves towards unification of the two territories, which was now presented as a long-term goal. The conference re-elected President Pereira and President Cabral secretary-general and assistant secretary-general respectively, and approved a policy of 'non-involvement with ideological blocs'. Radical reforms were proposed in the party structure to transform it from a mass liberation movement into an ideological 'vanguard' party. Changes in the Central Committee redressed the balance of representation in favour of Cape Verde.

There had been a certain cooling of relations with the Soviet Union since independence—the Russians had been over-fishing Guinean waters— and a measure of rapprochement with France and Senegal. Both Guinea-Bissau and Cape Verde were represented at the Franco-African summit in Dakar in April. An agreement for educational cooperation between Cape Verde and Senegal was concluded in June; Cape Verde was admitted to membership of ECOWAS in September. Guinea-Bissau received development aid from the UK (£1 million), Sweden ($10 million), the Netherlands ($8 million), and the European Development Fund ($8 million for harbour improvements). The first Catholic Archbishop of Bissau, an Italian Franciscan, was installed in June.

SÃO TOME AND PRINCIPE

Improved production on the nationalized cocoa plantations still failed to reach pre-independence levels, and the islands' dependence on food imports made the diversification of agriculture an urgent priority. The non-aligned Government of President Pinto da Costa welcomed aid from any quarter—doctors from Cuba and Romania, agricultural advisers from France and North Korea.

MOZAMBIQUE

The country's desperate domestic problems were compounded and overshadowed by the confrontation with Rhodesia. As the most actively engaged of the 'front-line' states, Mozambique continued to be the focus of much international attention.

The third conference of the ruling party, the Front for the Liberation of Mozambique (Frelimo), was held in Maputo from 3 to 7 February and attended by fraternal delegates from the USSR, Cuba, East Germany, the Palestine Liberation Organization and Tanzania as well as all the lusophone African states. President Machel, re-elected as party president, strengthened his hold on its secretariat and defined its future role as that of a militant marxist-leninist elite, dedicated to the promotion of 'scientific socialism' and 'democratic centralism'. Increased agricultural production was to be the immediate economic priority, but long-term hopes were to be placed in the development of heavy industry.

President Castro's visit of 21 to 23 March was followed on 29 March by President Podgorny's historic progress and the conclusion of a treaty of friendship and cooperation with the Soviet Union. As the year progressed, however, there were indications that the Government, which received considerable military aid from China, was seeking to maintain a genuinely non-aligned stance and to achieve a *modus vivendi* with South Africa. In October President Machel visited Cuba, where he concluded a 20-year treaty of friendship—there were already a thousand Mozambican students in Cuban schools: but he then went on to New York where his meeting with President Carter was said to have inaugurated 'a new era' in the relations between their two countries.

The decision in March to expel all Mozambicans who had opted for Portuguese nationality at independence, together with the impending departure of many Portuguese on short-term contracts, aggravated the already desperate shortage of skilled manpower and necessitated a two-year shortening of high-school courses and the labour direction of all school-leavers. On 10 March a limited amnesty was announced for certain categories of offenders, but large numbers of the politically 'unreliable' remained in detention, and in April the Archbishop of Maputo, on behalf of all the bishops, protested against the conditions in the so-called 're-education camps'.

It had meanwhile become clear that all was not well in the northern provinces of Niassa and Tete when a number of senior army officers and political commissars were arrested in March on charges of corruption and abuse of power. In May there were reports of rebellion among the Makonde of this region, and of guerrilla activity by the United Democratic Front of Mozambique (FUMO).

The choice of Maputo as the venue for the UN conference of 16 to 21 May on the crisis in Southern Africa was a recognition that the country was the most seriously involved of Rhodesia's neighbours. The Rhodesian Government's hopes of an acceptable settlement greatly depended on its demonstrable ability to contain the guerrillas of Mr Mugabe's Zimbabwe African National Liberation Army (ZANLA), whose activities were largely directed from bases in Mozambique. It was alleged that Rhodesia's policy of 'hot pursuit' had entailed more than 70 violations of Mozambique's frontier since the beginning of the year.

The more hopeful mood which had seemed to be developing with the visit of the Anglo-American conciliation mission was shattered when the Rhodesians launched their biggest raid so far on 29 May, the very day on which that mission left Salisbury for Maputo. A strong force of Rhodesian commandos with air support overran four guerrilla camps with little resistance and occupied their base at Mapai, in the north-western corner of Gaza province, more than 50 miles beyond the frontier. They withdrew on 2 June, virtually unopposed according to their own account, having captured large quantities of war material. This attack and reports of lesser raids in Manica and Tete provinces aroused widespread indignation in Africa and were immediately condemned by Britain, the USA, the Soviet Union and the OAU. On 30 June the Security Council called on all UN members to lend assistance to Mozambique's defence against Rhodesian aggression. A UN mission which visited the country in July reported that Rhodesian raids had inflicted great loss of life and that $87 million of aid would be needed to make good the destruction they had caused.

Hostile world opinion did not, however, deter Rhodesia from a still heavier raid on 23 to 24 November, when an airborne force destroyed the operational headquarters of ZANLA, ten miles north of Chimoio. A similar attack upon another camp at Tembue, 140 miles beyond the frontier, followed on 26 November, and the Rhodesians were able to claim, at a crucial stage in the internal talks, that they had destroyed the guerrilla's capacity for an early offensive. There were reliable reports of heavy civilian casualties.

Severe import restrictions had failed to halt the deterioration of the unfavourable balance of trade, and on 5 November the Government took control of all foreign exchange operations and payments abroad to prevent further 'sabotage in the financial sector'.

On 28 November the President opened the first National Youth Conference in Maputo and announced the formation of the Organization of Mozambique Youth, which was to take the forefront of the class struggle. The first elections since independence began on 25 September with those for local councils; district councils were elected in November, and the National People's Assembly in the first week of December.

Mozambique was to receive loans of £15 million from Britain under an agreement for economic cooperation concluded in July, and Britain also contributed 5,000 tons of wheat as part of the EEC's aid programme. In August the Nordic Council of Ministers approved a joint grant of 265 million Norwegian krone for agricultural development over the next two years.

Floods in February caused 'catastrophic' damage to crops in the fertile Limpopo valley. In August the country's worst-ever mining disaster at Moatize cost 150 lives.

ANGOLA

The first Portuguese ambassador to Angola was appointed in January, and diplomatic relations were established with France. Armed opposition remained a serious threat to the Government of the Popular Movement for the Liberation of Angola (MPLA). Despite President Mobutu's assurances, there were fears of an invasion from Zaïre by the forces of Mr Roberto's Front for the National Liberation of Angola (FNLA). More immediately dangerous were the guerrilla operations in the central and southern provinces mounted by Mr Savimbi's National Movement for the Total Liberation of Angola (Unita). Increasingly well-equipped with captured weapons and enjoying the support of South Africa and much sympathy from the local populations, the guerrillas faced the Government with a difficult problem in the early weeks of the year, especially through their ability to disrupt traffic on the vital Benguela railway. In March government troops, with Cuban support, mounted offensives against the guerrillas in Huila, Cunene and Cuando-Cubango, but all three bogged down in the heavy rains. Unita bands continued to dominate the south-east, and were said to be tying down 16,000 or more Cuban troops. Their attacks on communications and occupation of rich agricultural areas were causing severe food shortages in the towns, while each side accused the other of terrorism directed against the civilian population.

Meanwhile the Katangan invasion of Shaba, with whatever degree of Angolan connivance, had heightened tension in relations with Zaïre. Angola insisted on the purely internal character of the rebellion, denied that its own or Cuban forces were involved and regretted outside interference in favour of the Mobutu Government. On 23 March President Castro arrived in Luanda and on 29 March joined with President Neto and Foreign Minister Jorge in separate conversations with Mr Tambo of the (South) African National Congress and Mr Nkomo of the Zimbabwe Patriotic Front. As a gesture of solidarity with Angola and in reply to outside support for Zaïre, the 'front-line' states transferred their Rhodesian summit meeting from Dar es Salaam to Luanda, where it was held on 17 to 18 April.

On 27 May an attempted coup in the capital was led by Mr Nito Alves, a former Minister of the Administration, who had been expelled from the Central Committee of the party six days earlier, and was at least suspected of contacts with Unita. There was fierce fighting with heavy casualties as the rebels, who at one moment held the radio station, tried to storm the presidential palace and other public buildings. Repelled by Cuban troops and Soviet tanks, they held out for several days in the suburban townships, controlled by the popular militia loyal to Mr Alves. By 31 May the rising had been suppressed and its leaders had gone into hiding. (Mr Alves was eventually arrested in July.) A number of senior officers and at least ten members of the Government, including Mr Mingas, the Finance Minister, had been murdered by the rebels. The true inwardness of these violent events had not emerged by the year's end. The coup appeared to be the work of maoist extremists, who resented the dominance of mulattoes in the Government and the growing Cuban presence at every level of administration. It remained difficult to evaluate the paradoxical report that it had been promoted by Moscow.

The subsequent massive purge revealed the gravity of the rift in the ruling party, which extended far beyond the capital. The many hundreds arrested included several Portuguese marxists. President Neto's powers to appoint and dismiss Ministers were increased by the Central Committee of the MPLA, but he was now more dependent than ever upon Cuban and Soviet support. From 23 to 26 August he visited Havana and obtained a further reinforcement of Cuban troops and technical personnel; his talks in Moscow with Soviet leaders in mid-October led to a new agreement for economic and technical aid and the dispatch of a Soviet trade delegation to Luanda.

There were now said to be more than 20,000 Cubans in the country, and General Valdes, one of Cuba's Vice-Presidents, visited Luanda in November. There was little improvement, however, in the general security position. A government offensive in September and October recaptured Cuangar and a number of smaller towns near the Namibian border which had been lost to Unita earlier in the year. Unita seemed now to moderate its demands. Its spokesman, who had earlier rejected all idea of negotiations with Mr Neto, was talking in November of its readiness to share power with MPLA after a Cuban withdrawal.

Its guerrillas, however, continued to be widely active in the southern provinces, and after the transfer of many Cuban troops to Ethiopia gained new successes with their hit-and-run tactics. In December they claimed responsibility for a number of bomb explosions in Lobito and the destruction of a Cuban garrison and hydro-electric installations at Bie. Though relatively quiescent, the FNLA also retained a footing in some areas near the north-eastern frontier, which became the object of a major government drive in the last weeks of the year. The Cabinda Enclave, too, had been the scene of sporadic fighting throughout the year. The dissident Front for the Liberation of the Cabinda Enclave was weakened by its own internal divisions, but claimed to control two-thirds of the territory. The Government continued to complain of frontier violations by both South Africa and Zaïre.

The economic situation was grim indeed, with a chronic shortage of foreign exchange and a drop of 65 per cent in industrial production. In August the Government took majority control of the giant Diamang Diamond Company. In November it was announced that Britain and Angola had agreed to establish diplomatic relations at ambassadorial level. The MPLA congress which opened in Luanda on 4 December re-elected President Neto and all the members of the Political Bureau and reaffirmed the party's doctrinal orthodoxy. All private medical practice was abolished and compulsory military training introduced for all men and women between the ages of 18 and 35.

Chapter 2

ZAMBIA—MALAWI—RHODESIA—BOTSWANA—LESOTHO—SWAZILAND

ZAMBIA

SEEMINGLY insoluble problems confronted the Government of President Kenneth Kaunda amidst deepening economic crisis at home and continuing tensions in southern Africa. With popular support at a low ebb, Zambia's one-party state faced crucial elections in 1978.

Export markets suffered persisting stagnation in demand for copper, normally the source of over 90 per cent of Zambia's foreign exchange earnings and over half the Government's revenue. As production costs rose, imports of essential mining materials consumed two-thirds of the foreign exchange earned. The mines made heavy losses and contributed little public revenue. Despite expenditure cutbacks, the Budget again recorded a substantial deficit; further borrowing requirements raised the spectre of long-term debt burdens. Though the new Tanzam railway helped ease pressures on external trade arteries, stringent import controls caused widespread shortages of basic household goods, boosted inflation, disrupted industrial production and increased unemployment. In November Kaunda told British journalists: 'If we don't take action, we will perish. We will collapse as a nation.'

The regime responded to the crisis in part by re-ordering priorities among existing policy goals, while also moderating its commitment to socialist objectives. Encouragement was given to both foreign and local private investors. The Budget eased controls on profit remittances abroad.

The new Industrial Development Act provided more attractive investment guidelines, while the Finance Minister stressed that Zambia accepted a mixed economy and would avoid further nationalization.

Calling the National Assembly into emergency session in October, the President outlined an ambitious strategy to end Zambia's dependence on copper, emphasizing the diversification of mineral production, a rationalization of the copper industry, and the rapid development of agriculture as an alternative export base. He warned that the emergency powers invoked because of the Rhodesia crisis would be retained 'to attack economic insecurity'. Redundant civil servants would be 'redirected' to the land to provide manpower for rural reconstruction, as would also the urban unemployed.

In a subsequent report on these proposals, a parliamentary select committee backed his programme (except over compulsory redirection of civil servants into agriculture), but went further in recommending the abolition of free schooling and medical services, an end to consumer subsidies, and expenditure cutbacks in defence and the social services. It also called for fewer political personnel on public salaries, the elimination of wasteful duplication of roles between the party and state organizations, and a somewhat reduced status for the Central Committee of the ruling United National Independence Party (UNIP).

While the pending national elections spurred factional manoeuvring within UNIP and added rancour to public debate, the regime also faced rising popular dissatisfaction over its performance. Labour militancy increased; so did student discontent. At a Copperbelt by-election in March a white businessman overwhelmed two black opponents on a sparse poll—an outcome seen as reflecting public frustrations. Key local party elections in August unexpectedly produced little response; many offices went unopposed or unfilled. Following poor turnouts in the 1973 general and 1975 local elections, there was concern that another low poll could destroy the one-party state's credibility, but President Kaunda ruled out postponing the 1978 elections.

Marked turnover at Cabinet and other levels indicated both factional tensions and pre-election concern over the Government's declining support. Three Ministers were sacked in April, two for links with supporters of the banned United Progressive Party (UPP). The Prime Minister, Elijah Mudenda, was dismissed in July over recurring food shortages on the Copperbelt, and replaced by Mainza Chona, Prime Minister from 1973 until his surprise resignation in 1975. August brought the suspension of Aaron Milner, Home Affairs Minister and close presidential associate, over alleged corruption. In September Simon Kapwepwe and four former UPP colleagues agreed to rejoin UNIP. Kapwepwe, once Zambia's Vice-President and a formidable Bemba and Copperbelt politician, left UNIP in 1971 to lead the UPP.

Externally, Zambia continued its involvement in the search for a constitutional settlement in Rhodesia. Early in January, in the aftermath of the adjourned Geneva conference, Zambia and its 'front-line' partners—Tanzania, Mozambique, Botswana and Angola—pledged exclusive support to the Patriotic Front alliance between the two externally-based African groups, Joshua Nkomo's ZAPU and Robert Mugabe's ZANU. The decision in effect denied recognition to the more moderate, internally-based organizations, including Bishop Abel Muzorewa's UANC, with which Zambia had already suspended relations.

Mr Smith's rejection on 24 January of British compromise proposals brought Zambian warnings of intensified guerrilla pressures, and evidence of a rapid build-up of ZAPU forces in Zambia. On 16 May, after a Rhodesian diplomatic note threatened pre-emptive strikes against ZAPU bases should a guerrilla offensive be launched, Kaunda declared a 'state of war', sharply rebuking the British Foreign Secretary, Dr David Owen, for transmitting Smith's message.

Thereafter numerous shooting incidents disturbed the Zambezi River frontier, some serious; the respective roles of ZAPU, Zambian and Rhodesian forces were often unclear. In early June Rhodesia made, then withdrew, a threat to refuse Zambia electricity from its Kariba Dam facilities, apparently not realizing initially that Zambia had recently achieved self-sufficiency in power. When Rhodesian planes bombed Zambian troops at Feira on 31 August, Kaunda imposed a 17-day curfew and blackout on four towns, including Lusaka.

Boosting Zambia's role in Southern Africa, and overlooking its formerly strident opposition to Russian and Cuban involvement in Angola, Nikolai Podgorny, the Soviet President, visited Zambia in March. Despite Angolan complicity in the spring fighting in Zaïre's neighbouring Shaba province, Zambia strengthened links with the MPLA regime; ZAPU guerrillas were reported to be training in both countries. At the June Commonwealth Conference in London, Kaunda supported Britain over condemnation of Amin's Ugandan dictatorship but pressed for tougher measures against Rhodesia. His role was crucial in persuading the July OAU summit to recognize the Patriotic Front as sole Rhodesian liberation movement. The same month he warned that Zambia had accepted Cuban and Somali military aid in principle, and might seek troops from unspecified countries.

Zambia's most potent diplomatic weapon proved oil. With documentation provided by 'Tiny' Rowland, chairman of Lonrho, Kaunda accused Western oil companies of violating UN sanctions by supplying Rhodesia with fuel via South African subsidiaries. Zambia's announcement in April that it intended legal action helped prompt an official British inquiry; Kaunda was also instrumental in mobilizing Commonwealth and OAU concern. In August proceedings commenced in Zambia against 17 oil firms. Alleging conspiracy to deprive Zambia of fuel in 1965 in order to bolster Rhodesia's pre-UDI oil stocks, and continuing sanctions violations, Zambia demanded damages of £4,000 million; Shell and British Petroleum rejected their writs in November.

When the new Anglo-American plan for Rhodesia was unveiled on 1 September, Zambia gave only qualified endorsement. The disclosure of Smith's secret visit to Lusaka on 25 September exposed divisions within the Patriotic Front. Though Zambia dismissed the mission as having lacked fresh Rhodesian proposals on the Anglo-American scheme, Mugabe, the ZANU leader, accused Kaunda of dissembling over the meeting's purpose and Nkomo's actual presence.

In late October, Kaunda and Nkomo demanded a direct handover of power by Smith's Government to the Patriotic Front, with elections delayed until several years after Rhodesia's independence to forestall civil war should these be won by Muzorewa's UANC, as Zambian spokesmen privately admitted was likely. However, having checked the Anglo-American initiative's momentum, helped widen the Front's internal disagreements, and provoked opposition from its 'front-line' partners (notably Tanzania), Zambia quickly found itself isolated. On 6 December Kaunda angrily withdrew from further participation in the initiative, ostensibly over an 'insensitive' statement by the British Foreign Secretary regarding a recent Rhodesian raid into Mozambique (see pp. 241 and 251).

MALAWI

Malawi's economy achieved a 5 per cent growth in 1976-77, revealing considerable resilience in view of inflationary pressures, recession in Western export markets, an unstable southern African arena and the disruption to trade links caused by the Mozambique-Rhodesia border closure in March 1976. As in the previous year, agriculture underpinned economic expansion. To strengthen foreign exchange reserves and counter slowing industrial growth, labour recruitment for South African mines was quietly restarted in June. However, only 20,000 Malawians were expected to be needed, against the 130,000 employed there in April 1974, when Malawi banned further recruitment.

For plotting to assassinate Dr Kamuzu Banda, Malawi's Life President, a traditional court in Blantyre sentenced two prominent figures to death in February—Focus Martin Gwede, former head of the political police, and Albert Muwalo Nqumayo, a former Cabinet Minister and secretary-general of the ruling Malawi Congress Party, once considered second in influence only to the President. The official media also accused the two of responsibility for numerous illegal arrests since 1973; subsequently Banda freed most of Malawi's estimated 2,000 political prisoners and most of the Jehovah's Witnesses arrested in 1975-76.

Undoubtedly the President sought to refurbish his regime's image abroad and bolster support internally. Yet Nqumayo's downfall left questions regarding Banda's own role in silencing public dissent, while emphasizing, as had Aleke Banda's dismissal from public life in 1973, both his continuing political predominance and his sensitivity to the emergence of either rivals or heirs apparent.

RHODESIA

The year in Rhodesia was dominated more than ever before by the worsening guerrilla war and the search for a settlement of the constitutional dispute with Britain. Although the Prime Minister, Mr Ian Smith, had accepted the principle of majority rule as part of the Kissinger proposals in September 1976 (see AR 1976, pp. 249 and 492-94), little progress towards this eventuality had been made by the end of 1977, as Rhodesia entered its thirteenth year of illegal independence.

The Geneva conference, convened in October 1976 by the British Foreign Secretary in an attempt to reach agreement on proposals for the transition from a white-ruled Rhodesia to a black-ruled Zimbabwe, was adjourned on 14 December. Disagreements between Mr Smith and the African nationalist delegations, particularly on the nature of the interim government and the negotiability of the 'Kissinger package', threatened the scheduled recall of the conference on 17 January. Early in the new year Mr Ivor Richard, Britain's permanent representative at the United Nations and chairman of the conference, travelled to southern Africa to discuss the outstanding problems with the Presidents of the 'front-line' states, the nationalist leaders and the Governments of South Africa and Rhodesia. However, continuing differences of opinion over the implementation of the Kissinger principles and the extent of a British presence in the interim administration caused the prolongation of the Geneva adjournment *sine die*. On 24 January the Rhodesian Government declared the British proposals unacceptable 'even as a basis for negotiation' and announced plans for an internal settlement of the dispute.

The possibility of an internally negotiated settlement was considered on several occasions during the year, notably as hope of a British solution faded. The willingness of African nationalist leaders to participate in such talks reflected in part their lack of alternative options: the most resistant were those controlling active guerrilla armies. The Patriotic Front, an alliance of the Zimbabwe African People's Union (ZAPU), led by Mr Joshua Nkomo, and the Zimbabwe African National Union (ZANU), led by Mr Robert Mugabe, remained committed to the continuation of the guerrilla campaign and consistently rejected negotiation. It controlled virtually all the liberation forces, including the Zimbabwe African National

Liberation Army (ZANLA), which operated from bases within Mozambique, and the Zimbabwe People's Army, which operated from Zambia.

Bishop Abel Muzorewa, whose 'internal' wing of the African National Council (ANC) had been seriously weakened by the defection of senior officers at Geneva, spent much of the year within Rhodesia. He claimed substantial popular support, particularly in the Salisbury area, but failed to win significant international backing. By contrast Mr Nkomo obtained aid from the USSR, and Mr Mugabe from China, both men visiting those countries during the year. The fourth leader of a nationalist delegation at Geneva, the Reverend Ndabaningi Sithole, still claimed leadership of ZANU, while lacking demonstrable military or popular support. He returned to Rhodesia in July in the role of a moderate. At the end of the year both Bishop Muzorewa and Mr Sithole, together with Senator Chief Jeremiah Chirau, joint leader of the conciliatory Zimbabwe United People's Organization (ZUPO), were involved in direct negotiations with Mr Smith.

Earlier in the year, however, and despite the failure at Geneva, a considerable new settlement initiative had been launched by Dr David Owen, the newly-appointed British Foreign and Commonwealth Secretary. This approach deliberately incorporated a more active American participation, and followed discussions between President Carter and the British Prime Minister, Mr Callaghan, during the latter's visit to Washington in March. Shortly afterwards Dr Owen visited eight countries in central and southern Africa, including Rhodesia, and on his return to London announced the formulation of an Anglo-American plan to sponsor a constitutional conference on Rhodesia.

A consultative group of British and American officials was appointed to conduct discussions with all interested parties and, after two visits to Rhodesia, presented a 'definitive' settlement plan to Dr Owen and Mr Cyrus Vance, the US Secretary of State, in August. Later that month the Foreign Secretary, with the US permanent representative at the United Nations, Mr Andrew Young, visited Africa to discuss the proposals with the 'front-line' Presidents, the nationalist leaders and the South African Government. On 1 September the proposals were presented to Mr Smith in Salisbury and published simultaneously there, in Washington and in London, as *Rhodesia: Proposals for a Settlement* (Cmnd. 6919).

Central features of the Anglo-American proposals included Rhodesia's return to legality, an orderly transition to an independent Zimbabwe in 1978, and the establishment of an interim government, to be supervised by Britain and by a United Nations representative presence. The task of the British resident commissioner would be to administer the country for a period not exceeding six months, supervise the cease-fire, prepare for free elections under universal suffrage and head the armed forces. An Independence Constitution would provide for democratic government, the abolition of racial discrimination and the independence of the judiciary. A Development Fund, underwritten by a number of Western countries, would stimulate a revival of the country's economy. Field-Marshal Lord Carver, former chief of defence staff, was later named as resident commissioner designate, with Major-General Prem Chand, special representative of the UN Secretary-General, as his deputy.

The settlement proposals, intended as a coherent package, were received by the Rhodesian Prime Minister, by the 'front-line' Presidents and by the leading nationalists with caution. Mr Smith criticized several aspects of the White Paper, including the 'crazy suggestion' that the new Zimbabwe National Army be an amalgamation of sections of the Rhodesian security forces and of the guerrilla armies. He requested fundamental changes to portions of the plan, but invited Lord Carver to Salisbury to discuss military elements of the proposals.

The Carver talks, held early in November, accomplished little. A subsequent British proposition of a conference, to be held in Malta, to discuss the cease-fire upon which the whole of the settlement arrangements were predicated, was ignored both by the Rhodesian Government and by the Patriotic Front. At the end of the year the Anglo-American proposals were in abeyance. Dr Owen continued to promote their viability, though the Rhodesian Prime Minister chose to resurrect the option of an internal settlement. In exchange for announcing, on 24 November, his Government's commitment to the principle of majority rule based on 'one man, one vote', Mr Smith secured the participation in talks of Bishop Muzorewa, Mr Sithole and Chief Chirau. By Christmas the talks seemed set for slow but observable progress, the principal difficulty being agreement on the extent of white representation, and possible blocking device, within the future parliament.

Meanwhile all aspects of Rhodesian life were affected by the intensifying guerrilla war. On the military front the security forces were hard pressed to contain incursions over wide sections of the northern and eastern borders and prevent guerrilla penetration ever nearer urban areas. Two bomb attacks in the centre of Salisbury during August indicated that even the capital was vulnerable. In February the unpopularity of an announcement of extended military obligations for European, Asian and Coloured men between the ages of 38 and 50 precipitated the resignation of the Minister of Defence. Nationalist forces, however, particularly those of Mr Nkomo's ZAPU, increasingly recruited directly from within Rhodesia's borders. In January over 300 young Africans from the Manama Secondary School, in the south-west of the country, crossed the border into Botswana. Despite the intervention of the International Committee of the Red Cross, few were persuaded to return.

The Rhodesian army continued its counter-insurgency practice of pre-emptive strikes into neighbouring states sympathetic to the guerrillas. On

29 May it attacked supposed ZANLA camps inside Mozambique and occupied the town of Mapai for three days before withdrawing, apparently in response to South African pressure. Fears of similar 'hot pursuit' raids into Botswana and Zambia, and President Kaunda of Zambia's declaration in May that his country was 'in a state of war' with Rhodesia, emphasized the international dimension of the conflict. A further major strike into Mozambique between 23 and 26 November, during which Rhodesian forces claimed to have killed 1,200 members of the Patriotic Front at a guerrilla base near Chimoio, was widely condemned. Mozambique alleged at the UN Security Council that Rhodesian attacks had damaged property to the value of $13 million in a year. At the same time Rhodesian border installations and tourist resorts were frequent targets for guerrilla assault.

Repeated instances of extreme brutality were reported during the year. Farmers and missionaries in isolated areas appeared particularly susceptible to attack. In February three Jesuit priests and four Dominican nuns were assassinated at the Musami mission station, 43 miles east of Salisbury: security forces and nationalist groups each accused the other of the atrocity. Some missionaries left Rhodesia for fear of similar attack, while others were convicted of withholding information on guerrilla presence within their areas. The Most Rev. Donal Lamont, former Roman Catholic Bishop of Umtali, imprisoned on this charge in 1976 (see AR 1976, p. 251), was deported in March. Convicted 'terrorists' themselves were liable to the death sentence, and an unknown number were executed during the year.

Government casualty figures for 1977 claimed 1,759 guerrillas killed, for the loss of 244 members of the security forces; 1,111 civilians, of whom 56 were white, died as a result of the fighting. In country areas the conflict, and the widespread presence of guerrillas, seriously disrupted rural life: tribal Africans were intimidated and many ceased paying taxes, 300 schools were closed, agricultural jobs lost and more than 250,000 Africans resettled in 'protected villages'.

Signs of prevailing uncertainties emerged within domestic politics. On 23 February, in preparation for internal settlement talks with ZUPO and the ANC, Mr Smith announced plans to remove some of the grossest symbols of racial discrimination. The Quenet Commission of 1976 had recommended a relaxation of the Land Tenure Bill, by which almost half Rhodesia's land was reserved exclusively for white ownership. In March Mr Desmond Frost, the Rhodesian Front (RF) party chairman, opposed a change on these lines, and 12 RF MPs voted against the Government amendment in the House of Assembly. Following further disputes over policy Mr Frost resigned, and the dissident MPs were expelled from the party, thus removing the Government's two-thirds parliamentary majority, necessary for the passage of constitutional changes. On 17 July Mr Smith dissolved Parliament and called a general election for 31 August. Despite challenges from the Rhodesian Action Party on the right, and from the National Unifying Force on the left, Mr Smith easily regained all 50 white seats, secured a mandate for continued settlement negotiations and continued as Prime Minister for the fourteenth successive year. Out of Rhodesia's population of 6¾ millions, slightly more than 52,000 people voted. All African political parties boycotted the election.

The economy plainly reflected a society at war. Military costs consumed more than a quarter of the total national budget, equivalent to over £½ million a day, and contributed to a level of budgetary deficit which the Minister of Finance and Deputy Prime Minister, Mr David Smith, forecast the Government might have to exceed in the following year. Inflation remained close to ten per cent, while sanctions, and the decline in international commodity prices, badly affected the balance of payments. The foreign currency allocation to commerce and industry was heavily cut. Mineral output showed virtually no growth, while tourism fell by 25 per cent. The year saw the highest level of emigration in the country's history. About 17,000 Europeans, Asians and Coloureds, many of them in the productive or military age group, left Rhodesia. Fewer than 6,000 entered it.

BOTSWANA

Botswana, strategically placed between Zambia, Namibia, Rhodesia and South Africa, was again directly affected in 1977 by tensions and unrest in neighbouring territories. There was a steady influx of refugees from South Africa and Rhodesia and a number of incidents occurred on the Botswana-Rhodesia border. While Botswana was prepared to grant asylum to refugees, it refused to allow guerrillas to operate under arms from bases in its territory. In January, Botswana told the UN Security Council that its borders had been violated 36 times since 1966 in 'unprovoked acts of war' which, said Botswana, were designed to intimidate it from helping Rhodesian refugees. A UN report noted that the strain on Botswana as a result of its open-door refugee policy was very serious in relation to its size and resources.

In December, a spokesman for the office of the President, Sir Seretse Khama, said that plans were being made to establish a residential centre for South African refugees at which training would be given in horticulture and agriculture and eventually in building and allied trades. The main object of the scheme was to give refugees protection and the chance of employment in Botswana or overseas.

LESOTHO

Relations between Lesotho and South Africa continued on an uneasy footing during 1977. In February, the retiring South African Foreign Minister, Dr H. Muller, said in Parliament that Lesotho was creating border incidents and then complaining about them in 'outrageous' terms. In June a meeting took place between the Republic's new Foreign Minister, Mr Pik Botha, and Mr C. D. Molapo, Foreign Minister of Lesotho. It became clear that Lesotho had not abandoned its claim to the so-called 'conquered territories' along Lesotho's border with South Africa.

Another point of friction between the two countries was Lesotho's refusal to grant diplomatic recognition to Transkei, her south-eastern neighbour, which had been conceded independent status by the Pretoria Government. A UN commission, which visited the country in January to investigate the Transkei border problem, recommended that about R100 million be channelled into Lesotho to back the Government's decision to have nothing to do with Transkei.

SWAZILAND

Swaziland, like Botswana, gave a welcome to large numbers of refugees from South Africa during the year. The Prime Minister, Colonel Maphevu Dlamini, told a UN investigating committee that his country needed international support to take care of refugee students. But Swaziland also had its own problems of internal unrest in 1977. In October, police opened fire on rioting students in Manzini, and three people were wounded. The unrest, which was preceded by a teachers' strike over pay, quickly lost momentum. It appeared to reflect deep-rooted grievances against the Government and the ruling Dlamini family.

In March, King Sobhuza II abandoned the country's Westminster-style Constitution, which had been suspended since 1973, pending the introduction of a new system in keeping with Swaziland's tribal traditions.

It was announced that Swaziland would be spending R134 million in the next two years to extend its sugar-milling facilities. A R13 million contract was also awarded during the year for the construction of a railway line linking the Swaziland and South African rail systems.

Chapter 3

THE REPUBLIC OF SOUTH AFRICA AND NAMIBIA

IN 1977 South Africa moved rapidly away from the Western community of nations. The movement was foreshadowed by the Prime Minister, Mr B. J. Vorster, in his New Year message in January, when he said that any onslaught on the country would have to be faced alone.

The deterioration in relations between South Africa and the West became marked in May after a meeting in Vienna between Mr Vorster and Mr Walter Mondale, Vice-President of the United States of America. South Africa's domestic policies were on the agenda as well as the Western effort to promote peaceful settlements in Namibia and Rhodesia. Following the meeting, it became evident that Mr Mondale and Mr Vorster had clashed on the question of apartheid. From this date, the speeches of Mr Vorster, the Minister of Foreign Affairs, Mr Pik Botha, and their Cabinet colleagues were often anti-American in tone. It was repeatedly stated that South Africa would never capitulate to Western demands for one-man-one-vote in South Africa and would fight 'to the last man' against Western interference in the country's domestic affairs. American officials asserted that the United States had no wish to prescribe specific political formulas for South Africa's internal policies but was concerned to make it clear that American support for South Africa at the United Nations and elsewhere could not be expected as long as South Africa maintained policies of racial discrimination. Late in May, the South African Government agreed to a visit by Mr Andrew Young, the outspoken US ambassador at the United Nations, who surprised South Africa by the moderate and conciliatory spirit of his remarks in Johannesburg.

In spite of the increasingly acrimonious note in relations with the US, South Africa continued to lend support and cooperation to the five leading Western powers—the United States, Britain, Canada, France and Germany —in their diplomatic drive for negotiated solutions in Namibia and Rhodesia. South Africa agreed to elections in Namibia under UN supervision. Mr Justice M. T. Steyn was appointed to administer the territory in the interim and to prepare for the elections. One of his first moves was to abolish the law forbidding inter-racial marriages. Contacts continued throughout the year between representatives of the five Western powers and the South African Government until it eventually became clear that one major stumbling-block remained in preparing the way for an independent Namibia.

The South West African Peoples Organization (Swapo), which was conducting guerrilla warfare in Namibia from bases in Angola, refused to take part in elections until South African troops had been withdrawn from the territory. Acts of terrorism continued in the second half of the year, both the security forces and guerrillas suffering casualties. The South African Government appeared determined to retain troops in the territory unless and until the terror war ceased but appeared open to compromise on their numbers and location. As the year closed, the Western powers were making renewed efforts to reach a compromise between the Swapo and South African positions. If Swapo was to continue to refuse to take part in the elections, the South African Government intended to push ahead with them, aiming at an internal settlement rather as Mr Ian Smith was seeking to do in Rhodesia.

On the Rhodesia question, there were contacts throughout the year between Western diplomats and the South African Government. The British Foreign Secretary and Mr Andrew Young, on behalf of the USA, engaged in shuttle diplomacy which brought them to Pretoria to see Mr Vorster. Publicly, Mr Vorster was insistent that he would not put pressure on Mr Smith, but behind the scenes, it appeared, he was still using his good offices in the interests of a speedy settlement.

On the domestic front, sporadic unrest continued in the urban black African townships such as Soweto and the boycott of schools continued. The new development was the emergence of urban terrorism as a real threat to the safety of whites, bomb explosions occurring in the Carlton Centre shopping mall, Johannesburg, outside the Benoni railway station and at the Germiston police station. Nobody was killed in these explosions. Throughout the country security measures were tightened in supermarkets and shopping centres. There were also sabotage attempts on railway lines and bridges with varying degrees of success. In June, two whites were shot dead by African youths in a random terror attack in central Johannesburg. A security police sergeant was shot dead while asleep at his home near Durban.

In countering terrorism and anti-apartheid protest, the security police had detained an estimated 778 people by November. In December, the South African Institute of Race Relations said that 144 people had been convicted under the security laws in the first 11 months of the year and were sentenced to a total of 898 years' imprisonment. In this period, more than 400 people faced charges in 95 separate security trials. Of the people charged, 198 were either acquitted or had the charges against them withdrawn. Most of the trials related to activities or alleged activities of the banned African National Congress (ANC). There were 38 trials involving charges of sabotage.

In August, the security police said they had wiped out a number of terrorist bases, some close to Durban and others on the Witwatersrand, and had seized caches of Russian-made arms, explosives, booby traps and ammunition. The arms included machine guns, rocket launchers and grenades. In a notable trial in Maritzburg, Natal, five African men were sentenced to terms of imprisonment for life for offences relating to the security laws. Addressing the court in mitigation of sentence, the accused men spoke of their involvement in trade unionism and their resentment of the oppression of blacks, of racial and wage discrimination, apartheid, the pass laws, exploitation by employers, job reservation, influx control, poor working conditions and the standard of schooling for blacks. Mr Justice Howard dismissed claims by the men and by witnesses that they had been maltreated while in the hands of the security police as fabricated or grossly exaggerated in most cases.

The political storm of the year blew up when the commissioner of police announced the death in detention of Mr Steven Biko, a moderate and widely respected black leader, the founder of the 'black consciousness' movement in South Africa and the hero of the younger generation of township blacks. A statement by the Minister of Justice, Mr Kruger, that Mr Biko had died after going on hunger strike was greeted with scepticism by South African newspapers and notably by the *East London Daily Dispatch*. The editor, Mr Donald Woods, began an outspoken campaign on platforms around the country, demanding a full inquiry into Mr Biko's death and offering to resign his editorship if it was demonstrated that Mr Biko had in fact died of a hunger strike. An inquest into Mr Biko's death eventually began in November. In the course of the proceedings, there were disclosures which shocked public opinion in the country and caused an outcry of unprecedented intensity abroad. It emerged in evidence that Mr Biko had been kept naked and in shackles while in detention and had been driven, naked, in the back of a light truck from Port Elizabeth to Pretoria while suffering from serious brain damage. The inquest magistrate, in a brief finding, said that Mr Biko died of a head injury but that on the available evidence he could not determine that the death was brought about by an act or omission involving an offence on the part of any particular person.

A British lawyer, Sir David Napley, a former president of the Law Society in England, attended the inquest at the invitation of the Association of Law Societies of South Africa. In a subsequent report, Sir David said the police investigation into Mr Biko's death had been 'perfunctory in the extreme' and that security policemen who gave evidence at the inquest were guilty of 'mendacity'. Sir David said that he accepted that the inquest magistrate, on the available evidence, could not apportion blame for Mr Biko's death.

In the wake of Mr Biko's death, there was a renewed wave of unrest in urban black townships, notably in his home area of the Eastern Cape. On 19 October, the authorities declared the 'black consciousness' organizations—the Black Peoples Convention, the South African Students' Organization and others—to be prohibited organizations, and banned and detained leaders of the movement in many parts of the country. At the same time, the Christian Institute, an ecumenical organization, was proscribed and its leaders, including the Rev. C. F. Beyers Naude and the Rev. Theo Kotze, subjected to banning orders. But probably the greatest shock to liberal opinion at home and abroad was caused by a crackdown on free expression—the banning of Mr Donald Woods, and the closing-down of *The World*, a daily newspaper, whose editor, Mr Percy Qoboza, was at the same time taken into detention under the Internal Security Act. *The World*, a moderate voice of black opinion, which had distinguished itself in coverage of the Soweto riots and their aftermath, was owned by the Argus group of newspapers.

The prohibition of *The World*, the detention of Mr Qoboza and the banning of Mr Woods were seen as a direct threat to the freedom of the press, foreshadowing a similar fate for other newspapers sympathetic to the black cause. Mr Woods, in terms of his banning order, was forbidden to write for publication or to speak in public or to attend any social or political meetings. He was confined to East London. On 31 December he fled to Lesotho, having dyed his hair and disguised his appearance, hitch-hiking from East London to the Lesotho border where he swam a flooded river to enter the country. He planned to travel to Britain and to publish a book on the Biko affair, which he had written in secret defiance of his banning order.

At home and abroad, the reaction to the 19 October bannings and detentions was fierce and sustained. Together with the outcry against the treatment of Mr Biko and the spate of deaths in detention—more than one a month in an 18-month period—the international clamour against South Africa reached hurricane force. In the circumstances, no Western nation was prepared to exercise the veto when a resolution calling for a mandatory arms embargo against South Africa came before the Security Council. The resolution—and its support by the Western powers—marked a watershed in South Africa's relations with its erstwhile friends in the West and the Commonwealth, of which it had been a leading member until 1961. The Canadian Government, in a gesture symbolizing South Africa's breach with its old Commonwealth associates, suspended its official trade pro-motion activities in South Africa. By the end of 1977, South Africa was standing alone.

When the international uproar about South Africa was at its height, Mr Vorster called a snap general election to demonstrate, he said, that South Africans rejected interference in their domestic affairs. Assisted by state control of television, Mr Vorster won a massive victory at the polls, also winning appreciable support in the English-speaking community. Only whites were on the voters' roll. The election also saw the emergence of the Progressive Federal Party as the official opposition, replacing the old United Party, which had earlier disbanded itself.

The Progressive Federal Party, led by Mr Colin Eglin, did very well in the traditionally liberal Cape Peninsula and in the affluent suburbs of

I

Johannesburg but made little impact elsewhere in the country. The result of the election was as follows: National Party 134; Progressive Federal Party 17; New Republic Party 10; South African Party 3. The National Party gained 18 seats.

As the year ended, there was some expectation that Mr Vorster, armed with a comfortable majority, would feel free to introduce domestic reforms. Earlier, a commission of inquiry had been appointed to review South Africa's racially discriminatory labour legislation and it appeared that job reservation provisions would be steadily phased out. The University of Stellenbosch, intellectual fountainhead of Afrikaner nationalism, threw open its doors to non-white post-graduate students, a move of great symbolic importance. On the eve of the election Mr Vorster announced plans for constitutional reform, involving two new 'parliaments'—one for Coloured (mixed race) South Africans and one for Indians—in addition to the existing (whites only) Parliament. While it was not clear how sovereignty could be shared by three separate legislatures in a unitary state, the new proposals were thought to represent a significant admission that Coloured people and Indians could no longer be excluded from the process of government.

The new constitutional proposals made no provision for the urban blacks, however, who were expected to regard themselves as citizens of the rural 'homelands' such as the Transkei and Bophutatswana. The latter joined the Transkei in gaining independent status in November. Leaders of the Coloured and Indian communities, meanwhile, were expressing great reserve about the new constitutional proposals. Government spokesmen emphasized that the details were negotiable. It seemed clear that a process of modest change and reform was getting under way. But it was also clear that any reforms would take place within the ideological framework of separate development, which insists that the South African Parliament remain representative of whites only and that Africans should exercise political rights only in the rural homelands.

However, the Government did commit itself to granting municipal autonomy to urban black townships such as Soweto as soon as possible. There were also promises of drastic revision of the pass laws and influx control, the measures restricting the freedom of movement of Africans which have caused bitter resentment in the African community. Meanwhile, the conservative Minister of Bantu Administration, Mr M. C. Botha, had announced his intention to retire. Much would depend on Mr Vorster's choice of a successor to Mr Botha in this key portfolio. As the year ended, Mr Vorster was well placed to introduce significant reforms. But there was also a possibility of intensified urban terrorism in 1978 which could harden white attitudes and go counter to the mounting pressures for change and reform. Much would also depend on the prospects of peaceful settlement in neighbouring Namibia and Rhodesia.

VIII SOUTH ASIA AND INDIAN OCEAN

Chapter 1

IRAN—AFGHANISTAN

IRAN

An important change took place in the political establishment on 6 August 1977 when Mr Amir Abbas Hovaida resigned as Prime Minister after twelve and a half years in office. Dr Jamshid Amouzegar, aged 54, was appointed as Prime Minister by the Shah on 7 August. He had been active in political life since 1958. In addition to holding ministerial portfolios for Health, Labour, Finance and Interior, Dr Amouzegar had been for many years the Shah's principal oil negotiator. The entire Hovaida Cabinet resigned on 6 August but most senior Ministers were reappointed to the new Cabinet, including, among others, Mr Khalatbari as Minister of Foreign Affairs and Mr Ansari as Minister of Economic and Financial Affairs. Ten new Ministers entered the Cabinet formed by Dr Amouzegar, all drawn from the Rastakhiz (Resurgence) Party.

The change of Government came at a time of crisis. Slowing-down of the rate of expansion of the economy and dislocation of the infrastructure, particularly in Teheran where electricity and water supplies became intermittent, created an atmosphere of tension and criticism. The new Government was charged with the task of restoring economic order and recreating confidence. On 18 August the Shah announced that his reform programme, consisting of seventeen points, was to be augmented by principles 18 and 19 which called, respectively, for control of land prices and the declaration by all holders of public office of their wealth and financial interests.

Assadolloh Alam, the Imperial Court Minister, resigned on 5 August after a long and worsening illness. Mr Alam was a stalwart servant of the Shah throughout his life and was regarded as among the Shah's few real confidants.

The Shah's twin sister, Princess Ashraf, was the object of an attempted assassination in September. The attack on the Princess was made in the south of France and was thought to be politically motivated. Political opposition to the regime grew appreciably during 1977. The professional classes, particularly lawyers and academics, raised their voices against the more repressive aspects of the Government's policies and called for a return to constitutional monarchy, abandonment of press censorship, and disbandment of the State Security Organization (Savak). The Government encouraged a measure of liberalization during the year in response to pressure from the United States for improved human rights.

Iran had a successful year in its foreign relations. Iranian forces assisted in the defeat of the rebel groups in Oman (see p. 198) and on 26 January 1977 it was announced that Iranian military forces would be withdrawn. The Shah paid an official visit to Oman on 5-8 December. Relations with Pakistan were developed through guarantees of further Iranian investments, while Iran adjusted rapidly to the change of regime in Pakistan. General Zia ul-Haq, the Chief Martial Law Administrator of Pakistan since the coup against Mr Bhutto, visited Teheran in September and October to emphasize Pakistan's continuing commitment to the Iranian alliance. Final documents confirming an agreement with Afghanistan on the division of the Hirmand river waters were exchanged in June, thereby ending the long-standing dispute on the joint boundary and the sharing of irrigation water on the river system.

The Shah gave strong financial and diplomatic support to President Sadat of Egypt during 1977, culminating in public backing for the Egyptian peace initiative begun by Sadat's visit to Jerusalem. Elsewhere in the Middle East, the Shah sought to achieve a formal agreement on the security of the Persian Gulf and to extend economic relations with Iraq, with which a number of agreements governing trade, cultural affairs and tourism were signed.

On 15 November the Shah began a two-day visit to the United States. The occasion was marked by noisy and violent demonstrations by rival Iranian factions but the Shah completed the important business of his meeting with President Carter and gained unequivocal support for his policies from the authorities in Washington. An oil-for-arms agreement was signed with US companies in November under which Iran would acquire 160 F-16 aircraft against supply of crude oil.

The state Budget for 1977-78 was set at 2,188,600 million rials for revenue, 2,311,200 million for expenditure, with a deficit of 122,600 million. Of the total outlays, the Budget allocated 38 per cent to economic affairs, 14 per cent to social affairs, 9 per cent to defence and the balance to public affairs. Development expenditures were allotted above all to reducing bottle-necks in the infrastructure (379,200 million rials), though industry (115,700 million) and petroleum (115,000 million) were also given priority.

Iran's financial position remained stable through 1977. International liquidity improved, to stand at $11,547 million by October 1977. A considerable achievement of the Government was a reduction in the rate of price inflation. By the first half of 1977 the inflation rate had dropped to 16 per cent per annum. Foreign borrowing was enlisted to support individual development projects, while bartering oil for goods was widely adopted as a means of financing imports of industrial and defence materials.

Industrial performance was impeded by general failures in the electricity and water supply services during the year. Many plants worked at less than 50 per cent capacity as a direct result of disruption of power supply. Petro-chemical development was accelerated through construction of new Irano-Japanese ventures in the south and the adoption of a programme for expenditure of $3,500 million on the industry over a five-year period. In the automobile sector an agreement was signed with Peugeot–Citroen of France for production in Iran at a rate of 100,000 cars per year.

In the oil sector, production fell severely to 5·8 million barrels per day in the first quarter of 1977, and to 5·5 million barrels per day in the second and third quarters, respectively. Oil revenues in the first six months of 1977 amounted to $7,108 million. Nuclear power developments began to take shape and two nuclear power stations were ordered from France and four from West Germany during the year.

Foreign trade expanded in the first eight months of 1977, with imports rising to $9,410 million, though exports of non-oil goods showed little improvement at $64 million.

AFGHANISTAN

On 16 February Mr Mohammed Daud Khan was sworn in as President of the Republic before the Parliament that had elected him. The President then dissolved the Loya Jirgah, which had met on 30 January to adopt the Republic's first Constitution. The first legislative elections would be held in 1979. Mr Daud also approved the civil code which incorporated 'the fundamentals of the Islamic shariat'.

Afghanistan concluded with Bangladesh, on 1 March, a trade protocol for exchange of commodities worth 40 million Taka each way in 1977. On 17 July President Daud expressed the hope that the overthrow of Mr Zulfikar Ali Bhutto in Pakistan would lead to an early settlement of the dispute over the Pathan tribesmen living in Pakistan's North West Frontier province and Baluchistan.

Chapter 2

INDIA—PAKISTAN—BANGLADESH—SRI LANKA—NEPAL

INDIA

THE year began with the announcement, on 18 January, of fresh elections to the Lok Sabha, India's lower House of Parliament. The detainees were also released batch by batch. A nation which had gone through a near-totalitarian regime since the imposition of the Emergency on 25 June 1975 heaved a sigh of relief. The four opposition parties—Jana Sangh (Hindu Nationalist), Bhartiya Lok Dal (pro-agriculturist), the 'old guard's' Congress Party and the Socialists—took up the challenge and came together on 20 January to work as a single party under the label of the Janata Party. They were joined by the Congress for Democracy (CFD) which Mr Jagjivan Ram, the former Defence Minister, formed on 1 February by resigning from the Government of Mrs Indira Gandhi, then Prime Minister, and getting the support of some Congress Party leaders, including two former state Chief Ministers, Mr H. N. Bahuguna from Uttar Pradesh and Mrs Nandini Satpathy from Orissa, and Mr K. R. Ganesh, former Minister of State for Finance.

All the parties took a left-of-centre stance in their election manifestos; so much so that the Janata declared that private property protected under the Constitution was not a fundamental right and promised the 'right to work'. The Congress Party opposed any incursion on property. However, no economic issue ever came to the fore. It was 'dictatorship *versus* democracy'—a call sounded by Mr Jayaprakash Narayan, a respected follower of Mahatma Gandhi, who had been detained during the Emergency. The excesses committed during the Emergency, particularly forced sterilizations in rural areas, also came to light. The role played in the Administration by Mrs Gandhi's second son, Mr Sanjay Gandhi, became public. The press, even though not completely free from the shackles of censorship, shed its fear as days went by.

Mrs Gandhi and her Congress Party were on the defensive and vindicated the Emergency in the name of discipline, which they claimed was necessary because of the unrest in university campuses and strikes in industrial units that followed the speeches and actions of opposition leaders. It was an intensive election on both sides and even the death of India's President, Fakhruddin Ali Ahmed, on 11 February did not distract the attention of either.

Mrs Gandhi and her party paid the price of the excesses during the Emergency and of belittling India's faith in democracy. She, her son and many top Congress leaders, including Mr V. C. Shukla, the Information Minister, lost their seats.

The defeat of the Congress was dismal. It managed to muster only 153 seats as against 350 won in the 1971 elections. The Janata Party and its ally, the CFD, won 298 seats. The Congress did not win a single seat out of 84 in Uttar Pradesh, 54 in Bihar, 13 in Punjab, 11 in Haryana and 6 in Delhi. It won a single seat in Madhya Pradesh, one in Rajasthan, three in West Bengal, four in Orissa and ten each in Assam and Gujarat.

The percentage of votes polled by the Congress in the various states (1971 percentages in brackets) was: West Bengal 29·39 (28·23), Uttar Pradesh 25·04 (48·56), Tamil Nadu 22·28 (12·51), Rajasthan 30·56 (45·96), Punjab 35·87 (45·96), Orissa 38·18 (38·46), Manipur 45·71 (30·02), Maharashtra 46·93 (63·18), Madhya Pradesh 32·5 (45·6), Kerala 29·12 (19·75), Karnataka 56·74 (70·87), Himachal Pradesh 38·3 (75·79), Haryana 17·95 (52·56), Gujarat 46·92 (44·85), Bihar 22·90 (40·06), Assam 50·56 (56·98), and Andhra Pradesh 57·36 (55·73).

While the Janata Party swept the north, it did badly in southern India.

It won one seat each in Andhra Pradesh, Tamil Nadu and Karnataka. Obviously, the Janata wave did not seep through the Vindhyas; evidently the excesses in the south were fewer and stories of torture had not yet become common currency.

In the two states (Kerala and Tamil Nadu) and one Union territory (Pondicherry) which went to the polls along with the Lok Sabha the Janata fared badly. The Kerala United Front, comprised mainly of the Congress Party and the pro-Soviet Communist Party, won 111 out of 140 assembly seats and formed the Government under Mr K. Karunakaran. In Tamil Nadu, the All India Anna Dravida Munnetra Kazhagam won 130 seats out of 234 and formed the Government under Mr M. G. Ramachandran, a noted film actor. In Pondicherry, the All India Anna-DMK won 14 out of 30 seats and formed the Government.

On 24 March the Janata elected Mr Morarji Desai, aged 82, as its leader at the Centre and he became Prime Minister. His Cabinet members were: Chaudhuri Charan Singh, Minister of Home Affairs; Mr Jagjivan Ram, Minister of Defence; Mr L. K. Advani, Minister of Information and Broadcasting; Mr Parkash Singh Badal, Minister of Agriculture and Irrigation; Mr H. N. Bahuguna, Minister of Chemicals, Petroleum and Fertilizers; Mr Sikandar Bakht, Minister of Works and Housing, and of Supply and Rehabilitation; Mr Shanti Bhushan, Minister of Law, Justice and Company Affairs; Mr Pratap Chandra Chunder, Minister of Education, Social Welfare and Culture; Professor Madhu Dandavate, Minister of Railways; Mr Mohan Dharia, Minister of Commerce and Civil Supplies and Cooperation; Mr George Fernandes, Minister of Communications; Mr Purushottam Kaushik, Minister of Tourism and Civil Aviation; Mr Raj Narain, Minister of Health and Family Planning; Mr H. M. Patel, Minister of Finance and Revenue and Banking; Mr Biju Patnaik, Minister of Steel and Mines; Mr P. Ramachandran, Minister of Energy; Mr Atal Bihari Vajpayee, Minister of External Affairs; Mr Ravindra Varma, Minister of Parliamentary Affairs and Labour; Mr Brij Lal Verma, Minister of Industry. Subsequently, Mr Verma was shifted to Communications and Mr Fernandes to Industry.

Mr Sanjiva Reddy was elected as the Speaker of the Lok Sabha. On 21 July he was replaced by Mr K. S. Hegde, and four days later became the President of India.

The new Cabinet revoked the Emergency, abolished the press censorship and withdrew the Baroda Dynamite case in which the underground leader, Mr George Fernandes, was involved. The 'family planning' programme, which had been anathema to villagers, was renamed 'family welfare'. Compensation of Rs 5,000 (£300), it was announced, would be awarded to each victim of forcible family planning operations.

One by one, the instruments used during the Emergency were dismantled: Bills were passed to repeal the Prevention of Publication of

Objectionable Matters Act, 1976, and to protect the publication of reports of proceedings of Parliament. Three Commissions of Inquiry were appointed, one under the former Chief Justice of India, Mr J. C. Shah, to look into the abuse of authority and the excesses committed during the Emergency, the second under Mr Jaganmohan Reddy, a former judge of the Supreme Court, to examine the affairs of Mr Bansi Lal, the former Chief Minister of Haryana, and the case of Mr Nagarwala who had died in gaol during Mrs Gandhi's regime, and the third under Mr Alok Chandra Gupta, a Supreme Court judge, to look into the concerns owned by Mr Sanjay Gandhi.

The suspended assembly of Gujarat was revived (11 April) and a nine-member Janata Front Ministry headed by Mr Babubhai Patel was sworn in. The Central Government felt that there should be fresh elections for the assemblies of those states where the Congress Party had been rejected in the Lok Sabha elections. The Governors of nine states were advised by New Delhi to dissolve the legislative assemblies to facilitate fresh elections. This move was challenged in the Supreme Court, which unanimously dismissed the suit. The elections were held in nine previously Congress-ruled states. The Janata won in seven states, the Sikh Akalis in Punjab and the Communist Party of India (marxists) in West Bengal.

Mr Badal resigned on 20 June from the Central Cabinet to become Chief Minister of the Punjab, and was replaced by Mr Surjit Singh Barnala.

The Planning Commission was reconstituted on 24 May with the appointment of Dr D. T. Lakdawala as deputy chairman and Mr V. G. Rajadhyaksha and Professor Raj Krishna as members.

On 13 August the Kuldip Nayar committee submitted its report on the future of Samachar, the combined Indian news agency which the Government had brought about through intimidation during the Emergency. The Committee proposed the bifurcation of Samachar into an exclusively English-language news agency and another for vernacular languages plus English. However, the Government decided to revert to the pre-Emergency arrangement—two agencies in English, the Press Trust of India and United News of India, and two in Hindi, Hindustan Samachar and Samachar Bharati. The Government also issued a white paper on the misuse of mass media, describing how the press, radio and television were controlled and abused by Mrs Gandhi and her Information Minister, Mr Shukla, during the emergency.

The killings of the ultra-radical Naxalites during Mrs Gandhi's regime came to light. A non-official committee in Andhra Pradesh reported that the death of Naxalites in the state following encounters with the police were plain murders. In Kerala, one Naxalite, Mr P. Rajan, had died in police custody, as the state Chief Minister, Mr Karuna Karan, admitted. Mr A. K. Antony replaced him as Chief Minister on 28 May.

Ten persons, including Mr P. C. Sethi, former Union Minister, Mr Yashpal Kapoor, MP and Mr R. K. Dhavan, Mrs Gandhi's additional private secretary, were arrested on 15 August on charges of corruption and criminal conspiracy to misuse their official positions. They were released on bail. Mrs Gandhi was arrested on 3 October on allegations of corruption, along with four former Union Ministers, Mr K. D. Malaviya, Mr H. R. Gokhale, Mr D. P. Chattopadhyaya and Mr P. C. Sethi. The next day Mrs Gandhi was released unconditionally on the ground that there was no charge against her. The Union Government filed an appeal in Delhi High Court which was still pending at the end of the year.

Mrs Gandhi refused to appear before the Shah Commission, which she said had already denigrated her reputation by holding public sittings. The Commission issued a summons to her to appear on 9 January 1978.

The Government introduced on 23 December a composite Bill to repeal the Maintenance of Internal Security Act and simultaneously to provide for preventive detention.

The Congress Party suffered internal tensions and looked like splitting. Mr Bansi Lal was turned out of the party and Mr D. K. Barooah, the Party's president, resigned on 13 April to make way for the acting president, Mr Swaran Singh. He was later replaced by Mr Brahmananda Reddy. Mrs Gandhi resigned on 18 December from the Congress Working Committee.

Economically, conditions did not brighten; in fact, prices rose and investment remained sluggish. The Janata Party changed the industrial policy to lay more emphasis on small industry and rural crafts: 40 per cent of the revenue was to be spent on agriculture. The Foreign Exchange Regulation Act, which obliged all foreign companies to have at least 51 per cent of Indian equity, forced some multinationals like Coca Cola and IBM to quit operations in India.

The five-year plan was pushed into the background and an annual plan, called the 'rolling plan', took its place. The food position remained satisfactory and the buffer stock stood at 20 million tonnes. The population grew by 10 million, and because of the Janata Party's reluctance to renew the family planning programme in the wake of forced sterilization the population looked like rising more steeply than before.

In foreign affairs, India redressed the previous tilt in favour of the Soviet Union. It was stated officially that the country now followed a 'real' non-alignment policy. Mr Desai attended the Commonwealth conference (7 June), visited the Soviet Union (26 December) and Nepal (9 December). The trips to the Soviet Union and Nepal were described as 'very successful'. At least one thing was obvious, that New Delhi was trying to live down its reputation of being more friendly to the Eastern bloc than the Western. The Western world, representing the democratic form of government, seemed in favour.

I*

PAKISTAN

In a year of political frustration and accompanying economic stagnation, Pakistan's democratic electoral processes, so painstakingly acquired since before independence, culminated in crisis and the reimposition of martial law on 5 July, four months after the first general election in the country held on the basis of adult franchise with a civilian Government already in power. Martial law restored confidence and introduced a number of economic measures designed to stimulate the economy. With new elections promised in due course, but with the two main political parties themselves showing signs of splitting, Pakistan ended the year on a note of political and economic uncertainty.

The decision to go to the polls by Mr Bhutto's Pakistan Peoples Party (PPP), when the National Assembly could have prolonged its life by one more year, had seemed right at the time although it was realized it might well open a Pandora's box. The economy was showing some signs of improvement, including a promised self-sufficiency in wheat and an encouraging oil discovery. Admittedly the balance of payments seemed vulnerable, but with new economic relations with India and Bangladesh, and with representative Government restored in the problem province of Baluchistan and at work in the remaining provinces, an election seemed to hold few political risks for Mr Bhutto's Government.

The country went to the polls on 7 March to elect 200 members of the National Assembly for a new term of five years; three days later elections would be held for the four provincial assemblies of the Punjab, Sind, North West Frontier Province and Baluchistan. The opposition was a dramatically formed alliance of nine parties, the Pakistan National Alliance (PNA), created, it seemed, with the object of opposing but with few constructive policies. Its election manifesto was rightist but touched on issues only peripherally. The PPP manifesto was a more workmanlike document.

As the election campaign proceeded, however, it became clear that Mr Bhutto's party might not have the kind of walkover that had been predicted. With no past record for comparison, the size of PNA meetings surprised many, being due perhaps to a long-suppressed desire to hear alternative policies. The result nevertheless was a sweeping victory for the PPP, who won 156 seats against the PNA's 35, including 108 out of 155 in the Punjab alone, thus giving Punjab PPP members a majority of their own in the Assembly.

From the evening of election day there were widespread allegations of official interference with the balloting in favour of PPP candidates. The PNA boycotted the ensuing provincial elections. A strong belief among many people that rigging had taken place generated a wave of resentment which erupted in widespread agitation, resulting in heavy loss of life and property as well as loss of production in industry, though confined to the main towns. Prohibition for Pakistani Muslims was introduced and gambling prohibited by the Government. It was found necessary to call in the army in a number of places and impose local martial law. Only four election petitions alleging rigging were judicially decided but these did disclose a pattern of official interference.

A long period of unrest followed and the opposition leaders were arrested. Mr Bhutto, confronted with an erosion of his constitutional authority and finding it more and more difficult to maintain law and order both at the centre and in the provinces, wisely entered into a dialogue with the opposition leaders, offering to re-hold the provincial elections and to make his own position as Prime Minister subject to a referendum, for which purpose the Constitution was especially amended. But although the talks continued for a month no agreement was reached. A serious crisis had developed for which the Constitution provided no solution.

It was in these circumstances that the armed forces of Pakistan, led by the chief of staff of the army, General Mohammed Zia ul-Haq, intervened to separate the two factions. This extra-constitutional act was welcomed by many sections of the community after four months of civil strife. The four-year-old Constitution was held in abeyance, the national and provincial assemblies were dissolved and Ministers and Governors ceased to hold office. The President remained as head of state, but was to act on the advice of the Chief Martial Law Administrator. Pakistan was to be governed as nearly as might be in accordance with the Constitution, and a Laws Continuance in Force Order was published on the same day. The courts were to continue normally but fundamental rights under the Constitution were suspended.

Later, in November, the proclamation of martial law was challenged in a habeas corpus petition from Mr Bhutto's wife against his detention and that of others under a martial law regulation. Dismissing this petition, a full bench of the Supreme Court held that the Chief Martial Law Administrator had validly assumed power by means of an extra-constitutional act in the interest of the state and the welfare of the people, and that the military take-over was justified under the doctrine of necessity.

Although the Chief Martial Law Administrator had announced that it was the intention to hold elections on 18 October, he later postponed the elections as being 'an invitation to a new crisis' and announced a ban on political activity. The elections would now take place after cases against politicians and others charged with misconduct had been decided by the courts.

The rate of growth of GNP fell during Pakistan's financial year ending June 1977 to 1·2 per cent from an average of 4·5 per cent in the previous five years. The growth had been due to an expansion more of the service sectors than of the commodity-producing sectors, and the sharp rise in monetary demand led to pressure on the balance of payments. Prior to the elections there had been some grounds for hoping that Pakistan's economy during 1977 might improve despite a very poor cotton crop at the end of 1976. There were hopes of self-sufficiency in wheat, which subsequently proved over-optimistic, and increased production of cash crops gave ground for confidence, although the balance of payments continued to be sustained by foreign aid, including generous contributions from Muslim OPEC countries. Per capita income showed a small decline to $55 per annum at constant 1961 factor prices. With a fairly liberal import policy imports increased, while export earnings remained static, partly through a shortage of cotton available for export. The largest-ever trade gap which resulted was financed by increases in international borrowing, higher private remittances from Pakistanis working abroad, and a draw-down in the foreign exchange reserves.

Both agriculture and industry accounted for the deterioration in the growth of the economy, agricultural production slowing down to 2·2 per cent growth from 4·5 per cent and falling considerably short of the annual plan target of 8 per cent, mainly because of the steep fall in cotton production. However, the production of wheat, rice and sugar increased substantially, thanks to increased supply of water from the Tarbela dam and greater use of fertilizers and other agricultural inputs. Industrial production, which had shown a mild increase in the previous year, declined, and value added fell by 0·8 per cent; but this drop was confined to large-scale industries, being due in the main to constraints in the textile industry arising from the shortfall in cotton production and the international recession in cotton textiles. Cotton yarn and cotton cloth production fell by 19·5 and 16·5 per cent respectively, offsetting comfortable gains in other industries. The overall level of investment rose substantially as in preceding years, but this was due largely to increased public sector investment.

In the annual Budget, even though gross revenue showed an improvement, the resource gap widened mainly because aid was not received on the expected scale. The improvement in revenue receipts, which accrued notwithstanding a notable fall in the proceeds from cotton export duties, was mainly attributable to a better return on investment in state-owned enterprises, especially the nationalized banks, increased realization of income tax and recovery of arrears of tax on hitherto undisclosed income, and higher receipts from government domestic loans.

The high rate of inflation which had characterized previous years but had subsided in 1975-76 moderated further to 9 per cent as against 30 per cent in 1973-74. A fall in the velocity of money, the continuation of a monetary policy designed to discourage the undue building-up of inventories, adequate supplies of wheat and the maintenance of price controls were factors restraining price pressures.

BANGLADESH

At the start of 1978 the 80 million people of Bangladesh were promised not only a return to democracy but also a new deal under which politics would be conducted for the benefit of the people and not of the politicians. The man holding out those hopes was Major-General Ziaur Rahman, who after two years still clung to the helm of state. During 1977 he added the job of President to those of administering martial law, serving as chief of army staff and heading the Ministries of Finance and Home Affairs. General Zia was often popularly described as the 'strong man' of Bangladesh, but at times during 1977 his grip seemed somewhat shaky. The main challenge came not from the politicians but from General Zia's own power base, the army.

Throughout the year there were murmurs of disaffection between different branches of the army, dissension between soldiers who had fought in the liberation war and those who returned from Pakistan after Bangladesh had won its independence, and intense personal jockeying among the eight major-generals at the very top. The most serious challenge, however, emerged from the rank and file of the troops.

The bizarre events of late September and early October started in the garrison of Bogra, where soldiers mutinied and broke into the town, opening the gaol. That attempt was put down, but only after considerable delay. And two days later similar troubles spread to Dacca, where senior members of the Government were preoccupied with negotiations over a hijacked Japan Air Lines DC-8. For several hours mutinous soldiers and airmen were able to take over the radio station and kill air force officers. Strangely, however, the mutineers did not show the leadership needed to consolidate their advantage and after hesitation they were overcome. Hurried summoning of courts martial and executions of those judged to be the mutinies' leaders testified to the Government's sense of shock.

Several conundrums remained. Were these the first shots fired by Bangladesh's 'have-nots'? Might the mutinies not be merely the first signs of a long battle in which the multitudinous millions of the very poor would assert themselves? There were also questions about the activities of some senior officers. No known figure was implicated in either mutiny but there were rumours about the role of three major-generals. These were intensified when General Zia retired the commanders of the Bangladesh Rifles and the air force and reshuffled two major-generals in what were taken to be demotions. Nevertheless, although the violence came from within the military cantonments, it was still the army which at the end of 1977 manned the roadblocks at strategic points, enforced the curfew and generally made it clear who called the shots in Bangladesh.

In the countryside there was no sign that the 'have-nots' would follow the example of the soldiers and rise in revolt, perhaps because their intense poverty made survival a full-time task for 90 per cent of the population. Overall per capita income remained between $80 and $100. The excellent harvest of 1976 was followed by another good one in 1977, so starvation on a massive scale was kept at bay, though real GNP showed but a modest rise after a 10 per cent increase in 1976.

Behind the seemingly charming country scene there was an intense system of deprivation of the very poor. There were growing numbers of landless people and smallholders whose strips of land were fragmented into holdings far too small and poor to farm economically. At the top, besides the privileged westernized elite typical of a developing country, a good number of large landowners were doing well by the system.

General Zia, after two years in power, declared himself in 1977 for 'the people'. He began to visit the villages and declared: 'We are going to change the whole approach of politics. From now on anyone who wants to go into politics will have to go to the people. In the past the politicians did not bother with the people: they just fought one another for what they could get. We have got to work hard, go to the villages, go to the people.'

In December, to commemorate the sixth anniversary of independence, General Zia announced that he was going to form a new political grouping. The politicians of the established parties like the Awami League and Muslim League, however, largely shunned him, and he had mixed success in trying to attract well-known non-politicals to his banner, so the new political grouping was clearly going to have problems in establishing its identity. The President also framed laws to disqualify corrupt old-time politicians.

There were still questions about President Zia's political ability. Under his rule law and order had been restored and some useful reforms applied; the Social Welfare Department was beginning to try to provide work opportunities for vagrants and to penetrate to the poorest villages. General Zia proudly pointed out that near Jessore villagers had built a canal to straighten the river and assure better irrigation. He was alive to the possibilities of work and crops—and taxes for the Government—from projects like these, and said he wanted more of them.

By bearing and training a military man, General Zia liked to get things done, expected quick successes and reacted testily if his orders were not carried out. It was open to question whether Bangladesh with its pernicious social system would allow the rapid change that would satisfy a military ruler, let alone produce a metamorphosis radical enough to give the millions of 'have-nots' a real chance.

SRI LANKA

In the first general election for seven years Mrs Bandaranaike's Sri Lanka Freedom Party (SLFP) Government was defeated and replaced by a United National Party (UNP) Administration led by Mr J. R. Jayawardene with an absolute majority which allowed it to begin radical economic and constitutional changes immediately.

The year began with a crisis for Mrs Bandaranaike produced by a railway strike and by disagreement with her Communist Party (CP) allies in the Government. Emergency powers were adopted between 5 January and 16 February and a press censorship imposed for most of January. Parliament was prorogued between 10 February and 18 May and in the intervening period the CP withdrew their support from the Government and were supported by six defectors from the SLFP, who later formed a People's Democratic Party to contest the July elections. Mrs Bandaranaike attempted to come to an agreement with the newly-formed Tamil United Liberation Front (TULF) (see AR 1976, p. 272), but this failed and her party faced the voters alone for the first time since 1960.

The lifting of emergency powers allowed the republication of the Dawasa newspapers, closed in 1974 (see AR 1974, p. 298) and the reappearance of the Janatha Vimukthi Peramuna (JVP), which led the insurrection of 1971 (see AR 1971, pp. 282-84). The left parties united at May Day to launch a United Left Front (ULF), comprising the Lanka Samasamaja Party (LSSP), the CP and the defectors from the SLFP, to fight as a bloc at the elections. The parties began issuing election policies generally promising various forms of socialism. The UNP offered a free trade zone and changes to the Constitution to create an executive presidency. The SLFP Government revalued the rupee upwards by 20 per cent, began to liberalize imports, promised to nationalize monastic property and announced the impending nationalization of three British-owned banks. The new ULF led by Mr T. B. Subasinghe promised to introduce 'real socialism' and to end the alleged nepotism practised by Mrs Bandaranaike. June saw another railway strike and disturbances on the plantations, both directed against the Government.

The elections on 21 July resulted in a landslide for the UNP, the crushing defeat of the SLFP and the total elimination of the marxist left for the first time in 40 years. The results were:

	UNP	SLFP	ULF	TULF	Others
Seats (2 vacant)	139	8	0	17	2
Percentage vote	51	29·6	7·1	6·4	5·9

The elections were conducted peaceably but were followed by serious rioting in July, directed against supporters of the SLFP, and in August against the Tamil minority. Thirty-six were reported killed in the first riots and a curfew was imposed on 23 July. More serious disturbances led to 125 deaths after a fight in Jaffna had sparked national rioting against the Tamils. A curfew was imposed between 18 August and 31 August and by the end of the month 40,000 Tamils were in refugee camps under protection. Nevertheless the rioting subsided and Mr A. Amirthalingam became the first Tamil ever to lead the parliamentary opposition.

The new UNP Cabinet had 24 members, of whom one was a Tamil and two were Muslims. Seats had been offered to representatives of the SLFP, the TULF and the LSSP but they had declined. The new Parliament adopted a constitutional amendment on 5 October, after the opposition had walked out, inaugurating a presidential system from 1 January 1978. The new President, who would be Mr J. R. Jayawardena, had power to nominate Ministers and would be subject to popular election rather than parliamentary control. He was also empowered to appoint district ministers outside the Cabinet, could dissolve the Assembly but could be removed by it only with a two-thirds majority. This marked a major departure from prime ministerial and parliamentary focus of power as embodied in the Constitution of 1972 (see AR 1972, p. 286).

The Budget of Finance Minister Ronnie de Mel, presented on 2 December, devalued the rupee by 85 per cent, liberalized trade, abolished food subsidies for half the population, lifted price controls and introduced unemployment assistance. A salary ceiling was retained and the guaranteed price of rice was increased for farmers. This Budget marked a turn away from a controlled welfare economy towards policies long advocated by the World Bank.

The leader of the TULF, Mr S. J. V. Chelvanayakam, died in April. The new Government released from prison Mr H. P. Jayawardene, convicted of planning the assassination of Mr S. W. R. D. Bandaranaike (see AR 1959, pp. 113-14), and Mr Rohan Wijeweera, leader of the JVP insurrection of April 1971 (see AR 1971, pp. 282-84).

NEPAL

On 27 January the mountain kingdom of Nepal reduced customs and excise duties by 10 to 50 per cent on a large variety of consumer goods and abolished export duty on 179 of the 200 export items. On 21 February a divisional bench of the Supreme Court upheld the death penalty imposed on Captain Yagya Bahadur Thapa and Mr Bhim Narayan Shrastha for trying to overthrow the Nepal Government.

Mr B. P. Koirala, former Prime Minister, was released on 26 April and rearrested within minutes on a treason charge. The Supreme Court dismissed the habeas corpus petition challenging his detention. Subsequently, he was given permission to go to the United States for treatment; he returned on 8 November to Kathmandu and was put in gaol again. Mr Jayaprakash Narayan, the Gandhian leader in India, urged the King to release Mr Koirala and initiate the process of democratization in his country.

India's Foreign Minister, Mr Atal Bihari Vajpayee, visited Nepal on 5 July and discussed the possibilities of expediting three India–Nepal hydro-electric projects, namely Karnali, Pancheshwar and Rapti. India's Prime Minister, Mr Morarji Desai, visited Kathmandu on 9 December and removed the impression created during Mrs Gandhi's regime that New Delhi was out to force Nepal to accept a junior position. He assured the Nepalese that they could have two separate treaties, one for trade with India and the other for free transit through India for the goods Kathmandu wanted to import.

Bhutan decided on 11 November to regulate the entry, stay and employment of Nepalese nationals.

Chapter 3

SEYCHELLES—MAURITIUS—BRITISH INDIAN OCEAN TERRITORY—
MALAGASY REPUBLIC

SEYCHELLES

ON 7 June 1977, the Seychelles, which had become an independent republic in 1976, underwent a coup d'etat while President Mancham was in London for the Commonwealth Prime Ministers conference (see Pt. XI, Ch. 2). He could not be seated at the conference and Seychelles was unrepresented. The coup was in fact mainly directed against the President himself, and he was forbidden to return. But the democratic constitution, Assembly and courts of justice were swept away, and the country was thereafter ruled as a semi-marxist state by a seven-man Government led by Mr Albert Réné, who was previously Prime Minister in the coalition of Mr Mancham's Seychelles Democratic Party (SDP) and his own left-wing Seychelles Peoples United Party (SPUP).

A small force of about 40 men trained in guerrilla or revolutionary operations flew in and joined up with revolutionaries in the island, and seized the police stations and armoury (killing two policemen), the radio and government offices. According to Mr Réné's account they then bargained with him for two hours on the conditions on which he would head a new regime, and he agreed upon undefined terms; but it was elsewhere alleged that he masterminded the entire operation. Though the invading force was never identified, there is clear evidence that the men were trained in Zanzibar, and therefore with President Nyerere's connivance. Once they had disarmed the police there could be no further resistance, and Mr Mancham announced that he would attempt no counter-coup.

Mr Réné defined his regime as socialist, but not on Russian lines, and not opposed to private enterprise; he promised that elections would be held in 1979. Some of his colleagues sounded more militant, especially Mr Hodoul. Whether or not the Russian or Chinese embassies played a role, they tactfully refrained from congratulating the new Government. On the pretext of a Mancham counter-coup, Hodoul and Réné set up a 1,000-man People's Militia with fifty Tanzanian advisers; they were to stand behind the police and patrol the islands at night, the police being visible by day.

The split between Mancham and Réné was an old one, originating in Mancham's earlier resistance to independence. When the coalition was formed Mancham took on himself the development of high-class tourism, and during his lengthy absences his party decayed. The SPUP leaders accused him both of moral laxity and of a policy of enslaving the people to the capitalists, whereas priority should be given to revitalizing agriculture, to developing fisheries in the huge area embraced by the archipelago's 200-mile zone, and land reform—in all of which, however, Réné had had the initiative, and in fact he had alienated more land to hotels. Mr Réné ruled out a 'Scandinavian' welfare state, did not push land reform, reassured the expatriate retired people about their property, and called for socialist hard work. This had little effect. The islanders had forsaken the land for the hotels, and copra production had fallen by 60 per cent. The Government established minimum wages, a state transport system and price control. But in effect the quasi-marxist state remained dependent on bourgeois tourists of the richer variety. The American tracking station, which was paying £500,000 a year in rentals, was not ejected, while British aid, mainly for tourism under a soft loan of £10 million, continued. Seychelles catered to 50,000 visitors in 1976 and its development plan required 75,000 by 1980. Thus economically the Mancham policy persisted little changed, but rule was by decree, and surveillance and censorship were on the usual lines of a 'people's democracy'. There was a considerable exodus of private capital. Mr Réné's survival seemed to depend on his balancing act; his colleagues were much more doctrinaire and maintained close contacts with the Russians.

MAURITIUS

In Mauritius the marxist challenge, which seemed menacing when the Mouvement Militant Mauricien (MMM) won 34 of the 70 assembly seats in November 1976, receded steadily in 1977.

After recovering from his illness, to which some of his party's bad showing in the elections might be attributed, the Prime Minister, Sir Seewoosagur Ramgoolam, took vigorous charge of the coalition with Mr Gaetan Duval's party, the Parti Mauricien Social Democratique (PMSD), cemented its unity, helped by Duval's rebuff by the electorate and the rise of marxism, which worried Duval's supporters most of all, since the PMSD represented the *'population générale'* and in particular the propertied and managerial classes. The (mainly Hindu) Labour Party remained solid, and several MMM members crossed the floor to join the Government side.

Mr Paul Bérenger's association with Kim Il Sung of North Korea and M Ali Solih of the Cormoro semi-marxist regime had given him a marxist image, which he had confirmed by declaring that his party aimed to make Mauritius into another Cuba, and would rely on Russia, but he steadily moderated his statements in the course of the year. His proposals for a socialist society with a mixed economy finally differed from the Labour Party's only in emphasis. His team showed considerable parliamentary incompetence. The MMM's strength remained the discontent produced by poverty and unemployment, its weakness the fact that it appealed to disparate communal elements in a multiracial society still structured by communalism.

Though strikes continued to reveal the stresses in this society, Mauritius had suffered less from the world stagnation than might have been expected, notably as the result of Sir Seewoosagur's prudent arrangements with EEC on sugar prices and quotas, under which Mauritius did nearly as well as Réunion, and had not suffered from the slump in the world free-market sugar price. The industrial sector, though only 5 per cent of the economy, was now employing 30,000 wage-earners, planned to rise to 60,000 by 1980. The reduction of the birth-rate from 40 to 25 per thousand promised, in time, an alleviation of the malthusian threat.

The Bishop of Stepney, Father Trevor Huddleston, was appointed Bishop of Mauritius in 1977, and Princess Alexandria made a popular visit to the island.

BRITISH INDIAN OCEAN TERRITORY

The future of the British island of Diego Garcia, leased to the US for development as a permanent Indian Ocean naval, air and communications base, hung in the balance throughout 1977 as the result of suggestions put forward by President Carter to the Russians for creating a demilitarized zone in the Indian Ocean as a sweetener for the Salt II negotiations. Discussions between Mr Paul Warnke and Mr Mendelevich for Russia took place in Geneva, Moscow, Washington and Berne. The President's proposals seemed originally to involve the abandonment of Diego Garcia (of which Mauritius would then claim restitution) in return for a Russian withdrawal from the base at Berbera in Somalia. But in the course of the year Russia's support for the Mengistu regime in Ethiopia forced its withdrawal from Berbera, which left it without a bargaining card. Indeed, the Russians then made overtures to the Maldive Republic to take over Gan island, relinquished by the RAF as an Indian Ocean pied-a-terre, but was refused. By the end of the year the discussions turned on a limitation of the number of warship visits to the Indian Ocean and a mutual ban on the deployment of 'multiship task forces'. However, the work on Diego Garcia was rushed forward day and night. Though smaller than Berbera or Aden, used by the Russian fleets, it was planned to have a naval dock, a deep anchorage for the largest ships, a lengthened runway, a jet fuel farm and storage. Though it would not be finished until 1979-80 it became a substantial bargaining counter for Indian Ocean disarmament.

MALAGASY REPUBLIC

The 'great red island' off the coast of south-east Africa continued to be one of the hardest of the states of Africa, so-called, to categorize (Malagasies themselves deny that they are African). President Didier Ratsiraka, while remaining publicly marxist-inclined, and given to denouncing France, continued to give indications of his willingness to deal with Paris, and towards the end of 1977 this fact was emphasized by the cordial visit of the French Cooperation Minister, Robert Galley. Despite widespread nationalizations, considerable French business interests remained. The President continued his ardent advocacy of neutralization of the Indian Ocean and maintained the hostility towards South Africa that was one of the marked changes after the revolution of 1972.

Internally President Ratsiraka seemed to have consolidated his position with a series of elections (on the village, commune, federation of communes, provincial and national levels). Ratsiraka's party, the Avant-Garde de la Révolution Socialiste Malgache (AREMA), won a landslide victory, although it governed as part of a coalition movement, the Front Nationale pour la Défense de la Révolution; this embraced all the other parties except the MONIMA (Madagascar aux Malgaches) of Monja Joana, an elderly but respected political figure, whose revolt in the Tulear province in 1971 paved the way for the fall of the *ancien régime*. Joana's party split after the elections, and by the end of the year the rump he led had virtually collapsed.

IX SOUTH-EAST AND EAST ASIA

Chapter 1

MALAYSIA AND BRUNEI—SINGAPORE—HONG KONG—BURMA—THAILAND—
INDONESIA—PHILIPPINES—VIETNAM—CAMBODIA—LAOS

MALAYSIA AND BRUNEI

A major political crisis within the ruling National Front coalition occurred in December when Party Islam (PAS) was expelled. The crisis originated in the state of Kelantan where PAS commanded a majority in the legislature. In October the central leadership of the party inspired a vote of no confidence in the Chief Minister of Kelantan, Datuk Mohamed Nasir, who was appointed by the late Prime Minister Tun Abdul Razak, leader of the rival United Malays National Organization (UMNO). As a consequence major rioting broke out in the state capital, Kota Bahru, where demonstrators demanded the dissolution of the Kelantan legislature. In November the Federal Parliament passed a Bill which dissolved the state legislature and imposed emergency rule; the secretary general of Malaysia's Defence Ministry, Hashim Aman, was appointed federal administrator for Kelantan. With one exception, all PAS members of the Government and Parliament voted against the Bill. The expulsion of PAS from the National Front took place when the former party refused to comply with the latter's demand that it dismiss all of its members of Parliament who voted against the Bill.

In January Datuk Harun Idris, the former Chief Minister of the state of Selangor, was sentenced to six months' imprisonment for forging the minutes of the investment committee of the People's Cooperative Bank in order to secure letters of credit which enabled him to stage a world heavyweight boxing contest in Kuala Lumpur in 1975. In December this sentence was increased to four years when the Federal Court ruled on his appeal.

The death occurred in January of the controversial former secretary general of UMNO, Tan Sri Syed Jaafar Albar. In July 1976 he had been elected at the age of 62 to the leadership of the youth wing of the Organization in defiance of the known wishes of Prime Minister Datuk Hussein Onn. In February two former deputy Ministers, Abdullah Ahmad and Abdullah Majid, who had been detained in 1976 confessed on television to communist sympathies which they recanted. In confessing they implicated officials of the Soviet embassy in Kuala Lumpur.

In December all 93 passengers and 7 crew were killed when a Malaysian Air Services (MAS) Boeing 737 exploded in mid-air at low altitude near Johore Bahru. The aircraft had been on a flight from Penang to Kuala Lumpur when its captain reported the presence on board of a hijacker with explosives. Among the dead was the Malaysian Minister of Agriculture, Datuk Ali Haji Ahmad.

In January Malaysian security forces took part in an unprecedented combined operation with their Thai counterparts against communist insurgents in Thailand. The operation (named Big Star) concentrated on the western sector to the north of the border in Sadao district of Songkhla province, where the Revolutionary Faction of the fractured Malayan Communist Party had been deployed. In March Prime Minister Datuk Hussein Onn visited Bangkok and signed a revised joint border agreement which incorporated provision for hot pursuit but did not permit the permanent stationing of one country's security forces on the other's territory. In July a second combined operation (named Sacred Ray) was launched in the Betong and Weng districts along the central and eastern sectors of the border. Its object was to disrupt the long-established infrastructure of the mainstream insurgent Malayan Communist Party.

In August a 14-year-old Malaysian Chinese boy was sentenced to death for unlawful possession of a pistol and ammunition under a mandatory provision of the amended Internal Security Act. The rejection of his appeal for clemency in October caused considerable controversy among the legal profession which was not fully abated by the commutation of his sentence by the Pardons Board.

In August the five heads of government of the Association of South-East Asian Nations (Asean) met in Kuala Lumpur under the chairmanship of Prime Minister Datuk Hussein Onn to commemorate the association's tenth anniversary. The meeting was marked by the announcement by President Marcos of the Philippines that he was taking definite steps to terminate his country's longstanding territorial claim to Sabah in Northern Borneo. He and Mme Marcos travelled to the disputed territory after the conclusion of the Kuala Lumpur summit; it was the first visit by a Philippino head of government. Malaysia's attempt to act as a bridge between the Asean states and the communist countries of Indochina was underlined by the visit to Hanoi in May of its Foreign Minister Tengku Ahmad Rithauddeen who also visited Cambodia and Burma in December.

The new Concorde service between London and Singapore via Bahrein was suspended in December after only three flights because of the refusal of the Malaysian Government to countenance passage through its air space. The service had been inaugurated after the Indonesian Government had permitted three flights in each direction over its air space in the Strait of Malacca, but negotiations in Kuala Lumpur failed to change the position of the Malaysian Government, which had sole responsibility for coordinating air traffic control over all the air space in the Malacca Strait region.

In June the Sultan of BRUNEI, Sir Hassanal Bolkiah, and his father, Sir Omar Ali Saifuddin, held inconclusive discussions in London with a Minister of State at the Foreign and Commonwealth Office over the British intention to change its treaty relationship with the Sultanate and to withdraw the battalion of Gurkhas stationed there. In November the UN General Assembly approved a resolution which called on the Government of the United Kingdom 'to take all steps within its competence to facilitate expeditiously the holding of free and democratic elections' in the Sultanate.

SINGAPORE

In January Ho Kwon Ping, correspondent of the *Far Eastern Economic Review*, was arrested and charged with possessing and disseminating 'sensitive information'. He was heavily fined on the charge of possession and subsequently resigned his job. In February a prominent lawyer, Gopalan Raman, was detained under the Internal Security Act and accused of working with a group of 'Euro-Communists' to exert pressure through the Socialist International for the release of hard-core communist detainees. He disclosed the names of 11 people allegedly associated with him in pro-communist activities. Among those consequently arrested was Arun Senkuttuvan, correspondent for the *Financial Times* and the *Economist*, while a British teacher, Brian Maurice, implicated by Raman, was expelled from the country. In March Senkuttuvan admitted in a 'public confession' that he had used his position to portray the Government of Singapore as undemocratic and oppressive. Shortly afterwards Ho Kwon Ping was re-arrested under the Internal Security Act. Senkuttuvan was released from detention in April but deprived of his citizenship; Ho was released at the end of the month following his confession of how he had tried to depict Singapore as elitist, racist, fascist and dictatorial.

In January the British financier Jim Slater was cleared by London's Chief Metropolitan Magistrate of six charges of fraud and conspiracy brought against him by the Singapore Government concerning the affairs of Haw Par Brothers International. In April the Singapore Government once more sought his extradition but the application was rejected by the Queen's Bench Divisional Court, which in July ordered the extradition of his business associate Richard Tarling to face trial in Singapore on six charges related to the affairs of Haw Par and the Melbourne Unit Trust.

In October four men hijacked a Vietnamese airliner on a domestic flight and killed two crew members before forcing it to land in Singapore. The Vietnamese Government demanded the return of the hijackers but Singapore refused to comply because of the absence of an extradition treaty and also because Vietnam was not a party to any of three international conventions covering hijacking. The hijackers were tried in Singapore in December and given the maximum sentence of 14 years in prison, together with 30 strokes of the cane, for crimes under the Arms Offences Act.

HONG KONG

In December the EEC imposed a five-year agreement transferring part of Hong Kong's share of EEC markets to other exporting countries and requiring shipments of major textile and clothing lines to be sharply reduced from 1977 levels, which were already below those for 1976. Continued growth in United States, Latin American, Middle Eastern and Asian markets, diversification and rising quality enabled exports to grow overall in nominal terms by about $8\frac{1}{2}$ per cent. The trade deficit, customarily balanced by invisible earnings, increased by three-quarters. Tourist traffic rose by a seventh. Real GDP growth fell back from the 1976 recovery rate of 17·8 per cent to 8 per cent or less, largely generated by increased investment and consumption and by large public and private building programmes, especially of housing. A state low-cost home ownership scheme was launched. The underground railway progressed and a $6\frac{1}{2}$-mile extension to Tsun Wan was approved, to be completed in 1982.

The population passed $4\frac{1}{2}$ million, a third of the increase coming from refugees, mostly from Indochina. The cost of living rose by $5\frac{1}{2}$ per cent. In March industrial wages had improved in real terms by $5\frac{1}{2}$ per cent over the previous 12 months and this movement was expected to continue, alongside virtually full employment and labour shortages in industries with below-average wages or working conditions. Further changes in labour and social security legislation were introduced or proposed, including the ending by 1979 of overtime for women and 16- and 17-year-olds, an improved sickness benefit scheme and higher fines for those found employing children in industry. Legislation was announced to extend compulsory education to include 14-year-olds and to abolish fees in government junior schools. In October severe pressure on police corruption led to loss of morale and rank-and-file demonstrations which caused the Government to indicate that only the more heinous offences committed in earlier years would be prosecuted.

There were further hints that China had no wish to see any early change in the status of Hong Kong, from which it was thought to receive US$2,200 million a year as payment for exports and invisible earnings.

BURMA

Early in February fighting sharply escalated in eastern Burma, largely against well-armed Burma Communist Party forces apparently operating from bases in China, and continued on a smaller but still substantial scale thereafter. Nevertheless relations with China improved. Chou En-lai's widow paid a visit in February and U Ne Win subsequently twice visited China. It was suggested that the Chinese had agreed to reduce, or even end, support for BCP guerrillas in return for expulsion of a pro-Soviet group from the Burma Socialist Programme Party (BSPP) and Burmese support for Chinese objectives, notably a visit to Cambodia late in November by Ne Win himself. There were generally improved relations with Thailand and India and visits by the President of Laos and the Prime Minister of Japan.

The third Congress of the BSPP met in February. Ne Win was re-elected Chairman and General San Yu Secretary-General. Over half of those elected to the Central Committee were newcomers. Failure of the economic plan was attributed to faulty implementation rather than to policy, and the Prime Minister and the Finance and Planning Minister were amongst those who resigned. There were subsequently complaints of lobbying at this Congress and a purge of 'opportunists and schemers', possibly pro-Soviet. An extraordinary Congress met on 14 November and a new Central Committee was elected. Amongst those removed were the new Finance and Planning Minister and others installed after the third Congress.

Within the regime there was criticism of corruption, inefficiency and opulent living and a greater willingness to admit to economic shortcomings, but a continuing reluctance to attribute these to the *dirigiste* policies being followed or wholeheartedly to adopt more market-oriented policies. In September, however, a law on private enterprise was promulgated after months of debate. This approved a list of activities in manufacturing and distribution still open to small entrepreneurs, in order to promote production in fields with which the state system could not yet cope. Activity by foreign firms declined after unpromising offshore oil drilling results, but a large commercial loan was raised for oil development and consultations were held with a World Bank consultative aid group.

THAILAND

The Government of Thanin Kraivichien pursued campaigns against corruption, tax evasion, drug trafficking, moral decay and communist influence in an unimaginative manner which lost it support. There was an unsuccessful attempt at a right-wing coup on 26 March—its leader, un-characteristically for Thailand, was executed. Field officers and other influential groups increasingly felt that the Government was alienating important elements within society—civil servants, the press, peasants, industrial workers and students—although restraint was induced by a wish not to appear unstable to foreign governments and investors.

In September the annual promotions brought into the post of supreme commander General Kriangsak Chamanand, who had the support of field officers and more pragmatic views than the Government on social and political issues and on foreign policy, especially towards communist states. On 20 October the Thanin Government was removed, Thanin himself later being appointed to the Privy Council; the 1976 Constitution was abrogated and an interim Constitution was introduced with a new advisory assembly to prepare for elections within 18 months, a far more rapid return to representative government than Thanin had envisaged. On 11 November Kriangsak became Prime Minister and began to move to secure wider national support for Government policy.

The new Cabinet adopted a more positive attitude to the Indochinese countries and was prepared to revive trade with Laos. Since Vietnam and Laos had simultaneously reason to seek detente with Asean, this markedly improved the atmosphere. On 2 December Vietnam and Thailand announced that they would normalize relations and a Vietnamese representative arrived in Bangkok on 13 December to discuss trade and commercial aviation. On 12 December an air service agreement with Laos was signed in Bangkok. The Laotians also announced appointment of an ambassador—a new Thai ambassador had already arrived in Vientiane in September. In December Kriangsak was invited to visit China. It was made clear, however, that these developments would not preclude closer cooperation with Malaysia and other Asean states, with Burma and with the USA.

Early in the year there was greater military activity against armed insurgency and some infiltration of guerrillas from Laos and Cambodia, but no clear increase in guerrilla effectiveness. Field officers stressed the importance of political, social and economic measures rather than military in dealing with insurgency, as did Kriangsak. He urged the return of students and intellectuals who had joined the insurgents or retired abroad, and based his economic and social policy on emphasizing development in the rural areas and provincial towns rather than Bangkok, on reducing social and regional inequities and, in urban areas, on slum clearance, more public housing and facilities, free medical care for the poor and assisted family planning.

INDONESIA

Elections were held on 2 May. There was some pressure by local officials in favour of the official party, Golkar, and violence by the youth groups of both Golkar and PPP (Partai Persatuan Pembangunan) was alleged. PPP provided the main challenge to Golkar, basing its appeal on stricter adherence to Muslim ideals and attributing social and economic problems to Western, especially Christian, influences. PDI (Partai Demokrasi Indonesia), the third grouping, was an uneasy amalgam of the old Nationalist Party and various Christian and other parties. Golkar gained just over 62 per cent of total votes, fractionally less than in 1971, while PPP increased its share by nearly 2 per cent to over 29 per cent and the PDI share fell less than expected, from 10 per cent to $8\frac{1}{2}$ per cent. There were considerable regional variations, Golkar receiving only about two-fifths of the vote in Jakarta and in Aceh, Sumatra, but over nine-tenths in parts of eastern Indonesia. Golkar secured almost 65 per cent of elected seats, with the result that Government support, including appointed members, was over 72 per cent in Parliament and 78 per cent in the larger Assembly.

After the election Adam Malik left the Foreign Ministry to become Chairman of the Assembly, a move which was expected to give the two parliamentary bodies greater influence, also to help ensure the re-election of President Suharto for a third term in March 1978. The prospect of this election sustained political debate. Student criticism, especially of corruption and abuse of position, grew markedly. A new official campaign against corruption was started in July, but there was no evidence that it would reach the more important national leaders and their families. On 14 November the Supreme Advisory Council joined in this criticism, as did the armed forces journal, and this encouraged demonstrations by student and Muslim groups. On 15 December, however, leaders of the armed forces announced that they would deal firmly with anyone trying to undermine the national leadership or frustrate the Assembly plenary session.

Budget estimates were again balanced, but large proposed increases in official salaries and pensions swung the emphasis from capital to recurrent expenditure. Inflation, which on official figures had fallen from 33 per cent in 1974 to 13 per cent in 1976, subsided a little further. Improved commodity trade, apart from mineral oil, and a rather better harvest in 1976-77 enabled a lower level of external aid to be proposed for 1977-78, while progress with clearing up the Pertamina debacle (see AR 1976, p. 284) permitted outstanding loan support to be restructured at lower rates of interest. Harvest conditions for 1977-78 were, however, less favourable, and new oil search and development activity and foreign investment generally were again limited and were not encouraged by insistence that all trading activities must be transferred into Indonesian hands by 31 December. To revive interest, the Government announced on 4 October that investment approval would be concentrated in the Capital Investment Coordinating Board.

PHILIPPINES

A rice surplus was produced and crop prospects were encouraging. Despite sluggish demand for some export commodities, the trade deficit was reduced and the balance of payments was in surplus for the first time since 1974. The 1978 Budget directed 70 per cent of overall expenditure to the regions, mostly to depressed areas. Real growth was again over 6 per cent, but inflation rates ceased to fall.

President Marcos was recorded as receiving 89·53 per cent support in a referendum on 18 December for remaining President and assuming also the powers of Prime Minister. Progress was announced on the issue of the American bases, including agreement that they should in principle be commanded by Philippine officers. In November the chairman of the maoist Communist Party of the Philippines was captured. Earlier activity in Luzon by the CPP military arm, the New People's Army, had revived, while the authorities claimed that the NPA was collaborating with the Moro National Liberation Front in the south.

Negotiations with the Muslim MNLF proved difficult. They demanded control of a region comprising 13 provinces in which most people were not Muslims. Marcos insisted on popular consultation. The MNLF rejected this, realizing that all Christians in the region and many Muslims would oppose their proposals, and threatened to resume hostilities. A referendum was nevertheless held on 17 April, voters being offered choices ranging from MNLF control to limited autonomy under central supervision. A substantial turnout was officially reported, with an overwhelming majority for continued central control, although it seemed doubtful that many Muslims had thought it wise to vote in areas where MNLF forces were strong.

The MNLF rejected the referendum on 20 April and, through Islamic Conference representatives, demanded a regional government composed of seven MNLF members and four others, including two Muslims, chosen by itself, to hold power for a six-year transitional period, backed by a 15,000-strong MNLF security force. A ministerial meeting of the Islamic Conference in May, however, persuaded the MNLF to drop its demand for independence. In the belief that MNLF support, both abroad and amongst southern Muslims, was declining, the Government subsequently encouraged defections, while promoting economic development in Muslim areas. The cease-fire had sharply reduced casualties, but by September it was breaking down and there was renewed fighting, especially in Jolo and around Zamboanga.

Criticism of the effects of martial law on human rights continued, notably in the Roman Catholic church and the USA. In June Marcos spoke of ending military tribunals, releasing detainees not charged and transferring other cases to civilian courts. He stated that 4,764 people were held by the military, mostly for common crimes, and 2,000 were released in the following three months. In August, he promised a selective amnesty for political prisoners and on 30 December an amnesty for 1,646 people was announced. He also eased overseas travel restrictions, lifted the night curfew in most areas and promised local elections in 1978. Two leading detainees escaped into exile in October, but another, Benigno Aquino Jr, was sentenced to death by a military tribunal on 25 November (see AR 1976, p. 285). Marcos ordered the case to be reopened so that the defendants could present a defence. On 15 December, however, the Supreme Court called on the army to suspend this trial, which it did, and castigated the tribunal for passing sentence while a habeas corpus application was pending.

VIETNAM

Economic difficulties and conflicts with communist countries induced a more conciliatory attitude to Asean and the USA. There were shortages of food, raw materials and production goods, and inadequate performance in the electricity, building, transport and communications industries. On 2 September the Prime Minister spoke of these difficulties as being inevitable in the march to socialism. A basic problem was insufficient grain production, the shortfall being about 1·2 million tons in 1975-76 and 2 million tons in 1976-77. It was officially stated in May that 'the grain situation is generally critical' and there was no subsequent indication of improvement. The deficit was reduced by food aid or commercial purchases, but also by cuts in consumption.

These difficulties were due partly to unfavourable weather and reduced economic aid, but primarily to organizational failings. The party newspaper spoke of 'exceedingly low labour productivity in both agriculture and industry' and stated that 'leadership and management have often been lax, sluggish and inflexible'. Official comments indicated that peasants, in reaction to the low prices offered for produce and shortages of fuel, fertilizers and consumer goods, were disinclined to exert themselves or to sell to the state. Industry was hampered by shortages of managers, technicians and materials and the conduct of Party officials. The Prime Minister spoke of 'people whose revolutionary nature has changed or decayed' and another Politburo member of 'theft, bribery, speculation, smuggling', failings which were said to be tending 'to increase in both frequency and seriousness'. Changes were announced in economic ministries, in March and again in November, and greater emphasis was placed on agriculture and light industry, with heavy industry giving more support to agriculture.

Official journals reported action against armed resistance groups, while a member of the National Assembly elected in April 1976 spoke of being ostracized in his home town after being picked for the Assembly. Flight abroad increased again, despite the dangers. Reasons cited for flight were various, including the growing hardships of life, denial of the right to work or to have children educated, religious persecution, anger at the 'colonization' of the south or the privileged status and greed of Party officials, and loss of freedom. Opponents of former President Thieu who escaped spoke of little food and no medicine in prison camps, of large-scale executions and of deaths from hunger, overwork and disease. Estimates of the numbers of political prisoners ran from 200,000 upwards, ranging from former servants of the Thieu regime to its active opponents. The flight or imprisonment of technical, managerial and professional people seriously reduced economic efficiency. The exodus also caused difficulties abroad, especially as a rising proportion of refugees were illiterate fishermen, peasants and hill tribesmen.

Efforts to secure Western, Japanese and other markets, capital and technology increased. The IMF granted a loan of US$36 million in January and projects were investigated for World Bank, Asian Development Bank and OPEC Special Fund support. Compensation for French and Japanese assets was discussed and in April the Prime Minister paid a successful visit to France. Malaysia was asked for technical assistance with rubber and palm oil, posts, telecommunications, roads and road transport, while greater use was made of trade, financial and servicing facilities in Hong Kong. Joint ventures with up to 49 per cent foreign participation were proposed, cheap labour being Vietnam's main attraction; it seemed, however, that improved terms would be needed to attract much investment. It was claimed that French, Italian and West German companies had signed oil search agreements.

Contacts with the United States revived. A US mission visited Hanoi in March. In May talks began in Paris and continued thereafter. The US Administration seemed more interested in restoring relations than was Congress or the American public, and it ceased to oppose Vietnamese efforts to join international bodies. Vietnam was admitted to the UN on 20 September and in December made gestures of goodwill in Paris. Delegations also visited Thailand and other Asean countries, both for economic reasons and to avoid being isolated. Relations with China remained cool, despite a visit by the Party Secretary-General in November, while border disputes with Cambodia were publicly admitted in December to have developed into full-scale warfare.

CAMBODIA

Self-sufficiency in rice was claimed, although still, it appeared, at a low level of consumption, and further efforts were made to extend irrigation. It was said that some factory production, including cement, had been restarted and that the highway from Phnom Penh through Svay Rieng to Saigon and the railways to Battambang and Kompong Som port had been reopened. There was some revival of export of rice, rubber, kapok and pepper and of imports of spares and equipment, mainly to make further export possible, and of medical supplies—it had been intended to rely on herbal remedies, but severe outbreaks of malaria, cholera and dysentry forced a change in policy. A substantial loss of population appeared to have resulted from the brutality of the regime, malnutrition and disease.

A greater interest was shown in contacts with non-communist states. Ministerial visits were made to Burma, Ceylon, Malaysia and Singapore and received from Burma and Malaysia. Relations with China remained close. The Prime Minister, Pol Pot, twice visited Peking, in September and October, and a Chinese Vice-Premier made an extensive tour of Cambodia, including sensitive border and off-shore areas, in December. The Laotian head of state arrived in Phnom Penh on 17 December, in an effort perhaps to improve Vietnamese as well as Laotian relations with Cambodia. He was told that the Khmer regime expected mutual non-interference and that a country should not allow foreign troops to use its territory for aggression against neighbours—substantial Vietnamese forces remained in Laos.

Incidents continued along the border with Thailand. One massacre of Thai villagers was met with the claim that the area belonged to Cambodia which 'was arranging its internal affairs in these three villages'. The regime appeared to be depopulating a strip of territory along its borders and also to be eliminating non-Khmer groups. Purposes other than territorial claims suggested for these border raids included seizure of food and supplies, opening of routes into Thailand for guerrillas, punishment of smugglers or of Khmer peasants who had fled the country and inhibition of activity by Khmer resistance groups. The Thai authorities made only a restrained response, noting that the line of the border was unclear and that local officials might be ignoring Cambodian Government instructions, but in December it was indicated that future raids would provoke military operations.

Fighting along the Vietnamese border was much heavier, and in late December each country was openly denouncing the other. The Vietnamese launched a major armoured thrust into the 'Parrot's Beak' area of Svay Rieng province, penetrated deep into Cambodian territory and inflicted heavy losses, while elsewhere Vietnamese towns were bombarded. There were mutual accusations of atrocities and from the Khmer side of Vietnamese imperialist ambitions. A struggle for power, which pro-Vietnamese elements had lost, had taken place earlier in the year and it appeared possible that the Vietnamese wished to force a more compliant attitude upon the Khmer regime.

LAOS

The communist leadership under Kaysone Phomvihan increasingly excluded influences other than those of Hanoi and Moscow. Kaysone again visited Moscow in May and expressed support for Soviet policy. He also emphasized the crucial part the Vietnamese Communist Party had played in moulding his party and in enabling it to secure and maintain control of Laos, stating in July that 'every success of the Lao revolution has been possible thanks to a direct contribution of the Vietnamese revolution'. A trial in November concerned attempts to assassinate Kaysone and overthrow the regime; there may have been a division of opinion within the regime itself, while some of the armed resistance to Kaysone and Vietnamese influence was led by Pathet Lao men. In March, the former King was detained and removed from Luang Prabang to a prison nearer the Vietnamese border for fear that he might become a focus for resistance.

On 15 July many of the senior leaders of the Vietnamese Communist Party arrived in Vientiane, including the party Secretary-General, the Prime Minister, the leading Deputy Premier, the political commissar of the army and other members of the Central Committee. They signed agreements tying Laos closely to Vietnam, including a 25-year treaty of friendship and cooperation; the agreements provided for mutual support, border arrangements, economic aid and consultation on foreign relations. Vietnamese forces remained in Laos, engaged both in developing communications with Vietnam and in suppressing resistance. With Pathet Lao troops they engaged in a major offensive against Meo tribesmen who had consistently resisted communist forces; they were said to be destroying villages and forcing the Meos out of the hills in order to deny their support to the guerrillas. Non-communist foreigners, including technicians working for UN and other aid programmes, were further restricted or excluded.

For much of the year the border with Thailand was virtually closed, relations deteriorated and there were border incidents. This was largely due to the mutual fear that each was assisting guerrilla activity in the other's territory. Reduced trade with Thailand greatly hampered economic performance in Laos, already depressed by inept policies, inexperienced management due largely to the flight of competent personnel, and the imposts needed to support large numbers of party officials and troops. On 2 December Kaysone complained that production did not meet the needs of consumption and that the regime was 'compelled to allocate the main part of our forces and budget to defending the country and maintaining peace and public order'. To man-made problems was added a drought which increased food shortages and malnutrition. By December, however, the promptings of necessity in Laos and Vietnam, and a new Government in Thailand, seemed likely to lead to improved relations and trade, and an air service agreement was signed on 12 December in Bangkok.

Chapter 2

CHINA—TAIWAN—JAPAN—SOUTH KOREA—NORTH KOREA

CHINA

AFTER the chaos and high political drama of the previous year, for China 1977 was marked by what was officially designated as the restoration of 'great order throughout the land'. In many ways a new political order was established in China. For the first time in nearly 20 years the central leadership was not divided into contending factions and there was general agreement about the need to concentrate both on the application of the Maoist political norms that had obtained before their distortion by ultra-leftist forces during the Cultural Revolution and on the goal of modernizing China by the end of the century. The fifth volume of Mao's *Selected Works* covering the period 1949-57 was published in April. This provided an ideological framework for the current period. Interestingly, the volume not only brought out Mao's concern for economic development and for sensible democratic order (within a centralized mould), but also included passages of great revolutionary fervour. This in many ways set the tone for Chinese political life; for revolution was no longer counterposed to production.

One of the main features of the new order was the running of the country by way of convening national conferences on the specific aspects of economic and social life which the leadership decided were in need of redirection. This began with the convening of the national conference on Taching—the huge oil field enterprise in the north-east which had been singled out by Mao from 1964 onwards as embodying the best principles of socialist management and as therefore the model for all other industrial enterprises to emulate. Other conferences of note included those on national defence, science, transport, education and even on postal services.

K

The year was also dominated by the continued criticism of the 'gang of four'. In that process many of the cadres judged to have been unfairly dismissed as the result of the factional and conspiratorial politics of the 'gang' were rehabilitated. The most prominent of these was Teng Hsiao-p'ing, who returned to all the posts from which he had been dismissed in the wake of the Tian An Men square incident of April 1976 (see AR 1976, p. 292). It was a measure of Teng's political significance that he was able to insist that before his public rehabilitation the political programmes which he had promoted in the previous two years and which had been the object of massive public criticism orchestrated by the 'gang' should first be totally and publicly exonerated. Thus the Chinese media devoted much space in May and June to justifying the 1975-76 programmes for the modernization of the economy, the advancement of China's scientific research institutes to standards comparable to the best in the world and the restoration of its systems of education to a pattern where attention would again be paid to promotion of high academic standards.

Teng also insisted that he be publicly exonerated from all blame for the Tian An Men affair. This raised problems for some of the other senior leaders. While they were all committed to the modernization of China along the lines promoted by Teng, they had all been involved in issuing the April 1976 communique by the Party Centre which had condemned Teng. Moreover Wu Teh and Ch'en Hsi-lien (respectively the mayor and the commander of the Peking military district) had played an active role in suppressing the masses, who it was now revealed had been demonstrating support for the memory and line of the much-loved Chou En-lai and expressing opposition to the 'gang', and they were now placed in a particularly embarrassing position. From time to time throughout the year wall posters attacking these two appeared in Peking. But neither of them lost his high position. Nevertheless Teng was publicly exonerated from all blame in early July and it was only then that the third plenary session of the tenth Central Committee of the Communist Party of China which formally rehabilitated Teng was held in Peking from 16 to 21 July.

This was the first session of the Central Committee to have been held since the overthrow of the 'gang' and it predictably normalized the constitutional position of Hua Kuo-feng as Chairman of the Party—a position which he had assumed late in 1976. The Plenum also adopted a resolution dismissing the 'gang of four' from all their posts and expelling them 'once and for all' from the Party.

The eleventh Party Congress was held in Peking from 12 to 18 August. It was attended by 1,510 delegates representing 'more than 35 million Party members'. The Congress symbolized the return to proper Maoist party norms. In his political report Chairman Hua formally announced that the Cultural Revolution had in fact ended in October 1976 with the overthrow of the 'gang'. A new Party constitution was promulgated (see

DOCUMENTS) which, unlike its predecessor of 1973, once again made a probationary period of one or two years a necessary condition of membership. No more would particular factions within the Political Bureau be able to induct their favourites and acolytes directly into high Party positions without training or experience. A further practical indication of the return to proper Maoist institutional norms was this description in the formal communique of the Congress of the way in which delegates had been selected: 'They were formally elected to the Congress by the Party organizations in different areas and units which, strictly implementing the Party's principles of democratic centralism and earnestly following the mass line, had held repeated deliberations and consultations and sought opinions extensively from Party members and the masses outside the Party.' The delegates for the previous two Congresses of 1969 and 1973 had been simply nominated from above.

The Congress heard a four-hour-long political report by Chairman Hua Kuo-feng which dwelt at length on the struggle against the 'gang of four', set out the main lines of China's domestic and foreign policies and outlined 'eight main fighting tasks for the present and for some time to come'. These emphasized continuing the criticism and exposure of the 'gang of four', rebuilding and consolidating the Party, developing the economy, making a success of education, 'strengthening the people's state apparatus', promoting democratic norms and mobilizing 'all the positive forces' to develop socialism. Vice-Chairmen Yeh Chien-ying and Teng Hsiao-p'ing also addressed the Congress.

The new leadership line-up of the Party excluded all those associated with ultra-leftism and the 'gang'. The predominant quality of the new Political Bureau and Central Committee was experience allied to functional expertise in leadership of important departments of state and the armed forces. The Congress elected a Central Committee of 201 members and 132 alternate members.

The new Committee held its first plenary session on 19 August, immediately after the Congress. It elected as its Chairman Hua Kuo-feng and as Vice-Chairmen Yeh Chien-ying, Teng Hsiao-p'ing, Li Hsien-nien and Wang Tung-hsing. These five also constituted the Standing Committee of the Political Bureau. Of particular note was the rise of Wang Tung-hsing, whose primary functional responsibilities were the secretarial and organizational work of the Central Committee. In addition to these five men the Political Bureau consisted of the following: Wei Kuo-ching, Ulanfu, Fang Yi, Liu Po-cheng, Hsu Shih-yu, Chi Teng-kuei, Su Chen-hua, Li Teh-sheng, Wu Teh, Yu Chiu-li, Chang Ting-fa, Chen Hsi-lien, Keng Piao, Nieh Jung-chen, Ni Chih-fu, Hsu Hsiang-chien and Peng Chung. Three people were listed as alternate members: Chen Mu-hua (a woman), Chao Tzu-yang and Saifudin. Interestingly, no other central organs were mentioned. Before the onset of the Cultural Revolution in

1966 there had been several, such as the Secretariat and the Control Commission. Mao's constant injunctions against a top-heavy bureaucracy had clearly taken root. This was also instanced by the brief, streamlined quality of the Party constitution (see DOCUMENTS).

The Economy. According to official Chinese accounts the economy registered 14 per cent growth in 1977 over the previous year. This was due almost entirely to the industrial sector. Despite some of the most adverse weather conditions, especially in north and central China during the spring and summer months, the total agricultural output reached the same levels as in 1976. Nevertheless in the course of the year China imported about 11 million tonnes of grain, which exceeded the usual total by several millions. It was also revealed that the chaos in many of China's factories caused by the 'gang's' activities had not been finally settled until the end of March. Likewise it was stated that the state revenue showed an increase of 6 per cent upon that planned in the Budget—this was the first up-turn after three successive years of failure even to reach the planned target.

As from October 46 per cent of the total number of workers and staff received wage increases. These were generally the lower paid; the increases were also designed to remove many of the anomalies which had inevitably built up over a long period. Apart from a small rise in wages for a limited number of people in 1971 this was the first increase since before the Cultural Revolution. More controversial was the officially-inspired debate as to whether bonuses and piece-rates should be restored. After all, these tended to increase the differentials between workers and they also emphasized material incentives. But the debate illustrated the extent of the Chinese determination to build up the economy as quickly as possible.

Education and Culture. The educational situation was totally transformed in the course of the year. It was recognized that standards had been allowed to fall to appalling levels since the onset of the Cultural Revolution 11 years earlier. The reformers of 1975 who had been persecuted by the 'gang of four' were rehabilitated. An official campaign was begun to restore prestige and respect to the teaching profession. Particular attention was paid to the fields of science and foreign languages. Examinations were reintroduced as a means of determining whether satisfactory standards had been attained and also as a criterion for entry to universities.

The year saw the re-emergence of much of the rich diversity of Chinese culture long suppressed by the arbitrary intervention of the 'gang'. Thus films, theatrical performances, concerts and many features of highly popular entertainment like comic cross-talks and strong-man acts which had been kept from the public eye for more than a decade were once again seeing the light of day. Famous artists, musicians, dancers and writers who had suffered much returned to active life. By the end of the year China stood poised on the verge of the blossoming of a new 'Hundred Flowers' period. At the same time the Chinese stressed that this should not be mistaken for liberalization. Culture should still serve socialism.

Foreign Policy. This was one area where policy did not change as compared with the previous year, except to suggest that henceforth there would be a more open attitude to the outside world from which it was recognized that China had much to learn. The American Secretary of State, Mr Cyrus Vance, visited Peking in August. His suggestion that Peking should demonstrate flexibility over the Taiwan question caused his hosts to suspect the new American Administration of seeking to amend the terms of the Shanghai communique (see AR 1972, pp. 305-6). Teng Hsiao-p'ing later told Western reporters that Sino-American relations had suffered a setback.

A month earlier the schism which had been simmering behind the scenes in Sino-Albanian relations was made public by the Albanian publication of a theoretical critique of the ideological basis of China's foreign policy (see p. 120). State relations were not immediately affected, although they naturally lacked the effusiveness which had characterized the relationship in the 1960s. By contrast the burgeoning relationship between China and Yugoslavia was further boosted by the visit of President Tito from 30 August to 8 September. He received the most rapturous reception given to any foreigner for many years.

Foreign relations in the last quarter of the year were dominated by concern for the situation in Indochina. Although the leaders of first Cambodia and then Vietnam visited Peking, the Chinese were unable to prevent the deterioration of their relations to the point that the warfare between them was made public by the Cambodian side in Peking on 31 December, when they openly accused the Vietnamese of aggression.

Sino-Soviet relations continued along much the same lines as they had exhibited in the last years of Mao's life. The Chinese continued to criticize the Soviet Union as an imperialist superpower which tried to mask its true features in the cloak of socialism. If anything, the Chinese became even more vehement in their insistence that as the newest imperialist on the scene the Soviet Union was in an expansionist phase and as a result it was the most dangerous source of war in the world today. Indeed the Chinese repeatedly warned that detente was in fact a form of appeasement and that the only way to delay the onset of a new world war was to pay far more attention to defence preparedness, especially in Europe. By late spring the Soviet leaders evidently despaired of a change of heart in Peking following the death of their great antagonist Mao, and after a six month's grace they too resumed polemics. The new Chinese leadership was depicted as maoist without Mao. But in fact the ideological hostility was not fully reflected in Sino-Soviet state relations. Although the border negotiations broke down the two sides were able to reach agreement on navigation rights in certain disputed parts of their riverine borders.

TAIWAN

Events in Taiwan continued to be influenced by external political developments, among which the most important was the visit of the US Secretary of State, Cyrus Vance, to Peking from 22 to 26 August. It became evident that the Carter Administration was giving its China policy higher priority than earlier in the year, the shift being linked to the emergence and consolidation of the new leadership in China. On Taiwan, reaction to the visit included both re-emphasizing the significance of America's political and economic commitment to the island and, indirectly, preparing the population for the possibility of an American diplomatic withdrawal on China's terms, namely, removal of all US troops, abrogation of the defence treaty and severance of all diplomatic relations between Washington and Taipei.

The possibility of imminent de-recognition by the US accounted for the emergence of a much clearer picture of some of the financial aspects involved. It showed that, on current estimates, commitments by foreign banks to Taiwan would reach US$7-8,000 million by 1981. This was the result of the Government's pursuing a policy of reducing Taiwan's future reliance on foreign loans and key intermediate goods while greatly increasing its current levels of foreign borrowing, giving international banking, especially US banking, a continuing interest in the status quo. In this context, the ten major projects (see AR 1974, p. 322) appeared as a response to the long-term implications of the 1972 Shanghai communique on Sino-American relations (see AR 1972, p. 306): they created a sense of purpose as Taiwan became more isolated diplomatically, broadened the economic base to cope with more isolation, and gave suppliers of equipment and capital a vested interest in Taiwan's future, while forming an extended capital-spending programme that helped Taiwan to weather the worst impact of world recession.

Another outcome was an attempt to use the human rights issue to gain support in the US for retarding the normalization of US-China relations. The defection of a Chinese pilot flying a MiG19 on 7 July was used as propaganda to boost morale and to emphasize the relevance of the human rights question. The placing of full-page advertisements in major American newspapers coincided with a 'one person one letter' campaign that inundated the White House with over 50,000 letters protesting against the Carter Administration's China policy. Similarly, Taiwan Rotary Club members wrote to their American counterparts to seek support for the protest. By raising the human rights issue it became necessary for the Government to be seen to show respect for human rights on Taiwan. This appeared to have influenced the political climate; preparations were under way for the island's largest local elections ever held for mayors, magistrates, Taipei city councillors and provincial assemblymen. The political climate favoured the launching of a new monthly, *The New Generation*, on 1 July by Chang Chun-hung, who had been on the staff of the *Taiwan Political Review*, banned permanently in October 1976, only weeks after the *China Humanist Monthly* had been suspended for one year.

The local elections held on 19 November thus appear to have been conducted at a time of increased tolerance of differing political views. While the Nationalists had won an overwhelming 85 per cent of the 1,318 provincial posts, among the independent politicians' gains were four of the 20 mayoral and magistrates posts, 21 of the 77 provincial assembly seats and eight of the 51 new Taipei municipal council seats. These results, compared with the distribution of local power before the elections, were a significant and unexpected development, likely to enhance the position of independent politicians in matters affecting, in particular, county, city, municipal and provincial budgets. Encouraged by some of the most outspoken campaign speeches ever heard, over 75 per cent of the electorate voted, the only adverse incident being a riot sparked off by accusations of ballot tampering at Chungli, Taoyuan.

Industrial production grew by 12 per cent during the year, and the value of foreign trade for the first 11 months was US$16,003 million, an increase of 14 per cent on the same period in 1976. Exports were valued at US$8,333 million and imports at US$7,669 million. Industrial products accounted for 87·2 per cent of the exports, followed by processed agricultural products (7·5 per cent) and agricultural products (5·3 per cent). The US took 39·2 per cent of total exports, followed by Japan (12·3 per cent). Japan with 30·8 per cent remained the main source of imports, followed by the US (23·6 per cent). A notable feature was the important links forged with Saudi Arabia, which supplied 40 per cent of Taiwan's oil and extended substantial low-interest loans for development. In return, Taiwan provided assistance in industrial and rural development plans. President Yen Chia-kan paid a three-day state visit to Saudi Arabia in July.

During the first 11 months, overseas investments amounted to US$86·41 million, including US$58·983 million from foreign investors (mostly from the US, Japan and Europe), largely in the electrical and electronics industries, the remainder coming from overseas Chinese. At the same time the tourist industry continued to expand, the number of visitors reaching 1,030,000. These economic statistics failed, however, to dispel anxiety about the unforeseeable economic consequences of any change in Taiwan's political status or about the continuing effects of world recession on export markets, where, notably in the USA and EEC, protectionist sentiment was growing and increasing competition, notably from South Korea, was being encountered.

JAPAN

'The Year of the Economy' was how Mr Takeo Fukuda, newly-elected Prime Minister, defined 1977 in his New Year message to Japan. That was about the only forecast which came out right during the ensuing 12 months in this land of computers, calculators and abacuses. For the economy was never off the newspaper front pages or out of the television and radio headlines. But the news was rarely inspiring, and the biggest surprise was not forecast at all—the 22 per cent appreciation of the yen.

Perhaps the nation was paying the price of over-reacting throughout 1976 to the Japanese connexion with the Lockheed Aircraft pay-offs (see AR 1976, pp. 298-300) and the running battle for the Liberal Democratic Party presidency (and therefore Premiership), won by Mr Fukuda, when it should have been studying its trade and industrial problems more closely. Except for bureaucrats and businessmen, people had seemed indifferent to the domestic economic malaise, which refused to go away all through 1977.

As in previous times of trouble, Japan sought salvation through exports, because there seemed no point in keeping the wheels of industry turning just to pile up goods in the warehouses (inventories were large enough already). This proved an effective move; for Japanese high-quality products at competitive prices no longer needed a hard sell anywhere. Japan's rivals could bear witness to that. Overseas sales leapt by 20 per cent.

Somehow, the much-heralded and hoped-for boost in imports scarcely kept pace with the export drive and registered only a 9 per cent increase. Not even the strong yen helped, and Japan ended the year with a huge trading surplus. Of its purchases abroad, 80 per cent consisted of industrial raw materials, fuels and food, expanding and contracting in volume and value according to economic activity. The United States of America, Japan's chief trading partner, supplied a substantial proportion, but it joined the European Community in attacking Japan's restricted import of manufactured products—only 20 per cent of the total, compared with as much as 50 per cent by other major developed countries. As a fervent advocate of free trade, it was argued, Japan ought to open its doors wider to competition.

Japan, which no longer took criticism resignedly, responded that it had to buy much more raw materials and fuels than other countries because it had none of its own; how else could it turn out manufactures to earn a living? In any case, foreign exporters had never paid much attention to the Japanese market and over the years the nation had been obliged to manufacture its own needs. Because of this, it had become expert at manufacturing and its products had become acceptable to the world at large. 'We worked hard to overcome our shortcomings; now it is the West's turn to strive for marketing success in Japan' was a popular turn of phrase—though not in Western circles, which momentarily forgot how much easier it had always been to export to somewhere near home than thousands of miles away.

This export–import controversy provided the backdrop for almost every event in which Japan was concerned on the domestic or world stage: the continuous trade rumbles and grumbles from the EEC and USA, accompanied by the demand that Japan, with the USA and West Germany, should 'engine' world economic recovery; Japan's much publicized, criticized and doubtless envied year's surpluses on trading and current account and its $22,848 million gold and foreign exchange reserves; the 22 per cent revaluation of the yen in the course of the year, but half of it in little over a month; the restructuring of many sectors of Japanese industry whose future had been jeopardized by the quadrupling of oil prices; the people's consequent concern for their jobs and their incomes, with one million unemployed becoming the norm; and the Government's efforts to give the economy a new head of steam by spending more on public works and housing and easing credit terms, though many Japanese were convinced that the fundamental trouble came more from without than within Japan (that is, only world economic recovery could solve their and other nations' problems).

Because he was Prime Minister, Mr Fukuda—chided as 'Fukuda, the economic expert'—had to take the blame for some rather faulty forecasting, though no Japanese leader worth his salt would dare to deny his people a regular set of targets. The catalogue of false promises and premises read by the year's end like a crystal-gazer's nightmare—principally, Mr Fukuda was lumbered with an alleged 6·7 per cent economic growth that proved to be nearer 5·3 per cent in actuality; an expected $700 million deficit on current overseas account had to be revised to a $6,500 million surplus; and the confident expectation that imports would grow faster than exports was entirely falsified.

Mr Fukuda's '6·7 per cent' was echoed and re-echoed throughout the year by him and his colleagues. It impressed the London summit of major powers in May, and was still being put forward as late as November, when the Prime Minister suddenly remarked that the yen's rising value had 'damped the prospects a bit'. Thereafter the descent to 5·3 per cent was rapid. The fall-off in growth was also due, of course, to lack of business spending on new plant and equipment and to the tight rein kept by the man-in-the-street on his expenditure at a time of uncertainty.

After many years of high growth, Japan had been precipitated into a low growth era—figures down to half—by the oil crisis and its various repercussions. No country had had to adjust its ideas so quickly. Industry was in top gear when the crisis came for the Japanese, who do not take easily to violent gear changes. It was inevitable that many industries would have to scrap a large portion of their facilities—with shipbuilding, pride

K*

of Japan for two decades, losing perhaps 50 per cent—and this was a dire threat to an industrial country which overall was possibly the best-equipped in the world. Japan was paying a penalty not for carrying on too long with out-of-date machinery and methods, but for over-efficiency. It would take the Japanese some years of anguish to learn to live an industrial life-style that had been the way of the West for a generation. More immediately, the yen's appreciation dealt a severe blow to industries with poor competitive strength, and bankruptcies numbered around 1,500 a month.

Still, all that was Japan's business. The USA and EC simply wanted to know when Japan was going to cut its trade and current account surpluses (if Noel Coward's ditty 'Poor Little Rich Girl' was translatable into Japanese, it could have become top of the pops). The USA became particularly insistent and Japan knew it had to show willing. Washington wanted Japan to go back into the red on current account, which seemed a bit hard on a nation that had managed to achieve an overall payments balance only the year before, for the first time for four years. The Japanese promised to 'do everything possible' to hold down the surplus to $6,000 million in fiscal 1978 from an estimated $10,000 million in fiscal 1977, with 'the red' as fiscal 1979's target. Moreover, they would try to attain 7 per cent economic growth in fiscal 1978 (whose finger on the computer keys?).

Being very familiar with Gilbert and Sullivan's 'The Mikado', the Japanese must often wish their economic forecasts could be identified with the sentiments expressed by Ko-Ko, the Lord High Executioner: 'If Your Majesty orders a man to be killed, the man is already as good as dead, since Your Majesty's will is law; and if a man is as good as dead, why not say so?' Some Westerners may believe that W. S. Gilbert had a certain percipience!

If Mr Fukuda found time to read opinion polls, he would have noted that 51 per cent of the public thought his Cabinet had made a poor showing on economic recovery and 49 per cent thought the same about their price stabilization policy—and this when Tokyo's consumer price index in December was a mere 5 per cent higher than in December 1976; wholesale prices had fallen, for the first time since 1971, by 1·5 per cent; and industrial production was staging a gain.

The 'fresh and powerful' Cabinet he had presented to the country on Christmas Eve 1976 was radically changed in November 1977, to give emphasis to economics. But frequent Cabinet changes were usual in Japan: the most notable development now was the appointment of Mr Nobuhiko Ushiba, former ambassador to the USA, as Minister for External Economic Affairs. He at any rate needed no introduction to Washington, and had a penchant for things economic; he would need every ounce of diplomacy as Japan's trade trouble-shooter.

It seemed likely that Mr Fukuda would pay his second visit to Washington as Prime Minister when trade topics loomed less large; he had met President Carter soon after both of them had taken office, and was gratified to get Carter's assurance that the USA would phase out its ground troops in South Korea in a way that would not disturb peace and upset the balance of power on the Korean peninsular. Japan had not liked the original announcement of US intentions.

Mr Fukuda also stepped outside Japan to visit the five Asean state, and Burma, and Japan was gratified that there was no repetition of former Prime Minister Kakuei Tanaka's rough ride in the area in 1974. Mr Fukuda was exploring 'ways to contribute to peace and prosperity of Asia' and conveying promises of $1,000 million assistance to industrial projects. Japanese newspaper readers found the 'Fukuda Doctrine' making the headlines: this meant creation of a relationship of mutual confidence and trust based on 'heart-to-heart understanding' and determination to cooperate with ASEAN 'as an equal partner while aiming at fostering ties with Indo-chinese nations on the basis of mutual understanding'.

The Prime Minister knew that his biggest political hurdle during the year would be to lead his Liberal Democrats to victory in the House of Councillors (upper House) election in July. His chance of success was not highly rated; for the opposition thought they had the LDP on the ropes after their almost unbroken post-war reign. However, it was the opposition, in particular the Japan Socialist Party and the Japan Communist Party, that suffered the setbacks, and the country obviously decided to remain on its middle-of-the-road course.

If the election was a hurdle, Mr Fukuda was to experience an ordeal two months later. A Japan Air Lines DC8, en route from Paris to Tokyo with 142 passengers and 14 crew, was hijacked by five Japanese 'Red Army' guerrillas over Bombay and ordered to land at Dacca, Bangladesh. The hijackers demanded the release of seven leftist radicals and two criminals imprisoned in Japan, plus $6 million ransom. While the Japanese Cabinet and some of its top officials were in agitated debate, the passengers and crew were entering upon a 135-hour drama that was to take the aircraft to Kuwait, Damascus and finally Algiers. The Government released six prisoners—the others did not want to go—and the ransom, and the hijackers allowed all their captives off the aircraft in parties at each place of call. Formally, if not exactly hopefully, the Japanese Government asked the Algerian Government to turn over to them the five hijackers and six ex-prisoners and the $6 million. This did not happen.

Such an event had perforce to be marked by an opinion poll, this time on an official basis. It showed that 64 per cent of Japanese people favoured the Government's decision to comply with the hijackers' demands and 23 per cent were against. The rest were 'don't knows'. Just to be alive was important to the Japanese.

SOUTH KOREA

In South Korea 1977 began with the official launching of the fourth five-year development plan. Based, like its highly successful predecessor, on the proven policy of 'nation-building by export', it promised further massive industrialization and sweeping social advances to provide a more affluent way of life for the republic's 36 million citizens. The export drive was not without its problems, in particular the growing protectionist trends in Europe and the United States which threatened to impede South Korea's efforts to diversify its markets. But though it appeared that the US, and to a lesser extent Japan, would remain South Korea's chief trading partners for the time being, the resolve persisted to expand trade with West European countries and in the new markets which typically thrusting economic diplomacy had been opening up in the Middle East, Africa and Latin America.

Performance during the first 12 months of the plan gave good grounds for optimism. The 1977 export target was comfortably exceeded, reaching US$10,363 million by the year's end. At just over 10 per cent the economic growth rate was still one of the highest in the world. There was an increase in per-capita GNP from US$692 in 1976 to an estimated US$850, with a late-year forecast by the Economic Planning Board that it would reach US$1,050 in 1978 and US$1,800 by 1981. Though prices rose the Government managed to hold the inflation rate to around ten per cent. There were substantial increases in industrial production and a record rice harvest. International confidence in the South's economy and future stability was reflected in continuing foreign investment and in the establishment by six major international banks of branches in Seoul, bringing to 17 the number of such banks operating in the country.

Defence assumed a new and more urgent priority as South Korea faced up to President Jimmy Carter's decision to withdraw some 33,000 American ground troops over a period of four or five years. Development of the armaments industry, at the new Changwon industrial estate and elsewhere, proceeded apace and no less than 35·6 per cent of the 1978 national Budget of more than US$7,252 million, approved by the National Assembly in December, was earmarked for defence. President Park Chung Hee had declared early in the year that by 1980 South Korea would be capable of producing most of the weapons it needed. Reassuring pledges that the United States remained committed to the defence of South Korea were made and repeated by President Carter and his Administration.

The withdrawal continued to give concern, however, not only in South Korea and Japan but in the United States also, where military opinion in particular warned against its inherent dangers. Throughout the year discussions continued between the South Korean and American Governments, centred on the timing of the withdrawal and the 'compensatory measures' (military aid) which South Korea might receive from the United States. Negotiations were made more difficult by strained relations between the two countries—the result of the influence-buying scandal ('Koreagate') in which the central figure was Park Tong-sun (no relation to President Park), a wealthy South Korean businessman, who was alleged to have bribed a number of Congressmen. The question whether or not Park Tong-sun should return to Washington to give evidence at the trials of indicted Congressmen and before the House Committee on Ethics had not been fully resolved by the year's end, although both sides seemed then to be working towards an agreement.

Human rights were another stumbling-block, and it was perhaps as a concession to President Carter's views that the South Korean authorities released some 47 dissidents during the year.

NORTH KOREA

North Korea entered 1977 facing grave economic difficulties, including international debts in excess of an estimated US$2,000 million. Although completion of the six-year plan (1971-76) was claimed on several occasions, the plan was evidently far from successful, for the North Korean leader, Kim Il Sung, was forced to designate 1977 'a year of readjustment'. An ambitious seven-year plan (1978-84) was approved by the sixth Supreme People's Assembly at its first session on 15 December.

Attempts by Kim Il Sung to have his eldest son, Kim Chong Il, recognized as 'heir apparent' met with strong opposition and were widely believed to account for the power struggle in the Korean Workers Party and drastic purge of the armed forces which occurred in December. In foreign affairs a new-found politeness to the United States was discernible, not unconnected with North Korea's persistent but futile attempts to out-flank South Korea and negotiate the peninsula's future with the United States alone.

X AUSTRALASIA AND SOUTH PACIFIC

Chapter 1

AUSTRALIA—PAPUA NEW GUINEA

AUSTRALIA

THE economy continued sluggish, partly because of the world depression, and partly because of structural weakness in Australian manufacturing industry. The world depression affected mainly rural and mining industries, the worst to suffer being beef farmers. The Russian and Chinese markets enabled the wheat industry to remain reasonably prosperous, but the crop was reduced (and other primary producers handicapped) by prolonged, widespread droughts. Wool prices remained above the guaranteed floor price (A$2·84 per kg), and unsold stocks were small. Iron ore exports were affected by Japanese economic conditions. Shipments of iron ore and sugar were held up by disputes with Japanese buyers who claimed that long-term contracts should be renegotiated because of declining world market prices. The dispute caused tension between the Governments, and was settled by a compromise under which Australian suppliers had to accept lower rates. The coal trade remained buoyant, and substantial local and overseas investment went into opening up new coal measures in Queensland and New South Wales. There was also a substantial increase in prospecting for oil and natural gas off the north-west coast of Western Australia.

The devaluation of the Australian dollar in 1976 did not materially affect import levels. The external trade balance was in deficit for most of the year, and overseas reserves fell; the situation was mitigated by re-valuing the undervalued gold reserves and by government borrowing overseas exceeding A$1,700 million. The domestic economy did not improve significantly. Retail sales and average company profits increased a little, car registrations and housebuilding decreased. Unemployment increased markedly from under 5 per cent to an average for the year of 5·6 per cent of the work-force. There was considerable pressure on the federal Liberal–National Country Party (LNCP) Government of Mr Malcolm Fraser to attempt some pump-priming, but it resisted the pressure and continued to make its first priority a reduction in the rate of inflation; it argued that even a small 'reflation' would endanger that policy, and that economic recovery would be best served by getting the inflation rate down to well below 10 per cent.

The Budget opened on 16 August anticipated a deficit of $2,217 million for 1977-78, $500 million less than the outturn in 1976-77, a result achieved mainly by further small economies in detail. The most important feature of the Budget was the abandonment of the steeply-graded progressive rate system of income tax assessment in force since the 1940s, and substitution of a 'plateau' system with a relatively high untaxed band (up to $3,756 per annum), and three steps above, each at uniform rates. The system was criticized by the Australian Labor Party (ALP) opposition because it reduced the element of redistribution of wealth in the former system. It was defended on the ground that it would cut the total tax burden by about $406 million in a full year, the greater part of which benefited the lowest income earners, now completely exempted, and a median range of wage and salary earners in the $10-16,000 per annum band whose energy and enterprise were particularly important to the economy.

The Government contended that the largest single factor in the inflation was an excessively high average wage rate of employed workers, and that this also promoted unemployment. Accordingly at successive quarterly wage-adjustment inquiries by the Conciliation and Arbitration Commission the Government opposed full 'indexation' of wages in proportion to price increases. The Commission granted higher increases than the Government liked, but less than the trade unions requested, and in some cases graded them so as to benefit lower-paid earners. This produced industrial disputes based on loss of margins for skill.

Working days lost by strikes were the lowest in a decade, although a public and political impression of union unruliness was maintained because of the political background of some disputes. The federal and the non-Labor state Governments passed legislation intended to coerce unions into abandoning strikes, but in no case was it actually applied, the two sides repeatedly approaching a show-down and then reaching a negotiated settlement. By December it was clear that the Government's strategy had reduced both the average level of real wages and the rate of inflation. The latter was then a little below 10 per cent, as compared with about 13 per cent at the end of the previous year.

In February, the Fraser Government introduced four Bills to amend the Constitution in ways recommended by the Australian Constitutional Convention in 1976. The two important ones were brought forward at this time in order to lessen the risk that the Government might be sufficiently unpopular to lose control of the Senate at a half-election held apart from elections for the House of Representatives; if both had been carried, the result would have been to continue the existing Senate until the next Representatives elections, normally due at the end of 1978. One proposal was to require half-elections for the Senate to be held at the same time as elections for the Representatives, and the other to ensure that casual vacancies would be filled by a person from the same party as that (if any) to which the departed Senator belonged when elected, and for the term of that Senator. The former proposal was the more important.

At the referendum in May, the two minor proposals (retirement age for federal judges, Territory residents to have votes for constitutional referendums) were carried, as was the provision about casual Senate vacancies, but the simultaneous elections proposal, while obtaining a substantial majority of the electors as a whole, did not acquire the necessary majority in four states and so was defeated. Mr Fraser then decided that, unless conditions at the time were unfavourable, he would dissolve the House of Representatives towards the end of 1977, a year earlier than constitutionally necessary, in order to hold an election for that House at the same time as an election for half of the Senate as still required before May 1978.

Through 1977, the political outlook was equivocal. In Western Australia, a general election on 19 February returned the LNCP coalition headed by Sir Charles Court to power with a slightly increased majority in both Houses. On 17 September an election for the lower House only in South Australia gave the ALP Government of Mr D. Dunstan, previously dependent on the Speaker's casting vote, a clear majority of 7. On 12 November an election for Queensland's single House again returned the LNCP coalition Government of Mr J. Bjelke Petersen with a comfortable majority; the ALP vote increased substantially, but this was from a record low figure in 1974. In Victoria, the Liberal Government was in trouble from scandals connected with land development, and in October it lost a by-election to the ALP.

In May, a prominent Liberal back-bencher in the federal House of Representatives, Mr D. Chipp, who had for long been critical of what he considered the excessive conservatism of Mr Fraser's outlook and policies, resigned from the Liberal Party and formed a new political group called the Australian Democrats. Most of the remaining supporters of the Australia Party merged with the Australian Democrats, as did a dissident Liberal group in South Australia. The Democrats formed a movement with a loose constitutional structure and a populist policy, and attracted up to 20 per cent of the first-preference votes in outer suburban divisions at state elections after May; preference voting was left to individual discretion, and slightly favoured the ALP. Public opinion polls showed a small margin of support for Mr Fraser's Government, and suggested that neither Mr Fraser nor Mr Whitlam (re-elected to ALP leadership in May by a small margin) was regarded with confidence by a majority of voters.

Accordingly the political prospects were not clear when in October Mr Fraser called an election for the House of Representatives to be held on 10 December, and at the same time the election for half the Senate which had to be held by May 1978. He gave as his main reasons the business uncertainty caused by continual speculation about electoral plans, the desirability of keeping Senate and House elections in phase with each other, and the need for specific mandates to deal with industrial unrest and with the uranium question.

The latter question had gradually become more important during the previous four years, because of the development of substantial opposition to the mining, treatment or export of Australia's uranium deposits—about a quarter of the world's known resources. The opposition was strongest in the ALP and in the communist-led trade unions, but also had considerable religious and left-Liberal backing. The Whitlam ALP Government had appointed Mr Justice Russell Fox of the Australian Capital Supreme Court as chairman of a Royal Commission of three to investigate the possibilities and dangers of uranium mining and export. The Fraser Government was in general favourable to the industry, and its Country Party wing headed by Mr D. Anthony particularly so, but it continued the Fox Commission's inquiry and undertook to be guided by its report.

In 1977 the Commission issued two reports which discounted some of the popular grounds for fear of uranium as a source of power and gave full weight to the likely world importance of nuclear power plants as oil disappeared. However, the reports said that only after the fullest public discussion and well-considered political decision should the country regard itself as satisfied on three questions which no expert body could at that time resolve: first, the danger of proliferation of nuclear arms as a by-product of nuclear energy development; second, the problem of safe disposal of nuclear wastes; third, the impact of uranium mining on the life and culture of the Australian Aboriginals in whose remaining ancestral lands some of the main deposits lay.

The ALP resolved that, while the few existing mining commitments should be respected, no new ones should be permitted until the next federal conference of the Party in 1980. The Australian Council of Trade Unions, on the other hand, resolved that an early referendum of the people should be held on the question, and the decision at that referendum respected. The trade unions threatened that in the absence of a referendum (opposed by both major political groups) they would use strike action in order to prevent mining and transport of uranium, and it seemed probable that the communist-led unions would try to prevent mining by such tactics in any event.

In the early part of the election campaign, it seemed possible that the ALP could make up the great leeway caused by the 1975 election. A redistribution of seats for the House of Representatives, constitutionally required because of population changes, reduced their number from 127 to 124, and handicapped the National Country Party while advantaging both Liberals and the ALP. During the campaign, the Treasurer, Mr P. Lynch, was obliged to resign because his name was mentioned in connexion with the Victorian land deal enquiries. Mr Fraser stood mainly on his record, which was not inspiring.

In the latter part of the campaign, however, the ALP leaders threw away their advantage by proposing some unpopular measures and showing both disunity and incompetence in an attempt to explain and modify them. First, they proposed to persuade the states to abandon pay-roll taxes, as an inducement to employers to take on more hands; however, it soon appeared that only the larger and wealthier concerns were subject to the taxes, and that in the absence of appropriate government pressure, probably beyond federal power, it was uncertain whether the tax saved would be translated into jobs. Next, to compensate the states for what they lost in pay-roll tax, it was proposed that the tax reductions promised in the Fraser Budget (which were to become effective only in February 1978) would be cancelled and the higher tax levels of the previous system restored. This was resented by the skilled work-force as well as by business. Last, when a number of industries in which unemployment was particularly high, in particular textiles, footwear and small engineering, demanded undertakings that they would be given special short-term tariff assistance, this was promised by Mr Fraser (who had showed increasingly protectionist tendencies during the year) but the replies of ALP leaders were equivocal.

The election victory of the LNCP coalition was expected, but not its magnitude. The coalition obtained about 55 per cent of the votes, a very small reduction on it sweeping 1975 victory. The ALP's vote was up only about 1 per cent while the Australian Democrats polled more than 8 per cent—remarkable for a new group with a scratch organization. The NCP suffered most, because of the disappearance of rural seats in the redistribution, but the failure to make significant headway was a serious blow to the ALP and suggested, more than had the 1975 result, a distinct turn right by the electorate. The results in detail were:

House of Representatives: Liberal Party 67, National Country Party 19, Australian Labor Party 38; LNCP majority 48.

Senate (effective from 1 July 1978): Liberal Party 29, National Country Party 6, Australian Labor Party 26, Australian Democrats 2; LNCP majority 7.

Mr Whitlam at once resigned the ALP leadership, and was succeeded by his former Treasurer, Mr Tom Hayden. Mr Fraser enlarged and reshuffled his Ministry, and rearranged departments in a manner accentuating his personal control of policy.

PAPUA NEW GUINEA

The first national elections since independence dominated public affairs in Papua New Guinea. The ruling coalition Government, composed of the Pangu and Peoples' Progress Parties, was returned to office with a parliamentary majority of 30 seats over the United Party which again formed the opposition. Pangu leader Michael Somare was easily re-elected Prime Minister.

The state of the economy, buoyed by continued Australian aid, high prices for commodity exports and a revaluation of the Kina which kept the cost-of-living down, had generally worked to the Government's advantage. The Government's record of political management throughout the transition period, Somare's popularity, astute patronage politicking by the Ministry, a notion among MPs that being 'in government' regardless of its political hue was essential for access to the resources of the state, and the absence of credible opposition policies further accounted for the coalition's success.

The elections themselves illustrated a number of aspects of the evolving polity. Democratically conducted, they produced a 60 per cent turnout of those eligible and a 65 per cent turnover of incumbent MPs. Kinship affiliation and a demonstrated ability by MPs to deliver material resources to their constituencies were prime determinants in voting behaviour, considerations of national policy and party membership being largely irrelevant for voters. A survey of the socio-economic backgrounds of candidates further demonstrated the consolidation of a political elite, with men of business or professional wealth largely replacing the older-style, traditional 'big men'. Political parties were revealed as weak institutions which existed mainly to link successful candidates together at the national parliamentary level. All party platforms were similar in orientation and emphasized development strategies premised on foreign investment and the extension of state services. The difficulty of maintaining discipline and a stable majority under this type of party system was made immediately obvious by the emergence in Parliament of a small, informal, cross-party alliance which became a more effective critic than the opposition.

One result of the election from which both the Government and supporters of the new state alike took heart was the relatively poor showing by secessionist candidates in Bougainville and Papua. The authority of the Government, however, was challenged immediately after the elections by two internal disputes involving the heads of the defence and police forces. In October the disciplining of the commander of the defence force by the Cabinet for an unapproved meeting with a West Irianese guerrilla leader sparked rumours of a possible coup. In November the Cabinet refused to renew the term of office of the police commissioner, whose subsequent allegations of political interference in his area of responsibility won him support within the police force and from sections of the public service.

The two areas of policy which provided major long-term concern for the Government were the maintenance of friendly relations with Indonesia in the face of continued crossings of refugees from Irian Jaya and of considerable public sympathy for the Irianese cause; and the implementation of a quasi-federal system of government with its attendant adminis-trative, legal and financial difficulties.

Chapter 2

NEW ZEALAND

IN New Zealand, pessimism hardened as it was realized belatedly and reluctantly, if still only partially, that the country's worsening economic plight was truly deepseated. One response was legislation centralizing more powers with the Government, the focus here being its dominating figure, Prime Minister Robert Muldoon. In turn, there was considerable apprehension about such executive mastery, and a loss of faith in the legislative process, and this during a year which saw New Zealanders clamorously at odds with each other over many issues.

The economy presented a picture of increasing gloom, especially when its performance was matched against the rhetoric of the ruling National Party's President, George Chapman, who claimed during the year that the current parliamentary term would be remembered as the 'Muldoon economic miracle'. Despite reasonable pastoral export earnings, the balance of payments deficit on current account was running at $750 million by late 1977, when an OECD forecast claimed it would reach $1,000 million in 1978. Contributory factors included static levels of farm production, poor and deteriorating terms of trade for pastoral exports, rising levels of world agricultural protectionism (especially in the European Community) and rising costs of both domestic export production and international transportation charges. Furthermore, the amount New Zealand had to earn abroad just to service the interest payments on its foreign loans reached record levels in 1977.

Domestically, productivity and growth remained sluggish, and inflation was still running at 14 per cent by the year's end. Business confidence waned sharply, with closures and redundancy hitting particularly the apparel, car assembly and construction industries. By December unemployment had reached 25,000 (a total disguising many women out of work, but not registered as unemployed), a post-depression record. In the year to 30 November 1977 the country sustained a permanent and long-term net migration loss of 26,000, including many skilled, younger workers.

Although persisting with its attempts to rectify the economy through retrenchment, the Government nevertheless permitted a return to free wage bargaining, increased the subsidies for agricultural producers and slightly eased its previously tight hold on public spending. For most New Zealanders, the Government's promise of a 5 per cent cut in income tax, to take effect in February 1978, was too little and too late.

The Government rationalized previously separate energy agencies into one Ministry and also began its own on-shore drilling programme for oil and gas. Despite optimism from the Prime Minister, the Hunt off-shore drilling operation in the deep south basin failed to discover commercially exploitable condensate. In December, after protracted talks, the Government announced that it had concluded a mutually satisfactory renegotiation with Comalco (the conglomerate that was running the Bluff aluminium smelter) involving a five-fold increase in the electricity tariff to approximately half the amount charged to local consumers.

In its external relations, the Government rediscovered the advantages of Commonwealth political collaboration by willingly subscribing to the Gleneagles agreement (see p. 325). To the chagrin of some of his own backbenchers, Foreign Minister Talboys took positive steps to implement this agreement by advising local sports bodies about the consequences of competing against South African teams selected on criteria other than merit.

This area of confrontation was to some extent shaded by another: the Government's determination to demand greatly improved access of New Zealand beef exports to the Japanese market or, failing that, to shut the Japanese out of New Zealand's new 200-mile extended maritime economic zone, declared in October and constituting the fourth largest in the world. Reports from the August ASEAN summit (at Kuala Lumpur), which Mr Muldoon and Mr Fukuda both attended, indicated that the latter insisted upon treating these issues separately while the former was adamant that they remain linked. Despite numerous ministerial consultations this impasse remained, Japan being excluded from negotiations such as those completed in 1977 with South Korea, and begun with the Soviet Union, concerning future fishing access to the extended economic zone.

Interestingly, it was learned in August that Australian Prime Minister Fraser had complained in a letter to President Carter that Mr Muldoon was 'playing with fire' by excluding the Japanese from New Zealand's 200-mile zone, because this afforded greater Soviet leverage throughout the South Pacific. Yet the coolness that was apparent between the two trans-Tasman Prime Ministers was perhaps less significant than the difficulties and protectionism that New Zealand exports of clothing, forest products and whiteware encountered on the Australian market.

This protectionism, however, loomed less ominously for New Zealand than that facing it in the European Community. A 10 per cent price rise in September for butter sales still represented only half the increase paid to Community producers, a point Trade Minister Talboys emphasized when he visited Brussels in July. Apprehension strengthened about the introduction of a Community sheep–meats policy, which would disadvantage New Zealand lamb sales, and fading butter market prospects in the Community beyond 1980.

Throughout the year, and particularly abroad, the Government attempted to identify with less developed, primary-producing nations and articulate their claims, trade interests providing the common bond. Mr

Muldoon, for example, told IMF and World Bank meetings that 'it was not in the interests of wealthy oil and industrial countries to drive primary producing countries into the ground'. And, while remaining critical about some of its aspects, the Government in 1977 gave a more positive endorsement to proposals for a 'common fund' to finance the purchase of buffer stocks of agricultural products with the aim of stabilizing commodity prices.

The parliamentary session (which equalled a record of 118 sitting days) was easily one of the most contentious and badly managed in recent memory. For example, in passing the substantial and complex Town and Country Planning Bill, which established a structure of advisory regional planning committees, the Government provoked widespread discontent through its refusal to allow local interests sufficient opportunity to present submissions during this legislation's committee stages. However, 1977 saw New Zealand's ramshackle structure of local government receive yet a further lease of life. By weakening the Local Government Commission and placing it under direct ministerial control, the Government effectively drew the teeth from this agency—a move, it subsequently transpired, motivated by partisan interests, since in certain Government-held marginal constituencies opposition was manifest to amalgamations proposed by the formerly-constituted Commission.

In its handling of legislation designed to reorganize the Security Intelligence Service and authorize its controlling Minister (Mr Muldoon) to issue warrants permitting the interception or seizure of any communication, the Government aroused widespread vocal protest, demonstrations, and even arrests in the galleries of Parliament. Public suspicion intensified when the Prime Minister claimed that sending this legislation to a Select Committee for hearings would merely provide a forum for 'fringe elements'. The legislation subsequently passed placed no statutory time-limit for the expiry of interception warrants, which might be used against 'potential' subversives and 'include such other terms and conditions, if any, as the Minister considers advisable in the public interest', whilst it was also made a criminal offence to disclose publicly the identity of a Security Service agent.

Protest from a Government backbencher on a controversial public affairs television programme to the effect that this legislation seemed like the apparatus of a police state (he was then instantly and publicly threatened by Mr Muldoon with a withdrawal of party endorsement for future parliamentary candidacy) signified the widespread misgivings about the concentration of unrestrained powers manifest in the Bill. As retired Supreme Court Justice Wilson in Dunedin put it, 'Parliamentary control of the Executive is almost entirely lost.'

That this measure was strenuously opposed by the Labour opposition did little to enhance its standing in 1977. Still stung by the aftermath of the

Moyle affair (see AR 1976, p. 314), prevaricating but then finally refusing future candidate endorsement to an embarrassingly 'accident prone' parliamentarian, Mr Gerald O'Brien, uneven in its parliamentary performance and led by Mr Rowling whose standing in the opinion polls continued to slide, the opposition failed to capitalize on numerous opportunities either to attack the Government or to boost its own credibility.

Finally Parliament, on a so-called 'free conscience' vote, introduced abortion legislation deemed so restrictive as to provoke threats of open defiance by professional gynaecologists amidst general condemnation about its unworkability. It became unlawful to conduct an abortion in New Zealand unless a doctor 'believes that the woman's health would be endangered by continued pregnancy and that the danger cannot be averted by any other means'. Under the new law, foetal abnormality is not a ground for abortion, neither is a pregnancy resulting from rape. Deep, bitter and unresolved, the social, moral and religious fissures dividing New Zealanders over the abortion issue seemed almost certain to assume electoral salience in 1978.

New Zealand's 1977 also saw controversy over the appointment of a former Prime Minister (Sir Keith Holyoake) as Governor General, the ordination of women as priests in the Anglican Church, a wave of arson against schools, and a box office success for a locally-produced feature film, 'Sleeping Dogs'.

Chapter 3

THE SOUTH PACIFIC

AMONG the most significant developments in the South Pacific during 1977 were the practical steps adopted by South Pacific Forum member countries to coordinate their approach to, and declarations concerning, a 200-mile extended economic zone. At an August meeting in Port Moresby, these Governments established a Regional Fisheries Agency charged with pooling information, orchestrating regional policies for management, licensing, harvesting and surveillance, and taking part in negotiations with distant fishing nations such as Japan 'without detriment to the sovereign rights of coastal countries'. Despite some objections from Western Samoa and Fiji, the United States was excluded from participating in the Agency, *via* its links with American Samoa, since it opposed sovereign rights being exercised in respect of highly migratory species of fish, this being a principle insisted upon by Papua New Guinea.

In response, Japan quickly reacted by negotiating grant agreements for fisheries research and joint commercial exploitation with Tonga and

Western Samoa. In neither country, however, did the Soviet Union appear to follow up its 1976 overtures for fisheries operating facilities.

In FIJI, the ruling Alliance Party, headed by Ratu Sir Kamisese Mara, was returned to office with a comfortable majority in a September election. However, this followed an earlier April poll which resulted in a stalemate, when the Indian-dominated National Federation Party narrowly won most seats in the 52-member Lower House, but was not asked to form a Government by the Governor General because of the severe rifts that subsequently split the Party into competing electoral factions.

In NAURU, President Dowiyogo's failure to get his Budget through Parliament precipitated a November poll which Mr Dowiyogo's faction won, taking a two-seat majority in the 18-member Assembly.

In the NEW HEBRIDES there was confrontation when the dominant Vanuaaku Party (formerly National Party), headed by Father Walter Lini, boycotted November elections for a 39 member Assembly. It did so when the Condominium's joint French and British authorities rejected the Party's demands that it form a provisional Government and hold an immediate referendum on full independence. The Party also boycotted Paris talks held in July, claiming that the Franco-British timetable for a referendum on internal self-government late in 1980 was a delaying tactic. Police using tear gas broke up demonstrations in Vila in November involving anti-Vanuaaku Party crowds, as they had done earlier in June when differences erupted over future recognition of bilingualism (English and French) in the colony.

For the SOLOMON ISLANDS, arrangements for full independence in July 1978 were finalized with the British Government in September at a London conference. Mr Peter Kenilorea's delegation managed to win more aid from the British, and announced that the Solomons would remain in the Commonwealth and maintain links with the Crown, thus abandoning previous plans for republican status.

In TUVALU, a newly-elected (August) House of Assembly unanimously voted for a February 1978 London conference with a view to independence later in the same year.

In NEW CALEDONIA, elections for the 35-member Assembly saw auto-nomist support fragment, allowing the party favouring continued links with France to win most members.

The year also saw severe earthquakes causing property damage in the SOLOMONS and TONGA; a cholera outbreak costing 18 lives on Tarawa in the GILBERT ISLANDS; the rising political stature of WESTERN SAMOA's Prime Minister Tupuola Efi as a regional figure; difficulties between Fiji and New Zealand over air landing rights; a strong possibility of oil being discovered in Tonga; a political assassination in TAHITI; crop damaging drought in NIUE, Tonga, Western Samoa and Fiji; and the victory of Mr Peter Coleman as the first locally-elected Governor of AMERICAN SAMOA.

XI INTERNATIONAL ORGANIZATIONS

Chapter 1

THE UNITED NATIONS AND ITS AGENCIES

INTRODUCTION

THE essential evolution of the United Nations, claimed Secretary-General Dr Kurt Waldheim in his annual report, is to harmonize short-term national interests with the long-term interest of the world community. In those terms progress in 1977 was patchy. The problems of the Middle East and Southern Africa were unresolved, despite accelerated efforts. Cyprus remained a stalemate. Conflict between immediate national interests and world concerns continued in regard to disarmament, the economic order and the law of the sea. Lip-service was paid to interdependence while national considerations were over-riding.

Yet there were symptoms of change: greater willingness to use the UN, including proposals for a UN presence in Namibia, Rhodesia and more extensively in the Middle East; recognition of the Secretary-General's complementary role while member states undertook bilateral diplomacy, and a trend towards negotiating through the UN when the Conference on International Economic Cooperation (CIEC) dialogue achieved little more than emphasizing to the North the greater need of the South.

A contributing factor was the changed attitude of the US. President Jimmy Carter and his Secretary of State sought consultations with the UN. The choice of Mr Andrew Young as American ambassador to the UN eased the antagonism felt by many Third World leaders towards the US.

From 13 to 19 September the General Assembly reconvened in its 31st session, suspended in December 1976, to consider any progress towards development and economic cooperation. From 20 September to 21 December the Assembly held a very busy 32nd session with less polarization on issues. Uppermost in its considerations were the Middle East, Southern Africa, disarmament and a new economic order.

The Assembly adopted a budget of $985·9 million for 1978-79. It increased UN membership to 149 by admitting the Republic of Djibouti, formerly the French Territory of the Afars and Issas, and the Socialist Republic of Vietnam. A US veto had blocked the admission of Vietnam in 1976, but the American attitude changed and the Security Council recommended membership for both in July. The Assembly also chose five non-permanent members of the Security Council for two-year terms from January 1978: Bolivia, Czechoslovakia, Gabon, Kuwait and Nigeria; the non-permanent members with a year to serve were Canada, India, Mauritius, Venezuela and West Germany.

The Security Council held its 2,000th meeting on 6 April; of these 470 had been on problems of the Middle East. In 1977 it held 73 meetings of which the largest number—21—were on Southern Africa.

POLITICAL

MIDDLE EAST. Throughout the year there were repeated efforts to re-convene the Geneva conference, ending with President Sadat's dramatic visit to Jerusalem on 19 and 20 November (see pp. 179-81). From 31 January to 14 February Dr Waldheim toured the Middle East and then reported to the Security Council that Israel wanted a Geneva conference reconvened on the original basis, while the Arabs insisted that the Palestine Liberation Organization (PLO) must participate.

After the Israeli elections on 17 May the formation of Mr Menachem Begin's Government dampened hopes for Geneva, especially as he described the occupied territories as 'liberated' ones. In response the US and European Community issued statements reasserting UN Resolution 242 of 1967 on withdrawal.

The General Assembly session provided an opportunity for consulta-tions, which culminated in an American–Russian declaration of 1 October on terms for reconvening the Geneva conference, including consideration of demilitarized zones with UN forces or observers. Three days later President Carter and Israel's Foreign Minister Moshe Dayan, both in New York for the Assembly, worked out a formula to present to the Israeli and Arab Governments.

On 28 October the Assembly approved a resolution against any demographic changes, including settlements, in the occupied territories. Also the Security Council extended the mandates of the UN Emergency Force in Sinai until 24 October 1978 and of the UN Disengagement Observer Force on the Golan Heights until 31 May 1978.

When President Sadat went to Jerusalem the General Assembly was debating the Middle East; there was much comment but no effect on the resolutions it adopted. On 25 November it called for the reconvening of the Geneva conference with the PLO participating, withdrawal from all territories occupied in 1967, and attainment of the 'national rights' of the Palestinians.

As so few accepted President Sadat's invitation to the Cairo conference Dr Waldheim proposed (29 November) a pre-Geneva meeting on neutral ground of all those who had been invited to Cairo, including the PLO. The Israelis saw no purpose to this. At the Cairo conference which opened on 14 December the UN was represented by Lieut.-General Ensio Siilasvuo, chief coordinator of the UN Middle East peacekeeping operations.

SOUTH AFRICA. Pressure mounted amongst UN members to attack apartheid, while Western countries feared this might jeopardize efforts towards majority rule in Namibia and Rhodesia. Sanctions against South Africa were urged at the Maputo and Lagos conferences (see pp. 318-19). Demands were fanned by reported evidence of South African preparations for a nuclear test, the banning of certain organizations and newspapers, and arrests of black leaders.

When the Security Council met, France, the UK and US vetoed draft resolutions for economic sanctions, but all members voted on 4 November for a mandatory arms embargo, and then on 9 December established a watchdog embargo committee.

The General Assembly debated South Africa at length, adopting 14 resolutions on 14 December, including a call for an oil embargo against South Africa and a request to the Security Council for consideration of mandatory economic sanctions.

RHODESIA/ZIMBABWE. The UN role over Rhodesia was a supporting one during the efforts to get the Geneva and later the Anglo-American proposals accepted (see pp. 248–49). The UN became directly involved in September when the Anglo-American plan, which included proposals for a UN presence and force, was conveyed to the Security Council. The UK won approval (29 September) for sending a UN Special Representative to Rhodesia to discuss, together with the British Resident Commissioner designate Field-Marshal Lord Carver, the security arrangements for transition to majority rule. The Secretary-General appointed Major-General D. Prem Chand of India.

Pressure for wider and stronger sanctions increased, although the US in March repealed the Byrd amendment which permitted import of Rhodesian chrome. On 27 May the Security Council extended its mandatory sanction to the use of funds by Rhodesia for its offices abroad.

NAMIBIA. UN involvement over Namibia's independence centred on negotiations by the five Western members of the Security Council— Canada, France, the UK, US and West Germany. They consulted the five front-line states, had talks with Swapo (South West Africa People's Organization) and with Prime Minister B. J. Vorster and his aides from April onwards, and kept Dr Waldheim regularly informed.

The Western states felt they had forestalled the Turnhalle constitution. South Africa was ready for some concessions but insisted that a reduced number of its troops should remain for the transition period, while Swapo held they should all be withdrawn. On 31 August South Africa announced that Walvis Bay—the only deep-water port on the coast—would belong to South Africa although surrounded by Namibia. In November the General Assembly condemned this claim and insisted that Swapo be represented at independence talks under UN auspices. It urged the Security Council to act on sanctions and called for a special session of the Assembly on Namibia.

CYPRUS. Early in 1977 there were encouraging moves over Cyprus. The UN Special Representative Mr Javier Perez de Cuellar arranged a meeting between Archbishop Makarios and the Turkish Cypriot leader Mr Rauf Denktash on 27 January. Two weeks later Dr Waldheim met the Archbishop and Denktash in Nicosia when it was arranged to resume intercommunal talks. These were held in Vienna from 31 March to 7 April. Both sides presented plans known to be unacceptable to the other on territorial withdrawal and a weak central government. There was no progress. The Turkish elections were followed by long uncertainty over a Turkish Government and over the naming of a successor to Archbishop Makarios, who died on 3 August; in the interlude the Turks were reported to be developing the former Greek Cypriot part of Famagusta, which was expected to be returned through negotiations. Cyprus asked the Security Council to consider the 'threatened colonization of Famagusta'. On 15 September the Council expressed concern at recent developments and called for renewed negotiations under the auspices of the Secretary-General. In November the General Assembly called for the resumption of talks and for the Security Council to 'adopt all practical means' to implement its resolutions on Cyprus.

The mandate of the UN force in Cyprus (UNIFCYP, about 2,500 men) was renewed for six months in June and from 15 December. But Dr Waldheim warned in his report for June–November 1977 that if additional contributions were not received by 15 December 1977 the deficit accumulated since March 1964 would be $56·7 million.

COMPLAINTS TO THE UN. A number of complaints were taken to the UN, some with requests for action, some without as a matter of record and warning. Zaïre complained at the invasion of its Shaba province from Angola, but did not ask for action for fear that Russia would exercise its veto. Mauritania charged that mercenaries, paid by Algeria, had attacked its capital, and later accused Algeria of a policy of aggression. Angola alleged that South African troops from Namibia had violated its border, and Libya complained of 'acts of aggression' from Egypt and French air raids against the people of Western Sahara.

Often African states preferred to settle their conflicts through the Organization of African Unity, an effort they attempted, without success, over the fighting in the Horn of Africa. But the Security Council was asked to investigate the airborne attack on the capital of Benin on 16 January. Its mission reported in March that the attackers were mostly mercenaries, believed to have been recruited in Europe, trained in Morocco, and flown from Gabon; France and the other two countries denied involvement. The Council condemned the aggression, called for action against mercenaries, asked the help of the Secretary-General in assessing damage and of member states in making up losses. On 24 November the Council adopted a similar follow-up resolution.

In January Botswana complained of border violations by Rhodesia necessitating expansion of its mobile police unit at the expense of development plans. On 14 January the Security Council condemned Rhodesia for its harassment, demanded an end to 'hostile acts' and asked the Secretary-General to send a mission to assess Botswana's needs.

As the Council, a few weeks earlier, had requested the Secretary-General to organize assistance for Lesotho after the closure of several border posts with Transkei, Dr Waldheim decided that the same mission should evaluate the needs of both states. In May the Council endorsed the findings of the mission. Botswana needed $53·5 million in the next three years for security, refugees and development, and Lesotho needed $66 million for an emergency programme and an accelerated development programme to lessen dependence on South Africa.

Following the deep incursion of Rhodesian forces into Mozambique the Security Council held an urgent meeting and on 30 June adopted a resolution strongly condemning the aggression and calling on all states to provide aid to Mozambique to offset its losses from these attacks and its observance of sanctions, also for defence. It asked the Secretary-General to organize assistance. Subsequently a UN mission of experts reported that $50 million in aid was needed to resettle refugees and rebuild the areas.

DECOLONIZATION ISSUES. Apart from Southern Africa few remnants of the colonial era remained, but some still involved the UN. A UN three-member team observed voting in the French territory of Afars and Issas on 8 May and the steps towards independence as the Republic of Djibouti on 27 June. The General Assembly gave increasing support for the self-determination and territorial integrity of Belize, which the UK wanted to see independent provided it was not taken over by Guatemala. The Assembly reaffirmed its view that the people of East Timor had not chosen freely to become part of Indonesia, and asked the Secretary-General to send a representative to study the situation. Regarding the Comoros, a UN member since 1975 but without the island of Mayotte which opted to stay French, the General Assembly favoured the 'political unity and territorial integrity' of the archipelago. It requested Dr Waldheim to help negotiations in consultation with the Comoros and France.

Reaffirming its past principle of self-determination for Western Sahara, the Assembly hoped that the OAU special summit—so long delayed—would reach a solution for the area. The Secretary-General helped secure the release of eight Frenchmen working in Mauritania taken hostage by the

Polisario independence movement based in Algeria, accompanying them from Algiers to Paris on 23 December, where he received a letter of thanks from President Giscard d'Estaing.

DISARMAMENT. On 18 May 34 states signed a Convention prohibiting use of 'environmental modifications' for hostile purposes which would give the Secretary-General a unique verification role. At the end of June a review conference concluded that the 1972 treaty banning nuclear and mass-destructive weapons from the seabed had been observed, but asked the Conference of the Committee on Disarmament (CCD) to consider how to prevent an arms race on the seabed.

Nuclear test ban drafts were submitted to the CCD which reconvened in February. Subsequently the UK, US and USSR held a series of talks on comprehensive banning of tests. Their work was facilitated when President Brezhnev offered on 2 November to suspend underground tests for peaceful purposes.

The General Assembly, anticipating its special session of 23 May 1978, called as previously for a ban on all nuclear tests and chemical weapons, steps to prevent the development of new mass-destructive weapons, nuclear-weapon-free zones in Latin America, the Middle East, Africa and South Asia, and a zone of peace in the Indian Ocean. The Assembly also asked for studies on disarmament and development, and disarmament and international security.

HIJACKING. Following the hijacking of the Lufthansa plane to Mogadishu (see p. 131) and the murder of its pilot the International Federation of Airline Pilots Associations planned a 48-hour strike. Dr Waldheim immediately conferred with the Federation's head and the President of the General Assembly, Mr Lazar Mojsov. The strike was postponed pending urgent consideration by the Assembly. On 3 November it called on states to improve security and to accede to the Conventions on safeguarding civilian aircraft of Tokyo 1963, The Hague 1970 and Montreal 1971.

CONFERENCES

Of the five large UN conferences in 1977 two were designed to awaken public opinion on the rights of blacks in Southern Africa, two were to awaken the world on problems of resources, and the fifth was a continuation of the Law of the Sea Conference.

MAPUTO CONFERENCE. The conference in support of the peoples of Zimbabwe and Namibia from 16 to 21 May saw a significant change in attitudes towards Southern Africa. Instead of confrontation the spokesman for the five Western delegations (France, Canada, the UK, US and West

Germany) reported an unprecedented depth of solidarity on these issues, although they could not subscribe to all the conference's declaration and programme of action. The conference called for stronger sanctions against Rhodesia, aid to liberation movements and front-line states and a mandatory arms embargo against South Africa, amongst other measures.

APARTHEID. The World Conference for Action against Apartheid met at Lagos from 22 to 26 August. It considered measures to combat apartheid and aid for those suffering from it. It called for self-determination in South Africa, the removal of its forces from Namibia, and strict compliance with sanctions against Rhodesia, and asked the Security Council for a mandatory arms embargo against South Africa.

WATER CONFERENCE. The UN Water Conference in Argentina from 14 to 25 March was intended to arouse nations to tackle the problems of water. But developed countries were concerned chiefly with waste of water and pollution, and developing countries were concerned with shortage of water. The conference approved recommendations on community water supplies, pollution and water for industrial uses. It designated 1980-90 as the decade for provision of adequate drinking water and sanitation for all peoples.

DESERTS. The UN Conference on Desertification met in Nairobi from 29 August to 9 September. On the basis of reports and feasibility studies it adopted 26 detailed recommendations. It concentrated on human society in an arid environment and ran into the age-old clash between nomadism and settled agriculture. The Conference decided to establish a special UN fund rather than finance measures through existing UN organizations.

THE THIRD LAW OF THE SEA CONFERENCE. The sixth session was held from 23 May to 15 July, to be followed by another in March 1978 as the powers of the international authority, particularly in mining the seabed, were in dispute. The president of the conference, Mr H. Shirley Amerasinghe, prepared a new 'informal composite negotiating text', but its seabed mining provisions did not satisfy the American delegate. Progress was reported on the extent of the territorial sea, freedom of navigation, passage through straits, and sharing resources with landlocked states. But the clash of national and world interest over unclaimed areas of the globe was pronounced.

ECONOMIC, SOCIAL AND HUMANITARIAN

COMMON FUND, COMMODITY AGREEMENTS AND INDEBTEDNESS. The 31st session of the General Assembly adjourned from December 1976 to September 1977 to assess progress on a new economic order, including a

Common Fund and relief of Third World indebtedness. UNCTAD's negotiations for a Common Fund ended on 3 April with no real progress and so did the 'North–South' (CIEC) dialogue at its top-level meeting from 30 May to 1 June, although the Western countries committed themselves to a Common Fund.

When the General Assembly resumed on 13 to 19 September the Third World registered its disappointment, while the Western countries insisted that some advance had been made. The 32nd Assembly decided that a special session should be held in 1980 to assess progress. UNCTAD reopened negotiations on the Common Fund from 7 November until 1 December, when the developing countries decided they were no longer meaningful. The Third World favoured a large independent fund as part of an integrated programme for a number of commodities, while a hard core of Western nations favoured a limited fund to overcome price fluctuations of a few commodities which could be stock-piled and provide much of the financing.

In December financial experts held a meeting organized by UNCTAD on Third World debt problems. The two sides did not agree. The Third World proposed that official loans to 29 least developed countries should be cancelled, amounting to about 1 per cent of the total Third World debts. A few Western countries were already writing off some debts, but others opposed this for fear of the effect on commercial loans. In August the IMF had established a new fund, 'the Witteveen Facility', of about $10,000 million for loans especially to help developing countries.

To tackle problems of the 'North–South' dialogue Mr Robert McNamara, president of the World Bank, proposed in January 1977 that an independent group of leading people should consider problems of world development. The commission met on 9 to 11 December with former Chancellor Willy Brandt in the chair and with outstanding personalities from developed and developing countries participating.

In October a sugar agreement was finally reached under the auspices of UNCTAD, representing a step towards an integrated programme of commodity agreements. It provided for a price range, 'special stocks' and export quotas from 1 January 1978.

THE ECONOMIC AND SOCIAL COUNCIL. The ECOSOC meetings considered the broad scope of social and development issues for which it is responsible to the General Assembly, from corrupt practices of transnational companies to human rights. But at the meeting from 12 April to 13 May its chief concerns were combating racial discrimination, a draft Convention on the Elimination of Discrimination against Women and a code of conduct for law enforcement officials. At the summer meeting, 6 July to 4 August the Council turned its attention to hastening a new economic order, to providing adequate water and sanitation for all by 1990, and building up food reserves. It approved the 22-point plan of the World Food Council and a 13-point plan to improve disaster relief.

UN DEVELOPMENT PROGRAMME. Guidelines for UNDP's future were provided by two sessions of its Governing Council—to concentrate on food production, energy, technology, employment, trade, world research into tropical disease, and the importance of integrating its work with other specialized agencies. At a pledging conference on 2 November over $455 million was pledged for UNDP of the estimated requirement of $600 million for 1978. In its five-year programme it was expected to concentrate nearly half its activities in countries with $150 or less GNP per capita and over 30 per cent of its expenditure in the least developed countries.

AGRICULTURE AND FOOD. FAO reviewed the world food situation at its annual conference on 12 November to 1 December. The situation appeared precarious but had improved in the last two years, although the grain harvest for 1977 was down on the 1976 record, and drought threatened in the Sahel. The conference called for contributions towards its World Food Programme, which in 1977 provided help for survivors of the Turkish and Romanian earthquakes, of drought in Sri Lanka and Vietnam and a tornado in Bangladesh, displaced persons in Angola, refugees from Rhodesia and Western Sahara, and others.

The recently established agency against food deficiencies—the World Food Council—held its third ministerial meeting from 20 to 24 June and adopted a 22-point programme of recommendations to help developing countries achieve a yearly 4 per cent growth in food production: other objectives were a ten million ton target of cereal aid in 1977-78, and emergency reserves of half a million tons of grain by the end of 1977.

The new financial spearhead for agricultural development—the International Fund for Agricultural Development (IFAD)—held its first governing council meeting from 13 to 16 December and chose Abdelmushin Al-Sudeary of Saudi Arabia as president. The Fund was established as a specialized agency channelling its aid largely through existing UN organizations, especially to small farmers in the poor, food-deficient countries. It was given a unique tripartite voting system, divided equally between industrial, oil-producing and recipient countries.

ENERGY. The Secretary-General repeatedly pressed for an international institute to disseminate information on all sources of energy and related technologies, and to provide intensive training programmes and promote regional projects. He put the proposal to ECOSOC, which took no action.

In February an agreement on nuclear safeguards came into force between the International Atomic Energy Agency (IAEA) and seven of the Common Market members and EURATOM whereby IAEA would apply

L

the safety measures of EURATOM and IAEA to prevent 'diversion of nuclear energy from peaceful uses to nuclear weapons'. Under IAEA auspices 2,000 experts attended an International Conference on Nuclear Power and its Fuel Cycle in Salzburg on 2 to 13 May. Discussions covered the role of nuclear energy, fuel cycle planning, safety, waste disposal, and the transfer of nuclear technology to developing countries. Delegates were concerned by President Carter's announcement that he would slow down the fast breeder reactor programme and defer development of reprocessing techniques, a move to stop 'the premature entry into a plutonium economy'.

UN ENVIRONMENT PROGRAMME AND HABITAT. UNEP approved 21 goals for 1982, at its meeting in Nairobi on 9 to 26 May. These included a global environmental monitoring system, a warning system for natural disasters, a plan for the conservation of wildlife and parks, and measures for combating deserts. The meeting also considered problems of the remnants of war.

In its last days the General Assembly decided to set up Habitat—a Centre for Human Settlements—in Nairobi.

INTERNATIONAL LABOUR ORGANIZATION. The US withdrew from the ILO on 5 November after a two-year notice. Its chief objections were alleged politicizing in the organization, application of dual standards and the erosion of the principle of tripartite representation. Because the US contributed about a quarter of the budget the ILO had to consider stringent economies.

HUMAN RIGHTS. In no area of UN deliberations were selective standards more obviously applied than in human rights. This appeared truer of the Commission on Human Rights than of its sub-commission of experts. At its meeting on 7 February to 11 March the Commission side-stepped an investigation into human rights in Uganda and discouraged a request for information on arrests of activists in Russia. But it devoted attention to Israeli-occupied territory, Southern Africa and Chile. Its Yugoslav chairman said that the session decided to commence exposing violations of cultural, economic and social rights as well as civil and political. The sub-commission on prevention of discrimination and protection of minorities in August condemned violations of human rights in Uganda as well as Chile, Ethiopia, Indonesia, Paraguay and Uruguay.

The Human Rights Committee came into being to supervise the implementation of the International Covenant on Civil and Political Rights and to consider individual complaints of violations under the Optional Protocol. It held its first two sessions and considered reports of parties to the Covenants.

The General Assembly adopted a resolution condemning the violation of human rights in Chile. But its Third Committee decided against voting on the proposal for creating a UN High Commissioner of Human Rights.

WHO AND UNICEF. The WHO adopted a strategy for increasing co-operation with developing countries aimed at 'health for all by the year 2000'. It decided to increase technical cooperation and health services from about 51·2 per cent of its budget to at least 60 per cent by 1980, to prune outdated projects, to continue efforts on cancer control and to undertake a programme of research into tropical diseases. The organization's global drive to eradicate smallpox scored a near success, with India and Bangladesh reported free since 1975, but pockets of a mild form occurred during 1977 in Somalia and Ethiopia.

The UN Children's Fund (UNICEF) approved assistance of $113·6 million to benefit children in more than 50 developing countries. Much of the special funding was for child health, nutrition and supplying water and sanitation. Together with WHO it planned to expand programmes of primary health care and immunization. Mr Ferdinand Oyono of Cameroon was chosen as chairman, the first African in the post.

REFUGEES. On retiring as High Commissioner for Refugees, Prince Sadruddin Aga Khan criticized the lack of concern for refugees in a world professing interdependence. UNHCR became responsible for refugees from new areas—Indo-China, Southern Africa and the Horn of Africa. Sadruddin Aga Khan became a special consultant, the General Assembly chose Mr Poul Hartling, former Prime Minister of Denmark, as UNHCR, and extended the life of the organization through 1983.

Sir John Rennie retired as commissioner-general of the UN Relief and Works Agency for Palestinian refugees, and his deputy—Mr Thomas McElhiney—succeeded him. Mr McElhiney reported that a $12 million deficit in the budget had forced the Agency to reduce basic rations to 800,000 refugees for the last quarter of 1977. The General Assembly extended the Agency's life for three years from 30 June 1978.

Chapter 2

THE COMMONWEALTH

LEADERS of the Commonwealth gathered in London and Gleneagles in Scotland from 8 to 15 June, the first time its members had met in Britain at heads of government level since 1969. In what the Secretary-General, Mr Shridath Ramphal, later described as a low-key, practically-orientated conference, the leaders addressed three main issues: world economic problems; the situation in Southern Africa; and the excesses of the Amin regime in Uganda.

In the debate on international economic problems, Third World members expressed their disappointment that attempts to establish a 'new world economic order' had so far produced meagre results. The London conference met shortly after the disappointing outcome of the so-called North–South dialogue in Paris. It had before it the final report of a Commonwealth expert group headed by Mr Alister McIntyre which had been asked at the previous heads of government meeting in Kingston, Jamaica, in 1975 (see AR 1975, p. 316) to prepare an analysis of world economic problems, together with practical proposals for action by the Commonwealth. The group's findings urged member governments to renew their efforts to improve the lot of poor countries, stressing the vital importance of establishing a Common Fund for trade in commodities. The heads of government agreed to set up a technical working group on the Common Fund. They also urged the European Community to improve its trading arrangements with Commonwealth countries in Asia. The conference agreed to give financial support to a fund for Commonwealth industrial cooperation and to spend more on technical cooperation.

The discussions on Southern Africa formed part of year-long attempts by the Commonwealth, particularly its Secretariat, to find a solution to the Rhodesian problem. In the debate, President Kaunda of Zambia emerged as the most outspoken African leader, and his views found clear representation in a final conference communique notable for its bleak forecast of what was likely to happen in Rhodesia in the absence of a negotiated settlement. After some hesitation, Britain agreed to subscribe to a declaration stating that the guerrilla war had become 'complementary to other efforts' towards achieving a Rhodesian settlement and that 'its maintenance was inevitable'. It was the first time a British Government had adopted such a statement on Rhodesia. Britain did not, however, wholly support Commonwealth moves to tighten oil sanctions against the Smith regime. Its Prime Minister, Mr Callaghan, noted that it would be difficult to establish that oil company subsidiaries in South Africa were assisting in the flow of petroleum products to Rhodesia and pointed out that a special study of the legal and other issues involved was being carried out by the Foreign and Commonwealth Office. The conference instructed the Commonwealth sanctions committee to investigate breaches in sanctions already applied against the Salisbury regime.

In the weeks leading up to the London conference, President Idi Amin attempted to create confusion over whether or not he intended to be present. Earlier, the British Government had made contact with other Commonwealth Governments, asking for their views on the situation in Uganda and on the desirability or otherwise of President Amin's attending. Shortly before the conference was due to begin, the British Government made public its view that his presence would be unwelcome, and in the end Amin stayed away. The debate on Uganda produced an agreed statement of unprecedented severity. The statement spoke of 'accumulated evidence of sustained disregard for the sanctity of life and of massive violation of human rights in Uganda'. These excesses were 'so gross as to warrant the world's concern and to evoke condemnation by heads of government in strong and unequivocal terms'.

Another troublesome issue for the Commonwealth—sporting ties with South Africa—found its reflection in pressure applied to the New Zealand Prime Minister, Mr R. D. Muldoon, to persuade him to condemn attempts by New Zealand sporting bodies to retain active links with their counterparts in the Republic. New Zealand's policies had earlier produced a series of threats by African and Asian members of the Commonwealth to boycott the Commonwealth Games due to be held in Edmonton, Canada, in 1978. At a special informal weekend session of the conference held at Gleneagles, Mr Muldoon agreed to a joint statement pledging member Governments to do everything possible to prevent their teams playing against teams from South Africa not representative of all communities.

The Commonwealth leaders decided that the next heads of government conference would be held at Lusaka, Zambia, in 1979.

Throughout the year a vigorous programme of Commonwealth activity continued in a wide variety of fields. Commonwealth Finance Ministers met in Barbados in September to discuss the state of the world economy and to review developments since the heads of government meeting. They noted that the twin evils of high inflation and sluggish growth, coupled with unacceptably high levels of unemployment, were creating widespread uncertainty and impeding a recovery of the international economy. They renewed Commonwealth support for a Common Fund for commodities and for the use of buffer stocks to minimize fluctuations in world commodity prices.

The Commonwealth Secretariat, during the year, carried out technical studies aimed at preparing for the time when Rhodesia eventually secured legal independence under majority rule. A central part of the work was a manpower survey to identify students and others who would be suitable to return to Rhodesia after independence and play a part in the country's development. The Secretary-General reported that considerable talent was available.

At a meeting in Ottawa, members of the Commonwealth Parliamentary Association took steps to broaden the scope of their work and to make it more effective. A new constitution was adopted; in future greater emphasis would be laid on CPA activities in member countries.

New Commonwealth activities in the sphere of functional cooperation were begun. A special Commonwealth study for improving food production in rural areas was set in motion. The Commonwealth Science Council established a programme for investigating alternative sources of energy, and great interest was shown in this by the very poor Commonwealth members whose balance of payments problems had in some cases taken on crisis proportions because of high petroleum prices.

Acting on a proposal by the Australian Prime Minister, Mr Malcolm Fraser, the Secretariat made arrangements for a gathering of Asian and Pacific Commonwealth heads of government. The meeting, the first of its kind, was scheduled to take place in Sydney, Australia, early in 1978.

Chapter 3

DEFENCE NEGOTIATIONS AND ORGANIZATIONS

TALKS ON MUTUAL FORCE REDUCTIONS

DURING the year virtually no progress at all was made in the continuing East–West negotiations on mutual force reductions. After four years of negotiating the two sides remained substantially deadlocked on most of the issues which had divided them earlier.

Western delegates continued to press the East to abandon its insistence that all 11 direct participants, regardless of their actual circumstances, should be treated as identical in respect of military importance and geographical situation, and should therefore submit to an identical percentage reduction formula. From the outset the West had been against equal percentage reductions, which it believed would freeze Soviet advantages, and in favour of reductions aimed at reaching parity in ground forces. According to the Western plan, equality would be reached by reduction to a common collective ceiling in ground manpower, and by a substantial reduction of the large Eastern superiority in main battle tanks. The year ended without any sign of resolution of those differences of approach.

The discrepancy between Nato and Warsaw Pact statistics on force levels in Europe, which first came to light in 1976, continued to trouble the negotiators, who realized that without agreement on basic data there could be no agreed basis for calculating equitable reductions. At the heart of the discrepancy was the Western claim that the Warsaw Pact had a 150,000-man advantage in ground force deployments in Central Europe. This was countered by Warsaw Pact figures claiming approximate equality in the manpower of the two sides.

Throughout the year the Warsaw Pact countries continued to accuse Nato of seeking unilateral advantages by asking the communist countries to make the biggest cuts, while the Nato states accused the Warsaw countries of seeking to maintain their superiority in manpower. The differences of perspective between the two alliances were profound. 'Lack of tangible progress' was how the Warsaw Pact described the end of the 121st round of talks. Western spokesmen described it as 'an unsatisfactory overall situation'.

THE SALT TALKS

In March, US Secretary of State Cyrus Vance took two new proposals to Moscow in an attempt to make progress in the SALT II negotiations which had occupied the two superpowers on and off since 1972. The first proposal was 'comprehensive' and ambitious. It sought to reduce existing missile arsenals and to curb the qualitative arms race by restricting the modernization or replacement of existing weapons systems. The plan envisaged reducing the total number of delivery vehicles from the Vladivostok level of 2,400 to between 1,800 and 2,000. Of these only 1,100-1,200 could be MIRVed (compared with 1,320 under the Vladivostok terms), and only 550 of those MIRVed could be land-based ICBMs. In addition, the proposal required the Soviet Union to reduce the number of its very heavy ICBMs from the 308 permitted by the SALT I Interim Agreement to 150. The second proposal was a fall-back, 'deferral' plan which merely confirmed the Vladivostok ceilings, leaving for future discussion the awkward issues raised by the 'Backfire' bomber and the cruise missile—both weapons which had stalled the negotiations under the Ford Administration.

The Russians rejected both proposals. They rejected the 'comprehensive' proposal for a number of reasons: first, because they believed, quite rightly, that it discriminated against the land-based ICBMs which carry over 80 per cent of the Soviet strategic deterrent; secondly, because it would have made it impossible for them to MIRV all their missile force; thirdly, because the proposal would have compelled them to halve the number of their heavy missiles capable of carrying up to eight warheads; fourthly, because the American proposal sought to freeze the inferior state of Soviet MIRV technology; and fifthly, because, if implemented, the proposal would have prevented the Soviet deployment of mobile missiles.

The Russians were also unhappy about the suggestion included in the comprehensive proposal that only cruise missiles with a range in excess of 1,500 miles should be controlled. They pointed out that cruise missiles with much lesser ranges were capable of threatening strategic targets in the USSR. In essence, the comprehensive proposal sought to curb the weapons valued most highly by the Russians while permitting those favoured by the Americans.

The 'deferral' proposal was rejected by the Russians largely because they were unwilling to postpone consideration of the cruise missile.

After the breakdown of the Moscow talks at the end of March the dialogue was not resumed until May when Mr Vance and Mr Gromyko agreed on a new framework for the negotiations. They favoured a three-part agreement. The first part would be a treaty lasting till 1985 based upon the Vladivostok proposals. The second part would be a three-year protocol dealing with more controversial issues like the cruise missile and 'Backfire' bomber. And the third part would outline the plans for a new round of SALT III negotiations.

As the year moved to its end, both sides claimed that agreement was near. This caused considerable disquiet in some American circles, where it was feared that the Carter Administration was on the verge of accepting an agreement which would leave the United States with a 'second best' defence system.

NATO

The growing power of the Warsaw Pact and continuing internal disarray within Nato preoccupied the allies throughout the year. In May, Mr Harold Brown, the US Secretary of Defense, reminded his European allies that Warsaw Pact military capability continued to develop at a disturbing rate, particularly in the deployment of new weapons systems. Soviet expenditure in real terms had been rising by 3 to 4 per cent annually over the past ten years, and the cumulative effects of this posed a serious threat to Western security. Senators Sam Nunn and Dewey Bartlett, both members of the Senate's armed services committee, had already warned that the Warsaw Pact countries were rapidly moving towards a decisive conventional military superiority over Nato, and their concern was shared by Lord Home of the Hirsel, who declared that the Nato allies had reduced expenditure on conventional arms to such an extent that they were back to the 'trip wire' doctrine of the 1950s.

Aware of the dangers and acutely conscious of American pressure to do something about them, Nato Defence Ministers, at the conclusion of their spring meeting, announced that an annual increase in defence spending of about 3 per cent in real terms should be aimed at by all alliance members in the four-year period starting in 1979.

Dr Luns, Secretary General of Nato, warned of the dangers caused by political disunity and economic weakness. He noted the 'festering sore' of the Greek-Turkish conflict, and the economic problems facing many Nato countries. His concern about the alliance's political problems was echoed by Dr Henry Kissinger, who dwelt upon the dangers of Eurocommunism and urged a firm stand against this new threat. Dr Kissinger hinted that the consequence of communists' acquiring power in Nato countries could conceivably be the collapse of the alliance and the withdrawal of US troops 'who could hardly be maintained for the object of defending some communist governments against other communist governments'.

One of the most controversial issues facing the alliance in 1977 was the question whether or not to deploy the 'neutron bomb', a weapon which killed by radiation rather than concussion. This weapon, with its potential for killing people but leaving property intact, was savagely attacked in left-wing circles as the ultimate capitalist weapon. Many allies acknowledged the military usefulness of the neutron bomb, but at the end of 1977 no final decision on deployment had been taken.

Throughout the year many Europeans expressed fears about the possible outcome of the SALT talks. Allies were particularly anxious that the United States should not reach any agreement with the Soviet Union which would either jeopardize their option to acquire long-range cruise missiles or undermine the so-called 'forward based systems' in Europe. In the Nato Council meeting held in December Mr Vance promised that the US would continue to resist Soviet pressures in that direction.

At the end of the year it seemed likely that the US Government would end its partial embargo on arms deliveries to Turkey, in exchange for some political 'gesture' from the Turks to break the deadlock in the Cyprus talks. It was hoped that the restoration of military aid and supplies would quickly strengthen a particularly weak frontier with the Soviet Union.

THE WARSAW PACT

The military strength of the Warsaw Pact continued to grow throughout the year. As new Soviet equipment replaced ageing military systems, the qualitative gap between Nato armaments and those of the Warsaw countries steadily diminished. Long-term plans to modernize and integrate the armed forces of the Warsaw Pact continued to be implemented.

On 9 January, Marshal of the Soviet Union V. G. Kulikov was appointed commander-in-chief, Warsaw Pact joint armed forces. He succeeded Marshal I. I. Yakubovsky, who died in November 1976. During the year a number of military exercises were conducted. In March, Exercise SOYUZ-77, a command/staff exercise, was held in Hungary and Czechoslovakia, and immediately afterwards there were reports of a Soviet ground/air exercise in the Soviet Union. Observers were not invited but it was notified under CSCE rules as involving about 25,000 men. Joint naval exercises were held in the South Baltic in July, and in the same month a further Soviet ground/air exercise practising cooperation between various arms was held in Russia. This exercise was notified as involving 27,000 men, and observers from several Nato countries were invited.

The Political Consultative Committee (PCC), the highest organ of Warsaw Pact decision-making machinery, did not meet in 1977. But the year did see the first meeting of the Committee of Foreign Ministers formally instituted by the PCC in 1976. This new committee, which paralleled the existing Committee of Defence Ministers, met in Moscow in May, and although its functions remained unclear it was reported that the main business of the meeting related to clarifying and concerting Warsaw Pact views on the Belgrade review conference. During the year

L*

the Military Council met twice (in Prague during May and in Sofia during October), and the chairmen of parliaments of the Warsaw Pact member countries held their first consultative meeting.

CENTO

The annual conference of the Central Treaty Organization held in Teheran in the middle of May was attended by Mr Cyrus Vance, Dr David Owen, the Foreign Ministers of Iran and Turkey, and Pakistan's ambassador in Teheran. In reviewing the international situation the Ministers called for renewed efforts to reach 'a just, honourable and durable peace in the Middle Eastern area as a whole'. They hoped that the forthcoming Belgrade conference would lead to a further relaxation of international tension.

A statement issued after the two-day meeting reported progress against threats of subversion in the CENTO region and gave a pledge to go on trying to eliminate them. Ministers 'reaffirmed the vital importance they attach to the preservation of the independence and territorial integrity of each of the member states'.

ASEAN

In August, leaders from Thailand, Malaysia, Singapore, Indonesia and the Philippines gathered for a summit meeting of the Association of South-East Asian Nations. Ostensibly called to survey ASEAN's ten years of progress, the summit reviewed the economic progress made by the organization. Mindful of their suspicious neighbours in Indo-China, the leaders stressed the socio-economic purposes of the association and played down the subject of future security arrangements. Even so, problems of security provoked a good deal of private discussion, since all the five partners except Singapore had insurgency problems on their hands. Understandably, however, the leaders of ASEAN were reluctant to discuss openly the concept of a formal military alliance, which they knew would strengthen Hanoi's entrenched opinion that the organization was designed to promote American military interests in South-East Asia.

The summit meeting was expanded into an eight-nation conference on trade and economic development, where Mr Takeo Fukuda, the Japanese Prime Minister, agreed to provide £588 million to finance five major industrial projects in ASEAN countries. He also reassured ASEAN leaders that Japan had totally relinquished its military ambitions in the area and would not attempt to rearm as a result of American withdrawals.

THE BELGRADE CONFERENCE

President Carter's firm stance on the human rights issue, and the Belgrade conference to review the Helsinki agreement of 1975, made it inevitable that the human rights issue would continue to ruffle the surface of East–West relations in 1977.

Sustained Western attacks on the way in which the Soviet Union treated its dissidents provoked a vigorous response. In March, Mr Brezhnev reminded Western countries that the Helsinki agreement bound its signatories to refrain from all kinds of interference in each other's internal affairs. He also hinted that continuing criticism might jeopardize detente and American–Russian relations.

The Carter philosophy—which seemed to soften slightly as the months went by—was elaborated by Secretary Vance in April. He said: 'It is not our purpose to intervene in the internal affairs of other countries, but, as the President has emphasized, no member of the United Nations can claim that violation of internationally protected human rights is solely its own affair.' The implication was that, whereas the Russians persistently sought to separate the human rights issue from that of detente, the Americans insisted that the connexion between the two was vital, and they sometimes came close to treating progress on the human rights issue as a condition for continuing detente.

During the summer, the diplomats in Belgrade devoted themselves to the task of working out the ground rules and agenda for the 35-nation review conference in the autumn. Differences between East and West were apparent from the start. While the Western states sought a separate and thorough examination of how the Helsinki agreement had been implemented during the last two years, the Russians were anxious to avoid a specific agenda item on implementation. They preferred a more general agenda based on the relevant paragraph of the Final Act, largely because they believed this might enable them to slide over awkward and specific questions about human rights issues within the Soviet Union.

In the end, a fudged but ingenious compromise was reached, largely as a result of diplomatic initiatives taken by the neutral and non-aligned participants. It was decided to lift the relevant passage from the Helsinki Act—which pleased the Russians—but to put spaces between the sections so that it read:

A thorough exchange of views

both on the implementation of the Provisions of the Final Act and the tasks defined by the conference

as well as, in the context of the questions dealt with by the latter, on the deepening of their mutual relations, the improvement of security and the development of cooperation in Europe, and the development of the process of detente in the future.

This formula satisfied the West that a full discussion of the implementation of the Final Act could take place.

The other major disagreement to manifest itself in this initial skirmishing was the question whether or not to set a terminal date for the main conference. The Russians wanted a final cut-off date, after which the delegates would disperse, but most Western states favoured an open-ended conference, believing that a fixed terminal date might tempt the Russians into filibustering or 'talking out' controversial issues. In the end a target date of 22 December was set, but the end of the conference was left nominally open so that, if necessary, it could be resumed in mid-January for a further month.

The conference proper began in October, and, as expected, the human rights issue dominated the discussions and provoked a series of acrimonious exchanges. It became quite clear that, although Western delegates did not wish to provoke a Soviet walkout, they were determined to confront the Russians with some awkward questions about their treatment of minority groups and dissidents. On 6 October Mr Arthur Goldberg, chairman of the American delegation, delivered a firm and detailed condemnation of violations of human rights, and although he did not mention the Soviet Union by name it was quite clear from his examples which country he was talking about.

The Russian response was equally sharp. The Americans were accused of hypocrisy. Mr Vadim Loginov insisted that the United States 'has no moral right to teach other countries about human rights. Life in the United States is not perfect. It includes the right to go without expensive medical care and the right of minorities to be discriminated against.' He went on to question the right of those who used napalm and killed hundreds of thousands of people in Vietnam, and whose CIA agents tried to assassinate foreign statesmen, to judge others on the question of human rights. The conference was still continuing at the end of the year.

Chapter 4

THE EUROPEAN COMMUNITY

THE year saw the formal applications by Portugal (28 March) and Spain (28 July) to join the EEC—Greece had already applied in June 1975—and the bid by the new President of the European Commission, Mr Roy Jenkins, to revive the ambitious idea of monetary union, which had been agreed in the early 1970s and then quietly shelved. The two events were not unrelated. As Mr Jenkins said in his speech of 28 October in Florence, 'the prospect of EEC enlargement will face us with the clear choice either of strengthening the sinews of the Community or of tacit acceptance of a loose customs union, far removed from the hopes of its founders, and without much hope of recovering momentum'.

While Mr Jenkins acknowledged that something as radical as monetary union could not be achieved 'at a stroke', he believed that the run-up to direct Community-wide elections to the European Parliament was the time to launch a major debate on the issue. But by the end of the year that run-up looked like being prolonged beyond the planned election date of May/June 1978. Belgium, France, and Denmark had already passed the necessary legislation for direct elections, and Germany, Italy, Luxembourg the Netherlands and Ireland were expected to follow suit early in the new year. But in December the British House of Commons chose the most time-consuming means (the traditional 'first past the post' system) of setting out the new Euro-constituencies (see p. 17). It had earlier been agreed that a delay in one member state would mean a delay in all.

At their Rome summit meeting in March the EEC heads of government celebrated the twentieth anniversary of the signing of the Treaty of Rome, establishing the Common Market. The 13 Brussels Commissioners, however, apart from launching one or two major new initiatives, devoted most of their energies over the year to such issues as helping Europe's 'crisis' industries of steel, shipbuilding and textiles, trying to bring some order out of the chaos of the EEC fishing policy, and redesigning the Common Agricultural Policy (CAP), particularly with a view to the likely entry of the three Mediterranean applicant countries.

By rota, for the first time since its accession, Britain took the chair of the Council of Ministers in the first half of 1977, and Belgium in the second half. The British presidency provoked some controversy. Although businesslike in the organization of Council work, some British Ministers were criticized for allowing strong national interests on energy, farming and fish to divert them from the neutral role of chairmen. The UK Labour Government was accused by British Conservatives of 'trying to bend the rules to get any kind of short-term national advantage'. This was said to have been counter-productive.

By contrast, the Belgian Government, with fewer pressing national interests at stake, found it easier to avoid criticism of its presidency. It concentrated on promoting its relatively uncontroversial plans for closer short-term economic and monetary cooperation.

Enlargement. Although the entry applications of Greece, Portugal and Spain were being technically processed separately by Brussels, the Commission said it was working on a policy covering the global implications of expanding the Community from nine members to 12. Greek Ministers complained that this was inevitably slowing down the pace of their negotiations with the Community. Greece said it sought full membership by 1981, Portugal by 1985, while Spain, which applied only very shortly after its 15 June general election, did not set any precise date.

Only Spain of the three being a major industrial producer, the immediate impact of enlargement was expected to be on French and Italian agriculture, which had most to fear from competition in Mediterranean agricultural products. Both Gaullists and French communists came out against the entry of Spain and Portugal on these grounds, while Italy also had to reckon with Greek competition in olive oil, among other things. In December the EEC Commission made the first of its proposals to give French and Italian agriculture more protection, in the shape of a minimum wine price and structural aids for southern European farms.

West Germany, which would have to foot a major share of the bill for bringing living standards of the three applicant countries up towards current EEC averages and for extending to Mediterranean farm products the full measure already given northern produce such as cereals and milk, urged caution about enlargement on economic grounds. Chancellor Helmut Schmidt also gave warning at the London EEC summit in June of the possible influx of migrant labour following enlargement.

Economic policies. The slight economic recovery of 1976 petered out in 1977, and as it did so unemployment in the EEC—$5\frac{1}{2}$ million, 5·5 per cent of the work-force, in the spring and some 6 million by autumn 1977— became a major concern. By the end of the year both the Community's social and regional funds had been increased, the latter to 1,800 million European units of account (Eua) for 1978-80. But the tripartite conference (unions, employers and EEC Governments plus the Commission) meeting on 27 June was forced to concede that the goals it had set the year before— 4 to 5 per cent inflation, 5 per cent growth of GNP and full employment, all to be attained by 1980—were no longer realistic. No new goals were set; instead it was decided to concentrate study on work-sharing schemes and job-creating investment.

EEC Finance Ministers, meeting in October, took a slightly bolder line, and decided to aim for 4 to $4\frac{1}{2}$ per cent growth in 1978 (about 1 per cent above EEC Commission predictions), compared to the $2\frac{1}{2}$ to 3 per cent level that the Commission estimated the Community achieved in 1977. Internal demand should be increased by 1 per cent, and the Community as a whole should continue to run a moderate current account deficit in 1978. EEC Governments initially looked with some scepticism on the Brussels Commission's proposal that it should raise up to 1,000 million Eua ($1,200 million) on the international capital markets for lending to energy and industrial restructuring projects. The Commissioner for financial affairs and past Commission President, M Francois Xavier Ortoli, argued that existing EEC borrowers (such as the European Coal and Steel Community or Euratom) were too limited in their field or, like the European Investment Bank (EIB), too restricted in their scope, and that there was room for the Commission itself to go to the capital markets. His EEC loan proposal found no favour at the Community's June summit in London, where instead it was agreed that the capital of the EIB should be raised in 1978. But heads of government gave it their blessing at their

December meeting in Brussels, with the proviso that detailed supervision of the loans should be carried out by the EIB.

More controversial was the Commission's plan for short-term economic and monetary cooperation and a longer-term bid for monetary union, put to the December summit. The heads of government merely took note of the plan, which embodied a modified version of Mr Jenkins's Florence speech. It still implied a European currency of some form, a central European authority to manage it, European reserves, a broad EEC monetary policy and a corresponding loss of national monetary decision-making.

The embryonic form of European monetary union known as the 'snake' lost one of its non-EEC members, Sweden, which decided to drop out of the joint currency float, and in April the two remaining Scandinavian members of the system, Denmark and Norway, devalued their currencies against those of West Germany, Belgium and the Netherlands. Later, the fall of the dollar against the mark set up strains between the Dmark and weaker snake currencies. But by the end of the year these had been successfully resisted.

External affairs. The Commission hailed as one of its major achievements in 1977 the Community's joint position presented to the final session of the Conference on International Economic Cooperation (CIEC, the 'North–South dialogue'), held in Paris at the end of May. Arrived at with some difficulty, it consisted of a $1,000 million special action fund for the poorest developing countries (of which the EEC would contribute about one-third), a Common Fund for commodity price support, a proposal that the Stabex scheme operated by the EEC under the Lomé convention might be used more widely, and some rescheduling of debts of developing countries.

For the Community, the main achievements in the run-up to the GATT multilateral trade negotiations were agreement with the US on the principles of how and when tariffs should be cut, and a promise by Japan that its tariff concessions would benefit the EEC equally with the US.

A major step in the slowly developing relationship with Comecon was taken in September (see p. 348), when EEC external affairs Commissioner Wilhelm Haferkamp and Romanian Vice-Premier Mihai Marinescu agreed that EEC–Comecon talks should begin in the first half of 1978. The major obstacle to closer relations was the refusal of both organizations to recognize any element of supranationality in the other. The Commission, for its part, viewed discussions with Comecon as mainly leading to a better exchange of economic, commercial and technical data. The Commission also got the go-ahead from the Council of Ministers to start negotiations for a framework trade agreement with China, after a visit by Brussels officials to Peking in July. Given the fact of full Chinese diplomatic recognition of the Community, this could well bear fruit more quickly than the planned talks with Comecon.

At their London summit in June, EEC heads of government issued a statement which among other things called for a 'homeland' for the Palestinian people. This was welcomed by the Arabs in the context of the continuing six-monthly meetings of Commission and Arab League officials in the so-called 'Euro-Arab dialogue'. But in Brussels in November Arab spokesmen expressed disappointment that the EEC would not move further towards political recognition of the Palestinian and Arab case. Nor did the Arabs win any satisfaction on their request for an overall preferential trade agreement with the Community, which had always seen the potential benefits of the Euro-Arab dialogue less in political terms than in those of better business and trade cooperation. The round of bilateral trade agreements between the EEC and Arab countries was completed in 1977 with agreements signed with Egypt, Syria, Jordan and Lebanon, following the Maghreb accords of 1976. A similar agreement was also signed with Israel, though Foreign Minister Yigal Allon criticized it in Brussels as 'very limited in its extent and unsatisfactory in its terms'.

At the instance of British Foreign Secretary Dr David Owen, EEC Foreign Ministers in September endorsed a code of conduct for European companies or subsidiaries operating in South Africa. It called upon such companies not to discriminate, to give equal pay for equal work, to recognize trade unions and so on. The EEC code was sharply criticized by the South African Government, and also drew some initial reservations from German and British employers' federations.

A constant theme of 1977, as of 1976, was the EEC's attempts to ward off the worst effects of Japanese competition and to redress its growing trade deficit with Japan, which in 1977 approached $5,000 million, compared to $4,200 million in 1976. Unlike the much larger deficit the EEC was running with the USA, less than half of Japanese exports to Europe were covered by EEC exports the other way. Tokyo made some concessions at the start of the year, notably exempting EEC cars for a time from the tough Japanese anti-pollution controls and allowing tests on cars destined for Japan to be done in Europe. In February the Commission started its biggest-ever dumping inquiry on Japanese ball bearings, which ended in August with a promise by Japanese companies to raise their prices by 15 per cent. It was followed, however, by another dumping investigation in November on Japanese bearing 'housings'.

Nevertheless, an increase in top-level contacts between the Commission (Mr Jenkins visited Tokyo in October) and the newly reshuffled Fukuda Government towards the end of 1977—in addition to the normal twice-yearly EEC-Japanese talks—seemed to bode better for the future. EEC officials calculated that the tariff cuts which in the autumn Japan promised to make in the GATT negotiations would benefit some $500 million or

15 per cent of EEC exports. Relations between the EEC and the incoming Carter Administration remained good throughout the year, despite some concern in the EEC about the number of dumping cases in the US against European steel companies and also about President Carter's policy, announced in April, of retarding the development of nuclear reprocessing (see p. 64).

Three industrial sectors were of particular concern in 1977:

Steel. In 1977 EEC crude steel production fell some 5 per cent below 1976 levels; unemployment and short-time working increased, an average of about 35 to 40 per cent of steel plant was idle, and prices were depressed by cheap imports. From the start of the year, the Commission had asked companies to observe voluntary limits on their steel sales inside the Community, in order to try to bring production and demand into better balance.

In May the new industry Commissioner Viscomte Etienne Davignon introduced minimum guideline prices for a range of steel products and one compulsory minimum price for concrete reinforcing bars, the market price of which had been particularly depressed by Italian undercutting. He also announced a longer-term restructuring policy for the industry, entailing EEC loans for modernization and surveillance of national aids to companies with the condition that they did not increase production capacity. But by December the Commission was forced to take tougher action against third countries. The Council of Ministers authorized the imposition of special minimum prices for steel imports for the first three months of 1978 —with a penal tariff if imports entered the Community below these prices. The system was remarkably similar to one introduced for the whole of 1978 by the US Administration. The Community planned to have a series of agreements on price and quantities with all its major steel suppliers by the end of March 1978.

Shipbuilding. Over-capacity and foreign competition particularly characterized this sector, Japan being singled out as the major competitor. The EEC, along with other members of the Association of West European Shipbuilders (Finland, Norway, Sweden, Portugal and Spain), continued to press Japan for a 50/50 share-out of future ship orders in the two regions. Japan agreed to raise its ship prices by 5 per cent, and not to take orders from particularly hard-hit EEC yards such as those of Germany or the Netherlands. But these concessions were later described by the Commission as inadequate.

The Commission announced in December its plans for restructuring the industry. EEC shipbuilding capacity would have to adjust to demand, with a reduction of 46 per cent by 1980 to a level of 2·4 million tonnes a year. Employment in EEC yards would have to continue to fall by 10-15,000 a year, and the Commission gave notice that it would try to block any big national subsidies to shipyards, like the controversial subsidy that won the

UK a £115 million order from Poland. As with the steel industry, the Commission said it would try to use EEC money to subsidize interest rates on loans for modernization.

Textiles. At the end of 1977 the EEC announced that it would sign for another five years a renewed Multi Fibre Arrangement (MFA), the agreement regulating most of the world's textile trade. But the EEC's statement was made after it had secured, in long-protracted negotiations, bilateral agreements with some 30 supplying countries. Despite considerable difficulties with Hong Kong, the EEC's biggest supplier, and some other big textile producing countries, EEC negotiators succeeded in ensuring that the 6 per cent annual growth in imports allowed by the MFA would not be in the most sensitive categories, such as cotton yarn and cloth, on which some member states had threatened to take unilateral measures if specific limits were not set.

The Commission also announced a ban for two years on the EEC money for investment in synthetic fibre capacity, which it claimed was already surplus.

Fishing. Probably on no other issue did EEC Ministers spend so much time in 1977 to so little effect. On 1 January, the EEC extended its fishing limits from 12 to 200 miles, thereby increasing its problems with third countries and also the scope for disagreement between member states. Countries such as Japan, Bulgaria and Romania with no reciprocal catches to offer EEC fleets were immediately banned from EEC waters, while the Soviet Union, Poland, East Germany, Spain and Portugal had their catch levels cut. With Norway, Iceland and the Faroes, the EEC sought to negotiate access to their waters for EEC fishermen.

The Soviet Union, which, slightly to the surprise of EEC officials, seemed willing to negotiate for the first time with the EEC over fish, appeared to have second thoughts later in the year. In the autumn it suddenly banned EEC trawlers from the Barents Sea, a move which led to its immediate exclusion from EEC waters.

But it proved in any case very difficult to make external fishing deals until the nine members first decided how much they wanted to reserve for themselves. Britain and Ireland, whose waters accounted for 80 per cent of the EEC's expanded fish pond, stood out against the other seven members plus the Commission for some sort of exclusive rights. Britain stuck to its demand for a 50-mile exclusive zone around its shores for most of 1977, only late in the year hinting that it might be willing to accept a quota. The Commission eventually produced a quota figure of 21 per cent of EEC catches for the UK—which the British Agriculture and Fisheries Minister Mr John Silkin dismissed as far too low. Ireland unilaterally banned all trawlers more than 110 feet long from areas off its coasts, a move that the European Court of Justice ruled was discriminatory.

Britain did score a victory for conservation by imposing a ban on

North Sea herring fishing from 1 July, which the Commission and Council later sanctioned as a Community measure. Fishing in an area off northeast Scotland, known as the Norway Pout Box, was also banned to protect immature species from industrial fishing.

Agriculture. The EEC Commission proposed average price increases of 3 per cent for 1977-78. The fact that this was well below the 7·4 per cent that the European farming organization, Copa, was demanding reflected a growing Commission awareness of both the disproportionate share of the EEC budget taken by agriculture and the need to reduce the Community's structural food surpluses. Britain held out for no increase at all, and Mr Silkin's opposition prevented any agreement until the end of April, when the UK agreed to settle for a 3·5 per cent average price rise for the Community, and a 2·9 per cent devaluation of the 'green pound'— in return for EEC finance for a butter subsidy in the UK.

Monetary compensatory amounts (MCAs), covering the difference between actual parity of currencies and the notional 'green' rates, continued to arouse controversy. In Britain's case, MCAs took the form of a subsidy on food imports, and the UK Government firmly refused to consider any further reduction in this windfall gain. A Commission proposal for the automatic phasing-out of MCAs over seven years did not win the Council of Ministers' approval.

Facing subsidized Danish bacon exports, the British pig producers demanded help, and Mr Silkin gave it to them in January in the form of a subsidy. The Commission then ordered Britain to stop paying this subsidy as a distortion of Common Market rules, pending judicial hearings.

In February a subsidized sale of EEC butter to the Soviet Union caused an outcry, leading the Commission to ban all butter sales to Eastern Europe and the USSR. The Commission's somewhat clumsy handling of the affair attracted a censure motion in the March session of the European Parliament. It was easily defeated, but the butter sale once again demonstrated the curious economic fact that it was cheaper to subsidize the sale of EEC surpluses abroad than at home. However, an attempt was made later in the year to reduce the chronic milk surplus through the introduction of a 'co-responsibility' levy on dairy farmers to help pay for the storage and marketing of the EEC 'milk lake'.

One small reform of the Common Agricultural Policy was discussed in the Commission in the second half of 1977, in the shape of a variable premium for beef. This would amount to a partial deficiency payment to beef farmers, and would constitute a major step away from the CAP system of support prices. But strong French opposition made its introduction unlikely. The main thrust of the Commission's policy was to keep existing support prices as low as possible.

Energy. The most publicized event was the classic tug-of-war over which member state would have the prestige JET nuclear fusion project sited on its soil. Only just in time before the scientists' contracts ran out, and after a personal agreement between Prime Minister James Callaghan and Chancellor Schmidt not to block a majority Council vote, it went to Culham in the UK, against the rival site of Garching in West Germany, by a Council vote of five to two, with Italy and Belgium abstaining. Expected to cost £160 million to build and run, and planned to employ over 300 scientists, JET was the first Community establishment of any size in the UK.

President Carter's avowed attempt to persuade America's allies that nuclear reprocessing should be stopped in order to prevent nuclear bomb proliferation aroused concern in the EEC, which argued that energy-short Europe had no other choice but to reprocess its nuclear fuel. Member states had invested heavily in reprocessing plants. But the Commission was moved to institute public hearings in November—to be continued in January 1978—to air some of the hopes and fears about nuclear energy.

By the end of 1977 the Commission had successfully negotiated an end to the year-long Canadian embargo on uranium supplies to the Community. Ottawa had expressed concern about the security aspects and the uses to which its uranium was being put. A major factor in alleviating this concern was the agreement by all member states—including France, which had not signed the non-proliferation treaty—to negotiate a safeguard agreement with the Vienna-based International Atomic Energy Agency.

Chapter 5

COUNCIL OF EUROPE—WESTERN EUROPEAN UNION—NORTH ATLANTIC
ASSEMBLY—EUROPEAN FREE TRADE ASSOCIATION—ORGANIZATION FOR
ECONOMIC COOPERATION AND DEVELOPMENT—NORDIC COUNCIL—COMECON

COUNCIL OF EUROPE

FOLLOWING the example of Portugal, which joined the Council of Europe in 1976, Spain became the 20th member of the organization on 24 November, when its Foreign Minister, Sr Marcelino Oreja, presented his country's instrument of accession and also signed the European Convention on Human Rights. This event was seen as a stepping-stone to Spain's eventual entry into the EEC, since membership of the Council of Europe confirmed the country's democratic credentials. On the other hand, Yugoslavia, which had fought shy of overtly political links with the EEC, expressed interest in closer contacts with the Council of Europe, and in June 1977 a Yugoslav delegation visited its seat at Strasbourg.

In January, a new building was inaugurated by President Giscard d'Estaing, designed to serve both the Council and also some of the sessions of the European Parliament. In the same month the important European Convention on the Suppression of Terrorism was signed by 17 of the then 19 members of the Council; Ireland did not sign, arguing that it would have had constitutional difficulties in doing so, while Malta gave no reason for not signing. Four countries signed with reservations. France said it would not ratify the convention until the EEC had completed its own agreement on terrorism, and in addition stated that any persecuted person would have the right of asylum in France. Norway and Italy reserved the right to use article 13 of the new convention, which allows states not to extradite suspected terrorists in certain circumstances; and Portugal said it would not extradite if the offence in question was of a purely political nature or to a country which retained capital punishment (France was one such).

In December, the Council members issued a declaration reaffirming that the grant of asylum, for humanitarian reasons, should be allowed by any member state and should not be regarded 'as an act unfriendly to any other state'. Concern for refugees was largely behind this declaration. The Council's Resettlement Fund, 20 years old in 1977, had spent some $330 million for refugees over those years. Particular attention was paid in 1977 to Portugal's problems in absorbing refugees from its former African colonies. Also in 1977 the European Convention on the Legal Status of Migrant Workers, concerned with the legal rights of migrant workers, in particular recruitment, work permits and conditions, dismissal and re-employment, was opened for signature by Council member Governments.

WESTERN EUROPEAN UNION

The extra dimension given to Western European Union by the participation of communist members, in particular Italian, became evident in 1977. One of the highlights of the Union's two parliamentary sessions was the report—debated in both the June and November sessions—presented by Mr Segre (Communist, Italy) on the application of the final act of the Helsinki Conference on Security and Cooperation in Europe (text in AR 1975, p. 474). Mr Segre, as rapporteur of the WEU general affairs committee, emphasized that the Belgrade review conference (held in autumn 1977) must not become a tribune where points were to be scored; what was important was to continue the process begun in Helsinki. In the June session, the Segre report was referred back to the committee because of the large number of amendments to it. But Mrs von Bothmer (SPD, West Germany) stressed that it was important for a communist representative to give his views on the CSCE and that the rapporteur's membership of the Communist Party should not lead other representatives to adopt a systematically negative attitude. After amendments had been considered, the Segre report was duly adopted at the November session.

Some of the problems raised by Eurocommunism were mentioned by General Alexander Haig, Nato's supreme allied commander, when he addressed the WEU November session. As a military man, he said, he would be concerned by the consequences that communist participation in a Nato Government would have, first on the communication of security information, and secondly in giving low priority to defence spending.

Some nervousness about the rivalry that newer bodies posed to WEU could be detected among parliamentarians in the 1977 sessions. While it was asserted that WEU was the only assembly directly charged with defence and security matters, some MPs expressed concern about the consequences of a directly elected European Parliament. Also, in view of the WEU revival in 1976 of its standing armaments committee, there was some puzzlement about what its future relationship should be with the newly-formed Independent European Programme Group (IEPG). But it was the view of Mr Dankert (Labour, Netherlands), in presenting a report on European armaments policy which was adopted in June, that the IEPG was the best institution in Europe for this.

Presenting a report on Mediterranean policy, Mr Urwin (Labour, UK) said that WEU was open to all European countries with democratic regimes, and that this now obviously included Spain. An official from the Spanish Ministry of Foreign Affairs replied that Spain followed WEU activities with the greatest interest, but the Madrid Government wished there to be a national debate on the question of joining defensive military alliances.

At the beginning of the June session, the WEU assembly elected a new President, Mr Kai-Uwe Von Hassel (CDU/CSU, West Germany), the only candidate.

NORTH ATLANTIC ASSEMBLY

The main features of the Nato Assembly plenary session held in Paris in September were a reaffirmation by the French Prime Minister, M Raymond Barre, that France would not return to the integrated military, structure of Nato, and an address by Nato secretary general Joseph Luns. M Barre's message, delivered by M Pierre Christian Taittinger, outlined the three principles of French defence policy: the continued independence of French nuclear power, freedom of decision in the use of French forces, and loyalty to the Nato alliance.

The main theme of Dr Luns's speech was the juxtaposition of the economic strength of Nato with its reluctance to spend more than 5 per cent of GNP on defence, compared with the 11 to 13 per cent of the Soviet

Union. He argued that there should be no correlation between Nato defence and the temporary vicissitudes of Nato economies.

Some 29 MPs had visited US military installations in August and were given, among other things, a demonstration of the cruise missile and a view of the F-16 aircraft assembly line at a General Dynamics plant—both of interest to Europeans given the possibility of Europe's one day acquiring cruise missile technology and the fact of the purchase of F-16s by four European members of Nato. The president of the Nato Assembly, Sir Geoffrey de Freitas, who was re-elected, also paid an official visit to Turkey in September, with a view to organizing a future Nato Assembly session there.

EUROPEAN FREE TRADE ASSOCIATION

For the seven Efta countries it was a year in which to take stock of past achievements and to try to map the road ahead. After the disappearance, on 1 July 1977, of all tariffs on industrial goods—except for some 'sensitive' products for a limited period—between the EEC and the Efta countries, a free trade zone comprising some 300 million West Europeans was created. This landmark date came just ten years after the achievement of the original goal—free industrial trade among Efta countries themselves.

Efta heads of government and ministers met in May in Vienna, under the chairmanship of Chancellor Bruno Kreisky of Austria, to decide on their association's strategy for the future. They agreed to enlarge their cooperation with the EEC by means of an increased exchange of information and closer consultations on economic questions. In particular they recognized that customs procedures could be simplified to the mutual benefit of both trading blocs. This statement was welcomed by EEC external affairs Commissioner Wilhelm Haferkamp.

The Efta countries expressed their support for the application of one of their number, Portugal, for EEC membership. It was also thought appropriate, in view of Spain's impending EEC application, to open negotiations with Madrid for a multilateral trade agreement. It was further agreed that talks with Greece, the third EEC applicant, would be held in due course.

The Vienna summit also pledged Efta Governments to further cooperation among themselves and to a continued commitment to liberal trading policies. The Yugoslav Government's wish for closer economic relations with Efta would receive attention.

A particular sphere of Efta activities was the establishment of a $100 million industrial development fund for Portugal, which came into operation in February 1977; by the end of the year some $13,600,000 500 million escudos) had been lent in 37 projects to help small and medium-sized enterprises. Another step was the creation of a new Efta consultative body composed of parliamentarians in Efta states. Finally, the European Patent Convention, which Efta experts had played a major part in the drafting, came into force in October.

ORGANIZATION FOR ECONOMIC COOPERATION AND DEVELOPMENT

At the end of January the OECD published its 'World Energy Outlook', projecting supply and demand to 1985. This report substantially revised and extended the assessment made two years earlier and pointed the way in which vigorous energy policy action could bring about a better balance between supply and demand. Effective measures designed to bring this about concerned conservation and increased indigenous and alternative energy supplies.

Responding to a proposal made at the meeting of the OECD Manpower and Social Affairs Committee at ministerial level in 1976, an experts' meeting on structural determinants of employment and unemployment was held in March, the main theme being: 'for a given level of economic activity, were there policies complementary to demand management which could contribute to achieving a better balance between the demand for and the supply of employment?'.

In April, the OECD Council adopted a recommendation calling on member countries to consider introducing legislation or regulations to strengthen consumer protection in the field of consumer credit. The recommendation covered consumer information, respect for basic human rights on access to credit, together with protection of the consumer's privacy, his economic interests and means of redress and sanctions.

In response to a joint initiative of the George C. Marshall Research Foundation and the Atlantic Institute for International Affairs, a conference was held at OECD headquarters in early June to commemorate the 30th anniversary of General Marshall's speech at Harvard in which he proposed a vast programme of aid to the European continent—an idea which gave rise to the Marshall Plan and to the OEEC (the predecessor of OECD). The theme of the conference was 'From Marshall Plan to Global Interdependence—new challenges for the industrialized nations'.

The OECD Council met at ministerial level on 23 and 24 June; the main issues discussed covered international economic relations, with special reference to developing countries, and reaffirmation of the strategy for a sustained economic expansion, aiming at a progressive return to full employment and price stability, which the Council had adopted in June 1976. In this connexion the Organization was charged by Ministers with monitoring the progress made during 1978. Ministers also decided to renew, for a further year, their Trade Declaration of 30 May 1974.

A report, 'Towards Full Employment and Price Stability', by a group of independent experts chaired by Professor Paul McCracken, was published in July. It analyzed the prevailing widespread unemployment accompanied by high rates of inflation, and also made short- and medium-term policy recommendations related to the attainment of non-inflationary growth and high levels of employment in the OECD area.

Also in July, the OECD Council decided to establish a multilateral consultation and surveillance mechanism for sea-dumping of radio-active waste. Its objective was to reinforce international cooperation and surveillance in relation to the disposal of radio-active waste other than highly active waste, the dumping of which is in any case prohibited.

Another resolution adopted by the Council called on member Governments to take action to combat the problems raised by ships which did not meet internationally agreed standards and to comply fully, within their jurisdictions, with the minimum standards and procedures laid down by the International Labour Organization in its Convention of October 1976 on the manning of ships and in the various conventions of the Intergovernmental Maritime Consultative Organization concerning ship design, maintenance, safety and antipollution provisions.

The Governing Board of the OECD International Energy Agency met at ministerial level in October. Ministers reviewed progress achieved, notably in the adoption of the IEA's long-term cooperation programme and in the implementation of the emergency oil-sharing system. After discussing prospects of energy demand and supply, Ministers concluded that the world was 'confronted with the serious risk that as early as the 1980s it would not have sufficient oil and other forms of energy available'. Ministers decided that IEA countries as a group should aim to hold their total oil imports to not more than 26 million barrels per day in 1985. In order to achieve group objectives between now and 1985, Ministers endorsed a set of 12 principles for action in the energy fields and agreed on a systematic annual review of national policies within IEA. By the end of the year, 28 research and development projects had been agreed upon between IEA member Governments, covering coal research, solar power, fusion power, geothermal energy, wind power and hydrogen production from water.

The rise in youth unemployment, with all its social, economic and political consequences, became a major preoccupation for OECD member Governments. In response to wide spread concern a high-level intergovernmental conference on youth unemployment was held on 15 and 16 December. Participants reviewed the situation in member countries and discussed policy measures aimed at reducing youth unemployment. Specific aspects examined included the development of employment opportunities, easing the transition to working life and improved access to labour markets.

NORDIC COUNCIL

The Council's session in Helsinki was postponed on account of the Danish elections (see p. 146) until 31 March, and was compressed into four days. The 25-year jubilee was nevertheless marked by a festivity in Finlandia House, at which a veteran Swedish member, Professor Bertil Ohlin, hailed the Council as 'a political innovation which so far as his knowledge went was unprecedented'. Eighteen recommendations were adopted—a fall of one-half in the course of the decade—but these included an important proposal that local government bodies in border districts should have authority to provide common facilities of an economic, social or educational character. Action on this would be the concern of the Ministerial Council, as was now the case with many of the initiatives taken by the main Council.

Mr Olof Palme introduced into the general debate a party programme arising out of a congress of Nordic Labour Parties and trade union organizations in the previous November, but this fell rather flat in a Council with a small non-socialist majority. The discord which party alignments might occasion was, however, illustrated when Mr Aarne Saarinen voiced a Finnish criticism of Norwegian foreign policy as allegedly disclosed by German participation in Nato manoeuvres in the far north. The former Norwegian Labour Premier, Mr T. Bratteli, repudiated with some warmth the claim to intervene in what was exclusively a Norwegian concern, whereas his compatriot, Mr Reidar Larsen of the Socialist Left Party (see AR 1975, p. 151), followed the communist line.

The Council's committees selected Åland and the Faeroes for some of their meetings, and on 19 April the Icelandic Foreign Minister assured the Allting that he would wholeheartedly support the further extension of the Council's interest in the smaller nations by allowing separate representation to the Greenlanders. Great interest was expressed during the year in a project for a Nordic television satellite, which would enable viewers to pick and choose among all Scandinavian programmes. The older forms of communication among the several peoples likewise appeared to flourish, with 35 items in the annual series of reports, etc., sponsored by the Council (including four in English) and the various cultural awards, such as the Nordic Literature Prize. However, when a lecturer at Stockholm University questioned 53 students, all of whom would later be teaching Scandinavian literature in secondary schools, he found that, of six non-Swedish candidates for the literary award, four were completely unknown names and the other two mustered one and seven readers respectively.

COMECON

The July issue of Comecon's official journal (No. 4, 1977) carried an article on 15 years of the work of the standing commission on statistics by its chairman (Lev Volodarsky, head of the USSR central statistical administration). He commented chiefly on his commission's role in formulating the statistics for the measurement of Comecon integration, in comparing data among member states, in supporting Comecon recommendations on plan coordination and in regular economic reporting on the economies of member states. He noted that the latest (28th) meeting of his commission had resolved that it should 'further widen and deepen mutual statistical information among member states of Comecon on their economic development directly through the Secretariat's abstracts and bulletins'.

Although Comecon's *Statistical Yearbook* was put before a much broader public by appearing in 1977 in English (from a London publisher) as well as in Russian, there was a certain reduction in data on external economic relations of Comecon states. This diminution was all the more significant in that it occurred when the Belgrade conference (see p. 330) was reviewing implementation of the Helsinki Final Act, whereby the participating States undertook to 'promote the publication and dissemination of economic and commercial information' and 'in particular . . . foreign trade statistics drawn up on the basis of comparable classification including breakdown by product with indication of volume and value, as well as country of origin or destination'. It lent added force to the demand for the exchange of statistics by the EEC in its resumed contacts with Comecon.

Only a selection of the suspension of standard statistical series need be made to illustrate the trend. Comecon's own *Statistical Yearbook* succumbed to presumably Romanian pressure in withholding 1976 returns of that country on its aggregate trade with the industrial West and with developing countries, publishing only exchanges with the socialist group and within Comecon itself. Because the Romanian central statistical directorate had suspended publication of its own *Foreign Trade Yearbook* since 1974 (and returns in the general abstract were abbreviated), those data were effectively concealed. Romania was bound by membership to communicate trade and payments information to the IMF, but insisted that it remain unpublished. The Polish *Statistical Yearbook* for 1977 was also slimmer than in 1976; a series, for example, on retail sales in foreign currency (the Pewex shops) was dropped.

On 17 November 1976 an EEC proposal that its relations with Comecon be formalized in information exchange (notably on standardization, statistics and environmental protection) was delivered to the Comecon executive committee, a phase in a relationship which remained at arm's length (see AR 1976, pp. 348-49). A Comecon reply was received in Brussels on 18 April 1977, proposing preliminary discussions between the ministerial bodies, to which the Community agreed on 21 June. It made the provisos that the agenda should be restricted to the procedure for subsequent negotiations and to the inclusion of the EEC Commissioner for external affairs as the agent of the Community for matters falling within the Common Commercial Policy. The ministerial delegations met in Brussels on 21 September, led on the Comecon side by the chairman of its executive committee, Mihai Marinescu, a Deputy Chairman of the Romanian Council of Ministers, and on the EEC side by the President of the European Council, Henri Simonet, the Belgian Minister of Foreign Affairs. The EEC Commissioner for external affairs, Wilhelm Haferkamp, and a deputy secretary of Comecon, A. Velkov, also took part (see p. 335).

They agreed to initiate negotiations about an inter-organization agreement during the first half of 1978, but each side left open its form. The EEC envisaged a 'framework agreement' without direct commercial provision but fostering working relations between the two organizations, perhaps on the lines of Comecon's treaty with Finland (see AR 1973, p. 377); it pointed out that a draft long-term, non-preferential agreement, circulated in November 1974, remained on the table and could be signed by any Comecon member individually, after ratification of a framework agreement. The Comecon delegation on the other hand urged commercial negotiations which could eventuate in MFN treatment, the liquidation of non-tariff discrimination, mutual protection against domestic market disruption, the stable long-term marketing of agricultural produce and the improvement of credit relations.

The USSR had taken a step towards 'recognizing' the EEC (with which by the end of the year it had not established diplomatic relations) on 16 February, when its Minister for the Fisheries Industry, Aleksandr Ishkov, opened negotiations in Brussels for permission to trawl within the Community's new 200-mile limits. No agreement on fishing quotas materialized during the year because the Soviet delegation could not formally take the step of recognition. But in an interview with Le Monde (16 June) the Soviet President, Leonid Brezhnev, observed that 'we regard the Common Market as a reality and believe it important that the West should take a similar view of the Council for Mutual Economic Assistance'. EEC talks with the USSR, which came to include quotas in the Soviet waters of the Barents Sea, reached the stage of an 'understanding' in Warsaw in September, but a statement by Ishkov on 8 December claimed that 'the EEC representatives had introduced supplementary provisions into the draft which were of a purely political nature'.

Compared with the importance of the break-through in mutual recognition implicit in the September talks in Brussels, intra-Comecon relations were of a more routine nature. The 31st session of the Council was held in Warsaw from 21 to 23 June, all members save Cuba (whose delegate is invariably a Deputy Premier, Carlos Rodriguez) being represented by its Prime Minister, and with observers from Yugoslavia, Vietnam, North Korea, Angola and Laos (in that order in the communique). The Council resolved on 'measures to accelerate economic growth' in Cuba and Mongolia, its two least-developed members, and, for its industrialized economies, on stepping up investment for the exploitation of energy and raw-material resources, including nuclear power (a multilateral programme on which should be established during 1978 for 1981-90). It recorded satisfaction with the trade flows so far generated under the 'agreed plan of multilateral integration measures' (SPIM) of 1975 and approved a 'work programme for the coordination of 1981-85 plans' which would take account both of the 'long-range special-purpose programmes' (DTsP) of 1976 and 'of mutual interests arising therein'. Commitments under DTsP should be signed by June 1980. Vietnam, Laos and Angola were all recorded as partners in multilateral cooperation with member states, and the communique spoke in general terms of 'widening and deepening economic relations with developing countries'. The session left open the form of an agreement with the EEC ('between CMEA and its members and the EEC and its members'), while stressing that it should promote East–West exchanges on the basis of mutual advantage and equality of rights. The communique made no mention of Romania's advocacy, on the second day, of a 15- to 20-year programme to equalize development levels throughout Comecon; as in the case of a similar proposal to the 1975 Council, it did not command general assent.

The Executive met just before and after the Council (without communiques) and on three other occasions. The first of the year (the 79th Executive, 17-19 January) was held in Havana: Cuba had not previously been host and it was surprising in view of the political relationship that no Angolan diplomat attended (though Yugoslavia, Vietnam and Korea were represented). Fidel Castro opened the meeting, which was chaired by Rodriguez and devoted almost exclusively to members' relations with Cuba. The Executive asked them to conclude by the end of April the supply protocols concerning construction of a nickel-cobalt plant at Las Camariocas, under a multilateral agreement of June 1975. The outlines were established for setting up a cellulose-paper mill using Cuban bagasse, but the communique passed over in silence the disposal of the sugar itself. Cuba had sought assurances that it would become the sole cane-sugar supplier to Comecon, and the Guyana Minister for Economic Development, Desmond Hotye, came specially to the meeting, doubtless to argue that Cuba should not.

The Executive was back in its usual Moscow venue for a meeting on 12-14 April, which adopted programmes for numerically-controlled machine-tools, and (by some states only) for ferrous metallurgy. A corporation in Sofia, Intervodoochistka, was set up to design sewage equipment. The 83rd Executive (21-23 November) approved a plan running to 1990 for linking electricity grids.

The April Executive had taken measures 'further to develop the system of settlements and credit in transferable roubles', but neither Comecon nor the International Bank for Economic Cooperation (IBEC) (at its Council, in Moscow, 13-14 October) published details. IBEC and the International Investment Bank (IIB) reported to the Comecon Currency and Finance Commission (32nd meeting, Miskolctapolca, Hungary, 24-27 May), which drafted a double-taxation agreement applicable to personal incomes and property of member-state nationals. IIB raised a $500 million loan in June on the Frankfurt market to fund the gas pipeline from Orenburg (USSR) to East European terminals, after the failure of an IBEC flotation on the London market earlier in the year due to doubts about the bank's accountability under United Kingdom law.

Chapter 6

AFRICAN CONFERENCES AND INSTITUTIONS—SOUTH-EAST ASIAN ORGANIZATIONS—CARIBBEAN ORGANIZATIONS

AFRICAN CONFERENCES AND INSTITUTIONS

FOR the Organization of African Unity, 1977 was a year of rearguard action, of trying to keep the organization intact in the face of new great-power interest in the continent. Although there was no dramatic confrontation within the OAU on the pattern of Angola in 1976, a series of smouldering crises—over the Western Sahara, the Horn of Africa and Southern Africa—all raised the temperature of inter-state relations in Africa and affected all African organizations, not only the OAU.

In general, perhaps because of the diligent and discreet diplomacy of the OAU secretary-general, William Eteki-Mboumoua, but more because of the desire of the majority of states to keep the organization on the rails, the OAU's regular meetings managed to conduct a fair amount of business and even score one or two modest successes, but there were still many areas of tension.

On Rhodesia, the OAU's policy for the year was virtually set by the meeting of the key OAU Liberation Committee in Lusaka from 29 January to 4 February. The 22-state committee approved the decision of the 'front-line' states to give 'full political, material and diplomatic support to the Patriotic Front', while leaving the door open for all groups of 'Zimbabwean nationalists fighting for majority rule in their country to join the Patriotic Front'. Although this was not endorsed by the OAU Council of Ministers (the annual budgetary session) which met in Lomé, capital of Togo, from 21 to 28 February, by the summer the situation was different. At the heads of state and government meeting, held in Libreville, Gabon, a similar resolution was passed, giving the summit's own seal of approval to the Patriotic Front. The leaders were doubtless swayed by the powerful advocacy of President Kaunda, the only 'front-line' head of state to attend.

Generally, on Southern African questions such as Namibia and South Africa itself unity was achieved without too much difficulty, but this was not the case with other issues. The vexed question of Ethiopia's dispute with Somalia was referred once more to an existing but apparently impotent committee, whose paralysis was made clear in the weeks after the Libreville meeting when fighting flared up over the Ogaden (see p. 214). It did seem, however, that the majority of African states were sympathetic to Ethiopia, regardless of ideological affiliations, simply because there appeared to have been a threat to its frontiers, and, as had been proved several times in the past 15 years, the sanctity of frontiers inherited from the colonial period remained one of the most significant points of the OAU Charter.

Impotence again seemed to prevail in regard to the fighting in the Western Sahara, based on the claims of the Sahraoui people, inhabitants of the former Spanish Sahara, which was partitioned (with blessing from Spain, but not the UN or OAU) in 1976 between Morocco and Mauritania (see p. 218). At the 1976 OAU summit, an emergency meeting of heads of state was suggested, but had never taken place. The Libreville meeting simply re-endorsed this call, and agreed that it would take place in Zambia in October. The Zambians subsequently called the conference off: there were rumours of hidden pressures from all sides, but it seemed that there had been a dispute about the cost of the conference.

The quarrel between Chad and Libya over the alleged Libyan occupation of the Aouzou strip in northern Chad was also referred to a special OAU commission, apparently without result, but a small success was registered by a similar commission which mediated between Sudan and Ethiopia, which had been in dispute over Sudanese support for Eritrean rebels: a meeting in Freetown in December effected a reconciliation and helped to calm at least a part of the troubled Horn. In view of all these disputes and others in the background, such as the Zaïre–Angola row over Shaba and Cabinda, and the fracas between Benin and Gabon, Togo and Morocco over the abortive invasion of Benin in January, which led to Benin's boycotting the Libreville meeting (the Lomé meeting in February had already been disrupted over this issue), the Nigerian head of state, General Olusegun Obasanjo, proposed that the OAU should have its own Security Council—a representative body of standing which would be in virtually permanent session to consider disputes as they arise. This proposal was rejected, but the subject was taken very seriously, and highlighted the stress now placed on the OAU's most valuable role in the past, that of a safety-valve for the defusing of inter-African disputes before they become internationalized.

The OAU also accepted the new Republic of Djibouti as its 49th member (see p. 214), and called on its new chairman, President Bongo of Gabon, to discuss the issue of the continued French presence in Mayotte (one of the Comoro Islands) with President Giscard d'Estaing. The budget of $9 million (an increase of 20 per cent over 1976) approved by the Council of Ministers in February was accepted by the heads of state. Cape Verde, São Tome and Principe, Angola and Mozambique were exempted from contributions in 1977-78 because of their recent arrival to independence.

The other major conference in Africa was the first-ever Afro-Arab summit, which was held in Cairo from 7 to 9 March, and like the OAU summit was preceded by a meeting of Foreign Ministers. Sponsored jointly by the OAU and the Arab League, it was attended by representatives of sixty countries, including many heads of state and government, as well as the Palestine Liberation Organization. The conference concluded with the signing of a charter of political and economic cooperation. This document, known as the 'Cairo Declaration', endorsed Palestinian and Southern African guerrilla movements as 'Afro-Arab causes' and promised them renewed support, including arms and money. Another declaration promised Afro-Arab cooperation in finance, mining, trade, industry, agriculture, transport, energy and communications. Two other documents covered the mechanics of cooperation, including the need for the establishment of preferential trade agreements and an increase in the capital of both the Arab Bank for Development in Africa (ABEDIA) and the African Development Bank (ADB). At the conference $1,500 million was committed as further Arab aid to Africa—two-thirds by Saudi Arabia and the rest by Kuwait, Qatar and the United Arab Emirates—of which $250 million would go straightaway to the two banks.

The 'France–Africa' summit, which had become an annual event, was held in April in Dakar, and was attended by President Giscard d'Estaing and the heads of state or government of the vast majority of French-speaking Africa, as well as Cape Verde and Guinea-Bissau: there were still, however, four notable absentees—Mauritania, Malagasy, Congo-Brazzaville and Cameroon, as well, of course, as Guinea-Conakry. Held against the background of French logistic support for the Moroccan troops sent to assist President Mobutu in Zaïre, security questions dominated the meeting, despite ostensible discussion of only economic issues. The conference, however, did not endorse President Senghor's reported proposal for a Common Defence Force. This was referred to the six-nation West African Economic Community, which met later in the year and produced an agreement on a mutual defence pact. President Giscard d'Estaing also pressed on with the security idea, and at the moment of Djibouti's independence in June he proposed a 'Solidarity Pact' between Europe and Africa.

The Dakar meeting overshadowed the earlier summit of the Afro-Malagasy Common Organization (OCAM) in Kigali, capital of Rwanda, in February: its leaders also held a meeting while they were in Dakar. The ten-nation grouping, now largely an umbrella for specialized agencies, suffered no new walkouts, although one of the agencies, Air Afrique, was in financial difficulties following the 1976 departure of Gabon. The Paris-based francophone Cooperation Agency was also reported to be suffering from internal strains, but its executive secretary, Kouloudo Dan Dicko, had his mandate renewed at a ministerial meeting in November in Abidjan.

Of other regional groupings, the 16-nation West African Economic Community (ECOWAS) saw progress in consolidation, although some tensions existed between the secretariat headed by the Ivoirien Dr Boubacar Outtara and the Compensation Fund headed by the Liberian banker Romeo Horton. ECOWAS also signed a technical cooperation agreement with the UN Economic Commission for Africa. The Senegal River Development Organization (OMVS) faced problems as the costs of its main projects (two dams on the Senegal River) escalated dramatically. In December the presidents of Mali, Mauritania and Senegal toured the Middle East trying to raise the missing funds.

The East African Community

Though continuing to exist legally, the East African Community virtually collapsed. In the first half of the year harbours, railways and air services operated separately for the three partner states and the East African Posts and Telecommunications Corporation was effectively divided into three separate organizations. In April, Kenya took over the civil aviation and meteorological services formerly operated by the Community. The death-blow came when none of the partner states provided the Shs.800 million necessary to keep the Community general fund services going in the financial year starting on 1 July. Institutions adversely affected were concerned with research, legal affairs and education. Kenya workers at the Community headquarters in Arusha (northern Tanzania) were allowed to return home with their effects and without harassment; Ugandan employees were treated similarly, though over 100 of them sought, and were granted, political asylum in Tanzania. Both Kenya and Uganda blamed Tanzania for the final collapse of the Community. President Nyerere, as current chairman, had refused to convene a meeting of the Authority, the supreme organ of the Community comprising the heads of the three partner states, which had not met since President Amin came to power in January 1971 and which, it was claimed, could alone have resolved the major problems facing the Community.

M

SOUTH-EAST ASIAN ORGANIZATIONS

Vietnamese hostility again stimulated the cohesion of the Association of South-East Asian Nations (Asean) and an interest in defence, although member countries, especially Malaysia, denied any intention of creating a defence pact. The Malaysian Prime Minister, however, stated on 6 March that the security of the Asean countries was indivisible and that Malaysia would try to help Thailand if it were threatened. In practice, member states promoted cooperation, usually bilaterally, but sometimes multilaterally—the Asean national defence colleges jointly conducted courses for military staff. Late in the year pressing economic problems, the need for wider trading contacts and the war with Cambodia seemed to have persuaded Hanoi to abandon, for the time being, its efforts to isolate Thailand and to express less hostility to Asean.

The Asean Economic Ministers met on 20 January in Manila and drafted an agreement on the principle of preferential trade for products with 60 per cent local content. Indonesia and Malaysia, however, were against a rapid extension of preferences, and subsequently it was possible to agree to extend preferential margins to only 71 products comprising rather over $2\frac{1}{2}$ per cent of Asean mutual trade, itself only about one-eighth of the total trade of the five countries. Conflicts of interest also emerged over the five proposed Asean major industrial enterprises, notably the diesel plant for Singapore whose preference was therefore limited in scope: in consequence some thought was given to less ambitious industrial projects. Agreement on the emergency sharing of oil supplies was reached in March and on a foreign exchange 'swap' system in August, while another meeting in September made further progress.

An Asean heads of government meeting on 4 and 5 August, based on earlier meetings of Foreign and Economics Ministers, reflected growing political cohesion and influence, especially as it was followed by joint meetings with the Prime Ministers of Japan, Australia and New Zealand, during which Mr Fukuda took the opportunity to assert Japan's willingness to play a greater part in promoting stability and economic development in the region. There was, in general, greater formal contact between Asean as a body and those three countries, the EEC and the USA. At the opening session President Marcos announced his intention of renouncing the Philippine claim to Sabah as a contribution to Asean unity, while the communique stated the 'desire of Asean countries to develop peaceful and mutually beneficial relations with all countries in the region, including Cambodia, Laos and Vietnam'.

Indonesia, Malaysia and Singapore agreed in February on the regulation of shipping in the Malacca Straits, while a revival of the Mekong Committee seemed to be foreshadowed by a communique signed by Laos,

Thailand and Vietnam on 29 April at the Escap annual meeting, by a meeting of these countries in Vientiane in July and by the setting-up of a working group to examine a programme for 1978. Asean Ministers of Industry, meeting in November, called for greater emphasis on rural development, as did the Colombo Plan annual session in December, while the Ministers, and the Asean summit, stressed the value of stimulating the flow of private investment.

The last formal meeting of Seato was held on 22 June and the organization was wound up on 30 June, although the Manila Treaty remained in force.

CARIBBEAN ORGANIZATIONS

The two effective government-supported organizations for regional cooperation were the Caribbean Development Bank and the Caribbean Economic Community (Caricom). The Bank had the support and interest of the United Kingdom, Canada and the United States and its membership included Colombia and Venezuela. Caricom grew out of the Caribbean Free Trade Association (Carifta) and was managed by a Council of Ministers. The Bank had an established policy for loans for development, which aimed at strengthening the financial capability of members; and it was the policy of the Board of Governors to give special attention to the less developed countries. It focused on areas basic to development, such as agriculture, training in managerial skills and increasing the productivity of small enterprises. It was staffed by a group of well-qualified West Indians and, while sensitive to local needs, it was better insulated against local political pressures than was Caricom.

Caricom ran into great difficulty during the year. The less developed countries had always complained that the 'Haves' got more and the 'Have-nots' always got less. The secretariat of the organization was usually able to sort out the problems since they had to do with trade and production. But the widening gap between prosperous Trinidad and Tobago and needy Guyana and Jamaica, and the ideology which underlay the economic policies of both the latter, set the chief partners in Caricom at loggerheads with each other.

In some respects Caricom had a satisfactory record. In education it had brought proposals for a Caribbean examination system to the point where, in 1978, school children would write a number of subjects in the new CXC Examination. In health, valuable work had been done through the Caribbean Nutrition Institute. Unfortunately the Caribbean Food Plan made little progress. But any hope that the new nations of the Caribbean might develop a common foreign policy was frustrated, Jamaica and Guyana appearing much closer to Cuba than to Trinidad and Tobago or Barbados.

XII RELIGION

DIVERSE DOCTRINES. Reviewed in June in *The Observer* under the headline 'Clerics doubt Christ's Divinity', 'The Myth of God Incarnate' got off to a *succès de scandale*; the reviewer singled out Canon Maurice Wiles and Professor Dennis Nineham of Oxford as contributors and failed to mention the editor, Professor John Hick of Birmingham. 'Myth' was perhaps an unfortunate choice by the publisher, for it was used in the technical sense of symbol and not with the popular meaning of fiction. The work included seven essays at reinterpreting the nature of Christ for modern theology. A counter-blast in August, 'The Truth of God Incarnate', collected five scholars to state an assorted conservative case, the editor, Canon Michael Green of Oxford, writing more than half. Canon Wiles had been chairman of the Archbishops' Commission on Doctrine, but in December a new Commission was announced from which both Wiles and Nineham were dropped.

On 11 July the journal *Gay News* and its editor Denis Lemon were found guilty of blasphemous libel at the Central Criminal Court, for publishing a poem by Professor James Kirkup implying the Roman centurion's homosexual love for Christ at the crucifixion. Although intent to blaspheme was denied by the defendants, Judge King-Hamilton ruled that literary and theological evidence was not admissible, since 'all that is necessary to show is that the blasphemy tends to cause a breach of the peace'. Following the verdict, however, the poem was printed in other places for a wider public.

In June Archbishop Marcel Lefèbvre ordained 30 priests, in defiance of an order by the Pope, and attacked the reforms of the Second Vatican Council (see AR 1976, p. 358). In Paris traditionalists claimed that the Latin Mass was being suppressed but the Archbishop, Cardinal Marty, said that there were 26 Latin masses in Paris every week and tolerance should prevail.

In September a breakaway synod of the American Episcopal Church in St Louis claimed that it had not left the church but the church had left the faith. It opposed the ordination of women and changes in the Book of Common Prayer.

A joint Anglican–Roman Catholic commission recommended in 'Authority in the Church' that the Church of England should recognize the primacy of the Pope, and this was supported by the former Archbishop of Canterbury, Dr Michael Ramsey, who said that the Pope should be accepted 'not as infallible but as president bishop'. In 'Ordination Services' a commission proposed simplification of wording and return to primitive practices in ordination, to remove obstacles to union with both Roman Catholics and the Free Churches. On a visit to Pope Paul VI in April the

Archbishop of Canterbury, Dr Donald Coggan, called for joint services of Communion, but a Common Declaration signed by both dignitaries at the end of the visit pledged work towards unity without mention of inter-communion.

Both the Church of Scotland and the Methodist Church reported continuing decline of membership, but research at Nottingham University indicated that more than 60 per cent of the adult population of Britain claimed to have had some form of religious experience, and American surveys reported over 70 per cent. An opinion poll found that 95 per cent of teenagers in the USA believed in God or a supreme spirit. Protestant agencies in the USA and Canada increased the number of their foreign missionaries from 35,070 in 1953 to 36,950 in 1976.

PERSECUTION. The murder of Archbishop Janani Luwum of Uganda on 17 February provoked international protest. An official claim that he was killed in a car crash was denied by Bishop Leslie Brown, formerly of Uganda, among others, stating that eye-witnesses had seen bullet holes in the archbishop's body. A few days earlier his house in Kampala had been ransacked by armed men, and on 8 February the archbishop met with 18 bishops and drafted a letter to President Amin accusing security officers of torture, saying 'we have buried many who have died as a result of being shot' and this was 'a gun pointed at every Christian in the church'. This letter was sent to the President and a copy smuggled out to Kenya, whither many refugees had fled from Uganda. With Archbishop Luwum two senior Cabinet Ministers were killed, the last Christian members of the Cabinet. Bishop Brown claimed that a purge of Christians was in progress and more arrests were reported in December.

On 22 March Cardinal Emile Biayenda of Brazzaville was kidnapped and murdered, ostensibly in a 'family vendetta', though the cardinal was a noted advocate of social reforms. On 6 February seven white Roman Catholic missionaries, including four nuns, were shot by guerrillas in Rhodesia. In September members of a Catholic Commission for Justice and Peace in Rhodesia were arrested and an American nun, Janice McLaughlin, was deported.

Charter 77 in Czechoslovakia (see DOCUMENTS), called for religious freedom as guaranteed by the Constitution though it was 'continually curtailed by arbitrary official action'. Religious instruction was suppressed in schools, priests were threatened, and persons who showed religious faith lost their jobs or suffered disabilities. But new hopes for religious toleration appeared under China's new rulers, and in the USSR a Baptist leader, Alexei Bichkov, claimed record figures of adult baptisms.

JUDAISM. In his retiring address as president of the World Jewish Congress, which he helped to found 41 years ago, Dr Nahum Goldmann in Washington warned of the 'internal danger' resulting from Jewish emancipation and the disappearance of ideals, which was 'more destructive than pogroms or persecutions'. The growing indifference of the young, ignorance of history and alienation from the Jewish community were the product of material prosperity but religious weakness.

Small but important in the Israeli coalition Government was the Agudat Israel Party, representing ultra-orthodox quarters of Jerusalem and Tel Aviv and Yeshivot Talmudic colleges that flourished all over the country. They sought exemption for their students from army service, protection from vehicular traffic on the Sabbath, and maintenance of marriage and divorce laws by rabbinical courts. The mayor of Jerusalem, Teddy Kollek, warned in August against violence by zealots which had damaged homes where electricity was consumed on the Sabbath.

In March, for the first time since 1917, the USSR agreed to allow a shipment of 10,000 copies of the Torah from the USA to the Moscow synagogue, secured by the Appeal of Conscience Foundation. Permission was also obtained for five Russian rabbinical students to train in the USA and for others to enrol in a seminary in Budapest, the only Jewish seminary in eastern Europe.

ISLAM AND SIKHISM. In September the Egyptian Coptic Church held a four-day fast to protest against proposed harsh Islamic laws which would include death for a Muslim who changed his religion. This was the first serious clash between Copts and Muslims for years. In Saudi Arabia foreigners were warned that women's bare arms and ankles were offensive to Islam and would be punished. In February there were bloody clashes between army and people in the Shi'ite holy cities of Karbala and Nasaf in Iraq on a festival of the martyr Hussein. Shi'ites claimed oppression by the Sunni Muslim Ba'athist Government.

In March gunmen from a black Hanafi Muslim sect held 134 hostages in Washington, until persuaded to release them by the ambassadors of Egypt, Iran and Pakistan. Most of the hostages were Jewish, held in the B'nai B'rith building, but the terrorists asked for a ban on the film 'Mohammed the Messenger of God' from cinemas throughout the USA. The Hanafi group was a breakaway from the Black Muslims of the late Elijah Muhammad and stressed its Islamic orthodoxy by claiming to follow the Sunni law school of Abu Hanifa of the eighth century.

From a four-acre ranch in New Mexico Yogi Bhajan styled himself 'Supreme Religious and Administrative Authority of the Sikh Religion in the Western Hemisphere', with 110 ashrams for a movement which began in a garage in Los Angeles in 1968. He taught three H's: Healthy, Happy, Holy, and yoga of a form to improve physique. But in India the Sikh historian Trilochan Singh called Bhajan's teaching 'a sacrilegious hodge-podge' and was shocked at the 'sexual practices' of tantric yoga.

FAR EAST. Church membership in South Korea rose from 800,000 in 1964 to four million Protestants and one million Roman Catholics. There were 18,300 church buildings and a church in every village. The number of Buddhists in the same period was claimed to have grown from one million to 12 million, though methods of counting were questionable. Korean Christians, having supported some previous regimes, now emphasized human rights and social reform.

Korea, like Japan, produced sects with charismatic founders, proclamation of new heaven and earth, and worldly enterprise in big business. Much debated was the Unification Church, founded in 1954 by a Korean business man and pastor Sun Myung Moon. Its basic scripture, *The Divine Principle*, taught a mixture of biblical, scientific and evolutionary theories and was strongly anti-communist. The movement spread to Japan, America and Europe and claimed two million members in 120 countries. An academic activity of this church was the formation in 1968 of the International Cultural Foundation which sponsored conferences, attended by eminent academics, on the unity of the sciences, the sixth being held in San Francisco in November. Anti-semitism was denied by Jewish scholars who attended and 'Moon' propaganda was not evident at these conferences. Demonstrators outside the fine hotels where the conferences met claimed that 'Moonies' were brain-washed, or were political agents of the CIA. The Unification Church claimed that there was no brain-washing and that American parents were too possessive. Its teachings, besides loosening family ties, emphasized the role of its leader and looked towards national and world rule.

In Japan the religious and national role of the Emperor was often debated and on 24 August, speaking 'with remarkable candour—and authority', he gave an unprecedented press conference. A key question was the Rescript of 1946, known as the 'Human Declaration', in which the Emperor renounced claims to 'divinity'. In explanation he said that the primary purpose was the constitutional Charter Oath, and that negation of divinity was 'of secondary importance'. This shocked some hearers but the Emperor's position appeared secure.

Official religious statistics for Japan gave 84 million Shintoists, 83 million Buddhists and less than a million Christians, among a total population of some 110 million, a discrepancy explained by the fact that many people practised both Shinto and Buddhism. At the New Year 67 million were said to visit Shinto shrines and Buddhist temples to pray for blessings. Japan was variously described as the most secularized and one of the most religious countries of Asia. Ten million pilgrims visited the Ise shrines annually, but pilgrimage was boosted by a great tourist industry. Some of the most ardent and organized religious bodies were the 'New Religions', Buddhist and Shinto, with about 32 million members. Of these Soka Gakkai (Nichiren Shoshu) claimed between 7 and 16 million, Rissho

Koseikai and Reiyukai 4 million each, and Tenri-Kyo 2 million. The last had a complete religious town at Tenri near Nara, with splendid modern buildings and library and the finest collection of bibles in Japan.

Soka Gakkai, from its foundation in 1951, had been allied to a controversial political party, Komeito, but in 1970 the party convention declared the separation of politics and religion and dropped slogans like 'Buddhist democracy' and 'the unity of politics with Buddhist law'. Komeito seemed to veer to the left and in 1975 made an agreement of mutual respect with the Japanese Communist Party, but in the 1976 and 1977 elections the communists lost heavily to middle-of-the-road parties, including Komeito, and warnings were given of ending the truce agreement.

Soka Gakkai seemed to have reached a plateau of increase but parallel organizations like Rissho Koseikai, which also revered the Buddhist reformer Nichiren, increased rapidly, with huge religious and social buildings, schools, hospitals, publishing houses and spectacular festivals. Buddhist principles were emphasized but simplified for wide appeal, with regular recitation of 'salvation in Buddhism', and appeals to work 'in the spirit of Buddhist laymen'.

Japanese Christians were small in number but were said to have widespread influence, though chiefly among intellectuals, and their services were often formal. The National Christian Council centre at Kyoto brought together scholars of different religions, and journals such as *Japanese Religions* and *The Japan Christian Quarterly* considered modern theological and inter-religious questions. In February an Anglican service was held at Ayabe in the Grand Sanctuary of Omoto-Kyo, a 'new religion' with Shinto background, in return for an Omoto-Kyo visit to the cathedral of St John the Divine in New York in 1975.

BOOKS. A best-seller in German was Hans Küng's '*Christsein*', translated into English as *On Being a Christian*, in which the turbulent Roman Catholic priest and professor at Tübingen sought to reconcile fidelity to the Gospel with the doctrines of the church, facing problems of belief in a scientific age but staying in the church in 'critical solidarity'. The first volume of *Paul Tillich: his Life and Thought*, by Wilhelm and Marion Pauck, was largely biographical. *Zwingli* by G. R. Potter was hailed by *The Guardian* as 'in the highest traditions of our scholarship', its production expensive but representing 'the Cambridge Press at its splendid best'. The long-awaited four-volume work on *The Temple Scroll*, the longest and most recently discovered of the Dead Sea Scrolls, was celebrated in Israel by presidential invitations to a public lecture by the author, Yigael Yadin. The scroll gave new material on ancient Jewish feasts, sacrifices and laws, from the sect of the Essenes who, according to Yadin, influenced early Christianity in its rejection of the sacrifices.

In *Iconography of Religions* A. C. Moore showed the importance of image and picture to the expression of faith, and Wendy O'Flaherty continued her studies of Indian theodicy in *The Origins of Evil in Hindu Mythology*. Raimundo Panikkar in *The Vedic Experience* made a massive anthology of classical Indian scriptures with translations, notes and extensive commentary. Daisaku Ikeda, head of Soka Gakkai, in *The Living Buddha*, expressed a 'certain feeling' for the Buddha in a simple manner, and Julia Ching in *Confucianism and Christianity* made a scholarly analysis of the teachings and similarities of the two religions.

In *The Christians* Bamber Gascoigne made a quizzical survey of these complex subjects to accompany his television series of the same name. It was a year of religious programmes, with a dramatized study of *Jesus of Nazareth* also on British independent television, while the BBC explored world religions in *The Long Search* on television, followed by a radio series on *The Long Search Continued*. The BBC and the Open University prepared a further inter-religious series in *Man's Religious Quest*.

XIII THE SCIENCES

Chapter 1

SCIENCE, MEDICINE AND TECHNOLOGY

THE ENERGY DEBATE. The price of extending the search for oil was made clear when a disaster such as environmentalists had always feared struck in the North Sea. On 22 April there was a major blow-out of oil and gas on a production platform in the big Ecofisk field, roughly equidistant from the British, Danish and Norwegian coasts.

There were fears that it might take six months to block the gush. But in the event Mr Red Adair, the Texan oil disaster expert, and his team succeeded in fitting a special valve to contain the flow before more than 20,000 tons of oil had escaped. Fortunately the oil did not catch alight, the wind directed the slick away from fishing areas, and the blow-out came just too soon to affect the spawning of mackerel. Within a week the slick had been broken up into minute droplets, which could be consumed by sea-living micro-organisms. But the incident was a warning of the risks involved in exploiting deep-water oil reserves.

New support was given to studies of the formation of oil from buried organic material in pursuit of clues to the location of new oilfields. In September geologists of the London Institute of Geological Sciences and Sheffield University published a theory, borne out by studies on oil-bearing strata in Dorset, of the chemical reactions involved in each stage of the oil-forming process. Measurements of the isotopic composition of carbon and oxygen in carbonates formed from gases given off during the break-down of organic matter to form oil showed that strata where oil had been formed relatively rapidly were those most likely to be commercially exploitable, because in such circumstances the breakdown would have been less likely to proceed to the point of reducing the oil to gas; secondly, the more rapid the formation of oil the greater the storage space remaining for it in the porous sandstone and limestone of the surrounding rocks. Where oil had been formed slowly, these pores tended to become blocked with sludge.

The problems and dangers of nuclear power were highlighted by the enquiry held at Whitehaven, England, from July to October 1977 into an application by British Nuclear Fuels Ltd (BNFL), the state-owned concern responsible for providing fuel for Britain's nuclear power stations, to build an extension to its reprocessing plant at Windscale, Cumbria (see p. 377).

BNFL's arguments went as follows: in 20 years or so the world's extractable oil and gas would be close to exhaustion, while expanding coal production raised problems, technological and environmental, as severe as those involved in the expansion of nuclear power. Other sources of energy could not be exploited quickly enough or on a sufficient scale. A huge expansion of nuclear power was thus the only realistic means of avoiding a catastrophic slump in living standards. But uranium reserves were limited, as well as those of oil and gas. The only sound energy policy was therefore to invest in fast breeder reactors which, by converting uranium to plutonium, enabled fifty or sixty times as much energy to be extracted from a given quantity of uranium. The plutonium had to be extracted from spent uranium fuel rods in plants like that at Windscale; hence the need for the extension.

The case for the opposition was based partly upon the dangers of proliferation. Plutonium could be used as a nuclear explosive as well as a fuel. World-wide trade in plutonium, inevitable as more countries built fast breeders, would inevitably multiply the numbers of small nations able to make nuclear weapons, and hence to an increase in the risk of nuclear war. Plutonium might be stolen by terrorist groups, and used to make weapons to hold governments to ransom. Other objections centred round problems in disposing of long-lived highly radioactive wastes, and dangerous accidents which might be caused if the very rapid fission in the fast reactor core got out of control. The report from the Inspector, Mr Justice Parker, was expected early in 1978.

During the year, American high-energy physicists at the Brookhaven laboratory, and the British physicist Dr John Davies at the Rutherford laboratory, put forward detailed proposals for an alternative long-term nuclear power strategy, based upon a uranium/thorium cycle instead of the fast breeder's uranium/plutonium cycle. The system, worked out in every detail, involved transforming thorium into the fissile isotope uranium 233 by bombarding it with radiation. The uranium 233 would then produce almost enough radiation itself to convert an equivalent amount of thorium into more uranium 233. The extra radiation required to make the process self-sustaining would be provided, at intervals, by irradiating fuel rods with intensive neutron radiation, created by a powerful particle accelerator like that at the Rutherford laboratory.

The system had several potential advantages. It would be very much more difficult for terrorists to steal the fuel. Very much smaller quantities of long-lived radioactive wastes would be produced and it might be possible to eliminate them altogether. The reaction in the reactor core would proceed much more slowly, making it easier to control. Nor would any new technology be required. There seemed to be real weight behind the claim that the original need to make plutonium for weapons had to some extent shackled the thinking of nuclear power reactor designers, and prevented them from looking at all the possible alternatives.

French scientists, at a conference at Salzburg in May, announced their development of a process which could help to stop the proliferation of nuclear weapons. By using the different speeds at which various isotopes diffused through a semi-permeable membrane to separate uranium isotopes, uranium could be sufficiently enriched with the fissile isotope to make it usable as reactor fuel, but not sufficiently for making weapons.

It was by no means certain in 1977 that commercial power from nuclear fusion, the next logical step after atomic fission, would ever be feasible. But a very important step towards the harnessing of fusion power was taken when the EEC member nations, after years of wrangling, finally agreed on a site for JET, the Joint European Torus, in Oxfordshire, England. This was to be a big expensive research machine, in which scientists would extend the periods for which ionized gas could be contained at the very high temperatures at which the fusion process began. The building of JET was beyond the realistic resources of any one of the European nations, but through a joint effort they hoped to prevent the USA or USSR establishing a lead in what could become the world's chief source of energy from around the middle of the next century.

A step towards a different way of exploiting fusion power was taken at the Rutherford laboratory, where the new laser facility was opened. Lasers able to concentrate into beams of light, for a fraction of a second, power equal to that produced by all England's power stations were being focused upon tiny spheres containing deuterium and tritium. The ultimate aim of the research was to see whether the pressure of the intense laser light beams could create the conditions for nuclear fusion in the spheres, and whether such a concept, already being studied intensively in the USA, could be a feasible alternative to the much larger fusion reactor concept to be studied in JET.

Work on alternative energy sources continued. The USA voted to provide the funds required to build the world's biggest power windmill. Research at the Camborne School of Mines in Cornwall showed that granite rocks could be extensively cracked by drilling holes, detonating small explosive charges and then pumping in water, under high pressure, to expand the cracks linking the holes. The network of holes and cracks could then be used to heat water pumped down to the 'hot rocks' one or two miles down. Researchers visualized the process being used to provide warm water for district heating and agriculture, and, from greater depths, boiling water for industrial processes and power stations. Results showed that the extraction of heat could be economically combined with the extraction of valuable metals, leached from the rich ores commonly found in granite rocks.

Rising fuel costs, plus growing shortage of tipping space, led to the development of the fluidized bed system as a means of using domestic refuse as a fuel. A circulating fluidized bed, designed by London consulting engineers, in which refuse was burnt in a bed of sand kept in motion by air currents, proved ideal for burning rubbish, without polluting smoke or fumes, at low cost and in a conveniently small area.

THE EARTH SCIENCES. Research on volcanoes in the Azores and elsewhere, carried out by Dr Basil Booth of Imperial College, London, demonstrated the possibility of predicting future eruptions. By measuring the thicknesses as well as the depths of ash layers indicating past eruptions, it was possible to draw up a map of the areas most at risk from ash falls and lava flows around the volcano. Charts prepared from such surveys, together with the use of seismometers buried around those volcanoes most liable to erupt in the near future, could give several weeks' early warning of eruptions.

Another means of investigating past volcanic activity was demonstrated by Danish scientists of Copenhagen University, who analyzed ice cores from the Greenland ice cap. They demonstrated that the amounts of volcanic dust, and of sulphuric acid derived from sulphur dioxide emitted by volcanoes, found at different depths, could be used to provide an index of volcanic activity at least as far back as ten thousand years. Radio-isotope techniques could be used to date the ice. Dust and gas, transformed to acid, would have been precipitated in snow and frozen into ice in concentrations proportional to those in the atmosphere at that time. Dr C. Hammer thought it would be possible to correlate overall volcanic activity with climatic changes, and then to see whether, as some scientists suspected, both climate and volcanic activity could, in turn, be correlated with solar and planetary events.

Rubber springing showed great promise as a means of preventing earthquake damage to large buildings. Springs made from layers of natural rubber sandwiched with steel plates, designed and made at the laboratory of the Natural Rubber Producers Association at Hertford, were tested in a unique Californian research facility, in which model buildings mounted upon the springs could be vibrated exactly as though they were undergoing a real earthquake, using tape-recorded earthquake tremors to control the vibrations. The springs reduced the stress on the models to an average of about one-tenth of that caused when the models were bolted directly to the floor.

An international conference on dendrochronology, held at Greenwich in July, showed how far the science of dating of wooden objects from their tree rings had advanced. For a number of years it had been possible, by microscopic examination of the annual rings in a sample of wood, to deduce something about the weather in each year represented by each ring. Growth rings are thin in years of drought, thick in wet years and there are some other, more complex, variations in structure which can also be related to temperature and climate. The problem had been to put a date to the years represented by each ring, but it was now being overcome. For example, the year 764 AD had been characterized in Europe by a very severe winter, followed by a very severe drought, and both had left their mark in the trees of the time. The signature of 764 AD had been recognized in enough wooden samples, dated by other means, for it and others like it often to be recognizable in fresh undated samples. Once one year had been fixed in this way it was possible to fix all the rest. Dendrochronology could then be used to investigate early human settlements by their surviving wooden walkways, to follow climatic cycles in very great detail, and, in more recent historic times, to estimate the effects of atmospheric pollution due to industrial activity against a baseline of wooden samples from long before the Industrial Revolution.

More results from the continuing voyage of the sea-bed-drilling research ship *Glomar Challenger* were published in 1977, giving a fascinating picture of the repeated filling and emptying of the Mediterranean basin. Examination of core samples of the bottom of the Mediterranean Sea, collected in 1975, showed successive layers of salty deposits, proving clearly that about five and a half million years ago the sea had dried up, emptied, and then been refilled, probably as often as seven or eight times over a period of around ten thousand years. Each refilling had been due to the Atlantic repeatedly breaking through a barrier formed at the Straits of Gibraltar.

The repeated drying and refilling explained the interchanges of African and European animals which had long been a mystery to palaeontologists. It was even suggested that the associated climatic changes could have led to the replacement of forest by savannah type grasses and that this, in turn, could have forced man's ancestors down from a way of life in the trees to the ground, where they evolved to an upright position enabling them to see over the tall savannah grasses.

Close examination of photographs, taken by the American experimental 'Landsat' survey satellite, revealed traces of previously-unsuspected cracks in the Earth's crust, running almost due north and south across Nigeria. About 13 of the cracks appeared, spaced evenly about 30 kilometres apart all the way from the eastern to the western borders of Nigeria.

Dr John Norman, who identified the cracks, explained them by an intriguing theory. About 550 million years ago some cosmic body—planet, moon or asteroid—had strayed close enough to the Earth to brake the Earth's spin somewhat. The effect would have been to throw the surface of the Earth into wrinkles. Later the wrinkles would have cracked, producing the cracks revealed by Landsat. Valuable deposits of minerals, and hot rocks which could be tapped for geothermal power, were likely, geologists believed, to be found associated with the cracked regions.

Landsat also revealed similar cracks in Brazil, tilted at an angle of

52 degrees to the Earth's north–south axis, whereas those in Africa were tilted at only eight degrees. Both sets of cracks having been formed when Brazil and West Africa were one landmass, this showed that South America had swung round much more than Africa in the process of continental drift.

Dr Norman asked himself why South America and Africa had not split apart along the line of one of the cracks which preceded the separation by many millions of years. Instead separation had occurred along the curved line of the West African coast and the corresponding curves on the east coast of South America. Dr Norman concluded that the continents had split apart along the line of a much older crack, the edge of a gigantic crater, nearly as big as the whole of north-west Africa, which had been formed when a very large meteorite struck the Earth about three thousand million years ago. That had been the date, as established by the Apollo missions, of the biggest meteorite impacts upon the Moon. Close-up pictures of Mars and Mercury and radar pictures of Venus, taken over the past two years, had indicated that they had all suffered similar bombardments, probably the result of a swarm of asteroids passing through the solar system. Dr Norman and his colleagues identified segments of several other 'astrons' (as they called the remains of such gigantic craters), including parts of the Atlantic coast of Norway, of the coast of eastern Australia, and of north-western Latin America.

The case for the astrons was based upon several other lines of evidence besides the shapes of coastlines. One was the similarity of the geological features around the astrons to those around equivalent-size craters on the Moon. Another was a set of calculations showing that the impact of a big meteorite would have produced a central disc of hardened rock with concentric circles of cracks around it; there was evidence in West Africa of hardened disc as well as concentric cracks. And an experiment in Canada, in which 500 tons of TNT had been detonated to simulate a meteorite impact, had produced remarkably similar structures.

THE PHYSICAL SCIENCES. The most sensational reports during the year were those, from three separate laboratories, of considerable success in silencing noise by the use of anti-sound. In all cases the technique used depended upon generating sound similar in amplitude and frequency to the sound which was to be silenced but exactly out of phase with it, so that the respective sound waves cancelled out. The theory had been around for many years, but in 1977 it was reported to have been successfully used, by Southampton University's Noise and Vibration Institute, to quieten aircraft noise heard by pilots in their headsets in order to make conversations easier for them to follow. The system was under test by the RAF. It involved playing back the aircraft sound, picked up by a small microphone in the headset, out of phase with the original sound. Further applications of the same system, to aid ear protection while permitting communication in noisy industrial situations, were being considered.

Another research group, at Chelsea College of Technology, had developed the same principle to silence unwanted noise travelling through ventilation and other ducts in houses and offices. In Cambridge a third group, in the department of engineering, was preparing to test the same principle in the more difficult conditions of the open air, to see if it could be used to silence a noisy generator.

In fundamental particle physics the event of the year was the opening, on 7 May, of the world's largest particle accelerator, second in power only to the one at the Brookhaven National Laboratory in the USA. The Big Machine, as the accelerator was dubbed, was built and paid for by the combined efforts of the 12-member nations of the CERN organization.

One of the principal tasks facing it was to try to unearth evidence of the existence of quarks, hypothetical nuclear particles out of various combinations of which, most physicists believed, all the other nuclear particles were built. In April physicists at Stanford University, California, announced that they had found what could be the first real evidence of the existence of quarks. Their experiments suggested that certain observed electrical charges must belong to quarks which were no longer buried inside other particles but were 'free quarks', contrary to a previous theory that quarks would never be observed independently, being always unbreakably locked up in combinations comprising other particles.

Around July American military authorities announced they had developed the so-called 'neutron bomb'. This was a small fusion (hydrogen) device, the development of which had been made possible by using a very small fission (atomic) bomb as trigger to start the also relatively small-scale fusion reaction. The fusion device produced about 80 per cent of its energy in the form of very high-energy neutron radiation, as compared to only 5 per cent of the energy of a comparable fission device. The intention was to develop a weapon able to do more damage to troops in its vicinity and less to buildings and other civilian property. Heated debate followed over whether the development of such a weapon was unethical, because it saved property at the expense of life, or ethical, because it reduced the involvement of any but fighting soldiers in a battle.

X-ray telescopes, mounted in orbiting satellites, continued to accumulate evidence making the existence of 'black holes' in space seem increasingly likely. One theory predicted a limited life span for black holes because they must continually absorb negative energy, which would be transformed into negative mass, until, eventually, they ceased to have any mass and so ceased to exist.

ASTRONOMY, COSMOLOGY AND SPACE RESEARCH. Professor Sir Fred Hoyle and his colleague Professor Wickramasinghe of Cardiff together

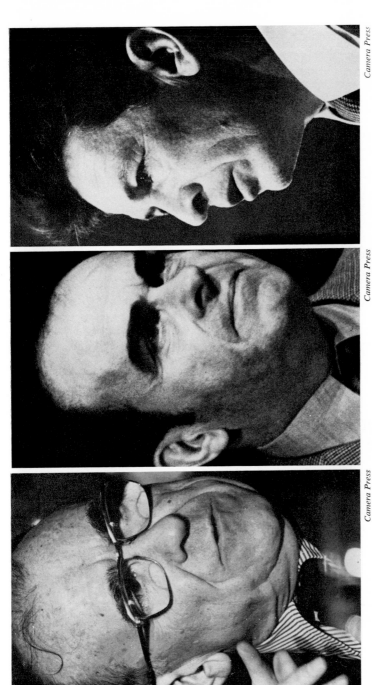

The three leaders of Western European Communist parties who met in Madrid on 5 March 1977 and issued a declaration on 'Eurocommunism' (see DOCUMENTS): left to right, Santiago Carillo, secretary general of the Spanish CP, Georges Marchais, secretary general of the French CP, and Enrico Berlinguer, secretary general of the Italian CP.

Camera Press   *Camera Press*

Camera Press   *Camera Press*

Four elder statesmen, each of whom left a permanent mark on history, who died in 1977 (see OBITUARY): top left, Anthony Eden, Earl of Avon, former British Foreign Secretary and Prime Minister; right, Dr Ludwig Erhard, former West German Federal Chancellor; bottom left, Archbishop Makarios, President of Cyprus; right, Sir Alexander Bustamante, first Prime Minister of independent Jamaica.

The world of music and entertainment lost a number of internationally famed figures in 1977, among them (top left) the operatic soprano Maria Callas, (right) the conductor Leopold Stokowski, (bottom left) the film comedian Sir Charles Chaplin and (right) the singer Bing Crosby (see OBITUARY).

Popperfoto

Two contrasting events of 1977 in aviation: above, the craft designed by Paul McCready of California and pedal-manned by Bryan Allen which on 23 August completed the first man-powered flight of 1¼ miles over a figure-8 course at a height of 18 ft or more and so claimed a prize of $86,000; below, the remains of a KLM Boeing 747 which crashed into a similar Pan Am aeroplane on the runway of Tenerife airport on 27 March, with the loss of 582 lives.

Press Association

published a sensational theory of the continuous creation of life (analogous to Hoyle's theory of the continuous creation of matter in the universe). Basically, it stated that the conditions for the evolution, not just of complex organic molecules, but of complete sub-units of living cells, existed in clouds of interstellar dust, and that such complex molecules and assemblies were continually coming into being throughout the universe wherever conditions were suitable, as stars condensed out of dust clouds. Life could then seed itself on any suitable planet in the vicinity.

Evidence for the theory was provided by spectroscopic readings indicating that the complex polysaccharide cellulose, the principal constituent of plant cell walls, was to be found in interstellar dust clouds. Other research had revealed the existence of other complicated organic compounds in space, but the molecular structure of cellulose was orders of magnitude more complex than anything found hitherto. Hoyle and Wickramasinghe went on to suggest that the first development of primitive life forms out of the 'proto-life' in the dust clouds might have proceeded upon the outer planets, Uranus and Neptune, at an early stage in the development of the solar system.

Measurements made briefly, for just four minutes, from an ultraviolet telescope mounted upon a Skylark space rocket indicated that the expansion of the universe was slowing down and that eventually it would probably stop expanding and begin to shrink. This remarkably comprehensive conclusion from observations of such short duration was based upon observations of ultraviolet light from two quasars, one relatively close, the other among the most distant objects ever observed. The observations showed that the rate at which the quasars were moving away from the rest of the universe, which could be taken as an index of the rate of the general expansion of the universe, was slowing down with time. The astronomers responsible, at Johns Hopkins University in Baltimore, did not claim certainty for their deduction, but they had demonstrated the value of quasars, the most distant and so furthest-back-in-time objects ever observed, as cosmological probes, able to reveal happenings in the history of the universe back perhaps nine-tenths of the way to the supposed Big Bang.

Several interesting discoveries were made and theories put forward concerning our own solar system. The American astronomer Charles Kowal discovered a previously-unknown heavenly body orbiting the Sun between Saturn and Uranus, at a distance of 2,400 million kilometres. With a diameter of only 640 kilometres at most, Planet X, as it was nicknamed, presented something of a mystery. Some astronomers believed it might be just the first member to be discovered of a second asteroid belt of minor planets, much further away from the Sun than the known asteroid belt between Mars and Jupiter.

Another group of American astronomers discovered that the outer planet Uranus had rings like Saturn, but probably dark rather than light in colour. The five rings of Uranus were first observed using a telescope mounted in a large transport aircraft, in order to get above the denser layers of the Earth's atmosphere. Later the rings were also seen from at least one observatory on Earth.

The elaborate European scientific satellite GEOS, designed to study the interrelationship between the Earth's magnetic field and the 'solar wind' of charged particles which blows out from the Sun, was put into the wrong orbit by an American Delta rocket on 20 April. While the satellite could still be used for some of its planned purposes, much of its value was lost. Then on 13 September the launch of the equally important European Orbital Test Satellite, OTS, an experimental geostationary communications satellite system, failed completely. The satellite had to be destroyed by radio command. Once again a Delta rocket was responsible. These disasters followed the earlier failure of a Delta to orbit Skynet Two, a British military communications satellite.

Apart from the continued launching of military satellites, Soviet space activities centred around their orbiting space station Salyut 6. The first effort, in October, to put a two-man crew into the space station ended in failure at the last moment, when the attempt to dock the Soyuz ferry ship with Salyut was abandoned when the Soyuz was only a few hundred feet away. The official explanation was shortage of fuel, believed to refer to electrical power, but suspicions that a fault had been suspected in the docking port grew when the second crew to be sent up to Salyut 6 used a second separate docking port to board the space station and when, after making a successful entrance, one of the crew went outside the space station to inspect the first docking port from the outside and reported that all was, in fact, well. Salyut 6 was the first of its kind to be equipped with two docking ports.

Expert sources agreed that much of the time on most Salyuts' missions was spent on surveillance of military and other movements in the West, a purpose for which the Soviet Union used manned spacecraft because of its relative backwardness in imagery using unmanned satellites. Meanwhile there were new developments in the use of space for military purposes. Although there was no official announcement, the *Washington Post* reported that the United States had developed and was testing a proto-type of a 'satellite killer', a highly manoeuvrable rocket-powered spacecraft able to home on to enemy satellites and destroy them by the force of its impact. There were unconfirmed reports that the Soviet Union was attempting to develop a proton beam to destroy missiles and even perhaps satellites from the ground, by converting the energy of nuclear explosions into a focused beam of atomic particles, protons. Physicists found it hard to see how sufficient power could be developed to drive such a beam through hundreds of miles of dense air, every atom of which would absorb protons from the beam. There was, however, no doubt that the USA and the USSR were continuing to develop space weaponry, as well as increasingly elaborate spy satellites.

Meanwhile the first re-usable spacecraft, the Space Shuttle, made its first free flights to successful, if at first rather bumpy, landings. Europe and America were already preparing for the first flights of Spacelab, the European-built orbiting laboratory due to be carried into space by the Shuttle for Spacelab's first mission in 1980. A short list of four European and five American scientist-astronauts was announced, in December, from which a pair, one American and one European, to travel on the first mission was later to be selected.

A pair of unmanned space probes, Voyagers One and Two, were launched by NASA in August and September on a long journey. They were designed to pass Jupiter in 1979 and Saturn in 1980 and 1981, and to send back the first-ever close-ups of Saturn and its rings. No evidence of life came from the two Viking landers still functioning intermittently on the surface of Mars, though biologists still did not regard its existence as disproved.

BIOLOGY AND MEDICINE. Perhaps the most important discoveries reported during the year concerned the biochemical basis of a mental illness, schizophrenia. Dr Edward Bird and his colleagues at Cambridge reported the results of a post-mortem study in which brains from severely schizophrenic patients had been compared with those of normal people. The brains, obtained within 48 hours of death, had been frozen and dissected and laboratory tests conducted on different regions of the brains, to determine the levels of various enzymes and other chemicals in them. The results showed that the schizophrenic brains had three consistent abnormalities. There was an abnormally high concentration of the neurotransmitter dopamine in one brain centre, the nucleus accumbens, which was largely responsible for the control of emotional behaviour and aggression. And there were abnormally low concentrations of two enzymes (GABA and choline acetyl transferase) responsible for manufacturing other neurotransmitters. The abnormally high concentrations of dopamine explained the success of dopamine-repressing drugs already used in treating schizophrenia. The abnormally low concentrations of other brain chemicals opened up the possibility of developing new treatments, based upon restoring normal concentrations.

Doubts remained, principally concerning the possibility that the abnormalities were not a root cause of schizophrenia but had merely been brought about by the long-term use of powerful drugs to treat the condition in the affected brains. Nor was there as yet any clue as to what else might have caused the abnormalities in brain chemistry.

Meanwhile doctors reported startling success in treating some cases of severe schizophrenia with a drug normally used to treat heart conditions. Four years earlier a group of heart patients, who happened also to be schizophrenic, were being treated for a heart condition with propranolol, a drug which protects a weak or arrhythmic heart from dangerous over-stimulation by adrenalin. Completely to the surprise of the doctors involved, at the Friern and Royal Northern hospitals in London, some of the patients showed a remarkable improvement in their schizophrenic symptoms. Subsequently the same doctors treated 14 severely schizo-phrenic patients, all failing to respond to other treatments and all suffering from severe delusions. Six patients lost all their symptoms, five showed moderate improvement, two slight improvement. Only one completely failed to respond. However, the doctors involved fended off publicity until they had carried out further trials, designed to ensure that the effects were not, as had proved to be the case with some earlier, apparently successful drugs, in reality only temporary and due simply to the unusual attention paid to the patients under treatment. These trials were completed and reported in September 1977. Of 12 patients treated over 12 weeks, six had lost all their symptoms and were able to return to normal life, but six showed only partial relief. Other similar results were reported later from other hospitals.

The discovery of the value of propranolol had been accidental, and its mode of action in the brain was unknown. But it seemed very probable that, just as propranolol damped down the action of adrenalin hormones in the heart by blocking up the receptors through which they would normally stimulate heart muscle, so in the schizophrenic brain they damped down the action of overactive neurotransmitters. Some neuro-transmitters belonged to the same family as adrenalin hormones. Pro-pranolol appeared to return some—not all—patients who had been severely schizophrenic to complete normality, though it was in no sense a cure, the symptoms returning soon after patients stopped using the drug. The difference between those who responded and those who did not was so striking as to suggest two separate biochemical defects. The indefinable quality of this recovery appeared different from that brought about by other drugs. Without prompting, patients using propranolol said that for the first time they were feeling as they had felt before they became ill. Over the periods, up to four years, for which the drug had been used, there appeared to be no harmful side-effects.

Professor Geoffrey Burnstock of the University of London reported the discovery of what, some believed, amounted to a third class of nerves to set beside the two already known. Those were cholinergic nerves, using acetyl choline to transmit their impulses, and adrenergic nerves, using noradrenalin. The newly-discovered class used a third transmitter sub-stance, one of the class of chemicals called purines, so they were called purinergic nerves. Professor Burnstock found that purinergic nerves were involved in controlling the contraction of the bladder and major blood vessels. Purinergic nerves also appeared to control the contraction of blood vessels in the skin and eyes, and to be involved in information transmission inside the brain.

A new mobility aid for the blind was introduced, which made use of a 'heat ray', a beam of infra-red radiation projected ahead of the blind person to locate obstacles, instead of the more usual beam of ultrasonic vibrations. The advantages of the infra-red blind aid, developed by Dr Yeshwant Sunthankar, working at Sunderland Polytechnic, were its lightness and compactness, low cost and accuracy in delineating obstacles. During the year it was tested by about 150 blind people in the Sunderland area and by the end of the year there were tentative plans for commercial production. The possibility that the device could be marketed for as little as £20 per set, about one-third the cost of comparable ultrasonic devices, made it of considerable potential interest to the developing world.

Patients suffering from bone cancer and other conditions benefited from the development, at the National Orthopaedic Hospital in Stanmore, of a complete thigh bone (femur) replacement, a titanium bone fitted with an artificial knee joint at one end and hip joint at the other. These unique prostheses, fitted to three patients, made it possible to avoid amputation of the affected leg and to restore complete mobility to the patient.

Dr Wan Jun Tze of Vancouver developed and tested, in animals, a new type of artificial pancreas which promised to bring real benefits for diabetics when judged safe for implantation in humans. The pancreas consisted of insulin-producing tissue taken from animals, enclosed in a so-called millipore membrane with pores big enough to allow insulin to leak out but too small to allow white cells from the recipient's blood stream to get inside the membrane. Animal trials showed that in this way recognition of the implant as foreign and subsequent rejection could be avoided.

Genetic engineers in the US, working towards the target of engineering bacteria into living factories to synthesize vital compounds like insulin, had inserted animal genetic material, DNA, into bacteria, and shown that it was accepted and duplicated along with the bacteria's own DNA, but they had not shown that the bacteria would make animal-type proteins to the instructions of the foreign DNA. This was demonstrated during 1977. The bacteria used were shown to have made somatostatin, a protein hormone produced in the brains of humans and mammals by the hypo-thalamus, to the instructions of the appropriate sections of DNA. Even this small-scale experiment gave an indication of the potential of genetic engineering as a means of producing hormones. When the experiment was reported, eight litres of bacterial culture had produced five milligrammes of hormone. The researchers who had first isolated somatostatin, from the brains of sheep, would have needed half a million sheep to obtain the same amount.

Also in the field of genetics, a very important but totally puzzling discovery was made by molecular biologists working cooperatively in several countries. It had always been logically supposed that the instructions for making a particular protein, contained in a particular length of DNA, ran from end to end of that length of DNA without interruption. But conclusive reports from several years of research now demonstrated that this was not by any means always so. Interspersed at intervals along stretches of DNA responsible for coding for, for example, haemoglobin were lengths of DNA with no relevance to the code required for haemoglobin at all. Their presence made it clear that gene mapping and genetic engineering were going to be more difficult and perhaps more hazardous than had been thought.

A disturbing medical discovery was that of the emergence, in South Africa, of a strain of pneumococci, bacteria responsible for pneumonia, which appeared to be resistant to every drug used to treat the disease. Some infected children died in spite of the use of every possible antibiotic. Laboratory tests showed that the pneumoccoci grew normally surrounded by high concentrations of every possible antibiotic. It was found that many medical staff already harboured the resistant bacteria. Unless new drugs could be found to attack the resistant pneumoccoci they seemed bound to spread and to cause many deaths among those most susceptible to pneumonia, the very young, the elderly and those in ill health.

A number of important advances were made against other diseases and especially tropical diseases. Workers in a Nairobi laboratory developed for the first time a means of growing, outside the body, the parasites which cause sleeping sickness. This opened the way to much swifter progress in developing badly-needed new drugs, and perhaps to a vaccine. Swedish scientists at the University of Goteborg developed and tested a new and more effective vaccine to protect against cholera. This protected patients against the toxins produced by cholera bacteria, as well as against the bacteria themselves.

The organism responsible for the mysterious death of a number of American ex-servicemen at a convention in Philadelphia organized by the American Legion in 1976 proved to be an unusually slow-growing bacterium. The virus responsible for Lassa fever, which had killed hundreds of people in north Zaïre and the south Sudan in 1976, was also identified. It proved to be a new variant of the virus which had been responsible for the outbreak of so-called 'green monkey' disease in Marburg in West Germany nine years earlier. The disease had been given its name because it was carried to Germany by monkeys exported from Uganda as laboratory animals. The identification of the virus made it possible for scientists to begin to search for carriers, and to begin to develop a vaccine to protect against it. The virulence of the virus had meant that only two laboratories, at Porton Down in Britain and Atlanta, Georgia, in the USA, were judged sufficiently secure to work upon its identification, and later growing it for research purposes. Equally important was the development and successful testing of a drug, praziquantal, in West Germany, able to cure the common tropical worm disease bilharzia with a single dose and with fewer side effects than other treatments.

The adoption of a 'high fibre' diet, including large quantities of the plant cell wall constituents pectin and guar, was shown, in trials at the West Middlesex Hospital, to be of real benefit to diabetics. The results indicated that those suffering from mild forms of diabetes might be able to dispense with insulin injections if they kept to the high fibre diet, while the onset of more serious symptoms in severe diabetes might be delayed.

Research reported in 1977 suggested that a third class of living things, the methanogens, might have to be added to the two great existing divisions of life, prokaryotes and eukaryotes. Prokaryotes were the simplest single-celled living things, distinguished by having no true nuclear membrane or nucleus, mainly bacteria and blue-green algae. Eukaryotes included all other living things. There was a known group of micro-organisms which died if they came into contact with oxygen, and could live on carbon dioxide, hydrogen and minerals, producing methane as a by-product. These so-called methanogens had been classified as prokaryotes, though somewhat eccentric ones. But genetic analysis of the methanogens, carried out by Dr Carl Woese in the USA, showed that there were such profound differences between the methanogens and the rest of the prokaryotes as to suggest that the methanogens represented a form of life which had survived virtually unchanged from the earliest days of life on Earth, around three thousand million years ago. The methanogens appeared to be as different from prokaryotes or eukaryotes as either from the other.

TECHNOLOGY. It is possible only to select a few developments which demonstrated important trends during the year. Among such was the development of an 'intermediate technology' knitting machine at the textile machinery design and development centre at Leicester. Having only two moving parts instead of the hundreds used in typically sophisticated and expensive modern knitting machines, and able to make use of a much wider variety of materials in its products, it typified a trend away from ever more expensive and specialized factory machinery. This trend, so the designer was convinced, was one which neither the industrialized nor the developing world could any longer afford.

The increasing effects of the oil crisis, coupled with the introduction of new coal-burning technology in the shape of the fluidized bed, led to engineers putting forward detailed designs for new steam locomotives in which low-grade coal could be burnt, producing less polluting smoke than a diesel locomotive. The English designers of the new steam locomotives had held or were planning talks with railway authorities in the USA, South America and China. A return to the age of steam, initially for long-distance freight, later for passenger trains, seemed inevitable for many countries well before the end of the century, though Britain, with North Sea oil, might postpone it longer than most.

THE NOBEL PRIZES. The prize for medicine was awarded jointly to three American scientists, Dr Rosalyn Yalow, Dr Roger Guillemin and Dr Andrew Schally, for their discoveries of the nature and functions of hormones produced by the hypothalamus in the brain. These hormones were the means by which the human brain responded to the world around it, by giving appropriate chemical instructions to its ductless glands. The prize for chemistry went to Professor Ilya Prigogine, a Moscow-born scientist working in Belgium, for his work on thermodynamics, particularly on theories explaining how the organization of living things had been able to emerge in a universe in which physical laws dictated the steady increase of disorder. The physics prize went to a trio of scientists, Dr Philip Anderson of Bell Telephone laboratories, Professor Sir Neville Mott of Cambridge and Professor John Van Vleck of Harvard University, for their work on the behaviour of electrons in non-metallic solids. Their research had exploited, among other things, the transparency of glass, the magnetism of magnets, and the functioning of solar cells.

Chapter 2

THE ENVIRONMENT

AT Easter-time President Jimmy Carter announced that he would seek to halt the development of plutonium as a fuel (see pp. 35 and 64). In doing so, he gave the environmental movement its greatest encouragement for years and gravely disappointed and disturbed the world's nuclear industry. He made his announcement a few days after the publication of a particularly significant study carried out by the Mitre Corporation for the Ford Foundation. It voiced particular concern about nuclear proliferation and concluded that the economic benefits both of reprocessing and of the fast breeder had been exaggerated, saying that any net economic benefit from reprocessing during the twentieth century was 'questionable', and that fast breeders were not likely to prove competitive even in the first decades of the twenty-first. The President announced that he wanted to defer reprocessing in the United States nuclear industry indefinitely, to scale down the research programme on fast breeders, and to defer their introduction while other, less dangerous models were investigated. He hoped that the rest of the world would follow the United States, and suggested that spent fuel elements could be stored under international control with the plutonium still mixed in with intensely radioactive wastes.

The United States had the power to enforce compliance with such a policy, for it supplied almost all the non-communist world's nuclear fuel and could lay down what happened to it after it was used in reactors. Shortly after the President's announcement, the US told the world's nuclear industry that it would permit its fuel to be re-exported for reprocessing only under exceptional circumstances, as when reactors were threatened with closure because of 'extreme congestion' in their spent fuel storage. It also delayed Japanese plans to start testing a small reprocessing plant. As no nation had yet begun regularly reprocessing modern nuclear fuel on a large scale, and as the viability of plans to do so (in Britain and France, for example) depended on secure foreign business, this seemed to be an attempt to halt development altogether. At the same time Canada, who with the US supplied two-thirds of the West's uranium ore, was taking a similar line.

Almost all the other main industrialized countries, however, vigorously opposed these policies. Europe and Japan believed that they had more need of plutonium than the US, since they had smaller energy resources; and many such countries also seemed to think that by pioneering the fast breeder they had won a rare technological lead over the US, one which they would be foolish to relinquish. Several declared that they would proceed with both reprocessing and fast breeders—as did the Soviet bloc. As the year went on, the President seemed gradually to modify his approach, though at the end of it the industrial nations did begin a series of meetings to discuss alternatives to plutonium.

Against this background a remarkable public inquiry into the British nuclear industry's reprocessing plans was taking place in the remote Cumbrian town of Whitehaven. Champions and opponents of British Nuclear Fuel Ltd's application to build a big new plant for reprocessing modern, oxide fuel at Windscale argued their cases for 100 days before the inspector, Mr Justice Parker, and his two distinguished assessors. BNFL, who were supported by the local county council, put forward a competent case. Foremost among the opponents, who included the Government of the Isle of Man and a wide range of environmental groups, were Friends of the Earth, who concentrated particularly on the economics of reprocessing and the risks of the spread of nuclear weapons and argued for a ten-year delay on building the plant while long-term storage of fuel elements was researched. Among highlights of the inquiry were evidence by Dr Alice Stewart that research carried out at Hanford, the American equivalent of Windscale, showed that working in such a plant was 20 times more dangerous than had previously been supposed; the disclosure by Professor Arnold Wohlstetter of Chicago University that the US had tested, and exploded, a bomb made from reactor-grade plutonium; and the submissions by Dr Peter Chapman, of the Open University, and Mr Gerald Leach, of the International Institute for Environment and Development, that simple energy conservation measures, and the natural slackening of the growth of demand as various energy uses approached saturation point, showed government projections of energy growth to be far too high and the reprocessing plant to be unnecessary. At the end of the year the inspector's report had yet to reach the Secretary of State for the Environment. (See also pp. 362-3).

Meanwhile the Government announced that there would be another, similar inquiry before any decision was taken to build Britain's first commercial fast breeder reactor. And in May it published its response to the 1976 report of the Royal Commission on Environmental Pollution on nuclear power and the environment (see AR 1976, p. 377). This contained little that was surprising, but it did announce that in future the Department of the Environment instead of the Department of Energy would assume control of research and development on the disposal of nuclear waste.

The greatest contrast to the gentlemanly, almost friendly atmosphere at the British nuclear inquiry was provided when, on 31 July, a man was killed and 100 people injured during a mass demonstration at the site where France's first commercial fast breeder was being built at Creys-Malville near Lyon. A subsequent demonstration at Kalkar, the site of Germany's prototype fast breeder, passed off peacefully, although some previous encounters in the Federal Republic had been violent. Public opposition virtually halted the nuclear programme in Germany during the year, and it continued to intensify elsewhere. In Australia, where the Government lifted a four-year ban on the export of uranium during the summer, the Labour Party and the trades union movement campaigned against the decision—ineffectively, in terms of the general election result (see pp. 305-6). On 15 July 200,000 people marched against nuclear power in Bilbao, Spain.

Meanwhile more than twenty of America's leading authorities warned that increasing use of fossil fuels could have 'adverse, perhaps even catastrophic' consequences on climate. Their two-and-a-half year study for the National Academy of Sciences predicted that the increased levels of carbon dioxide emitted by burning the fuels would intensify the 'greenhouse effect' of the gas in the atmosphere so that the climate would warm up by several degrees centigrade, shifting agricultural zones towards the poles (including moving the great American corn belt to less fertile Canadian soils) and eventually raising the sea level by nearly 20 feet (which would inundate countless coastal cities).

Support for alternative, environmentally less dangerous, energy sources increased. In January a prototype solar power station began feeding energy into the grid in France. The number of solar-heated homes in the United States grew dramatically, and researchers both there and in Britain claimed that the breakthrough to economic competitiveness for solar cells was close. Windpower attracted increasingly distinguished support, while the British Government, less than halfway through a two-year study on wave-power, was so encouraged by the results that it doubled the research budget. Scientists at Los Alamos, New Mexico, made significant progress in developing the technology needed to exploit the massive amounts of energy stored in hot dry rocks in the earth's crust.

Besides campaigning for energy conservation, President Carter committed himself to do more than any of his predecessors to preserve the environment and combat pollution. His Administration paid particular attention to strengthening protection from hazards at work. Reports published during the year showed that one out of every four US workers was exposed to one or more substances that caused disease or death, but fewer than 5 per cent of US factories had active industrial hygiene schemes. A government survey of British firms, meanwhile, found that 85 per cent had neither a doctor nor a nurse for their work-force. The British Health and Safety Executive proposed a scheme, less rigorous than that enacted in the US in 1976, to test substances for toxic effects.

Once again asbestos attracted special concern. The British standard for workers' exposure, two fibres per cubic centimetre of air, which had been adopted as a model by countries all over the world, looked increasingly shaky. One authoritative study suggested that between 5 and 10 per cent of the people who worked for a lifetime in exposures permitted by this standard would die of asbestosis or cancer. Both the British Trades Union Congress and the European Parliament called for the use of asbestos to be phased out altogether. Sweden announced that it would do precisely that.

There was also increasing concern about cancer hazards to the general public. In 1976 the US National Cancer Institute had published an atlas showing the incidence of death from various forms of the disease in every county in the nation. Preliminary analyses published during 1977 showed that deaths from bladder, liver and lung cancers were particularly prevalent in the counties where chemical industries were concentrated; more nasal, lung and skin cancers were found around petroleum refineries; and increased lung cancer was also noticeable near copper, lead and zinc smelting works.

More evidence accumulated that some types of hair dye could cause cancer, and another suspected carcinogen, used for flame-proofing children's night-clothes, was banned in the United States. On the other hand Congress postponed a ban on saccharine despite evidence that it could cause cancer in man and animals; since cyclamates, the other main artificial sweetener, had been banned some years before, there was enormous public resistance to being left with no alternative but to embrace the different health risks associated with sugar.

Meanwhile the US Food and Drugs Administration, the Consumer

Product Safety Commission and the Environment Protection Agency ruled jointly that no aerosol cans containing 'fluorocarbons' as propellants should be sold after April 1979, except for essential medical uses; it was generally believed that these gases caused partial depletion of the world's protective ozone layer. Concern grew, however, that nitrous oxides given off by nitrogenous fertilizers might also threaten the ozone, and this was a major preoccupation of a special UN Environment Programme (UNEP) conference in the spring.

There was widespread relief when babies born to women from Seveso, the Italian town which had been the site of an accidental release of highly poisonous TCDD in 1976 (see AR 1976, p. 362), showed few malformations. But the long-term effects of the poison on people were still unknown. The first evacuated families were allowed to return to their homes in October, but the chemical itself and cases of poisoning were meanwhile turning up in Milan, more than ten miles away.

International conferences proved somewhat disappointing during the year. Major UN assemblies on water and on deserts made some progress but little impact. And the remarkable series of meetings of Mediterranean states, which brought normally hostile countries together to talk about the pollution of their common sea, saw a slowing of progress during the year. This was scarcely surprising, however, since the umbrella convention and two protocols (on dumping and cooperation in pollution emergencies) which had been previously agreed cost the participating nations little, while the convention discussed in 1977 concerned discharges from the land (the source of four-fifths of the sea's pollution) and would, it was estimated, cost $10,000 million to implement.

In September Dr E. F. Schumacher, the author of 'Small is Beautiful', one of the leading philosophers of the environmental movement and an increasingly powerful force in contemporary thinking, died in Switzerland (see OBITUARY).

XIV LAW

Chapter 1

INTERNATIONAL LAW—EUROPEAN COMMUNITY LAW

INTERNATIONAL LAW

THE Diplomatic Conference on the reaffirmation and development of international humanitarian law applicable to armed conflicts had met each year since 1974. In 1977 its efforts reached fruition in the conclusion of a Final Act, comprising two Protocols which are intended as additions to two existing conventions—the Geneva Conventions on the Protection of Victims of International and of Non-International Armed Conflicts respectively. These Protocols were adopted by the Diplomatic Conference in June 1977 and opened for signature, for a 12-month period, in December 1977. The Final Act also contained adopted resolutions.

Throughout the Protocols there is evidence of the changing realities since the Geneva Conventions were signed in 1949. In Protocol I, Article 1 describes its scope as including armed conflicts against 'colonial domination and alien occupation and against racist regimes in the exercise of [the] right of self determination'. The conference was faced with the difficult task of providing better protection for the civilian population while acknowledging that guerrilla warfare made the old rules on identification of combatants outdated. Article 44 provides a somewhat ambiguously worded attempt to deal with this problem. Certain clauses, made necessary by the grim realities of contemporary hostilities, break new ground. Thus Articles 46 and 47 contain provisions on prisoner of war status in respect of spies and mercenaries respectively. Interestingly, Article 47 attempts a definition of a mercenary, which, because of six concurrent requirements, is very restrictive.

Other important principles are reaffirmed and elaborated. It is prohibited to carry out medical or scientific experiments on prisoners even with their consent (Article 11). Reprisals against protected persons are forbidden (Article 20). There is a much more detailed procedure than in the Geneva Conventions dealing with parties' duties in respect of notifications about missing persons (Article 33).

Protocol II substantially expands the very limited—albeit important—protections that international law has hitherto afforded in non-international armed conflicts. It contains a particularly significant, lengthy article on the prosecution and punishment of criminal offences related to them.

Certain technical resolutions are appended, while another calls for a further conference of governments to be convened by 1979 to deal with the problem of indiscriminate and excessively injurious weapons, on which it had not been possible to reach agreement within the ambit of this Act.

The UN Conference on the Law of the Sea could make only limited progress at its 1977 sessions. It did, however, produce an 'informal composite negotiating text', which—while moving away from the format of the revised negotiating text (see AR 1976, p. 386)—provided a basis for negotiations without ruling out further revisions.

On 30 June a Court of Arbitration specially constituted under an agreement reached between France and the United Kingdom in 1975 handed down its award on the delimitation of certain portions of the continental shelf in the English Channel. From 1970 to 1974 the two countries had conducted negotiations to delimit their respective continental shelves. It was, however, necessary to turn to arbitration for assistance on unresolved problems. The Court was asked to decide 'what is the course of the boundary (or boundaries) between the portions of the continental shelf appertaining to the United Kingdom and the Channel Islands and to the French Republic, respectively, westward of 30 minutes West of the Greenwich meridian as far as the 1,000 metre isobath?'

The parties had found particular difficulties in the area of the Channel Islands and in the Atlantic sector; but before it could assist in resolving these the Court had first to decide what principles of law would be applicable. This in itself was a task of the greatest complexity, and international lawyers were likely to find the Award as important for its observations on principles of treaty law—especially interpretation, continuing validity and reservations—as for the specific delimitations which it made. The Court rejected the French contention that the Continental Shelf Convention of 1958 had been rendered legally obsolete by subsequent events, including a consensus that was emerging, so France claimed, from the Third UN Conference on the Law of the Sea. It further found that the UK's objections to certain reservations that France had entered to that Convention did not render it inapplicable as between France and the United Kingdom. But it also rejected the UK contention that France's reservations to Article 6 of the Convention were inadmissible, or not proper reservations, and should therefore be left out of account altogether.

Article 6 (1) of the Continental Shelf Convention provides:

(1) Where the same continental shelf is adjacent to the territories of two or more states whose coasts are opposite each other, the boundary of the continental shelf appertaining to such states shall be determined by agreement between them. In the absence of agreement, and unless another boundary line is justified by special circumstances, the boundary is the median line, every point of which is equidistant from the nearest points of the baselines from which the breadth of the territorial sea of each state is measured.

France's reservations thereto provided that, in the absence of a specific agreement, it would not accept the invocation against it of a continental shelf boundary determined by the equidistance principle if such boundary was calculated from post-1958 baselines, or one so determined if it extended beyond the 200 metre isobath. The Court found that the combined effect of the French reservations and their rejection by the United Kingdom was to render Article 6 inapplicable to the extent of the reservations. Where this was so, the rules of general international law governing delimitation of the continental shelf applied.

The first French reservation was found by the Court to be immaterial (in the sense that straight baselines were not invoked by the United Kingdom). Looking back to the evidence of the 1970-74 negotiations, the Court further declared that the second reservation did not have the effect of making Article 6 in principle inapplicable to the Atlantic region. But, even outside the Channel Islands region, general international law would also have its place, for Article 6 did not define the *conditions* for applying the 'special circumstances' rider to the equidistance rule.

In applying the relevant legal principles to the particular geographical circumstances, the Court emphasized that the most fundamental norm was that of delimitation in accordance with equitable principles, no matter what method was used. Leaving aside for the moment the specific problems of the Channel Islands, the Court found that a delimitation of the shelf between 'opposite' states was called for in three segments of the English Channel and that the median line would be generally equitable. Nor were its views altered by the UK contention that the Hurd Deep to Hurd Deep Fault zone could offer an alternative boundary.

Was the Eddystone Rock to be used as a base point in delimiting that segment of the median line? France objected, both on the grounds of past practice and because it claimed that the Rock was a low-tide elevation rather than an island; for it to be an island capable of having its own territorial sea it needed to be above the water line at even the highest tides. The UK both interpreted differently the significance of past practice and claimed that the high-water line must be taken to mean the ocean high-water spring tides, which was the only precise measurement available. The Court, preferring to rely on what flowed from the past practice of the parties, and avoiding any pronouncement on the precise legal status of Eddystone Rock, found that it was a relevant base point for delimiting the continental shelf boundary in the Channel.

The Channel Islands clearly presented great difficulties, because they 'are situated not only on the French side of a median line drawn between the two mainlands but practically within the arms of a gulf on the French coast' (*Award*, para. 183). The Court was thus faced with the problem of deciding the course of the boundary of the shelf of two opposite states, one of which possesses island territories close to the coast of the other state. The Court was particularly mindful that the Channel Islands had a fisheries zone of 12 miles which had been recognized by the French Republic. The UK also made the point that, while the Channel Islands had at present a territorial sea of three miles, it would be lawful to extend it to 12 miles.

The United Kingdom, while not claiming that the Channel Islands were a projection of its mainland, urged that there was a portion of continental shelf appertaining to the Channel Islands which merged, in mid-Channel, with that portion which appertained to the south coast of England. It therefore asked that the Channel median line should deviate southwards around the Channel Islands. In a statement that is important for other comparable international controversies, the Court said:

The principle of natural prolongation of territory is neither to be set aside nor treated as absolute in a case where islands belonging to one state are situated on continental shelf which would otherwise constitute a natural prolongation of the territory of another state . . . it is rather dependent not only on the particular geographical and other circumstances but also on any relevant considerations of law and equity (para. 194).

In a novel solution, the Court, having decided that the primary boundary should be a median line, indicated a second boundary in the area of the Channel Islands, to the south of the mid-Channel median line, 12 nautical miles from the established baselines of the territorial sea of the Channel Islands. Thus the Channel Islands were left with a zone of seabed and subsoil to their north and west, while France secured a band of continental shelf in mid-Channel continuous with its shelf to the east and west of the Channel Islands region.

Finally, the Court had to address itself to the problems of the Atlantic sector. Article 6 of the Continental Shelf Convention in principle was applicable to this sector. However, because the United Kingdom coast extends further westward than does the French coast, the Court had to decide whether the Atlantic region was a case of 'opposite' or 'adjacent' states, or rather a case which fell (as France claimed) outside Article 6 altogether. The Court held that Article 6 did apply. Did the prolongation of the Scilly Isles further westward than the French island of Ushant render unjust or inequitable an equidistant boundary delimited from the baselines of the French and United Kingdom coasts?

The Court thought that the position of the Scilly Isles south-west of England did constitute a special circumstance, but it declined to accede to France's proposal that a median line therefore be delimited by reference to prolongation of the general directions of the Channel coasts of the two countries. Instead, it decided 'to take account of the Scilly Isles as part of the coastline of the United Kingdom but to give them less than their full effect in applying the equidistance method' (*Award*, para. 249). The method consisted of delimiting the line equidistant between the two coasts, first without the use of the offshore island as a base point, and secondly with its use as a base point: a boundary could then be drawn mid-way between these two equidistance lines.

The United Kingdom has now addressed certain questions to the

Court concerning the compatibility of the principles of the Award with the techniques used by the Court's expert for drawing the boundaries.

In an arbitration treaty of 1902 Chile and the Argentine Republic had designated His Britannic Majesty's Government as arbitrator. In 1971, in fulfilment of its duties in relation to the Beagle Channel dispute between Chile and Argentina, the Government appointed a Court of Arbitration— five members—interestingly drawn from the International Court of Justice. The members were Mr Hardy Dillard (USA), Sir Gerald Fitzmaurice (UK), M André Gros (France), Mr Charles Onyeama (Nigeria) and Mr Sture Petrén (Sweden). After lengthy written and oral pleadings the Court of Arbitration handed down its Award in February.

The Argentine Republic had argued that the boundary line between the respective maritime jurisdictions of that country and the Republic of Chile from meridian 68° 36′ 38.5 W of Greenwich runs along the median line of the Beagle Channel, deviating 'only where inflexions are necessary so that each country may always navigate the waters of its own' (*Award*, p. xiv). It claimed in consequence that Picton, Nueva and Lennox Islands and adjacent islands and islets belonged to Argentina. Chile claimed these islands and islets as its own. Indeed, it claimed that listed islands and islets appurtenant to the southern shore belonged to Chile; and asked that, even if that argument were rejected, the Court should find that all other islands and islets whose entire land surface is situated between certain indicated latitudes and longitudes belonged to Chile.

The islands of Picton, Nueva and Lennox are situated at the eastern end of the Beagle Channel where it meets the open sea. Although Argentina framed its claim in primarily maritime terms, and Chile in territorial terms, the Court was faced in each case with the question of title to the three islands. The Court thus had a great deal of historical evidence to consider, with particular emphasis on the boundary treaty of 1881. Attention was also paid to a protocol of 1893 and to acts and incidents (including those of cartography) which each of the parties claimed to be corroborative of its own views.

The Award represented a substantial victory for Chile. The Court unanimously found (although Judge Petrén died before the Award was announced, he had taken part in all the deliberations) that Picton, Nueva and Lennox Islands, together with their immediate appurtenant islets and rocks, belong to the Republic of Chile. It indicated the proper boundary between the territorial and maritime jurisdictions of Argentina and Chile respectively, and directed the parties to inform it of the administrative and technical steps necessary to be taken by either of them. Her Majesty the Queen then—in her formal capacity as Arbitrator—ratified the Award of the Court of Arbitration, thus concluding an innovative and imaginative use of third-party settlement in the resolution of disputes.

N

EUROPEAN COMMUNITY LAW

In spite of some very significant single events, 1977 was a somewhat brooding year for Community law, as it digested measures thrown up in 1976 and waited in appalled expectancy for what 1978 was going to bring. There was a subconscious awareness that the Community was hovering on the threshold of irreversible legal changes which, because of their radical nature, would blot out much that was familiar and dear to its citizens. The one clear embodiment of this during the year itself was the enactment of the UK Patent Act 1977, which implemented the European and the Community Patent Conventions and in the process completely rewrote British patent law. Another symptom was the prolonged debate in the various member states on the implementation of direct elections to the European Parliament.

For the new member states the same awareness of impending change could be detected in a sudden realization of the powers of foreign courts and of Community 'police authorities'. The discussions on their accession to the EEC 'full faith and credit' Convention on Jurisdiction and Enforcement of Judgments, which had been conducted in great secrecy since 1973, finally surfaced in mid-year with a report from the House of Lords scrutiny committee and a later, rather farcical, debate in the House of Commons just after the year's end. The matter was so advanced that the treaty of accession to the Convention would almost certainly be signed by the new member states early in 1978. The impact of the EEC anti-trust investigators was more immediate, as companies began to submit to searches of their files and archives; and the first two formal decisions to compel recalcitrant companies (in these cases both German) to admit investigators were published by the Commission. Apart from the pure civil liberties aspect, attention in Britain was especially concentrated upon the question of lawyers' privilege against such searches, particularly in the case of in-house lawyers, who do not enjoy such privilege in other member states.

Another event, the true significance of which was only dimly perceived, was the enactment by the Council in May of the 6th Value Added Tax Directive. This unified the major part (except the actual rates) of the VAT systems throughout the Community, creating in effect, despite some discretion left to member states, the first branch of taxation to be wholly controlled by the Community, even though it was not a 'Community tax' in the strict sense. This was passed in the nick of time for its implementing provisions to be included in the British Finance Act 1977, whereby the UK became the only member state to apply the new EEC provisions from their intended date of commencement on 1 January 1978. Because the other member states were not so prompt, the remaining part of the Community revenue system could not be brought under the VAT umbrella (as projected a decade previously in the Budgetary Treaty), and so the 'block grant' principle had to be continued for one further year instead.

The tendency (see AR 1976, pp. 388-89) of Community legislative effort to move into more substantive areas of law and life continued with the publication of controversial draft directives on the rights of commercial agents *vis-à-vis* their principals and on restrictive regulation of doorstep consumer sales. It had particularly striking effect in the application, at last, of full freedom of movement to the professions with the coming into full force on 19 December 1976 of the Doctors Directive, the enactment the following June of two Nurses Directives and in March of the Lawyers' Services Directive and a series of judgments of the European Court in *Thieffry* and *Razanatsimba* (lawyers) and *Patrick* (architects), all developing the principles laid down in *Reyners'* case. The result of all these events was that doctors and nurses would have virtually free movement throughout Community territory, that in other professions nationality restrictions would not apply to Community nationals, nor would ancillary discriminatory requirements unless they could be justified objectively. Thus, if relevant foreign qualifications had been accepted internally by the profession as equivalent to a domestic qualification there would to that extent be a right of full establishment. However, this applied only to citizens of member states and did not extend to nationals of the ACP states under the Lomé Convention.

A great deal of the Commission's legislative attention was being directed to labour matters, and directives were enacted on the rights of workers in cases of collective bargaining and on transfer of ownership of their enterprise. The draft Commission Agents Directive was also initiated as part of the 'social policy', as were the provisions restricting hours of driving in commercial road transport (including the fixing of tachograph meters in drivers' cabs). The latter continued to receive scant respect in the UK (largely because of the opposition to the 'spy in the cab' from the trade unions), and by the end of the year the Commission was threatening to sue the UK before the European Court. On this subject the Court itself issued a further judgment to the effect that where a company supplied drivers, but not vehicles, to a transport enterprise the latter and not the former should be criminally responsible for ensuring compliance with the rules.

The importance of these and other directives was enhanced by two judgments of the European Court—in *Verbond van Nederlandse Ondernemingen* and *Enka*—holding that directives were self-executing and consequently that individuals could rely on them before their national courts without having to wait for national implementing legislation, and that even where there was national legislation the litigant might go behind it straight to the underlying directive if there was a discrepancy between the two. It is difficult to over-emphasize the importance of these rulings for the future of Community law.

The year was also remarkable for the first action ever to be brought before the European Court (under article 170 EEC) by one member state against another, when Ireland sued France for failure to allow free entry to Irish lamb. This was, however, withdrawn in January 1978 after the two countries had agreed on a compromise. Whereupon the UK asked the Commission to intervene against France for the latter's restrictions on import of British lamb, but it continued itself to impose from 1 January 1978 (*i.e.* after the relevant accession transitional period had expired) a total ban on import of Dutch potatoes into the UK. The Commission in effect said 'A plague on both your houses!' and indicated that it might bring proceedings against both France and the UK. Earlier in the year the Commission had brought its first actions against new member states under article 169 and in the process won from the European Court interim injunctions against the UK (for unlawfully subsidizing pig-meat producers) and Ireland (for introducing no-trawl areas off its coasts).

The main focus of interest on the anti-trust side was the position of joint ventures, and the Commission issued several decisions to help clarify this very complex issue. It also gave signs of applying EEC article 86 (on dominant positions) more actively, and it gave a decision holding that a BP company in the Netherlands had abused its dominant position by refusing to supply a non-regular customer during the OPEC petrol crisis. Just before Christmas, in an exceptionally large flood of anti-trust decisions, the Commission also fined a Swedish enterprise, Hugin Kassaregister AB, a substantial sum for refusing to supply its spare parts to an independent English firm, holding that even though Hugin had no dominant position in the EEC on the cash register market it had one on the market for its own spare parts.

Finally, the Community institutions solemnly signed a joint declaration in which they undertook to respect human rights. This followed on the concern arising out of the judgment of the German Constitutional Court in May 1974 in the *Internationale Handelsgesellschaft* case, and also a more immediate concern to reinforce the recent emergence of the three new applicants for membership from autocratic rule. The European Court in *Bouchereau* supplemented this with an important gloss on its restrictive interpretation of 'public policy' as a ground for restricting entry of Community nationals, which resulted in an English magistrate's holding that he could not recommend the deportation of a Frenchman who had pleaded guilty to possession of small quantities of soft drugs, since that was not sufficiently serious to fall within the proviso.

Chapter 2

LAW IN THE UNITED KINGDOM

No case gave rise to greater interest in 1977 than *Gouriet* v. *Union of Post Office Workers*,[1] which involved a question of major constitutional importance. Do the English Courts have jurisdiction to entertain an action at the instance of a private person for an injunction to restrain threatened conduct because it would constitute a criminal offence? The plaintiff obtained interim injunctions from the Court of Appeal preventing two post office unions from calling on their members to disrupt mail and other communication with South Africa (a statutory offence) despite the Attorney-General's refusal to lend his name to the proceedings in a relator action. The House of Lords, however, unanimously overturned the Court o Appeal, stressing the distinction between public and private law. Where a plaintiff is not claiming the infringement of a private legal right, only the Attorney-General is entitled to represent the public in the courts, and the exercise of his discretion is unreviewable. Nor should injunctions be requested from the Civil Courts to enforce the criminal law except in exceptional circumstances. Lord Denning's view that the Courts had a residual power to allow an individual to seek an injunction when the Attorney-General had refused or delayed consent to relator proceedings was rejected as lacking in authority and contrary to principle.

Another public law issue of fundamental importance involved sovereign immunity[2] (see AR 1976, pp. 384-85). Adopting the 'incorporation' rather than the 'transformation' approach, the Court of Appeal held that the rules of international law which formed part of English law were not confined to those adopted by the Courts or by Acts of Parliament, and the rule of binding precedent had no application to such rules. Accordingly the 'restrictive' theory of sovereign immunity, which, unlike the 'absolute' theory, refuses immunity to state commercial activities, was applied, since this reflected current international law. Some earlier cases had decided that once a rule of international law was 'fixed' in English law by the Courts it prevailed over later international developments, and the point still awaited an authoritative decision from the House of Lords.

Noteworthy House of Lords decisions included *Birkett* v. *James*,[3] where it was decided that only in rare and exceptional circumstances should a judge exercise his discretion to dismiss an action for want of prosecution within the prescribed limitation period; and *Anns* v. *Merton London Borough Council*[4] which, applying the *Donoghue* v. *Stevenson* good neigh-

---

[1] [1977] 3 W.L.R. 300.
[2] *Trendtex Banking Corp.* v. *Central Bank of Nigeria* [1977] 2 W.L.R. 356.
[3] [1977] 3 W.L.R. 38.
[4] [1977] 2 W.L.R. 1024.

bour principle, imposed liability on local authorities which have negligently exercised their statutory powers of inspection during building operations. In *D.* v. *National Society for Prevention of Cruelty to Children*[1] the House had to consider when it was justifiable to withhold information in legal proceedings because its production would be contrary to the public interest. Someone had made a wholly unfounded accusation to the NSPCC that the respondent had been ill-treating her child and she suffered nervous shock as a consequence. Instituting proceedings in negligence against the Society, she sought discovery of documents revealing the identity of the informant but this was resisted on the grounds of confidentiality. Overruling the Court of Appeal, the House of Lords extended by analogy the established rule protecting the identity of police informers, on the ground that if an organization performs a valuable public function then it should be able to withhold information if that is absolutely necessary to enable it to operate effectively.

In the first case on unfair dismissal to come before them their Lordships agreed that an industrial tribunal had correctly disallowed a company's attempt to introduce evidence of misconduct which had come to light only after they had dismissed the respondent manager.[2] The statutory rules concerning unfair dismissal were therefore significantly different from the common law rules for assessing damages for wrongful dismissal.

The Courts also became involved in the Grunwick affair (see pp. 28-31), a *cause célèbre* involving a London film processing laboratory and a union, the Association of Professional, Executive, Clerical and Computer Staff (APEX). The House of Lords decided in December that an ACAS report recommending that the company should recognize APEX for the purposes of collective bargaining was *ultra vires* and void because the recommendation was made without ACAS first ascertaining the opinions of those workers at Grunwick who had continued to work throughout the troubles.[3] Section 14(1) of the Employment Protection Act 1975 imposed a mandatory duty on ACAS to ascertain these opinions despite the refusal of the company to cooperate by supplying names and addresses of employees. An earlier Court of Inquiry conducted under Lord Scarman had reported in August that the company's action in dismissing a number of workers who had gone on strike for union recognition, though within the letter, was outside the spirit of the law. The report welcomed the announcement of a Government review of the law relating to picketing, mass picketing at Grunwick having led to violent confrontation with the police.

Industrial matters also concerned the Court of Appeal, which ruled

[1] [1977] 2 W.L.R. 201.
[2] *W. Devis & Sons Ltd* v. *Atkins* [1977] 3 W.L.R. 214.
[3] *Grunwick Processing Laboratories Ltd* v. *ACAS* and others. *The Times*, 15 December 1977.

that the Association of Broadcasting Staff should not interfere with the television broadcast of the Cup Final. Although a 'trade dispute' would be immune from proceedings in tort this was merely a threat of coercive action.[1] The Employment Appeal Tribunal decided numerous cases and pushed back frontiers particularly in the area of sex discrimination and equal pay.

The doctrine of precedent received further attention from the Courts during the year. In a tax case which 'leap-frogged' the Court of Appeal,[2] the House of Lords held that the 1966 Practice Statement whereby the House of Lords could review and depart from one of its earlier decisions did not permit an appellant to argue that an earlier decision (even if decided by a narrow majority) should not be followed merely because it was wrong! Some other ground, such as a material change of circumstances, had to be shown before the House would be justified in adopting such a course. Of even more interest was the 'battered mistress' case, *Davis* v. *Johnson*,[3] in which a full Court of Appeal by a 3-2 majority disagreed with two of its own earlier decisions[4] and added a new exception to the rule laid down in *Young* v. *Bristol Aeroplane Co. Ltd*,[5] that the Court of Appeal was bound to follow its own previous decisions. Now, if it appeared that a previous decision was wrong, the Court was at liberty to depart from it in exceptional circumstances. The House of Lords' opinion of this doctrine was awaited with interest, as was its decision on the substantive issue. Lord Denning believed that justice required that, in a proper case, personal rights should be given priority over rights of property. Thus the Matrimonial Proceedings Act 1976 should not prevent the courts ordering the eviction of a man who had battered his mistress merely because he owned a share of the house. If the new doctrine were to be upheld by their Lordships there could be substantial repercussions on property law.

Other noteworthy decisions in the Court of Appeal included *Hosenball's* case,[6] where an American journalist was deported for security reasons. In security cases it appears that it is not necessary for the authorities to comply fully with the rules of natural justice and inform the person concerned of the exact nature of the charges against him. In *Goldsmith* v. *Sperrings Ltd*[7] Lord Denning's brethren strongly disagreed with his view that the actions brought by Sir James Goldsmith against the distributors of *Private Eye* should be stayed as an abuse of process and also that the newsagents were not liable in any case. That distributors could be liable had been assumed by counsel and not argued before the Court.

[1] *BBC* v. *Hearn, The Times*, 21 May 1977.
[2] *Fitzleet Estates Ltd* v. *Cherry* [1977] 1 W.L.R. 538.
[3] *The Times*, 29 November 1977.
[4] *B* v. *B, The Times*, 14 October 1977 and *Cantliff* v. *Jenkins, The Times*, 25 October 1977.   [5] [1944] 1 K.B. 718.
[6] [1977] 1 W.L.R. 88.   [7] [1977] 1 W.L.R. 478.

Two cricketing cases aroused considerable interest. In the first, the Court of Appeal held that, although a cricket club was ordinarily liable in negligence and nuisance for balls landing on neighbouring properties, an injunction would not be granted in this case since the preservation of the cricket ground for public recreation prevailed over the interests of the plaintiffs, who must have realized that cricket balls would sometimes land on their properties.[1] In the second, the High Court decided in favour of Mr Kerry Packer and his World Series cricketers by holding that the new International Cricket Conference rules were an inducement to players to break their contracts, and also an unlawful restraint of trade in that they denied Tony Greig and others the right to practise their profession.[2] The case left the ICC with a large bill for legal costs (see pp. 443-4).

In July the homosexual newspaper *Gay News* was prosecuted (at the instigation of Mrs Mary Whitehouse) for publishing a blasphemous poem and convicted.[3] The case caused controversy both as to the desirability of protecting orthodox religion in this way and also with respect to the judge's finding that a necessary element of the offence, the likelihood of a breach of the peace, had been proved. The European Court of Human Rights also held that the suppression of the avant-garde *Little Red Schoolbook* did not breach the European Convention on Human Rights since restrictions on freedom of speech are permissible for the 'protection of morals'.[4] An important decision of the European Court of Justice granted the Commission's request for interim measures and ordered the UK to suspend forthwith its £1 million per week subsidy to pig farmers.

A suspended sentence of a two years imprisonment for indecent assault and grievous bodily harm on a 17-year-old girl handed down in the guardsman's case *R* v. *Holdsworth* raised some eyebrows. It appeared that the Court of Appeal's Criminal Division was under the misapprehension that this lenient course would save the young officer's army career.

Parliament was heavily tied up with successive devolution Bills (see pp. 8, 16 and 41) but it found time to enact some important legislation. The Criminal Law Act was a complex mixture of substantive and procedural reform. The law of conspiracy was put on a statutory footing, with the exception of conspiracy to defraud and the vague common law offences of conspiracy to corrupt public morals or outrage public decency which will eventually be superseded by specific statutory offences also. Squatting was also dealt with. Anyone who required property for his own residential occupation might require a trespasser to leave and constables could enter and remove persons reasonably suspected of committing the

---

[1] *Miller* v. *Jackson* [1977] 3 W.L.R. 20.
[2] *Greig and Others* v. *Insole and Others: World Series Cricket Pty. Ltd* v. *Same. The Times*, 26 November 1977.
[3] *R* v. *Lemmon, The Times*, 12 July 1977.
[4] *Handyside Case*, European Court of Human Rights [1977] N.L.J. 1064.

offence. The jurisdictional rules concerning offences triable summarily or on indictment were simplified and penalties were adjusted. One amendment required the police to notify the prisoner's friend immediately after arrest unless delay is necessitated 'in the interest of the investigation or the prevention of crime or the apprehension of offenders'. This topic and the vexed question of the Judges' Rules adverted to by the Fisher Report on the Confait murder case were to be further considered by a new Royal Commission on the criminal process. The Patents Act gave legislative effect to several international conventions, streamlined the procedures for obtaining patents and conferred greater validity on UK patents.

The Unfair Contract Terms Act, described by Lord Denning as a 'gratifying piece of law reform', provided that a person could not contract out of or limit his liability in negligence for causing death or personal injury, and could exclude or restrict liability for other negligent loss or damage only where this was reasonable in the circumstances. Liability in contract could not be excluded or restricted where one party is a consumer or where there is a standard-form contract. Nor could a negligent manufacturer or distributor of goods exclude his liability towards a consumer by the terms of a guarantee.

The Torts (Interference with Goods) Act abolished the old tort of detinue and made the law relating to conversion and trespass to goods more intelligible and more rational to apply. This Act, a model of clarity, extended to Northern Ireland but not to Scotland. Several Orders amended the law of Northern Ireland. In particular it was made an offence to place or dispatch an article intending to make anyone believe that it is likely to explode or ignite or falsely communicate information to this effect; illegitimate children were given the same rights of intestate succession to property as legitimate children.[1]

The Marriage (Scotland) Act abolished the calling of banns as a method of giving notice of an intended marriage and instead required notice to be given to the district registrar in all cases, with a normal waiting period of 14 days. The Act enabled marriages to be celebrated by ministers or priests of religious bodies which were not Christian or Jewish; and it removed the bar on marrying one's great-uncle or aunt!

[1] Statutory Instruments 1977/124g and 1250.

N*

XV THE ARTS

Chapter 1

OPERA—BALLET—THE THEATRE—MUSIC—THE CINEMA—
TELEVISION AND RADIO

OPERA

IT was a good year for new operas. On 7 July the Royal Opera gave the premiere of Sir Michael Tippett's *The Ice Break*, a philosophical yet admirably concise treatment of tensions between races, generations and political systems. Sam Wanamaker's production seemed over-complex to some, but for the cast, the conducting of Colin Davis and the work itself there was little but praise. *Mary, Queen of Scots*, Thea Musgrave's third opera, was first performed at the Edinburgh Festival by Scottish Opera on 6 September. A nineteenth-century grand opera in content but twentieth-century in form, this was an unqualified success both in Edinburgh and subsequently in the company's repertory.

The English National Opera staged two premieres during the year. David Blake's *Toussaint* (28 September), an epic-didactic-documentary study of the Haitian revolutionary, was long (4½ hours) and prolix, but none could deny the composer's talent for the stage, the brilliance of David Pountney's production, or the uncomfortable parallels with today. This was preceded on 2 February by Iain Hamilton's *The Royal Hunt of the Sun*, which found less favour; it was felt that the austere music added little to Peter Shaffer's successful play.

On 18 June Peter Maxwell Davies's *The Martyrdom of St Magnus* was premiered at the first St Magnus Festival, Orkney. It was commissioned by the BBC and later performed at the Proms. The Bath Festival saw the first performance of John Tavener's *The Gentle Spirit* on 6 June; this one-acter was based on a short story by Dostoyevsky about a suicide, and although written for limited forces it packed a genuinely operatic punch, in contrast to Nicola LeFanu's *Dawnpath* (New Opera Company, 29 September), which seemed an insubstantial example of the music-theatre genre that flourished five years ago.

Elsewhere, the New York City Opera gave the first performance of Leon Kirchner's *Lily* (10 April), a loose—too loose many thought—adaptation of Saul Bellow's novel *Henderson the Rain King*. Rudolf Kelterborn's faithful operatic setting of Friedrich Dürrenmatt's *Ein Engel kommt nach Babylon* was launched at the Zurich Festival on 6 June. The Holland Festival set some sort of record by giving the first performance of

Axel (10 June), an opera by two composers (Reinbert de Leeuw and Jan Van Vlijmen) and in two languages (French and German); the work was based on a symbolic play by Villers de l'Isle Adam, and parallels with contemporary events were thought to be too laboured.

The autumn schedules of London's two opera houses were bedevilled by industrial disputes with orchestra and chorus. These caused the abandonment of one half of *The Trojans* and the shortening of *Don Carlos* at Covent Garden, and at the Coliseum some performances of *Toussaint* and the excellent ENO new production of *Werther* (first seen on 16 March) were cancelled. The latter company's new staging of Weber's *Euryanthe* (2 November) was thus sadly underprepared musically, but their fine new version of *La Bohème* (9 September) by Jean-Claude Auvray emerged unscathed. At the end of the year Charles Mackerras relinquished the post of musical director for the company, a post he had held with the utmost distinction for eight years.

The Royal Opera's new productions were less seriously affected. They were: *Der Freischütz* (27 January) in a serious but generally convincing socio-critical production by Götz Friedrich; *La fanciulla del West* (24 May) in spectacularly realistic sets by Ken Adam and production by Piero Faggioni (this, hitherto the poor relation in the Puccini canon, was given many new airings in both Europe and America); a wholly successful *Lohengrin* (17 November) produced by Elijah Moshinsky and conducted by Bernard Haitink; and on New Year's Eve a lavish and popular version of *Die Fledermaus*, which was televised live virtually world-wide.

Among other notable new productions in the UK was the Edinburgh Festival *Carmen* (22 August), thoughtfully produced by Faggioni in exquisite decor by Ezio Frigerio; Teresa Berganza sang the title-role for the first time, with fascinating and refreshing results, and Claudio Abbado conducted. Jonathan Miller's searching production of *Eugene Onegin* for Kent Opera (29 September) was also greatly admired, as was Julian Hope's energetic staging of the early Verdi opera *I masnadieri* for the Welsh National Opera (29 March); the latter company's *Queen of Spades* was something of a disaster, but their new *Bohème* (24 November, produced by William Gaskill) and *Marriage of Figaro* (15 November, Michael Geliot) were sound. The Arts Council cut the English Music Theatre Company's subsidy by two-thirds, and after new productions of *The Fairy Queen* (7 June) and *The Magic Flute* (13 June) the company went into suspended animation. On the other hand the Arts Council made funds available for the Welsh National Orchestra to establish a touring base in Birmingham, and for the ENO to launch a new company—English National Opera North—in Leeds.

Perhaps the most startling event of the year was the *Don Giovanni* that opened the Glyndebourne Festival on 31 May. In a stark but utterly compelling production by Peter Hall and designed by John Bury, the opera was exceptionally well sung by two casts and conducted by both John Pritchard and Haitink. It later played for six performances at the National Theatre, and toured the regions. This was one of those productions after which the work in question will never quite seem the same. Glyndebourne also mounted a deft and witty new staging by John Cox of Strauss's *Die schweigsame Frau* (29 June).

In Europe the trend away from Wieland Wagner's abstract stage style towards extreme pictorialism was more than ever marked (Jean-Pierre Ponnelle's first attempt at the *Ring* in Stuttgart and Luca Ronconi's *Nabucco* in Florence are just two examples), as was the idea of setting operas in the period of their composition (Virginio Puecher's *Aida* in Cologne and John Neumeier's *Otello* in Munich). The Paris Opéra remained the scene of the world's most eccentric productions, with a *Cenerentola* set amidst plexiglass and steel lifts, and a comic-strip *Zauberflöte*. By contrast, the Metropolitan in New York opted for a simpler style than in the past, with John Dexter's admired stagings of *Le Prophète* (18 January), *Dialogues des Carmélites* (5 February) and *Lulu* (18 March), although his *Rigoletto* (31 October) won less approval.

The year's obituary list was dominated by the tragic death of Maria Callas on 16 September aged only 53 (see OBITUARY). Through her unique artistry and vibrant personality she brought the very word 'opera' to the attention of people who would otherwise scarcely have heard of it. The deaths also occurred of the singers Rosette Anday, Joseph Hislop and Paul Schoeffler.

BALLET

The year saw an unprecedented expansion of ballet, in terms of its companies (especially the small groups), in the number of performances, length of seasons and size of audiences, and in the attendant 'industries' of schools, equipment and publications. All to the good, except that far too many students were being trained for a profession which, like music and the stage, was already greatly over-crowded.

In mid-season Kenneth MacMillan, director of the Royal Ballet, resigned in order to have more time for choreography: he was appointed the company's chief choreographer, and was replaced by Norman Morrice, formerly director of the Ballet Rambert. Two important works were added to the repertoire—Cranko's *Taming of the Shrew* (from the repertoire of the Stuttgart Ballet) and *Fourth Symphony* (by Mahler), specially created by John Neumeier and later performed by his own Hamburg Ballet. The Royal's *Sleeping Beauty*, which had long been thought unsatisfactory, was re-choreographed by Ninette de Valois and Frederick Ashton; though an improvement on the earlier version it fell short of expectations. The *première* was danced by Lesley Collier, the outstanding young dancer of the season, and Anthony Dowell, who returned after a year's sick-leave.

The remarkable Mikhail Baryshnikov danced with the company in *La Fille Mal Gardée* and *Romeo and Juliet*; indeed there were few major companies in the world of which he was not a guest during the year. As a dancer he eclipsed Nureyev, who spent much of the year guesting in ballets which he himself had choreographed (e.g. *Romeo and Juliet* and *Sleeping Beauty* for Festival Ballet) and in special programmes, 'Nureyev and Friends', in London and New York. Northern Dance Theatre acquired a new director, Robert de Warren, changed its name to Northern Ballet Theatre and mounted a new *Coppélia*, set in the North Country, with clog dancing, choreographed by Peter Clegg. Scottish Ballet danced in Paris with Nureyev and celebrated its excellence by being chosen to perform at the Edinburgh Festival (*La Sylphide* with Makarova and the brilliant Fernando Bujones). By scoring a great success in America, home of modern dance, the London Contemporary Dance Theatre established itself as the leading Martha Graham troupe outside New York.

Among the visitors to London were American Ballet Theatre (ABT)— their first visit for six years—and Roland Petit's Ballet de Marseille, who presented at the Palladium his eccentric *Coppélia* (with himself as Dr Coppelius) and his *Notre Dame de Paris* (himself as the Hunchback), starring Loipa Araujo. ABT gave London its first sight of the young prodigy Gelsey Kirkland and included Baryshnikov and Bujones, Martine van Hamel, Cynthia Gregory and Rebecca Wright. The *Giselle* of Kirkland and Baryshnikov was a performance to remember. The Béjart Ballet du XXme Siécle presented at the Coliseum, among other works, *Notre Faust* and *The Triumph of Petrarch*.

London Festival Ballet commissioned a *Romeo and Juliet* from Nureyev, with outstanding decor by Ezio Frigerio, which toured Australia with himself dancing all the Romeos. It was a production with good crowd and fighting scenes but lacking lyricism in the romantic moments.

The Paris Opéra Ballet performed in Leningrad and Moscow, while the Bolshoi Ballet danced at the Opéra and the Palais de Congrès, presenting their greatest dancers and including the young Nadezhda Pavlova and Ludmilla Semenyaka. The Opéra also did homage to Serge Lifar in a special programme of his *Suite en Blanc*, *Phèdre* and *Mirages*.

In Germany the Hamburg Ballet still dominated the scene, with Neumeier's new *Midsummer Night's Dream* added to their repertoire, while Stuttgart scored only a moderate success with Rosella Hightower's staging of *Sleeping Beauty*. In Berlin the Panovs found a sympathetic haven and mounted a successful *Cinderella*.

In New York the seasons were bedevilled by troubles with the unions, as they were in London too. However, for New York City Ballet Balanchine produced an hour-long masterpiece in *Vienna Waltzes*, to music by Johann Strauss the younger, Lehar and Richard Strauss. For ABT Mary Skeaping mounted a fine *Sleeping Beauty*, using the version produced by Sergueeff for the Sadlers Wells Ballet, with costumes by Oliver Messel which seemed disappointingly 'dated'. An interesting and popular revival was the reproduction of early ballets by Ruth St Denis and Ted Shawn of the time when Martha Graham was in the company—the first 'modern ballets'—presented by the Joyce Trisler company and called *The Spirit of Denishawn*, a production which also toured in Europe.

In Australia, the newly-appointed director, Anne Woolliams, resigned and Peggy van Praagh, the original director, returned to keep the company going. In England the year was clouded by the collapse, through lack of funds, of two very praiseworthy companies—Ballet International and the New London Ballet. The latter's founders and principal dancers were André Prokovsky, who then became director of the Rome Opera Ballet, and Galina Samsova, who resumed her career as a guest ballerina.

The outstanding ballet book of the year was David Vaughan's definitive work *Frederick Ashton and his Ballets*. Among the deaths were those of dancers Stanislas Idzikowsky, Nicholas Magellanes, Yuri Soloviev and André Eglevsky and the historian Natalia Roslavleva. (For Idzikowsky and Eglevsky, see OBITUARY). The Order of Merit was awarded to Sir Frederick Ashton.

THE THEATRE

Although a dispute between a plumber and his mate about how long it took to repair a washbasin led to the temporary closure of the National Theatre in the spring of 1977, and a few provincial theatres went 'dark' during the summer, the British theatre in general had a surprisingly successful year.

Leading the success was not the National Theatre, which besides its troubles with the plumbers was financially embarrassed by the costs of running the new building, but the Royal Shakespeare Company, which, under the direction of Trevor Nunn, expanded its already prodigious activities in several ways. It opened a new studio theatre in London, the Warehouse, Covent Garden, to accommodate small-scale productions in the way that The Other Place at Stratford-on-Avon put on plays unsuited to the main theatre there. With the Aldwych as its main London branch the RSC therefore had four theatres under its banner.

Moreover, two of its successful revivals, Shaw's *Man And Superman* and O'Keeffe's *Wild Oats*, moved into the West End, so that by the end of the year the company was occupying six theatres, four of them with repertories; and much of this impressive quantity, amounting to thirty productions, reached in quality a higher standard of performance than might have been expected from such an output. At Stratford-on-Avon the three parts of *Henry VI* and *Coriolanus* were much admired, especially Alan Howard's acting in the leading roles; and the best offerings at the Aldwych were Peter Nichols's new play *Privates on Parade*, which gave Denis Quilley a finely-taken opportunity to show life behind the scenes of troop entertainments, a revival of *The Alchemist* and David Edgar's political play *Destiny* (both of which had first been seen at the studio theatre at Stratford) and Ibsen's *Pillars of the Community*, directed by John Barton, which created a special stir of excitement because it was so seldom acted and was so well done.

In the rediscovery of neglected classics, such as Boucicault's *London Assurance* and O'Keeffe's *Wild Oats*, the Royal Shakespeare Company had a name for excellence which the Ibsen revival superbly sealed. Since it also had a name for encouraging new playwrights, notably Pam Gems, James Robson and C. P. Taylor, at both its studio theatres, where young directors such as Barry Kyle and Howard Davies were making a good impression, the diversity and strength of the RSC appeared to reach a new peak which was not so much Shakespearian as catholic.

Having only half as many theatres at its service the National Theatre under Sir Peter Hall's direction found itself comparatively in the doldrums. Although it proved more popular than ever with playgoers, it pursued a policy which gave no sign of that serious approach to its task which marked the style of the RSC. The haphazard tone was partly caused by an attempt to cut costs, but it was hard to discern in the choice of certain plays any distinction from the policy of an unsubsidized management staging plays in the West End. Alan Ayckbourn's *Bedroom Farce* and Feydeau's *The Lady from Maxim's* looked at the Lyttelton as if they ought to have been in Shaftesbury Avenue; and several of the plays put on at the Olivier, the open-stage auditorium shaped like an amphitheatre, looked as if they would have gone down better at the Lyttelton with its proscenium arch. An elaborate and generally welcome revival of Harley Granville-Barker's *The Madras House*, directed by William Gaskill, looked notably displaced at the Olivier. It was, however, brilliantly designed by Hayden Griffin, and with its large cast and rarity value constituted an evening worthy of a national theatre. The same qualities of intelligent, spectacular and old-fashioned emotional drama proved even more enjoyable earlier in the year when Maximilian Schell directed Odon von Horvath's *Tales from the Vienna Woods* at the Olivier with a young actress of high promise, Kate Nelligan, playing the unhappy Austrian heroine at odds with her lover and the world of 1931.

Revivals of *Julius Caesar* and *Volpone* at the Olivier were received with respect, and the presence in the first of John Gielgud and in the second of Paul Scofield was welcomed. Since the National Theatre's move to the South Bank there had been not only a change of leadership but also an almost complete change of company. It was not therefore to be expected that, with the financial worries too, any sort of daring or original approach to its work would yet be discernible; and indeed at its supposedly experimental auditorium, the Cottesloe, used mainly for visiting companies from the provinces or abroad, the only new work of quality was Julien Mitchell's *Half-Life*, an elegant, thoughtful comedy with John Gielgud as the former head of an Oxford College. It was due to transfer to the West End in 1978.

Meanwhile at the Old Vic, which had looked desolate since the National Theatre Company's departure, a brighter future appeared with the decision in the spring to let Prospect Productions, best known for touring the classics both at home and abroad, use the National's old home as a base with Toby Robertson in charge. The company promptly staged admirable revivals of Shaw's *Saint Joan*, with Eileen Atkins in the leading role, *Hamlet*, with Derek Jacobi, *Antony and Cleopatra*, with Alec McCowen and Dorothy Tutin, *All For Love*, Dryden's echo of that last play, with Barbara Jefford and John Turner, and an adaptation of Homer's *Iliad* by Christopher Logue which was called *War Music*. Here, almost immediately and without fanfares, was a repertoire worthy of a national theatre, produced on a fraction of the National Theatre's funds at the theatre it had lately quit.

If the standard of production at the Old Vic could not match that of its former tenants, the policy seemed exemplary, and with it went a firm undertaking to keep on touring. That was more than the National Theatre could promise, and even the Royal Shakespeare Company, wreathed in success, could not satisfy the needs of playgoers beyond the reach of Stratford-on-Avon and London except to descend triumphantly on Newcastle-upon-Tyne for a few weeks in the spring with parts of its repertoire. In the hands of other managements touring, in fact, continued to sustain many provincial theatres at a time when the repertory companies found their subsidies eroded by inflation; and several productions mounted in the provinces without the West End specifically in view ended up there, including J. B. Priestley's *Laburnum Grove* at the Duke of York's as a vehicle for Arthur Lowe, and *Hedda Gabler* with Janet Suzman at the same theatre.

But despite the initiative, and attraction for critics, of certain repertory theatres such as the Glasgow Citizens' Theatre, which turned up rare plays by Noel Coward and Balzac, or the Sheffield Crucible, which engaged a Russian director to stage *The Government Inspector* and mounted simultaneously a clutch of new plays in its studio, or the Royal Exchange, Manchester, which drew actors like Albert Finney and Michael Hordern to its unusual arena stage, where Michael Elliott was the artistic director and where the policy was as unpredictable as Peter Hall's, London remained the centre of theatrical attention and most ambition.

Long runs kept the majority of theatres stagnant and the need to cater for the tastes of tourists discouraged much serious enterprise. Four established playwrights kept their reputations ticking over satisfactorily for them if not for every playgoer. Apart from Mr Nichols's *Privates on Parade* (Aldwych) and Mr Ayckbourn's *Bedroom Farce* (Lyttelton), which have already been mentioned, Mr Ayckbourn's *Just Between Ourselves* (Queen's), William Douglas-Home's *The Kingfisher* (Lyric), Robert Bolt's *State of Revolution* (Lyttelton) and Alan Bennett's *The Old Country* made effective and sometimes interesting vehicles for their leading actors—Colin Blakely for Mr Ayckbourn, Ralph Richardson and Celia Johnson for Mr Douglas-Home, Michael Bryant for Mr Bolt and Alec Guinness for Mr Bennett. Mr Blakely later discovered in Eduardo de Filippo's Neapolitan comedy, *Filumena*, a delightful vehicle at the Lyric with Joan Plowright under Franco Zeffirelli's direction; and for its first London production in English Henri de Montherlant's *La Ville dont le Prince est un Enfant* took most touchingly to the stage of the Mermaid Theatre under the title of *The Fire That Consumes* and yielded a remarkable performance by Nigel Hawthorne.

Of the established successes *The Rocky Horror Show, Jesus Christ Superstar, Oh! Calcutta!, No Sex Please—We're British* and *The Mousetrap*, which reached its 25th year, seemed immortal; and the most obvious new hit was Mary O'Malley's *Once A Catholic*, which went from the Royal Court to Wyndham's as a brisk satire on adolescent attitudes to sex and religion in a London convent school.

Arnold Wesker's *Wedding Feast* was acted at Leeds Playhouse. Barrie Keeffe's *A Mad World, My Masters* was well received at the Young Vic in a production by the Joint Stock Company, which also offered Howard Brenton's *Epsom Downs* at the Round House, Chalk Farm; and Ken Campbell's *Illuminatus*, which started life at Liverpool as an eight-hour science-fiction epic, reached London at the Cottesloe and then the Round House at a more bearable length. But it was not a year for good new plays.

The best of a batch of bad new musical comedies came from Broadway and seemed destined to run. *Bubbling Brown Sugar* reopened the Royalty Theatre, which had been a cinema. Its high Harlem spirits and dancing made it fashionable. *I Love My Wife* at the Prince of Wales Theatre gave Richard Beckinsale a good comical opportunity to look glazed at the requirements of a sexually liberated society.

On 30 November Sir Terence Rattigan died, aged 66, just when it seemed as if a taste for his well-crafted plays was coming back (see OBITUARY). *Separate Tables* had just been revived with success at the Apollo, and his last play, *Cause Célèbre*, was enjoying a good run at Her Majesty's with Glynis Johns as the heroine in a version of the Rattenbury murder case.

The New York Theatre

Three phenomena distinguished 1977—the emergence of many new or hitherto budding playwrights, some with up to three productions on the boards; the predominance of female stars, including Anne Bancroft in *Golda* (Meir), Estelle Parsons in *Miss Margarida's Way*, Colleen Dewhurst in *An Almost Perfect Person*, Liv Ullman in *Anna Christie*, and Julie Harris giving an exquisite solo performance as Emily Dickinson in *Belle of Amherst*; and continued flourishing box office business.

The Beaumont Theatre at Lincoln Centre was finally abandoned by Mr Joe Papp, who stated he could not satisfy the upper middle class subscribers with the experimental new works he preferred, after a series of near triumphs—a long run of Brecht/Weill's *Threepenny Opera* staged by Richard Foreman, *Streamers*, a strikingly original *The Cherry Orchard*, directed by Andrei Serban with Irene Worth as a thrilling Ranevskaya, and Mr Serban's version of *Agamemnon* by Aeschylus, highly theatrical, but less subtle and effective.

Downtown at The Public Theatre, Mr Papp both originated productions and gave a home to other companies: Joseph Chaikin directed a new adaptation of S. Ansky's *The Dybbuk*, both passionate and ritualistic; Strindberg's *The Stronger* and *Creditors*, brought in from the new producer of the Hudson Guild Theatre, starred Rip Torn (who directed), and Geraldine Page; *Dressed Like an Egg*, adapted from Colette's writings, presented by the imaginative Mabou Mines Company, a series of surreal images exquisitely delicate and sensuous; *The Mandrake* (Machiavelli's *Mandragola* adapted into Commedia style); two plays by the much-admired John Guare, *Marco Polo Sings a Solo*, obscure despite a distinguished cast and the invention of a country with an inspired name, 'Saudi Israel'; and *Landscape of the Body*, a 'hard rock' absurdist play with strong language and Shirley Knight.

The Manhattan Theatre Club, which had been bringing chiefly new plays for about a decade offered two weak ones in 1977—*Wayside Motor Inn* by A. J. Gurney, and the New York premiere of Peter Nichols's *Chez Nous* from England. Three of Samuel Beckett's plays there were directed with genuine authority by Alan Schneider. Beckett's *Waiting for Godot*, directed by the author, was imported to the Brooklyn Academy of Music from the West Berlin Schiller Theatre (performed in German); it could be the definitive production.

Circle In The Square presented its first Shakespeare, *Romeo and Juliet*, impaired by violent excisions and direction which reduced the tragedy to a domestic tale. There followed John Wood as Moliere's *Tartuffe*, eccentric, but surrounded by a brilliant cast; Shaw's *St Joan* with Lynn Redgrave, intelligent, amusing and crafty but lacking a devoutly passionate drive.

The Circle Repertory Company staged an admirable production of

James Joyce's only play, *Exiles*; Albert Innaurato's comic *Gemini*, as well as his *Ulysses in Traction*, too melodramatic for success; Lanford Wilson's *Brontosaurus*; and Corinne Jacker's *My Life*, a play of memory and a search for the central character's roots.

A new producer turned the small Hudson Guild Theatre into a highly professional source, introducing the Strindberg plays taken over by the Public Theatre. Christopher Hampton's *Savages* was given an excellent production, as was his *Treats*.

The American Place Theatre offered a new Steve Tesich play, *Passing Game*; Jeff Wanshel's *Isadora Duncan Sleeps with the Russian Navy*, with the exquisite Marian Seldes; a new Ronald Ribman play, *Cold Storage*, starring Martin Balsam, slated for Broadway; and Jules Feiffer's *Hold Me!*.

Independent companies off Broadway continued to turn (or in some instances, grind) out the largest number of works, from Richard Foreman's continued saga of Rhoda, his eternal heroine, to the Actors' Studio Theatre's production of *Richard III* with Ron Leibman in the title role. Elsewhere there were fine revivals and new productions ranging from *Peg o' my Heart* through Brecht, David Storey, Albee and Elmer Rice to Miguel Pinero and Peter Handke.

Broadway offered Tennessee Williams's *Vieux Carre*, a feeble auto-biographical play filled with *déja vu* passages from his superior works. David Mamet's *American Buffalo*, dealing with small-time criminals, starred Robert Duvall. The Pulitzer Prize and Tony Award play was Michael Christofer's *The Shadow Box*—family visits to terminally ill patients, neither so maudlin nor gripping as it sounds. Al Pacino revived *The Basic Training of Pavlo Hummel*; Tom Stoppard's *Dirty Linen* and *New-Found-Land* opened. From Princeton came *The Night of the Tribades* by Per Olav Enquist, brilliantly cast with Max von Sydow, Bibi Anderson and Eileen Atkins. Neil Simon's annual new play, *Chapter Two*, was serious and somewhat autobiographical, but his addiction to funny one-liners weakened it. Two major directors returned: Jose Quintero reviving O'Neill's *Touch of the Poet*, and Mike Nichols with *The Gin Game* by newcomer D. L. Coburn, starring, in its only roles, Jessica Tandy and Hume Cronin.

Musicals were bounteous. Tony Award-winning *I Love my Wife* by Michael Stewart and Cy Coleman; *Side by Side by Sondheim* from London; *Annie*, based on the comic strip, 'Little Orphan Annie'. Liza Minelli was dynamic in *The Act*; and *A Party with Betty Comden and Adolph Green* was an engaging reprise of works by and with the authors themselves. Both *The King and I* and *Man of la Mancha* were revived with their original male stars.

Arnold Wesker in *The Merchant* wrote a tribute to Shakespeare's Shylock. It starred briefly a great theatre talent, Mr Zero Mostel, who died while working on the role out of town.

MUSIC

Commissions of various kinds enabled British composers to embark on an unusual number of large-scale works during 1977, and their success went a good way towards discounting the much-publicized theory that the conventional symphony orchestra now exists only for the purpose of playing music from the past. Not unnaturally in Silver Jubilee Year the busiest composer was Malcolm Williamson, Master of the Queen's Music. The burden of his official duties was in fact so heavy that he was unable to complete two of his major commissions. Less than two-thirds of his *Mass of Christ the King* had been orchestrated in time for the Three Choirs Festival, so that only 10 of its 16 sections were performed as planned in Gloucester Cathedral, while an eleventh, a moving *Agnus Dei* in memory of Benjamin Britten, was given with organ accompaniment. Even in this form, however, it proved an impressive work, suggesting that the complete Mass would constitute a major contribution to the music of our time. There was much grateful writing for the four soloists, two choruses and full orchestra involved, and the composer once again showed his ability to fuse varying styles into a satisfying whole. Passages of easy lyricism alternated with others that were arrestingly discordant, giving a new sense of drama to a traditional form.

Williamson's other major venture, his Fourth Symphony, did not get a hearing at all. Its first performance was scheduled for a London Philharmonic Orchestra concert attended by the Queen and the Duke of Edinburgh, but only three of its four movements were completed in time. The composer at first agreed that the symphony should be played in its unfinished state, but changed his mind two days before the concert. Never before has a symphony made newspaper headlines for so many days, and it is a sad thought that the national press should consider music interesting enough for front pages only when it is not performed.

In happier circumstances, Sir Michael Tippett's Fourth Symphony was commissioned and given its first performance by the Chicago Symphony Orchestra conducted by Georg Solti. That this orchestra, certainly one of the best not only in the United States but indeed in the whole world, should so honour Britain's most distinguished living composer was heartening in itself. Even more important was the fact that so much expertise and affection were lavished on a work of the utmost complexity and individuality. In recent years most essays in this form have been symphonies in name rather than conception, as in fact was Tippett's own Third. This time, though presenting the work in a single movement, he decided to follow the structural scheme of symphonic development, albeit on his own terms. He may not have followed the classical concept of resolving opposing elements, but he certainly achieved a fusion of contrasting ideas. The symphony began by stating three different 'tempi' which were then expanded by the addition of new melodic material. These diverse elements were subsequently developed and finally integrated with a fine sense of symphonic logic. Special features of the writing included climbing figures in the brass, imaginative use of harp, piano and glockenspiel, and an important role assigned to a wind-machine.

The most important private commission of the year was that offered to Priaulx Rainier by Yehudi Menuhin, who proceeded to give her Violin Concerto its first performance at the Edinburgh Festival with the Royal Philharmonic Orchestra. The composer forestalled objections that the work did not follow strict sonata form by giving it the title *Due Canti e Finale*. True to the spirit of this title, the music for the soloist was mainly song-like in character, though often energetic and always capable of holding its own against the lively orchestral opposition. Charles Groves conducted with such keen sense of balance that Menuhin was able to generate meditative warmth as well as virtuoso brilliance in his playing.

Another impressive new work on a large scale, though more radical in every way, was John Buller's *Proença*, commissioned by the BBC for its annual season of Promenade Concerts at the Royal Albert Hall. This represented a considerable act of faith, since Buller, though a man of 50, was virtually unknown. *Proença* took its name from the composer's special interest in thirteenth-century troubadour songs with Provençal texts. Scored for large orchestra, electric guitar and solo mezzo-soprano, this 40-minute piece created an exotic atmosphere. Its eleven sections alternated songs of intense passion with others denouncing the institutions of the day, the Church included. It made an immediate appeal, though one was left wondering why an English composer should choose to set a series of poems in the old Provençal tongue which not a single member of the audience was likely to understand. Mark Elder conducted the BBC Symphony Orchestra with easy confidence, and the accomplished soloists were Timothy Walker (guitar) and Sarah Walker.

Also a 'Prom' commission was a piece by Richard Rodney Bennett for solo horn and orchestra entitled *Actaeon*, based on the Greek legend of the huntsman turned into a stag by the offended goddess Artemis and then hunted to death by his own hounds. A concerto in all but name, with a haunting central Pastorale, it made pleasant listening and brought a dazzling show of virtuosity from soloist Barry Tuckwell, for whom it had been expressly written.

The Proms also gave two British premieres of works by major European composers, Hans Werner Henze and Luciano Berio. The former's *Raft of the Medusa*, an oratorio zestfully conducted by David Atherton, was an example of a work with a declared political purpose which turned out to be blatant propaganda. The words of the Narrator (Gerald English) were always clear, but those of the two singing soloists, John Shirley-Quirk and

Phyllis Bryn Julson, were sometimes obscured. The music was certainly forceful, but it seemed doubtful whether the didactic political approach would ultimately prove an advantage to the composer.

Berio himself conducted his *Coro*, an elaborate work for 40 solo voices and the same number of solo instrumentalists. Piano, electric organ and percussion were prominently featured. The skilfully constructed work, which lasted about an hour, drew on folk songs from all parts of the world, though these were not always sung in their original languages. The mood of the music ranged from primitive urgency to languorous stillness. There was no denying the composer's originality and integrity, but as so often with contemporary music one was left wondering whether it would ever win wide acceptance.

The London Sinfonietta continued to champion the younger British composer and successfully brought forward Brian Ferneyhough, whose music had hitherto been better known abroad than at home. His *Transit*, scored for vocal sextet and orchestra, was at least a *succès d'estime*, making it quite clear that he has a wholly individual creative talent. To help the audience to come to grips with the music, the composer was given the first half of the concert to discuss the music with 'live' illustrations. It was sad that the Sinfonietta, which had done so much pioneering work of this kind, should find itself at the end of the year in a worse financial state than ever before. Presenting new and experimental music is a costly business, and such programmes rarely draw big audiences. Ironically it was this British orchestra, which had received only a very small subsidy, that had perhaps done more than any other to win prestige abroad.

In general the standard of performance at concerts in London and the provinces remained encouragingly high. Most orchestras were able to break even at the end of the year, taking subsidies from various sources into account, some even showing slight profits. Attendance figures were gratifying too, though this was achieved only by tailoring programmes to public taste. Adventurousness was rarely rewarded.

Record companies again provided some of the most unusual, and lasting, pleasures. At long last *Boris Godunov* was recorded in the original Mussorgsky version, with Martti Talvela heading a fine cast conducted by Jerzy Semkow. Adrian Boult, conducting the London Philharmonic Orchestra, achieved what might well remain for all time the definitive reading of Elgar's First Symphony. On the avant-garde front, Karlheinz Stockhausen's *Trans*, a major work not yet performed in Britain, was featured twice on one disc. One side was devoted to the world premiere (1971), conducted by Ernest Bour, the other to a studio recording (1973) with Hans Zender conducting.

The deaths occurred during the year of conductors Leopold Stokowski (see OBITUARY) and Edouard Van Remoortel; composers Alexander Tcherepnin and Grace Williams; pianists Witold Malcuzynski and Lisa

Fuchsova; harpsichordist Lucille Wallace; organist E. Power Biggs; and violinist Reginald Morley.

THE CINEMA

The death of Sir Charles Chaplin on Christmas day 1977 ended a creative life that had spanned almost the entire historical development of the film and the cinema industry. Chaplin had first joined Mack Sennett's newly-established Keystone Studios in 1913, when Hollywood was still embryonic. In 1977 the American film industry was in a fragmented and much diminished state. American film-making sank to its lowest level quantitatively, with its remaining production increasingly dispersed round the world, the result largely of individual enterprise by well-established producer-directors, or by the brash and energetic younger generation anxious to seize the limelight.

Soaring costs had made production increasingly hazardous. *A Bridge too Far*, the British war epic made with American backing, cost its producer, Joe Levine, some $25 million. However, the American and European distribution rights and the first American television rights combined to cover the vast production commitment in advance of release. The new principle seemed to be the bigger the risk the surer the success. *Jaws*, for example, combining the fashion for disaster spectacles with those involving some sort of monster, took some $200 million at the box office. *Star Wars*, the American space fantasy, proved an all-time success. Like its predecessor, *2001*, it had made use of experienced British technicians to achieve its spectacular special effects; and costly successors were planned. In the smaller bracket of production costs, *Rocky*, at one million dollars, brought United Artists $50 million, while Mel Brooks's *Young Frankenstein*, which cost $2 million, grossed $52 million for Twentieth-Century-Fox.

British film-making remained small-scale precisely because it lacked over-all finance. The soundest backing came either from American sources or from television, led by Lord Grade, who in May claimed to be investing up to $125 million in future projects. Another sound source for finance was EMI (which in 1976 had absorbed British Lion), but its production interests lay primarily in America, though the Agatha Christie novel, *Death on the Nile*, was to be made largely in Britain as a successor to the profitable *Murder on the Orient Express*.

Meanwhile the British film-makers' trade union, the ACTT, continued to call for the establishment of a British Film Authority to secure the survival of the industry, and Sir Harold Wilson's official working party on the industry recommended that it should receive a government grant of not less than £5 million to assist its rehabilitation. Admissions to British cinemas, however, reached the lowest level ever in 1976, standing at 107 million for the year. But not all was negative in the film world— Canada, both French and English-speaking, and Australia, with much higher ratios of cinemas to population than in Britain, had begun to establish themselves as regular centres for feature production, while the West German Federal Film Board, with a fund amounting to $7·5 million supporting production, plus further subsidies from individual Länder and backing from television, ensured continuity of work for the new generation of German film-makers, such as Fassbinder, Herzog and Wenders.

Taking the English-language films first, the large-scale productions of the year included *King Kong* (John Guillermin) and *Star Wars* (George Lucas). The revival of interest in war films was shown in Sir Richard Attenborough's all-star film of the Arnhem debacle, *A Bridge too Far*, Sam Peckinpah's Anglo-German *Cross of Iron*, John Sturges's *The Eagle has Landed* and the Israeli film *Entebbe*, in the end the best of the three competing versions of the notorious hijack of July 1976. Films with a political background were Stuart Rosenberg's *Voyage of the Damned* (the Jewish refugee ship sailing from Hamburg in May 1939), John Frankenheimer's film of terrorism in the Middle East, *Black Sunday*, and Robert Aldrich's controversial thriller, *Twilight's Last Gleaming*, with its corrosive portrait of a fictional American President facing crisis on a rocket site.

Many films drew on historical, literary or theatrical sources. Fred Zinnemann's *Julia* (with Jane Fonda, Vanessa Redgrave) was based on Lillian Hellman's autobiographical story. Peter Bogdanovich's *Nickelodeon* returned nostalgically to the American cinema of 1910-15, while Abraham Polonsky's *Romance of a Horse-Thief* was set in a Jewish community in rural Poland at the turn of the century, conceived with the romantic nostalgia of an ancestral fairytale. John Huston's *A Walk with Love and Death* (from the novel by Hans Koningsberger) made protest against indiscriminate violence in a story of fourteenth-century Europe. Trevor Nunn's *Hedda* (Glenda Jackson) presented a savage portrayal of Ibsen's heroine, and Joseph Strick's *Portrait of the Artist as a Young Dog* proved a realistic rather than an imaginative or allusive rendering of Joyce's evocative story. Tony Richardson's *Joseph Andrews* (Peter Firth, Michael Hordern) was a pale sequel to his *Tom Jones*.

Elia Kazan's version of *The Last Tycoon*, with Robert De Niro heading an exceptionally distinguished cast, was adapted by Harold Pinter, but suffered by bringing the rich implications of Scott Fitzgerald's story too realistically down to earth. Similarly, Sidney Lumet's adaptation of *Equus* (Peter Firth, Richard Burton), with its realistic presentation of the horses and their blinding, deprived Shaffer's play of the effectively theatrical symbolism it achieved on the stage. In the area of the psychological film, Alfred Sole's *Communion*, with a virtually unknown cast, presented an extraordinary and complex study of subconscious guilt in the form of a thriller with significant undertones set in an Italian Catholic community in New Jersey. Another outstanding, if ambivalent, psychological study was Robert Altman's *3 Women*, concerning the interrelationship of three young therapists in a Californian rehabilitation centre. Sydney Pollack's *Bobby Deerfield* (Al Pacino, Marthe Keller) also exposed a nervous and confused relationship between a champion racing driver and his mistress. Another film, British and low-budget, Simon Perry's *Eclipse*, dealt subtly with the oppressive relationship of two brothers.

Sport featured in several films—notably in *Rocky* (John V. Avilsen) with Silvester Stallone, who wrote the brilliant script as well as starring, and won a notable Oscar on this initial showing of his talent. In *Slap Shot*, George Roy Hill with Paul Newman exposed dirty play in ice hockey, whereas *The Greatest* (Tom Gries) featured Muhammad Ali himself, but was more hagiography than biography. Show business received its airing in *Bound for Glory* (Hal Ashby, with David Carradine), based on Woody Guthrie's autobiography, in Martin Scorsese's *New York, New York* (Liza Minnelli; Robert De Niro), in Alan Rudolph's *Welcome to L.A.*, and in Paul Mazursky's *Next Stop, Greenwich Village* (Lenny Baker, Shelley Winters), in which an aspirant young actor strives for independence from his possessive mother. Ken Russell's much-publicized *Valentino* showed Rudolf Nureyev posing his way through a version of Valentino's chequered life in Hollywood of the 1920s.

For comedy and satire there were Orson Welles's *F for Fake*, Robert Benton's *The Late Show* (Art Carney, Lily Tomlin), Alan Arkin's comic misanthropy in *Fire Sale*, Ivan Passer's *Silver Bears* (Michael Caine heading a distinguished cast), and Jeff Lieberman's zany and paranoiac *Blue Sunshine*. Michael Schultz's first two films as director, *Cooley High* and *Car Wash*, revealed an original new talent in the modern-styled comedy of manners.

Outstanding for the bitterness of its attack on American commercial television, Sidney Lumet's *Network* (Faye Dunaway, William Holden, Peter Finch) was also notable for Peter Finch's final screen appearance in the unsuitable part of a latterday television prophet. Ted Kotcheff's *Fun with Dick and Jane*, while often entertaining, played a sour joke on the American dream of success at any price, while Woody Allen's *Annie Hall* (with himself and Diane Keaton) achieved wry humour out of contemporary disillusion. Though not strictly comedy, since it revealed deep frustration as well as ebullient humour in the black population of Brixton, London, Anthony Simmons's *Black Joy* was probably the best film yet about Britain's immigrant blacks.

It was an outstanding year for imported, foreign language films, with France, Italy, and West Germany in the lead for quality work, often in the form of co-productions. The marked revival in the West German cinema was further demonstrated by the continuous output of films by Rainer

Werner Fassbinder (*Wild Game*), Werner Herzog (*The Great Ecstasy of Woodcarver Steiner*, a short film, and *Heart of Glass*), Wim Wenders (*Wrong Movement; Kings of the Road*) and Hans Jürgen Syerberg (*Ludwig —Requiem for a Virgin King*). French-Swiss production continued to be led by the outstanding talents of Alain Tanner (*The Middle of the World*) and Claude Goretta (*The Lace-maker*). From France there were films from Jean-Luc Godard (*Number Two*), Georges Franju (a fantasy, *Shadowman*), François Truffaut (*The Story of Adele H; Small Change*), Michael Drach (*Les Violons du Bal*, an autobiographical film), Walerian Borowczyk (*Immoral Tales*, the iconography of lust; *The Streetwalker*, the purgatory of a man ensnared by erotic fantasies), Costa-Gavras (*Section Spéciale*— a study of French collaboration with the Nazis during the occupation), Bertrand Tavernier (*The Watchmaker of Saint-Paul*, an accomplished first film involving the relationship of father and son), Claude Chabrol (*Love Match*), Eduardo de Gregorio (*Sérail*, with Leslie Caron, Bulle Ogier, Corin Redgrave) and Marguerite Duras (*India Song*, with Delphine Seyrig). From Italy came Marco Bellocchio's *In the Name of the Father* (made in 1971), Bernardo Bertolucci's *The Spider's Stratagem* (with Alida Valli, made in 1970), and the *Padre Padrone* of Paolo and Vittorio Taviani, based on the extraordinary autobiographical novel by the former shepherd, Gavino Ledda. Francesco Rosi's study of conspiracy and assassination, *Illustrious Corpses*, added to his remarkable series of films uncovering political duplicity in Italy. Fellini's *Casanova*, with its fantastic decor and photography and a fine performance by Donald Sutherland, excited critical controversy between those who saw it as a fable of the *reductio ad absurdum* of sensuality and decadence and those who considered it only as an example of self-indulgent showmanship. Miklós Jancsó's *Private Vices and Public Virtues*, an Italian-Yugoslav co-production, abandoned his previous long-take technique in a political fable of rebellion within a romantic-seeming monarchy. Joseph Losey's *Mr Klein* (Alain Delon, Jeanne Moreau) exposed anti-semitism in French society in Kafka-like terms.

Lastly, in the Asian cinema, Satyajit Ray produced a characteristically quiet masterpiece in *The Middleman*, a study in disillusion in contemporary commercial practice in India made with great humour and forming a companion film to *Company Limited*, while a new Indian director, Girish Karnad, produced in *The Forest* (made in 1973) a work with a similar atmospheric richness of detail. Two outstanding films from Japan were Shuji Terayama's *Pastoral Hide-and-Seek* (1974) and Tadashi Imai's *Brother and Sister*.

Among the prominent personalities who died during 1977, in addition to Sir Charles Chaplin, were Sir Michael Balcon, Herbert Wilcox, Howard Hawks, Tay Garnett, Roberto Rossellini, Zero Mostel, Peter Finch, Bing Crosby, Joan Crawford, Elvis Presley, Henri Clouzot, John Hubley,

America's most imaginative animation director, and Henri Langlois, the eminent French film archivist. (For Chaplin, Rossellini, Finch, Crosby, Crawford and Presley, see OBITUARY).

TELEVISION AND RADIO

For those concerned with the business of communications, 1977 was the year which at last saw the publication of the long-awaited Annan report on the Future of Broadcasting. The fruit of three years' intensive labour, it proved to be a massive White Paper running to 522 pages and more than 250,000 words, presented to Parliament on 23 March.

The most important of its recommendations concerned the disposition of the fourth television channel, arguably the main reason for setting up the Committee under Lord Annan, Provost of University College, London. Since the late 1960s contending lobbies had pressed vigorously for the award of this rich prize. The most urgent pleas came from the independent television companies, who complained bitterly of unfair handicapping in their competition with the two BBC channels. Others wanted TV 4 to be allocated to some cultural use, such as education.

The Annan Committee adopted a proposal submitted to them by a number of broadcasters and academics. This was that the fourth channel should be put in charge of an entirely new body, the Open Broadcasting Authority (OBA), which would commission programmes from any suitable sources, such as the Open University, the existing ITV companies, and (particularly important, in the Committee's view) bona-fide independent producers. The OBA would be financed from 'block' advertising and rigidly-controlled, non-commercial sponsorship. It would be relieved of the obligations to 'balance' programmes and, above all, to compete with the other channels.

The Committee's aims in making this recommendation were to break the broadcasting 'duopoly' of the BBC and ITV and to encourage diversity. 'A great opportunity would be missed if the fourth channel were seen solely in terms of extending the present range of programmes', they wrote. 'In our belief an ITV-2 will result in worse television services than we have now, because the BBC and ITV will engage in a self-destructive battle for the ratings. To perpetuate the duopoly would be to stultify new initiatives. . . . We believe our recommendations could bring fresh air into the system and help broadcasting to evolve rather than ossify.'

Paradoxically, the Committee's proposal to put all local radio under another new institution, the Local Broadcasting Authority, seemed to be a move away from diversity and towards monopoly. It would mean the end of the 20 local stations at present run by the BBC and the 19 operated under the wing of the IBA. This was too much for three of the 16 committee members, who wrote notes of dissent chiefly in support of the BBC.

Two more new bodies envisaged by Annan were a Complaints Commission and a Public Enquiry Board, which would hold regular enquiries into the general conduct of broadcasting.

The Annan Committee, set up originally by the Labour Government in 1970, disbanded by its Conservative successor and reconvened in 1974, was given a brief to survey virtually every aspect of broadcasting in Britain, except the external services of the BBC. This remit was matched by an equally comprehensive response, covering in its elegantly written and highly readable pages almost every imaginable topic: screen violence, sexual permissiveness, audience ratings, cable TV, party political broadcasts (which the Committee suggested should not be put out simultaneously on all channels), advertising and technical research. Some of the Report's most trenchant prose set out the Committee's views of the present broadcasting institutions. They were especially scathing about the organizational shortcomings of the BBC, and of that institution's 'loss of nerve'. 'We are left with an uneasy feeling that some of the finest attributes of the BBC showed signs of decay. . . . We do not think that the BBC as it is organized at present can achieve its programming objectives. . . . The BBC sees itself as beleaguered, pressurized, lobbied and compelled to lobby.' BBC television handling of current affairs was particularly criticized as 'patchy, dull, and on occasions superficial to the point of banality'.

Despite this, a move by a six-strong minority on the Committee, headed by Philip Whitehead, MP (Labour), to advocate splitting the BBC into separate radio and television corporations, on the grounds that most of its ills stemmed from sheer size and the crushing effect of 'a vast, omnipresent bureaucracy', was warded off by the majority ten. In the end the Committee concurred in its overall view: 'The BBC is arguably the single most important cultural organization in the nation. It has over many years raised the level of taste and discrimination and such has been its success that austere critics bitterly attack the BBC for not raising it higher.'

In contrast ITV, while receiving praise for many individual achievements, and greatly improving its overall quality over the past decade, was found to be 'settled in well-worn grooves . . . safe, stereotyped, and routine in its production'.

The BBC's financial position was slightly eased by the announcement in July of new licence fees of £21 (previously £18) for colour and £9 (previously £8) for monochrome. It was expected that this would augment the BBC's income by some £38 million to about £300 million. As compensation for two and a half years of cost inflation on a fixed income, however, the increases were considered disappointing. By comparison, licence fees on the Continent (as at 1 December 1977) ranged from £30.50 in France to £61.50 in Denmark. The BBC were also alarmed by the apparent intention of the Government to award future increases on a yearly basis, effectively converting the licence to a government grant. They estimated that by mid-1978 their deficit would be running at £17 million. Colour licences at the end of the year numbered 10,604,874 against 7,483,492 for monochrone, as opposed to parity some 15 months before.

ITV's finances, derived almost entirely from advertising revenue, continued to flourish. At the end of 1977 the estimated income of the companies was just under £298 million, 29 per cent more than in 1976.

Prominent among programmes seen on British television in 1977 were several major adaptations from well-known literary classics. Of these the most ambitious, and by general consent the least successful, was *Anna Karenina*, screened as a ten-part serial on BBC-2. Despite some good detail and much effective location filming in Britain and Hungary, critics felt that neither Nicola Pagett's Anna nor Donald Wilson's script came close enough to the essence of Tolstoy's tragedy. In contrast there was little but praise for Granada's more compressed (four episodes) version of *Hard Times*, produced at a reputed cost of £500,000, which vividly re-created the living and working conditions of Dickensian industrial England. For sheer verbal brilliance, no screen drama in 1977 quite matched *Professional Foul* (BBC-2), Tom Stoppard's first TV play about a devious British professor caught up in ethical tangles in Czechoslovakia.

Religion featured strongly in the year's documentary output. On ITV there was Bamber Gascoigne's *The Christians*; on BBC-2 Ronald Eyre, hitherto best known as a theatre director, explored all the faiths in *The Long Search*. Apartheid, subject of many television investigations, was put under a highly personal microscope by Anthony Thomas in *The South African Experience* from ATV, while with *The Case Of Yolande McShane* Yorkshire Television pushed the boundaries of the permissible a stage further by screening police tapes of a woman incriminating herself. Zeffirelli's long-delayed biblical epic *Jesus of Nazareth* was seen in two three-hour parts on ITV, and won general approbation for its magnificent pictorial quality, though some found it too sentimental. Both ex-President Nixon and ex-Prime Minister Sir Harold Wilson made extended TV appearances, respectively on BBC-1 and ITV, in interviews with David Frost.

Ian Trethowan, former managing director of BBC Television, succeeded Sir Charles Curran as director-general of the BBC.

In Canada, the resounding victory won by Quebec nationalists in the provincial elections of 1976 led to a politically-inspired inquiry into Canadian broadcasting. The independent Canadian Radio-Television and Telecommunications Commission (CRTC) was charged by the Government to determine whether the Canadian Broadcasting Corporation (CBC) had fulfilled their statutory obligation to 'contribute to the development of national unity'. Some politicians alleged that the CBC's French network was 'riddled with separatists' who had produced biased, anti-federal programmes.

In the outcome, CBC were given a clean bill of health and congratulated on the public confidence they enjoyed. At the same time the CRTC recognized that there was insufficient interaction between the French and English communities in Canada, and that broadcasters must bear their share of blame in failing to promote this.

The civic responsibilities of broadcasters were also considered in the report of Sweden's three-year-old Committee on Broadcasting, published ten days after the Annan Report, which recommended an increase in television transmission from 80 to 100 hours weekly, and on radio from 360 to 440 hours. It also suggested that Sweden should apply for a frequency allocation for a fourth radio channel. The report laid much emphasis on broadcasting's role in providing Swedish citizens with the information they needed to take an active part in the democratic process. The Committee seemed uncertain, however, whether freedom of expression would best be served by decentralization or by continuing the present control of broadcasting by a single national organization.

In the United States a long-term battle over one of the major television events of 1980, the Moscow Olympics, was won by NBC, one of the 'big three' American networks. Bidding against the rival ABC and CBS, they agreed to pay the Russians a total of $72 million for rights and facilities, and a further $12·6 million to the International Olympic Committee. The victory was important to NBC, who had fallen badly behind ABC in the all-important audience ratings. But at a total price in excess of $100 million, including production expenses, it could be a costly one.

In Argentina an announcement by the military Government appeared to herald the return of some TV networks to private hands, after a four-year suspension of the main commercial licences. Meanwhile a special TV organization, Argentina 78 Televisora, was set up with help from the European Broadcasting Union to cover the 1978 World Cup. Some $3 million-worth of new equipment was ordered from the United States for the occasion. But it seemed likely that Argentinian audiences would still watch the matches in black and white.

In India the change of Government opened up the exciting possibility that a ten-year-old report advocating independence for the state-controlled broadcasting services might at last be implemented. Meanwhile both AIR (All-India Radio) and Door Darshan (Television) enjoyed greater freedom of operation than they had ever known under the Congress Party. For the first time, genuine political controversy was permissible on the Indian air waves.

A four-year-old BBC proposal for an independent, multilingual European news service looked as if it might come to fruition in 1978. Provisionally called 'EuroRadio', the service would pool facilities and expertise from all the EEC countries and would attempt to project a

European, as opposed to a national, perspective of events. For the time being, EuroRadio would be confined to one half-hour bulletin prepared in London and broadcast in the domestic services of the EEC countries.

An even more ambitious plan for regular news exchanges, covering television and radio, was announced by the Asian Broadcasting Union. Because of the vast distances and relatively limited microwave or satellite links involved, this would depend very considerably on the physical exchange of news film, with Teheran, Hong Kong, Kuala Lumpur and Tokyo as main staging posts.

On the technical front, Electronic News Gathering (ENG) using miniaturized cameras and tape-recorders became a reality in Britain. The BBC invested £120,000 in a year-long experimental use of the new system, which cuts out time-wasting film processes and can relay instant news, when required, via microwave links. In the United States, CBS had abandoned film entirely in favour of ENG.

The BBC also launched the first regular radio service in quadraphony, using a new, cheap system developed by BBC engineers and known as 'Matrix H'.

Two of the world's smaller states, Guinea and the Bahamas, inaugurated regular television services. The newly liberalized Spanish TV service announced plans to treble the transmission time of its second channel.

Chapter 2

ART

PARADOXICALLY, 1977 proved an unusually interesting year for the art public, while increasingly the effects of inflation-recession were felt by the art world behind the scenes, by artists and administrators.

For the public it was a year of great exhibitions, confounding the prophets of the end of the huge international show. Most typical perhaps was the totally untypical opening in Paris, in February, on schedule (seven years a-building) and on budget, the brainchild of President Pompidou, of the Centre National d'Art et de Culture Georges Pompidou, familiarly known as the Beaubourg, and nick-named the Pompidouleum. The building was almost universally acclaimed by art and architecture critics. Its arresting appearance, that of a glass box with an exo-skeleton of pipes and struts, external staircases, service pipes differentiated by brilliant colours, and a zig-zag escalator along one main façade, was devised by the Anglo-Italian team of Rogers and Piano. The building, as a place to go, was ahead of the Eiffel Tower. The culture-as-fun-palace-for-the-people had arrived (see also p. 421).

The Beaubourg houses not only one of Paris's first public reference libraries, but also the Centre de Création Industrielle, the National Museum of Modern Art, and the premier exhibition space for international contemporary art for all of France. In its first 11 months, massive exhibitions included the opening show devoted to Marcel Duchamp and a survey of artistic relationships this century between Paris and New York. The Beaubourg also initiated travelling exhibitions to the provinces.

The Beaubourg—which incidentally also houses Pierre Boulez's institute of experimental music, underground, and a replica of Brancusi's studio in the traffic-free square just outside—exemplifies to a rather heart-rending degree the strengths and weaknesses in the art world of the 1970s. Behind the Beaubourg is state money. To build and finance it was a political decision, taken during the turbulent but financially euphoric 1960s. To staff it, run it, and keep it solvent in the late 1970s is a major headache, exacerbated by a change in philosophy that may reflect economics and certainly affects art. Small is beautiful is a fairly new cry, as is decentralization and its corollorary, regionalism. So while the public flocks— in numbers five to ten times as great as the most optimistic forecasts—to the Beaubourg, its administrators face both worrying financial problems and ideological opposition to the kind of cultural imperialism that Beaubourg represents to many.

All over the West, museums public and private faced financial crises. The Museum of Modern Art in New York continued its fight to build a skyscraper in its own air-space in expectation of thus achieving financial solvency; the Metropolitan, New York, announced its highly controversial intention to make its new head (to be appointed in 1978) an administrator-cum-businessman rather than an art historian. In Britain, the Victoria and Albert closed every Friday, curtailed the opening times of its several out-posts (for example, Apsley House) by as much as one-fourth, cancelled several proposed exhibitions and promised further cuts in services. Its circulation department, which supplied the whole country with travelling exhibitions, was dismantled after over 130 years of service. Some university museums were in just as dire straits, the Fitzwilliam, Cambridge, opening only half its galleries at any one time. Paradoxically, the Royal Academy had an exceptionally active and successful year. Nearly 100,000 people visited its celebration of British painting to mark the Queen's Jubilee; another major exhibition there was that of the newly cleaned and beautifully mounted anatomical drawings by Leonardo da Vinci from the Queen's Collection.

Throughout the West gigantic exhibitions of art were held. A genuine 'first' was that of unofficial Soviet art at the Institute of Contemporary Arts, London, with which 1977 opened; and, in the late autumn, an extra Venice Biennale was devoted, despite political opposition and difficulty, to the art of dissent and dissidents, notably those from Eastern Europe and

Russia, in various media, from literature to the plastic arts. Meanwhile, West Germany's massive Documenta, the sixth since the concept was started in Kassel after World War II, brought together hundreds of contemporary artists in as many media as possible: video, performance, the artist's book, sculpture, environment, installations, as well as photography and even conventional easel painting. The most interesting, and dispiriting, section was that from East Germany, dubbed by irreverent Westerners as 'social surrealism'. However, over all the inevitable controversy and excitement raised by such a massive international compilation of today's art hung a sad sense of *déja vu*. A few outstanding works and artists were not sufficient to dispel an undeniable air of weariness, which indeed was to be found later in the year, in the autumn in Paris, in the 10th anniversary exhibition of the 'Biennale des Jeunes'. Young or old, everybody was looking more at whence than at whither.

This was typified by the three major autumn exhibitions in America. Intense excitement was justifiably generated by the exhibition of Matisse paper cut-outs (National Gallery, Washington, Detroit Institute of Arts) and the late paintings of Cézanne (MOMA, New York). The Jasper Johns retrospective (Whitney, New York) opened in an atmosphere of almost hysterical excitement, only to play to diminishing houses and rather carping later criticisms. Further, the exhibition of the year (if one excepts the remarkable collection devoted to early Christian and late classical art, 300-700 A D, that closed the year at the Metropolitan) was that held under the auspices of the Council of Europe in four parts in West Berlin, called 'Trends of the Twenties'. Dada, surrealism, constructivism and architecture were surveyed against their political, economic and social background. The exhibition was a popular success beyond any of the organizers' expectations. It could be seen as reflecting partly the view that the 1920s were a time of crisis for which parallels could be found now, and partly a growing admiration of, and understanding for, the purposeful energy and intelligence with which many artists met then the challenge of their times. Rosc, the Irish occasional international survey of contemporary art, was held in Dublin in August, and a feeble splutter it was, particularly pathetic when set against the fervour of the Berlin expositions.

It was becoming more evident in the 1970s, with the increasing importance of public money as the major source of subsidy and patronage for the visual arts, that a good deal of the concerns of contemporary artists, and the allied support-systems of specialist art magazines, contemporary public collections and state agencies, were becoming more rather than less remote from the interests of the majority. Consequently there was an air of uneasiness about the specific problem of spending public money on coterie interests, although public support of other spheres of minority interests was often not looked at so critically.

The celebration of the 400th anniversary of the birth of the great

O

Flemish artist Peter Paul Rubens was justly marked all over Western Europe; for during his activity as painter—and diplomat—there was hardly a country of Western Europe untouched by his talent. Germany (Cologne), Belgium (Antwerp) and England (the British Museum) were among the hosts and organizers of unusually splendid exhibitions of the art of Rubens.

Another anniversary, that of the so-called 'father of modern art', Gustav Courbet (1819-77), was marked by an Anglo-French exhibition at the Grand Palais in the autumn. Like Rubens, Courbet as an artist was still being radically re-assessed, and each may be taken as a pattern of one extreme or another: Rubens at the heart of the Establishment, Courbet's career based in part on being publicly anti-Establishment.

London remained the centre of the art market, although Christie's decision to open in New York as well, as Sotheby's had done several years ago, implied a further impetus to New York's challenge to London's post-war supremacy in the art market. The major auction houses each reported further records; most notable, however, was wild fluctuation in the prices obtained by artifacts and art of the nineteenth and twentieth centuries.

The sale of the contents of the Rothschild mansion, Mentmore, after the failure of a concerted campaign by interested parties to pressurize the British Government, in the name of the national heritage, to come to some arrangement whereby Mentmore could be saved for the nation, was conducted by Sotheby's and billed as the sale of the century with some accuracy, coming to a final total of over £6 million. Several paintings were purchased for the National Gallery. In Britain, the debate over the possible use of Somerset House, now refurbished, as a Turner Museum, continued; the Tate Gallery trustees resolutely refused to cooperate, partly on grounds of conservation and security requirements. Meanwhile, 20 rarely-seen Turner paintings, mostly early, and three only recently rediscovered, were exhibited at the Tate in the autumn, to mark the publication of the complete catalogue of Turner paintings (by Martin Butlin and Evelyn Joll, Yale University Press).

Nationalism and patriotism continued to help the arts expand. Examples from 1977 included the opening of the major Canadian wing of the Art Gallery of Ontario, and the first museum devoted to twentieth-century fine art, mainly European and American, in Teheran. Further indications of the spread of culture: the first touring exhibition from London's National Gallery (Venetian paintings from the permanent collection), which started in Wolverhampton; the increasing intellectual respectability of photography; and in general, through adult and further education and the cultural institutions, the promotion of culture including the visual arts over as wide a class and geographical area as the world had yet seen. However, there were seemingly intractable gaps. There seemed as yet in Europe to be no satisfactory manner of using contemporary art and artists for public works; the sculpture exhibited at Documenta was controversial and in the main ridiculed as both wasteful and pointless. Even so, in Yorkshire (Bretton Hall), England's first public sculpture park opened; in London, the Department of the Environment placed some contemporary sculpture in Regent's Park and Hyde Park; and in America corporations continued to fund public sculpture, although Oldenburg's latest piece, a baseball bat, called 'Batcolumn' and 100 feet tall, aroused bitter controversy in Chicago.

The deaths were reported of the constructivist sculptor, Naum Gabo, in August, at the age of 87; of the British painter Keith Vaughan, in November; and Jack Bush, Canadian colour-field painter.

A noteworthy contribution to the history of art was made by the largest-ever book prize, the Mitchell Prize, inaugurated in the autumn with an award of $10,000 to Professor Francis Haskell for *Re-discoveries in Art*. Other art books published in 1977 included:

Rubens and Italy by Michael Jaffe (Phaidon Press).
The Notebooks of Edgar Degas by Theodore Reff (Oxford University Press).
Sculpture by Rudolf Wittkower (Allen Lane).
Romanesque Art by Meyer Shapiro (Chatto and Windus).
Man Ray by Arturo Schwartz (Thames and Hudson).
Surrealism by Gaeton Picon (Macmillan).
Corregio by Cecil Gould (Faber).

ARCHITECTURE

The year was another gloomy one for the building industry, and architects in the UK were depressed about the future. In the spring it was predicted that 30 per cent of the architectural staffs in the south-west were surplus, and a survey had shown that 2,500 architects (90 per cent of whom had come from the private sector) had been laid off in the last 12 months. Architects' earnings over the past year had risen just over 6 per cent against an inflation rate of 17½ per cent. In December the figures for new commissions placed in the previous three months were the lowest ever recorded. Before that, however, the building industry, led by the Royal Institute of British Architects (RIBA), had decided that collective action was needed.

Headed by Eric Lyons, PRIBA, a high-powered delegation representing all sectors of the building industry met the Prime Minister, in June, explained the industry's plight, and what was needed. Mr Callaghan made it quite clear that the Government's main concern was the fight against inflation. There could be no immediate increase in public spending, but construction would be high on the priority list when times improved. In December the delegation, led by the RIBA's next president Gordon Graham, met the Chancellor of the Exchequer, Denis Healey, who accepted the moving-belt system of construction planning. This meant that road maintenance and some replanning could go ahead at once so that projects could start immediately they were given the green light. Previously, in his November mini-budget, the Chancellor had allowed an additional £400 million to be spent on public sector construction during 1978-79, half of which would go on housing in England, and enable construction programmes to be kept working steadily.

Economics aside, other influences were at work during the year to concern the architectural profession, and to pose problems for the future. A joint Commonwealth Association of Architects and International Union of Architects meeting in Kuala Lumpur in June concluded that changes should be considered to allow architects in South-East Asia to work as developers, if necessary, provided there were safeguards to ensure the integrity of architects working professionally for the public. In July the RIBA Council in England voted that its members could advertise themselves. This raised a hullabaloo amongst the membership, particularly in the provinces, and in October the Council rescinded its decision by 42 votes to 4. However, there was to be no respite for the membership, which received another shake-up in November when the Monopolies and Mergers Commission's report to the Government on the architectural profession stated that the profession's conditions of engagement and current scale of fees were against the public interest and should be abolished. Instead there should be a recommended fee scale, and fee quotation in competition should be allowed. The Secretary of State for Prices and Consumer Protection would discuss with the architectural bodies concerned the best way to bring the changes into force. The RIBA's reaction to the report's proposals was that they were completely unacceptable.

In regard to town planning policies, two events in the year centred around government action. Early on, the Government had stated its resolve to regenerate the economic activity of major city inner areas, reversing the policy of two decades ago when firms had been encouraged to leave them. The new aim was to create more jobs, mainly in industry, in order to reduce poverty and attendant problems. Studies carried out for the Government in Liverpool, Birmingham and London, respectively by Hugh Wilson and Lewis Womersley, Llewelyn-Davies, Weeks, Forestier-Walker & Bor, and Shankland Cox Partnership, in association with the Institute of Community Studies, were made public in January. All the advice emphasized that industrial regeneration must be integrated with appropriate housing, education and welfare services, and that development funds would need to be transferred from outer to inner city areas. In April the Chancellor of the Exchequer said he would provide £100 million for construction work in inner city areas to be spread over the next two years.

The other major planning issue was the Government's decision in November to allow, amongst other minor issues, houses to be converted into two and industrial buildings to be enlarged by 20 per cent (previously 10 per cent) without planning permission. The order, to be effective from 1978, was welcomed by the RIBA, and was expected to save between 10 and 20 per cent of the current stream of planning applications to local councils.

The most significant European building of the year, opened in January by President Giscard d'Estaing, was the Centre National d'Art et de Culture Georges Pompidou (previously Beaubourg Centre), by architects Piano and Rogers, in the old Beaubourg quarter of Paris. The building cost over £100 million. The design, hailed by the French press as hideous, was the winner (see AR 1971, p. 443) of an international competition with 491 entries. Externally the building displayed its aggressive structural forms and vast service tubes, coloured a vivid green, blue and orange, reminiscent of an oil refinery. The effect was to create a unique architectural experience amidst the old buildings of the area. Inside the building, clear floor spaces accommodated four major specialist activities: reference library, centre for industrial design, centre for music and acoustic research, and museum of modern art (see also p. 415).

In the UK a number of building projects indicated the advance of immigrant cultures in the country. A mosque by Godfrey Gilbert and Partners was opened at Wimbledon in the Greater London area in April. Sir Frederick Gibberd and Partners' Central London Mosque in Regent's Park was finished in July and clearly stated Islamic culture and form in a modern guise. In Scotland designs for mosques ran into trouble. W. M. Copeland and Associates' design for a mosque on the banks of the Clyde in Glasgow was rejected by the Royal Fine Art Commission for Scotland. A modified design was later approved by the Glasgow city council, and was expected to be built. In Edinburgh, G. Lindsay and Partners' design for a mosque with all its traditional elements was acceptable to the Royal Fine Art Commission, but planning permission was refused on the grounds that the building was too large for the site.

Notable buildings were completed in commerce, education and the arts. A conference centre offering 3,000 square metres of exhibition space, and with an auditorium to seat 2,700 people, was opened at Wembley in January (architects, Richard Seifert and Partners). The American Express European headquarters building (architects, Gollins, Melvin, Ward & Partners) was opened in Brighton in September. Also opened in September was the Army & Navy Stores' new building in Victoria Street. The stores and office floors above closely resembled the large south-side Victoria Street scheme by Elsom Pack and Roberts (see AR 1975, p. 404) but the outline was more varied. At the end of September, the new library for Wadham College (architects, Gillespie, Kidd & Coia) was opened at Oxford, and praised for the sympathy of its yellow-coloured exposed concrete frame with Wadham's existing stone-clad buildings. In October the Guildhall School of Music and Drama, part of Chamberlin, Powell and Bon's Barbican Development Arts Centre, was officially opened in the City of London.

An event significant for the trends it portrayed was the Greater London Council's exhibition 'New Directions in Housing', open to the public in February. The exhibition showed that the GLC, the largest housing authority in the UK, was now concentrating on low-rise infill development with plenty of open space and buildings no higher than three storeys. Indeed it was reported that the GLC had not designed a high-rise scheme for well over a decade. A month later the World's End housing scheme (architects, Eric Lyons, Cadbury-Brown, Metcalfe & Cunningham), stretching from the Thames to the King's Road, Chelsea, was completed, with its high-rise residential blocks (the tallest 21 storeys high), primary school, community centre, supermarket, shops, children's facilities and so on. The scheme was designed in the early 1960s and therefore contrasted with ideas of the late 1970s.

The 1977 Royal Gold Medal for Architecture was awarded to Sir Denys Lasdun for the splendid quality of his architecture. Among the internationally recognized buildings of great architectural merit were the Royal College of Physicians' headquarters and buildings for Cambridge and East Anglia universities. The *Financial Times* Industrial Architecture Award for 1977 went to the new furniture factory for Herman Miller Ltd, Bath, Avon, designed by Farrell/Grimshaw Partnership. The scheme was praised for the relationship of brilliant architectural skill, industrial engineering ability and management imagination. The Gold Medal of the American Institute of Architects, the AIA's highest award, not won since 1972, went to the late Richard J. Neutra, an Austrian by birth who, in 1923, was one of the first to bring the International Style to the USA. The Bronx Development Centre by Richard Meier of New York won the R. S. Reynolds Memorial Award for distinguished architecture using aluminium.

The new Palais de l'Europe, headquarters of the Council of Europe in Strasbourg, was opened in February (architects, Henry Bernard of France). In the USA the Yale Centre for British Art, Louis Kahn's last work and one-third built when he died in 1974, was completed in the summer, in most respects to the master's design, by Pellecchia & Meyers. The four-storey building, finished in stainless steel and glass, had shops at street level to suit the neighbourhood and contained the largest collection of rare books and British art outside the UK.

An important building nearing completion in the Middle East was Taliesin Associated Architects' Damavend College for 1,200 women students in the Alborz mountains, north of Teheran, which employed the Persian arch and vault using local bricks, and the curved roof glazed in turquoise blue tiles.

Germany's Kiel University Sports Hall, by Klaus Mickels of Hamburg, won in competition in 1966, was noted for its extensive use of glass, and structures such as the new Cambridge, Massachusetts, headquarters of Abt Associates in the USA, a social and policy research firm, for their use of solar heat to save 50 per cent of the building's winter fuel bill.

Los Angeles' Bonaventure Hotel by John Portman & Associates was opened in March and its five shining cylindrical towers, the tallest 35 storeys high, were acclaimed with enthusiasm. Similar skyscrapers continued to arise and dominate the US city skylines. In the summer office towers by Hugh Stubbins & Associates were opened: the $75 million Federal Reserve Plaza overlooking Boston Harbour, and the $128 million Citycorp Centre in New York's Manhattan. Both buildings had aluminium skins and incorporated new energy conservation features, thus echoing the USA's current concern about world energy problems.

FASHION

As the economic situation continued to restrict incomes and the price of clothes continued to rise, fashion tended to ignore radical change, and day clothes in particular became essentially classic and practical in style. The most popular garment worn by women throughout the year, at all price levels, was the blazer, the all-purpose tailored jacket that had long been an accepted part of the male wardrobe. The alternative, also a unisex garment, was the full and baggy blouson which was introduced by high fashion designers at the end of 1976 and continued to attract a big following by both sexes right up to the end of 1977.

In August, a warm tweed hacking jacket took the place of the blazer and was worn, by women of all ages, over full, gathered skirts in a different material or with the new, straight-leg trousers or jodphurs. This essentially English country look was complemented with tweed deerstalker hats or flat caps, and waistcoats emerged again to complete this conventional, if stylized, picture of classic English clothes.

Knitwear continued to be one of the strongest fashion trends, and big, soft sweaters stretched from the neck to well over the hips. Some of the more adventurous young wore these maxi-sweaters as mini-dresses, but generally they were worn over trousers or full skirts, giving a very ample look to the silhouette.

In the latter part of the year, trousers made a definite return to the fashion scene, the basic shape changing to a restrained jodphur with fullness at the hips and the mannish-inspired four-pleat style. Straight and narrow pants continued, however, to be worn by the majority and knickerbockers appeared among the avant garde.

Despite the tidiness of the universally-worn blazer and hacking jacket and the exaggerated fullness of the enormous sweater, it was a year when a free-wheeling mood prevailed, with an all-round look of oversized garments, whether they were shirts, blouses, flared or gathered skirts, sweeping tent-shaped coats or wide capes. The length of skirts varied considerably, but this particular problem no longer mattered and everything depended on how clothes were worn and with what accessories.

Blouses became almost as important as the well-established shirt; the big, floppy blouse gained prestige because it had the ability to transform trousers, skirts or tights from an informal to a formal mood, depending on the fabric in which it was made. An example of this transformation was seen when blouses in soft, silky fabrics trimmed with lace acted as good, if unusual, foils for the rustic tweeds and country checks.

Fabrics were soft, light and supple during all seasons. British tweeds for the sporting types included chevron, herringbone, Harris, all the tartans and checks. Corduroy was introduced as a new fashion fabric and quickly had a success when it was used, instead of blue denim, for jeans. Cashmere, mohair and fluffy angora brought a shaggy look in bulky knitwear, and fine materials, like velvet and silk, dominated the evening scene, which was a colourful if exotic free-for-all, in contrast to the hardwearing clothes worn during the day.

Colours concentrated on the pale naturals and spicy shades of saffron, ginger and caramel and, at the other extreme, strong shades like red berries, fir green, black and brown. Cosmetic colours followed suit, deep red nail varnish and lipstick being worn with summer and winter clothes. During the summer, a pale, khaki denim knocked the familiar blue into second place for jeans and other casual clothes.

Boots regained their popularity in the middle of the year and continued into winter as the most important accessory, the heel being abruptly lowered and thereby reversing the one-year-old trend for a high heel. The cost of boots and shoes rose astronomically during 1977, putting leather beyond the reach of many, and uppers and soles of man-made material appeared more frequently in fashionable shoe shops. There was every indication that people were making their shoes, as well as their clothes, last as long as possible.

Scarves continued to be favourites, and long mufflers or shawls were considered fashionable when worn wrapped around the season's big, soft dresses. The widespread introduction of small pieces of jewellery, with delicate settings and small gems, was another pointer towards the need for lowering costs in order to sell.

In January, the Queen bestowed a knighthood (KCVO) on Norman Hartnell, setting a seal on the work of a lifetime that had brought admiration for Britain from the rest of the world. Hartnell, the most famous British couturier of his time, designed clothes for four generations of the Royal Family, including the Queen's wedding and coronation dresses and Princess Margaret's wedding dress.

Chapter 3

LITERATURE

IT might have been thought that with the continuing rise in the price of books and the cutback in spending by national and local government, affecting the grants to public libraries and educational institutions, the main buyers of books, the number of titles published would have fallen sharply during 1977. In fact the steep decline of 1974 and the small decline of 1976 were not continued. Indeed more books were published in Britain during 1977 than in any previous year—27,684 new titles appeared and, in addition, there were 8,638 reprints and new editions, making a grand total of 36,322, very nearly double the figure for 25 years earlier, and an increase of 5·5 per cent on 1976.

The most astonishing increase was in the number of works of fiction published, up by 11·5 per cent to 4,487. This new total was achieved in the teeth of assertions by academic critics that the novel was dead, the complaints by publishers that they could not make money by issuing 'literary' novels and the general assumption that printed fiction had lost its place to television as a main provider of entertainment. A large public was still seeking escapist reading in the fantasy story, the thriller, the gothic novel and the historical romance.

The ultimate in escapist reading was achieved by the publication of J. R. R. Tolkien's unfinished, and so far as the author was concerned unfinishable, effort to create a literature, history and mythology for an imaginary parallel world to the real one, in *The Silmarillion*. The English language editions of this work, published in Britain and the United States, sold in the last three months of the year a total of more than a million copies, even though the reviews, most of them written more in sorrow than in anger, had been almost universally poor. The reason why the work was incomplete was to be discovered from a reading of Humphrey Carpenter's skilfully written biography, *J. R. R. Tolkien*, in which he explained that his subject had begun work on his imaginary world in 1917, when recovering from an illness contracted while serving in the trenches in World War I, and thereafter it had been his refuge from the stresses of academic life, which he did not particularly enjoy, an unhappy marriage and a real world of which he never really wished to be part. Tolkien's trilogy, *The Lord of the Rings*, had become, a decade after its publication, the cult book first of American university students and then of teenage school children in many parts of the world. Its rejection of reality and its compelling plot had made it an immense success. The formlessness, even after much editing by the author's son Christopher, of *The Silmarillion* led to its rejection by reviewers.

o*

A feeling of nostalgia that permeated many aspects of social life was pointed by the almost incredible success of *The Country Diary of an Edwardian Lady*, the nature notes written in the first decade of the century by Edith Holden, describing her observations in a West Country village, and reproduced in supposed facsimile. Although this book sold more copies than most other works of non-fiction, its appeal was almost entirely non-literary and it was bought more as an object to display than as a work to be read.

In fiction the trend was away from the large-scale novel. It was a time for miniaturist writing in novels that would have been regarded, a decade earlier, as uncommercially short. Now these were welcomed by publishers, particularly those of paperback reprints who had found in the spring of the year a strong consumer resistance to the high prices they were forced to charge for longer novels, and blessed by the award of the major British fiction prizes to works of this scale. The Booker Prize, often the subject of controversy, was, to general satisfaction, given to Paul Scott for his novel of post-Raj Indian life, *Staying On*. Mr Scott's major work, a four-novel sequence known collectively as *The Raj Quartet*, published over a decade from the late 1960s, had been ignored by the donors of prizes. This smaller-scale, greatly accomplished though intentionally minor work, found favour. It was a gentle study of an impoverished couple trying to retain their dignity in a changing India. Mr Scott had been criticized previously for a certain heaviness in his writing. In *Staying On* he displayed a delicacy previously foreign to him.

The other major British novel prize, the Whitbread Award, went also to a short novel, *Injury Time* by Beryl Bainbridge. This author had several times appeared on short lists but had always been passed over in previous years. *Injury Time* showed her skill at portraying the intricacies of the domestic scene, the tiny signals that pass between married people and lovers, and contrasting this superficial calm with a sudden outburst of violence—in this case, the arrival of a gang of criminals to disrupt a suburban dinner party.

When in the early months of the year the *Times Literary Supplement* celebrated its 75th birthday, a number of writers were asked to nominate those of their kind who they felt were the most over- and under-rated. One of those picked twice as the most under-rated was Barbara Pym, who in the 1940s and 1950s had published a series of pithily witty novels about suburban life but who, faced with a rejection from her customary publisher, had stopped writing. Given new confidence by her selection in the *TLS* list, she offered a novel she had put to one side to another publisher who welcomed it. Her *Quartet in Autumn*, a realistic study of professional people facing retirement, was one of those shortlisted for the Booker Prize. Others selected by the Booker judges for the short list were Paul Bailey's *Peter Smart's Confession*, Jennifer Johnston's study of the stresses of living in contemporary Ulster, *Shadows on Their Skin*, and Caroline Blackwood's study of the varying forms of madness that afflicted three generations in a family, *Great Granny Webster*.

It should not be thought that there were no long novels. Perhaps there was most controversy about John Fowles's first novel for seven years, *Daniel Martin*. In Britain it was denounced by nearly all critics as overlong, self-indulgent and brilliant only in flashes, while in the United States it was almost without exception hailed as a master work with at most only the smallest blemishes. Its long introspective passages were more in tune with American methods of writing fiction, but it was also true that British critics thought Mr Fowles was capable of better, as he showed in the same year by issuing a revised version of his earlier novel, *The Magus*, which was generally regarded as a great improvement on the original. Had Mr Fowles delayed and made to *Daniel Martin* the sort of revisions that he had to *The Magus*, which, incidentally, included a totally new ending, it would have been a much better book.

Daniel Jacobson's long Kafkaesque novel, *The Confessions of Josef Baisz*, an allegorical presentation of the tyranny operating in Mr Jacobson's native South Africa, received mixed notices but the power of the writing was widely acclaimed. Margaret Drabble, in *The Ice Age*, broke away from her customary delineation of the problems of the intellectual woman trapped in domesticity to try a larger canvas showing the middle classes at bay and introducing an international terrorist. The most ambitious change of direction was by John le Carré, the author over the previous 15 years of a number of tightly-written spy stories stressing the murkiness rather than the glamour of the calling of undercover agent. In *The Honourable Schoolboy* he took a number of characters and situations set up in earlier novels and tried to magnify the spy-story formula into a novel of Victorian length and complexity. The general opinion was that he would have been wiser to stick to his customary length, but to enthusiasts this seemed not only the best spy story for a generation but a major novel in its own right.

It was not a year for the great names but a number of regular performers published novels: Olivia Manning's *The Danger Tree* revived the characters of her Balkan trilogy; Edna O'Brien's *Johnny I Hardly Knew You* proved a great disappointment, and Richard Adams's *The Plague Dogs*, an allegory about cruelty to animals, sold largely on the reputation of his cult book, *Watership Down*, a children's book about rabbits published five years earlier that had created the sort of following enjoyed by Tolkien. At his death P. G. Wodehouse left a portion of a novel. This was published, together with his working notes for the rest, as *Sunset at Blandings*. Not perhaps vintage Wodehouse but a remarkable effort for a man in his 94th year.

In the non-fiction field, the greatest fuss was created by books that could in no way be considered of lasting literary interest. The publication of the third volume of Richard Crossman's *Diary of a Cabinet Minister* completed this singular undertaking, revealing in considerable detail not only the goings-on in the Cabinet Room but also a Minister's often stormy relations with his senior civil servants. Had not this series of books been published, it is unlikely that Joe Haines, Harold Wilson's press officer while Prime Minister, would have considered writing an account of the intricate happenings inside Wilson's 'kitchen cabinet', his personal circle of advisers. Mr Haines's revelations, particularly about the power of Lady Falkender, the Prime Minister's sometime secretary, caused much discussion and no little sensation. This was equalled only by the reception of the autobiography of Tom Driberg (Lord Bradwell), *Ruling Passions*, which described in copious detail his casual homosexual relationships and his use of his status as a Member of Parliament to avoid prosecution. The book was unfinished and the prurient interest in its revelations might have been less had the author been able to spend more time in discussing his other 'ruling passions'—politics and religion.

Among the political biographies the most notable were David Marquand's massive study of *Ramsay MacDonald*, certain to be the definitive work on a previously enigmatic figure, J. A. Cross's *Sir Samuel Hoare* and a first book by a young historian, John Campbell's *Lloyd George: the Goat in the Wilderness*, a well-researched study of a statesman in decline. The convolutions, doubts and enthusiasm of those who were to form the intellectual wing of the fledgling Labour Party were analysed with understanding by Norman and Jeanne Mackenzie in *The First Fabians*, while Lord Butler headed a team of historians producing an uneven but generally accomplished history of *The Conservatives*. The different methods used by the Conservatives during the twentieth century in choosing their leader were discussed by an MP, Nigel Fisher, in *The Tory Leaders*, a book that gained greatly in interest as the author's personal knowledge grew closer. It provided the clearest picture available of the 'ditching' of Edward Heath in favour of Margaret Thatcher.

Over a period of years controversy had surrounded the writing of David Irving, whose studies of incidents in World War II seemed to have placed more credence on German sources than Allied ones and had tended to question Allied motives, particularly those of Winston Churchill. This industrious researcher published two long books during the year. One, *The Trail of the Fox*, a biography of the Afrika Korps commander, Erwin Rommel, was widely praised for the way it solved the apparent contradictions in Rommel's career, though Mr Irving's accounts of the battles in North Africa were found to be one-sided. The other, *Hitler's War*, caused outrage by his insistence that Hitler was totally unaware of and did not authorize the extermination of the Jews. The refusal of many reviewers to believe this theory, based though it was on much research and the demonstration of a total absence of documentary evidence, and indeed its inherent improbability, tended to lead readers to ignore the book's other merits in its careful analysis of the part that Hitler played in the successes and failure of German arms.

Other works of contemporary history included Alistair Horne's detailed examination of the events leading up to the French withdrawal from Algeria, *A Savage War for Peace*, and Robert Blake's *History of Rhodesia*, written from the point of view of the white settlers. Dealing with less publicized events were Anthony Sampson's *The Arms Bazaar*, describing the arms dealers' activities, and Geoffrey Moorhouse's *The Diplomats*, a thoughtful account of the history and workings of the British Foreign Service.

It was not an important year for major works of history, though three stood out: *Gold and Iron: Bismarck, Bleichröder and the Building of the German Empire* by Fritz Stern, a work of original research showing how much the 'Iron Chancellor' had relied on the advice and support (moral and financial) of a Jewish banker whose name was hitherto barely known to historians; the second volume of Theodore Zeldin's *France, 1848-1945*, a masterly *omnium gatherum* of all aspects of French life, and Lawrence Stone's study of the changing patterns in English society after the Reformation in *The Family, Sex and Marriage in England*.

The major literary biography was undoubtedly Angus Wilson's *The Strange Ride of Rudyard Kipling*, remarkable not perhaps for any new revelations about the novelist and poet but rather for its description of the close relationship between Kipling's life and his writings. P. N. Furbank produced the first volume of the long-awaited life of *E. M. Forster*. Why it should have been found necessary to use two volumes to describe a life so devoid of incident puzzled many. Paul Ferris produced an adequate, unspectacular life of *Dylan Thomas* and Victoria Glendinning described well the various tugs of loyalty (personal and geographical) that shaped the life and writings of *Elizabeth Bowen*.

Much interest centred on the writers of the 1930s. There was, for instance, the definitive edition of W. H. Auden's early work, largely in verse but with some passages of prose criticism, *The English Auden*. Auden's collaborator as a playwright in this period, Christopher Isherwood, published a second volume of autobiography describing his time in Berlin, already featured in his early novels, and his and Auden's travels, *Christopher and His Kind*. Martin Green published an analysis of the writings of those who, like Auden and Isherwood, were at Oxford and Cambridge in the 1920s, emphasizing the influence on their views of the homosexuality of some of the group, *Children of the Sun: a Narrative of 'Decadence' in England after 1918*. Those who felt that Mr Green was arguing from the particular to the general preferred the more scholarly study of the same period *Seeing through Everything: English Writing, 1918-40* by William H. Pritchard, which emphasized the general scepticism of this generation of writers. The wartime activities of the same group, in particular those involved with Cyril Connolly in producing the literary magazine *Horizon*, were discussed by Robert Hewison in *Under Siege: Literary Life in London, 1938-1945*.

Three notable biographies of Russian literary figures appeared: V. S. Pritchett's study of Turgenev, *The Gentle Barbarian*; Laurence Kelly's *Lermontov: Tragedy in the Caucasus* (a notable 'first' biography) and Joseph Frank's *Dostoevsky: the Seeds of Revolt, 1821-69*, the opening volume of a remorselessly detailed study.

In an age when specialization is widely practised it was strange to find Christopher Hill, the Master of Balliol and a historian, writing of *Milton and the English Revolution*. It proved, however, not to be primarily a work of criticism but an effort to explain Milton's attitudes by a discussion of contemporary events and to show in detail that the poet was essentially a product of his times and that some of his references were less transcendental than local.

No new poets emerged during the year, and, while a number of existing ones confirmed their reputation, it was not a splendid year for poetry, though its practitioners could take comfort from the fact that one of their number, the Spanish writer of free verse, Vincente Aleixandre, had been awarded the Nobel Prize for Literature; but it was probably of less comfort that he who had been publishing his work for more than 50 years should have to wait until his 90th year before he received the award.

Both J. B. Priestley and F. R. Leavis had to wait until they were well in their eighties before they were honoured in their own country. Mr Priestley was made a member of the Order of Merit and Dr Leavis, on the last day of the year, a Companion of Honour. Mr Priestley published a short work of autobiographical sketches during the year, *Instead of the Trees*. Among other autobiographies were two by Mitford sisters, written from very different points of view, Diana (Lady Mosley) described her life with the former leader of the British Union of Fascists, her husband Sir Oswald Mosley, and her wartime internment in *A Life of Contrasts*, while in *A Fine Old Conflict* Jessica explained her involvement with the American Communist Party and her appearances before the McCarthy Committee during the 1950s. Kenneth Clark completed his autobiography with *The Other Half* and A. J. Ayer began his with *Part of My Life*.

Agatha Christie's *Autobiography* was published posthumously, and Dennis Wheatley, a popular novelist whose sales most nearly among English writers matched those of Mrs Christie, lived only to see the publication of the first volume of his, *The Time has Come* . . . . Other writers who died during the year were the leading American poet Robert Lowell and the English writer of popular verse, John Pudney. The novelists, William Gerhardie, Phyllis Bentley, James M. Cain, Carl Zuckmayer and Hans Habe were also among those whose deaths were

LITERATURE 431

announced. Lost from the ranks of historians were Sir Keith Feiling and one of the last great 'amateurs', Mrs Cecil Woodham-Smith. (For Lowell, Zuckmayer, Feiling and Woodham-Smith, see OBITUARY).

There was still no good news for British writers of the establishment of a Public Lending Right, but as a result of a Consent Decree in the American courts the exclusive rights of British and American publishers in the Commonwealth and American markets respectively were ended. During the year British firms began setting up subsidiaries to sell their books on the other side of the Atlantic, while books with American imprints appeared in British and Commonwealth bookshops. In future authors and their agents would think in terms of world rights and the pattern of publishing could change.

Among the books published during the year were:

FICTION: *The Plague Dogs* by Richard Adams (Allen Lane); *Peter Smart's Confession* by Paul Bailey (Cape); *Injury Time* by Beryl Bainbridge (Duckworth); *The Squire of Bar Schachor* by Chaim Bermant (Allen & Unwin); *Great Granny Webster* by Caroline Blackwood (Duckworth); *Sombrero Fallout* by Richard Brautigan (Cape); *Abba Abba* by Anthony Burgess (Faber); *Beard's Roman Women* by Anthony Burgess (Hutchinson); *The Wife* by Judith Burnley (Heinemann); *Fires on the Mountain Side* by Anita Desai (Heinemann); *The Ice Age* by Margaret Drabble (Weidenfeld); *A Loving Eye* by Janice Elliott (Hodder); *The Sin Eater* by Alice Thomas Ellis (Duckworth); *Daniel Martin* by John Fowles (Cape); *The Magus* by John Fowles (Cape); *Terra Nostra* by Carlos Fuentes (Secker & Warburg); *Enemies: a Novel about Friendship* by Giles Gordon (Harvester); *Edith's Diary* by Patricia Highsmith (Heinemann); *The Confessions of Josef Baisz* by Dan Jacobson (Secker & Warburg); *Shadows on Their Skin* by Jennifer Johnston (Hamish Hamilton); *A Victim of Aurora* by Thomas Keneally (Collins); *The Honourable Schoolboy* by John le Carré (Hodder); *The Danger Tree* by Olivia Manning (Weidenfeld); *The Autumn of the Patriarch* by Gabriel Garcia Marques (Cape); *But Answer Came There None* by Yvonne Mitchell (Constable); *Kith* by P. H. Newby (Faber); *Johnny I Hardly Knew You* by Edna O'Brien (Weidenfeld); *God Perkins* by David Pownall (Faber); *Quartet in Autumn* by Barbara Pym (Macmillan); *Staying On* by Paul Scott (Heinemann); *The English Lover* by Jonathan Smith (Hutchinson); *The Silmarillion* by J. R. R. Tolkien (Allen & Unwin); *Marry Me* by John Updike (Deutsch); *In a Dark Wood* by Marina Warner (Weidenfeld); *Sunset at Blandings* by P. G. Wodehouse (Chatto).

POETRY: *Self-portrait in a Convex Mirror* by John Ashberry (Carcanet); *Geography III* by Elizabeth Bishop (Chatto); *Song of the Battery Hen* by Edwin (Secker & Warburg); *Selected Poems* by George Mackay Brown (Hogarth Press); *Implements in Their Places* by W. S. Graham (Faber); *Dreams of the Dead* by David Harsent (Oxford); *Gaudete* by Ted Hughes (Faber); *The Oxford Book of Welsh Verse in English* edited by Gwyn Jones (Oxford); *Tree of Strings* by Norman MacCaig (Chatto); *The English Auden* edited by Edward Mendelson (Faber); *Poisoned Lands* by John Montague (Oxford); *State of Justice* by Tom Paulin (Faber); *The Oval Portrait* by Kathleen Raine (Hamish Hamilton); *Selected Poems of Leopold Sedar Senghor* (Cambridge); *The Awful Rowing toward God* by Anne Sexton (Chatto); *In the Middle* by Iain Crichton Smith (Gollancz); *Prussian Nights* by Alexander Solzhenitsyn (Collins/Harvill); *Enough of Green* by Anne Stevenson (Oxford); *A Portion of Foxes* by Anthony Thwaite (Oxford).

LITERARY CRITICISM: *Thackeray: Prodigal Genius* by John Carey (Faber); *In Pursuit of Coleridge* by Kathleen Coburn (Bodley Head); *Dylan Thomas* by Paul Ferris (Hodder); *Dostoevsky: the Seeds of Revolt, 1821-69* by Joseph Frank (Robson); *E. M. Forster:*

a Life. Vol. I by P. N. Furbank (Secker & Warburg); *Elizabeth Bowen: Portrait of a Writer* by Victoria Glendinning (Weidenfeld); *Children of the Sun: a Narrative of 'Decadence' in England after 1918* by Martin Green (Constable); *Under Siege: Literary Life in London, 1938-45* by Robert Hewison (Weidenfeld); *Milton and the English Revolution* by Christopher Hill (Faber); *Lermontov: Tragedy in the Caucasus* by Laurence Kelly (Constable); *Seeing through Everything: English Writers, 1918-40* by William H. Pritchard (Faber); *The Gentle Barbarian: the Life and Works of Turgenev* by V. S. Pritchett (Chatto); *Handbook of Anthony Powell's Music of Time* by Hilary Spurling (Heinemann); *The Strange Ride of Rudyard Kipling* by Angus Wilson (Secker & Warburg).

BIOGRAPHY: *Whom the Gods Love: Boyd Alexander's Expedition from the Niger to the Nile and His Last Journey* by Joan Alexander (Heinemann); *Frederick Rolfe, Baron Corvo* by Miriam J. Benkovitz (Hamish Hamilton); *King without a Crown: Albert Prince Consort of England* by Daphne Bennett (Heinemann); *Liddell Hart: a Study of his Military Thought* by Brian Bond (Cassell); *The Riddle of Erskine Childers* by Andrew Boyle (Hutchinson); *Lloyd George: the Goat in the Wilderness* by John Campbell (Cape); *J. R. R. Tolkien* by Humphrey Carpenter (Allen & Unwin); *Sir Samuel Hoare: a Political Biography* by J. A. Cross (Cape); *Nellie and Sissie: the Biography of Ethel M. Dell and her Sister Ella* by Penelope Dell (Hamish Hamilton); *The Cousins: the Friendship, Opinions and Activities of Wilfred Scawen Blunt and George Wyndham* by Max Egremont (Collins); *Ned's Girl: the Authorised Biography of Dame Edith Evans* by Bryan Forbes (Elm Tree); *Isabella and Sam: the Story of Mrs Beeton* by Sarah Freeman (Gollancz); *Marie Stopes: a Biography* by Ruth Hall (Deutsch); *Spooner: a Biography* by William Hayter (W. H. Allen); *The Trail of the Fox: the Life of Field Marshal Erwin Rommel* by David Irving (Weidenfeld); *Remember You Are an Englishman: a Biography of Sir Harry Smith* by Joseph H. Lehmann (Cape); *Ramsay MacDonald* by David Marquand (Cape); *Ada, Countess of Lovelace: Byron's Illegitimate Daughter* by Doris Langley Moore (Murray); *Caught in a Web of Words: James A. H. Murray and the Oxford Dictionary* by K. M. Elizabeth Murray (Yale); *Mary Curzon* by Nigel Nicolson (Weidenfeld); *Trelawny: the Incurable Romancer* by William St Clair (Murray).

AUTOBIOGRAPHY AND LETTERS: *Part of My Life* by A. J. Ayer (Collins); *O America: a Memoir of the 1920s* by Luigi Barzini (Hamish Hamilton); *A Postillion Struck by Lightning* by Dirk Bogarde (Bodley Head); *In Patagonia* by Bruce Chatwin (Cape); *Autobiography* by Agatha Christie (Collins); *The Other Half: a Self Portrait* by Kenneth Clark (Murray); *Diaries of a Cabinet Minister. Vol. III* by Richard Crossman (Hamish Hamilton and Cape); *Ruling Passions* by Tom Driberg (Cape); *Growing Pains: the Shaping of a Writer* by Daphne du Maurier (Gollancz); *The Country Diary of an Edwardian Lady* by Edith Holden (Webb & Bower with Michael Joseph); *Christopher and His Kind* by Christopher Isherwood (Eyre Methuen); *A Fine Old Conflict* by Jessica Mitford (Michael Joseph); *A Life of Contrasts: an Autobiography* by Diana Mosley (Hamish Hamilton); *When the Indus was Young* by Dervla Murphy (Murray); *Instead of the Trees* by J. B. Priestley (Heinemann); *Dear Me* by Peter Ustinov (Heinemann); *The Time Has Come . . . the Memoirs of Dennis Wheatley. Vol. I* (Hutchinson); *Letters on Literature and Politics, 1912-72* by Edmund Wilson (Routledge).

HISTORY: *A History of Rhodesia* by Robert Blake (Eyre Methuen); *The Conservatives: a History* edited by Lord Butler (Allen & Unwin); *Four Fine Gentlemen* by Hesther Chapman (Constable); *Fighter* by Len Deighton (Cape); *The Tory Leaders* by Nigel Fisher (Weidenfeld); *Facing the Nation: Television and Politics* by Grace Wyndham Goldie (Bodley Head); *Politics of Power* by Joe Haines (Cape); *Montrose: the King's Champion* by Max Hastings (Gollancz); *A Savage War of Peace* by Alistair Horne (Macmillan); *Shakespeare by Hilliard* by Leslie Hotson (Chatto); *Hitler's War* by David Irving (Hodder); *Enemies of Society* by Paul Johnson (Weidenfeld); *Napoleon and the*

Restoration of the Bourbons by Thomas Babington Macaulay, edited by Joseph Hamburger (Longman); *The First Fabians* by Norman and Jeanne Mackenzie (Weidenfeld); *The Diplomats* by Geoffrey Moorhouse (Cape); *India: a Wounded Civilization* by V. S. Naipaul (Deutsch); *The British Revolution. Vol. II: from Asquith to Chamberlain* by Robert Rhodes-James (Hamish Hamilton); *Churchill and the Admirals* by Stephen Roskill (Collins); *The Arms Bazaar* by Anthony Sampson (Hodder); *Gold and Iron: Bismarck, Bleichröder and the Building of the German Empire* by Fritz Stern (Allen & Unwin); *The Family, Sex and Marriage in England* by Lawrence Stone (Weidenfeld); *France, 1848-1945, Vol. II* by Theodore Zeldin (Clarendon Press: Oxford).

XVI SPORT

RUGBY UNION FOOTBALL

FRANCE won the international championship, beating all rivals for its second Grand Slam in rugby history, becoming the first country to win the title with an unchanged team, and the first for over 60 years to do it without conceding a try. But the undoubted merits of the achievement were marred by the charge of unnecessarily rough play. When they beat Scotland by 23 points to 3 in Paris, the French XV were described as 'brutal' in the *Observer*, and the *Sunday Times* summed up their ultimate victory with the headline 'A Slam, but not so Grand'. Much of the credit for the success must go to their 5 ft 4 in captain and scrum-half Jacques Fouroux, often called 'le petit Napoleon' by his admirers but just as often severely criticized in the French Press for the tactics he initiated; his detractors said they had resulted in France's abandoning its traditional handling and running game in favour of 'pressure rugby'. The arguments continued to rage, and in December Fouroux, complaining bitterly, announced his retirement from the international game.

The French conceded only 21 points during the championship and nine of those went to Wales, beaten 16-9 in its first international defeat for two years. However, Wales did collect Triple Crown triumphs over England, Scotland and Ireland, and Welshmen filled over half the places in the British Lions touring party to New Zealand in the summer. Unfortunately they did not include three of the best, Gareth Edwards, Gerald Davies and J. P. R. Williams, who all refused the invitation to tour for various reasons.

The trip was not a happy one. Before the four Test matches were begun, the Lions crashed 21-9 to New Zealand Universities for their first non-international defeat for nine years. They lost the Test series by three games to one—the last by 10-9 after leading 9-3 at half time. New Zealand even survived the retirement of two of its greatest players, scrum-half Sid Going and wing Grant Batty, during the season. On the way home the Lions were beaten 25-21 in their first-ever match against Fiji. Their only consolation came when, brought together again in the autumn, they crushed the Barbarians 23-14 in a great match which provided the Rugby Union's contribution to the Queen's Jubilee Appeal.

SWIMMING

The indoor swimming world appeared to be taking a breather after the hectic excitements of the previous year's Montreal Olympics. The European championships in Jonköping, Sweden, in August were the year's only major multi-national event and proved something of a disappointment in this record-hungry sport.

Only three new world marks were set—all by Germans. Gerald Morken, of the Federal Republic, clocked 1 min 02·86 sec in the 100 metres breaststroke, and two East German women, Petra Thumer and Ulrike Tauber, clocked 4:08·91 and 2:15·95 in the 400 metres freestyle and 200 metres medley respectively.

The East Germans confirmed their overall superiority in Europe by taking the Europa Cup by 297 points from the Soviet Union (231) and the GFR (169). The British were satisfied to retain fourth place with a total of 120 pts, but what did come as a surprise, at least to those outside this particular branch of the sport, was the success of the British women's synchronized swimming team. They took the overall trophy and also won gold medals through Jackie Cox in the solo event and Miss Cox and Andrea Holland in the duet.

A two-country meeting between the major Montreal adversaries, East Germany and the USA, in East Berlin, produced five world records in an American victory by 176 points to 168. The German girl Christiane Knacke by clocking 59·78 sec became the first to break the one-minute 'barrier' in the women's 100 metres butterfly, and her colleague Ulrike Tauber broke the 200 metres individual medley record for the third time in the year, in 2:15·85. Other records were set by the USA 400 metres men's freestyle relay team, by Brian Goodell (USA) in the individual 400 metres freestyle and by Joe Bottom in the 100 metres butterfly, which he swam in 54·18 sec to knock nine-hundreths of a second off the last world record standing in the name of the Munich Olympic phenomenon, Mark Spitz.

In rougher waters, a number of notable achievements were notched in long-distance swimming. On 26 July a schoolboy from Scarborough in Yorkshire, David Morgan, at the age of 13 years and 10 months, became the youngest ever to swim the Channel between England and France, taking 11 hours and 10 minutes. A 19-year-old Canadian from Scarborough in Ontario, Cynthia Nicholas, with her non-stop two-way swim between the English and French coasts in 19 hours 55 minutes, became the first woman to achieve the feat, knocking 10 hours and five minutes off the previous record.

Linda McGill, a 32-year-old Australian, made the first nonstop swim between Saudi Arabia and Bahrein—14 miles in 8 hours 25 minutes.

ATHLETICS

While the international federation (IAAF) was still dithering, as it had done for many years, over the introduction of official world championships other than the Olympic Games, a step along the way was taken by the innovation of a track and field World Cup in Düsseldorf, West Germany, on 2-4 September.

Eight teams of men and women represented countries or areas—USA, Americas, Asia, Africa, Oceania, East Germany, West Germany and Europe. East Germany won the men's competition with 127 points from the USA (120), while the polyglot European women's team finished ahead of East Germany by five points. There were a number of fine performances which confirmed Olympic form of the year before, notably by the giant Cuban Alberto Juantorena in the 400 and 800 metres, Irena Szewinska of Poland in the women's 400 metres and Ed Moses of the USA in the 400 metres hurdles. For Britain the outstanding achievement came from Steve Ovett, who won the 1,500 metres to add to his victory in the European Cup finals in Helsinki a few weeks previously.

However, for many the athlete of the year was the East German high-jumper Rosemarie Ackermann, who broke the women's world record four times and became the first to clear the 'magic' two metres (6 ft 6¾ in).

British athletics prospered on the domestic front, with a welcome return of capacity crowds at events as far apart as London, Gateshead and Edinburgh. In Scotland they were able to cheer a first-ever victory by both the British men and women over teams from the Soviet Union, including many athletes who, earlier in the summer, had crushed the USA for the fifth successive time in the annual Soviet-American meetings.

Among the world record-breakers were Samson Kimombwa, of Kenya, with a time of 27 min 30·5 sec in a 10,000 metres race in Helsinki, and New Zealand's Dick Quax with 13:12·9 in a 5,000 metres event in Stockholm. Overall, East Germany confirmed its superiority in Europe by taking both the men's and women's team titles in the European Cup, over West Germany and the Soviet Union respectively, Britain coming fourth in both.

But the tardiness of the IAAF in putting its full world championship plans into operation—the earliest date was now said to be 1983—meant that in 1978 there would be no event of true world class, and this may have tempted the professional promoters back into the arena. In October it was announced that Arabian money would be poured into a series of events in 1978 to be called the Dubai International Championships, crowned by a first prize of nearly £180,000 for the winner of the Dubai 'Golden Mile'.

TENNIS

The world's oldest lawn tennis championships celebrated their centenary at Wimbledon in as fitting a manner as possible on 1 July—in front of the Queen in her Silver Jubilee year and with a British winner in the women's singles.

It was a long-awaited victory for 31-year-old Miss Virginia Wade, who had several times come very near to the title in 15 years of trying. This time she beat the reigning champion, Chris Evert, of the USA, in a stirring semi-final match to face the 32-year-old Dutchwoman, Betty Stove, at the last hurdle. For the British, the only disappointment was that Miss Stove had proved unexpectedly too good for young Sue Barker in her semi-final and thus deprived them of an all-British women's final. Almost incredibly, it seemed possible that Miss Wade would once more fail when she lost the first set 4-6 and then saw a 3-0 lead disappear in the second. But then she won seven games in a row amid mounting excitement which burst into a crescendo of cheers when Miss Stove finally volleyed the match point into the net for a 4-6, 6-3, 6-1 victory to the British player.

Most of the surviving champions from the past had taken part in a nostalgic parade to celebrate the centenary on the first day, but one noticeable absentee was the 1975 men's singles winner, Jimmy Connors, who appeared to prefer to spend the time testing an injured hand on an outside court. As a result, he was booed on his first appearance on the Centre Court and was forgiven only when he produced a superb game against the holder, Bjorn Borg of Sweden, before losing in the men's singles final. They reached that stage after semi-finals in which Borg had had to struggle manfully for three hours to beat a young American, Vitas Gerulaitis, by three sets to two, and Connors had to overcome the extraordinary challenge of an 18-year-old fellow-countryman, John McEnroe, who came to Wimbledon originally to take part in the junior singles, qualified for the championships proper and then became the only unseeded man in the last four.

The women's singles also saw its youngest-ever entry when another American, Tracy Austin, got through a round at the age of 14 before bowing to Miss Evert. A few weeks later, Miss Austin became the youngest-ever to reach the quarter-finals of the US championships, beating Miss Barker on the way. This was the last year in which the US championships would be held at Forest Hills, after 53 years. They were to be moved about five miles away to new stadia built at Flushing Meadow.

The fact that Wimbledon survived as the only major championship still played on grass was recognized by the international federation (formerly ILTF) when it voted to delete the word 'Lawn' from its title and became instead the International Tennis Federation. One of the first acts

of the new ITF was to ban a double-stringed racquet—called the 'spaghetti'
—which by imparting enormous top spin and killing the velocity of serves
caused several upsets of form and tempers in some tournaments.

BOXING

It was more of a retiring than a fighting year in British professional
boxing; for three former heavyweight champions, Joe Bugner, Richard
Dunn and Danny McAlinden, all quit the ring for the second time after
brief, inglorious comebacks. Bugner was stripped of his European title for
failing to defend, and went to Italy to make films. Dunn had only one,
long-delayed fight during the year and after being beaten decided again to
quit. McAlinden's comeback lasted just over two minutes against a comparative novice. World light-heavyweight champion John Conteh had a
lengthy battle in the High Court against the British Boxing Board of
Control and the World Boxing Club for depriving him of his title. But
having won that fight he had to concede his championship when illness
prevented him from making a comeback.

As Dave Green was forced to forfeit his European light-welterweight
crown, and Alan Minter lost the European middleweight title to Gratien
Tonna of France, British hopes at the end of the year were pinned on
Charlie Magri, a London flyweight who won the British title in his third
bout only 43 days after turning professional.

World heavyweight champion Muhammad Ali defended his title twice,
winning on points against an 'unknown' Spaniard, Alfredo Evangelista,
and fellow-American Earnie Shavers, better known during a long career as
a supporting-bout fighter than as a title contender. Ali's major preoccupation during the year, however, was completing and promoting the
film of his life, predictably titled *The Greatest*.

Boxing gave a scant farewell to another fighter who deserved to share
that title with Ali, when the name of Carlos Monzon, of Argentina,
disappeared into the record books. He announced his retirement on 30 July
after defending his world middleweight title successfully for the 14th time
in eight years. Monzon was 35 when he quit. He had had 100 professional
fights since his debut in February 1963, and had not been beaten in any
contest since October, 1964. Such was his supremacy that when, in his last
fight, he was brought briefly to his knees by a punch, neither his followers
nor Monzon himself could remember the last time he had been off his feet
in the ring.

In the United States a grandiose series of televised contests designed to
establish an American champion in every weight division, called the US
Boxing Championships, came to grief in a major scandal culminating in a
grand jury investigation.

GOLF

While Johnny Miller was suffering one of his worst seasons (he did not win a single title and ended 48th in the money-winning list) it soon became clear that Tom Watson was going to be the one to beat among United States and world golfers. It was the now nearly-veteran Jack Nicklaus who picked up the challenge and chased Watson all the way home. Their clashes in major title tournaments alone made the year memorable, beginning in the US Masters, which Watson won, and reaching a high point in the British Open, held for the first time on the links at Turnberry. Watson cracked this course with an all-time Open record of 268, but Nicklaus was never far behind and over the last two days they played each other stroke for stroke in what was described in the *Sunday Times* as 'probably the greatest "match" in medal-play history'.

So far were these two ahead on the final day that the match-play analogy was by no means out of place. The lead swung precariously between them, each making superb recoveries or putts when threatened with more than a single stroke deficit, before Watson edged home one stroke ahead. Their fellow American, Hubert Green (later to win the US Open), who finished third 10 strokes behind Nicklaus, commented: 'I'm the winner of the 1977 British Open. Those other two guys were playing an entirely different game.'

Watson, 27-year-old Kansas City professional, won three other US tournaments and the Spanish Open to top the earnings for the year at $310,653; Nicklaus apart, the only other rival to come near him was fellow-American Lanny Wadkins, who won the US PGA and World Series titles.

Al Geiberger became the first man to break the magic 60 on the official US circuit, shooting a 13-under-par 59 in the Memphis Open. At the other end of the scale, Takashi Kobayashi, of Japan, created a record in the British Open by returning 199 in the first two rounds.

In Europe, the dominating figure continued to be the young Spaniard Severiano Ballesteros, who played a major part in his country's winning the World Cup team trophy and also had notable victories in Asia and Australasia. Britain waited keenly on the development of its latest rising star, Nick Faldo, who had a notable—and unrivalled—debut in the Ryder Cup. That event, at Royal Lytham, saw Tony Jacklin dropped from the final day's singles and ended in a five-points victory for the US team. The British Walker Cup team also never recovered from a 9-3 deficit on the first day against the US in America.

Perhaps the most significant move in world golf came from the ubiquitous Mr Kerry Packer. He 'bought out' the Australian Open at a cost of £1·5 million, got Nicklaus to redesign the course, turned it into an

8-hours-a-day television spectacular and offered six-figure prize-money that few could resist. Many thought it might well turn out to be a better long-term venture than his excursions into cricket (see p. 443).

MOTOR SPORT

On 2 October, 14 months to the day after his near-fatal crash in the German Grand Prix last year, the remarkable Austrian driver Nicki Lauda completed his comeback by regaining the world championship he had held in 1975. Fourth place in the US (East) Grand Prix at Watkins Glen, New York, sufficed to give Lauda the title although two more championship Grand Prixs had still to be run. His superiority was already complete; he had won three of the 15 races, finished second in six others and amassed 72 points with an enormous lead of 25 over his nearest rival, Mario Andretti of the USA. To cap it all, Lauda included among his victories that of the German Grand Prix at Hockenheim, held only two days before the anniversary of his accident there which had resulted in such severe injuries that he had been given the Last Rites.

At the same time, Lauda also 'won' his battle with Ferrari and his critics among the Italian press and Italy's fanatical motor-racing addicts. Some had even accused him of cowardice when, still scarred from his injuries, he had retired from the last Grand Prix in 1976 and thus forfeited his chance of retaining the world title for himself and Ferrari.

Lauda's disenchantment with Italian motor-racing took the most provocative turn when he announced his decision to quit Ferrari only a few days before the Italian GP at Monza in September, when he held a 21 points lead but was not yet absolutely sure of the title. For that, some of the more outraged Italians pelted him with rotten fruit, while the press went into paroxysms of speculation over whether Lauda's final 'revenge' would take the form of allowing the championship to escape his and Ferrari's grasp in the last races. It was all very nasty indeed.

Then Lauda deflated them all by not only driving superbly in the race, but also, in finishing second, taking himself within one point of an unbeatable lead in the championship. Typically, the relieved Italian fans went wild in their adoration of him at Monza and had to be held back by baton-charging police and soldiers. But Lauda remained uncompromising to the end. 'The engine you gave me for this race was a joke', he was quoted as telling a Ferrari engineer: 'I was struggling all the time.'

It was not a very happy year all round. Andretti's Lotus-Ford had several embarrassing breakdowns and he lost his second place to South Africa's Jody Scheckter in a Wolf by failing to score in the last two races. The reigning champion, Britain's James Hunt, steered his Marlboro-McLaren to victory in only two races, the British and Japanese GPs, and finished fifth in the championship.

THE TURF

The Queen's love of horses and racing were suitably celebrated in her Jubilee year by her filly Dunfermline, which won both the Oaks and the St Leger, while eleven of Her Majesty's other horses contributed towards her 17 victories during the season, bringing her a total of £135,038 in prize money and third place—her highest ever—in the owners' table for the flat season. She was also voted Owner of the Year by the Horse Race Writers' Association. Royal jockey Willie Carson won the title Jockey of the Year, although he finished second to reigning champion Pat Eddery in the winning jockeys' table.

The royal successes were part of an important year for women in racing. Charlotte Brew, aged 21, became the first woman to ride in the Grand National, reaching the 25th fence on her mother's gelding Barony Fort before the horse refused. She also took part in the famous Czech steeplechase, said to be an even tougher test of horse and rider than the National.

Then, on 12 December, the Jockey Club, for the first time in its history (even longer than that of the Annual Register, at least 225 years), elected three women members—the Countess of Halifax and Mrs Priscilla Hastings, both well-known breeders of horses, and Mrs Helen Johnson-Houghton, a twin sister of the trainer Fulke Walwyn and herself a trainer of considerable success going back long before women were officially granted trainers' licences in 1968. Among the racing fraternity, indeed, Mrs Johnson-Houghton had always been given credit for training the 1956 Two Thousand Guineas winner Gilles de Retz, although her name does not appear in the record books because women trainers were not then recognized by the Jockey Club.

Dunfermline was the only horse to beat the American-bred, Irish-trained colt Alleged during the flat season, but although Alleged included the Prix de l'Arc de Triomphe (worth £140,845) among his victories he was outdone as Horse of the Year by The Minstrel, which won the English and Irish Derbys and the King George VI and Queen Elizabeth Stakes. Both these horses were largely owned by Mr Robert Sangster and contributed a great deal towards his top-owner winnings of £348,023. Both Alleged and The Minstrel were ridden by Lester Piggott in their major victories, making his 20th year in the saddle one of his most successful, although he was lucky to escape serious injury when his Oaks mount, Durtal, threw him before the start and bolted into the rails.

In the USA there were only two names on everyone's lips—the teenage jockey Steve Cauthen and the colt Seattle Slew. Cauthen, son of a Kentucky blacksmith and virtually unknown at the start of the year, had ridden 84 winners by the middle of February and set a record by hitting the million-dollar prize-money mark. A month after being taken to hospital in May with fractures to ribs, fingers and right arm after a collision of horses, he was back on the race-course, still with a lead of over 100 victories over his nearest rival. In November, he completed a first year unmatched in US racing history by winning the $200,000 Washington International. Seattle Slew added his page to history by becoming the first colt to chalk up ten successive victories, including the Triple Crown races, the Kentucky Derby, Preakness Stakes and Belmont Stakes.

But for prolonged re-writing of the record books no horse on the flat or over the sticks could match the 12-year-old steeplechaser Red Rum. Winning the Grand National for an unprecedented third time (by 25 lengths), he had now finished in the first two in all his five successive starts. Since at the end of the year the future of the National at Aintree yet again seemed to be in doubt, the Liverpool-trained horse could be said to have set records on his home course which would never be surpassed.

ASSOCIATION FOOTBALL

On the morning of 12 July, England—including the Football Association—was given the news by the *Daily Mail* that it no longer had a national team manager. Tired, apparently, of the criticism attending his three-year reign, Mr Don Revie had for some time been in negotiation with the rulers of the United Arab Emirates over a post in Dubai as national soccer organizer. To conclude the talks, he had allowed the England team to undertake the first part of an important tour of South America without him while he travelled to the UAE in disguise and under an assumed name, returning with assurances of a four-year contract worth about £340,000 tax-free. By the time his employers learnt of his resignation from the *Daily Mail*, which was reported to have paid him a large sum for the scoop, he was already in the UAE.

A caretaker manager, Mr Ron Greenwood, was appointed to pick up the pieces, but although he succeeded in producing a team to beat Italy 2-0 in a vital World Cup game it was not by a sufficient margin to get England to the finals in Argentina the following year. However, on 12 December, Mr Greenwood was confirmed in the post on a two-and-a-half-year contract taking him up to the end of the next European championship.

In Scotland, the more formal resignation of team-manager Mr Willie Ormond had far less traumatic results, although he left the job in May, shortly before the home international championship and a tour of South America, and when an all-important World Cup qualifying game against the reigning European champions Czechoslovakia was on the horizon. Mr Ally MacLeod, manager at Aberdeen for less than two years, accepted the national post with enthusiasm and swept all before him, winning the home championship by beating Revie's England soundly at Wembley and adding victories over both Czechoslovakia and Wales to clinch a World Cup finals place.

In Argentina, in addition to the host nation and West Germany (the holders), Scotland would be joined by Poland, Austria, Netherlands, France, Sweden, Spain, Hungary, Italy, Brazil, Peru, Mexico, Iran and Tunisia—the last two competing in the finals for the first time.

It was symptomatic of Mr Revie's problem that he had been unable to produce an England team as cohesive or consistently successful as the country's leading club side, Liverpool, which again dominated the domestic and European scene. Liverpool retained the League championship and reached both the FA Cup and European Cup finals, playing the last two finals in the space of five days.

They lost the FA Cup 1-2 to Manchester United but then went to Rome to beat Borussia Münchengladbach, champions of West Germany, 3-1 in the European Cup final. They became only the second English club to win this trophy in its 21 years of existence and the first to be victorious in a final outside England. Liverpool followed up this outstanding success by claiming the European Super Cup with a 6-0 victory at home over the European Cup-Winners' Cup holders, Hamburg FC, after drawing 1-1 in Hamburg, despite the fact that in the meantime their leading player, Kevin Keegan, had been transferred to Hamburg for a British record fee of £500,000.

The differences between national and club managership were no better shown than when Mr Greenwood picked seven of this Liverpool team (including Keegan on loan from Hamburg) for his first England selection against lowly Switzerland at Wembley in September but saw them stumble to a goalless draw.

CRICKET

The controversies aroused by the intervention of Mr Kerry Packer, an Australian newspaper and television tycoon, dominated what should otherwise have been a cricket year chiefly memorable for the celebration of the Centenary Test between England and Australia in Melbourne and another Ashes series in England.

Mr Packer entered the scene as a result of a dispute between himself and the Australian Board of Control when the latter refused to give him exclusive rights for his TV company to cover Tests in Australia. With the object of competing against the official Tests between Australia and India during the 1977-78 season, Mr Packer began recruiting players from all over the cricket world for his own series of 'Super Tests' between Australian, West Indian and Rest of the World XIs. His campaign apparently started during the Centenary Test in March, and by the time his players took the field for the first time on 24 November in Melbourne he had secured enough to field four full teams playing simultaneously at different venues. They included all the Australians (except fast bowler Geoff Thomson) who had played most of the Tests in England the previous summer, two former England captains (Tony Greig and Mike Denness) and at least four other English internationals, virtually the whole of the West Indies team, five top players from Pakistan and several South Africans.

They played on pitches grown in greenhouses and transported in bulk to such venues as were available (mostly football grounds). They played under 'Packer's Rules', which involved not only time-limit cricket but also additions to the pitch markings and changes in the field placings 'to speed up the game and make it more entertaining'. On 14 December, again in Melbourne, they inaugurated floodlit cricket when an Australian XI beat a World XI by six wickets in a 40-over match watched by 3,000 people. However, despite massive publicity in Mr Packer's newspapers and magazines, the public response was not as great as anticipated, and blanket coverage on Mr Packer's television stations did not justify his claim that he was attracting more viewers than the official Tests between Australia and India going on at the same time.

Mr Packer's most vociferous critics accused him of setting out to destroy the character of the game and its proper organization and control, and the England headquarters at Lord's was quick to react on behalf of the International Cricket Conference. Soon after he had admitted operating as a recruiting agent for Packer, Tony Greig was dismissed from the England captaincy and he and others who had signed for the Packer 'circus' were banned from playing elsewhere. The row ended in a lengthy and expensive action in the English High Court in which some of the players, backed by Packer, successfully sought an injunction against the ban. At the end of the year, the authorities were still undecided whether to appeal.

The Court action served to bring into the open the major reason for such massive defections. Alan Knott, the England wicket-keeper for over 70 Tests and universally recognized as probably the best in the world at his job, went into the witness box to reveal financial circumstances which caused many people who had originally regarded him as a kind of traitor to change their minds. He was going to be paid, he said, nearly twice as much playing for a few months for Packer as he earned in a whole year of almost continual cricket at home and abroad from his county (Kent) and country. He had a three-year contract with Packer; he would not have to pay his wife's air-fare to join him in Australia; and she would not be restricted to a 21-day visit as was rule for the wives of players in England touring parties.

Greig and Knott had been leading players in an England team which became the first to win a series in India for 43 years; they had also taken part in the Centenary Test which, by extraordinary coincidence, Australia won by 45 runs—exactly the same result and margin as in the first Test between the two countries in Melbourne 100 years previously.

Both also played in the Ashes series in England, but like every other player, English and Australian, from the third Test onwards they were overshadowed by the return of Geoffrey Boycott. Self-exiled from Test cricket for three years and 30 matches, the Yorkshire captain and opening bat came back to score a century in his first innings and another in the fourth Test before his own crowd at Headingley, becoming the first player to complete a century of first-class centuries in a Test match and helping England regain the Ashes with an average of 147·33. On top of that, he turned down Packer, flat.

XVII ECONOMIC AND SOCIAL AFFAIRS

Chapter 1

BUSINESS INVESTMENT

A marked feature of the faltering world recovery from the 1974-75 recession was the weakness of business investment. The level of capital spending in almost all the leading industrial countries was well below that recorded in similar phases of previous economic upturns, with the only partial exception of the USA.

A rise in investment played no more than a small part in the recoveries of the other main economies between 1975 and 1977, even those of Japan and West Germany. Gross fixed investment, including spending by the public sector as well as manufacturing and service industries, declined by 4 per cent in real terms in 1975 in the area of the Organization for Economic Cooperation and Development, after rising at an annual rate of 6¾ per cent in the previous decade. Such spending increased by 5 per cent in 1976 and came up to the previous annual average rise only in 1977. But on the evidence of previous cycles a larger acceleration would have been expected at this stage, and anyway a substantial part of the rise of investment was in housebuilding, especially in the US.

That was important because consumer spending and restocking of finished goods and raw materials by industry and distributors could generally support only the first period of recovery from the trough of a recession, as occurred in 1975-76. These components of demand were reckoned normally insufficient for sustained expansion of an economy. Consequently a strong rise in fixed capital formation was required to give some substance to lasting growth. An increase in investment would help to prevent bottlenecks and supply shortages emerging in key sectors at an early stage of recovery. Additional investment was also needed to make changes in plant and machinery to adapt to the sharp rise in the cost of energy and structural changes in the world economy. More new capital would boost productivity and thus lessen the pressure on capacity ceilings and thereby reduce the impact of a potentially major source of further inflation. The gains achieved here would also help to provide jobs in other sectors.

The main reason for the low level of investment in 1977 was probably the obvious one of the slow and hesitant growth of demand and the large margin of unused capacity in many sectors of industry in the leading industrialized countries. Professor Lawrence Klein of the Wharton Econometric Forecasting Associates at the University of Pennsylvania, in the October 1977 issue of *The World Economy*, published by the Trade Policy Research Centre in London, pointed out that in most major industrial countries the rate of capacity utilization—reflecting the margin of unused and under-used plant—peaked in 1973 or early 1974 and reached a trough in 1975. As long as capacity utilization rates were rising or stayed close to their high values—above 95 per cent—capital formation was going to be strongly stimulated, as indeed happened in 1973. Thereafter the level of capacity utilization fell back sharply throughout the industrialized world, down to levels of around 80 per cent on average in the major economies by mid-1975. The rate was slightly lower in Japan and somewhat higher in the UK and Canada.

This level was unusually low by the standard of past recessions and indicated a considerable amount of idle or spare capacity. Consequently the demand for output could be met with existing facilities and there was little inclination to expand capital plant or equipment. Overall capacity utilization increased during 1976, but in 1977 declined in several countries, notably Japan and Italy, in face of stagnant industrial production. The result was that throughout much of the OECD area the pick-up in activity and in capacity utilization had not yet reached the point where there was any real need for new plant. So, given the continuing doubts about the strength of the recovery in demand, many businessmen preferred to hold back from new investment. The only main exception was the US, where, according to a Federal Reserve Board estimate, the level of capacity utilization by the end of 1977 was just below the average level of 1964-73. On the basis of past trends this should be sufficient to produce higher investment in the US.

Apart from these cyclical restraints on the growth of investment, certain additional influences appear to have acted as a barrier in 1975-77, notably the slow progress made in reducing inflation in many countries. Mr Emile van Lennep, the secretary-general of OECD, pointed out in a speech in London in January 1978 that 'high rates of inflation inhibit investment primarily because they generate uncertainty about future rates of inflation, and hence about the future course of government policy and the likelihood of continuing expansion. Empirical work done at the OECD shows that, discounting the influence of other factors, investment has tended to recover more strongly in countries which have made the most progress in reducing inflation, and vice versa.'

Mr van Lennep also pointed out that the weakness of investment reflected the slow rate at which it had been possible to shift the underlying relationship between costs and prices in such a way as to increase the rate of return on investment. However, there had been some progress; for there was evidence that a number of countries had seen a reversal of the secular down-trend in profitability, which in many cases went back as far as the mid-1960s. However, this improvement in cost/price relationships was offset by the high, and in some cases rising, burden of fixed costs resulting from the prevailing low levels of capacity use. Thus while the level of profitability at full employment levels of activity might have improved, actual profits in the current depressed state of business recovered by a much smaller amount. This remained the position at the end of 1977.

The overall result of these constraints was that the element of risk in investment calculations expanded. According to Mr van Lennep again, 'the future has become more uncertain. Businessmen require the prospect of a higher rate of return than in the past if they are to be tempted into incurring the risks associated with investment in productive capacity—particularly productive capacity with a long lead-time and long life-time.'

Political uncertainty also became a limiting factor in certain countries, notably France and Italy, where business was concerned about a possible leftward shift in the balance of the Administrations. Even in other countries with greater political stability there was often uncertainty about legislative programmes important for investment, especially the long-delayed Energy Bill in the US.

Outside the leading Western industrial countries the heavy burden of private debt and difficulties of financing had also become a restraint. Private banks were taking an increasingly close look in 1975-77 at applications for new loans from both industrializing less-developed countries and from the centrally-planned economies. Both groups had been large-scale investors which had been obliged to cut back imports of capital goods for financial reasons.

A shortage of external finance did not appear to have been a restraint in the main industrialized countries, where capital markets were more developed and domestic savings relatively much greater. There was certainly a phase of restraint by the banks during 1974, when the prospect appeared of a much larger number of bankruptcies than actually occurred. But, apart from the profit and liquidity squeeze of this period, little evidence was found of a major long-term restraint on capital spending for this reason. In the UK, for example, almost all the submissions to the inquiry into City of London institutions by a committee headed by Sir Harold Wilson, the former Prime Minister, confirmed the availability of finance for worthwhile investment projects—with the sole exception of a possible financial barrier for certain smaller companies.

The response of Governments to the slow pick-up in investment varied. In the US, for example, the incentive of investment tax credits was used, and, in order to improve the post-tax return for companies, proposals for accelerated depreciation, reduced taxes on corporate profits and more favourable treatment of capital gains were all considered. But in the UK the tax incentives to investment through allowances of various kinds were already large before the recession, with the result that a comparatively small amount of tax was paid by many industrial companies.

In this position, Governments sought to encourage a continued improvement in cost/price/profit relationships and to minimize uncertainty by their actions—or lack of action. But the general view of most economists and policy-makers at the end of 1977, after two-and-a-half years of partial recovery, was that the best stimulus to investment remained the prospect of a sustained rise in demand.

Chapter 2

INTERNATIONAL ECONOMIC DEVELOPMENTS

THE recovery of the world economy from the recession of 1974-75 proved to be both hesitant and long-drawn-out. After the initial vigorous upturn, the rate of growth of activity generally faltered, while differences in performance resulted in growing imbalances in the current accounts of some of the major industrial economies and consequent instability in exchange markets.

These disappointments can be measured against the objectives set in June 1976 at a ministerial meeting of the Organization for Economic Cooperation and Development. The leading industrial countries then agreed on a strategy for non-inflationary growth involving 'a determination to restore full employment gradually but securely over a number of years rather than to risk a dramatic front-loaded recovery'. This strategy was based on the view that an annual rate of economic growth, for member countries collectively, of 5 per cent or somewhat more during the five years 1976-80 would be feasible. At the time the main Western economies were expanding fairly rapidly—at the annual rate of around 6 per cent in the first half of 1976.

Then, however, there was then a definite slowdown. This was partly because the effects of fiscal stimulus wore off and there was little follow-up to the initial recovery from the bottom of the economic cycle. By the end of 1976, the OECD talked merely about a 'pause in the recovery' rather than a new recession. It forecast a growth of nearly 4 per cent in total Gross National Product in OECD countries, with a fairly strong pick-up in the US, Japan and Germany in the next few months, followed by some slow-down in the second half of 1977 if existing policies continued. Accordingly, in order both to boost the level of activity generally and to reduce the spread between the performances of the more and less successful economies, the OECD secretariat advocated some new boost to domestic demand by the stronger economies.

The general pattern of activity turned out broadly as expected in 1977 but the extent of the slowdown was much greater than had been forecast. The recovery in activity in early 1977 was short-lived and growth weakened markedly in the second quarter, remaining sluggish during the rest of the

P

year. Overall, industrial production was stagnant from April onwards: the US was the best performer with only a certain slackening in the growth of output. In Europe, production fell sharply in the second quarter and showed no significant improvement during the rest of the year. This partly reflected an adjustment to the high level of stocks of finished goods which were built up in face of a general retreat of consumer spending from the spring onwards. The recovery in business investment was also hesitant in most Western countries.

Percentage increase in real Gross National Product from previous year

	Average 1964-65 to 1974-75	1976	1977 (estd)	1978 (estd)
USA	3·0	6·0	4¾	4¼
Japan	8·6	6·3	6	5
W. Germany	3·6	5·7	2¾	3¼
France	5·0	5·2	3	3¼
UK	2·3	2·1	¼	3
Canada	5·2	4·9	2¼	3¾
Italy	4·5	5·6	2	1
Other OECD	4·5	2·9	1½	2
All OECD	4·3	5·2	3½	3½

Source and estimates: *Organization for Economic Cooperation and Development.*

The rate of growth in real Gross National Product throughout the OECD area braked from an annual increase of 4 per cent to 3¼ per cent between the two halves of 1977. The increase over the year as a whole was only 3½ per cent, even after expansionary action by Governments. Consequently unemployment in the main industrialized countries continued to rise. A total of about 16·3 million at the end of 1977 was around 500,000 higher than at the trough of the 1975 recession. This was equivalent to 5·4 per cent of the civilian work-force. The leading economies had contrasting experiences. In the US the faster rate of economic growth was reflected in a decline in the numbers out of work, but in Europe there was a steady rise in unemployment from about 4·7 million at the beginning of 1975 to more than 7 million by the end of 1977. In many countries the weakness of the labour market led not only to a fall in employment but also to a rise in the under-utilization of employees.

A series of international meetings was held through the year in an attempt to produce an agreed policy to implement the medium-term strategy pronounced in June 1976. Their achievement was limited; the growth projections made by West Germany and Japan at the Downing Street summit of world leaders in early May were not fulfilled. The calls by the US and other countries on the Governments of the surplus economies to reflate might be held, however, to have strengthened the pressures for the expansionary action eventually taken during the autumn. These moves opened the prospect of a slight acceleration of output as 1977 ended. But the evidence of a pick-up was still slight and there was increasing resistance, notably by the West German Administration, to appeals for yet further action to boost domestic demand.

Another result of the slow growth in total output in the industrialized countries was that world trade expanded only modestly following the sharp rise in 1976. Consequently the aggregate current account deficit of the OECD countries, which had jumped by $20,000 million in 1976, increased by only a further $5,500 million in 1977 to $32,000 million. Indeed the aggregate deficit fell slightly between the first and second halves of 1977. At the same time the current account surplus of the oil-producing states declined slightly during 1977 from $42,250 million to $40,000 million, or just two-thirds of the record figure of 1974. This mainly reflected an improvement in the position of the non-oil developing countries.

Chart 1. World Current Accounts

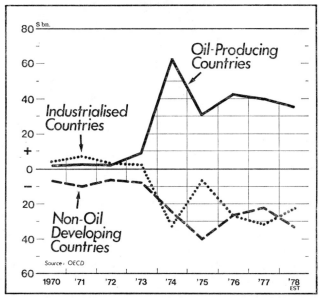

Within the group of industrialized countries there were striking contrasts in current account performance. France, Italy and the UK, which had had to adopt tough stabilization policies during 1976 at the cost of slow growth in 1977, all achieved considerable improvements in their current balances. Meanwhile, the surpluses of West Germany and Switzerland continued at a high level while that of Japan was multiplied three times. The contrasting feature was the sharp increase in the deficit of the US as a result of its relatively faster rate of recovery. Out of a near $40,000 million adverse swing on its trade, close on $10,000 million was with other industrialized countries but $15,000 million was with oil-producing countries and a further $15,000 million with non-oil developing countries.

The emergence of this deficit, and the prospect that it would persist, led to growing instability in foreign exchange markets. Whereas in 1976 the main attention was on sterling and the lira in face of the delayed economic stabilization programmes of the UK and Italy, the focus switched to other currencies in 1977. The yen, in particular, appreciated sharply against other major currencies, while the Swiss franc also gained ground. In contrast, both the Canadian dollar and the Swedish krona fell by a large percentage. Because of these divergent movements the effective value of the US dollar against a basket of other currencies did not alter significantly. The dollar was much weaker, however, against the yen and the stronger European currencies. All the major changes essentially represented a delayed response to current account imbalances.

The main long-term solution to the US deficit was generally seen as the adoption of effective energy policies which would also help to reduce the surpluses of the oil-producing countries. In the short-term, however, it was agreed that any significant reduction in the deficit depended on narrowing the differences in the rate of economic recovery between the US and other countries.

Most of the Finance Ministers of the leading countries were agreed that if the US deficit continued at a high level then the dollar would remain weak. The resulting uncertainties and volatility in the exchange markets were clearly feeding on themselves and limiting the overall recovery in both the appreciating and depreciating economies. This was shown, for example, by the increased complaints in West Germany about worsening export prospects.

Against this background of currency movements, slow growth and high unemployment, there was increasing pressure for intervention by Governments to protect the most vulnerable industries and sectors, of which steel was the most notorious case. This defensive approach was directed not only against the more successful industrialized economies, as shown by the protracted trade negotiations between the US and Japan, but also against the rapidly rising exports of manufactured goods of the newly emerging industrial countries in the developing world.

At the end of 1977 there was agreement among most of the leading industrial countries that there should be coordinated action, including monetary, fiscal and, in some cases, prices and incomes policies, to encourage and maintain a sustained recovery without reactivating inflation. Similarly, there should be a differentiation of monetary, fiscal and exchange rate policies coupled with more effective energy policies, to reduce payments disequilibria and to promote structural readjustments.

One of the few moderately encouraging features of 1977 was that the fears of an acceleration in the rate of inflation were not fulfilled. Overall in the West, the rate of increase in consumer prices remained around an annual rate of 8 per cent in 1977, as in 1976. Indeed, the underlying annual rate was down to around 6 per cent by the autumn of 1977, compared with a rate of 11 per cent earlier in the year. Falling commodity prices in response to the weakness of demand and good harvests were the main influence. The rate of increase of earnings had also edged downwards in many countries, though it was generally proving to be very difficult to cut the rate of inflation to the levels experienced before the 1973-74 oil price rise.

Chapter 3

THE ECONOMY OF THE UNITED STATES

THE USA was the only major industrialized country to fulfil its hopes of above-average economic growth in 1977. But the pattern of expansion and its consequences for both the current account and the dollar were very different from what had been expected. The US economy had recovered strongly during 1976 from the 1974-75 recession but the rate of advance slowed down during the autumn of that year. This reflected hesitant consumer spending, notably on durable goods. By the start of 1977 indicators such as new orders in manufacturing, retail sales and industrial production raised doubts about the underlying strength of the recovery. There were, however, hopes that this might be no more than a pause, since there were signs of a recovery in investment, real incomes and government spending.

Most economists expected that, despite the depressed outlook for world trade, any renewal of expansion would result in only a small deterioration in the US current account. Both business confidence and market sentiment were, however, affected by uncertainty about the policies of the new Carter Administration, which took office in mid-January 1977 and was committed to expansionary fiscal action.

Output and Investment. The optimistic view of the short-term outlook proved to be correct. Consumer demand grew at an exceptionally strong pace as households drew on their personal savings. Both residential and industrial investment also rose sharply, so real Gross National Product rose at an annual rate of 7·5 per cent in the first three months of 1977 and by 6·2 per cent in the second quarter. The result was a substantial rise in employment and a decline in the seasonally adjusted unemployment rate from 7·8 per cent in December to 6·9 per cent by the middle of the year.

The strength of the first quarter recovery also resulted in a change in the Carter Administration's policy. In early January, a two-year $31,600 million fiscal stimulus was proposed. Initially this would have largely consisted of a once-and-for-all tax rebate of $11,400 million, while increased public spending would provide the main impetus in the following year. Subsequent changes reduced the size of the package to between $17,000 million and $18,000 million and shifted the main impact to the end of 1977 and early 1978.

The recovery in output slackened during the summer and the annual rate of increase in real GNP slowed to 5·1 and 4·2 per cent in the final two quarters of the year. This reflected a weakening in consumer demand as the percentage of personal income saved rose from the unusually low level recorded earlier in 1977. Residential construction fell slightly after the spring and the expansion of industrial fixed investment lessened.

The overall result was still up to expectations: according to Commerce Department estimates, real GNP rose by nearly 4·9 per cent in 1977 as a whole compared with 6 per cent in the previous year. Private consumption increased by about 4½ per cent in real terms in 1977 and industrial investment was around 8½ per cent higher. Unemployment remained at around 7 per cent between the early summer and the autumn but there was a sharp fall in December, taking the rate down to 6·4 per cent, the lowest level since the start of the recession. During the year employment rose by 4,100,000, the largest annual gain since World War II, while about 3 million people entered the labour force.

The overall prospects for output appeared to be improving at the end of 1977 after the earlier slackening in growth. This was reflected in a sharp rise in new orders for non-defence capital goods, an increase in housing starts and a strong upward trend in the Commerce Department's index of leading indicators. However, the prospects for automobile sales were less encouraging and business confidence was still uncertain, with the result that fixed investment was still not recovering at a pace sufficient to ensure a sustainable rate of expansion.

Inflation. The early months of 1977 were marked by renewed concern about an acceleration in inflation, but in the event the fears were not fulfilled. The problem arose because of the impact of the severe 1976-77 winter on food and fuel prices. This pushed up the annual rate of increase in wholesale prices to nearly 10 per cent in the first few months of 1977.

The outlook improved during the year as a result of abundant harvests and a decline in commodity prices, with the result that the annual rate of increase in wholesale prices was down to between 2 and 3 per cent by the autumn. The annual rate of increase in earnings in manufacturing remained within the range of 8 to 9 per cent for most of the year. The net outcome was that after a marked acceleration in the rate of consumer price inflation in the first few months of the year the underlying rate of increase was down to less than 5 per cent per annum by the late autumn of 1977.

Monetary Policy. The dangers of a possible acceleration in the growth of the main monetary aggregates dominated much of the discussion of the economy during the year. At the beginning of the year the money supply expanded more rapidly than the target levels, and this led to a tightening of monetary policy and a rise in the Federal Funds rate—up to 5⅜ per cent at the end of May compared with 4⅝ per cent in December 1976. Short-term interest rates rose further later in the year in face of a continuing unexpectedly large rise in the narrowly-defined money supply. Long-term interest rates, however, remained relatively stable.

Current account and the dollar. The continued expansion of the US economy in contrast with the sluggish growth in other industrialized countries led to a sharp deterioration on the current account. At the beginning of the year a rise in the visible trade deficit from around $9,000 million to $10,500 million in 1977 had been widely expected. But the position soon became very much worse, a deficit of nearly $15,000 million being recorded in the first half of 1977 alone. At first it appeared that the deterioration could be explained largely by temporary factors such as the high level of fuel demand during the severe winter, but it quickly became apparent that the problems were more fundamental and that a high level of deficit might persist as long as the US led the world recovery. The pattern of consumer-led growth in the US and weak investment activity abroad compounded the problem, capital goods being a large component of US exports and consumer goods featuring prominently in imports. Moreover, the good harvests throughout the world limited the scope for boosting agricultural exports.

The trade deficit for 1977 turned out to be $26,700 million, four-and-a-half times as much in the previous year, though slightly less than the range of $27-30,000 million forecast by the Administration in the late summer. There were fears that this might strengthen the growing protectionist forces within the US.

Much of the discussion of the deficit focused on the rise in oil imports—up nearly one-third during 1977 to $42,140 million. This was cited by the Administration as the main reason why Congress should pass a comprehensive Energy Bill, but at the end of the year the measure was still held up in Congress and had been heavily modified.

The absence of any effective action to cut oil imports contributed to the weakness of the dollar which developed during the summer as the actual and prospective scale of the trade deficit became clear. There was intense pressure during July and again towards the end of the year. The Administration initially appeared to be content with the decline in the rate, and its later policy of 'benign neglect' did little to restore confidence. The result was that the dollar fell by 18 per cent against the Japanese yen during 1977 and by more than a tenth against the DMark.

The deteriorating position in late 1977 forced President Carter to produce a statement on 21 December insisting that the currency was 'fundamentally sound'. But this made little difference, and in face of intense pressure a switch to a policy of active support to stabilize the rate was implemented by the announcement on 4 January 1978 of a new swap agreement with West Germany and the activation of existing swap lines. This move was, however, widely seen as providing only a breathing-space until the fate of the Energy Bill was decided and it could be seen whether President Carter and his advisers (including Mr G. William Miller as chairman of the Federal Reserve Board in place of Dr Arthur Burns) could provide more effective economic leadership than in 1977.

Chapter 4

THE ECONOMY OF THE UNITED KINGDOM

THE UK economy entered 1977 in a battered state after the repeated sterling crises of the previous year, but with the hope that the worst was over. This expectation was fulfilled in one respect at least—the dramatic improvement in both the external and internal financial position during the following twelve months. However, what Mr Denis Healey, the Chancellor of the Exchequer, liked to call the 'real economy' remained sluggish, with Gross Domestic Product still below the 1973 peak and unemployment continuing to rise.

The note of faint optimism at the beginning of 1977—at least in contrast to the previous widespread gloom about the economic prospects— reflected hopes that the series of measures, including a monetary squeeze and public spending cuts, introduced during the previous three months might stabilize the financial position and form part of a 'medium-term programme for national recovery'. The Government's approach had been summed up in a letter of intent sent by Mr Healey to the International Monetary Fund (see AR 1976, p. 28) requesting a standby credit of $3,900 million. The success of negotiations for this loan had already stemmed the outflow from the official reserves by the end of 1977. It was recognized, however, that the priorities were cutting the rate of price inflation, which had been boosted by the earlier fall in sterling, and strengthening the balance of payments, and that the stabilization measures would check the growth of output.

External finance. The turn-round in foreign confidence, already apparent at the end of 1976, was consolidated in early 1977 when central bankers, meeting at Basel, reached an agreement arrived at removing the threat to the reserves from a sudden withdrawal of sterling balances by official holders, notably the oil-producing states. The capital inflows started almost from the New Year onwards and continued, with only one check, until late October when the pound was allowed to float freely (see p. 27). As a result, the official reserves rose by nearly five times during 1977 to $20,557 million, easily a record for the UK and the fourth largest total in the industrialized world. However, the net reserves position was much less favourable, since the Government and other public bodies had incurred massive overseas borrowings between 1973 and the end of 1977 in order to finance the large current account deficits of the past four years and the capital outflows of 1975-76.

The improvement in the external financial position allowed the UK to limit its drawings from the IMF to about half the December 1976 facility, or $1,900 million. But this still left total overseas debts of around $20,000 million due by 1984, and the Bank of England, in particular, stressed the need for a continuing current account surplus in order to permit an appreciable net reduction in debt. The Government's approach, which emerged towards the end of 1977, was based on spreading the burden of repayment away from the peak maturity dates of the early 1980s by repaying debt early and by seeking new loans lasting into the late 1980s.

Such repayments had been made possible not only by the rise in the official reserves but also by the sharp turn-round on the current account. This occurred much more rapidly than had been expected; instead of the deficit of £1,500 million forecast at the beginning of 1977, the year's outcome was estimated at a deficit of only £35 million, compared with £1,107 million in 1976.

The improvement reflected the build-up of North Sea oil production— contributing about £1,200 million to the current account—combined with a sharp growth in the volume of exports. Indeed the UK improved its share of world trade in manufactured goods for the first time in many years. The prospects for the current account looked reasonably good at the end of 1977 but there was growing concern, especially in industry, about the slow growth in world trade and the effect of the rise in the pound in the late autumn on the competitive position of Britain's exports.

Domestic finance. The attempt to reassert control over domestic monetary conditions through higher interest rates and a squeeze on bank lending also succeeded quickly. Interest rates fell sharply during the early months of 1977 and sales of gilt-edged stock were at record levels. Consequently the growth of sterling M3, the broadly-defined money stock, was kept within the target range of a 9 to 13 per cent annual increase until the last two months of 1977, and domestic credit expansion was well below the ceiling agreed with the IMF.

Since private sector demand for bank loans remained slack, the only threat to the control of the money supply, apart from government finance, came from inflows from overseas. The increased importance attached by

P*

the Government to monetary policy was shown when the M3 target rather than preserving the price competitiveness of exports was made a priority in late October after inflows of $3,040 million in a month had forced the authorities to stop holding down the exchange rate.

The public sector was a favourable influence on monetary policy throughout the period as a result not only of the cutback in planned expenditure but also of substantial underspending—by more than 4 per cent in 1976-77 and, according to an estimate in a White Paper published in January 1978 (Cmnd 7049), an even larger margin in 1977-78. This reflected both various financial changes and the tightening of controls, notably the extension of the cash limits system.

The result, when coupled with buoyant tax revenue, was a much lower than expected public sector borrowing requirement (PSBR)—an outturn of £8,770 million in 1976-77 against £11,000 million forecast in December 1976. The projections for 1977-78 were also revised downwards, permitting net tax cuts in the spring 1977 budget costing £1,000 million, followed by further cuts in late October costing just under £1,000 million in 1977-78. At the same time, increases in public spending, mainly on construction and child benefits, were announced for 1978-79 and the later White Paper projected a resumption of growth of public spending at a rate of about 2 per cent a year in volume terms—below the forecast expansion of the economy.

Chart 2. The Recovery of Sterling

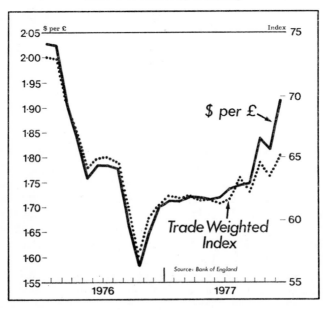

Source: Bank of England

Inflation. The inflationary position and prospects throughout the year were dominated by the exchange rate. The sharp fall in sterling during 1976 accelerated the 12-month rate of increase in retail prices up to a peak of 17·6 per cent by mid-July. However, the improvement in sterling coupled with a decline in world commodity prices after the spring resulted in a sharp decline in the underlying rise by the late summer. Indeed the Government was, for once, able to meet its inflation target—a 12 to 13 per cent increase of prices during 1977—and a single figure rate was just over the horizon.

Labour costs remained under control for most of the period. A measure of the success of Phase 2 of the Government's incomes policy, which gave way to Phase 3 in August, was a fall in the annual rise in average earnings from 13·9 to 8·9 per cent during 1976-77. The Government's failure to reach agreement with the TUC on formal policy after July 1977 (see p. 21) aroused early fears of runaway wage increases, but by the end of 1977 a qualified optimism had emerged. Although average earnings still looked like rising by more than the 10 per cent official guideline, the outcome was widely forecast at between 12 and 14 per cent, not over 15 per cent. The result of this containment of higher earnings, coupled with a faster increase in prices, was that living standards, as measured by real personal disposable income, declined sharply until the late summer. The income tax cuts, followed later by a rise in real earnings, then stabilized the position, giving a net fall of 1½ per cent in 1977.

Output and employment. The overall impact of the squeeze on living standards and the cutbacks in public spending was that total output hardly increased during the year, after beginning to recover from the depths of the 1975-76 recession. In contrast to a rise in Gross Domestic Product of 2 per cent between the second halves of 1976 and 1977 which had been forecast in December 1976, the actual outcome was estimated at no more than a ½ per cent increase. Export growth was strong until the autumn, but personal consumption fell and the rise in manufacturing investment was smaller than expected, before signs of an improvement in both respects appeared towards the end of the year.

The slow growth in the economy had a surprisingly small effect on unemployment. The number of people out of work fell during the winter and early spring, then rose sharply during the summer before falling slightly in the autumn. The result was a rise during the year of 102,400 to 1,428,000 in the number of adult unemployed in the UK, on a seasonally adjusted basis. Both the pattern of the change and the limited extent of the overall rise were somewhat puzzling, but were probably influenced in part by the Government's special job creation and preservation measures. An encouraging feature at the end of the year was the rise in the number of vacancies, indicating a possible upturn in the labour market during 1978.

NOTES ON ECONOMIC AND SOCIAL DATA

The statistical data on the following pages record developments from 1972 to the latest year, usually 1977, for which reasonably stable figures were available at the time of going to press. Year headings 1972 to 1977 are printed only at the head of each p age and are not repeated over individual tables unless the sequence is broken by the inserti on of series of figures recording developments over a shorter (or longer) period than is shown on the remainder of the page. Shorter-term or longer-term data are separated by fine rules from the main tables which they follow.

Those pages in the three sections of statistics to which the point is relevant include a comparative price index, allowing the figures given on a current-price basis to be reassessed against the background of inflation.

Unless figures are stated as indicating the position at the *end* of years or quarters, they should be taken as annual or quarterly *totals* or *averages*, according to context.

Tables 2, 3, 4 and 21. Statistics which are normally reported or collected separately in the three UK home jurisdictions (England and Wales, Scotland, and Northern Ireland) have been consolidated into UK series only to show general trends. As the component returns were made at varying times of year and in accordance with differing definitions and regulatory requirements, the series thus consolidated may therefore be subject to error, may not be strictly comparable from year to year, and may be less reliable than the remainder of the data.

Symbols. — = Nil or not applicable .. = not available at time of compilation.

Sources

A. THE UNITED KINGDOM
   Government Sources
   Annual Abstract of Statistics: Tables 1, 2, 3, 4, 13, 14, 18, 20, 21, 25, 26.
   Monthly Digest of Statistics: Tables 1, 5, 6, 7, 8, 9, 16, 17, 18, 19, 20, 23, 25, 26, 28, 30.
   Financial Statistics: Tables 5, 6, 9, 10, 22.
   Economic Trends: 11, 12, 15, 22, 24.
   Social Trends: Tables 2, 3, 4, 21.
   Department of Employment Gazette: Tables 27, 28, 29, 30.
   Housing and Construction Statistics: Tables 13, 21.
   Additional Sources
   National Institute of Economic and Social Research, *National Institute Economic Review:* Tables 11, 12, 15.
   Bank of England Quarterly Bulletin: Tables 5, 7.
   Midland Bank: Tables 8, 9.
   United Nations, *Monthly Bulletin of Statistics:* Tables 1, 6.
   The Financial Times: Tables 5, 8.
   British Insurance Association: Table 14.

B. THE UNITED STATES
   Government and other Public Sources
   Department of Commerce, *Survey of Current Business:* Tables 31, 32, 33, 34, 35, 36, 41, 42.
   Council of Economic Advisers, Joint Economic Committee, *Economic Indicators:* Tables 35, 40.
   Federal Reserve Bulletin: Tables 37, 38, 39.
   Additional Sources
   A. M. Best Co.: Table 39.
   Insurance Information Institute, New York: Table 39.
   Bureau of Economic Statistics, *Basic Economic Statistics:* Tables 42, 44.

C. INTERNATIONAL COMPARISONS
   United Nations, *Annual Abstract of Statistics:* Tables 45, 46, 47, 55, 56, 57, 58.
   UN *Monthly Bulletin of Statistics:* Tables 45, 46, 55, 56, 58.
   IMF, *International Financial Statistics:* Tables 46, 48, 49, 50, 51, 52, 58, 59.
   OECD, *Main Economic Indicators:* Tables 46, 52.
   Institute of Strategic Studies, *The Military Balance:* Table 54.

Chapter 5

ECONOMIC AND SOCIAL DATA
A. THE UNITED KINGDOM

1. Population	1972	1973	1974	1975	1976	1977
Population, mid-year est. ('000)	55,781	55,913	55,922	55,900	55,886	55,852
Density (persons per sq. km.) (1)	231	232	232	232	232	232
Live births registered ('000)	834·0	779·5	737·1	697·5	675·5	656·0
Crude birth rate (per 1,000 pop.)	14·9	13·9	13·2	12·5	12·1	11·8
Deaths registered ('000)	673·9	669·7	667·4	662·5	680·0	655·0
Crude death rate (per 1,000 pop.)	12·1	12·0	11·8	11·2	12·1	11·7

(1) Based on land area of 241,042 square kilometres.

2. Health

	1972	1973	1974	1975	1976	1977
Public expenditure on National Health Service (£ million)(1)	2,597	2,939	3,847	5,181	6,182	6,567
Hospitals:						
staffed beds, end-year ('000)	523·4	516·7	506·0	497·0	488·8	480·0
ave. daily bed occupancy ('000)	431·2	415·1	410·4	396·3	393·0	390·0
waiting list, end-yr. ('000)	596·0	624·0	629·0	704·0	722·0	700·0
Certifications of death ('000) by:						
ischaemic heart disease	175·5	175·5	177·0	177·4	180·8	..
malignant neoplasm, lungs and bronchus	35·8	36·4	37·4	37·2	38·0	..
road fatality	8·1	8·2	7·6	7·0	6·8	6·6
accidents at work (number)(2)	784	826	753	730	646	..

(1) Central government and local authority, capital and current. (2) Great Britain.

3. Education

	1972	1973	1974	1975	1976	1977
Public expenditure (£ million)(1)	3,414	3,949	4,601	6,561	7,340	8,053
Schools ('000)	38·3	38·1	38·3	38·1	38·2	..
Pupils enrolled ('000) in schools	10,453	10,635	11,070	11,143	11,203	..
maintained primary(2)	6,001	6,072	6,040	5,986	6,010	..
maintained and aided secondary(3)(4)	3,866	3,944	4,407	4,588	4,558	..
direct grant(5)	120	121	122	122	122	..
independent(5)	410	414	419	422	426	..
Pupils per full-time teacher at:						
maintained primary schools	26·2	25·6	24·9	24·2	23·8	..
maintained secondary schools(4)	17·4	16·9	17·3	17·0	16·8	..
direct grant schools(4)(5)	16·4	16·3	16·3	17·4(6)	17·4(6)	..
recognized independent schools(5)	14·1	14·1	14·1	} 15·1	15·2	..
other independent schools(5)	17·2	17·2	17·2			
Further education: institutions(7)	8,401	8,192	8,562	8,299	8,046	..
full-time students ('000)	342	348	352	392	392	..
Universities(8)	51	51	51	52	52	52
University students ('000),	266	270	276	283	269	..
in mainly arts faculties(9)	115·3	118·3	122·5	127·5	135·3	..
in mainly science faculties(10)	127·3	128·4	128·7	130·1	133·4	..
First degrees awarded (number)	51,286	52,472	54,813	55,650	55,920	..
Open University graduates ('000)	0·9	3·6	5·2	5·5	6·0	..

(1) Central government and local authority, capital and current. (2) Including nursery schools. (3) Including special schools. (4) 1976 estimate excludes some voluntary maintained or aided grammar schools which became independent. Pupils at middle schools have been allocated to primary or secondary series according to whether they were aged 8-11 or 11-14. (5) England and Wales. (6) Direct grant grammar (secondary) schools only. (7) Great Britain. (8) University College, Buckingham, added 1975. (9) Including economics, social sciences, law. (10) Including medicine.

4. Law and Order	1972	1973	1974	1975	1976	1977
Public expenditure (£ million)(1)	693	827	1,060	1,386	1,704	..
Police	479	558	695	909	1,137	..
central government grants	206	226	258	..	..	..
Prisons	89	107	148	193	234	..
Administration of justice(2)	125	162	217	284	332	..
local authority expenditure	63	57	66	79	..	..
Police establishment ('000)(3)	122·3	124·4	127·7	129·2	130·0	..
Full-time strength(3)	111·4	112·5	114·3	120·0	122·2	..
Ulster, full-time strength	4·3	4·4	4·6	4·9	5·3	..
Offences known to police ('000) (4)(5)	1,905	1,858	2,189	2,375	2,450	..
Persons convicted ('000)(4)(6)	2,055	2,179	2,201	2,245	2,320	..
Burglary or robbery	72	64	75	81	81	..
Fraud, forgery	20	18	20	22	25	..
Theft, unauthorized taking	209 ⎫	184	207	222	229	..
Handling stolen goods/receiving	22 ⎭					
Violence against the person	44	49	49	52	55	..
Murders (number)	121	132	173	217	266	..
Intoxicating liquor laws	110	121	127	139	148	..
Criminal/malicious damage	28	35	38	42	45	..
Traffic (excl. drunken driving)	1,314	1,331	1,306	1,316	1,357	..
Prisons: average population ('000)	47	44	44	45	47	..

(1) Gross expenditure, capital and current, by central government (direct and by grant to local authorities) and by local and police authorities. (2) Includes expenditure on parliament and courts. (3) Police establishment and full-time strength: Great Britain only. (4) Because of differences in juridical and penal systems in the three UK jurisdictions (England and Wales; Scotland; Northern Ireland), totals of offences and convictions are not strictly comparable from year to year: they should be read only as indicating broad trends. Crimes and offences are in general described by the terms applicable in England from 1972 onwards. (5) Series revised to cover indictable offences and (Scotland) crimes only. (6) Series revised to include non-indictable and (Scotland) miscellaneous offences.

5. Interest Rates and Security Yields(1)

(% per annum, end of year)						
Bank rate/minimum lending rate(2)	9·00	13·00	11·50	11·25	14·25	7·00
Treasury bill yield	8·48	12·82	11·30	10·93	13·98	6·39
London clearing banks base rate	7·50	13·00	12·00	11·00	14·00	7·03
Finance houses base rate	8·00	14·00	12·00	12·00	15·00	5·50
2½% consols, gross flat yield (3)	9·11	10·85	14·95	14·66	14·25	12·32
10-year government securities (3)	8·45	10·65	14·21	13·18	13·61	12·02
Ordinary shares, dividend yield (3)	3·26	4·12	8·23	6·81	5·96	5·42
Local authority bonds, 2 years	9·40	14·30	14·50	12·25	14·75	8·63
Local authority 3-month deposits	8·75	16·63	13·25	11·31	14·88	6·75
Interbank 3-month deposits	8·72	16·19	12·44	11·16	14·38	6·66
US $ 3-month deposits in London	5·91	10·19	10·06	5·87	5·06	7·19
Clearing bank 7-day deposits	5·75	9·50	9·50	7·00	11·00	4·00

(1) Gross redemption yields, unless stated otherwise. For building society rates see Table 13. (2) Bank of England MLR replaced bank rate on 13 October 1972. (3) Revised series.

6. Prices and Costs (index 1970 = 100)

Total home costs per unit of output(1)	121·6	131·8	153·7	197·6	225·4	255·3
Labour costs per unit of output	118·5	128·1	158·6	206·5	231·0	258·4
Mfg. wages, salaries/unit of output	113·4	121·2	150·0	195·7	221·1	251·6
Import unit values	109·1	138·1	210·3	235·9	288·6	333·6
Wholesale prices, manufactures	114·8	123·2	152·0	188·7	219·6	261·8
Consumer prices	117·2	127·9	148·4	184·4	215·0	249·1

(1) Used as 'Overall price index' on remaining pages of UK statistics.

7. Banking(1)
(£ million, at end of period)

	1972	1973	1974	1975	1976	1977
Current and deposit accounts	50,936	71,490	84,615	129,073	163,476	177,275
Advances to	44,674	64,285	76,134	115,978	149,964	161,722
local authorities	2,154	2,335	2,094	3,932	4,025	4,368
public corporations	435	1,207	1,442	1,918	2,340	2,365
financial institutions	2,003	2,648	2,640	3,781	4,436	4,702
property companies(6)	892	1,669	2,716	2,956	2,785	2,505
companies	9,730	14,219	18,026	19,993	23,335	25,651
manufacturing(6)	4,790	5,923	8,426	7,126	8,545	9,380
construction(6)	843	1,320	2,207	1,715	1,560	1,583
personal sector	2,182	3,270	4,077	7,127	7,723	9,020
for house purchase(2)(6)	661	1,011	1,233	1,291	1,364	1,470
overseas residents(3)(7)	25,614	38,134	46,222	62,126	85,505	85,924
Eligible liabilities (4)	20,582	26,574	30,584	32,686	36,876	40,833
Special deposits(5), cumulative(%)	3	5	4	3	6	3

Overall price index (1970 = 100)	*121·6*	*131·8*	*153·7*	*197·6*	*225·4*	*255·3*

Shorter-term data	*1975*	*1976*	*1977:I*	*II*	*III*	*IV*
Current and deposit accounts	129,073	163,476	163,470	168,350	174,190	177,275
Advances	115,978	149,964	151,753	155,446	159,762	161,722

Overall price index (1970 = 100)	*197·6*	*225·4*	*245·6*	*249·5*	*261·5*	*264·6*

(1) Unless otherwise stated, this table covers all banks in the UK observing the common 12·5 per cent reserve ratio introduced on 16 Sept. 1971 and includes the accepting houses (merchant banks), discount houses and, for deposits, the National Giro and the banking department of the Bank of England. Except in the case of overseas advances, inter-bank transactions have been omitted. (2) 1971-75: excluding Northern Ireland banks. (3) Individuals, corporations, financial institutions; revised series to give gross advances outstanding, in sterling and other currencies, at current prices and allowing for effects of exchange rate changes. (4) Sterling deposit liabilities excluding those having original maturity of over two years, and sterling resources obtained by switching out of foreign currency holdings: special deposits called in by the Bank of England are expressed as a percentage of banks' eligible liabilities. (5) Including supplementary deposits from July 1974. (6) 1977 figure: November.

8. The Stock Market
(£ million, unless otherwise stated)

	1972	1973	1974	1975	1976	1977
Turnover(1) (£000 mn.)	57·2	55·7	56·8	94·0	106·4	173·3
ordinary shares (£000 mn.)	20·7	13·7	12·6	17·6	14·2	20·2
New issues, less redemptions (value)	1,100·2	168·7	78·2	1,551·0	1,114·3	926·2
Government securities	156	1,778	1,127	5,706	5,927	11,168
Local authority issues (2)	83·1	−15·6	27·2	186·0	107·8	239·0
UK companies (gross)	956·4	210·5	162·1	1,578·4	1,160·9	947·3
by ordinary shares	649·9	153·6	119·3	1,320·7	1,023·9	819·6
preference shares	10·9	14·0	—	44·9	44·5	33·9
convertible loan stock	96·4	21·6	25·6	117·0	14·8	2·0
other debt	199·2	21·3	17·2	95·8	77·7	91·8
FT ordinary share index (1935 = 100)(3)	503·8	435·6	251·2	311·0	368·0	452·3
FT-Actuaries index (1962 = 100)(3)	212·66	184·61	106·75	133·11	153·04	191·91
Industrial, 500 shares	213·97	185·26	108·84	135·97	162·91	208·79
Financial, 100 shares	218·19	188·85	102·45	122·85	124·18	145·68

(1) London and Scottish Stock Exchanges to March 1973; thereafter The Stock Exchange. (2) Includes public corporation issues. (3) Average during year.

Overall price index (1970 = 100)	*121·6*	*136·8*	*153·7*	*197·6*	*225·4*	*255·3*

9. Companies
(£ million)

	1972	1973	1974	1975	1976	1977
Total income	13,016	18,411	21,388	21,106	25,561	29,180
Gross trading profit in UK	7,769	9,833	9,962	9,677	12,445	13,780
Investment income in UK	2,453	2,945	4,218	5,286	9,444	9,677
Total overseas income	1,436	2,562	2,760	2,518	3,043	3,385
Dividends on ord. and pref. shares	1,613	1,695	1,566	1,520	1,846	2,221
Net payments of UK tax	1,518	1,718	2,404	1,887	1,493	2,087
Net profit	6,104	9,188	9,873	9,994	12,942	12,676
Companies taken over (number)	1,331	1,313	570	388	402	482
Total take-over consideration	2,938	1,742	640	460	557	812
of which in cash (%)	19	51	66	51	67	63
Liquidations (number)(1)	3,063	2,575	3,720	5,398	5,939	5,815
Receiverships (number)(1)	4,337	3,917	5,718	7,271	7,207	4,505

(1) England and Wales.

10. Money and Savings
(£ million, amounts outstanding at end of period, unless otherwise stated)

Money stock M_1(1)	12,657	13,303	14,739	17,481	19,467	22,639
Money stock M_3(2)	26,245	33,478	37,698	40,573	45,124	48,223
Sterling M_3	25,443	32,046	35,300	37,595	41,160	44,066
Notes and coins in circulation	4,079	4,377	5,085	5,903	6,714	7,525
Domestic credit expansion	6,674	8,066	6,936	4,462	7,439	7,844

Shorter-term data	1975	1976	1977:I	II	III	IV
Money stock M_3	40,573	45,124	44,421	43,342	47,219	48,223
Domestic credit expansion	4,462	7,439	−1,857	2,040	−473	695

	1972	1973	1974	1975	1976	1977
Personal savings ratio (%)(3)	10·4	11·6	13·9	15·1	14·6	13·4
National savings	10,062	10,391	10,565	11,275	11,618	13,179
Trustee savings bank	3,155	3,366	3,535	3,849	4,064	4,542
National savings bank	1,984	2,065	2,087	2,141	2,200	3,030
National savings certificates	2,642	2,567	2,467	2,630	2,978	4,027
Premium bonds	962	1,016	1,049	1,110	1,186	1,263
Save as You Earn	98	147	190	221	290	317

(1) M_1 = Notes and coins in circulation with the public plus resident private sector sterling current accounts with the banks minus 60 per cent of transit items. (2) M_3 = notes and coins in circulation plus total deposits of the domestic sector. (3) Personal savings as a percentage of personal disposable income.

11. Personal Income and Expenditure
(£ million, seasonally adjusted, current prices unless otherwise stated)

Wages and salaries	33,141	38,024	45,856	59,300	67,185	73,354
Current grants	5,853	6,445	7,873	10,208	12,822	15,334
Forces' pay	862	928	1,078	1,296	1,440	1,747
Other personal income	10,777	15,039	15,483	17,311	20,680	23,342
Personal disposable income(1)	44,593	51,156	60,455	74,865	86,241	96,843
Real personal disposable income (2)	38,562	40,813	41,443	41,533	41,454	40,656
Consumers' expenditure	39,944	45,201	51,977	63,552	73,656	83,758

Overall price index (1970=100)	121·6	131·8	153·7	197·6	225·4	255·3

Shorter-term data	1975	1976	1977:I	II	III	IV
Real personal disposable income (2)	41,533	41,454	10,210	9,970	10,084	10,392
Consumers' expenditure (2)	35,257	35,405	8,761	8,665	8,796	8,840

Overall price index (1970 = 100)	197·6	225·4	245·6	249·5	261·5	264·6

(1) From rent, self-employment (before depreciation or stock appreciation provisions), dividend and interest receipts and charitable receipts from companies. (2) At 1970 prices.

12. Fixed Investment	1972	1973	1974	1975	1976	1977
(£ million, 1970 prices, seasonally adjusted)						
Total, all fixed investment(1)	9,797	10,253	10,287	10,062	9,724	8,996
Dwellings	1,834	1,752	1,705	1,820	1,806	1,500
public	703	715	834	905	922	726
private	1,151	1,037	871	915	884	774
Mainly private industries & services(2)	4,423	4,888	4,880	4,229	4,473	4,632
manufacturing	1,739	1,872	2,024	1,737	1,659	1,776
other(2)	2,684	3,016	2,856	2,492	2,813	2,856
Mainly public industries & services(3)	3,244	3,348	3,332	3,340	3,158	2,572

Shorter-term data (Quarterly average rates)	1975	1976	1977:I	II	III	IV
Total, all fixed investment(1)	2,515	2,431	2,248	2,231	2,262	2,255
Public dwellings	226	231	205	179	172	170
Private dwellings	229	221	168	191	205	210
Mainly private manufacturing	434	415	419	432	455	470
Mainly public industries	835	790	724	612	601	625

Overall price index (1970 = 100)	*197·6*	*225·4*	*245·6*	*249·5*	*261·5*	*264·6*

(*1*) *Includes investment in North Sea oil platforms and equipment (from 1975 onward) and in mining and quarrying (all years), not allocated to sectors. (2) Includes distribution, agriculture, shipping. (3) Excludes the nationalized steel industry, which is included in manufacturing.*

13. Building Societies	1972	1973	1974	1975	1976	1977
(Condition at end of financial year ended in year indicated, unless otherwise stated)						
Societies on register (number)	456	447	416	382	364	357
Interest rates (%):						
Paid on shares, ave. actual	4·88	6·51	7·33	7·21	7·02	..
BSA(1) recommended, end-year	5·25	7·50	7·50	7·00	7·80	6·00
Paid on deposits, ave. actual	4·61	6·04	6·88	6·74	6·61	..
BSA recommended, end-year	5·00	7·25	7·25	6·75	7·55	5·75
Mortgages, ave. charged	8·26	9·59	11·05	11·08	11·06	..
BSA recommended, end-year	8·50	11·00	11·00	11·00	12·25	9·50
Shares and deposits, net (£ mn.)	2,193	2,162	1,993	4,172	3,405	5,808
Government advances (£ mn.)(2)	35	32	358	23	20	20
Mortgage advances, net (£ mn.)	2,215	1,999	1,490	2,768	3,618	3,760

(*1*) *BSA: Building Societies Association. (2) Excludes 3-month bridging grant in 1973.*

14. Insurance(1)	1972	1973	1974	1975	1976	1977
(£ million)						
Life assurance(1)(2), net premiums	2,226	2,464	2,758	3,111	3,825	..
investment income	1,130	1,340	1,580	1,830	2,230	..
benefits paid to policyholders	1,460	1,620	1,970	2,180	2,560	..
life funds, end-year	16,010	18,286	18,293	21,877	23,342	25,131
Non-life(1)(2), net premiums	2,862	3,360	3,858	4,641	6,043	..
underwriting profit/(—)loss(3)	42·3	19·0	−107·0	−183·0	−151·0	..
Lloyd's (4), premiums	957	1,191	1,539	1,661	690	..
balance(5)	92	110	82	1,229	531	..

(*1*) *Companies only; excludes Lloyd's. (2) World-wide business of UK companies and authorized UK affiliates of foreign companies. (3) Including net transfers of marine, aviation and transit branch revenues to/from profit and loss accounts. (4) 1975 and 1976; years 2 and 1 only of three-year open account. (5) Including net interest on underwriting funds, less claims, expenses and other outgo.*

Overall price index (1970 = 100)	*121·6*	*131·8*	*153·7*	*197·6*	*225·4*	*255·3*

15. National Income¯and Expenditure(1)
(£ million, 1970 prices, seasonally adjusted, quarterly averages or rates)

	1975	1976	1977	1977:I	II	III	IV
GDP(2), expenditure basis	11,682	12,049	12,049	11,987	12,121	12,123	11,963
income basis	23,232	27,266	30,613	29,451	30,068	31,419	31,515
output basis (1970 = 100)	107·4	108·7	110·4	110.6	109·5	110·6	110·8
average estimate (1970 = 100)	107·2	109·7	110·6	110·0	110·7	110·9	110·8
Components of gross domestic product:							
Consumers' expenditure	8,817	8,851	8,783	8,758	8,644	8,831	8,900
Public authorities' current spending	2,699	2,763	2,757	2,751	2,766	2,759	2,751
Gross fixed investment	2,410	2,361	2,268	2,260	2,293	2,265	2,254
Exports, goods and services	3,609	3,855	4,086	3,977	4,075	4,252	4,038
Total final expenditure, excluding stocks	17,306	17,854	17,994	17,979	18,006	18,076	17,936
Stockbuilding	−842	97	425	33	228	−31	−7
Imports of goods and services	3,422	3,552	3,687	3,738	3,709	3,686	3,615
Adjustment to factor cost	2,202	2,253	2,264	2,254	2,176	2,267	2,358

(*1*) *The longer-term development of the UK gross domestic product is recorded in Table 46 of the international comparative data, page 475.* (2) *At factor cost.*

16. Industrial Production
(Index, average 1970 = 100, seasonally adjusted)

All industries	101·5	102·0	102·3	103.3	101·9	102·6	101·5
Mining and quarrying	86·0	89·4	104·1	103·1	104·5	105·3	104·4
Coal mining	81·1	74·7	72·8	74·5	73·8	72·7	71·2
Manufacturing industries	102·2	103·1	103·6	105·3	102·7	103·5	102·5
Food, drink and tobacco	108·7	110·9	112·6	113·2	111·9	110·4	113·7
Chemicals	113·3	124·3	126·9	129·6	128·3	127·7	122·3
Oil and coal products	92·0	96·3	93·2	96·0	94·4	92·8	89·7
Metal manufacture	78·6	85·3	80·4	84·2	80·8	83·7	74·2
Engineering and allied	103·1	98·8	99·3	100·0	98·6	99·2	98·9
Mechanical	104·2	97·4	95·0	98·1	94·2	94·3	92·8
Electrical	113·4	110·8	114·4	115·6	110·7	116·0	118·0
Shipbuilding and marine	79·7	92·0	93·5	79·9	89·7	82·2	82·4
Vehicles and aircraft	95·3	91·9	92·8	91·6	93·6	92·5	92·9
Textiles	99·5	101·7	101·5	105·1	99·2	102·6	100·1
Bricks, pottery, glass	107·9	111·1	108·9	109·2	106·8	108·4	110·6
Timber, furniture, etc.	110·2	112·3	105·3	110·7	99·6	103·1	107·2
Paper, printing, publishing	95·6	98·0	102·1	102·7	101·0	101·4	102·9
Construction	92·6	88·9	..	80·8	82·4	83·6	..
Gas, electricity, water	120·8	123·5	128·0	128·3	131·8	130·4	124·1

17. Productivity
(Index of output per head, 1970 = 100)

All production industries	110·9	114·2	114·3	115·4	113·6	114·4	113·8
Manufacturing	113·4	118·1	117·6	119·8	116·5	117·3	116·6
Mining and quarrying	100·2	105·2	123·3	121·3	122·7	124·5	125·3
Metal manufacture	93·5	106·8	100·0	104·5	99·9	103·3	92·8
Engineering	120·4	119·4	119·0	122·0	117·3	118·8	118·3
Vehicles	105·2	103·3	101·2	101·2	102·5	100·8	100·3
Textiles	119·9	128·5	123·2	129·8	120·3	122·6	120·3
Gas, electricity, water	133·0	136·2	142·4	142·5	146·4	142·9	138·2
Overall price index (1970 = 100)	*197·6*	*225·4*	*255·3*	*245·6*	*249·5*	*261·5*	*264·6*

18. Energy	1972	1973	1974	1975	1976	1977
Coal, production (million tons)	120·0	130·0	108·7	126·7	121·8	120·2
Stocks, end-year (mn. tons)(1)	30·0	27·5	21·5	30·7	32·6	31·0
Power station consumption (mn. tons)	55·5	75·6	70·0	73·4	76·6	78·7
Power stations' demand for oil (million tons coal equivalent)	31·2	28·1	28·6	21·3	16·6	17·7
Electricity generated ('000 mn. kwh.)	242·7	258·8	250·4	251·2	254·8	262·1
by nuclear plant ('000 mn. kwh.)	25·3	23·7	29·4	27·1	32·2	40·0
Natural gas sent out (mn. therms)	7,702	9,188	13,104	13,692	14,217	15,252
Town gas sent out (million therms)	2,558	2,433	1,602	754	229	73
Crude oil output ('000 tonnes)(2)	336	372	408	1,560	11,678	37,884
Oil refinery output (mn. tons)(3)	97·8	104·3	101·4	85·3	90·3	86·3
Inland deliveries (mn. tons) of:						
Petrochemical feedstock	6·2	7·1	7·2	4·8	5.7	5·8
Motor spirit(4)	15·9	16·9	16·5	16·1	16·9	17·3
Other vehicle/engine fuels(5)	23·9	24·6	22·4	21·9	22·6	23·8
Vehicle miles travelled (1970 = 100)(1)	112	118	115	117	122	118
Other fuel oils	41·6	42·7	39·6	33·1	30·5	30·4

(*1*) *Excluding Northern Ireland.* (*2*) *Including natural gas liquids.* (*3*) *All fuels and other petroleum products.* (*4*) *Including aviation spirit (for piston-engined aircraft).* (*5*) *Including diesel-engined road vehicle fuel (Derv) and other gas/diesel oils, and jet (aviation turbine) kerosene.*

19. Industrial products and manufactures, output

Crude steel (million tonnes)	25·3	26·7	22·3	19·8	22·3	20·4
Aluminium, UK smelted ('000 tonnes)	370	462	499	498	541	549
Sulphuric acid (million tonnes)	3·45	3·89	3·85	3·17	3·27	3·40
Synthetic resins (million tonnes) (1)	1·61	2.39	2.28	1·95	2·45	2·52
Man-made fibres (million tonnes)	0·53	0·73	0·63	0·56	0·62	0·55
Cars ('000)	1,921	1,747	1,534	1,268	1,334	1,316
Motor vehicles, cars imported ('000)(2)	490	414	401	423	488	1,347
Commercial vehicles ('000)	408	417	402	381	372	398
Merchant ships(3) completed ('000 gr.t)	1,208	1,069	1,189	1,203	1,460	1,007
Tankers(4) completed ('000 gr.t)	412	221	457	592	720	426
Aircraft delivered (number)	246	293	364	339	341	..

(*1*) *Wider coverage from 1973 had effect of increasing reported output by about 30%.* (*2*) *Including imported chassis.* (*3*) *100 gross tons and over.* (*4*) *300 gross tons and over.*

20. Agriculture
(Production, '000 tons, unless otherwise stated)

Wheat	4,704	4,923	6,033	4,365	4,740	5,227
Barley	9,098	8,865	8,989	8,303	7,648	10,777
Sugar, refined from UK beet	1,018	922	758	655	595	886
Beef and veal	902	865	1,061	1,202	1,070	998
Mutton and lamb	216	230	248	254	248	222
Pork	644	670	680	560	595	648
Milk, disposals (million Litres)				13,092	13,128	13,620	14,400

Prices(1), farm years ended June (index 1968/69–71/72 average = 100)

Wheat	97·5	141·8	241·0	236·8	266·3	347·0
Barley	101·4	125·6	219·4	244.4	254·0	349·3
Cattle, clean	117·8	159·8	172·8	162·1	203·2	276·5
Pigs, clean(2)	105·5	125·2	163·2	192·4	248·9	251·2
Milk	111·6	114·3	136·4	173·7	212·4	243·1
Chemical fertilizers(3)	120·5	139·9	161·4	251·5	266·1	300·9
Compound feedingstuffs(3)	106·6	124·6	191·9	203·9	216·8	291·1
Farm net income (£ million)(4)	684	866	1,275	1,263	1,357	1,566

(*1*) *Based on producer prices after subsidy or intervention; barley, market prices.* (*2*) *1972–June 75, at bacon factory. July 1975 onwards all clean pigs, excluding subsidy in 1977.* (*3*) *Based on manufacturers' average prices.* (*4*) *Years to 31 May.*

Overall price index (1970 = 100)	121·6	131·8	153·7	197·6	226·4	255·3

21. Housing	1972	1973	1974	1975	1976	1977
Public expenditure (£ million)(1)	1,498	2,346	4,110	4,322	5,190	..
by local housing authorities(2)	1,032	1,331	1,961	2,966	2,528	..
Dwellings completed ('000)	331	305	280	322	325	313
by and for public sector(3)	130	114	134	167	170	170
by private sector	201	191	145	155	155	143
Dwellings: sold by local housing authorities(2)(4)('000)	61·5	41·8	5·4	3·0	5·8	..
Housing land, private sector, weighted ave. price (£/acre)	15,980	24,760	24,644	17,018	16,713	..
Dwelling prices, average (£)(5)	7,850	10,690	11,340	12,406	13,164	14,478

(1) Capital and current, net of rents, etc., received, and adjusted to eliminate double counting of grants and subsidies paid by central government and expended by local authorities. (2) Including new town development corporations. (3) Including government departments (police houses, military married quarters, etc.) and approved housing associations and trusts. (4) England and Wales. (5) Of properties newly mortgaged by building societies. See also Table 13 above.

22. Government Finance
(£ million)

Revenue(1)	20,805	23,095	29,230	35,783	43,825	50,609
taxes on income	8,083	9,295	12,548	16,537	18,724	21,227
corporation tax(2)	1,554	1,533	2,262	2,859	1,996	2,655
taxes on expenditure	9,264	10,122	11,435	14,146	16,660	19,383
purchase/value added tax(2)(3)	1,429	1,388	1,848	2,507	3,452	3,766
taxes on capital(4)	756	823	860	829	885	873
selective employment tax(5)	1,009	39	3	—	—	—
Expenditure(6)	20,188	23,144	29,537	39,742	47,695	52,232
social services(7)	11,658	13,119	16,219	21,975	26,337	..
defence	3,014	3,339	4,053	5,123	6,109	6,763
net lending(8)	2,213	2,292	3,184	4,417	2,916	..
Deficit(−) or surplus	−1,596	−2,341	−3,491	−8,376	−6,786	−1,623
Domestic borrowing, net	209	2,870	2,006	7,873	5,475	..

(1) Total current receipts, taxes on capital and other capital receipts. (2) Financial years ended 5 April of year indicated. (3) 1973/74 figure includes first net receipts of VAT, introduced April 1973 (£1,469 million), plus outstanding receipts of purchase tax, abolished at that date. (4) Capital gains tax and estate/death duties. (5) Abolished 1973. (6) Total government expenditure, gross domestic capital formation and grants. (7) Including expenditure by public authorities other than central government. (8) To private sector, local authorities, public corporations, and overseas. For external reserve and official borrowing overseas, see Table 24, page 469.

23. Terms of Trade
(Index 1970 = 100)

Volume of exports(1)	111·3	126·5	132·9	129·8	139·4	152·3
manufactures	112·0	128·0	135·0	130·0	140·0	151·6
machinery/transport equip't.	106·0	117·0	125·0	133·0	133·0	138·3
Volume of imports(1)	116·0	132·7	133·8	124·4	133·6	136·6
food	102·0	102·0	99·0	98·0	101·0	101·0
fuels	109.0	112.0	106·0	89·0	87·0	72·2
Unit value of exports(2)	111·1	126·0	162·7	198·5	240·6	283·9
manufactures	111·0	124·0	155·0	193·0	234·0	276·6
machinery/transport equip't.	118·0	128·0	153·0	196·0	245·0	299·2
Unit value of imports(2)	109·6	139·6	210·3	235·9	288·6	333·6
food(3)	114·0	150·0	193·0	220·0	247·0	288.5
fuels(3)	123·0	164·0	468·0	535·0	704·0	795·4
Terms of trade(4)	101·3	90·3	75·1	81·0	80·4	81·9

(1) Seasonally adjusted; f.o.b. (2) Not seasonally adjusted. (3) c.i.f. (4) Export unit value index as percentage of import unit value index, expressed as an index on the same base.

Overall price index (1970 = 100)	121·6	131·8	153·7	197·6	225·4	255·3

24. Balance of Payments
(£ million: current transactions seasonally adjusted; remaining data unadjusted)

	1975	1976	1977	1977:I	II	III	IV
Exports (f.o.b.)	19,462	25,422	32,176	7,502	7,930	8,540	8,204
Imports (f.o.b.)	22,667	28,932	33,788	8,449	8,694	8,486	8,159
Visible balance	−3,205	−3,510	−1,612	−947	−764	54	45
Gov't services/transfers (net)	−999	−1,459	−1,901	−452	−474	−502	−473
Private(1) services/transfers (net)	1,690	2,644	3,195	722	844	874	755
Public sector interest etc (net)	−517	−652	−688	−190	−204	−146	−148
Private sector interest etc (net)	1,417	1,960	971	362	234	203	172
Invisible balance	1,591	2.403	1,577	442	400	429	306
Current balance	−1,614	−1,107	−35	−505	−389	483	351
Current balance (unadjusted)	−1,614	−1,107	−35	−530	−336	455	376
Capital transfers(2)	—	—	—	—	—	—	—
Official long-term capital	−288	−158	−302	−24	−16	−17	−245
Overseas investment in							
UK public sector	43	203	2,179	498	921	291	469
UK private sector	1,719	2,062	2,953	847	799	779	528
UK private investment overseas	−1,383	−2,154	−1,734	−465	−652	−255	−362
Overseas borrowing/lending (net) by UK banks to finance:							
UK investment overseas	320	165	620	85	195	210	130
other loans/credits (net)	−85	−271	−355	336	−901	−26	236
Exchange reserves in sterling(3):							
British government stocks	7	14	5	−165	−4	31	143
Bank/money market liabilities	−624	−1,421	−24	355	−394	43	−28
Other external stg. liabilities	550	255	1,471	199	350	323	599
Import credit(4)	224	242	68	40	95	−27	−40
Export credit(4)	−570	−1,178	−211	91	−101	−86	−115
Other short-term flows	290	−565	132	122	20	−122	112
Total investment/capital flows	203	−2,806	4,802	1,919	312	1,144	1,427
Balancing item	−54	285	2,596	524	932	1,011	129
Total official financing(6)	1,465	3,628	−7,363	−1,913	−908	−2,610	−1,932
Foreign liabilities (5) net	4,409	8,320	9,404	9,532	9,786	10,258	9,404
Overall price index (1970 = 100)	*197·6*	*225·4*	*255·3*	*245·6*	*249·5*	*261·5*	*264·6*

(1) Including transfers made by and to public corporations. (2) Payments under the sterling guarantee agreements. (3) Sterling reserves of overseas countries and international organizations, other than the IMF, as reported by banks, etc., in the UK. (4) Excluding trade credit between 'related' firms, after deducting advance and progress payments to suppliers. (5) Includes eurodollar facility (1974-75) and public sector exchange cover scheme. (6) From 1972, transactions with the IMF were included as changes in the official reserves. Total official financing is the reverse counterpart of the item 'Total currency flow' or overall current/capital balance omitted from this table for space reasons (see table below). Total official financing less foreign borrowing produces amount by which official reserves were added to or drawn down.

Longer-term data (£ million)(1)	*1972*	*1973*	*1974*	*1975*	*1976*	*1977*
Current surplus (+)/deficit (−)	+131	−1,752	−3,380	−1,614	−1,107	−35
Overall surplus (+)/deficit (−)	−1,141	−771	−1,646	−1,465	−3,628	+7,363
Official reserves, end of year	2,404	2,787	2,890	2,683	2,426	10,715
Foreign liabilities (2), net, do.	156	1,283	3,018	4,409	8,320	9,404
Overall price index (1970 = 100)	*121·6*	*131·8*	*153·7*	*197·6*	*225·4*	*255·3*

(1) Reserves and borrowings calculated at $2.40 = £1.00, December 1967–September 1971; $2.60571 ('Smithsonian' parity) October 1971–May 1972, and at closing market rate from June, 1972; gold and SDRs at closing dollar parity throughout $2.6057 from January 1972. (2) To IMF and foreign monetary authorities and institutions; includes foreign currency borrowing by government and, under exchange cover scheme, by public sector.

25. Trade by Areas and Main Trading Partners

(£ million; exports f.o.b.; imports c.i.f.)	1972	1973	1974	1975	1976	1977
All countries: exports	9,746	12,454	16,494	19,761	25,909	32,952
imports	11,138	15,840	23,117	24,037	31,170	36,493
E.E.C.: exports	2,941	4,030	5,508	6,349	9,197	12,041
imports	3,521	5,197	7,222	8,686	11,386	14,035
Other Western Europe: exports	1,720	2,225	2,877	3,268	4,287	5,547
imports	1,816	2,694	3,420	3,518	4,579	5,519
North America: exports	1,599	1,936	2,258	2,319	3,137	3,824
imports	1,783	2,358	3,237	3,203	4,225	4,924
Other developed countries: exports	944	1,218	1,700	1,890	1,967	2,098
imports	1,141	1,460	1,594	1,784	2,119	2,671
Oil exporting countries: exports	609	800	1,209	2,280	3,144	4,282
imports	1,024	1,494	3,785	3,324	4,207	3,691
Other developing countries: exports	1,561	1,809	2,368	2,934	3,381	4,159
imports	1,412	2,042	2,591	2,665	3,514	4,247
Centrally planned economies: exports	308	409	514	680	730	904
imports	423	598	748	741	1,110	1,353
United States: exports	1,096	1,219	1,522	1,770	2,478	3,087
imports	1,095	1,180	1,622	2,254	3,048	3,663
West Germany: exports	534	590	785	1,016	1,843	2,501
imports	647	841	1,351	1,892	2,757	3,574
France: exports	394	511	678	914	1,712	2,148
imports	445	604	979	1,349	2,090	2,660
Netherlands: exports	409	451	604	983	1,501	2,139
imports	508	615	912	1,637	2,426	2,492
Belgium-Luxembourg: exports	340	394	620	838	1,402	1,837
imports	224	316	442	730	1,300	1,683
Ireland: exports	501	469	625	821	2,255	1,640
imports	507	445	527	810	1,004	1,283
Switzerland: exports	367	521	601	805	1,003	1,421
imports	369	592	717	736	932	1,319
Italy: exports	249	284	386	510	827	978
imports	282	353	504	724	1,104	1,532
Sweden: exports	383	405	515	724	1,048	1,197
imports	407	513	740	929	1,187	1,260
Canada: exports	349	380	414	488	638	713
imports	637	605	736	983	1,162	1,223
Saudi Arabia: exports	45	59	120	200	400	577
imports	184	318	1,176	857	978	1,095
Denmark: exports	241	330	429	444	657	797
imports	350	477	577	621	705	812
Norway: exports	190	241	334	390	476	762
imports	219	326	428	605	623	847

26. Trade by Selected Product Groups

(£ million)

	1972	1973	1974	1975	1976	1977
Exports: transport equipment	1,300	1,555	1,839	2,455	3,065	3,749
chemicals	962	1,296	2,146	2,153	3,045	3,867
textiles	698	929	1,176	1,147	1,606	2,053
beverages	266	305	384	437	525	629
oil and petroleum products	219	341	696	721	1,162	1,953
Imports: food and livestock	2,104	2,714	3,372	3,931	4,495	5,383
oil and petroleum products	1,169	1,682	4,533	4,169	5,512	5,064
wood, paper and products	878	1,307	1,866	1,654	2,165	2,359
transport equipment	670	919	933	1,179	1,749	2,593
mineral ores	285	390	675	632	683	691
Overall price index (1970 = 100)	121·6	136·8	153·7	197·6	225·4	

27. Employment	1972	1973	1974	1975	1976	1977
(millions of persons, in June each year)						
Working population(1)	25·19	25·54	25·60	25·83	26·09	26·33
Employed labour force(2)	23·86	24·43	24·51	24·41	24·76	24·88
Employees: production industries	9·81	9·92	9·81	9·53	9·26	9·32
Including mining	0·38	0·36	0·35	0·36	0·35	0·35
manufacturing	7·78	7·83	7·77	7·55	7·25	7·35
construction	1·30	1·38	1·34	1·28	1·31	1·27
Transport and utilities(3)	1·90	1·86	1·85	1·87	1·83	
Distributive trades	2·64	2·74	2·76	2·76	2·72	
Financial, professional, scientific	4·10	4·30	4·49	4·66	4·76	} 11·72
Catering and other services	2·04	2·15	2·13	2·20	2·30	
Public service(3)	1·55	1·58	1·60	1·66	1·63	1·62
Total employees	22·12	22·66	22·79	22·71	22·54	22·66
of whom, females	8·51	8·89	9·13	9·17	9·15	9·28

(1) Including registered unemployed and members of the armed services. (2) Including employers and self-employed. (3) Excludes employees of nationalized industries and public sector transport and utilities.

28. Demand for Labour

Average weekly hours worked, manu- facturing industry, men over 21(1)	44·1	44·7	44·0	42·7	43·5	43·6
Manufacturing employees:						
Total overtime hours worked ('000)(2)	12,884	15,504	14,655	12,947	13,459	15,447
Short time, total hours lost ('000)(2)	452	215	348	2,449	968	592
Unemployed, excl. school-leavers, adult students (monthly ave., '000)(3)	854·9	611·0	599·7	929·0	1,269·8	1,378·2
Percentage of all employees	3·7	2·6	2·6	3·9	5·3	5·8
Unfilled vacancies, end-year ('000)	228·3	462·1	496·8(4)	153·8	163·1(5)	171·5

(1) October. (2) Great Britain, June. (3) Seasonally adjusted. (4) End-November. (5) 8 October.

29. Industrial Disputes

Stoppages (number)(1)(2)	2,497	2,873	2,922	2,262	2,016	2,627
Known official stoppages (number)	160	132	125	139	69	80
Workers involved ('000)(3)	1,722	1,513	1,622	789	666	1,143
in official stoppages ('000)	635	396	467	80	46	..
Work days lost ('000), all inds., services	23,909	7,197	14,750	6,012	3,284	9,935
Mining and quarrying	10,800	91	5,628	56	78	85
Metals, engg., shipbdg., vehicles	6,636	4,799	5,837	3,932	1,977	6,126
Textiles and clothing	274	193	255	350	65	251
Construction	4,188	176	252	247	570	295
Transport and communications	876	331	705	422	132	298
All other industries/services	1,135	1,608	2,072	1,006	461	2,931

(1) Excluding protest action of a political nature, and stoppages involving fewer than 10 workers and/or lasting less than one day except where the working days lost exceeded 100. (2) Stoppages beginning in year stated. (3) Directly and indirectly, where stoppages occurred; lay-offs elsewhere in consequence are excluded.

30. Wages and Earnings

Basic hourly rates (31 July 1972 = 100), all manual employees(1)	101.4	115.6	138·7	179·8	214·5	228·4
women(1)	100·5	116·5	145·9	198·8	243·0	..
Ave. weekly earnings (£)(2): mfg.	36·20	41·52	49·12	59·74	67·83	73·56
food industries(3)	35·75	40·24	47·97	60·29	66·81	72·46
coal and oil products(3)	38·88	42·41	57·01	69·74	76·75	82·36
mechanical engineering(3)	34·73	40·51	48·49	58·86	66·11	73·38
construction(3)	36·59	41·41	48·75	60·38	65·80	72·91

(1) In all industries and services. (2) Of male manual workers, aged 21 and over. (3) October.

Overall price index (1970 = 100)	121·6	136·8	153·7	197·6	225·4	255·3

B. THE UNITED STATES

31. Population	1972	1973	1974	1975	1976	1977
Population, mid-year est. (mn.)	208·85	210·41	211·90	213·54	214·12	216·82
Density (persons per sq. km.)(1)	22·31	22·47	22·63	22·81	22·87	23·16
Crude birth rate (per 1,000 pop.)	15·7	15·0	15·0	14·8	14·7	15·3
Crude death rate (per 1,000 pop.)	9·4	9·4	9·2	8·9	9·0	8·8

(1) Based on land area of 9,363,345 sq. km.

32. Gross National Product
('000 million current dollars)

Gross national product	1,171·1	1,306·6	1,412·9	1,528·8	1,706·5	1,890·1
Personal consumption	733·0	809·9	889·6	980·4	1,094·0	1,211·4
Gross private domestic investment	178·8	202·1	205·7	200·6	230·0	276·4
Net exports, goods and services	−3·3	7·4	7·5	2·0	7·8	−10.1
Government purchases	253·1	269·5	302·7	338·9	361·4	394·9

33. Government Finance
('000 million dollars, seasonally adjusted)

Federal government receipts	228·7	265·0	288·2	286·5	330·6	365·2
from personal taxes(1)	107·9	114·5	131·2	125·7	145·3	170·7
Federal government expenditure	244·6	264·0	299·7	357·8	386·9	416·2
Defence purchases	74·4	73·9	77.3	84·3	88·2	99·6
Grants to state/local govts.	37·7	40·9	43·9	54·4	60·2	92·6
Federal surplus or (−) deficit	−15·9	1·0	−11·5	−71·2	−58·3	−51·0
State and local govt. receipts	177·2	194·5	210·4	235·7	264·7	294·3
from indirect business tax(1)	89·6	96·8	106·9	114·7	127·1	140·3
State and local govt. expenditure	164·0	184·0	202·8	229·8	246·2	265·5
State/local surplus/(−) deficit	13·1	10·5	7·6	5·9	18·5	28·8

(1) Includes related non-tax receipts on national income account.

34. Balance of Payments	1972	1973	1974	1975	1976	1977
(millions of dollars)						
Merchandise trade balance	−6,986	911	−5,367	9,045	−9,320	−31,401
Balance on current account(1)	−9,807	22	−5,028	11,552	−1,427	..
Current and long-term capital	−11,235	−744	−10,702	−9,191	−23,849	..
Net liquidity balance(2)	−13,856	−7,796	−18,109	3,324	..	..
Official reserves transactions(3)	−10,354	−5,304	−7,960	−2,037	−3,976	..

(1) Includes balance on services and remittances and US government grants other than military. (2) Includes net non-liquid short-term private capital flows and allocations of IMF special drawing rights (SDRs): series not compiled after 1975. (3) Includes net liquid private capital flows.

35. Merchandise Trade by Main Areas	1972	1973	1974	1975	1976	1977
(millions of dollars)						
All countries: exports (f.o.b.)	49,199	70,823	97,908	107,130	115,155	121,144
imports (f.o.b.)	55,583	69,476	100,251	96,115	121,009	147,491
Western Europe: exports	14,989	21,339	29,439	30,874	37,650	..
imports	15,648	22,109	24,048	21,200	23,180	..
Canada: exports	12,506	15,577	19,936	21,744	24,109	..
imports	14,403	17,442	21,924	21,747	26,238	..
Latin America/other western hemisphere:						
exports	7,241	9,948	14,501	15,670	15,492	..
imports	7,068	9,021	13,667	16,840	13,226	..
Japan: exports	4,978	8,356	10,679	9,563	10,144	..
imports	9,079	9,645	12,338	11,268	15,504	..
Dollar purchasing power (1967 = 100)	79·9	73·2	65·2	62·1	58·7	55·1

36. Merchandise Trade by Main Commodity Groups

(millions of dollars)	1972	1973	1974	1975	1976	1977
Exports:						
Machinery and transport equipt.	22,533	27,842	38,189	45,668	49,060	59,373
Motor vehicles and parts	4,709	5,989	7,878	10,028	10,949	11,741
Electrical machinery	3,698	5,031	7,019	7,582	9,278	10,161
Food and live animals	5,661	11,931	13,986	15,484	15,710	13,898
Grains and cereal products	3,501	8,495	10,331	11,642	10,911	10,939
Chemicals and pharmaceuticals	4,133	5,749	8,819	8,691	9,938	10,674
Imports:						
Machinery and transport equipt.	17,420	20,970	24,060	23,465	29,824	36,156
Motor vehicles and parts	7,946	9,216	9,216	9,921	13,104	15,367
Food and live animals	6,370	7,986	9,386	8,509	10,267	12,294
Meat and preparations	1,223	1,668	1,353	1,141	1,447	1,263
Coffee	1,182	1,565	1,505	1,561	2,632	3,984
Petroleum and products	4,300	7,549	24,270	24,814	31,795	41,026
Iron and steel	2,928	3,009	5,149	4,595	4,347	4,579

37. Interest Rates
(Per cent per annum, annual averages, unless otherwise stated)

Discount rate(1), end-year	4·50	7·50	7·75	6·00	5·25	6·00
Treasury bill rate	4·07	7·03	7·87	5·82	4·99	5·27
Government bond yields: 3-5 years	5·85	6·92	7·81	7·55	6·94	6·69
Long-term (10 years or more)	5·63	6·30	6·99	6·98	6·78	7·67
Banks' prime lending rate(2)	5·82	9·75	12·00	7·86	6·84	6·82

(1) Of Federal Reserve Bank of New York. (2) Predominant rate charged by commercial banks on short-term loans to large business borrowers with the highest credit rating.

38. Banking, money and credit
('000 million dollars, outstanding at end of year, seasonally adjusted)

Money supply M₃(1)	844·9	919·5	981·5	1,092·6	1,237·1	1,374·0
Currency	56·9	61·5	67·8	73·7	80·5	88·4
Deposits of commercial banks	616·0	681·9	741·7	789·5	838·2	908·5
Advances of commercial banks	414·7	494·9	549·2	542·1	576·0	625·7
Consumer credit	157·6	180·5	190·1	225·1	249·0	..
Instalment credit	127·4	148·3	158·1	165·0	185·5	216·6
Motor vehicle contracts	44·3	51·3	52·2	55·9	66·1	79·4
Non-instalment credit: retail charge						
accounts	7·1	7·8	7·7	7·5	7·3	
Credit cards	2·0	2·1	2·1	2·2	2·5	

(1) Demand deposits at banks, currency in circulation, deposits at mutual savings banks, and savings capital of savings and loan associations.

39. Insurance

	1972	1973	1974	1975	1976	1977
($million, unless otherwise stated)						
Property-liability, net premiums written	38,889	42,019	44,631	49,550	60,380	72,730
Automobile(1)	18,050	18,811	19,069	20,932	25,255	30,700
Underwriting gain/(−) loss (2)	1,073	−3	−2,643	−4,257	−2,210	1,034
Combined ratio(2)	96·2	99·2	105·4	107·9	102·4	97·1
Automobile(1)	94·7	98·6	102·0	110·4	103·9	95·6
General liability(3)	114·7	117·1	125·9	116·2	107·9	95·1
Life insurance, total assets, end-year	239,730	252,436	263,349	289,304	321,552	350,506

(1) Physical damage and liability, private and commercial. (2) After stockholder and policy-holder dividends and premium rebates. (3) Sum of ratios of losses and loss expenses to earned premiums, and underwriting expenses to written premiums.

Dollar purchasing power (1967 = 100)	*79·9*	*73·2*	*65·2*	*62·1*	*58·7*	*55·1*

40. Companies(1)

('000 million dollars)

	1972	1973	1974	1975	1976	1977
Net profit after taxes	54·6	67·1	74·5	73·5	92·2	101·7
Cash dividends paid	24·6	27·8	31·0	32·4	35·8	40·4

(*1*) *Manufacturing corporations, all industries.*

41. The Stock Market

(millions of dollars, unless otherwise stated)

Turnover (sales), all exchanges	9,647	186,173	124,891	166,606	194,969	183,563
New York Stock Exchange	8,877	8,012	105,372	142,754	169,807	158,354
Securities issued, gross proceeds	96,522	100,417	105,372	114,430	113,297	118,181
Bonds and notes: non-corporate	54,564	67,025	51,862	58,299	55,750	66,233
corporate	26,132	21,049	32,066	41,756	42,262	36,684
Corporate common stock	10,725	7,642	3,994	7,413	8,305	6,744

Stock prices (Standard and Poor's indices, 1941-43 = 10, end of year):

Combined index (500 stocks)	109·20	107·43	82.85	85·17	102·01	98·18
Industrials (400 stocks)	121·79	120.44	92.91	96·56	116·33	103·13

42. Employment

('000 persons)

Civilian labour force(1)	86,500	88,714	91,011	92,613	94,773	97,401
in non-agricultural industry	78,230	80,957	82,443	81,403	84,188	87,302
in manufacturing industry	19,090	20,068	20,046	18,347	18,958	19,560
in agriculture	3,472	3,452	3,492	3,380	3,297	3,244
unemployed	4,840	4,304	5,076	7,830	7,288	6,856
Industrial stoppages(2) (number)	5,010	5,353	6.074	5,031	5,600	5,590
Workers involved ('000)	1,714	2,251	2,778	1,746	2,508	2,296

(*1*) *Aged 16 years and over.* (*2*) *Beginning in the year.*

43. Earnings and Prices

Average weekly earnings per worker

(current dollars): mining	176·51	201·03	220·90	249·57	274·78	302·88
contract construction	222·51	235·69	249·08	265·35	284·56	295·73
manufacturing	154·69	166·06	176·40	189·51	208·12	226·90
Average weekly hours per worker in manufacturing	40.6	40.7	40·0	39·4	40·0	40·3
Farm prices received (1967 = 100)	125	179	192	186	186	183
Wholesale prices (1967 = 100)	119·1	134·7	160·1	174·9	182·9	194·2
Petroleum products	108·9	126·7	223·4	257·5	276·6	307·9
Consumer prices (1967 = 100)	125·3	133·1	147·7	161·2	170·5	181·6
Food	123·5	141·4	161·7	175·4	180·8	192·2
Dollar purchasing power (1967 = 100)(1)	79.9	73.2	65·2	62·1	58·7	55·1

(*1*) *Based on changes in retail price indexes.*

44. Production

Farm production (1967 = 100)	110	112	108	111	113	116
Industrial production (1967 = 100)	119·7	129·8	129·3	117·8	129·8	137·0
Manufacturing	118·9	129·8	129·4	116·3	129·5	137·1

Output of main products and manufactures

Coal (million tons)	546·6	523·6	544·5	635·4	665·0	670·1
Oil, indigenous (million tons)	532·2	517·9	492·0	469·0	443·7	472·9
Oil refinery throughput (mn. tons)	590	624	580	615	656	618
Natural gas (million cubic metres)	638·0	635·9	586·8	558·0	559·9	630·0
Electricity generated ('000 mn. kwh)	1,853	1,947	1,863	1,903	2,108	1,926
Steel, crude (million tonnes)	120·9	136·5	132·0	116·5	116·3	124·9
Aluminium ('000 tonnes)	4,608	4,968	5,306	4,360	4,984	5,166
Cotton yarn ('000 tonnes)	1,824	1,356	1,512	1,368	1,676	..
Man-made fibres (million lbs.)	7,294	8,329	8,085	7,167	7,317	8,201
Plastics/resins ('000 tonnes)	9,324	11,880	10,068	8,213	9,785	..
Motor cars, factory sales ('000)	8,824	9,658	7,331	6,713	8,497	11,040

C. INTERNATIONAL COMPARISONS

45. Population of Selected Countries	Area '000 sq. km.	Population (millions), mid-year estimate 1967	1976	1977	Annual Growth %	Persons per sq. km.
Argentina	2,777	22·49	25·72	26·06	1·3	9
Australia	7,695	11·60	13·80	14·03	1·7	1·8
Belgium	31	9·53	9·80	9·83	0·3	317
Canada	9,976	20·05	23·03	23·32	1·3	2
China	9,561	722·22	861·59	877·96	1·9	92
Denmark	34	4·80	5·07	5·09	0·3	150
France	552	49·16	52·89	53·12	0·4	96
Germany, Western (incl. W. Berlin)	248	59·68	61·53	61·40	−0·2	248
India (incl. Indian-admin. Kashmir)	3,268	493·39	612·45	627·15	2·4	192
Ireland	69	2·88	3.12	3·15	1·1	46
Israel (excl. occupied areas)	21	2·63	3·40	3·51	3·1	167
Italy	301	52·33	56·16	56·45	0·6	188
Japan	370	99·79	112·77	113·86	1·0	308
Netherlands	34	12·45	13·77	13·85	0·6	407
New Zealand	104	2·68	3·09	3·12	1·0	30
Norway	324	3·75	4·03	4·04	0·4	13
South Africa (incl. S.W. Africa)	1,221	20·84	26·79	27·73	3·5	23
Spain	505	32·39	35·97	36·35	1·1	72
Sweden	450	7·81	8·22	8·26	0·4	18
Switzerland	41	5·92	6·45	6·50	0·7	159
Turkey	781	32·02	40·16	41·17	2·5	53
USSR	22,402	233·53	256·67	258·70	0·8	12
UK	244	54·50	55·89	55·85	−0·1	229
USA	9,363	196·56	215·14	216·67	0·8	23

46. Gross Domestic Product, Expenditure Basis, Selected Countries
(current prices, '000 million national currency units)

	1972	1973	1974	1975	1976	1977
Argentina (new pesos)	217·0	364·6	497·1	1,345·0	..	..
Australia (Australian dollars)(1)	32·46	34·03	50·56	58·53	69·67	70·02
Belgium (Belgian francs)	1,566	1,655	1,721	2,081	2,158	2,212
Canada (Canadian dollars)	104·03	119·80	145·30	157·33	187·2	191·4
Denmark (kroner)	146·07	151·62	154·66	185·29	230·3	229·5
France (francs)	1,001·90	1,062·01	1,322·6	1,439·0	1,669·5	1,919·6
Germany, W. (Deutschemarks)	829·40	873·36	996.7	1,040·4	1,136·1	1,167·3
India (rupees)	467·35	573·54	681·09	..	..	..
Italy (lire)	69,026	80,818	97,427	112,358	136,745	139,753
Japan (yen)	90,603	111,003	132·486	145,619	163,903	173,737
Kuwait (dinars)(2)	1·20	1·77	3·20	3·45	3·28	..
Netherlands (guilders)	147·08	153·99	159·08	203·90	230·56	231·32
Norway (kroner)	96·67	100·00	128·76	147·93	166·42	173·49
Portugal (escudos)	233·30	284·80	338·30	373·50	..	..
Saudi Arabia (riyals)	28,257	40,551	99,517	135,048	..	..
South Africa (rand)	15·66	18·68	22·38	24·70	27·73	..
Spain (pesetas)	2,970	3,554	4,943	5,800	6,891	7,046
Sweden (kronor)	199·18	220·33	249·05	286·88	320·16	312·15
Switzerland (francs)	116·70	130·10	141·10	139.80	143·74	147·69
USSR (roubles)	313·20	337·20	353·70	362·80	375·50	388·64
UK (£)	61·95	70·41	73·50	78·51	108·25	108·52
USA (dollars)	1,147·30	1,279·40	1,413·2	1,516·3	1,691·4	1,771·7

(*I*) Years beginning 1 July. (2) Years beginning 1 April. (3) Years ended 30 June.

World trade prices (1970 = 100)(1)	113·5	137·5	184·0	202·0	203·5	212·6

(*I*) Unweighted average of IMF series for US dollar import and export prices in developed countries.

47. Disposable Income per head

(US dollars)	1972	1973	1974	1975	1976	1977
Sweden	4,623	5,545	6,100	7,036	8,364	..
USA	4,946	5,523	5,918	6,207	..	..
Canada	4,260	4,818	5,673	6,120	..	..
Denmark	3,765	4,989	5,412	6,242	..	..
Germany, West	3,690	4,878	5,363	5,922	..	..
Australia	3,464	4,994	5,856	..	..	..
Norway	3,229	4,146	4,886	5,887	..	..
France	3,301	4,204	4,423	4,440	..	..
Switzerland	4,155	5,760	6,687	7,710	..	..
Belgium	3,332	4,271	4,889	5,802	..	..
Netherlands	3,125	4,044	4,670	5,308	..	..
Iceland	3,180	4,280	4,457	4,677	..	..
New Zealand	2,890	3,703	4,040	..	..	..
Japan	2,414	3,283	3,559	..	..	..
UK	2,540	2,831	3,036	3,642	..	..
Spain	..	1,901	2,259	..	..	..
Portugal	..	1,402	1,589	..	..	..
Saudi Arabia	753	814	2,514	..	..	..
South Africa	..	969	1,151	1,178	..	..
India	..	123	137	..	..	..

48. World Trade(1)

(millions of US dollars. Exports fob; imports cif)

	1972	1973	1974	1975	1976	1977
World(1): exports	376,600	524,700	778,100	779,700	903,500	1021,670
imports	388,300	535,300	782,400	801,900	924,400	1049,640
Industrial Countries: exports	275,710	376,280	503,270	534,000	596,460	676,150
imports	281,080	386,030	543,610	544,000	630,340	716,860
USA: exports	49,758	71,339	98,507	107,652	114,997	120,164
imports	58,862	73,575	107,996	103,414	129,565	156,695
Germany, West: exports	46,698	67,502	89,055	90,107	101,977	118,054
imports	40,187	54,552	68,897	74,255	88,209	101,446
Japan: exports	28,591	36,982	55,596	55,817	67,167	81,126
imports	23,471	38,347	62,075	57,853	64,748	71,326
France: exports	26,451	36,659	46,473	52,951	57,162	64,997
imports	27,001	37,727	52,914	53,964	64,391	70,497
UK: exports	24,345	30,657	38,885	44,127	46,300	57,553
imports	27,859	38,841	54,530	53,522	55,981	63,715
Other Europe: exports	16,510	22,810	30,360	31,940	35,160	39,900
imports	24,670	34,260	52,750	56,480	56,890	64,060
Australia, NZ, S. Afr: exports	10,950	15,710	18,440	19,910	23,800	26,200
imports	10,610	15,030	23,920	22,920	22,830	23,260
Less Developed Areas: exports	73,300	109,900	225,900	267,200	246,370	278,673
imports	71,900	100,000	162,100	185,900	210,870	244,402
Oil exporters: exports	28,700	44,900	135,900	116,700	130,500	144,024
imports	15,500	22,000	37,700	41,700	66,600	84,682
Saudi Arabia: exports	5,492	9,071	35,654	29,602	35,622	40,894
imports	1,136	1,944	3,473	6,701	11,759	17,196
Other W. Hemisphere: exports	14,960	21,610	30,610	32,920	38,290	44,458
imports	18,680	25,250	48,115	49,273	50,312	51,913
Other Middle East(2): exports	2,910	3,780	5,310	6,002	8,030	8,931
imports	5,560	8,060	12,370	16,760	17,660	..
Other Asia: exports	18,920	28,810	39,170	38,570	52 550	62,718
imports	23,370	33,240	51,940	53,070	57,660	69,178
Other Africa: exports	7,790	10,870	14,960	15,660	15,180	..
imports	8,810	11,410	16,520	19,830	18,500	..

(1) Excluding trade of centrally planned countries (see Table 49). (2) Including Egypt.

World trade prices (1970 = 100)	113·5	137·5	184·0	202·0	203·5	212·6

49. World Trade of Centrally Planned Countries

(millions of US dollars)	1972	1973	1974	1975	1976	1977
European(1): *exports*	40,510	53,200	65,500	78,300	85,200	..
imports	40,295	56,300	70,900	92,100	96,700	..
USSR: *exports*	15,361	21,463	27,405	33,316	37,168	..
imports	16,047	21,112	24,890	36,971	38,109	..
China: *exports*	2,900	4,900	6,300	7,025	6,915	..
imports	2,700	5,000	7,400	7,360	5,975	..
Cuba: *exports*	803	1,393	1,691	3,551	3,246	..
imports	1,292	1,701	1,674	3,751	3,093	..

(*1*)*Except Yugoslavia (included in Other Europe in Table 48), and Albania.*

50. International official reserves(1)
(millions of US dollars, end-year)

World	150,720	183,910	220,418	227,737	233,620	315,813
Industrial countries	103,728	115,027	119,899	121,880	131,910	169,332
USA	13,150	14,378	16,056	15,883	18,320	19,390
UK	5,647	6,476	6,939	5,459	4,230	21,057
Industrial Europe	62,517	76,148	77,557	87,856	91,612	121,471
Germany, West	23,785	33,171	32,398	31,034	34,801	39,737
France	10,015	8,529	8,852	12,593	9,728	10,194
Canada	6,050	5,768	5,825	5,326	5,843	4,608
Japan	18,366	12,246	13,519	12,815	16,605	23,261
Less developed areas	32,125	44,740	79,438	87,952	101,710	127,305
Middle East	7,630	11,595	32,603	39,622	53,748	59,142

(*1*) *Excluding convertible reserves held by centrally-planned countries.*

World trade prices (1970 = 100)	*113·5*	*137·5*	*184·0*	*202·0*	*203·5*	*212·6*

51. Exchange Rates
(middle rates for overseas settlements, end of year, unless stated)

	Currency units per US dollar					per £
	1973	1974	1975	1976	1977	1977
Australia (Australian dollar)	0·6723	0·7576	0·7955	0·9205	0·8761	1·6812
Austria (schilling)	19·90	17·50	18·51	16·77	15·14	28·93
Belgium-Luxembourg (franc)	41·32	36·87	39·53	35·98	32·94	62·72
Canada (Canadian dollar)	0·9958	0·9980	1·0164	1·0092	1·0944	2·0987
China (yuan)(1)	2·04	2·04	2·04	2·04	2·04	1·90
Denmark (krone)	6·294	5·788	6·178	5·788	5·778	11·075
Finland (markka)	3·85	3·55	3·85	3·77	4·02	7·7144
France (franc)	4·708	4,537	4·486	4·970	4·705	9·007
Germany, W. (Deutschemark)	2·703	2·458	2·622	2·363	2·105	4·014
Israel (Israel £)	4·20	6·00	8·31	8·90	15·39	29·53
Italy (lira)	607·92	658·89	683·55	875·00	871·60	1,672·0
Japan (yen)	280·0	300·4	305·2	292·8	240·00	459·25
Netherlands (guilder)	2·824	2·535	2·688	2·457	2·280	4·340
New Zealand (NZ dollar)	0·7001	0·7692	0·9581	1·0530	0·981	1·8925
Norway (krone)	5·74	5·40	5·59	5·19	5·14	9·869
Portugal (escudo)	25·96	24·87	27·47	31·55	39·86	76·52
South Africa (rand)	0·6712	0·6897	0·8696	0·8696	0·8696	1·6688
Spain (peseta)	56·95	57·20	59·77	68·2	80·91	155·27
Sweden (krona)	4·590	4·199	4·386	4·127	4·670	8·961
Switzerland (franc)	3·244	2·619	2·620	2·504	2·000	2·8025
USSR (rouble)(1)	0·746	0·746	0·746	0·746	0·734	1·4086
UK (£)(2)	2·323	2·349	2·024	1·702	1·919	—
Yugoslavia (dinar)	15·60	17·05	17·99	18·23	18·30	35·12

(*1*) *Official fixed or basic parity rate.* (*2*) *US dollars per £.*

478   ECONOMIC AND SOCIAL DATA

52. Money Supply(1), selected countries

'000 million national currency units, end of year)

	1972	1973	1974	1975	1976	1977
France (francs)	302·5	332·1	382·6	431·2	465·2	475·0
Germany, West (Deutschemarks)	131·9	132·9	149·1	169·9	176·6	208·1
Japan (yen)	34,526	40,311	44,950	49,948	56,179	60,786
Saudi Arabia (riyals)	3·78	5·29	7·48	14·18	24·65	30·00
Switzerland (francs)	56·7	56·6	56·0	58·4	62·9	62·0
UK (£ sterling)	12·66	13·30	14·74	17·48	19·47	23·66
USA (dollars)	262·9	278·2	286·9	302·3	319·2	345·4

(1) Currency in circulation and demand deposits of the private sector only: figures for the UK and USA are therefore not compatible with those in Tables 10 and 38.

53. Central Bank Discount Rates

(per cent per annum, end of year)

Belgium	5·00	7·75	8·75	6·00	9·00	7·00
Canada	4·75	7·25	8·75	9·00	8·50	7·50
France	7·50	11·00	13·00	8·00	10·50	9·50
Germany, West	4·50	7·00	4·00	3·50	3.50	3·00
Italy	4·00	6·50	8·00	6·00	15·00	11·50
Japan	4·25	9·00	9·00	6·50	6·50	4·25
Sweden	5·00	5·00	7·00	6·00	8·00	8·00
Switzerland	3·75	4·50	5·50	3·00	2·00	1·50
UK(1)	9·00	13·00	11·50	11·25	14·25	7·00
USA(2)	4·50	7·50	7·75	6·00	5·25	6·00

(1) Minimum lending rate from 1971. (2) Federal Reserve Bank of New York.

54. Defence Expenditure

	Expenditure or budget (US $ mn.)				$ per caput 1977	% of GNP 1976
	1974	1975	1976	1977		
Egypt	4,071	6,103	4,859	4,365	112	37·0
France	9,970	13,984	12,857	13,740	256	3·7
Germany, East	2,373	2,550	2,729	2,889	167	6·0
Germany, West (incl. W. Berlin)	16,668	19,540	18,758	21,092	333	4.2
Greece	807	1,435	1,249	1,100	120	5·5
Iran	5,550	8,800	9,500	7,898	227	12·0
Israel	3,869	3,552	4,214	4,268	1,178	35·3
Japan	4,300	4,620	5,058	6,090	49	0·9
Portugal	1,000	1,088	748	508	52	3·9
Saudi Arabia	1,808	6,771	9,038	7,538	1,005	..
South Africa	1,052	1,332	1,494	1,897	70	4·7
Sweden	1,903	2,483	2,418	2,833	343	3·7
Turkey	1,173	2,200	2,800	2,653	64	5·6
USSR(1)	111,000	124,000	124,000	..	..	13+
UK	10,041	11,118	10,734	11,214	201	5·1
USA	85,906	88,983	102,691	113,000	523	6·0

(1) Data, at dollar purchasing power (not official exchange) rates, based on reconciliation of CIA, W. T. Lee's figures.

55. Industrial Ordinary Share Prices

(Index 1970 = 100, daily average, unless otherwise stated)

	1972	1973	1974	1975	1976	1977
Amsterdam	114	126	98	97	92	83
Australia, all exchanges	100	94	70	65	81	78
Canada, all exchanges(1)	123	139	115	108	112	100
Germany, West, all exchanges(2)	106	101	84	95	101	100
Hong Kong (31 July 1968=100)(3)	..	438	118	338	444	387
Johannesburg	106	125	99	99	99	92
New York	133	132	102	106	125	119
Paris	107	119	88	95	94	76
Switzerland, all exchanges(4)	111	103	78	70	77	81
Tokyo	173	222	188	191	213	231
UK(5)	150	130	76	96	114	147

(1) Average of Thursday quotations. (2) Average of four bank returns each month. (3) Hang Seng index for Hong Kong Stock Exchange only: last trading day of year. (4) Average of Friday quotations. (5) Average of closing prices on last Tuesday of each month.

56. World Production

(Index 1970 = 100)	1972	1973	1974	1975	1976	1977
Food (1)	103	108	110	112	116	118
Industrial production (2)	112	122	126	125	136	143
OECD	109	119	120	110	120	125
EEC (3)	107	115	115	108	115	118
France	115	120	123	113	123	126
Germany, West	106	114	111	105	113	116
Italy	104	114	119	108	121	121
UK	102	110	109	103	104	106
Japan	110	129	123	110	125	130
Sweden	104	111	117	115	114	111
USSR (4)	115	123	133	143	150	160

(1) Excluding China. (2) Excluding China, USSR, Eastern Europe. (3) Community of nine.

57. Energy Surpluses and (−) Deficits
(million tons coal equivalent)

World	558	615	668	553	..	..
Africa	359	376	349	298	..	..
America, North	−185	−266	−267	−271	..	..
America, Central	210	228	288	157	..	..
America, South	−39	−41	−45	−49	..	..
Asia: Middle East	1,286	1,506	1,548	1,432	..	..
Asia, Other	−339	−377	−368	−351	..	..
Europe, Western	−871	−948	−914	−815	..	..
Oceania	11	12	15	15	..	..
Centrally planned economies	127	143	167	184	..	..

58. Prices of Selected Commodities

Aluminium, Canadian (US$/lb.)	26·8	27·2	34·7	39·4	40·4	56·1
Beef, Irish (London) (pence/lb.)	63·4	79·9	81·7	89·8	92·0	96·3
Copper, wirebars (London)(£/tonne)	428	727	878	537	781	752
Cotton, Egyptian (L'pool) (US cents/lb.)	65·29	98·44	153·61	129·39	136·53	159·73
Gold(London) (US $/fine oz.)	59·14	100·00	162·02	160·47	124·03	148·79
Newsprint, S. Quebec (US $/short ton)	144·2	153·1	202·4	245·0	262·8	281·01
Petroleum, Ras Tanura (US $/barrel)	2·47	3·27	11·58	11·53	12·38	12·70
Rice, Thai (Bangkok) (£/ton)	60·1	—	237·0	166·0	186·3	189·4
Rubber, Malay (Singapore) (cents/lb.)	15·12	30·67	33·81	25·82	35·52	39·22
Steel bars (Oberhausen) (DM/tonne)	502	550	646	737	828	734
Soya beans, US (R'dam) (US$/tonne)	140	291	277	220	231	279
Sugar, f.o.b. Carib/Brazil (US cents/lb.)	7·43	9·63	29·96	20·50	11·57	8·00
Tin, spot (London) (£/tonne)	1,506	1,967	3,495	3,090	4,242	6·113
Wheat, Manitoba, No. 2 N. (£/ton)	34·7	71·3	103·8	94·7	97·0	75·8
Wool, greasy (Sydney) (cents/lb.)	53	96	62	59	91	83

(1) Irish.

59. Consumer Prices, Selected Countries
(index 1970 = 100)

Argentina	209·0	335·0	425·0	6,517·0	17,993	49,672·9
Australia	112·4	122·9	141·5	162·8	184·9	207·6
France	112·0	120·2	136·7	152·8	166·9	182·7
Germany, West	111·1	118·8	127·1	134·7	140·8	146·3
India	109·8	128·3	163·0	172·8	159·0	172·5
Japan	110·9	124·0	154·1	172·4	188·4	203·5
South Africa	112·5	123·2	137·5	156·0	173·4	193·0
Sweden	113·8	121·5	133·5	146·6	161·7	180·2
UK	117·2	127·9	148·4	184·4	205·0	249·0
US	107·7	114·4	127·0	138·6	146·6	156·1
World trade prices (1970 = 100)	*113·5*	*137·5*	*184·0*	*202·0*	*203·5*	*212·6*

XVIII DOCUMENTS AND REFERENCE

CHARTER 77

Charter 77 Manifesto was dated 1 January 1977 and issued in Prague.

In the Czechoslovak Register of Laws No. 120 of 13 October 1976, texts were published of the International Covenant on Civil and Political Rights, and of the International Covenant on Economic, Social and Cultural Rights, which were signed on behalf of our Republic in 1968, reiterated at Helsinki in 1975 and came into force in our country on 23 March 1976. From that date our citizens have enjoyed the rights, and our state the duties, ensuing from them.

The human rights and freedoms underwritten by these covenants constitute features of civilised life for which many progressive movements have striven throughout history and whose codification could greatly assist humane developments in our society.

We accordingly welcome the Czechoslovak Socialist Republic's accession to those agreements.

Their publication, however, serves as a powerful reminder of the extent to which basic human rights in our country exist, regrettably, on paper alone.

The right to freedom of expression, for example, guaranteed by Article 19 of the first-mentioned covenant, is in our case purely illusory. Tens of thousands of our citizens are prevented from working in their own fields for the sole reason that they hold views differing from official ones, and are discriminated against and harassed in all kinds of ways by the authorities and public organizations. Deprived as they are of any means to defend themselves, they become victims of a virtual apartheid.

Hundreds of thousands of other citizens are denied that 'freedom from fear' mentioned in the preamble to the first covenant, being condemned to the constant risk of unemployment or other penalties if they voice their own opinions.

In violation of Article 13 of the second-mentioned covenant, guaranteeing everyone the right to education, countless young people are prevented from studying because of their own views or even their parents'. Innumerable citizens live in fear of their own, or their children's, right to education being withdrawn if they should ever speak up in accordance with their convictions.

Any exercise of the right to 'seek, receive and impart information and ideas of all kinds, regardless of frontiers, either orally, in writing or in print' or 'in the form of art' specified in Article 19, Clause 2 of the first covenant is followed by extra-judicial and even judicial sanctions, often in the form of criminal charges as in the recent trial of young musicians.

Freedom of public expression is inhibited by the centralized control of all the communication media and of publishing and cultural institutions. No philosophical, political or scientific view or artistic activity that departs even slightly from the narrow bounds of official ideology or aesthetics is allowed to be published; no open criticism can be made of abnormal social phenomena; no public defence is possible against false and insulting charges made in official propaganda—the legal protection against 'attacks on honour and reputation' clearly guaranteed by Article 17 of the first covenant is in practice non-existent; false accusations cannot be rebutted and any attempt to secure compensation or correction through the courts is futile; no open debate is allowed in the domain of thought and art.

Many scholars, writers, artists and others are penalized for having legally published or expressed, years ago, opinions which are condemned by those who hold political power today.

Freedom of religious confession, emphatically guaranteed by Article 18 of the first covenant, is continually curtailed by arbitrary official action; by interference with the activity of churchmen, who are constantly threatened by the refusal of the state to permit them the exercise of their functions, or by the withdrawal of such permission; by financial or other sanctions against those who express their religious faith in word or action; by constraints on religious training and so forth.

One instrument for the curtailment or in many cases complete elimination of many civic rights is the system by which all national institutions and organizations are in effect subject to political directives from the machinery of the ruling party and to decisions made by powerful individuals.

The constitution of the Republic, its laws and legal norms do not regulate the form or content, the issuing or application of such decisions; they are often only given out verbally, unknown to the public at large and beyond its powers to check; their originators are responsible to no one but themselves and their own hierarchy; yet they have a decisive impact on the decision-making and executive organs of government, justice, trade unions, interest groups and all other organizations, of the other political parties, enterprises, factories, institutions, offices and so on, for whom these instructions have precedence even before the law.

Where organizations or individuals, in the interpretation of their rights and duties, come into conflict with such directives, they cannot have recourse to any non-party authority, since none such exists. This, of course, constitutes a serious limitation of the right ensuing from Articles 21 and 22 of the first-mentioned covenant, which provides for freedom of association and forbids any restriction on its exercise; from Article 25 on the right to take part in the conduct of public affairs; and from Article 26 stipulating equal protection by the law without discrimination.

This state of affairs likewise prevents workers and others from exercising the unrestricted right to establish trade unions and other organizations to protect their economic and social interests, and from freely enjoying the right to strike provided for in Clause 1 of Article 8 in the second-mentioned covenant.

Further civic rights, including the explicit prohibition of 'arbitrary interference with privacy, family, home or correspondence' (Article 17 of the first covenant), are seriously vitiated by the various forms of interference in the private life of citizens exercised by the Ministry of the Interior, for example by bugging telephones and houses, opening mail, following personal movements, searching homes, setting up networks of neighbourhood informers (often recruited by illicit threats or promises) and in other ways.

The Ministry frequently interferes in employers' decisions, instigates acts of discrimination by authorities and organizations, brings weight to bear on the organs of justice and even orchestrates propaganda campaigns in the media. This activity is governed by no law and, being clandestine, affords the citizen no chance to defend himself.

In cases of prosecution on political grounds the investigative and judicial organs violate the rights of those charged and of those defending them, as guaranteed by Article 14 of the first covenant and indeed by Czechoslovak law. The prison treatment of those sentenced in such cases is an affront to their human dignity and a menace to their health, being aimed at breaking their morale.

Clause 2, Article 12 of the first covenant, guaranteeing every citizen the right to leave the country, is consistently violated, or under the pretence of 'defence of national security' is subjected to various unjustifiable conditions (Clause 3). The granting of entry visas to foreigners is also treated arbitrarily, and many are unable to visit Czechoslovakia merely because of professional or personal contacts with those of our citizens who are subject to discrimination.

Some of our people—either in private, at their places of work or by the only feasible public channel, the foreign media—have drawn attention to the systematic violation of human rights and democratic freedoms and demanded amends in specific cases. But their pleas have remained largely ignored or been made grounds for police investigation.

Responsibility for the maintenance of civic rights in our country naturally devolves in the first place on the political and state authorities. Yet not only on them: everyone bears his share of responsibility for the conditions that prevail and accordingly also for the observance of legally enshrined agreements, binding upon all individuals as well as upon governments.

It is this sense of co-responsibility, our belief in the importance of its conscious public acceptance and the general need to give it new and more effective expression that led us to the idea of creating Charter 77, whose inception we today publicly announce.

Charter 77 is a loose, informal and open association of people of various shades of opinion, faiths and professions united by the will to strive individually and collectively for the respecting of civic and human rights in our own country and throughout the world— rights accorded to all men by the two mentioned international covenants, by the Final Act of the Helsinki conference, and by numerous other international documents opposing war, violence and social or spiritual oppression and which are comprehensively laid down in the UN Universal Charter of Human Rights.

Charter 77 springs from a background of friendship and solidarity among people who share our concern for those ideals that have inspired, and continue to inspire, their lives and their work.

Charter 77 is not an organization; it has no rules, permanent bodies or formal membership. It embraces everyone who agrees with its ideas and participates in its work. It does not form the basis for any oppositional political activity. Like many similar citizen initiatives in various countries, West and East, it seeks to promote the general public interest.

It does not aim to set out its own platform of political or social reform or change, but within its own field of impact to conduct a constructive dialogue with the political and state authorities, particularly by drawing attention to individual cases where human and civic rights are violated, to document such grievances and suggest remedies, to make proposals

Q

of a more general character calculated to reinforce such rights and machinery for protecting them, to act as intermediary in situations of conflict which may lead to violation of rights, and so forth.

By its symbolic name Charter 77 denotes that it has come into being at the start of a year proclaimed as Political Prisoners' Year—a year in which a conference in Belgrade is due to review the implementations of the obligations assumed at Helsinki.

As signatories, we hereby authorize Professor Dr Jan Patočka, Dr Václav Havel and Professor Dr Jiří Hájek to act as the spokesmen for the Charter. These spokesmen are endued with full authority to represent it vis-à-vis state and other bodies, and the public at home and abroad, and their signatures attest the authenticity of documents issued by the Charter. They will have us and others who join us as their colleagues, taking part in any needful negotiations, shouldering particular tasks and sharing every responsibility.

We believe that Charter 77 will help to enable all the citizens of Czechoslovakia to work and live as free human beings.

There followed 242 signatures. Many others were added later.

THE CONSTITUTION OF THE USSR

Approved by the Supreme Soviet on 7 October 1977

(The document, for reasons of space, has been slightly abbreviated, the omissions being indicated in the text. They comprise paragraphs in the Preamble consisting of historical narration and laudation of the Soviet socialist society; parts of Articles 40, 41, 42, 43, 45, 47, 48, 49, 50 and 53 which are descriptions (as, e.g., in Articles 44 and 46) of how the Articles are implemented, not mandatory clauses; Article 83, which is repetitive, and Articles 85 and 87, which enumerate the Autonomous SSRs and Regions; much of Part VI dealing with subordinate jurisdictions; and the four short Articles of Part VIII.)

(English text supplied by Novotny Press.)

The Great October Socialist Revolution, made by the workers and peasants of Russia under the leadership of the Communist Party headed by Lenin, over threw capitalist and landowner rule, broke the fetters of oppression, established the dictatorship of the proletariat, and created the Soviet state, a new type of state, the basic instrument for defending the gains of the revolution and for building socialism and communism. Humanity thereby began the epoch-making turn from capitalism to socialism. . . .

The supreme goal of the Soviet state is the building of a classless communist society in which there will be public, communist self-government. The main aims of the people's socialist state are: to lay the material and technical foundation of communism, to perfect socialist social relations and transform them into communist relations, to mould the citizen of communist society, to raise the people's living and cultural standards, to safeguard the country's security, and to further the consolidation of peace and development of international cooperation.

The Soviet people . . .

hereby affirm the principles of the social structure and policy of the USSR, and define the rights, freedoms and obligations of citizens, and the principles of the organization of the socialist state of the whole people, and its aims, and proclaim these in this Constitution.

I. PRINCIPLES OF THE SOCIAL STRUCTURE AND POLICY OF THE USSR

Chapter 1. The Political System

Article 1. The Union of Soviet Socialist Republics is a socialist state of the whole people, expressing the will and interests of the workers, peasants, and intelligentsia, the working people of all the nations and nationalities of the country.

Article 2. All power in the USSR belongs to the people. The people exercise state power through Soviets of People's Deputies, which constitute the political foundation of the USSR. All other state bodies are under the control of, and accountable to, the Soviets of People's Deputies.

Article 3. The Soviet state is organized and functions on the principle of democratic centralism, namely the electiveness of all bodies of state authority from the lowest to the highest, their accountability to the people, and the obligation of lower bodies to observe the decisions of higher ones. Democratic centralism combines central leadership with local initiative and creative activity and with the responsibility of each state body and official for the work entrusted to them.

Article 4. The Soviet state and all its bodies function on the basis of socialist law, ensure the maintenance of law and order, and safeguard the interests of society and the rights and freedoms of citizens. State organizations, public organizations and officials shall observe the Constitution of the USSR and Soviet laws.

Article 5. Major matters of state shall be submitted to nationwide discussion and put to a popular vote (referendum).

Article 6. The leading and guiding force of Soviet society and the nucleus of its political system, of all state organizations and public organizations, is the Communist Party of the Soviet Union. The CPSU exists for the people and serves the people. The Communist Party, armed with Marxism-Leninism, determines the general perspectives of the development of society and the course of the home and foreign policy of the USSR, directs the great constructive work of the Soviet people, and imparts a planned, systematic and theoretically substantiated character to their struggle for the victory of communism.

All Party organizations shall function within the framework of the Constitution of the USSR.

Article 7. Trade unions, the All-Union Leninist Young Communist League, cooperatives, and other public organizations, participate, in accordance with the aims laid down in their rules, in managing state and public affairs, and in deciding political, economic, and social and cultural matters.

Article 8. Work collectives take part in discussing and deciding state and public affairs, in planning production and social development, in training and placing personnel, and in discussing and deciding matters pertaining to the management of enterprises and institutions, the improvement of working and living conditions, and the use of funds allocated both for developing production and for social and cultural purposes and financial incentives. Work collectives promote socialist emulation, the spread of progressive methods of work, and the strengthening of production discipline, educate their members in the spirit of communist morality, and strive to enhance their political consciousness and raise their cultural level and skills and qualifications.

Article 9. The principal direction in the development of the political system of Soviet society is the extension of socialist democracy, namely, ever broader participation of citizens in managing the affairs of society and the state, continuous improvement of the machinery of state, heightening of the activity of public organizations, strengthening of the system of people's control, consolidation of the legal foundations of the functioning of the state and of public life, greater openness and publicity, and constant responsiveness to public opinion.

Chapter 2. The Economic System

Article 10. The foundation of the economic system of the USSR is socialist ownership of the means of production in the form of state property (belonging to all the people), and collective farm-and-cooperative property. Socialist ownership also embraces the property of trade unions and other public organizations which they require to carry out their purposes under their rules. The state protects socialist property and provides conditions for its growth. No one has the right to use socialist property for personal gain or other selfish ends.

Article 11. State property, i.e. the common property of the Soviet people, is the principal form of socialist property. The land, its minerals, waters, and forests are the exclusive property of the state. The state owns the basic means of production in industry, construction and agriculture; means of transport and communication; the banks; the property of state-run trade organizations and public utilities, and other state-run undertakings; most urban housing; and other property necessary for state purposes.

Article 12. The property of collective farms and other cooperative organizations, and of their joint undertakings, comprises the means of production and other assets which they require for the purposes laid down in their rules. The land held by collective farms is secured to them for their free use in perpetuity. The state promotes development of collective farm-and-cooperative property and its approximation to state property. Collective farms, like other land users, are obliged to make effective and thrifty use of the land and to increase its fertility.

Article 13. Earned income forms the basis of the personal property of Soviet citizens. The personal property of citizens of the USSR may include articles of everyday use, personal consumption and convenience, the implements and other objects of a small-holding, a house, and earned savings. The personal property of citizens and the right to inherit it are protected by the state. Citizens may be granted the use of plots of land, in the manner prescribed by law, for a subsidiary small-holding (including the keeping of livestock and poultry), for fruit and vegetable growing or for building an individual dwelling. Citizens are required to make rational use of the land allotted to them. The state and collective farms provide assistance to citizens in working their small-holdings.

Property owned or used by citizens shall not serve as a means of deriving unearned income or be employed to the detriment of the interests of society.

Article 14. The source of the growth of social wealth and of the well-being of the people, and of each individual, is the labour, free from exploitation, of Soviet people. The state exercises control over the measure of labour and of consumption in accordance with the principle of socialism: 'From each according to his ability, to each according to his work'. It fixes the rate of taxation on taxable income. Socially useful work and its results determine a person's status in society. By combining material and moral incentives and encouraging innovations and a creative attitude to work, the state helps transform labour into the prime vital need of every Soviet citizen.

Article 15. The supreme goal of social production under socialism is the fullest possible satisfaction of the people's growing material, and cultural and intellectual requirements. Relying on the creative initiative of the working people, socialist emulation, and scientific and technological progress, and by improving the forms and methods of economic management, the state ensures growth of the productivity of labour, raising of the efficiency of production and of the quality of work, and dynamic, planned, proportionate development of the economy.

Article 16. The economy of the USSR is an integral economic complex comprising all the elements of social production, distribution, and exchange on its territory. The economy is managed on the basis of state plans for economic and social development, with due account of the sectoral and territorial principles, and by combining centralized direction with the managerial independence and initiative of individual and amalgamated enterprises and other organizations, for which active use is made of management accounting, profit, cost, and other economic levers and incentives.

Article 17. In the USSR, the law permits individual labour in handicrafts, farming, the provision of services for the public, and other forms of activity based exclusively on the personal work of individual citizens and members of their families. The state makes regulations for such work to ensure that it serves the interests of society.

Article 18. In the interests of the present and future generations, the necessary steps are taken in the USSR to protect and make scientific, rational use of the land and its mineral and water resources, and the plant and animal kingdoms, to preserve the purity of air and water, ensure reproduction of natural wealth, and improve the human environment.

Chapter 3. Social Development and Culture

Article 19. The social basis of the USSR is the unbreakable alliance of the workers, peasants and intelligentsia. The state helps enhance the social homogeneity of society, namely the elimination of class differences and of the essential distinctions between town and country and between mental and physical labour, and the all-round development and drawing together of all the nations and nationalities of the USSR.

Article 20. In accordance with the communist ideal—'The free development of each is the condition of the free development of all'—the state pursues the aim of giving citizens more and more real opportunities to apply their creative energies, abilities, and talents, and to develop their personalities in every way.

Article 21. The state concerns itself with improving working conditions, safety and labour protection and the scientific organization of work, and with reducing and ultimately eliminating all arduous physical labour through comprehensive mechanization and automation of production processes in all branches of the economy.

Article 22. A programme is being consistently implemented in the USSR to convert agricultural work into a variety of industrial work, to extend the network of educational, cultural and medical institutions, and of trade, public catering, service and public utility facilities in rural localities, and transform hamlets and villages into well-planned and well-appointed settlements.

Article 23. The state pursues a steady policy of raising people's pay levels and real incomes through increase in productivity. In order to satisfy the needs of Soviet people more fully social consumption funds are created. The state, with the broad participation of public organizations and work collectives, ensures the growth and just distribution of these funds.

Article 24. In the USSR, state systems of health protection, social security, trade and public catering, communal services and amenities, and public utilities, operate and are being extended. The state encourages cooperatives and other public organizations to provide all types of services for the population. It encourages the development of mass physical culture and sport.

Article 25. In the USSR there is a uniform system of public education, which is being constantly improved, that provides general education and vocational training for citizens, serves the communist education and intellectual and physical development of the youth, and trains them for work and social activity.

Article 26. In accordance with society's needs the state provides for planned development of science and the training of scientific personnel and organizes introduction of the results of research in the economy and other spheres of life.

Article 27. The state concerns itself with protecting, augmenting and making extensive use of society's cultural wealth for the moral and aesthetic education of the Soviet people, for raising their cultural level. In the USSR development of the professional, amateur and folk arts is encouraged in every way.

Chapter 4. Foreign Policy

Article 28. The USSR steadfastly pursues a Leninist policy of peace and stands for strengthening of the security of nations and broad international cooperation. The foreign policy of the USSR is aimed at ensuring international conditions favourable for building communism in the USSR, safeguarding the state interests of the Soviet Union, consolidating the positions of world socialism, supporting the struggle of peoples for national liberation and social progress, preventing wars of aggression, achieving universal and complete disarmament, and consistently implementing the principle of the peaceful coexistence of states with different social systems. In the USSR war propaganda is banned.

Article 29. The USSR's relations with other states are based on observance of the following principles: sovereign equality; mutual renunciation of the use or threat of force; inviolability of frontiers; territorial integrity of states; peaceful settlement of disputes; nonintervention in internal affairs; respect for human rights and fundamental freedoms; the equal rights of peoples and their right to decide their own destiny; cooperation among states; and fulfilment in good faith of obligations arising from the generally recognised principles and rules of international law, and from the international treaties signed by the USSR.

Article 31. The USSR, as part of the world system of socialism and of the socialist community, promotes and strengthens friendship, cooperation, and comradely mutual assistance with other socialist countries on the basis of the principle of socialist internationalism, and takes an active part in socialist economic integration and the socialist international division of labour.

Chapter 5. Defence of the Socialist Motherland

Article 31. Defence of the Socialist Motherland is one of the most important functions of the state, and is the concern of the whole people. In order to defend the gains of socialism, the peaceful labour of the Soviet people, and the sovereignty and territorial integrity of the state, the USSR maintains Armed Forces and has instituted universal military service. The duty of the Armed Forces of the USSR to the people is to provide reliable defence of the Socialist Motherland and to be in constant combat readiness, guaranteeing that any aggressor is instantly repulsed.

Article 32. The state ensures the security and defence capability of the country, and supplies the Armed Forces of the USSR with everything necessary for that purpose. The duties of state bodies, public organizations, officials, and citizens in regard to safeguarding the country's security and strengthening its defence capacity are defined by the legislation of the USSR.

II. THE STATE AND THE INDIVIDUAL

Chapter 6. Citizenship of the USSR: Equality of Citizens' Rights

Article 33. Uniform federal citizenship is established for the USSR. Every citizen of a Union Republic is a citizen of the USSR. The grounds and procedure for acquiring or forfeiting Soviet citizenship are defined by the Law on Citizenship of the USSR. When abroad, citizens of the USSR enjoy the protection and assistance of the Soviet state.

Article 34. Citizens of the USSR are equal before the law, without distinction of origin, social or property status, race or nationality, sex, education, language, attitude to religion, type and nature of occupation, domicile, or other status. The equal rights of citizens of the USSR are guaranteed in all fields of economic, political, social, and cultural life.

Article 35. Women and men have equal rights in the USSR. Exercise of these rights is ensured by according women equal access with men to education and vocational and professional training, equal opportunities in employment, remuneration, and promotion, and in social and political, and cultural activity, and by special labour and health protection measures for women; by providing conditions enabling mothers to work; by legal protection, and material and moral support for mothers and children, including paid leave and other benefits for expectant mothers and mothers, and gradual reduction of working time for mothers with small children.

Article 36. Citizens of the USSR of different races and nationalities have equal rights. Exercise of these rights is ensured by a policy of all-round development and drawing together of all the nations and nationalities of the USSR, by educating citizens in the spirit of Soviet patriotism and socialist internationalism, and by the opportunity to use their native language and the languages of other peoples of the USSR. Any direct or indirect limitation of the rights of citizens or establishment of direct or indirect privileges on grounds of race or nationality, and any advocacy of racial or national exclusiveness, hostility or contempt, are punishable by law.

Article 37. Citizens of other countries and stateless persons in the USSR are guaranteed the rights and freedoms provided by law, including the right to apply to a court and other state bodies for the protection of their personal, property, family, and other rights. Citizens of other countries and stateless persons, when in the USSR, are obliged to respect the Constitution of the USSR and observe Soviet laws.

Article 38. The USSR grants the right of asylum to foreigners persecuted for defending the interests of the working people and the cause of peace, or for participation in the revolutionary and national-liberation movement, or for progressive social and political, scientific or other creative activity.

Chapter 7. The Basic Rights, Freedoms, and Duties of Citizens of the USSR

Article 39. Citizens of the USSR enjoy in full the social, economic, political and personal rights and freedoms proclaimed and guaranteed by the Constitution of the USSR and by Soviet laws. The socialist system ensures enlargement of the rights and freedoms of citizens and continuous improvement of their living standards as social, economic, and cultural development programmes are fulfilled. Enjoyment by citizens of their rights and freedoms must not be to the detriment of the interests of society or the state, or infringe the rights of other citizens.

Article 40. Citizens of the USSR have the right to work (that is, to guaranteed employment and pay in accordance with the quantity and quality of their work, and not below the state-established minimum), including the right to choose their trade or profession, type of job and work in accordance with inclinations, abilities, training and education, with due account of the needs of society. . . .

Article 41. Citizens of the USSR have the right to rest and leisure. This right is ensured by the establishment of a working week not exceeding 41 hours, for workers and other employees, a shorter working day in a number of trades and industries, and shorter hours for night work. . . . The length of collective farmers' working and leisure time is established by their collective farms.

Article 42. Citizens of the USSR have the right to health protection. This right is ensured by free, qualified medical care provided by state health institutions. . . .

Article 43. Citizens of the USSR have the right to maintenance in old age, in sickness, and in the event of complete or partial disability or loss of the breadwinner. . . .

Article 44. Citizens of the USSR have the right to housing. This right is ensured by the development and upkeep of state and socially-owned housing; by assistance for cooperative and individual house building; by fair distribution, under public control, of the housing that becomes available through fulfilment of the programme of building well-appointed dwellings, and by low rents and low charges for utility services. Citizens of the USSR shall take good care of the housing allocated to them.

Article 45. Citizens of the USSR have the right to education. This right is ensured by free provision of all forms of education, by the institution of universal, compulsory secondary education, and broad development of vocational, specialized secondary, and higher education, in which instruction is oriented toward practical activity and production. . . .

Article 46. Citizens of the USSR have the right to enjoy cultural benefits. This right is ensured by broad access to the cultural treasures of their own land and of the world that are preserved in state and other public collections; by the development and fair distribution of cultural and educational institutions throughout the country; by developing television and radio broadcasting and the publishing of books, newspapers and periodicals, and by extending the free library service; and by expanding cultural exchanges with other countries.

Article 47. Citizens of the USSR, in accordance with the aims of building communism, are guaranteed freedom of scientific, technical, and artistic work. . . . The rights of authors, inventors and innovators are protected by the state.

Article 48. Citizens of the USSR have the right to take part in the management and administration of state and public affairs and in the discussion and adoption of laws and measures of All-Union and local significance. This right is ensured by the opportunity to vote and to be elected to Soviets of People's Deputies and other elective state bodies, to take part in nationwide discussions and referendums, in people's control, in the work of state bodies, public organizations, and local community groups, and in meetings at places of work or residence.

Article 49. Every citizen of the USSR has the right to submit proposals to state bodies and public organizations for improving their activity, and to criticise shortcomings in their work. Officials are obliged, within established time-limits, to examine citizens' proposals and requests, to reply to them, and to take appropriate action. Persecution for criticism is prohibited. Persons guilty of such persecution shall be called to account.

Article 50. In accordance with the interests of the people and in order to strengthen and develop the socialist system, citizens of the USSR are guaranteed freedom of speech, of the press, and of assembly, meetings, street processions and demonstrations . . . .

Article 51. In accordance with the aims of building communism, citizens of the USSR have the right to associate in public organizations that promote their political activity and initiative and satisfaction of their various interests. Public organizations are guaranteed conditions for successfully performing the functions defined in their rules.

Article 52. Citizens of the USSR are guaranteed freedom of conscience, that is, the right to profess or not to profess any religion, and to conduct religious worship or atheistic propaganda. Incitement of hostility or hatred on religious grounds is prohibited. In the USSR, the church is separated from the state, and the school from the church.

Article 53. The family enjoys the protection of the state. Marriage is based on the free consent of the woman and the man; the spouses are completely equal in their family relations. . . .

Article 54. Citizens of the USSR are guaranteed inviolability of the person. No one may be arrested except by a court decision or on the warrant of a procurator.

Article 55. Citizens of the USSR are guaranteed inviolability of the home. No one may, without lawful grounds, enter a home against the will of those residing in it.

Article 56. The privacy of citizens, and of their correspondence, telephone conversations, and telegraphic communications is protected by law.

Article 57. Respect for the individual and protection of the rights and freedoms of citizens are the duty of all state bodies, public organizations, and officials. Citizens of the USSR have the right to protection by the courts against encroachments on their honour and reputation, life and health, and personal freedom and property.

Article 58. Citizens of the USSR have the right to lodge a complaint against the actions of officials, state bodies and public bodies. Complaints shall be examined according to the procedure and within the time-limit established by law. Actions by officials that contravene the law or exceed their powers, and infringe the rights of citizens, may be appealed against in a court in the manner prescribed by law. Citizens of the USSR have the right to compensation for damage resulting from unlawful actions by state organizations and public organizations, or by officials in the performance of their duties.

Article 59. Citizens' exercise of their rights and freedoms is inseparable from the performance of their duties and obligations. Citizens of the USSR are obliged to observe the Constitution of the USSR and Soviet laws, comply with the standards of socialist conduct, and uphold the honour and dignity of Soviet citizenship.

Article 60. It is the duty of, and a matter of honour for, every able-bodied citizen of the USSR to work conscientiously in his chosen, socially useful occupation, and strictly to observe labour discipline. Evasion of socially useful work is incompatible with the principles of socialist society.

Article 61. Citizens of the USSR are obliged to preserve and protect socialist property. It is the duty of a citizen of the USSR to combat misappropriation and squandering of state and socially-owned property and to make thrifty use of the people's wealth. Persons encroaching in any way on socialist property shall be punished according to the law.

Article 62. Citizens of the USSR are obliged to safeguard the interests of the Soviet state, and to enhance its power and prestige. Defence of the Socialist Motherland is the sacred duty of every citizen of the USSR. Betrayal of the Motherland is the gravest of crimes against the people.

Article 63. Military service in the ranks of the Armed Forces of the USSR is an honourable duty of Soviet citizens.

Article 64. It is the duty of every citizen of the USSR to respect the national dignity of other citizens, and to strengthen friendship of the nations and nationalities of the multinational Soviet state.

Article 65. A citizen of the USSR is obliged to respect the rights and lawful interests of other persons, to be uncompromising toward anti-social behaviour, and to help maintain public order.

Article 66. Citizens of the USSR are obliged to concern themselves with the upbringing of children, to train them for socially useful work, and to raise them as worthy members of socialist society. Children are obliged to care for their parents and help them.

Article 67. Citizens of the USSR are obliged to protect nature and conserve its riches.

Article 68. Concern for the preservation of historical monuments and other cultural values is a duty and obligation of citizens of the USSR.

Article 69. It is the internationalist duty of citizens of the USSR to promote friendship and cooperation with peoples of other lands and help maintain and strengthen world peace.

III. THE NATIONAL-STATE STRUCTURE OF THE USSR

Chapter 8. The USSR—A Federal State

Article 70. The Union of Soviet Socialist Republics is an integral, federal, multinational state formed on the principle of socialist federalism as a result of the free self-determination of nations and the voluntary association of equal Soviet Socialist Republics. The USSR embodies the state unity of the Soviet people and draws all its nations and nationalities together for the purpose of jointly building communism.

Article 71. The Union of Soviet Socialist Republics unites: the Russian Soviet Federative Socialist Republic [*and 14 named Soviet Socialist Republics*].

Article 72. Each Union Republic shall retain the right freely to secede from the USSR.

Article 73. The jurisdiction of the Union of Soviet Socialist Republics, as represented by its highest bodies of state authority and administration, shall cover:

(1) The admission of new republics to the USSR; endorsement of the formation of new autonomous republics and autonomous regions within Union Republics.

(2) Determination of the state boundaries of the USSR and approval of changes in the boundaries between Union Republics.

(3) Establishment of the general principles for the organization and functioning of republican and local bodies of state authority and administration.

(4) The ensurance of uniformity of legislative norms throughout the USSR and establishment of the fundamentals of the legislation of the Union of Soviet Socialist Republics and Union Republics.

(5) Pursuance of a uniform social and economic policy; direction of the country's economy; determination of the main lines of scientific and technological progress and the general measures for rational exploitation and conservation of natural resources; the drafting and approval of state plans for the economic and social development of the USSR, and endorsement of reports on their fulfilment.

(6) The drafting and approval of the consolidated Budget of the USSR, and endorsement of the report on its execution; management of a single monetary and credit system; determination of the taxes and revenues forming the Budget of the USSR; and the formulation of prices and wages policy.

(7) Direction of the sectors of the economy, and of enterprises and amalgamations under Union jurisdiction, and general direction of industries under Union-Republican jurisdiction.

(8) Issues of war and peace, defence of the sovereignty of the USSR and safeguarding of its frontiers and territory, and organization of defence; direction of the Armed Forces of the USSR.

(9) State security.

(10) Representation of the USSR in international relations; the USSR's relations with other states and with international organizations; establishment of the general procedure for, and coordination of, the relations of Union Republics with other states and with international organizations; foreign trade and other forms of external economic activity on the basis of state monopoly.

(11) Control over observance of the Constitution of the USSR, and ensurance of conformity of the Constitutions of Union Republics to the Constitution of the USSR.

(12) Settlement of other matters of All-Union importance.

Article 74. The laws of the USSR shall have the same force in all Union Republics. In the event of a discrepancy between a Union Republic law and an All-Union law, the law of the USSR shall prevail.

Article 75. The territory of the Union of Soviet Socialist Republics is a single entity and comprises the territories of the Union Republics. The sovereignty of the USSR extends throughout its territory.

Chapter 9. The Union Soviet Socialist Republic

Article 76. A Union Republic is a sovereign Soviet socialist state that has united with other Soviet Republics in the Union of Soviet Socialist Republics. Outside the spheres listed in Article 73 of the Constitution of the USSR, a Union Republic exercises independent authority on its territory. A Union Republic shall have its own Constitution conforming to the Constitution of the USSR with the specific features of the Republic being taken into account.

Article 77. Union Republics take part in decision-making in the Supreme Soviet of the USSR, the Presidium of the Supreme Soviet of the USSR, the Government of the USSR, and other bodies of the Union of Soviet Socialist Republics in matters that come within the jurisdiction of the Union of Soviet Socialist Republics.

A Union Republic shall ensure comprehensive economic and social development on its territory, facilitate exercise of the powers of the USSR on its territory, and implement the decisions of the highest bodies of state authority and administration of the USSR. In matters that come within its jurisdiction, a Union Republic shall coordinate and control the activity of enterprises, institutions, and organizations subordinate to the Union.

Article 78. The territory of a Union Republic may not be altered without its consent. The boundaries between Union Republics may be altered by mutual agreement of the Republics concerned, subject to ratification by the Union of Soviet Socialist Republics.

Article 79. A Union Republic shall determine its division into territories, regions, areas, and districts, and decide other matters relating to its administrative and territorial structure.

Article 80. A Union Republic has the right to enter into relations with other states, conclude treaties with them, exchange diplomatic and consular representatives, and take part in the work of international organizations.

Article 81. The sovereign rights of Union Republics shall be safeguarded by the USSR.

Chapter 10. The Autonomous Soviet Socialist Republic

Article 82. An Autonomous Republic is a constituent part of a Union Republic. In spheres not within the jurisdiction of the Union of Soviet Socialist Republics and the Union Republic, an Autonomous Republic shall deal independently with matters within its jurisdiction. An Autonomous Republic shall have its own Constitution conforming to the Constitutions of the USSR and the Union Republic with the specific features of the Autonomous Republic being taken into account.

Article 83. [*Repeats the phraseology of Article 77,* mutatis mutandis].

Article 84. The territory of an Autonomous Republic may not be altered without its consent.

Article 85. [*Names the 20 Autonomous Republics*].

Chapter 11. The Autonomous Region and Autonomous Area

Article 86. An Autonomous Region is a constituent part of a Union Republic or Territory. The Law on an Autonomous Region, upon submission by the Soviet of People's Deputies of the Autonomous Region concerned, shall be adopted by the Supreme Soviet of the Union Republic.

Article 87. [*Names the 8 Autonomous Regions*].

Article 88. An Autonomous Area is a constituent part of a Territory or Region. The Law on an Autonomous Area shall be adopted by the Supreme Soviet of the Union Republic concerned.

IV. SOVIETS OF PEOPLE'S DEPUTIES AND ELECTORAL PROCEDURE

Chapter 12. The System of Soviets of People's Deputies and the Principles of their Work

Article 89. The Soviets of People's Deputies, i.e., the Supreme Soviet of the USSR, the Supreme Soviets of Union Republics, the Supreme Soviets of Autonomous Republics, the Soviets of People's Deputies of Territories and Regions, the Soviets of People's Deputies of

Q*

Autonomous Regions and Autonomous Areas, and the Soviets of People's Deputies of districts, cities, city districts, settlements and villages shall constitute a single system of bodies of state authority.

Article 90. The term of the Supreme Soviet of the USSR, the Supreme Soviets of Union Republics, and the Supreme Soviets of Autonomous Republics shall be five years. The term of local Soviets of People's Deputies shall be two and a half years. Elections to Soviets of People's Deputies shall be called not later than two months before expiry of the term of the Soviet concerned.

Article 91. The most important matters within the jurisdiction of the respective Soviets of People's Deputies shall be considered and settled at their sessions. Soviets of People's Deputies shall elect standing commissions and form executive-administrative, and other bodies accountable to them.

Article 92. Soviets of People's Deputies shall form people's control bodies combining state control with control by the working people at enterprises, collective farms, institutions, and organizations. People's control bodies shall check on the fulfilment of state plans and assignments, combat breaches of state discipline, localistic tendencies, narrow departmental attitudes, mismanagement, extravagance and waste, red tape and bureaucracy, and help improve the working of the state machinery.

Article 93. Soviets of People's Deputies shall direct all sectors of state, economic and social and cultural development, either directly or through bodies instituted by them, take decisions and ensure their execution, and verify their implementation.

Article 94. Soviets of People's Deputies shall function publicly on the basis of collective, free, constructive discussion and decision-making, of systematic reporting back to them and the people by their executive-administrative and other bodies, and of involving citizens on a broad scale in their work. Soviets of People's Deputies and the bodies set up by them shall systematically inform the public about their work and the decisions taken by them.

Chapter 13. The Electoral System

Article 95. Deputies to all Soviets shall be elected on the basis of universal, equal, and direct suffrage by secret ballot.

Article 96. Elections shall be universal: all citizens of the USSR who have reached the age of 18 shall have the right to vote and to be elected, with the exception of persons who have been legally certified insane. To be eligible for election to the Supreme Soviet of the USSR a citizen of the USSR must have reached the age of 21.

Article 97. Elections shall be equal: each citizen shall have one vote; all voters shall exercise the franchise on an equal footing.

Article 98. Elections shall be direct: Deputies to all Soviets of People's Deputies shall be elected by citizens by direct vote.

Article 99. Voting at elections shall be secret: control over voters' exercise of the franchise is inadmissible.

Article 100. The following shall have the right to nominate candidates: branches and organizations of the Communist Party of the Soviet Union, trade unions, and the All-Union Leninist Young Communist League; cooperatives and other public organizations; work collectives, and meetings of servicemen in their military units.

Citizens of the USSR and public organizations are guaranteed the right to free and all-round discussion of the political and personal qualities and competence of candidates, and the right to campaign for them at meetings, in the press, and on television and radio. The expenses involved in holding elections to Soviets of People's Deputies shall be met by the state.

Article 101. Deputies to Soviets of People's Deputies shall be elected by constituencies. A citizen of the USSR may not, as a rule, be elected to more than two Soviets of People's Deputies. Elections to the Soviets shall be conducted by electoral commissions consisting of representatives of public organizations and work collectives, and of meetings of servicemen in military units. The procedure for holding elections to Soviets of People's Deputies shall be defined by the laws of the USSR, and of Union and Autonomous Republics.

Article 102. Electors give mandates to their Deputies. The appropriate Soviets of People's Deputies shall examine electors' mandates, take them into account in drafting economic and social development plans and in drawing up the budget, organize implementation of the mandates, and inform citizens about it.

Chapter 14. People's Deputies

Article 103. Deputies are the plenipotentiary representatives of the people in the Soviets of People's Deputies. In the Soviets, Deputies deal with matters relating to state, economic and social and cultural development, organize implementation of the decisions of the Soviets, and exercise control over the work of state bodies, enterprises, institutions and organizations. Deputies shall be guided in their activities by the interests of the state, and shall take the needs of their constituents into account and work to implement their electors' mandates.

Article 104. Deputies shall exercise their powers without discontinuing their regular employment or duties. During sessions of the Soviet, and so as to exercise their Deputy's powers in other cases stipulated by law. Deputies shall be released from their regular employment or duties, with retention of their average earnings at their permanent place of work.

Article 105. A Deputy has the right to address inquiries to the appropriate state bodies and officials, who are obliged to reply to them at a session of the Soviet. Deputies have the right to approach any state or public body, enterprise, institution, or organization on matters arising from their work as Deputies and to take part in considering the questions raised by them. The heads of the state or public bodies, enterprises, institutions or organizations concerned are obliged to receive Deputies without delay and to consider their proposals within the time-limit established by law.

Article 106. Deputies shall be ensured conditions for the unhampered and effective exercise of their rights and duties. The immunity of Deputies, and other guarantees of their activity as Deputies, are defined in the Law on the Status of Deputies and other legislative acts of the USSR and of Union and Autonomous Republics.

Article 107. Deputies shall report on their work and on that of the Soviet to their constituents, and to the work collectives and public organizations that nominated them. Deputies who have not justified the confidence of their constituents may be recalled at any time by decision of a majority of the electors in accordance with the procedure established by law.

V. HIGHER BODIES OF STATE AUTHORITY AND ADMINISTRATION OF THE USSR

Chapter 15. The Supreme Soviet of the USSR

Article 108. The highest body of state authority of the USSR shall be the Supreme Soviet of the USSR. The Supreme Soviet of the USSR is empowered to deal with all matters within the jurisdiction of the Union of Soviet Socialist Republics, as defined by this Constitution. The adoption and amendment of the Constitution of the USSR; admission of new Republics to the USSR; endorsement of the formation of new Autonomous Republics and Autonomous Regions; approval of the state plans for economic and social development, of the Budget of the USSR, and of reports on their execution; and the institution of bodies of the USSR accountable to it, are the exclusive prerogative of the Supreme Soviet of the USSR.

Laws of the USSR shall be enacted by the Supreme Soviet of the USSR or by a nation-wide vote (referendum) held by decision of the Supreme Soviet of the USSR.

Article 109. The Supreme Soviet of the USSR shall consist of two chambers: the Soviet of the Union and the Soviet of Nationalities. The two chambers of the Supreme Soviet of the USSR shall have equal rights.

Article 110. The Soviet of the Union and the Soviet of Nationalities shall have equal numbers of deputies. The Soviet of the Union shall be elected by constituencies with equal populations. The Soviet of Nationalities shall be elected on the basis of the following representation: 32 Deputies from each Union Republic, 11 Deputies from each Autonomous Republic, five Deputies from each Autonomous Region, and one Deputy from each Autonomous Area.

The Soviet of the Union and the Soviet of Nationalities, upon submission by the credentials commissions elected by them, shall decide on the validity of Deputies' credentials, and, in cases in which the election law has been violated, shall declare the election of the Deputies concerned null and void.

Article 111. Each chamber of the Supreme Soviet of the USSR shall elect a Chairman and four Vice-Chairmen. The Chairmen of the Soviet of the Union and of the Soviet of Nationalities shall preside over the sittings of the respective chambers and conduct their affairs. Joint sittings of the chambers of the Supreme Soviet of the USSR shall be presided over alternately by the Chairman of the Soviet of the Union and the Chairman of the Soviet of Nationalities.

Article 112. Sessions of the Supreme Soviet of the USSR shall be convened twice a year. Special sessions shall be convened by the Presidium of the Supreme Soviet of the USSR at its discretion or on the proposal of a Union Republic, or of not less than one-third of the Deputies of one of the chambers. A session of the Supreme Soviet of the USSR shall consist of separate and joint sittings of the chambers, and of meetings of the standing commissions of the chambers or commissions of the Supreme Soviet of the USSR held between the sittings of the chambers. A session may be opened and closed at either separate or joint sittings of the chambers.

Article 113. The right to initiate legislation in the Supreme Soviet of the USSR is vested in the Soviet of the Union and the Soviet of Nationalities, the Presidium of the Supreme Soviet of the USSR, the Council of Ministers of the USSR, Union Republics through their higher bodies of state authority, commissions of the Supreme Soviet of the USSR and standing commissions of its chambers, Deputies of the Supreme Soviet of the USSR, the Supreme Court of the USSR, and the Procurator-General of the USSR. The right to initiate legislation is also vested in public organizations through their All-Union bodies.

Article 114. Bills and other matters submitted to the Supreme Soviet of the USSR shall be debated by its chambers at separate or joint sittings. Where necessary, a Bill or other matter may be referred to one or more commissions for preliminary or additional consideration. A law of the USSR shall be deemed adopted when it has been passed in each chamber of the Supreme Soviet of the USSR by a majority of the total number of its Deputies. Decisions and other acts of the Supreme Soviet of the USSR are adopted by a majority of the total number of Deputies of the Supreme Soviet of the USSR.

Bills and other very important matters of state may be submitted for nationwide discussion by a decision of the Supreme Soviet of the USSR or its Presidium taken on their own initiative or on the proposal of a Union Republic.

Article 115. In the event of disagreement between the Soviet of the Union and the Soviet of Nationalities, the matter at issue shall be referred for settlement to a conciliation commission formed by the chambers on a parity basis, after which it shall be considered for a second time by the Soviet of the Union and the Soviet of Nationalities at a joint sitting. If agreement is again not reached, the matter shall be postponed for debate at the next session of the Supreme Soviet of the USSR or submitted by the Supreme Soviet to a nationwide vote (referendum).

Article 116. Laws of the USSR and decisions and other acts of the Supreme Soviet of the USSR shall be published in the languages of the Union Republics over the signatures of the Chairman and Secretary of the Presidium of the Supreme Soviet of the USSR.

Article 117. A Deputy of the Supreme Soviet of the USSR has the right to address inquiries to the Council of Ministers of the USSR, and to Ministers and the heads of other bodies formed by the Supreme Soviet of the USSR. The Council of Ministers of the USSR, or the official to whom the inquiry is addressed, is obliged to give a verbal or written reply within three days at the given session of the Supreme Soviet of the USSR.

Article 118. A Deputy of the Supreme Soviet of the USSR may not be prosecuted, or arrested, or incur a court-imposed penalty, without the sanction of the Supreme Soviet of the USSR or, between its sessions, of the Presidium of the Supreme Soviet of the USSR.

Article 119. The Supreme Soviet of the USSR, at a joint sitting of its chambers, shall elect a Presidium of the Supreme Soviet of the USSR, which shall be a standing body of the Supreme Soviet of the USSR, accountable to it for all its work and exercising the functions of the highest body of state authority of the USSR between sessions of the Supreme Soviet, within the limits prescribed by the Constitution.

Article 120. The Presidium of the Supreme Soviet of the USSR shall be elected from among the Deputies and shall consist of a Chairman, First Vice-Chairman, 15 Vice-Chairmen (one from each Union Republic), a Secretary, and 21 members.

Article 121. The Presidium of the Supreme Soviet of the USSR shall: (1) name the date of elections to the Supreme Soviet of the USSR; (2) convene sessions of the Supreme Soviet of the USSR; (3) coordinate the work of the standing commissions of the chambers of the Supreme Soviet of the USSR; (4) ensure observance of the Constitution of the USSR and conformity of the Constitutions and laws of Union Republics to the Constitution and laws of the USSR; (5) interpret the laws of the USSR; (6) ratify and denounce international treaties of the USSR; (7) revoke decisions and ordinances of the Council of Ministers of the USSR and of the Councils of Ministers of Union Republics should they fail to conform to the law; (8) institute military and diplomatic ranks and other special titles; and confer the highest military and diplomatic ranks and other special titles; (9) institute orders and medals of the USSR, and honorific titles of the USSR; award orders and medals of the USSR; and confer honorific titles of the USSR; (10) grant citizenship of the USSR, and rule on matters of the renunciation or deprivation of citizenship of the USSR and of granting asylum; (11) issue All-Union acts of amnesty and exercise the right of pardon; (12) appoint and recall diplomatic representatives of the USSR to other countries and to international organizations; (13) receive the letters of credence and recall of the diplomatic representatives of foreign states accredited to it; (14) form the Council of Defence of the USSR and confirm its composition; appoint and dismiss the high command of the Armed Forces of the USSR; (15) proclaim martial law in particular localities or throughout the country in the interests of defence of the USSR; (16) order general or partial mobilization; (17) between sessions of the Supreme Soviet of the USSR, proclaim a state of war in the event of an armed attack on the USSR, or when it is necessary to meet international treaty obligations relating to mutual defence against aggression; (18) and exercise other powers vested in it by the Constitution and laws of the USSR.

Article 122. The Presidium of the Supreme Soviet of the USSR, between sessions of the Supreme Soviet of the USSR and subject to submission for its confirmation at the next session, shall: (1) amend existing legislative acts of the USSR when necessary; (2) approve changes in the boundaries between Union Republics; (3) form and abolish Ministries and State Committees of the USSR on the recommendation of the Council of Ministers of the USSR; (4) relieve individual members of the Council of Ministers and appoint persons to the Council of Ministers on the recommendation of the Chairman of the Council of Ministers of the USSR.

Article 123. The Presidium of the Supreme Soviet of the USSR promulgates decrees and adopts decisions.

Article 124. On expiry of the term of the Supreme Soviet of the USSR, the Presidium of the Supreme Soviet of the USSR shall retain its powers until the newly elected Supreme Soviet of the USSR has elected a new Presidium. The newly elected Supreme Soviet of the USSR shall be convened by the outgoing Presidium of the Supreme Soviet of the USSR within two months of the elections.

Article 125. The Soviet of the Union and the Soviet of Nationalities shall elect standing commissions from among the Deputies to make a preliminary review of matters coming within the jurisdiction of the Supreme Soviet of the USSR, to promote execution of the laws of the USSR and other acts of the Supreme Soviet of the USSR and its Presidium, and to check on the work of state bodies and organizations. The chambers of the Supreme Soviet of the USSR may also set up joint commissions on a parity basis.

When it deems it necessary, the Supreme Soviet of the USSR sets up commissions of inquiry and audit, and commissions on any other matter. All state and public bodies, organizations and officials are obliged to meet the requests of the commissions of the Supreme Soviet of the USSR and of its chambers, and submit the requisite materials and documents to them. The commissions' recommendations shall be subject to consideration by state and public bodies, institutions and organizations. The commissions shall be informed, within the prescribed time-limit, of the results of such consideration or of the action taken.

Article 126. The Supreme Soviet of the USSR shall supervise the work of all state bodies accountable to it. The Supreme Soviet of the USSR shall form a Committee of People's Control of the USSR to head the system of people's control. The organization and procedure of people's control bodies are defined by the Law on People's Control in the USSR.

Article 127. The procedure of the Supreme Soviet of the USSR and of its bodies shall be defined in the Rules and Regulations of the Supreme Soviet of the USSR and other laws of the USSR enacted on the basis of the Constitution of the USSR.

Chapter 16. The Council of Ministers of the USSR

Article 128. The Council of Ministers of the USSR, *i.e.*, the Government of the USSR, is the highest executive and administrative body of state authority of the USSR.

Article 129. The Council of Ministers of the USSR shall be formed by the Supreme Soviet of the USSR at a joint sitting of the Soviet of the Union and the Soviet of Nationalities, and shall consist of the Chairman of the Council of Ministers of the USSR, First Vice-Chairmen and Vice-Chairmen, Ministers of the USSR, and Chairmen of State Committees of the USSR. The Chairmen of the Councils of Ministers of Union Republics shall be ex officio members of the Council of Ministers of the USSR. The Supreme Soviet of the USSR, on the recommendation of the Chairman of the Council of Ministers of the USSR, may include in the Government of the USSR the heads of other bodies and organizations of the USSR. The Council of Ministers of the USSR shall tender its resignation to a newly-elected Supreme Soviet of the USSR at its first session.

Article 130. The Council of Ministers of the USSR shall be responsible and accountable to the Supreme Soviet of the USSR and, between sessions of the Supreme Soviet of the USSR, to the Presidium of the Supreme Soviet of the USSR. The Council of Ministers of the USSR shall report regularly on its work to the Supreme Soviet of the USSR.

Article 131. The Council of Ministers of the USSR is empowered to deal with all matters of state administration within the jurisdiction of the Union of Soviet Socialist Republics insofar as, under the Constitution, they do not come within the competence of the Supreme Soviet of the USSR or the Presidium of the Supreme Soviet of the USSR. Within its powers the Council of Ministers of the USSR shall:

(1) Ensure direction of economic, social and cultural development; draft and implement measures to promote the well-being and cultural development of the people, to develop science and engineering, to ensure rational exploitation and conservation of natural resources, to consolidate the monetary and credit system, to pursue a uniform prices, wages, and social security policy, and to organize state insurance and a uniform system of accounting and statistics; and organize the management of industrial, constructional, and agricultural enterprises and amalgamations, transport and communications undertakings, banks, and other organizations and institutions of Union subordination.

(2) Draft current and long-term state plans for the economic and social development of the USSR and the Budget of the USSR, and submit them to the Supreme Soviet of the USSR; take measures to execute the state plans and Budget; and report to the Supreme Soviet of the USSR on the implementation of the plans and Budget.

(3) Implement measures to defend the interests of the state, protect socialist property and maintain public order, and guarantee and protect citizens' rights and freedoms.

(4) Take measures to ensure state security.

(5) Exercise general direction of the development of the Armed Forces of the USSR, and determine the annual contingent of citizens to be called up for active military service.

(6) Provide general direction in regard to relations with other states, foreign trade, and economic, scientific, technical, and cultural cooperation of the USSR with other countries; take measures to ensure fulfilment of the USSR's international treaties; and ratify and denounce intergovernmental international agreements.

(7) When necessary, form committees, central boards and other departments under the Council of Ministers of the USSR to deal with matters of economic, social and cultural development, and defence.

Article 132. A Presidium of the Council of Ministers of the USSR, consisting of the Chairman, the First Vice-Chairmen, and Vice-Chairmen of the Council of Ministers of the USSR shall function as a standing body of the Council of Ministers of the USSR to deal with questions relating to guidance of the economy, and with other matters of state administration.

Article 133. The Council of Ministers of the USSR, on the basis of, and in pursuance of, the laws of the USSR and other decisions of the Supreme Soviet of the USSR and its Presidium, shall issue decisions and ordinances and verify their execution. The decisions and ordinances of the Council of Ministers of the USSR shall be binding throughout the USSR.

Article 134. The Council of Ministers of the USSR has the right, in matters within the jurisdiction of the Union of Soviet Socialist Republics, to suspend execution of decisions and ordinances of the Councils of Ministers of Union Republics, and to rescind acts of ministries and state committees of the USSR, and of other bodies subordinate to it.

Article 135. The Council of Ministers of the USSR shall coordinate and direct the work of All-Union and Union-Republican ministries, state committees of the USSR, and other bodies subordinate to it.

All-Union ministries and state committees of the USSR shall direct the work of the branches of administration entrusted to them, or exercise inter-branch administration, throughout the territory of the USSR directly or through bodies set up by them. Union-Republican ministries and state committees of the USSR direct the work of the branches of administration entrusted to them, or exercise inter-branch administration, as a rule, through the corresponding ministries and state committees, and other bodies of Union Republics, and directly administer individual enterprises and amalgamations of Union subordination. The procedure for transferring enterprises and amalgamations from Republic or local subordination to Union subordination shall be defined by the Presidium of the Supreme Soviet of the USSR.

Ministries and state committees of the USSR shall be responsible for the condition and development of the spheres of administration entrusted to them; within their competence, they issue orders and other acts on the basis of, and in execution of, the laws of the USSR and other decisions of the Supreme Soviet of the USSR and its Presidium, and of decisions and ordinances of the Council of Ministers of the USSR, and organize and verify their implementation.

Article 136. The competence of the Council of Ministers of the USSR and its Presidium, the procedure for their work, relationships between the Council of Ministers and other state bodies, and the list of All-Union and Union-Republican ministries and state committees of the USSR are defined, on the basis of the Constitution, in the Law on the Council of Ministers of the USSR.

Chapter 17. Higher Bodies of State Authority and Administration of a Union Republic

Article 137. The highest body of state authority of a Union Republic shall be the Supreme Soviet of that Republic. The Supreme Soviet of a Union Republic is empowered to deal with all matters within the jurisdiction of Republic under the Constitutions of the USSR and the Republic. Adoption and amendment of the Constitution of a Union Republic; endorsement of state plans for economic and social development, of the Republic's Budget, and of reports on their fulfilment; and the formation of bodies accountable to the Supreme Soviet of the Union Republic are the exclusive prerogative of that Supreme Soviet. Laws of a Union Republic shall be enacted by the Supreme Soviet of the Union Republic or by a popular vote (referendum) held by decision of the Republic's Supreme Soviet.

[**Articles 138** and **139** *establish for each Supreme Soviet of a Union Republic a Presidium and a Council of Ministers.*]

Article 140. The Council of Ministers of a Union Republic issues decisions and ordinances on the basis of, and in pursuance of, the legislative acts of the USSR and of the Union Republic, and of decisions and ordinances of the Council of Ministers of the USSR, and shall organize and verify their execution.

[**Articles 141** and **142** *deal further with the powers of the Council of Ministers of a Union Republic.*]

Chapter 18. Higher Bodies of State Authority and Administration of an Autonomous Republic

[**Articles 143** and **144** *establish for each Autonomous Republic a Supreme Soviet, a Presidium and a Council of Ministers.*]

Chapter 19. Local Bodies of State Authority and Administration

Article 145. The bodies of state authority in Territories, Regions, Autonomous Regions, Autonomous Areas, districts, cities, city districts, settlements, and rural communities shall be the corresponding Soviets of People's Deputies.

[**Articles 146** *to* **150** *deal with the powers of these local Soviets.*]

Chapter 21. Courts and Arbitration

Article 151. In the USSR justice is administered only by the courts. In the USSR there are the following courts: the Supreme Court of the USSR, the Supreme Courts of Union Republics, the Supreme Courts of Autonomous Republics, Territorial, Regional, and city courts, courts of Autonomous Regions, courts of Autonomous Areas, district (city) peoples' courts, and military tribunals in the Armed Forces.

Article 152. All courts in the USSR shall be formed on the principle of the electiveness of judges and people's assessors. People's judges of district (city) people's courts shall be elected for a term of five years by the citizens of the district (city) on the basis of universal, equal and direct suffrage by secret ballot. People's assessors of district (city) people's courts shall be elected for a term of two and a half years at meetings of citizens at their places of work or residence by a show of hands. Higher courts shall be elected for a term of five years by the corresponding Soviet of People's Deputies. The judges of military tribunals shall be elected for a term of five years by the Presidium of the Supreme Soviet of the USSR and people's assessors for a term of two and a half years by meetings of servicemen.

Judges and people's assessors are responsible and accountable to their electors or the bodies that elected them, shall report to them, and may be recalled by them in the manner prescribed by law.

Article 153. The Supreme Court of the USSR is the highest judicial body in the USSR and supervises the administration of justice by the courts of the USSR and Union Republics within the limits established by law. The Supreme Court of the USSR shall be elected by the Supreme Soviet of the USSR and shall consist of a Charman, Vice-Chairmen, members, and people's assessors. The Chairmen of the Supreme Courts of Union Republics are ex officio members of the Supreme Court of the USSR. The organization and procedure of the Supreme Court of the USSR are defined in the Law on the Supreme Court of the USSR.

Article 154. The hearing of civil and criminal cases in all courts is collegial; in courts of first instance cases are heard with the participation of people's assessors. In the administration of justice people's assessors have all the rights of a judge.

Article 155. Judges and people's assessors are independent and subject only to the law.

Article 156. Justice is administered in the USSR on the principle of the equality of citizens before the law and the court.

Article 157. Proceedings in all courts shall be open to the public. Hearings in camera are only allowed in cases provided for by law, with observance of all the rules of judicial procedure.

Article 158. A defendant in a criminal action is guaranteed the right to legal assistance.

Article 159. Judicial proceedings shall be conducted in the language of the Union Republic, Autonomous Republic, Autonomous Region, or Autonomous Area, or in the language spoken by the majority of the people in the locality. Persons participating in court proceedings, who do not know the language in which they are being conducted shall be ensured the right to become fully acquainted with the materials in the case; the services of an interpreter during the proceedings; and the right to address the court in their own language.

Article 160. No one may be adjudged guilty of a crime and subjected to punishment as a criminal except by the sentence of a court and in conformity with the law.

Article 161. Colleges of advocates are available to give legal assistance to citizens and organizations. In cases provided for by legislation citizens shall be given legal assistance free of charge. The organization and procedure of the bar are determined by legislation of the USSR and Union Republics.

Article 162. Representatives of public organizations and of work collectives may take part in civil and criminal proceedings.

Article 163. Economic disputes between enterprises, institutions, and organizations are settled by state arbitration bodies within the limits of their jurisdiction. The organization and manner of functioning of state arbitration bodies are defined in the Law on State Arbitration in the USSR.

Chapter 21. The Procurator's Office

Article 164. Supreme power of supervision over the strict and uniform observance of laws by all ministries, state committees and departments, enterprises, institutions and organizations, executive-administrative bodies of local Soviets of People's Deputies, collective farms, cooperatives and other public organizations, officials and citizens is vested in the Procurator-General of the USSR and procurators subordinate to him.

Article 165. The Procurator-General of the USSR is appointed by the Supreme Soviet of the USSR and is responsible and accountable to it and, between sessions of the Supreme Soviet, to the Presidium of the Supreme Soviet of the USSR.

Article 166. The procurators of Union Republics, Autonomous Republics, Territories, Regions and Autonomous Regions are appointed by the Procurator-General of the USSR. The procurators of Autonomous Areas and district and city procurators are appointed by the procurators of Union Republics, subject to confirmation by the Procurator-General of the USSR.

Article 167. The term of office of the Procurator-General of the USSR and all lower-ranking procurators shall be five years.

Article 168. The agencies of the Procurator's Office exercise their powers independently of any local bodies whatsoever, and are subordinate solely to the Procurator-General of the USSR. The organization and procedure of the agencies of the Procurator's Office are defined in the Law on the Procurator's Office of the USSR.

VIII. THE EMBLEM, FLAG, ANTHEM, AND CAPITAL OF THE USSR

[Four Articles omitted.]

IX. THE LEGAL FORCE OF THE CONSTITUTION AND PROCEDURE FOR AMENDING IT

Article 173. The Constitution of the USSR shall have supreme legal force. All laws and other acts of state bodies shall be promulgated on the basis of and in conformity with it.

Article 174. The Constitution of the USSR may be amended by a decision of the Supreme Soviet of the USSR adopted by a majority of not less than two-thirds of the total number of Deputies of each of its chambers.

EURO-COMMUNIST DECLARATION

Published in Madrid 3 March 1977

(translated from the French text)

On 2 and 3 March 1977 a meeting took place in Madrid between comrades Santiago Carrillo, secretary general of the Spanish Communist Party, Enrico Berlinguer, secretary general of the Italian Communist Party, and Georges Marchais, secretary general of the French Communist Party.

In responding to Santiago Carrillo's invitation, Georges Marchais and Enrico Berlinguer wished to confirm to the Spanish Communist Party and to all the democratic forces in Spain the solidarity of French and Italian Communists in their efforts for democracy and for the construction of a free Spain.

In this spirit, the French and Italian Communist Parties express their conviction that the Spanish people will proceed to the full establishment of democracy, of which an essential criterion at this time is the legalization of the Communist Party and all democratic parties, which is indispensable for the holding of truly free elections. They express their solidarity with all who strive in Spain for the liberation of political prisoners, and for countering the fascist provocations and crimes which seek to bar the advance to democracy. The end of the Franco dictatorship, after that of fascism in Portugal and Greece, has effected an important positive change in the European situation.

Democratic progress in Spain is of particular concern to the French and Italian peoples.

The three countries are today witnessing a crisis which is at the same time economic, political, social and moral. This crisis throws into relief the need for new solutions for the development of society. Aside from the diverse conditions which exist in each of the three countries, the Italian, French and Spanish communists declare the need, in order to manifest a positive alternative to the crisis and to combat reactionary moves, to effect the largest possible accord among the political and social forces prepared to contribute to a policy of progress and renewal. This requires the presence of the workers and their parties in the direction of political life. While the communists defend the immediate interests of the workers from day to day, they thus predicate profound democratic reforms.

The crisis of the capitalist system thus calls more forcibly than ever for the development of democracy and an advance to socialism.

The communists of Spain, France and Italy agree to work for the construction of a new society embracing a plurality of political and social forces, respect and guarantee for all collective and individual liberties and their development: freedom of thought and expression, of the press, of association and meeting, of demonstration, of personal movement within countries and abroad, trade union freedom, the independence of trade unions and the right to strike, inviolability of private life, respect for universal suffrage and the possibility of alternating democratic majorities, religious liberty, freedom of culture and of the expression of different philosophical, cultural and artistic schools and opinions. This wish to achieve socialism with democracy and liberty inspires the policies adopted in full independence by each of the three parties.

The three parties further agree to develop in the future their international and friendly solidarity on the basis of the independence of each, equality of rights, non-intervention and respect for the free choice of ways and original methods of constructing socialist societies in accordance with the conditions of each country.

This meeting in Madrid is also the occasion for the Spanish, Italian and French communists to reaffirm the vital importance that they attach to new steps forward on the road of detente and peaceful coexistence, to real progress in the reduction of armaments, to the comprehensive application by all states of all the provisions of the Final Act of the Helsinki conference and to a positive stance at the Belgrade meeting, to action towards overcoming the division of Europe into hostile military blocks, and to the creation of fresh agreements between developed and developing countries and of a new international economic order.

Thus the three parties conceive the prospect of a peaceful, democratic and independent Europe, without military bases or recourse to arms and of a Mediterranean sea of peace and cooperation among its bordering states.

The free Spain for which the communists and all Spanish democratic forces strive will be for Europe an important element of democracy, progress and peace. For these objects it is both possible and necessary that, notwithstanding a diversity of ideas and traditions, a dialogue and a search for common ground and joint understandings should proceed among the communists, socialists and Christian forces, indeed among all democratic forces. Over the years, the cause of freedom in Spain has been the battleground of communists. From the capital of a Spain now advancing on the road of democratic renaissance, the communists of the three countries call today for a united front of all those forces which seek democracy and progress.

CONSTITUTION OF THE COMMUNIST PARTY OF CHINA

Adopted by the 11th National Congress of the Communist Party of China on 18 August, 1977

(English text from the Peking Review No. 36 of 2 September 1977 by courtesy of the Novosti Press Agency)

GENERAL PROGRAMME

The Communist Party of China is the political party of the proletariat, the highest form of its class organization. It is a vigorous vanguard organization composed of the advanced elements of the proletariat, which leads the proletariat and the revolutionary masses in their fight against the class enemy.

The basic programme of the Communist Party of China for the entire historical period of socialism is to persist in continuing the revolution under the dictatorship of the proletariat, eliminate the bourgeoisie and all other exploiting classes step by step and bring about the triumph of socialism over capitalism. The ultimate aim of the Party is the realization of communism.

Marxism–Leninism–Mao Tsetung Thought is the guiding ideology and theoretical basis of the Communist Party of China. The Party persists in combating revisionism, and dogmatism and empiricism. The Party upholds dialectical materialism and historical materialism as its world outlook and opposes the idealist and metaphysical world outlook.

Our great leader and teacher Chairman Mao Tsetung was the founder of the Communist Party of China and the greatest Marxist–Leninist of our time. Integrating the universal truth of Marxism–Leninism with the concrete practice of the revolution, Chairman Mao inherited, defended and developed Marxism–Leninism in the struggles against imperialism and the domestic reactionary classes, against Right and 'Left' opportunist lines in the Party and against international modern revisionism. He led our Party, our army and our people in winning complete victory in the new-democratic revolution and in founding the People's Republic of China, a state of the dictatorship of the proletariat, through protracted revolutionary struggles and revolutionary wars, and then in achieving tremendous victories in the socialist revolution and socialist construction through fierce and complex struggles between the proletariat and the bourgeoisie, and through the unparalleled Great Proletarian Cultural Revolution. The banner of Chairman Mao is the great banner guiding our Party to victory through united struggle.

Socialist society covers a historical period of considerable length. In this period classes, class contradictions and class struggle, the struggle between the socialist road and the capitalist road and the danger of capitalist restoration invariably continue to exist, and there is the threat of subversion and aggression by imperialism and social-imperialism. The resolution of these contradictions depends solely on the theory and practice of continued revolution under the dictatorship of the proletariat.

China's Great Proletarian Cultural Revolution was a political revolution carried out under socialism by the proletariat against the bourgeoisie and all other exploiting classes to consolidate the dictatorship of the proletariat and prevent the restoration of capitalism. Political revolutions of this nature will be carried out many times in the future.

The Communist Party of China adheres to its basic line for the entire historical period of socialism. It must correctly distinguish and handle the contradictions among the people and those between ourselves and the enemy, and consolidate and strengthen the dictatorship of the proletariat. The Party must rely on the working class wholeheartedly and rely on the poor and lower-middle peasants, unite with the vast numbers of intellectuals and other working people, mobilize all positive factors and expand the revolutionary united front led by the working class and based on the worker-peasant alliance. It must uphold the proletarian nationality policy and strengthen the great unity of the people of all nationalities in China. It must carry on the three great revolutionary movements of class struggle, the struggle for production and scientific experiment, it must adhere to the principle of building our country independently, with the initiative in our own hands, and through self-reliance, diligence and thrift, and to the principle of being prepared against war and natural disasters and doing everything for the people, so as to build socialism by going all out, aiming high and achieving greater, faster, better and more economical results. The Party must lead the people of all nationalities in making China a powerful socialist country with a modern agriculture, industry, national defence and science and technology by the end of the century.

The Communist Party of China upholds proletarian internationalism and opposes great-nation chauvinism; it unites firmly with the genuine Marxist–Leninist parties and organizations the world over, unites with the proletariat, the oppressed people and nations of the whole world and fights shoulder to shoulder with them to oppose the hegemonism of the two super-powers, the Soviet Union and the United States, to overthrow imperialism, modern revisionism and all reaction, and to wipe the system of exploitation of man by man off the face of the earth, so that all mankind will be emancipated.

The correctness or incorrectness of the ideological and political line decides everything. All Party comrades must implement Chairman Mao's proletarian revolutionary line comprehensively and correctly and adhere to the three basic principles: practise Marxism, and not revisionism; unite, and do not split; be open and aboveboard, and do not intrigue and conspire. They must have the revolutionary boldness in daring to go against any tide that runs counter to these three basic principles.

The whole Party must adhere to the organizational principle of democratic centralism and practise centralism on the basis of democracy and democracy under centralized guidance. It must give full scope to inner-Party democracy and encourage the initiative and creativeness of all Party members and Party organizations at all levels, and combat bureaucracy, commandism and warlordism. The whole Party must strictly observe Party discipline, safeguard the Party's centralization, strengthen its unity, oppose all separatist and factional activities, oppose the assertion of independence from the Party and oppose anarchism. In relations among comrades in the Party, all members should apply the principle of 'Say all you know and say it without reserve' and 'Blame not the speaker but be warned by his words', adopt the dialectical method, start from the desire for unity, distinguish between right and wrong through criticism or struggle and arrive at a new unity. The Party must strive to create a political situation in which there are both centralism and democracy, both discipline and freedom, both unity of will and personal ease of mind and liveliness.

The Party must conscientiously follow the proletarian line on cadres, the line of 'appointing people on merit', and oppose the bourgeois line on cadres, the line of 'appointing people by favouritism'. It must train and bring up in mass struggles millions of successors in the revolutionary cause of the proletariat in accordance with the five requirements put forward by Chairman Mao. Special vigilance must be exercised against careerists, conspirators and double-dealers so as to prevent such bad types from usurping the leadership of the Party and the state at any level and ensure purity of the leadership at all levels.

The whole Party must keep to and carry forward its fine tradition of following the mass line and seeking truth from facts, keep to and carry forward the style of work characterized by integration of theory with practice, close ties with the masses and criticism and self-criticism, the style of modesty, prudence and freedom from arrogance and impetuosity, and the style of plain living and hard struggle; and the whole Party must prevent Party members, especially leading Party cadres, from exploiting their position to seek privileges, and wage a resolute struggle against bourgeois ideology and the bourgeois style of work.

A member of the Communist Party of China should at all times and in all circumstances subordinate his personal interests to the interests of the Party and the people; he should fear no difficulties and sacrifices, work actively for the fulfilment of the programme of the Party and devote his whole life to the struggle for communism.

The Communist Party of China is a great, glorious and correct Party, and it is the core of leadership of the whole Chinese people. The whole Party must always hold high and resolutely defend the great banner of Marxism–Leninism–Mao Tsetung Thought and ensure that our Party's cause will continue to advance triumphantly along the Marxist line.

CHAPTER 1. MEMBERSHIP

Article 1. Any Chinese worker, poor peasant, lower-middle peasant, revolutionary soldier or any other revolutionary who has reached the age of 18 and who accepts the Constitution of the Party and is willing to join a Party organization and work actively in it, carry out the Party's decisions, observe Party discipline and pay membership dues may become a member of the Communist Party of China.

Article 2. The Communist Party of China demands that its members should:

(1) Conscientiously study Marxism–Leninism–Mao Tsetung Thought, criticize capitalism and revisionism and strive to remould their world outlook.

(2) Serve the people wholeheartedly and pursue no private interests either for themselves or for a small number of people.

(3) Unite with all the people who can be united inside and outside the Party, including those who have wrongly opposed them.

(4) Maintain close ties with the masses and consult with them when matters arise.

(5) Earnestly practise criticism and self-criticism, be bold in correcting their shortcomings and mistakes and dare to struggle against words and deeds that run counter to Party principles.

(6) Uphold the Party's unity, refuse to take part in and moreover oppose any factional organization or activity which splits the Party.

(7) Be truthful and honest to the Party, observe Party discipline and the laws of the state and strictly guard Party and state secrets.

(8) Actively fulfil the tasks assigned them by the Party and play an exemplary vanguard role in the three great revolutionary movements of class struggle, the struggle for production and scientific experiment.

Article 3.   Applicants for Party membership must go through the procedure for admission individually. An applicant must be recommended by two full Party members, fill in an application form for Party membership and be examined by a Party branch, which must seek opinions extensively inside and outside the Party; he or she may become a probationary member after being accepted by the general membership meeting of the Party branch and being approved by the next higher Party committee.

Before approving the admission of an applicant for Party membership, the higher Party committee must appoint someone specially to talk with the applicant and carefully examine his or her case.

Article 4.   The probationary period of a probationary member is one year. The Party organization concerned should make further efforts to educate and observe him or her.

When the probationary period has expired, the Party branch to which the probationary member belongs must promptly discuss whether he or she is qualified for full membership. If qualified, he or she should be given full membership as scheduled; if it is necessary to continue to observe him or her, the probationary period may be extended by no more than one year; if he or she is found to be really unfit for Party membership, his or her status as a probationary member should be annulled. Any decision either to transfer a probationary member to full membership, to prolong the probationary period, or to annul his or her status as a probationary member must be adopted by the general membership meeting of the Party branch and approved by the next higher Party committee.

The probationary period of a probationary member begins from the day when the higher Party committee approves the applicant's admission. The Party standing of a Party member begins from the day when he or she is transferred to full membership.

A probationary member does not have the right to vote and to elect or be elected enjoyed by a full member.

Article 5.   When a Party member violates Party discipline, the Party organization concerned should give the member education and, on the merits of the case, may take any of the following disciplinary measures—a warning, a serious warning, removal from his or her post in the Party, being placed on probation within the Party, and expulsion from the Party.

The period for which the Party member concerned is placed on probation should not exceed two years. During this period, he or she does not have the right to vote and to elect or be elected. If the Party member concerned has been through the period of probation and has corrected his or her mistake, these rights should be restored; if the member clings to the mistake instead of correcting it, he or she should be expelled from the Party.

Proven renegades, enemy agents, absolutely unrepentant persons in power taking the capitalist road, alien class elements, degenerates and new bourgeois elements must be expelled from the Party and not be re-admitted.

Article 6.   Any disciplinary measure taken against a Party member must be decided on by a general membership meeting of the Party branch to which the member belongs and should be submitted to the next higher Party committee for approval. Under special circumstances, a primary Party committee or a higher Party committee has the power to take disciplinary action against a Party member.

Any decision to remove a member from a local Party committee at any level, to place on probation or to expel the member from the Party must be made by the said Party committee and be submitted to the next higher Party committee for approval.

Corresponding provisions on disciplinary measures against members of the Party committees at all levels in the army units should be laid down by the Military Commission of the Central Committee in accordance with the Party Constitution.

Any decision to take a disciplinary measure against a Member or Alternate Member of the Central Committee must be made by the Central Committee or its Political Bureau.

When a Party organization takes a decision on a disciplinary measure against a member, it must, barring special circumstances, notify the member that he or she should attend the meeting. If the member disagrees with the decision, he or she may ask for a review of the case and has the right to appeal to higher Party committees, up to and including the Central Committee.

Article 7. A Party member whose revolutionary will has degenerated, who fails to function as a Communist and remains unchanged despite repeated education may be persuaded to withdraw from the Party. The case must be decided by the general membership meeting of the Party branch concerned and submitted to the next higher Party committee for approval.

A Party member who fails to take part in Party life, to do the work assigned by the Party and to pay membership dues over six months and without proper reason is regarded as having given up membership.

When a Party member asks to withdraw from the Party or has given up membership, the Party branch concerned should, with the approval of its general membership meeting, remove his or her name from the Party rolls and report the case to the next higher Party committee for the record.

CHAPTER II. ORGANIZATIONAL SYSTEM OF THE PARTY

Article 8. The Party is organized on the principle of democratic centralism.

The whole Party must observe democratic centralist discipline. The individual is subordinate to the organization, the minority is subordinate to the majority, the lower level is subordinate to the higher level, and the entire Party is subordinate to the Central Committee.

Article 9. Delegates to Party congresses and members of Party committees at all levels should be elected by secret ballot after democratic consultation and in accordance with the five requirements for successors in the revolutionary cause of the proletariat and with the principle of combining the old, the middle-aged and the young.

Article 10. The highest leading body of the Party is the National Congress and, when it is not in session, the Central Committee elected by it. The leading bodies of Party organizations at all levels in the localities and in the army units are the Party congresses or general membership meetings at their respective levels and the Party committees elected by them. Party congresses at all levels are convened by Party committees at their respective levels. The convocation of Party congresses at all levels in the localities and in the army units and the composition of the Party committees they elect are subject to approval by the next higher Party committee.

Article 11. Party committees at all levels operate on the principle of combining collective leadership with individual responsibility under a division of labour. They should rely on the political experience and wisdom of the collective: all important issues are to be decided collectively, and at the same time each individual is to be enabled to play his or her due part.

Party committees at all levels should set up their working bodies in accordance with the principles of close ties with the masses and of structural simplicity and efficiency. Party committees at the county level and upwards may send out their representative organs when necessary.

Article 12. Party committees at all levels should report regularly on their work to Party congresses or general membership meetings, constantly listen to the opinions of the masses both inside and outside the Party and put themselves under their supervision.

Party members have the right to criticize Party organizations and working personnel in leading posts at all levels and make proposals to them and also the right to bypass the immediate leadership and present their appeals and complaints to higher levels, up to and including the Central Committee and the Chairman of the Central Committee. It is absolutely impermissible for anyone to suppress criticism or to retaliate. Those guilty of doing so should be investigated and punished.

If a Party member holds different views with regard to the decisions or directives of the Party organizations, he or she is allowed to reserve these views and has the right to bring up the matter for discussion at Party meetings and the right to bypass the immediate leadership and report to higher levels, up to and including the Central Committee and the Chairman of the Central Committee, but the member must resolutely carry out these decisions and directives.

Article 13. The Central Committee of the Party, local Party committees at the county level and upwards and Party committees in the army units at the regimental level and upwards should set up commissions for inspecting discipline.

The commissions for inspecting discipline at all levels are to be elected by the Party committees at the respective levels and, under their leadership, should strengthen Party members' education on discipline, be responsible for checking on the observance of discipline by Party members and Party cadres and struggle against all breaches of Party discipline.

Article 14. State organs, the People's Liberation Army and the militia and revolutionary mass organizations, such as trade unions, the Communist Youth League, poor and lower-middle peasant associations and women's federations, must all accept the absolute leadership of the Party.

Leading Party groups should be set up in state organs and people's organizations. Members of leading Party groups in state organs and people's organizations at the national level are to be appointed by the Central Committee of the Party. Members of leading Party groups in state organs and people's organizations at all levels in the localities are to be appointed by the corresponding Party committees.

CHAPTER III. CENTRAL ORGANIZATIONS OF THE PARTY

Article 15. The National Congress of the Party should be convened every five years. Under special circumstances, it may be convened before its due date or postponed.

Article 16. The plenary session of the Central Committee of the Party elects the Political Bureau of the Central Committee, the Standing Committee of the Political Bureau of the Central Committee and the Chairman and Vice-Chairmen of the Central Committee.

The plenary session of the Central Committee of the Party is convened by the Political Bureau of the Central Committee.

When the Central Committee is not in plenary session, the Political Bureau of the Central Committee and its Standing Committee exercise the functions and powers of the Central Committee.

CHAPTER IV. PARTY ORGANIZATIONS IN THE LOCALITIES AND THE ARMY UNITS

Article 17. Local Party congresses at the county level and upwards and Party congresses in the army units at the regimental level and upwards should be convened every three years. Under special circumstances, they may be convened before their due date or postponed, subject to approval by the next higher Party committees.

Local Party committees at the county level and upwards and Party committees in the army units at the regimental level and upwards elect their standing committees, secretaries and deputy secretaries.

CHAPTER V. PRIMARY ORGANIZATIONS OF THE PARTY

Article 18. Party branches, general Party branches or primary Party committees should be set up in factories, mines and other enterprises, people's communes, offices, schools, shops, neighbourhoods, companies of the People's Liberation Army and other primary units in accordance with the need of the revolutionary struggle and the size of their Party membership, subject to approval by the next higher Party committees.

Committees of Party branches should be elected annually, committees of general Party branches and primary Party committees should be elected every two years. Under special circumstances, the election may take place before its due date or be postponed, subject to approval by the next higher Party committees.

Article 19. The primary organizations of the Party should play the role of a fighting bastion. Their main tasks are:

(1) To lead Party members and people outside the Party in studying Marxism–Leninism–Mao Tsetung Thought conscientiously, educate them in the ideological and political line and in the Party's fine tradition and give them basic knowledge about the Party.

(2) To lead and unite the broad masses of the people in adhering to the socialist road, in criticizing capitalism and revisionism, in correctly distinguishing and handling the contradictions among the people and those between ourselves and the enemy and in waging a resolute struggle against the class enemy.

(3) To propagate and carry out the line, policies and decisions of the Party, and fulfil every task assigned by the Party and the state.

(4) To maintain close ties with the masses, constantly listen to their opinions and demands and faithfully report these to higher Party organizations and be concerned about their political, economic and cultural life.

(5) To promote inner-Party democracy, practise criticism and self-criticism, expose and get rid of shortcomings and mistakes in work, and wage struggles against violations of the law and breaches of discipline, against corruption and waste, and against bureaucracy and all other undesirable tendencies.

(6) To admit new Party members, enforce Party discipline, and consolidate the Party organizations, getting rid of the stale and taking in the fresh, so as to purify the Party's ranks and constantly enhance the Party's fighting power.

THE UNITED KINGDOM LABOUR ADMINISTRATION

(as at 31 December 1977)

Prime Minister, First Lord of the Treasury and Minister for the Civil Service .	Rt. Hon. James Callaghan, MP
Lord President of the Council and Leader of the House of Commons . .	Rt. Hon. Michael Foot, MP
Lord Chancellor	Rt. Hon. The Lord Elwyn-Jones
Chancellor of the Exchequer . .	Rt. Hon. Denis Healey, MBE, MP
Secretary of State for the Home Department	Rt. Hon. Merlyn Rees, MP
Secretary of State for Foreign and Commonwealth Affairs . . .	Rt. Hon. David Owen, MP[1]
Secretary of State for Education and Science and Paymaster General .	Rt. Hon. Shirley Williams, MP
Secretary of State for Energy . .	Rt. Hon. Anthony Wedgwood Benn, MP
Secretary of State for Industry . .	Rt. Hon. Eric Varley, MP
Secretary of State for the Environment .	Rt. Hon. Peter Shore, MP
Secretary of State for Northern Ireland.	Rt. Hon Roy Mason, MP
Secretary of State for Scotland . .	Rt. Hon. Bruce Millan, MP
Secretary of State for Wales . .	Rt. Hon. John Morris, QC, MP
Secretary of State for Defence . .	Rt. Hon. Frederick Mulley, MP
Secretary of State for Employment .	Rt. Hon. Albert Booth, MP
Secretary of State for Social Services .	Rt. Hon. David Ennals, MP
Secretary of State for Trade . .	Rt. Hon. Edmund Dell, MP
Lord Privy Seal and Leader of the House of Lords	Rt. Hon. The Lord Peart
Chief Secretary to the Treasury . .	Rt. Hon. Joel Barnett, MP[2]
Minister of Agriculture, Fisheries and Food	Rt. Hon. John Silkin, MP
Secretary of State for Prices and Consumer Protection. . . .	Rt. Hon. Roy Hattersley, MP
Secretary of State for Transport . .	Rt. Hon. William Rodgers, MP
Minister for Social Security . .	Rt. Hon. Stanley Orme, MP
Chancellor of the Duchy of Lancaster .	Rt. Hon. Harold Lever, MP

MINISTERS NOT IN THE CABINET

Minister of State, Ministry of Agriculture, Fisheries and Food . .	Rt. Hon. Edward Bishop, MP
Minister of State, Civil Service Department	Charles Morris, MP
Minister of State, Ministry of Defence .	Dr John Gilbert, MP
Ministers of State, Department of Education and Science (Arts). . .	Gordon Oakes, MP The Lord Donaldson of Kingsbridge, OBE
Minister of State, Department of Employment	Harold Walker, MP

[1] Succeeded, 21 February, the late Rt. Hon. Anthony Crosland; previously Minister of State, Foreign and Commonwealth Office.

[2] Promoted to Cabinet rank, 21 February.

Minister of State, Department of Energy	Rt. Hon. Dickson Mabon, MP
Minister of State (Sport and Recreation),	
Department of the Environment .	Rt. Hon. Denis Howell, MP
Ministers of State, Foreign and Common-	
wealth Office	Frank Judd, MP[1]
	Rt. Hon. The Lord Goronwy-Roberts
	Edward Rowlands, MP
(Overseas Development) . .	Rt. Hon. Judith Hart, MP[2]
Minister of State, Department of Health	
and Social Security . . .	Roland Moyle, MP
Ministers of State, Home Office . .	The Lord Harris of Greenwich
	Brynmor John, MP
Ministers of State, Department of In-	
dustry	Rt. Hon. Alan Williams, MP
	Gerald Kaufman, MP
Ministers of State, Northern Ireland	
Office	John Concannon, MP
	The Lord Melchett
Minister of State, Department of Prices	
and Consumer Protection . .	John Fraser, MP
Minister of State, Privy Council Office .	John Smith, MP
Ministers of State, Scottish Office .	The Lord Kirkhill
	Rt. Hon. Gregor MacKenzie, MP
Chief Secretary to the Treasury . .	Rt. Hon. Joel Barnett, MP
Parliamentary Secretary to the Treasury	
(Government Chief Whip) . .	Rt. Hon. Michael Cocks, MP
Financial Secretary to the Treasury .	Rt. Hon. Robert Sheldon, MP
Minister of State, Treasury . . .	Denzil Davies, MP

LAW OFFICERS

Attorney General	Rt. Hon. Samuel Silkin, QC, MP
Solicitor General	Rt. Hon. Peter Archer, QC, MP
Lord Advocate	Rt. Hon. Ronald King Murray, QC, MP
Solicitor-General for Scotland . .	The Lord McCluskey, QC

[1] Until 21 February Minister of State for Overseas Development.
[2] Succeeded, 21 February, Frank Judd.

OBITUARY

Adrian, Lord, OM (b. 1889), British scientist, was the greatest neurophysiologist of his time. In 1913 he became a fellow of Trinity College, Cambridge, where he had graduated, and of which he was Master from 1951 to 1965. After war service as a doctor he returned to Cambridge. He became Foulerton research professor of the Royal Society 1929-37 and professor of physiology at Cambridge 1937-51, president of the Royal Society 1950-55 and of the Royal Society of Medicine 1960-62. Among many other honours from his own and other countries he was awarded the Nobel prize for medicine in 1932. His monograph *The Basis of Sensation*, published in 1928, had marked him as a brilliant student of neurophysiology and he was a pioneer of electro-encephalography. The simplicity and wit with which he demonstrated and expressed his ideas in lectures and scientific papers masked the extreme sensitivity and originality of his research. He was a skilled fencer, skier and mountain-climber and a most popular and hospitable head of college and university vice-chancellor (1957-59). Died 4 August

Adu, Amishadia Larson, CMG, OBE (b. 1915), Ghanaian administrator, was one of the ablest international civil servants thrown up by post-colonial Africa. Educated at Achimota and Cambridge, he rose in public service to become President Nkrumah's senior official. He became head of the East African Common Services, served the UN development programme in East Africa 1964-65, and was deputy secretary-general of the Commonwealth Secretariat in London 1966-70. At the time of his death he was vice-chairman of the UN international civil service commission. A *Times* obituary tribute called 'Yaw' Adu 'the quintessence of African humanism'. Died 2 September

Ahmed, Fakhruddin Ali (b. 1905), was President of India from 1974 to his death. A conventional Congress supporter, with his base in Assam, he became successively Minister of Irrigation and Power, of Education and of Food and Agriculture in Mrs Gandhi's Cabinets and her party's candidate for the Presidency. Died 11 February

Avon, Earl of, (Robert) Anthony Eden, KG, (b. 1897), was British Foreign Secretary for twelve years and Prime Minister for nearly two. After active service on the Western Front 1915-18, when he won the MC, he took a first class in modern languages at Oxford. In 1923 he became MP for Warwick and Leamington, a seat he held until his resignation early in 1957. As parliamentary private secretary to Sir Austen Chamberlain at the Foreign Office 1926-28 he began his close association with foreign affairs, which led him through the offices of parliamentary under-secretary 1932-34, Lord Privy Seal in charge of disarmament and League of Nations policy 1934-35, Minister for League Affairs with a seat in the Cabinet 1935, and Secretary of State 1935-38, when he resigned in protest against Prime Minister Neville Chamberlain's intrigue with Mussolini behind his back. 'There seemed', wrote Winston Churchill of him, 'one strong young figure standing up against long, dismal, drawling tides of drift and surrender, of wrong measurements and feeble impulses'. Eden joined Chamberlain's wartime Government as Secretary of State for Dominion Affairs, then took over the War Office under Churchill in 1940 at a critical period of reorganization and redeployment after Dunkirk, and returned to the Foreign Secretaryship from the end of that year until the 1945 election, being also Leader of the House from 1942. Already he was seen as Churchill's heir, a status acknowledged in his deputy leadership of the Opposition 1945-51, and after serving again as Foreign Secretary from 1951 he succeeded his great chief as Prime Minister in 1955.

While his achievements in the foreign field before the war and in Churchill's wartime shadow—above all his part in the construction of the United Nations—were substantial, his claim to greatness as a Foreign Secretary rests primarily on the years 1951-55, when by his commitment of British forces to the Continent he rescued the defence of

Europe from chaos after France's rejection of the European Defence Community and brought Western Germany into the North Atlantic alliance; when he tenaciously held together the divergent policies of Western Europe and the United States; when with M Mendès-France he negotiated at Geneva the pact that ended the Indo-China war; and when he settled, it seemed, Anglo-Egyptian relations by withdrawing British troops from the Suez Canal area while retaining a civilian base. It was the last theatre, however, that caused his political downfall. His reaction to President Nasser's nationalization of the Suez Canal in July 1956 was to equate it with such pre-war coups by the European dictators as Hitler's reoccupation of the Rhineland, which had presaged world war; and, after various ploys had been attempted and the support of Secretary of State Dulles had proved perfidious, Eden colluded with the French and less directly the Israeli Governments to launch an invasion of Egypt on 5 November. He never retracted his belief that he had been right. The strain of these events, compounded by the breach in Anglo-American relations, gravely affected his health, and on 9 January 1957 he resigned as Prime Minister, never again to take part in political life. He subsequently published his memoirs under the titles *Full Circle*, *Facing the Dictators* and *The Reckoning*. The Garter was conferred on him in 1954 and an earldom in 1961. Died 14 January

Baden-Powell, Olave, Lady, DBE (b. Soames, 1889), as wife and (from 1941) widow of the founder of the Scout and Guide movement, whom she married in 1912, indefatigably shared and carried forward his work for boys and girls. In 1916 she became Chief Commissioner and in 1918 Chief Guide of the UK Girl Guides, and in 1930 was unanimously elected Chief Guide of the World. In that capacity she travelled half-a-million miles in the next 40 years, exerting through her high ideals and indomitable energy a unique influence over millions of the movement's members and supporters. Died 25 June

Balcon, Sir Michael (b. 1896) was a pioneer of the British film industry. He became director of production for Gaumont British and Gainsborough Pictures in 1932 and with *Rome Express* established the prestige of the British sound film. This was followed by *The Good Companions*, *39 Steps*, outstanding feature documentaries like *The Foreman Went to France* and *Next of Kin*, and the famous 'Ealing Comedies', including *Kind Hearts and Coronets*, *The Lavender Hill Mob* and *Whisky Galore*. In 1959 he went into independent production and made *The Long and the Short and the Tall*, followed by *Sammy Going South* in 1962. In 1969 he published his autobiography *A Lifetime of Films*. He was chairman of the Film Production Board (1963-71) and a governor of the British Film Institute. Died 17 October

Black, Sir Misha (b. in Russia 1910), came to England as a baby and practised as an independent designer from 1928. The height of his youthful reputation was demonstrated when he was engaged to design the interior of the British pavilion at the New York World's Fair in 1939. In partnership with Milner Gray he founded the International Design Partnership in 1935 and the still more comprehensive Design Research Unit after World War II. His work was visible in many public and commercial buildings as well as the exhibitions which were his speciality. He was a coordinating architect for the 1951 Festival of Britain on the South Bank. As professor of industrial design at the Royal College of Art 1959-75 he exerted a wide influence. Among other posts he was a trustee of the British Museum from 1968. Died 11 August

Bruce, David (b. 1898), was American ambassador in London 1961-69, having previously been ambassador in Paris 1949-52 and Bonn 1957-59. In World War II he also served in London as chief representative of the American Red Cross and later in charge of the US Office of Strategic Studies. He held important State Department posts between 1952 and 1957, and was called from diplomatic retirement to lead the US delegation to the Paris peace talks on Vietnam in 1970, then to take charge of the first US mission to Peking for 24 years in 1973, and finally to represent his country on the Nato Council 1974–75. All this diplomatic service under both Republican and Democratic Presidents expressed not only his great talent, wisdom and charm but also his belief that one born, as he was, to high social status and great riches owed a duty to serve the nation wherever it might call him. By profession a lawyer, he also managed large family estates and a wide spectrum of business interests. In the last 30 years of his active career he was brilliantly supported by his second wife, Evangeline, *née* Bell. Died 5 December

Bustamante, Sir Alexander, GBE (b. 1884), was Prime Minister and Minister of External Affairs of Jamaica 1962-67. Of mixed Irish and Jamaican parentage, he spent much of his early life abroad, changing his name from Clarke to Bustamante and returning only in 1932 to set up successfully as a money-lender. In 1938 he emerged as a radical champion of the unemployed and trade union organizer, often in grave conflict with authority, and was interned from 1939 to 1942. He then formed the Jamaican Labour Party and was elected to the House of Representatives in 1944 at the head of its sweeping majority. In 1953, under a new constitution, he became Chief Minister. Two years later, with the advent of internal self-government, his party was defeated by Norman Manley's People's National Party and he was leader of the opposition from 1955 to 1962, when he again triumphed at the polls and became first Prime Minister of independent Jamaica. Meanwhile he had formed a West Indies Democratic Labour Party to fight the newly-formed federation of West Indian colonies, for Jamaica's departure from which he had won a majority in a referendum under the Manley regime. He spent his eightieth birthday in office but resigned from political leadership in 1967. Despite his radicalism, his demagoguery and his clashes with colonial government, he was devoted both to free enterprise and to the British connexion. Died 6 August

Callas, Maria (b. 1923), Greek operatic soprano, was acknowledged as the greatest dramatic singer of her time, for she was as fine an actress as she was vocalist. Born in New York, she returned with her family to Greece in 1936, and made her debut in Athens. After World War I her marriage to Giovanni Meneghini took her to Italy, where she took the operatic world by storm in such roles as Aïda, Turandot, Isolde and Brünnhilde. Later, however, she made the *bel canto* heroines of the great Italian operas her speciality, impressing a passionate reality upon these romantic figures. A long liaison with Aristotle Onassis, the Greek shipowner, which ended with his marriage to Mrs Jacqueline Kennedy, took her from the operatic stage—she last appeared at Covent Garden in 1965—but in 1973 she toured Europe, including London, in a series of operatic recitals. Died 16 September

Chaplin, Charles (b. 1889), British comedian and film-maker (knighted 1975), was born at Walworth, London, his parents well-known music-hall singers, and spent his childhood in Kennington. Deserted by his father, the family experienced the acute poverty which was to make such a mark on his character and future work, and which he described later with Dickensian feeling in his *Autobiography* (1964). Educated in a workhouse school after his mother's mental collapse, he entered vaudeville as a child and was a well-established juvenile actor before becoming a clown in Fred Karno's celebrated troupe. After touring for Karno in America, he entered films at the invitation of Mack Sennett in 1913, acting and eventually directing Keystone comedy shorts. Immediately successful in applying his stage expertise to film, his desire to achieve artistic independence led him in successive years to other companies (Essanay, Mutual and First National) at ever-increasing salaries corresponding to his growing international fame. He refined slap-stick with brilliantly choreographed comic invention, and created a new comedy of sentiment and poetry in the ceaseless succession of shorts he produced during the years of World War I. Charlie the Tramp, the universal figure he created, represented not only would-be gentility and a romantic feeling for women but also a resolute capacity of 'the little fella' to survive in a world of extreme poverty and oppression. He finally achieved total independence as a founder member of United Artists (1919), and began to make his series of feature-length masterpieces— *A Woman of Paris* (1923, a serious drama), *The Gold Rush* (1925), *The Circus* (1928), *City Lights* (1931), *Modern Times* (1936). Essentially an artist of silent mime, he resisted spoken dialogue as long as he could. During World War II his complex character, mingling egocentricity with profound humanity, led him to dabble in political matters, introducing a passionate social message into such films as *The Great Dictator* (1940) and *Monsieur Verdoux* (1947). Ruthlessly ostracized in America during the McCarthy era as an alleged communist supporter and moral delinquent, he finally settled with his family in Switzerland, his permit to return to America officially withdrawn. His embittered film, *A King in New York* (1957), made in England, expressed his disillusionment with the country whose citizenship he had never acquired. He was reconciled only in 1973, when he returned to America with honour to receive a special Oscar award. His idyllic old age was spent with his fourth wife, the former Oona O'Neill, daughter of Eugene O'Neill, and their eight children. His last work, *A Countess in Hong Kong* (1966), showed all the signs of a fading talent, though his earlier British film, *Limelight* (1952), was a perfect expression of his rich, if sentimental humanity. Died 25 December

R.M.

Chick, Dame Harriette (b. 1875), British scientist, switched her interest from bacteriology to nutrition during World War I, while remaining with the Lister Institute of Preventive Medicine, of which she became secretary 1925-45, and whose annual meeting she attended at the age of 100, 70 years after she had first joined its staff. Her researches included the demonstration (1919-22) that rickets was a deficiency disease which could be prevented and even cured by nutritional means. She was secretary of a League of Nations committee on the physiology of nutrition 1934-37 and president of the Nutrition Society 1956-59. Died 9 July

Churchill, Lady, *see* Spencer-Churchill

Cobham, Charles John Lyttelton, 10th Viscount, KG, PC, GCMG, GCVO (b. 1909) was a highly successful Governor-General of New Zealand 1957-62. A keen cricketer (president of the MCC in 1948), an artillery officer in World War II, an active business man in his later years, Lord Steward to the Queen's Household 1967-72, he was keenly interested in the education and development of young people and was chairman of the Outward Bound Trust, as well as president of the National Institute for the Blind. Died 20 March

Cohen of Birkenhead, Lord, CH (b. 1900), British physician, came from a poor Jewish home in Birkenhead, across the Mersey from Liverpool, a city to which he remained devoted and on which was based his whole career. Through scholarships he graduated at its university as a doctor in 1924, and from 1924 to 1965 was consulting physician of the Liverpool Royal Infirmary. In 1934, already with a large and prosperous practice, he was elected professor of medicine at Liverpool University. His brilliance as clinician and diagnostician was matched by his administrative powers, and though taking no part in the creation of the National Health Service he soon became its principal adviser, as vice-chairman (from 1949) and chairman (from 1957) of the Central Health Services Council. He was the first physician from the provinces to be made a peer of the realm (1956). His administrative services and professional honours, British and foreign, were innumerable: he was president of the British Medical Association 1950-52, of the Royal Society of Health (from 1958), of the General Medical Council 1961-73, and of the Royal Society of Medicine (1964-66). Died 7 August

Conway, Cardinal William (b. 1913), Roman Catholic Archbishop of Armagh and Primate of All Ireland, was born in the notorious Falls Road working-class district of Belfast. He became a bishop in 1958, archbishop in 1963 and cardinal in 1965. A traditionalist in theology, moral doctrine and canon law, he presided over the modernizing reforms of Vatican II in an Ireland of change and turbulence. Died 17 April

Crawford, Joan, whose real name was Lucille Le Sueur (b. 1908?), American film actress, was one of the last of the great silent movie stars. Reaching Hollywood from the New York vaudeville stage in 1925, she first achieved fame in *Our Dancing Daughters* (1928) and never thereafter lost her star place. Among her most memorable performances were those in *Grand Hotel* (1932), *The Women* (1939), *Sudden Fear* (1952), *Torch Song* (1953), *Autumn Leaves* (1956) and *Whatever Happened to Baby Jane* (with Bette Davis, her long-time rival, 1962). She married four times. Died 10 May

Crosby, Bing (b. 1904), American singer and film-star, was affectionately admired all over the world not only by fans of the crooning style of vocalism in which he excelled but by all lovers of genial comedy and light music. Paul Whiteman, the famous dance band leader, who had spotted his talent in a band act in San Francisco, took him to Hollywood in 1930, where from the following year he sang solo in Mack Sennett comedy shorts and was taken up by gramophone companies and radio sponsors as well as film magnates. From then on he was the first and superlative singing film star. A long series of successful films, in which he played with such stars as Marion Davies, Carole Lombard, Miriam Hopkins, W. C. Fields, Bob Hope and Dorothy Lamour, included *Mississippi* (1935), *Pennies from Heaven* (1938), *Road to Singapore* (1940), *Going My Way* (1944) and *High Society* (with Frank Sinatra, 1955). They yielded songs of which many millions of copies were sold, the most popular of all being *White Christmas*. 'The old groaner', as he called himself, was still singing in his 60s and 70s and had just completed a season at the London Palladium when he died on a Spanish golf course. Golf was his great pastime, and he founded the Bing Crosby National Pro-Am tournament at Pebble Beach, California. From the great riches he earned he gave millions to charity. Died 14 October

Crosland, Anthony, PC, MP (b. 1918), British socialist politician and author, became Foreign Secretary in April 1976

and died in office. After war service on overseas fronts he returned to Oxford, where he had already taken his degree, and in 1947 was elected Fellow of Trinity College and lecturer in economics. He became Labour MP for South Gloucestershire 1950-55 and for Grimsby from 1959. The death of Hugh Gaitskell in 1963 deprived him of a close friend and political ally, but although he had openly opposed the succession of Harold Wilson the latter made him Minister of State for Economic Affairs 1964-65, Secretary of State for Education and Science 1965-67, President of the Board of Trade 1967-69, Secretary of State for Local Government and Regional Planning 1969-70, Secretary of State for the Environment 1974-76 and eventually Foreign Secretary; the Chancellorship of the Exchequer, however, which he had passionately coveted, was never his lot. An able administrator and creative thinker, he was disliked by the left for his cool fabianism yet was too intellectual to attract the personal loyalty of his party's right, and he came at the bottom of the poll for the leadership in 1976. His major book, *The Future of Socialism* (1956), followed by *The Conservative Enemy* (1962), had a deep effect upon British social-democratic thought. Died 19 February

Eden, Anthony, *see* Avon, Earl of

Eglevsky, André (b. 1917), Russian-born ballet dancer, was a star of the Ballets Russes de Monte Carlo and René Blum's Ballets Russes in the 1930s. From 1937 he lived in the USA and became an American citizen, dancing with the New York City Ballet and other American companies, as well as the Marquis de Cuevas's Ballet de Monte Carlo. In 1958 he opened a ballet school on Long Island and he also taught at the New York School of American Ballet. Powerfully built, he had such elevation as to appear to defy gravity. Fokine and Balanchine were among the masters who created roles for him in new works. Died 4 December

Elena, Princess (b. 1896?), was best known to the world as Magda Lupescu, her maiden name. She became the mistress of King Carol II of Romania in the early

1920s, and was a strong influence behind the scenes when Carol occupied the throne in the following decade. She accompanied him in exile in Mexico and then Brazil, where they were married in 1947, his two previous marriages having been dissolved; the ex-King thereupon endowed her with the title of Princess. Died 28 June

Eqbal, Dr Manuchehr (b. 1908), a former Prime Minister of Iran, was a distinguished physician and authority on infectious diseases. Between 1939 and 1949 he held a number of ministerial appointments. Appointed governor general of Azarbaijan in 1950 he was dismissed by the eccentric Premier, Dr Musaddiq, but became Prime Minister in 1957, from which office he was dismissed in 1960 because his liberal views had been creating problems for the Shah. In 1963, however, he was appointed chairman and managing director of the National Iranian Oil Company, which he guided to great size and influence. Died 25 November

Erhard, Professor Ludwig (b. 1897), German economist and statesman, was Minister of Economic Affairs of the Federal Republic 1949-63, under Dr Adenauer, and Federal Chancellor 1963-66. In the former role he presided over Germany's 'economic miracle' after the demoralization, devastation and depriva-tion of territory suffered through defeat in World War II. His famous currency reform was inspired by belief in a 'social free-market economy', the foundation of which was confidence in the economy and equation of money incomes to real output. As Chancellor, which he became after a bitter struggle with Adenauer, he was less successful, largely through misadventures in foreign policy, but it was his character-istic effort to redress a budget deficit by tax increases that caused the break-up of the coalition of his party, the CDU, with the Free Democrats and his resignation. Died 5 May

Faulkner, Lord, of Downpatrick, PC (b. 1921), was, as Brian Faulkner, the last Prime Minister of Northern Ireland (1971-72) before the imposition of direct rule from Westminster. A staunch Unionist, he became an MP in 1949, Chief Whip in

1956, Minister of Home Affairs in 1959, Minister of Commerce in 1963 and Minister for Development in 1969. As leader of his party he took part in the tripartite Sunningdale talks in December 1973, and, although he had lost much Unionist support, headed the new power-sharing Executive from January 1974 until its collapse in the following May, by which time he had been obliged to form a new party of his own. Died in a riding accident 3 March

Feiling, Sir Keith (b. 1884), British historian, was Student and tutor of Christ Church, Oxford, from 1909 to 1946, with a break for active military service in World War I, then Chichele Professor of Modern History 1946-50. His books included the *History of the Tory Party 1640 to 1714* (1924), with a sequel to 1832 (1938), a one-volume *History of England* (1950) and his *Life of Warren Hastings* (1954). Died 16 September

Finch, Peter (b. 1916 in England of Australian parentage), British actor, had his first part on the London stage in *Daphne Laureola* (1949), thanks to Lawrence Olivier who had seen him act in Australia. His stage parts included Iago in *Othello* (with Orson Welles, 1951), Mercutio in *Romeo and Juliet* (1952) and Trigorin in *The Seagull* (with Vanessa Redgrave, 1964). But he was far more widely known as a film actor, notably in *A Town Like Alice, The Battle of the River Plate, Robbery under Arms, The Nun's Story, The Trials of Oscar Wilde* (as Wilde) *No Love for Johnnie, Far from the Madding Crowd, Sunday, Bloody Sunday* and *Network,* for which he posthumously received an 'Oscar'. Died 14 January

Gouin, Félix (b. 1884), President of the French Constituent Assembly which drew up the Constitution of the Fourth Republic, became Prime Minister during the first half of 1946. In 1940 he was one of the 80 deputies who voted against demise of the Third Republic, and in exile he headed the French parliamentary group in London. After the Allied landings in North Africa, he was elected president of the Constituent Assembly first in Algiers and then in Paris. From June until

December 1946, Gouin was deputy Prime Minister and then Minister of State in M Ramadier's Cabinet. Although he was in the running for the Presidency, a wine scandal involving his staff ruined his chances. Died 25 October

Hill, Professor Archibald Vivian, CH (b. 1886), British scientist, won (with Otto Meyerhof) the Nobel prize for physiology and medicine in 1922 for his work on heat changes. His skills spread from mathematics through physiology to physical chemistry and instrument design, and he contributed to invaluable military-scientific studies in World Wars I and II. He was a Fellow of Trinity (1910-16) and King's (1916-25) Colleges, Cambridge, professor of physiology at Manchester University (1920-23) and University College, London (1923-25), and Foulerton research professor of the Royal Society (1926-51), and served the Royal Society as Secretary (1935-45) and Foreign Secretary (1945-46). He was also MP for Cambridge University 1940-45. Died 3 June

Idzikowski, Stanislas (b. 1894), Polish ballet dancer, danced in London before World War I and in 1915 joined the Diaghilev Ballet, with which he remained until his dissolution in 1929. Short in height, he rarely danced the noble roles in romantic ballet, but he was the company's most brilliant star in such productions as *La Boutique Fantasque* or *The Sleeping Beauty*, where he excelled in the Bluebird *pas de deux*. In the 1930s he danced with various companies in England, including the inauguration, with Markova, of Ashton's *Les Rendezvous*. He was equally famous in the ballet world as a teacher of the Cecchetti method in which he had been tutored, and on which he wrote with the critic Cyril Beaumont a standard textbook. Died 12 February

Ilyushin, Sergei Vladimirovitch (b. 1894), Russian aircraft designer, was best known outside the USSR for his late, somewhat conventional airliners the Il-18 (1957) and the Il-86 airbus (1976), but he had shown more originality with military aircraft in World War II. He was thrice awarded the Order of Lenin. Died 11 February

Johnson, Professor Harry G. (b. 1923), could well be called an Anglo-American economist. Born in Canada and graduating from Toronto, he then sat at Keynes's feet in Cambridge, England, and obtained his doctorate from Harvard in Cambridge, Massachusetts. After holding fellowships at Cambridge, he was professor of economic theory at Massachusetts 1954-59 and of economics at Chicago from 1959, combining this chair with one at the London School of Economics 1966-74, and was also a frequent lecturer at Canadian universities. He left his mark as much through his teaching, his articles and his engagements in controversy as through his books (among them, *Essays in Monetary Economics*, 1967, and *Aspects of the Theory of Tariffs*, 1971); but he made important original contributions to the theories of tariffs and of the relations of international trade and economic growth. Died 8 May

Jumblatt, Kamal (b. 1919), was long regarded as the *enfant terrible* of Lebanese politics. A Druze from the mountains, he feuded bitterly with the Maronite President Chamoun, and though a Christian sided with the mainly Muslim revolt in 1958 which was ended only by American armed intervention, and acted likewise in the civil war of 1975-76. A member of the Chamber of Deputies 1943-57 and from 1960, he founded the Socialist and Progressive Party and moving further and further to the left eventually became an ardent Maoist. He held various ministerial offices between 1960 and 1975 but ended as a spent force. Assassinated 16 March

Kirk, Sir Peter, MP (b. 1928), was leader of the Conservative delegation to the European Parliament from the start of British membership until his death. A journalist by profession, he became MP for Gravesend 1955-64 and for Saffron Walden from 1965. Before the UK joined the European Community, he had been an assiduous delegate to the Council of Europe and Western European Union. He was a parliamentary under-secretary of state in the Ministry of Defence in 1964 and 1970-72. In the Strasbourg Assembly he was widely respected, not least for his championship of reform in its procedures and enlargement of its authority. Died 17 April

Littlewood, Professor J. E. (b. 1885), Rouse Ball Professor of Mathematics at Cambridge 1928-50, was one of the outstanding pure mathematicians of his time—which extended, in terms of published innovative work, for over sixty years. For a large part of that time he collaborated with his mathematical peer G. H. Hardy, notably on the theory of series, the distribution of primes, the theory of functions and application of the Hardy–Ramanujan–Littlewood analysis to the theory of numbers. His principal works, apart from innumerable learned papers, were *Elements of the Theory of Real Functions* (1926), *Lectures on the Theory of Functions* (1944) and *A Mathematician's Miscellany* (1953). He was a life Fellow of Trinity, Cambridge, and three times a medallist of the Royal Society. After his retirement in 1950 he was a frequent lecturer in the USA. Died 6 September

Lowell, Robert (b. 1917), American poet, came from old-established New England stock on both sides of his parentage, but broke with family tradition in becoming a Roman Catholic and later joining a mainly Jewish intellectual circle in New York, though he never shed his background or his love of the northeastern lands. His wide fame and influence in the English-speaking world date from *Life Studies* (1959), poems with a mainly autobiographical theme. Other works included *The Mills of the Kavanaughs* (1951), *For the Union Dead* (1964), *Benito Cereno*, a verse play (1967), *Near the Ocean* (1967), *The Voyage* (1968) and *Notebook* (1970). *The Times* obituarist wrote: 'Perhaps no poet of our time, since the death of Yeats, has been more a master of what Saintsbury called "the grand style".' Died 12 September

Lunt, Alfred (b. 1893), American actor, was inextricably linked in the minds of American and British theatre-goers with his British-born wife Lynn Fontanne, whom he married in 1922. Thereafter they almost always acted together, starting with *Sweet Nell of Old Drury*

(1923) and *The Guardsman* (1924) in New York, where they also shared with Noel Coward the honours of *Design for Living*, which he had written for them. With *Reunion in Vienna* (1934) and *Amphitryon 38* (1938) they took London by storm. Later joint successes included Rattigan's *Love in Idleness* and Dürrenmatt's *The Visit*. Without Miss Fontanne he played in New York, among other parts, Marco Polo in O'Neill's *Marco's Millions*. Died 3 August

Lupescu, Magda, *see* Elena, Princess

Makarios III, Archbishop of the Autocephalous Church of Cyprus from 1950 (b. 1913), became President of the Cypriot Republic by overwhelming vote of both the Greek and Turkish communities in 1960, after Cyprus had gained independence within the Commonwealth on terms laid down in the London agreement reluctantly signed by him in the previous year. They included perpetual renunciation of *enosis* (union with Greece) and a constitution designed to share power between the two communities. In March 1956 Archbishop Makarios, ethnarch of the Greek Cypriots, had been exiled from the island by the British Governor as the inspiration for the pro-*enosis* Eoka movement, and in Greece he was acclaimed a national hero. Turkish resentment of his proposed constitutional reforms led to bloody violence at the end of 1963, and in 1964 the United Nations peacekeeping force was installed. He had to cope not only with Greek–Turkish animosity but also with the opposition, within his own community, of the communists and the passionate *enosist* General Grivas. In July 1974, after the death of Grivas, the Cyprus National Guard, a force ultimately controlled by the Colonels' regime in Greece, staged a revolt and claimed the death of Makarios in an air and tank attack on the presidential palace. The Archbishop, however, who had survived several previous attempts on his life, escaped by RAF helicopter to a British air base and thence to Britain and the United States, where he pleaded his case at the United Nations. The failure of the coup was followed by the fall of the Colonels in

Athens and the invasion and virtual partition of Cyprus by Turkish forces. Makarios returned as President, pledged to work, in vain, for peaceful coexistence of the two communities, which his own inevitable Greek sympathies had done much to sunder. He remained, through two decades as an industrious, powerful and subtle statesman, a dedicated and austere churchman and preacher. Died 3 August

Marx, Groucho (b. 1895), American film comedian, was the most talented of the famous Marx Brothers. His real first name was Julius and he was the son of a poor immigrant tailor in New York. With his brothers he formed a touring musical group, but his talent for burlesque acting soon emerged, and he was the star of their Broadway appearances. Brought to Hollywood by Paramount, the Marx Brothers promptly created some of their most famous films, including *Animal Crackers* (1930), *Monkey Business* and *Horsefeathers.* Transferring to MGM, under the direction of Irving Thalberg, they made such side-splitting films as *A Night at the Opera, A Day at the Races* and *A Night at Casablanca.* Groucho also appeared solo in a number of comedy films and on television and radio. He was the master of the ironic non-sequitur. Died 19 August

Massemba-Débat, Alphonse (b. 1921), was President of the Republic of the Congo 1963-68, after serving various government offices after independence in 1960. He was overthrown by the left-wing military coup of Major Ngouabi (*q.v.*), for complicity in whose assassination he was executed, 25 March

Masterman, Sir John (b. 1891), Provost of Worcester College, Oxford 1946-61, was a well-known and much-loved Oxford figure, but his interests and influence spread far beyond the university. Athlete, novelist, counter-spy, school governor, educational adviser, industrial personnel expert, he was an exemplar of the wide-ranging humane, tolerant intellect. His books included *Fate Cannot Harm Me* (novel, 1935), *Marshal Ney* (1937), *To Teach the Senators Wisdom* (1952), *The Double Cross System* (an account of

wartime-counter-espionage, 1972) and *On The Chariot Wheel* (autobiography, 1975). Died 6 June

Moran, Lord (b. 1882), British physician, was best known to a wide international public as Winston Churchill's personal doctor and constant companion, and as author of *Winston Churchill: the Struggle for Survival,* controversial for its disclosure of what many regarded as medical confidences, and of *The Anatomy of Courage,* a durable study of fear and stress based on his experiences as a Royal Fusilier doctor in World War I, when he won the MC and was twice mentioned in despatches. But he was in his own right a highly distinguished consultant and medical administrator. He was Dean of the Medical School of St Mary's Hospital 1920-45 and President of the Royal College of Physicians 1941-50. Reform of medical education and close collaboration between the different branches of the medical profession were his major causes. Died 12 April

Nabokov, Vladimir, b. 1899, Russian-born author, sprang to world fame with the publication in Paris in 1955 of *Lolita,* a story of obsession with immature girlhood which at first had the same sort of notoriety and surreptitious circulation as had *Lady Chatterley's Lover* but was, like Lawrence's book, a work of substantial and individual literary merit. His later novels, like *Pale Fire* (1962), and others resurrected from his earlier output, confirmed his repute as an original and imaginative artist, but had a much smaller and more discriminating readership. He also wrote poetry and translated works from the Russian, including Pushkin's *Eugene Onegin.* Rich and privileged, the Nabokovs had fled Russia after the revolution, and Vladimir graduated at Cambridge University. From Germany he went to the USA, where he became professor of Russian and European literature at Cornell in 1948, but later he settled in Switzerland. He was also a distinguished lepidopterist. Died 2 July

Nash, John, RA (b. 1893), British painter (brother of Paul Nash), became an original member of the London Group

R

of artists at the age of 20. He was an official war artist in both world wars, in which he also served in the army and navy respectively. His serene paintings of landscapes and flowers—he was essentially a countryman—won wide public and critical favour, and he was a fine book illustrator in line and woodcut. Died 23 September.

Ngouabai, Marieu (b. 1938), President of the People's Republic of the Congo from end of 1968, headed a coup which overthrew President Massemba-Débat (*q.v.*) in that year. A graduate of the Brazzaville preparatory military school and St Cyr, he had risen to the rank of major. His communist sympathies were not to the taste of some of the Congo's neighbours, notably Zaïre. Assassinated 18 March

Patocka, Professor Jan (b. 1908), Czechoslovak philosopher, was one of the three intellectual leaders who were spokesmen for Charter 77 in January 1977. An exponent of phenomenology, he directed the Educational Institute of the Academy of Sciences from 1948. His attitude was non-communist but non-political, and he was respected by communists as well as their critics, but he was persecuted at the end of his life for applying non-political criteria to promotions in the Academy. Died 13 March

Presley, Elvis (b. 1935), American popular musician, was known to devotees of 'rock and roll' music as The King, and was idolized by the infatuated youth of his own and other countries. He began as a Southern white boy who could sing the folk-songs of the blacks, but was launched by shrewd sponsors upon the national and world-wide scene in 1956, above all with a record-breaking disc *Heartbreak Hotel*. No great musician, he cultivated a wild style of animation which gave him the soubriquet of Elvis the Pelvis and earned him vast riches from the tributes of teenagers, who were reported to have bought 150 million copies of his records. Died 16 August

Printemps, Yvonne (b. 1895), French actress and singer, was married 1916-32 to the playwright and actor Sacha Guitry and gained her chief international fame as his partner; but her later marriage to the actor Pierre Fresnay was equally fruitful artistically. An enchanting stage personality and singer, she had owed her rise to stardom in 1915 to the perspicacity of the impressario Louis Verneuil. She appeared often in London, notably opposite Noel Coward in his *Conversation Piece* (1934), which gave her the song 'I'll follow my secret heart'. Died 18 January

Rattigan, Sir Terence, CBE (b. 1911), British dramatist, rose to sudden fame in 1936 with his second professionally performed play, *French Without Tears* (with Rex Harrison and Kay Hammond), which was as great a success on Broadway and as a film as it had been in London. After *Flare Path* (1942), *While the Sun Shines* (1943) and *Love in Idleness* (1944), he won success of a higher order with *The Winslow Boy* (1946), based on the Archer–Shee case, just as his last play, *Cause Célèbre*, drawing crowds in London when he died, was based on a famous murder trial. The most memorable of his other plays were *The Browning Version* (1948), *The Deep Blue Sea* (1952), *The Sleeping Prince* (1953), *Separate Tables* (1954) and *Ross* (1960), a portrait of T. E. Lawrence acted by Alec Guiness. Rattigan, sensitive and warm-hearted, felt himself displaced in critical favour by the 'kitchen-sink' school of drama which flourished in the 1960s, but he survived that dismal phase of British play-writing and never lost the acclaim of the theatre-loving public for whom he wrote. Died 30 November

Rosellini, Roberto (b. 1906), Italian film director, never fully recaptured the international acclaim that greeted his first major films, *Roma Città Apertà* (1945) and *Paisa* (1946), made with documentary realism and passionate sympathy amid the chaos of Italian society as the war ended. Of his many later films another war story, *Il Generale della Rovere* (1954), received the highest critical praise. Died 3 June

Sabah as-Salim as-Sabah, Shaikh (b. 1915), was Ruler of Kuwait from November 1965. He used the huge oil wealth of his country to create a modern state with lavish public amenities and a generous welfare system. He also successfully sustained Kuwait's independence against menacing Iraqi claims, after the withdrawal of British protection in 1961 when he was in charge of foreign affairs under his brother, Shaikh Abdullah. Died 31 December

Schleyer, Hanns-Martin (b. 1915), West German industrialist, was president of the national association of employers and of the Federation of Industry. As a former member of the SS he was interned by the Allies for three years after World War II. He swiftly rose to industrial power in the Daimler Benz company, and in the 1960s made a national reputation as a tough wage negotiator who believed in strong trade union power and strong employers' power, too. Kidnapped on 5 September, he was murdered in cold blood in France after the defeat of the Lufthansa hijack. Died 16 October

Schumacher, Dr Ernst, CBE (b. in Germany 1911), was the foremost champion of 'intermediate technology', the tailoring of modern industrial method and equipment to the needs of poorer countries or relatively small communities. Outside the development field he was best known for his book *Small is Beautiful* (1973), an exposition of a society neither capital- nor energy-intensive. A Rhodes scholar at Oxford, he adopted Britain as his home. He was economic adviser to the British side of the Control Commission in Germany 1946-50, and to the National Coal Board 1950-70. His other books included *Export Policy and Full Employment* (1945) and *Roots of Economic Growth* (1962). Died 4 September

Schuschnigg, Dr Kurt von (b. 1897), Austrian Chancellor, 1934-38, made his mark in 1919, as a young lawyer, by the successful organization of the *Ostmärkische Sturmscharen*, a para-military youth formation of strongly Roman Catholic character. A conscientious scholar and a devout monarchist, he was elected as a deputy to the Chamber in 1927 and became Minister of Justice and Education in 1932 and Chancellor in 1934. On 12 February 1938 he found himself threatened with German invasion unless, *inter alia*, he accepted installation of the well-known Austrian Nazi, Seyss-Inquart, as head of the Austrian police; on March 12 he was forced to resign in the latter's favour after a full-scale German attack. After years of confinement in concentration camps he was liberated by the US Army on 3 May 1945. He lived in Italy until appointed to a professorship of politics at the University of St Louis, USA, in 1948. His autobiography (1969) was translated into English as *The Brutal Takeover* (1971). Died 18 November

Spencer-Churchill, Baroness, GBE (b. 1885 Clementine Hozier), widow of Sir Winston Churchill, married him in 1908 when he was President of the Board of Trade and survived him by 12 years. Though they often differed on political issues, for she had a strong personality and opinions of her own, she was utterly devoted and loyal to him, as he was to her. Despite the cares of being wife and hostess to so great, so moody and so dynamic a man, she was also in her own right a talented organizer and active worker for welfare causes and was chairman of the Red Cross Aid to Russia Fund 1939-46. In old age her beauty was undiminished and adorned the calmness and wisdom of her spirit. Died 12 December

Stokowski, Leopold (b. 1882 in London of Polish parentage), was an autocrat of the conductor's podium. After musical education and a start to his career in London, he went to America and became conductor of the Cincinatti Orchestra (1909-12) and the Philadelphia Orchestra (1912-36). Not only did he build the Philadelphia into one of the finest orchestras in the world, but he compelled the introduction of many contemporary works, by composers like Bartok, Stravinsky, Schoenberg and Mahler, into the concert repertoire. His methods were idiosyncratic: he abandoned the baton, and the movement of his hands became virtually part of the composition; he was a complete dictator, imposing his interpretation upon every work and every artiste. He fostered young musicianship and in 1940 founded the All American

Youth Orchestra. He brought the symphony orchestra into the cinema, notably in *A 100 Men and a Girl* and Walt Disney's *Fantasia*. Still conducting major new works in his 80s, in 1972 he retired to the English countryside. Died 13 September

Thomson, Sir Arthur Landsborough, CB (b. 1890), British ornithologist, also served the Medical Research Council (originally Committee) as its second officer from 1919 to 1957. His books on bird migration are international classics, but his *magnum opus* was the editing of *A New Dictionary of Birds*. Among other posts he was president of the Royal Zoological Society 1954-60, chairman of the Home Office advisory committee on protection of birds 1954-69, chairman of the trustees of the Natural History Museum 1967-69, President of the British Ornithologists' Union 1948-55 and of the XIth International Ornithological Congress 1954. Died 9 June

Tredgold, the Right Hon. Sir Robert, KCMG, QC (b. in Southern Rhodesia 1899), practised at the Rhodesian bar until 1936, when he became Minister of Justice and Defence in the Huggins Government. From 1950 he was the colony's Chief Justice, and from 1955 Chief Justice of the Central African Federation. In 1960 he resigned in protest against a Law and Order Bill which he regarded as racially discriminatory and an affront to freedom of speech, of association and of the press. He denounced the unilateral declaration of independence and constantly pressed for gradual advance to majority rule. Died 8 April

Vassilyevsky, Marshal Aleksandr (b. 1895), was made a Marshal of the Soviet Union in 1943 for his planning, as chief of operations control of the general staff, of the battles of Moscow, Stalingrad and Kursk. He became chief of the general staff 1946-49, Minister of the Armed Forces 1949-50 and of Defence 1950-53, and first deputy Minister of Defence 1953-57. Died 5 December

Velasco, General Juan (b. 1910), was President of Peru 1968-75. It was as commander-in-chief of the army that he ousted the Belaunde Government in 1968, but his policies were left-wing, including the nationalization of US companies and far-reaching agrarian and political reforms in favour of the Indian peasants. His socialism was not to the taste of the ruling classes or the military, and he was overthrown seven years later by General Bermudez, his Prime Minister. Died 24 December

Von Braun, Dr Wernher (b. 1912), was the greatest rocket designer of his time, from the German V1s and V2s to American spaceship-launchers. An enthusiastic amateur in this science, he was eagerly recruited by the German army and Adolf Hitler, and in 1937 became technical director of the famous guided missile centre at Peenemünde. Escaping to the area of American advance in 1945, he was taken with much equipment to the USA, where he eventually became director of development operations for the army ballistic missile agency and later director of the space flight centre at Huntsville under the National Aeronautics and Space Administration. He was thus responsible for the USA's first ICBMs and for the Saturn V rocket which launched the first man to tread the moon. Died 16 June

Wand, the Right Rev. and Right Hon. William, KCVO (b. 1885), was Bishop of London 1945-55 and Canon Treasurer of St Paul's 1956-69. After pastoral cures and an army chaplaincy in World War I he became Dean of Oriel College, Oxford in 1925, but in 1934 was chosen as Archbishop of Brisbane, where he displayed high powers both of administration and of communication with the public. In 1943 he returned to England as Bishop of Bath and Wells, and in 1945 Sir Winston Churchill chose him to be Bishop of London. There he continued to display the same qualities, fortified by abundant energy, earning great popularity in the City and throughout the diocese, and he also took a leading part in the oecumenical movement and in national church affairs. He preached often and wrote much, from *Development of Sacramentalism* (1928) and *Westminster Commentary on I, II Peter and Jude* (1934) to *Reflections on the*

Gospels (1969) and *Letters on Preaching* (1974). Died 16 August.

Williams, Sir William Emrys, CBE (b. 1896) devoted his life to adult education and the public support of the arts. He was secretary of the British Bureau of Adult Education 1934-40, director of the Army Bureau of Current Affairs (ABCA) 1941-45 and of its foundation-funded civilian successor 1946-51, secretary-general of the Arts Council 1951-63 and secretary of the National Arts Collection Fund 1963-70. Indeed with the backing of General Sir Ronald Adam he was effectively the founder of ABCA and, with that of Dr Tom Jones, of the Arts Council (via the Council for the Encouragement of Music and the Arts). He was also editor-in-chief of Penguin Books for thirty years from 1935. Died 30 March

Woodham-Smith, Mrs Cecil Blanche, CBE (b. 1896), British biographer and historian, was Irish by ancestry (Fitzgerald) and sympathy. She stepped into fame with her life of *Florence Nightingale* (1950). This was followed by *The Reason Why* (1953), a study of the Crimean campaign woven round the lives of the Earls of Lucan and Cardigan, *The Great Hunger* (1962), the story of the Irish potato famine, and her two-volume *Queen Victoria: her life and times* (1972 and 1975), all works of moving humanity based upon deep research and scholarship. Died 16 March

Zuckmayer, Carl (b. 1896), German dramatist, incurred the wrath of the Nazis with his satire on German militarism, *Der Hauptmann von Köpennick* (1931); his plays were banned by the Hitler regime, and in 1939, having fled from Austria in the previous year, he went to America. He returned to Germany in 1945, however, and in 1955 received from the Federal Republic the national prize for literature. His other best-known plays were *Der Fröhliche Weinberg* (1925), *Der Teufels General* (1945), *Das Kalte Licht* (1955) and *Die Uhr schlägt Eins* (1961). His film scripts included that for the Jannings–Dietrich masterpiece *The Blue Angel* (1929). He was also a novelist and poet. His autobiography *Als wärs ein Stück von mir* appeared in 1966 (in English, as *A Part of Myself*, in 1970) and his collected works in 1961. Died 18 January

CHRONICLE OF PRINCIPAL EVENTS IN 1977

JANUARY

1 Gilbert Islands achieved self-government.
3 IMF approved Britain's application for a £2,300 million loan (see also 10 and 24 Jan.).
6 'Charter 77' manifesto smuggled into Germany; 31 Jan., Czech Govt declared Charter illegal.
  Roy Jenkins took over from Francois-Xavier Ortoli as President of European Commission.
  L. Tyler and family, held by Ethiopian guerrillas since May 1976, released.
7 French police arrested Abu Daoud, suspected leader of the assassins in Munich 1972 (see AR 1972, p. 540); 11 Jan., released and flown to Algiers.
9 In Lebanon, press censorship imposed.
10 The Bank for International Settlements arranged £1,765 million standby safeguard for sterling.
13 In UK, postal unions decided to boycott all mail to S. Africa for one week from 16 Jan.; 15 Jan., private litigant obtained injunction against postal interference; 27 Jan., Court of Appeal upheld right of an individual to a remedy in law when the Attorney General had refused consent for a relator action; 16 July, House of Lords reversed the judgment.
16 In Benin, coup attempt failed.
17 In USA, Gary Gilmore, at own request, executed by firing squad for murder in July 1976, in the first execution in ten years.
  Eighty killed when a bridge crashed on a train near Sydney, NSW.
  European Human Rights Commission found Turkey guilty of torture in Cyprus.
19 *Authority in the Church* issued by Anglican and Roman Catholic theological commission, stated that agreement had been reached on doctrine of authority.
20 In USA, Jimmy Carter inaugurated as 39th President.
23 In China, Teng Hsiao-ping reported to be appointed 1st Vice-Chairman of Party.
  West German Chancellor Helmut Schmidt arrived in London.
24 Britain negotiated loan of £873 million from 13 British, West German and American banks to aid economic recovery.
27 European Convention on the Repression of Terrorism signed by 17 member countries of Council of Europe.
  A first edition of *Moby Dick* fetched record price for fiction of £30,813 at auction in New York.
30 Mme Françoise Claustre, held hostage by Chad rebels for nearly three years, released.
31 In Rhodesia, guerrillas kidnapped nearly 400 schoolchildren; 6 Feb., parents persuaded 51 to return.
  In USA cold killed 75 and laid-off 1·5 million workers.
  Foreign Ministers of the EEC had two-day meeting in London.

FEBRUARY

3 In Ethiopia, General Taferi Bante, Chairman of the Military Council, killed; Colonel Mengistu Haile-Maryam succeeded him.
6 In UK, 25th anniversary of the Queen's accession to the throne.
  Irish President Dr Patrick Hillery arrived in Bonn for the first state visit from his country to West Germany.
  In Paraguay, 'office for life' poll for President Alfredo Stroessner, ruler since 1954.
7 At the European Court of Human Rights Britain admitted malpractice against prisoners in Ulster in 1971 and pledged never again to use deprivation techniques.
8 Soyuz 24 linked with orbiting Salyut 5 space laboratory.

9 HM the Queen and Duke of Edinburgh left London for six-week Jubilee tour of Western Samoa, Tonga, Fiji, New Zealand, Australia and Papua New Guinea.
Spain established diplomatic relations with the Soviet Union.

11 In India, President Fakhruddin Ali Ahmed died; 25 July, succeeded by Neelam Sanjiva Reddy.
In USA, Patricia Hearst refused retrial (see AR 1976, p. 515).

13 Partition formula for Cyprus drawn up at meeting of President Makarios and Rauf Denktash with Dr Waldheim.

14 EEC reached agreement on conservation of fish stocks.

15 In Denmark, PM Anker Jørgensen won clear victory in elections.

16 In UK, American journalists Philip Agee and Mark Hosenball received orders of deportation for reasons of national security.
In Uganda, after alleged plot to overthrow President Amin, Anglican Archbishop Dr Janani Luwum arrested; he and two Cabinet Ministers reported by Ugandan Government to have been killed in road accident while attempting to escape; report disbelieved and killings condemned throughout the world.
In Mozambique, flooding of Limpopo river killed hundreds.

17 In USSR, Andrei Sakharov received personal letter from President Carter.

18 In UK, General Synod of Church of England approved Anglican-Roman Catholic statement on Papal primacy.

19 In UK, Anthony Crosland, Foreign Secretary, died suddenly; 21 Feb. succeeded by Dr David Owen.

21 Representatives of the Argentine Commission for Human Rights claimed that under 11-month-old regime of General Videla 2,300 had been killed and between 20,000 and 30,000 had disappeared.

23 In Uganda, mass killings of Langi and Acholi tribes reported by refugees who had fled to Tanzania.

27 About 1,000 Roman Catholic supporters of the Latin Mass occupied church in Paris (see also 29 June).

MARCH

1 USA extended its fishing limits to 200 miles.

4 In Romania, severe earthquake in the Ploesti region killed 1,541 and injured more than 11,000.

6 Israeli PM Rabin in Washington on a six-day visit.

8 Five thousand mercenaries reported to have marched into Zaïre from Angola (see also 10 April).

9 In Pakistan, ruling Pakistan People's Party won general elections (see 10 April).

10 British PM Callaghan in Washington.

11 Brazil ended 1952 military aid pact with USA.

16 In Lebanon, Kamal Jumblatt, leftist leader, shot dead; more than 200 revenge killings later reported.
In India, Mrs Gandhi lost seat in elections, opposition Janata Party won absolute majority; President revoked 1975 emergency laws; 24 March, Morarji Desai became new PM.

18 In Congo, President Ngouabi assassinated; Massemba-Débat, former President, executed as being one of the murderers; 3 April, Colonel Yhombi-Opango elected head of state.

22 In the Netherlands, Cabinet resigned over land reform plan; 25 May, Socialist Party won the elections (see 15 Dec.).
83 died in earthquake which struck southern Iran.

23 In UK four-month pact with Liberals enabled Government to survive 'no confidence' motion in Commons; 28 July, pact renewed (see also 27 Sept.).

24 In UK Annan Committee report on broadcasting published.
USA and Cuba resumed official contacts after 18 years.

25 EEC leaders commemorated 20th anniversary of Treaty of Rome in Rome.
20 died in earthquake which struck eastern Turkey.
26 In Thailand, abortive attempt to overthrow Government.
In China, Beethoven rehabilitated; 25 May, ban on Shakespeare lifted.
27 582 killed when Pan-Am Boeing 747 collided with a KLM 747 taking off at Tenerife airport; £1,160 million claimed for disaster victims.
28 Portugal applied to EEC for membership.
29 In UK Budget Day: tax concessions estimated as equivalent to 4½ per cent pay increase—some conditional on union acceptance of wage restraint from 1 Aug.; dearer cigarettes; dearer petrol (revoked 9 May) (see also 15 July and 26 Oct.).
In Burma, PM U Sein Win dropped in Cabinet reshuffle and replaced by U Maung Maung Kha.

APRIL

1 In Chad, security forces crushed coup attempt; 6 April, 9 executed.
In Brazil, President Geisel dismissed Congress after opposition rejected judicial reform Bill; 11 April, Bill introduced under emergency powers.
2 In UK, Red Rum created record in winning Grand National for third time.
3 In Libya, 22 executed for anti-Qadafi plot in 1975.
4 3 per cent devaluation of Danish and Norwegian krone and 6 per cent devaluation of Swedish krona announced.
In Fiji, PM Ratu Sir Kamisese Mara's Alliance Party defeated in elections after 10 years in power; opposition National Federation Party won majority (see 1 June and 25 Sept.).
5 In Congo, constitution set aside and full powers assumed by ruling Military Committee headed by Colonel Joachim Yhomby Opango.
In China, Teng Hsiao-ping, former Deputy PM, restored to previous posts.
6 In the Gambia, head of state Sir Dawda Jawara re-elected.
7 In Israel, Yitzhake Rabin resigned as PM; succeeded by Shimon Peres (see also 17 May).
In Rhodesia, official figures of deaths to date, government forces 304, guerrillas 2,348.
In USA, President Carter proposed to stop nuclear reprocessing and scrap plans for commercial fast breeder reactors.
9 In Spain, Communist Party legalized after a 38-year ban.
10 Al-Qadi al-Hajri, former Yemeni PM, his wife and a colleague shot dead in London.
France supplied aircraft to fly 1,500 Moroccan troops to Zaïre to help fight rebels.
In Pakistan, over the weekend 42 killed in riots; 21 April, death toll 200 and martial law proclaimed; 24 April, opposition leaders arrested (see also 5 July).
11 Cuba and Malta established diplomatic relations.
13 Fiat chief, Luchino Revelli-Beaumont, abducted; 11 July, released after $2 million ransom paid.
15 British Foreign Secretary, Dr David Owen, met Ian Smith in Rhodesia.
17 Meeting of leading international socialists from 24 countries in Amsterdam.
In Liechtenstein, women voted for the first time in its history.
18 Foreign Ministers of EEC met in London.
In Belgium, Social Christian Party led by PM Tindemans won elections; 3 June, Government sworn in.
World auction record for a letter created when a page written by Galileo in 1612 fetched £17,500.
19 In San Salvador, Foreign Minister Mauricio Borgonovo Pohl kidnapped; 11 May, found shot dead.
20 In Sudan, President Nimeiry re-elected head of state with a 99·1 per cent vote.
In USA, President Carter announced details of national energy plan, with penalties for wasters and rewards for conservers (see also 13 Oct.).

22 In Algeria, first Cabinet reshuffle in 10 years.
24 In UK, the Prince of Wales launched the Queen's Silver Jubilee Appeal for fund to encourage service by young people.
25 In Jamaica, state of emergency of 19 June 1976 ended.
   Vietnamese PM Pham Van Dong in Paris, the first visit to a Western country since end of the war.
28 After trial of nearly two years in Stuttgart, German terrorists Andreas Baader, Gudrien Ensslin and Jan-Carl Raspe gaoled for life (see also 18 Oct.).

MAY

1 38 killed during May Day riots in Istanbul.
2 In Northern Ireland, general strike of 'loyalists' called for and partially enacted; 14 May, strike called off.
   In Indonesia, ruling party won majority in elections.
   Zaïre suspended diplomatic relations with East Germany.
4 Hundreds reported killed in anti-Government riots in Addis Ababa.
   In Argentina, General Alejandro Lenusse, ruler from 1971 to 1973, held on corruption charges; 13 June, freed.
5 President Carter arrived in London; 6 May, visited Newcastle and environs; 9 May, he met President Assad of Syria in Geneva.
6 In Sierra Leone, ruling All People's Party won elections.
7 Two-day summit conference of heads of government of Canada, France, W. Germany, Italy, Japan, Britain and USA opened in Downing Street.
8 Romania declared general amnesty affecting 28,500 people.
10 Two-day 15-nation Nato meeting opened in London.
   Salt II negotiations resumed in Geneva; ended 20 May.
11 In UK, former Scotland Yard chief detectives found guilty of receiving bribes, gaoled for 20 years.
   Peter Jay, Economics Editor of *The Times*, appointed British ambassador to US.
   In Finland, Government resigned and President Kekkonen invited Kalevi Sorsa, to head a new centre-left coalition; sworn in 15 May.
13 In Spain, Sra Ibarrari, 'La Pasionaria', returned after 38 years in exile.
   OPEC ministers, meeting in Nicosia, decided to drop plan for 5 per cent price rise.
14 Don Juan de Bourbon, father of King Juan Carlos, renounced claim to the Spanish throne.
15 Annual conference of Cento held at Teheran.
16 In Djibouti, Hassan Gouled, president of African People's League for Independence, elected PM.
17 In Israel, after 29 years in office Labour Party defeated in elections; 21 June, Menachem Begin, leader of Likud Party, succeeded as new PM.
   HM the Queen began first of her UK jubilee tours in Glasgow.
18 Report by the International Commission of Jurists estimated that during the first two years of President Amin's rule in Uganda 80,000 to 90,000 were killed.
   Convention banning 'weather warfare' signed by 33 nations in Geneva.
19 Guatemala and Panama broke diplomatic relations over Belize.
22 The Orient Express which began in 1883, made a late last arrival in Istanbul.
23 In the Netherlands, Moluccan terrorists held hostages in two sieges—105 schoolchildren and 50 in a hijacked train; 27 May, children released; 11 June, Dutch marines stormed the train and school; six terrorists and two hostages killed.
   US Vice-President Mondale in London.
24 In UK, a new Political Honours Scrutiny Committee appointed.
   In France, 24-hour general strike in protest against Government's austerity programme, the biggest strike since 1968.

R*

In USSR, President Podgorny dropped from the Politburo; 16 June, Brezhnev new President.

25 Spain and Vietnam established diplomatic relations.

26 Anglo-American consultative team on a constitution for Rhodesia began discussions with Rhodesian officials (see also 1 Sept.).

100 nations voted, in Geneva, to give prisoner-of-war status to captured guerrillas.

28 In USA, at least 200 died in a Kentucky night club fire.

Poland and East Germany signed treaty of friendship, cooperation and mutual assistance.

30 Rhodesian troops penetrated over 50 miles into Mozambique and killed 32 guerrillas.

Mrs Rosalyn Carter began two-week visit to seven South American countries as US President's personal envoy.

In Bangladesh, referendum affirmed policies of President Ziaur Rahman.

JUNE

1 In Fiji, Government defeated in confidence vote, Parliament dissolved.

2 Banabans offered to accept £6·5 million compensation from Britain in return for immediate independence for Ocean Islands.

3 27-nation North-South dialogue (CIEC) ended in Paris after 18 months, without significant agreement.

In Morocco, free elections, after 14 years, won by King Hassan's supporters.

4 In USSR, draft of new 147-article constitution, replacing that of 1936, published; 7 Oct., approved by Supreme Soviet.

5 In Seychelles, President Mancham deposed in a bloodless coup and replaced by Albert René.

In Turkey, Bulent Ecevit's Republican People's Party won in elections (see also 3 July and 31 Dec.).

7 In UK, a bank holiday to celebrate the Queen's Silver Jubilee; the Queen drove in state to St Paul's, and from there walked among crowds to Guildhall.

8 Commonwealth Conference open in London; 15 June, in the final communique, the 33 heads of government condemned regime of President Amin.

In Indonesia, five weeks after the elections, victory of ruling Golkar Party announced.

11 In Switzerland, in a referendum, plans for introduction of VAT rejected.

15 In Spain, in the first elections for more than 40 years, Senor Suarez's Democratic Centre Union obtained majority.

17 In the Republic of Ireland, Fianna Fail led by Jack Lynch won elections.

19 John Neumann, Bishop of Philadelphia 1850-60, canonized.

20 New Soviet head of state Brezhnev arrived in Paris on a three-day state visit.

21 Comecon summit meeting began at Warsaw.

22 Britain and USA initialled new North Atlantic air services agreement.

26 After 117 years of French rule, Djibouti became a republic.

29 Archbishop Lefèbvre ordained 30 priests in defiance of the Pope.

Heads of EEC met in London and supported call for a homeland for Palestinian people.

30 The Queen's first jubilee tour of London.

Trafalgar House Investments acquired Beaverbrook Newspapers for £14 million.

Seato expired.

JULY

1 In Zaïre, President Mobuto dismissed Cabinet in preparation for sweeping reforms.
   In Argentina, Sra Peron charged with $1 million charity fraud.
   In USA, President Carter cancelled B1 bomber production.
   Britain placed unilateral ban on herring fishing in the North Sea.
3 In Turkey, Ecevit Cabinet voted out by National Assembly; 21 July, Suleyman
   Demirel, chairman of Justice Party, formed Government.
5 In Pakistan, General Muhammad Zia al-Huq overthrew Bhutto Government in a
   bloodless coup; 10 July, Quranic penalty of amputation of the hand for theft
   introduced.
11 In UK, *Gay News* fined £1,000 and editor given suspended gaol sentence, after
   conviction of publishing a blasphemous libel, in first such trial for 56 years.
   In Papua New Guinea, in the first elections since independence, Michael Somare's
   coalition Government won.
12 In Spain, peseta devalued by 20 per cent.
13 In Spain, first democratic Cortes since the Civil War opened.
   24-hour power failure in New York led to looting; over 4,000 arrests.
14 In Ghana, it was announced that army rule would end on 1 July 1979.
   In Australia, Governor General Sir John Kerr resigned; replaced by Sir Zelman
   Cowen.
15 In UK, Chancellor of Exchequer's statement: increase in earnings in next 12 months
   should be limited to 10 per cent; breaches of guideline would bring penalties to
   companies; government would uphold limit in public sector; amendments to
   Finance Bill benefiting taxpayers.
18 Albania and Greece concluded air agreement, the only agreement between Albania
   and a Western country.
   In South Africa, new legislation, Criminal Procedure Bill and Lower Courts Amendment Act, replaced British trial system.
20 Security Council unanimously recommended Vietnam for UN membership.
   In the Bahamas, in the first elections since independence, landslide victory for
   Premier Lynden Pindling.
   In UK, record price of £62,000 paid at Sotheby's for a Qur'ān of 681AH (AD 1282).
21 In Sri Lanka, Mrs Bandaranaike's Freedom Party routed by United National Party
   of J. R. Jayewardene who became PM; before and after election, looting, riots
   and arson, causing some deaths.
   Clashes between Egypt and Libya developed into widespread air and ground battles.
22 PLO became member of Economic Commission for Western Asia, the first non-
   state to become member of a UN body.
25 In Pakistan, 50 died in floods in the North West Frontier Province.
   An international court of arbitration determined division of Western Approaches
   for Anglo-French undersea rights.
28 Spain applied to join the EEC.
   In Mexico, 106 parliamentarians from EEC and Latin America signed document
   called *The Act of Mexico* in favour of a new international economic order.
31 In France, one man died and 100 were injured when 20,000 demonstrators battled
   with police at nuclear reactor site at Creys-Malville.
   Summit meeting to mark tenth anniversary of Asean at Kuala Lumpur.
   In India, it was announced that alcoholic drink would be outlawed within four years.
   Ten killed when typhoon Vera swept across northern Taiwan.

AUGUST

3 In UK, *Review of Overseas Representation*, the 'think tank' report, proposed closing many overseas establishments and end of British Council.
  In Cyprus, Archbishop Makarios died; 31 Aug. succeeded by Spyros Kyprianou.
5 In India, 138 died in floods.
6 11 killed when bomb exploded in Salisbury; Bishop Muzorewa accused Nkomo's party, Zapu, of responsibility.
8 Ethiopia stated that its conflict with Somalia in the Ogaden was now a full-scale war; Organization of African Unity (OAU) rejected Somali claims to the region.
9 In Rhodesia, two white missionaries killed by guerrillas, bringing total of white RC missionaries killed in nine months to 13.
10 In UK, the Queen made a two-day visit to N. Ireland.
11 In Paraguay, 'butcher of Riga' reported dead.
13 In UK, 55 policemen and at least as many others injured, and 202 arrested, in a National Front march in Lewisham.
  From Thailand, reports of atrocities by Khmer Rouge troops on Cambodia border.
15 Former SS Colonel Herbert Kappler (70) escaped from Rome's military hospital; in consequence Italian-German summit meeting called off.
18 In China, Constitution of the Communist Party adopted by 11th national Party Congress.
19 In Cambodia, coup attempt foiled.
  In USA, three claimants awarded damages of $1,000 against CIA, in the first court decision over CIA surveillance of domestic mail.
  In Indonesia, about 100 died in severe earthquake and tidal waves.
21 In Ethiopia, call for general mobilization; both sides suffered heavy casualties in battle for Dire Dawa.
  In Lebanon, first clashes since March between Christians and Muslims left 17 dead.
26 World Conference for Action against Apartheid in Lagos adopted declaration calling for end of military links with South Africa.
28 In UK, despite efforts of the organizers, Notting Hill carnival marred by violence.
  Denmark and Norway devalued currencies by 5 per cent.
  In Peru, 14-month state of emergency lifted.
29 Anglo-American Rhodesia peace negotiators, meeting PM John Vorster in Pretoria, failed to obtain South Africa's support for proposals.
31 In Rhodesia, Ian Smith's Rhodesian Front won overwhelming victory in general election.
  In Nigeria, first civilian elections since 1966, with all candidates standing as independents because of ban on parties.

SEPTEMBER

1 In UK, Government's white paper on a settlement in Rhodesia published; FM Lord Carver nominated Resident Commissioner-designate; Ian Smith described Anglo-American proposals as 'insane'.
  World Psychiatric Association condemned Soviet Union for abusing psychiatry for political purposes.
3 In Pakistan, former PM Bhutto arrested in connexion with a murder in 1974; 6 Sept., sent to prison; 9 Dec., released on bail.
5 Dr Hanns-Martin Schleyer, head of West German Industries Federation, kidnapped near Cologne and four killed by terrorists; 19 Oct., body found in France.
6 In India, kalaazar (black fever) reported to have killed about 4,000.
7 USA and Panama signed two new Panama Canal treaties.
8 In Yugoslavia, President Tito returned after 24-day tour of Soviet Union, North Korea and China.
  Ethiopia severed diplomatic relations with Somalia.

9 15 publicly executed in Kampala for alleged plot against President Amin.
11 In Norway, general election resulted in deadlock; ruling Labour Party decided to
stay on in office.
12 Dr Waldheim presented Leonid Brezhnev with UN's peace medal.
In South Africa, black leader Steve Biko died in detention; 2 Dec., at the inquest,
no security police found responsible for his death—a verdict denounced in
London and Washington.
13 In USA, Massachusetts police released 50-year file on Sacco-Vanzetti case.
15 In UK, House of Commons report on civil service, the first since 1874, recommended
that its powers be subject to checks.
17 In UK, Dr Conor Cruse O'Brien contended that fewer than half the combined
population of N. Ireland and the Republic favoured a united country; he
resigned from Irish Parliamentary Labour Party.
20 Vietnam and Djibouti became 149th and 150th members of UN.
21 In USA, President Carter's Budget Director, Bert Lance, resigned following attacks
on his conduct as a banker.
22 Archbishop of Canterbury, Dr Coggan, on 12-day visit to Soviet Union.
25 Laker's first Skytrain service to New York began.
In Switzerland, electors voted for euthanasia.
Cambodia radio announced Pol Pot, former Premier, was the country's new leader.
In Fiji, PM Kamisese Mara's Alliance Party had landslide victory in election.
26 The Pope celebrated his 80th birthday.
27 Soviet Foreign Minister Gromyko in Washington to meet President Carter.
28 A Japan Air Lines DC8 hijacked off Bombay by Japanese Red Army terrorists; at
Dacca, the 144 hostages were released in return for nine prisoners in Japan and
£3·5 million.
29 Spain approved granting of home rule to Catalonia.
30 At Orly airport, Paris, police stormed hijacked Caravelle; a passenger was killed.
Soviet vessels banned from fishing in EEC's North Sea grounds.

OCTOBER

2 In Bangladesh, coup attempt crushed, claiming 230 lives; 20th, 37 executed.
3 In India, former PM Indira Gandhi arrested, to be released the following day.
4 In UK, at the Labour Party conference, 'back us or sack us', was the PM's challenge.
In Belgrade, 35 nations began review of 1975 Helsinki agreement (see also 4 Nov.).
9 Sharkel Makhouf (1828-98), a Lebanese hermit, proclaimed a saint.
Soviet Union and China, after eight years of talks, reached limited agreement on
Ussuri river frontier navigation.
10 In Sri Lanka, constitution amended in favour of presidential system.
In India, 61 killed in express train crash.
11 President Ibrahim al-Hamdi of N. Yemen assassinated.
12 In UK, record price for a camera—£21,000—was paid at Christie's.
13 US President Carter condemned oil companies for destruction of his energy policy.
In UK, memorial commemorating all those who 'laid down their lives for Christ and
conscience' during the Reformation unveiled in Westminster Abbey.
A Lufthansa Boeing 737 enroute from Majorca hijacked by two men and two women;
their demands were release of 11 terrorists held in Germany and two Palestinians
held in Turkey, plus $15 million; 16 Oct., pilot murdered at Aden; 17 Oct., at
Mogadishu, German commandos stormed aircraft and freed the 87 hostages;
three hijackers killed (see also 18 Oct. and 12 Nov.).
Dr C. H. Green, American philanthropist, gave £1 million towards founding new
medical college at Oxford.

14 The Queen and Duke of Edinburgh arrived in Ottawa on a six-day Silver Jubilee visit to Canada.

Spanish Government granted amnesty for political activists.

Heavy fighting broke out anew in southern Lebanon.

18 Prince of Wales arrived in Chicago to begin 13-day visit to USA.

In W. Germany, Andreas Baader and two fellow terrorists committed suicide in their cells in Stammheim gaol.

19 In South Africa, 18 anti-apartheid organizations banned, two newspapers closed and 50-70 black leaders arrested.

Former British PM Edward Heath on visit to China.

20 In Thailand, military under General Kriangsak Chamanand seized direct control in bloodless coup.

24 Somalis claimed 2,000 Cuban troops were aiding Ethiopia.

25 EEC chose Culham, Oxfordshire, for site of Joint European Torus.

26 In UK, autumn 'Budget': increase in personal allowances; £10 pensioners' Christmas bonus; disabled aided; increased holiday allowance.

27 In UK, Jeremy Thorpe denied he had ever been involved in plot to harm Norman Scott.

Five South African soldiers and 61 African guerrillas killed in clash on Angola-Namibia border.

28 M. Caransa, Dutch millionaire, kidnapped in Amsterdam; freed for £2 million.

31 USA, France and Britain vetoed motions in UN Security Council to impose economic and arms sanctions against S. Africa; 4 Nov., Council unanimously imposed mandatory sanctions on supply of arms.

NOVEMBER

1 In Surinam, in the first election since independence, PM Henk Arron's ruling coalition won.

In USSR, supersonic airliner TU144 opened regular passenger service.

In Burma, 500 rebels killed by army.

2 In UK, the Queen returned from Barbados on Concorde, having travelled 56,000 miles in 13 countries.

Russia offered to suspend peaceful nuclear explosions.

3 In Andorra, first elections in 700 years held.

New rules on mixed marriages drawn up by Roman Catholic and other churches.

4 In Belgrade, 14 Western countries called on Russia and its allies to recognize human rights.

5 USA withdrew from International Labour Office.

In USSR, amnesty, limited to criminals, proclaimed; 'prisoners of conscience' would not be freed.

India and Bangladesh signed agreement, after 25 years' dispute, on sharing Ganges waters.

In Italy, draft treaty with the Vatican proposed that Roman Catholicism would no longer be state religion.

9 Tyre in Lebanon bombed by Israeli aircraft; 65 bodies found.

In UK, European Assembly Elections Bill published (see also 13 Dec.).

11 In North Korea, President Kim Il Sung re-elected.

12 In W. Germany, Ingrid Schubert, sixth member of Baader-Meinhof gang, committed suicide in her cell.

13 Somalia expelled 6,000 Russian advisers; it also broke off diplomatic relations with Cuba.

In Nauru, President Bernard Dowiyoge voted back to power.

In Cyprus, Bishop Chrysostomos enthroned as Archbishop.

14 In UK, first official strike by firemen began after claim for 30 per cent pay increase was refused; 10,000 men of armed forces drafted to fight fires.

15 Mr Begin invited President Sadat to visit Israel (see also 17 and 19 Nov.).

In UK, son (Peter Mark Andrew) born to Princess Anne, to become fifth in succession to the throne.

17 Egyptian Foreign Minister and deputy resigned over President Sadat's proposed visit to Israel.

19 In Israel, President Sadat arrived; he addressed the Knesset the following day; 21 Nov., arrived back in Cairo amid cheering crowds (see also 27 Nov.).

8,000 to 10,000 reported killed when cyclone struck southern states of India.

In Portugal, 130 killed in national airline's first crash.

20 In Greece, PM Karamanlis's New Democracy won in election.

21 British shipbuilders signed £115 million order with Poland for 24 cargo ships; 12 Dec., the Government admitted it had given subsidy of £28 million.

22 After two years of legal argument, Anglo-French Concorde began operating London/Paris-New York service (see 9 Dec.).

Treaty of friendship and cooperation between Spain and Portugal signed, replacing 1939 Iberian Pact.

23 In Argentina, 70 killed and 250 injured when earthquake struck province of San Juan.

24 In Rhodesia, Ian Smith invited internal nationalist groups to immediate conference; he accepted principle of one man, one vote; Patriotic Front said it would fight on.

A tomb at Vergina, 40 miles west of Salonika, identified as that of Philip of Macedon (336 BC).

25 In Yugoslavia, amnesty for 218 political prisoners, including M. Mihajlov, announced.

In UK, *The Mousetrap* celebrated its Silver Jubilee.

27 President Sadat stated he was ready to negotiate with Israel alone; Begin accepted his call to a Cairo summit meeting (see also 14 and 25 Dec.).

28 In Japan, Cabinet resigned and new one appointed to deal with economic crisis.

In Rhodesia, it was claimed that in previous week 1,200 guerrillas were killed in air and ground raids in Mozambique, and denied that women and children were deliberately killed; Bishop Muzorewa declared week of national mourning.

Polish leader, Edward Gierek, arrived in Rome for a visit during which he was to see the Pope, the first time a Polish communist leader had visited Vatican.

In Upper Volta, overwhelming vote in referendum for return to civilian rule.

29 In UK, Home Secretary declared amnesty for immigrants who had entered country illegally before 1 Jan. 1976.

30 In South Africa, ruling National Party achieved overwhelming majority in general election.

DECEMBER

1 Commercial chartered flight from Hong Kong to China started, the first since 1939.

2 Israeli PM Begin began 5-day visit to Britain, the first official visit by an Israeli Premier.

In UK, two reports on Crown Agents gave details of mismanagement involving losses of at least £200 million.

In Bermuda, riots followed execution (the first in 30 years) of two men, one convicted of murder of Governor Sir Richard Sharples in 1973.

Leaders of Libya, Algeria, Iraq, South Yemen, Syria and PLO met in Tripoli to unify opposition to Egypt-Israel peace moves; 5 Dec., Sadat expelled their ambassadors (except Iraq's).

4 In Malaysia, 100 killed when plane hijacked by Japanese Red Army en route to Singapore crashed.

Jean-Bedel Bokassa crowned himself emperor of Central African Empire in ceremonies costing £14 million.

5 In South Africa, second tribal homeland, Bophuthatswana, came into being.

Two-day summit meeting of EEC heads of government opened in Brussels.

6 In Finland, 60th anniversary of independence celebrated.

8 In Portugal, M. Soares's Socialist Government voted out of office.

9 Concorde service to Singapore started; 16 Dec., suspended because of Malaysian refusal to allow overflights.

11 In Australia, after Fraser Government was returned to office in general elections, Gough Whitlam announced he would relinquish Labour leadership.

   Soyuz 26 docked with orbiting Salyut 6 space laboratory.

   In UK, President Giscard d'Estaing arrived for summit meeting with PM Callaghan.

12 West Germany confirmed that more than 1,000 Nato secret documents had been passed by agent to East Germany.

13 In UK, Government's recommendation of proportional representation for elections to European Assembly defeated by 97 votes.

14 Cairo conference opened with representatives of Egypt, Israel, USA and UN present.

   In the Netherlands, Pieter Menten, millionaire, gaoled for 15 years for part in massacre of Jews in 1944, after a trial which began in April.

15 In Cyprus, son of President Kyprianou kidnapped; 18 Dec., freed, after pledge of safe-conduct for gang leader.

   In the Netherlands, centre-right Government formed by Andreas Van Agt, ending 204-day political crisis.

16 President Carter and Israeli PM Begin met in Washington.

   In UK, the Queen opened new £300 million underground extension to Heathrow.

18 In San Marino, Communists invited by Captains Regent to form new coalition Government.

20 343 killed when severe earthquake struck south-eastern Iran.

   In Indonesia, 10,000 prisoners, held since 1965, freed.

25 Begin peace plan presented to President Sadat at Ismailia: Israel to withdraw from Sinai, occupied Jordan and Gaza strip to have councils, residents to have choice of citizenship, sovereignty to be left in abeyance; President Sadat reiterated objection to Israeli troops on West Bank.

29 US President Carter arrived in Warsaw at the start of seven-nation tour of Iran, India, Saudi Arabia, France and Belgium.

30 In Philippines, President Marcos granted amnesty to 1,646 prisoners.

31 In Turkey, Government of Suleyman Demirel resigned, after defeat on no-confidence motion; replaced by Ecevit's Republican Party.

INDEX